USE OF SURVEY DATA FOR INDUSTRY, RESEARCH AND ECONOMIC POLICY

Use of Survey Data for Industry, Research and Economic Policy

Selected papers presented at the 24th CIRET conference, Wellington, New Zealand, 1999

Edited by
KARL HEINRICH OPPENLÄNDER
Professor of Economics
Former President of the Ifo Institute
Munich, Germany

GÜNTER POSER
Professor of Economics
Darmstadt University of Technology
Darmstadt, Germany

BERND SCHIPS
Professor of Economics
Director of the Swiss Institute for Business Cycle Research
Swiss Federal Institute of Technology
Zurich, Switzerland

Ashgate

Aldershot • Burlington USA • Singapore • Sydney

Published by
Ashgate Publishing Ltd
Gower House
Croft Road
Aldershot
Hants GU11 3HR
England

Ashgate Publishing Company
131 Main Street
Burlington
Vermont 05401
USA

Ashgate website: http://www.ashgate.com

British Library Cataloguing in Publication Data
Use of survey data for industry, research and economic
policy : selected papers presented at the 24th CIRET
conference, Wellington, New Zealand 1999 - (CIRET
conference proceedings)
1. Business cycles - Congresses 2. Economic forecasting -
Congresses 3. Economic surveys - Congresses
I. Oppenländer, Karl Heinrich II.Poser, Günter III.Schips,
Bernd IV. CIRET. Conference (24th : 1999)
338.5'42

Library of Congress Control Number: 00-132599

ISBN 0 7546 1349 6

Printed in Great Britain by
Antony Rowe Ltd, Chippenham, Wiltshire

Contents

List of Contributors

Marlene Amstad, Research Economist, Swiss Institute for Business Cycle Research, Zurich, Switzerland.
Anirvan Banerji, Co-director of the Economic Cycle Research Institute (ECRI) headed by Geoffrey H. Moore, New York, USA.
Elena Belyanova, Director of the Moscow branch of the Netherlands Economic Institute/IMEMO, Moscow, Russia.
Pierre Beziz, Administrator, Organisation of Economic Co-operation and Development (OECD), Statistics Directorate, Paris, France.
Phillip Briggs, Head of the quantitative division, New Zealand Institute of Economic Research, Wellington, New Zealand.
Robert A. Buckle, Associate Professor of Economics and Head of the School of Economics and Finance, Victoria University of Wellington, Wellington, New Zealand.
John A. Carlson, Loeb Professor of Economics at Purdue University, West Lafayette, Indiana, USA.
Paolo Carnazza, Head of unit 'Business and Consumer Surveys', Institute for Studies and Economic Analyses (ISAE), Rome, Italy.
Philip Chen, Senior Economist, Foundation for International Business and Economic Research, New York, USA.
Marcella Corsi, Associate Professor of Economics, Liberal Universita Internazionale degli Studi Sociali 'G. Carli', Rome, Italy.
Pierre Crevits, Assistant Advisor Short Term Indicators, National Bank of Belgium, Brussels, Belgium
Enrico D'Elia, Senior Economist, Price Survey Unit of the Italian National Institute of Statistics, Rome, Italy.
Yves de Lombaerde, Assistant Quarterly National Accounts, National Bank of Belgium, Brussels, Belgium
Phoebus Dhrymes, Jr., Research Associate, Foundation for International Business and Economic Research, New York, USA.
Assunta Draicchio, Researcher, Survey Unit of the Institute for Studies and Economic Analyses (ISAE), Rome, Italy.
Luc Dresse, Assistant Advisor, Research Department, National Accounts and Business Surveys Cell, National Bank of Belgium, Brussels, Belgium.
Maria Drozdowicz-Biec, Senior Research Associate, Foundation for International Business and Economic Research, New York, and Research Institute of Economic Development at the Warsaw School of Economics, Warsaw, Poland.

Matthew Hassan, Economist, New Zealand Institute of Economic Research, Wellington, New Zealand.
David Haugh, Analyst, Budget Management Branch, The New Zealand Treasury, Wellington, New Zealand.
Harald A. Haupt, Research Assistant, Department of Economics and Econometrics, University of Regensburg, Regensburg, Germany.
Miklós Hegedüs, Managing Director, GKI Economic Research Company, Budapest, Hungary.
Lorene Hiris, Associate Professor of Finance, C. W. Post Campus of Long Island University in New York and Senior Research Scholar at the Economic Cycle Research Institute (ECRI), New York, USA.
Michel Houdebine, Institut National de la Statistique et des Etudes Economiques (INSEE), Paris, France.
Bengi Kibritcioglu, Assistant Expert of Treasury, Prime Ministry, The Undersecretariat of Treasury, General Directorate of Economic Research, Ankara, Turkey.
Franz-Josef Klein, Head of Unit 'Business Surveys and Publications', European Commission, Brussels, Directorate General 'Economic and Financial Affairs', Brussels, Belgium.
Philip A. Klein, Professor of Economics, Penn State University, Philadelphia, and Senior Research Scholar, Economic Cycle Research Institute (ECRI), New York, USA.
Yasuyuki Komaki, Senior Economist, Nippon Life Insurance Research Institute, Tokyo, Japan.
Bülent Kose, Expert of Treasury, Prime Ministry, The Undersecretariat of Treasury, General Directorate of Economic Research, Ankara, Turkey.
Jürg Dieter Lindlbauer, Senior Researcher, Ifo Institute for Economic Research, Munich, Germany.
Bianca Maria Martelli, Researcher, Survey Unit of the Institute for Studies and Economic Analyses (ISAE), Rome, Italy.
Zbigniew Matkowski, Senior Lecturer, Warsaw School of Economics and Professor of Economics, B. Janski School of Management and Business, Warsaw, Poland.
Gernot Nerb, Head of Survey Research, Ifo Institute for Economic Research, Munich, Germany.
Serguei Nikolaenko, Principal Analyst, Bureau of Economic Analysis, IMEMO, Moscow, Russia.
Karl Heinrich Oppenländer, Professor of Economics, former President of Ifo Institute, Munich, Germany.
Gábor Papanek, Managing Director, GKI Economic Research Company, Budapest, Hungary.

Raymund Petz, Research Manager, GKI Economic Research Company, Budapest, Hungary.
Günter Poser, Professor of Economics, Darmstadt University of Technology, Darmstadt, Germany.
Ricardo Reyes-Araiza, Deputy-Manager of the Productive Sector, Banco de Mexico, Mexico.
Paul Rodway, Manager, Tax Forecasting and Modelling Group, The New Zealand Treasury, Wellington, New Zealand.
Bernd Schips, Professor of Economics, ETH-Zurich, Director of the Swiss Institute for Business Cycle Research, Zurich, Switzerland.
Johan G. J. Snyman, Director of Medium-Term Forecasting Associates, Building Economists, Stellenbosch, South Africa.
Doug Steel, Economist, New Zealand Institute of Economic Research, Wellington, New Zealand.
Kurt Stock, Research Fellow, Ifo Institute for Economic Research, Munich, Germany.
Alex Sundakov, Director of the New Zealand Institute of Economic Research, Wellington, New Zealand.
Kari Takala, Economist, Economics Department, Bank of Finland, Helsinki, Finland.
Jukka Topi, Economist, Financial Markets Department of the Bank of Finland, Helsinki, Finland.
Giuseppe Travaglini, Researcher, University of Urbino, Urbino, Italy.
Sergey Tsukhlo, Head of Business Survey Department, Institute for the Economy in Transition, Moscow, Russia.
Pekka Tsupari, Head of department, Confederation of Finnish Industry and Employers, Helsinki, Finland.
Gamze Ugur, Expert of Treasury, Prime Ministry, The Undersecretariat of Treasury, General Directorate of Economic Research, Ankara, Turkey.
Yvonne M. van Everdingen, Assistant Professor of Marketing Management, Erasmus University Rotterdam, Rotterdam, The Netherlands.
George van Gastel, Head of the division 'Business tendency surveys and short term indicators' at the National Bank of Belgium, Brussels, Belgium.
Jean-Jacques Vanhaelen, Advisor, Research Department, National Accounts and Business Surveys Cell, National Bank of Belgium, Brussels, Belgium.
W. Fred van Raaij, Professor of Marketing Management, Erasmus University Rotterdam, Rotterdam, The Netherlands.
Sandra M. Waller, Research assistant to the executive board, Ifo Institute for Economic Research, Munich, Germany.

Thomas M. F. Yeh, Secretary-General of the Council for Economic Planning and Development of the Republic of China, Taipei, Republic of China.

Victor Zarnowitz, Professor Emeritus of Economics and Finance at the University of Chicago, and Research Director of the Foundation for International Business and Economic Research (FIBER) in New York, USA.

Preface

The Centre for International Research on Economic Tendency Surveys (CIRET) held its 24th conference and a workshop on capacity utilisation at the invitation of the New Zealand Institute of Economic Research (NZIER) in Wellington from March 16 to March 20, 1999.

For this volume thirty-one workshop and conference papers were selected and grouped into seven parts: Leading Indicators and Turning Points; Classification of Business Cycles; Survey Data and Policy Decisions; Attitudes and Behaviour of Firms; Capacity Utilisation; Stocks and the Business Cycle; and Survey Data and Economic Forecasts.

As in previous conferences, prominent speakers of the host country addressed the conference participants in plenary sessions. The editors wish to thank Len Cook (New Zealand Government Statistician) for his opening address on 'Challenges in Measuring Small Economies', and Sir Roger Douglas (Previously Minister of Finance), Arthur Grimes (Institute of Policy Studies, Victoria University of Wellington), Graham Scott (Previously Secretary to the Treasury) and John Yeabsley (NZIER) for their comments to the topic 'Deregulation and the New Zealand Economy', Rt Hon Bill Birch (Treasurer) and Alan Bollard (Secretary to the Treasury) for informing the plenum about the government's view of the economic and fiscal development in New Zealand as well as Donald T. Brash, Governor of the Reserve Bank of New Zealand for his dinner speech on New Zealand's monetary policy.

Our special thanks go to the Director of NZIER, Alex Sundakov, to Liz Hodgson and Corina Basher of the NZIER secretariate and to the Business Manager of NZIER, Alan Froggatt, who did a wonderful job in organizing conference, workshop and social events.

During the conference the CIRET Coordinating Committee decided to transfer the CIRET Bureau from the Ifo Institute in Munich to the Institute of Business Cycle Research at the ETH Zurich.

The editors wish to thank all persons who were engaged in the preparation of the 24th CIRET conference, especially the staff of NZIER as well as Sandra Waller and Christine Beckhäuser of the Ifo Institute.

They also thank Petra Freitag and Heiko Lenhard, Darmstadt University of Technology, for their efforts in formating the papers for publication.

Karl Heinrich Oppenländer, Günter Poser, Bernd Schips
Munich, Darmstadt, Zurich

Introduction

The objective of CIRET conferences is the utilisation and promotion of research in the field of business cycle analysis and economic forecasts using predominantly qualitative data. A world-wide network of institutes has been established for this purpose, which combines theoretical, econometric and empirical knowledge in an ideal fashion.

This volume contains 31 lectures presented and discussed at the 24th CIRET conference in Wellington (New Zealand), which have been divided into seven chapters. The topics of each of the chapters reflect current fields of interesting research.

Part I deals with the question of turning points in a business cycle and their predictability. It has been shown again and again that turning point analyses and forecasts are difficult tasks to master. A solution is probably most likely to be found by using leading indicators based on qualitative data collected within companies in connection with new econometric methods.

Part II deals with the issue of business cycle classification. Assistance for business cycle forecasts will also be given in this connection. Provided that the business cycle exists (which is assumed), defining 'Where are we located in the business cycle' would be helpful for forecasts. It would then be possible to roughly estimate how long the upturn or downturn will continue (compared to 'reference cycles' of the past) or when approximately the top or the bottom of the business cycle is expected to be reached.

Part III presents examples for the use of survey data for political decisions. This chapter serves firstly to show that this type of data leads to increased knowledge by virtue of its up-to-dateness and secondly, to clearly establish that additional information which is not gained from official statistics or other sources is a valuable addition and can assist in making political decisions.

Part IV provides a contribution to the analysis of the entrepreneurial decision-making process. The behaviour shown by each individual company depends to a crucial extent on additional information. The survival or success of a company in competitive surroundings is thus fostered and positions can be more firmly established. In addition, researchers – and incidentally also business enterprises – find analysing and understanding each decision-making process interesting, which, in turn, is especially successful with survey data which can be used for very specific purposes.

Part V draws attention to an important determinant in the development of the economic process - capacity utilisation. Information on capacity utilisation is rare. Surveys have the great advantage that the entrepreneur, who is answering specific questions on capacity utilisation of his plant knows what he is talking about. He is able to judge not only the future developments of demand with regard to the existing capacity, but is also able to correctly allocate changes on the supply side (shift operation, capacities becoming desolate due to new products etc.). When viewed on an aggregate level it is possible to compile series for potential growth (fully utilised capacities), which, in turn, provide assistance for the prediction of economic growth in the manufacturing sector. Each individual rate of capacity utilisation also is an indication of the performance of the current business cycle.

Part VI deals with a similarly interesting field of research: inventory movements and their influence on the development of business activity. Again, there is serious lack of statistical data so that qualitative data constitute valuable supplementary information. It goes without saying that the quality and accuracy of business forecasts benefit in particular from the availability of survey data on investments in inventories of goods, the course of such inventory investments, their assessment and their predictability by companies.

Part VII rounds off the insight given into the intricacies of carrying out business cycle research. Several examples are given in this chapter on how the prediction of economic phenomena such as inflation, stock market movements, building programmes etc. could be improved by means of qualitative data.

CIRET conferences combine two major aspects which are of decisive importance to scientific progress: they endeavour to win protagonists of new scientific knowledge as speakers and offer a platform for encounters and discussions which are also indispensable for scientific progress. Starting with the Budapest conference in 1991 more and more institutes from East European countries have participated in CIRET conferences. It turned out that during the first phase of transition qualitative data were almost the only information available on the economic process. Therefore, survey activities in transition economies were stimulated tremendously.

The following five papers presented by young authors were selected to give an overview of the variety of contributions to this volume.

Marlene Amstad presented a paper which is to lead to an improved predetermination of business cycle turning points by using Markov switching models with survey data. Data is used which is collected from the quarterly surveys of the industry in Switzerland. An indicator is constructed (H- signal) which is tested on the past. Result: 'The meanlead of the H-signal amounts to four quarters. Covering a period with ten turning points in GNP, four false signals occur.' This is viewed as progress with previous tests based on other methods. The tests to date with leading indicators were often carried out using linear methods, such as correlational analysis and spectral analysis. However, the test with the non-linear Markov switching approach demonstrates that it is wise to analyse various economical situations separately (e.g. boom phases and recession phases) and then to locate the probability of stable regimes.

In the course of his observation of business cycles for classification purposes, *Pierre Beziz* compares univariate methods for measuring business cycles (moving averages, annual growth rates, phase average trend method of the NBER, Hodrick Prescott Filter, Kalman Filter, probability methods for the trend) with multivariate methods (MVA). A 'set of economic indicators' is used as a starting point with the customary combination of quantitative and qualitative data. The initial combination is retained ('a different set of indicators will give different results'). Irregular components are able to be separated from the trend, which is constructed using a large number of indicators. Details of the theory, which is referred to as being 'rather complex', were not given. The method is currently being tested on the Mexican economy and is viewed as being trailblazing for OECD research ('The use of multivariate techniques is still relatively recent.').

Harald Haupt and *Sandra Waller* examine whether inflationary expectations, which are gained from qualitative survey data, can improve short-term forecasts of the inflation rate. The examination is based on data derived from the quarterly survey of experts 'Economic Survey International' carried out by the ifo Institute. Vector-error-correction (VEC) or autoregressive-distributed-lag (ADL) models are used, which consistently give a better performance than autoprojective approaches. It is concluded that 'survey respondents have relevant information about future inflation'. It has also been shown in the case of the existing set of data that co-integration tests provide better results than the classic approaches for checking the rationality of inflationary expectations.

Elena Belyanova and *Serguei Nikolaenko* take up an interesting issue which is decisive for the assessment of prospective growth in transformation countries. How can the existing savings funds of households encourage investments? The crisis in Russia in August 1998 is used as a setting. The situation before and after the crisis is compared. The analysis is based on a VAR model. The empirical information was gained by means of consumer surveys. It is demonstrated that as real income decreases the propensity to save is shifted from employees to the self-employed. Investment is influenced thereby, although the general situation remains 'very volatile'.

Paolo Carnazza and *Guiseppe Travaglini* examine the investment behaviour of Italian enterprises. The starting point is the establishment of the fact that 'different degrees of irreversibility of capital stock' exist that may influence the investment activity of companies. In order to gain additional information, a special survey is carried out focusing on this fact. Moreover, the real option theory of investment is applied. A second starting point for observations is the uncertainty of investment decisions. It appears that the combination of both factors ('uncertainty-irreversibility combination') constitutes a serious impediment to companies' investment programmes. The authors recommend that politicians be aware of the irreversibility problem.

These papers not only show the wide range of the programme of the 24th CIRET conference, but also demonstrate successful combinations of theoretical reflection and empirical survey research.

Karl Heinrich Oppenländer

Part I

Leading Indicators and Turning Points

1 On the Use of Markov Switching Models Applied to Business Survey Data for the Prediction of Turning Points

MARLENE AMSTAD[1]

Abstract

This paper investigates the use of Markov Switching Models (MSM) applied to Business Survey Data (BSD) as a predictor of business cycle turning points. Results of the quarterly Swiss industry survey are converted to a dichotomous signal by using Hamilton's Markov Switching Model. The derived series tends to coincide with phases of excess boom and the end of recessions, respectively. It thus leads the turning points in the growth cycle. After determining the potential contributors to a leading indicator, the corresponding filtered series are combined in a single variable (H-Signal), which can be considered to perform reasonably well. The H-Signal outperforms the barometer of the Swiss Institute of Business Cycle Research in terms of a longer lead and less false signals in forecasting growth cycle phases. The proposed method can easily be applied to other countries.

[1] I would like to express my gratitude for many valuable comments that were offered by the participants of the 24th CIRET conference. Any inadequacies that remain are my responsibility.

1 Introduction

This paper presents the first results of attempts at the KOF/ETH[2] to design a leading indicator for turning points using Markov Switching Models (MSM) applied to business survey data (BSD) for the case of Switzerland. The key feature of such an indicator is the possibility to derive a quantitative measure for probabilities of being in a recession or boom and, therefore, to predict switches between the regimes. As the business survey data used as input for the model is not subject to revisions, forecasts are bound to be more stable. Furthermore, as business survey data has become available for most industrial countries over several business cycles, the proposed method could prove to be applicable for other countries as well.

The structure of the paper is as follows: In section 2 the motivation for the design of an additional indicator at the KOF/ETH is given. Section 3 strikes the issue of different possible reference series indicating phases of recession and boom, which can be used as a benchmark for the new indicator. Section 4 gives a brief outline of the methodology of Markov switching models followed by a description of the data and model specification used in this paper (section 5). After applying a measure of prediction performance on the markov-switching-filters (MS-filters) in section 6, a signal for turning points in growth cycles is constructed and its forecasting power is evaluated (section 7). The paper ends with the summarized findings and an outlook for future research (section 8).

2 Motivation

The forecasting of economic activity in general and the advance perception of turning points is one of the key interests of business cycle research. Early signals of recession or recovery are of great interest to businessmen, policy makers and investors. Two elements of analyzing this topics will be stressed here: (a) the desire to gain further information on turning points to assist the interpretation of existing indicators and (b) getting more insight into business survey data by means of a nonlinear methodology.

---

[2] Institute of Business Cycle Research at the Swiss University of Technology (Konjunkturforschungsstelle (KOF) an der Eidgenössischen Technischen Hochschule (ETH)), Zürich.

2.1 Further Information on Turning Points

Currently, the KOF/ETH uses mainly two instruments[3] to describe and predict the economic activity in Switzerland. Firstly, there is the 'macro model' which was developed by Stalder (1991) in the eighties. It uses input data from both the official statistics and business survey data and generates detailed quantitative forecasts on consumption, investment and other macro variables. Predictions are made in the form of quarterly growth rates for the following two years and are published twice a year. The second instrument is the 'KOF/ETH-Barometer' (Spörndli (1977), Spörndli (1978)), which aims to condense the information on the general economic situation into a single leading indicator. It was first introduced in the seventies, but has been subject to several revisions with respect to the input data and methods used.[4] The results are published monthly as a qualitative number with the characteristics of an index.

While both models give information on expected turning points as a by-product, it can be seen from experience that they suffer from past and ongoing revisions of the input data. It goes without saying that improving the quality of forecasts of turning points is not a specifically Swiss issue. McNees (1991) looked at the predictive performance of a number of reputable forecasting firms in the post-war period and found that the turning points derived from the analyzed forecasts were far from satisfactory. From this point of view it is desirable to gain access to additional information which is independent of the time-consuming revisions of official statistics and which helps to find a better understanding of already existing indicators. In this respect, this paper focuses on the task to find an additional indicator which is specifically oriented towards detecting turning points. The paper presents the first proposal for such an early warning indicator, which shall be used in the future as an additional source of information to support the turning point predictions made by the KOF-Macro-Model and the KOF-Barometer.

2.2 More Insight into the Statistical Properties of Business Survey Data

Business surveys have become increasingly popular and have been conducted in most industrialized countries covering several business cycles. In the endeavor to increase the benefits of this valuable source of

---

3 Other ways and concepts in forecasting business cycles are discussed in Tichy (1994) and Niemira (1994).

4 For the latest revision in 1997 see Marty (1998).

information for forecasting economic activity, the statistical properties of business survey data and its behavior over time have been examined in different ways.[5] Up to today, analysts often employed systems of leading and lagging indicators designed by means of linear methods such as correlations and spectral analysis.[6] The non-linear Markov switching approach used in this work will allow to look at business survey data from a different perspective: the time series are divided into periods of different economic states and the probability of staying in a specific regime is estimated (see section 4).

3 The Forecasting Benchmark: Dating Turning Points

Every approach to develop an early warning signal needs 'a workable definition of a turning point' as a benchmark, 'which is by no means a trivial problem' (Lahiri and Moore (1991) p.8). The dating of turning points is influenced by (a) the chosen cycle concept (b) the implementation of the concept and (c) the data to which it is applied.

3.1 Turning Point Concepts

Three turning point concepts shall be considered here:

- The Classical Business Cycles (CC) which define states between times when growth rates change sign and
- Growth cycles (GC), which define different states between points of extreme deviation from an average trend. The growth cycle concept goes back to the work of Mintz (1969), who describes the difference between CC and GC: 'In those instances in which an absolute decline in activity has occurred, (growth cycles dates) will tend to differ from dates selected on the basis of the classical business cycle concept. Downturns will come earlier, upturns later in trend-adjusted series with upward trends than in unadjusted series. Therefore upswings will be shorter and downswings longer than in classical cycles.' The more pronounced the trend the greater the difference between CC and GC. The economy of most industrialized countries show a increasing trend, so classical recessions are rare and the GC-Concept is nowadays the most popular.

---

5 For an overview see e.g. Zimmermann (1997).

6 For Swiss business survey data see e.g. Spörndli (1978).

- Finally the concept of acceleration and deceleration (AccDec) looks at points of extreme growth rates, i.e. mathematical points of inflection of the original series.

The above concepts are illustrated in Figure 1.1 using a hypothetical reference series.

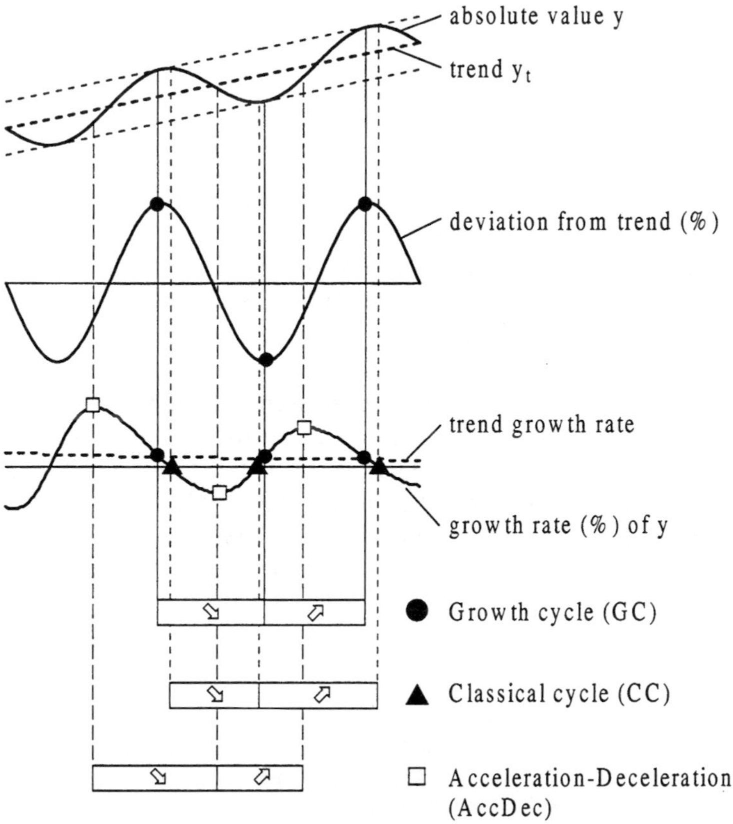

Figure 1.1 - Different Concepts for the Definition of Turning Points

3.2 Implementation of the Turning Point Concept

The implementation of the CC and the AccDec-Concept depends on the method of computing growth rates. A comprehensive discussion of different methods to compute growth rates can be found in Niemira (1994). The implementation of GC depends on the method to calculate the trend. The objective of all methods to calculate trends is to summarize the long-term pattern of development without eliminating too much of the structural information. One of the most popular techniques is the Hodrick-Prescott-Filter. The OECD uses the so called 'phase average trend' (PAT) which obeys the rules set by the Bry-Boschan procedure[7] to determine turning points with the growth cycle concept.[8]

In this paper the CC and AccDec-concept are applied to quarter-to-quarter growth rates and the GC-concept is applied to series smoothed by PAT.[9]

3.3 Series of Macroeconomic Performance - The Special Case of Switzerland

The business cycle concepts and their implementation define a method to date turning points. To derive a reference series they need to be applied to a time series which reflects macroeconomic performance. 'The single most important target variable in the OECD is GNP', but for reasons of comparison between different countries 'it was decided to settle on total industrial production (IP)[10] as the reference series' (OECD (1987)).

In the case of Switzerland three measures of performance are supplied from the official statistics which could be used as a reference series for dating turning points: (a) the GNP series valid today, which is adapted to the European System of Accounts ESA 1978 (GNP(ESA)). It was introduced in 1997 and is available from 1980; (b) the GNP series valid from 1970 to 1996 (GNP (OECE[11])) and (c) the industrial production (IP) available from 1970 to 1995.[12] In this paper the macroeconomic performance will be mainly represented by the GNP(ESA) (shorthand symbol GNP will be used).[13]

---

[7] The key feature on the Bry-Boschan technique of the turning point selection is the elimination of the following: (1) Turns within 6 months of beginning and end of series (2) Peaks (troughs) at both ends of series which are lower (higher) than values closer to end (3) Cycles shorter than 15 months (4) Phases shorter than 5 months (see Bry (1971)).

[8] It mainly consists of a 75-month centered moving average, where the NBER found for the US that 'it could be long enough to remove most of the cyclical fluctuation while leaving the underlying secular pattern intact' (OECD (1987)).

[9] Phase Average Trend Program - OECD Version 1995.

[10] The obvious disadvantage of the IP is that services which account for an ever-increasing percentage of economic performance are neglected.

[11] Organisation européennes de coopération économique (OECE).

[12] In 1995 a revised IP was introduced. Since this newer IP was only available since 1990 this series is too short for an analysis of turning points.

[13] Since this series is quite short for the analysis of turning points, the GNP(OECE) and IP were taken into account to substantiate the findings (see footnote 28 and 37). For the US Business cycle the NBER has a long tradition of dating turning points. For

4 The Markov Switching Model

Several attempts have been made to model the fact that in business cycles a long gradual expansion is usually followed by short steep contraction (asymmetry). It is usually assumed that the mechanisms governing the interrelations between different aspects of the macro-economy differ between the phases: 'There has been considerable interest in recent years in the question of whether the correlation properties of macroeconomic series differ across various phases of the 'business cycle'' (Mills (1991). Among the proposed approaches are the non-linear moving average considered by Robinson (1978), the model of Wecker (1981), and the algorithm of Neftçi (1982).[14] The latter algorithm was generalized by Hamilton (1989), who developed the Markov switching (MS-) approach based also on research by Quandt (1978).

For most techniques it is usually assumed that there is one[15] fixed data generating process throughout the whole sample period and over all phases of the business cycle. The significance of this assumption is reduced by the fact that model parameters may vary over time. The main feature of the MSM is that it allows for the different data generating processes for different states or regimes. Because the current state or regime cannot be directly observed,[16] it is necessary to deduce the probabilities with which a particular observation belongs to one of the different states or regimes. It is common to model two regimes which are interpreted as phases of expansion and contraction. For the MS-approach an iterative procedure using standard statistical techniques such as Bayes's rule and Markov chain dynamics will result in time series of probabilities which are indicative for the chances of being in one of the assumed states at any chosen point in time.

For the 2-regime case, a Markov switching model can be mathematically summarized by the following equations. Let y_t denote an observable

---

European countries the OECD collaborates with the different national bodies to assess business cycles turning points (see OECD (1987)). Dating of turning points for Switzerland are supplied by Béguelin (1976): CC in IP from 1950 to 1970; Spörndli (1977): GC in several macroeconomic series; OECD (1987): GC and CC in IP and GNP(OECE) for 1960 to 1983 and Amstad (forthcoming 1999): GC, CC, AccDec in GNP(ESA), GNP(OECE) and IP for 1970 to 1997.

14 For an important difference between Neftçi's and Hamiltons-approach see footnote 16.

15 Besides some unique structural exogenic breaks like a change of the monetary system.

16 According to Neftçi's model, the shifts can be observed directly and it is therefore not necessary to make a probabilistic inference about the underlying regimes as in the case of Hamilton's MS-models.

variable (e.g. the growth rate or 'balance' derived from BSD) in period t with t = 1,..,N. y_t is supposed to follow

$$y_t - \mu_{s^*_t} = \phi(y_{t-1} - \mu_{s^*_{t-1}}) + \varepsilon_t \qquad (1)$$

with $y_t | s_t \sim N(U_{s_t}, \Omega_{s_t})$ and an unobserved state variable s^*_t that assumes the value 1 for contraction and 2 for expansion.

$U_{s_t} = (\mu_1, \mu_2)$: mean value of the time series in expansion and contraction

$\Omega_{s_t} = (\sigma_1^2, \sigma_2^2)$: regime dependent variance-covariance matrix

This process entails two conditional densities, which are collected in a vector containing one element for each state or regime:

$$\eta_t = \begin{bmatrix} f(y_t | s_t = 1, \psi_{t-1}; \theta) \\ f(y_t | s_t = 2, \psi_{t-1}; \theta) \end{bmatrix} \qquad (2)$$

with the density-parameter vector $\theta = (\mu_1, \mu_{2,} \sigma_1^2, \sigma_2^2, \pi_1, \pi_2)$, containing the model parameters and the ergodic probabilities[17] $\pi_j = P(s_t = j), j = 1{,}2$, and ψ_{t-1} as a vector containing (N-1) observations y_t up to period (t-1).

In a Markov switching model the unobserved stochastic state variable s_t is assumed to follow an ergodic first-order[18] Markov chain with

[17] It can be shown that π is the eigenvector corresponding to the unit eigenvalue of P, which is unique for an ergodic Markov chain. Thus the ergodic probabilities π can be interpreted as the vector of unconditional probabilities.

[18] This means that the probability of s_t=j depends on the past only trough the lagged value s_{t-1}: $P(s_t = j | s_{t-1} = i, s_{t-2} = k, ...) = P(s_t = j | s_{t-1} = i) = p_{ij}$. Assuming a first order Markov process is not restrictive, as a N-state Markov process of order p can always be rewritten as a N^p-state first order Markov process.

$$P = \begin{bmatrix} p_{11} & p_{21} \\ p_{12} & p_{22} \end{bmatrix} = \begin{bmatrix} p_{11} & 1-p_{22} \\ 1-p_{11} & p_{22} \end{bmatrix}$$
$$\text{with} \quad P_t(s_t = j | s_{t-1} = i) = p_{ji} \qquad \text{i, j} = 1,2 \qquad (3)$$
$$\text{and} \sum_{j=1}^{2} p_{ij} = 1 \qquad i = 1,2$$

The inference about the value of s_t based on data trough observation t and knowledge of the population parameters θ is a conditional probability which is gathered in a Nx1-vector.

The optimal inference and forecast on $\hat{\xi}_{t|t}$ and $\hat{\xi}_{t+1|t}$ for each period t can be found by iterating trough the following equations:[19]

$$\hat{\xi}_{t|t} = \frac{\hat{\xi}_{t|t-1} \otimes \eta_t}{1'(\hat{\xi}_{t|t-1} \otimes \eta_t)} \qquad (4)$$
$$\hat{\xi}_{t+1|t} = P \cdot \hat{\xi}_{t|t}$$

The likelihood function L(θ) for the observed data evaluated at the value of θ that was used to perform the iterations can be calculated as a byproduct of the filter-algorithm:

$$L(\theta) = \sum_{t=1}^{T} \log f(y_t | \Psi_{t-1}; \theta) \quad \text{where } f(y_t | \Psi_{t-1}; \theta) = 1'(\hat{\xi}_{t|t-1} \otimes \eta_t) \quad (5)$$

MSMs can be further extended so that the transition probabilities, ARIMA parameters and the variance may depend on some exogenous information (e.g. to include duration dependence within a regime) or the regime itself.

Hamilton (1994a) gives a comprehensive treatment of Markov switching models. In another paper[20] he presents an intuitive way to understand MSM

[19] Given $\hat{\xi}_{1|0}$ and an assumed value for the population parameter vector θ. For a discussion of starting the algorithm see Hamilton (1994a), p.693.

[20] See Hamilton (1994b).

by introducing them as Kalman filters or state-space models.[21] Hamilton applied MSM with some success to the GNP of the USA. This encouraged a lot of research mainly with GNP or financial data and induced extensions and methodological refinements.

5 Application of MSM to Business Survey Data

In this paper business survey data (BSD) have been modeled using a Markov-Switching (MS) approach: Section 5.1 describes the used data and Section 5.2 the used model specification.

5.1 Used Business Survey Data

For this paper, data from the quarterly Swiss industry survey from 1970 to 1997 are used. Below, the 13 qualitative and two quantitative variables are listed. All qualitative questions yield data which are derived from the percentage of 'increasing/up/too high' over 'decreasing/down/too low' replies,[22] the so called balance. Answers that indicate a constant tendency ('unchanged/sufficient') are not taken into account, although they might provide further information on the economic activity.

Assessment

Q1 Employment compared with the previous quarter
Q2 Assessment of employment
Q4 Technical capacity compared with the previous quarter
Q5 Assessment of technical capacity
Q7 Stocks of material compared with the previous quarter
Q8 Assessment of stocks of material
Q9 Purchasing prices compared with the previous quarter
Q10 Selling prices at home compared with the previous quarter
Q11 Selling prices abroad compared with the previous quarter
Q12 Profit situation compared with the previous quarter

Expectation by the end of the next quarter

Q13 Purchasing prices
Q14 Selling prices expectations at home
Q15 Selling prices expectations abroad

Quantitative series

Q26 Share of overtime (in %)
Q27 Capacity utilisation (in %)

---

[21] This approach relates MS-models to the so called 'hidden Markov model' developed by Lindgren (1978).

[22] Weighted by the number of employees.

Composite indicator[23]

Q97 share of firms with upward trend (in %)
Q98 share of firms with stagnant trend (in %)
Q99 share of firms with downward trend (in %)

5.2 *Used Specification of Markov-Switching-Model*

Three MSM-AR-models with two states (MSM(2)) were considered as data generating processes: MSM(2)-AR(0), MSM(2)-AR(1) and MSM(2)-AR(4). The variance of innovative components in recessions and booms was assumed to be equal and a time-constant matrix of transition probabilities was used. The model thus allows for two regimes which generate data according to two normal distributions with different means and identical variance.

With most of the series, a 2-regime MSM with AR(0)-process[24] yields reasonable results. For all series the two regimes displayed clearly distinct means[25] and the recession probabilities derived from the BSD showed some correspondence with the recessions as defined by the 'growth cycle'-concept using the OECD-PAT method.

6 A Measure of Performance in Predicting Business Cycle Regimes

To analyze the usefulness of the estimated regime probabilities derived from business survey data in predicting the business cycle phases a measure of performance is required. So regions with 'increasing/up/too high'-regime probabilities larger than 0.5 are defined as states of contraction and those with probabilities less than 0.5 are defined as states of expansion.[26] Using this 50%-rule the recession probabilities $P(s_t = 1)$ for periods $t = 1 \ldots N$ are converted into a vector I_t of zeroes and ones

[23] Increasing, stagnating and decreasing business activity tendency are a combination of the series Q02 (Assessment of employment) and Q05 (Assessment of technical capacity) according to the following table:

upward trend		stagnant trend		downward trend	
Q02	Q05	Q02	Q05	Q02	Q05
too low	too low	too high	too low	sufficient	too high
too low	sufficient	too low	too high	too high	sufficient
sufficient	too low	sufficient	sufficient	too high	too high

[24] For some questions AR(1)-processes appear to give reasonable results as well, but for sake of brevity these will not be discussed here.

[25] A t-test for difference between these means was highly significant in all cases.

[26] The economic reasoning for this definition is given in section 7.

corresponding to expanding and contracting regimes, respectively. If the reference series is presented in a similar measure ($I_{R,t}$), the number of correctly classified quarters can be computed from

$$\text{Hit} = \sum_{t=1}^{n} \left| I_t + I_{R,t} - 1 \right| \text{ or as a frequency}$$

$$\text{Hit\%} = \frac{1}{n} \cdot \sum_{t=1}^{n} \left| I_t + I_{R,t} - 1 \right|$$

If the series I_t is shifted by k quarters with respect to the reference $I_{R,t}$, 'Hit' or 'Hit%' becomes a function of the shift k.

$$\text{Hit}(k) = \sum_{t=1}^{n-k} \left| I_{t+k} + I_{R,t} - 1 \right| \text{ for lags } k \geq 0 \text{ of series } I_t \text{ with respect to}$$

reference $I_{R,t}$ and

$$\text{Hit}(k) = \sum_{t=1}^{n+k} \left| I_t + I_{R,t-k} - 1 \right| \text{ for leads } k \leq 0 \text{ of series } I_t \text{ with respect}$$

to reference $I_{R,t}$

If only the number of correctly predicted states is used to compare the performance of different predictions, even notorious pessimists or optimists will score a certain number of hits if they choose to forecast recession or boom all the time. Hence the achieved number of hits is compared with one that indicates the expected hits for a random prediction. If the random predictor chooses recessions with probability α independently of the economic state and the reference series contains recessions with probability A, the probability that the random prediction for an individual quarter will be correct is

$$P_{\text{random hit}} = 1 - \alpha - A + 2 \cdot \alpha \cdot A = \text{Hit\%}_{\text{random}}$$

A measure for the difference between the prediction from the MS-Filter, which chooses recessions with probability α, and a random guess governed by chance is therefore

$$\text{Score\%} = \text{Hit\%} - \text{Hit\%}_{\text{random}}$$ [27]

Using Score%, the performance of the derived MS-filters from the BSD was determinated with reference to the GC, the CC and the AccDec-Concept applied to GNP. The best performance was reached with the GC-concept. Figure 1.2 shows the largest values of Score% for all series with the corresponding lag or lead to the GC-Concept in the GNP.

The achieved performance of the series differs depending upon the considered cycle concept. In conclusion, most of the MS-filters achieve the lowest value for Score% within the CC and the smallest lead with the AccDec concept. The majority of the MS-filters reach the best performance regarding the obtained value of Score% as well as the lead with the GC-Concept.[28] Since the MS-filters seem to correspond best with the pattern of boom and recession in the growth cycle, the analysis will concentrate on the investigation of the usefulness of the MS-filter to predict turning points in the growth cycle.

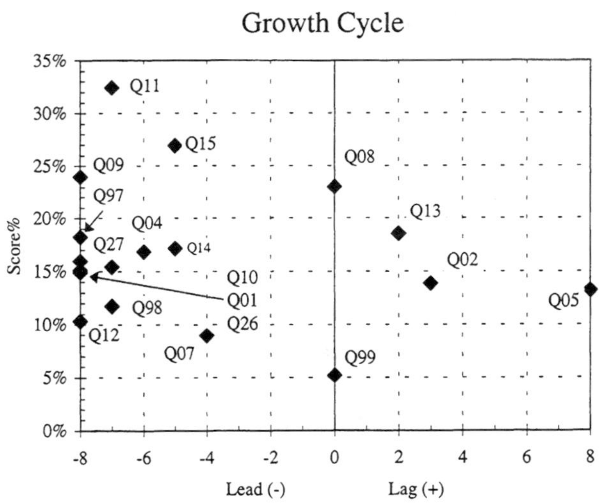

Figure 1.2a - Percentage of Correctly Classified Quarters

---

27 It should be noted that this method could be refined even further if the probability α and A are random entities as well. The distribution of random guesses can be calculated, and it is possible to assign probabilities for the observed scores based on the hypothesis of random guesses.

28 This conclusions remains the same when GNP (OECE) or IP are used instead of GNP (see section 3.3).

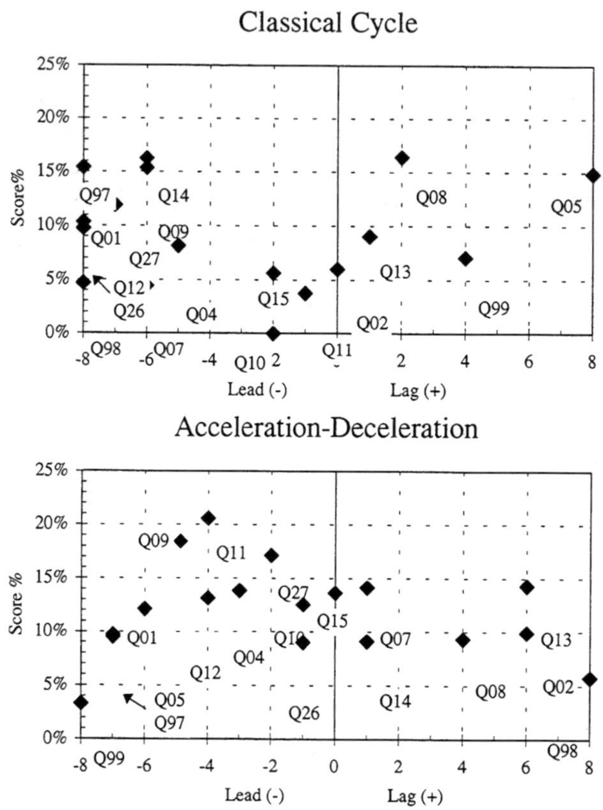

Figure 1.2b - Percentage of Correctly Classified Quarters Compared to a Random Guess (Score%) as a Function of (+8) Lag and (-8) Lead Quarters with Respect to the Growth Cycle, Classical Cycle and Acceleration-Deceleration in Swiss GNP.

7 Construction of a Signal for Turning Points in the Growth Cycle

With the help of Score% six series were chosen to build a leading indicator of turning points in the growth cycle: Q07, Q09, Q12, Q14, Q27 and Q97. In Figure 1.3, the series (dashed lines) are shown with their corresponding estimated MS-filter (solid line). The shaded areas indicate phases of recession according to the GC-concept applied to the Swiss GNP.

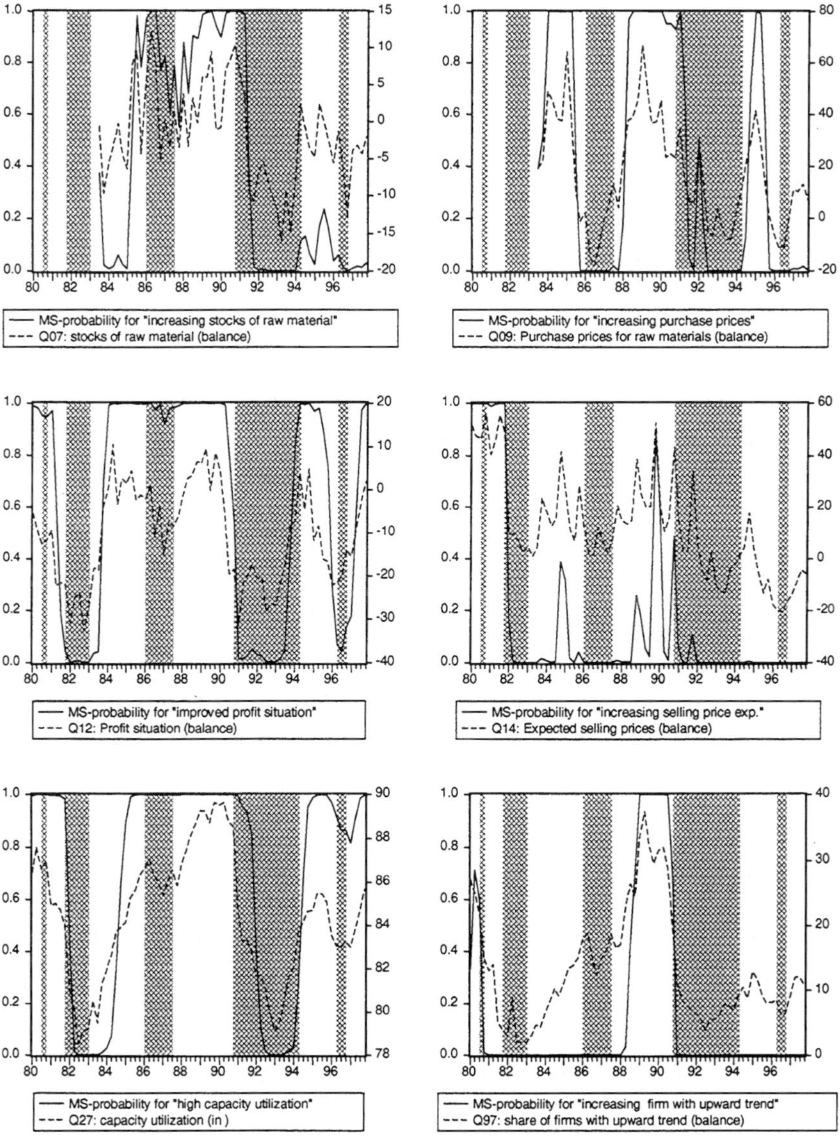

Figure 1.3 - Selected MS-Filter and Balances (Shaded Area: Recessions in Swiss GNP Growth Cycle)

In the following, an attempt to justify this technical choice of the six potential contributors to a leading indicator by economic reasoning is presented. The phase preceding a peak can be defined as a phase of economic 'strain' or 'overheating'. Similarly, the phase preceding a trough in the growth cycle could be seen as a situation with a small risk or probability of excess boom. The probability of an over-heated economy therefore leads the turning points in growth cycle, as it increases before a peak and decreases before a trough. The potential contributors to a leading indicator for growth cycle turning points appear to have the characteristic of an indicator which can be interpreted in the sense of a probability of strain or overheating:

(1) Overheating phases in the economic cycle are characterized by excess demand and the tendency to increase prices. An indicator of the price development is the entrepreneur's assessment of the purchase prices for raw materials and semi-manufactures (Q09). The MS-filter of Q09 switches into the 'high price'- regime when the corresponding balance is already quite high and a majority of the surveyed companies report increasing prices. On the other hand, the MS-filter or probability tends to switch into the regime with decreasing prices at a time when the balance is already quite low and the enterprises reporting price-curbing development are in a clear majority.

(2) The question on expectations regarding the development of the selling prices at home in the following quarter (Q14) appears to be answered with a pessimistic bias. Even in phases when the economic horizon lightens, there is but a low probability for the regime indicating an expectation of increasing selling prices. The duration in the regime 'decreasing price expectation' is therefore longer than that in the regime with 'increasing price expectation'. Only in periods just before a recession, when the economy is in high gear, the price expectations and thus the balance of Q14 rise high enough for the MS-filter to change it's state. On the other hand the enterprises seem to take back their price expectations as soon as a cooling of the economic activity shows up: The MS filters switches back to the regime with 'expectation of decreasing selling price' before a growth cycle recession occurs.

(3) The balance of the question on the profit situation (Q12) rises during boom phases. The MS-filter tends to change to the regime 'improved profit situation' when the balance is quite high, thus signaling a distinctive boom which has already progressed. However, the phase in the middle of the 1980s is an exception. Despite of a recession, the MS-filter remained in the

regime with 'improved profit situation' and the corresponding regime probability reduced only slightly, without dipping under the 0.5-limit.

(4) A further feature of overheating phases is a rise in the percentage of capacity utilization reported by the enterprises (Q27). Here the MS filter, according to its nature as a form of low-pass filters, tends to change only to the regime with high capacity utilization when the reported percentage is already quite high and the machines are 'running hot'. On the other hand, the MS-filter changes to the regime with low capacity utilization when the firms report a rather low capacity utilization. This switch may herald the coming end of the recession.

(5) From Q02 and Q05 of the quarterly business survey, the KOF/ETH calculates a combined indicator '% of firms with increasing business activity' (Q97).[29] The corresponding MS-Filter tends to be high in the final phase of a boom. At the end of a recession, the reported percentage of firms with increasing business activity tends to fall and the filter drops to low values.

(6) Not each phase in which the economic situation 'runs hot' leads to a recession. Only if the signals of overheated economic activity coincide with early signs of softness in demand or an excess supply can one conclude, that a boom is in its final state and will in the long run lead into a recession. Before a decline in demand is registered in the books and expresses itself in the profit situation, a tendency to overstock can be observed. If the enterprises report an increasing stock of raw materials and semi-manufactures (Q07) compared with the previous quarter, this can be seen as a first signal that sales were smaller than the enterprises expected. If the MS-filter changes into the regime with high stocks, the risk of an ending boom increases. On the other hand, a small probability for a excess boom together with a change of the MS filter to the regime with decreasing stocks indicates that a cooling of the economy will probably reach an end.

[29] see footnote 23.

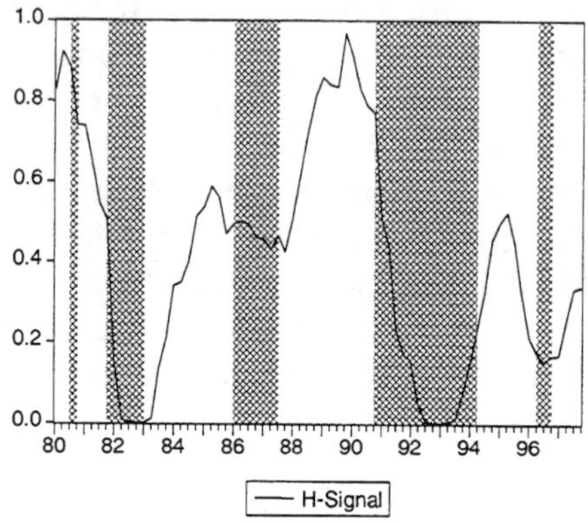

Figure 1.4 - Risk of Overheating Given By the Markov-Switching Signal H (Shaded Area Indicates Recession)

The above interpretation shows that six series used to build the H-signal could be interpreted to signal a economic constellation which coincides with the phase at the end of a boom or contraction and therefore leads the turning points in the growth cycle.

Each series reflects some information on the probability of turning points of the growth cycle, but none of them could be used as a reliable indicator of growth cycle recessions on its own. The series are therefore combined to the signal 'H' by calculating the mean of the MS-filters.

Figure 1.4 shows the values of the signal H compared to the turning points of the growth cycle in the Swiss economy (shaded areas indicate recessions). It gives a first impression of a leading indication of phases of recession (shaded areas) and an increase of signal H. Although a qualitative impression of the path of a recession probability may be quite useful, a strict rule is required to determine turning points. In the following, a simple '50%-rule' was applied: a peak P (trough T) is assigned to the quarter following a value of H increasing (decreasing) above (below) the 50%-mark. In Table 1.1 the resulting turning points are compared to those determined by the growth-cycle concept in GNP.

During the covered period (80:1 to 97:4) the H-signal predicts turning points with an average lead of 6 quarters with reference to the growth cycle in GNP. Two turning points were missed and two extra turning points were indicated. If a lead of 0 is assigned in theses cases, the average lead is reduced to about 4 quarters.

In addition to the average lead, another criterion to judge the performance of the prediction is the frequency of false predictions (Table 1.2). For an assessment, both the absolute number of false predictions and the relative frequency of false predictions can be considered (so called 'noise-to-signal–ratio').[30] For the H-signal, four false signals occurred during a period with 10 effective turning points. The resulting noise-to-signal-ratio is therefore 40%.

Table 1.1 - Comparison MS-Prediction and Dating According to GC-Concept Applied to GNP

	Growth Cycle GNP[31]	*H-Signal*[32]	*(+) Lead/(-) Lag*[33] *(Quarters)*	
P	80.2	79.4	2	
T	80.4	no	-	
P	81.3	no	-	
T	83.1	82.1	4	
P	85.4	84.4	4	
T	87.3	85.4	7	
P	no	86.2	-	
T	no	86.3	-	
P	90.3	88.1	10	
T	94.2	91.2	12	
P	96.1	95.2	3	
T	96.4	95.3	5	
			Unweighted	Error-weighted[34]
Mean			5.9	3.9
P			4.7	3.2
T			7.0	4.7

[30] The noise-to-signal-ratio can obtain any value above zero. The lower the noise-to-signal-ratio the better the performance. As the noise-to-signal-ratio can exceed 100% when many false predictions occur, it should not be confused with a probability to make false predictions.

[31] All turning points detected by PAT (see section 13.3).

[32] A peak P (trough T) is assigned to the quarter following a value of H increasing (decreasing) above (below) the 50%-mark.

[33] A positive (resp. negative) sign indicates that the turning point in the H-Signal appears before (after) the growth cycle peak or trough.

[34] Missing and extra signals are penalized by a lead of zero.

Table 1.2 - Extra and Missing Growth Cycle Signals Given by H-Signal

	P	**T**	*Total*
Extra signals	1	1	2
Missed signals	1	1	2
Total	2	2	4

To compare the forecasting performance of the H-Signal, the lead and the noise-to-signal-ratio of the KOF/ETH-Barometer (see section 2.1) in signaling growth cycle is shown in Table 1.3 and Table 1.4. To determine turning points with the barometer, the KOF/ETH usually uses the well-known rule proposed by Zarnowitz. After a change in direction, the third repeated step in this direction is considered as confirmation for that change, and a turning point is indicated. Table 1.3 summarizes the dates when turning points are perceived.[35]

Table 1.3 and Table 1.4 show that the H-signal is superior to the barometer in predicting growth cycle turning points in two respects: The error-weighted mean lead of the barometer on turning points is 1.5 quarters. However, the even more important disadvantage of the barometer as against the H-signal is the relatively high rate of false signals. During a period with 6 turning points in GNP, the barometer gives 8 false signals, namely in the form of extra signals (noise-to-signal-ratio = 133%).[36] The advantage of predictions of turning points derived from the barometer is the more stable lead.

---

[35] The ex post dated turning points lie (as a consequence of the Zarnowitz rule) three months before the listed date.

[36] These findings remain the same when GNP (OECE) or IP are used instead of GNP (see section 3.3).

Table 1.3 - Comparison KOF/ETH-Barometer and Dating According to GC-Concept

	Growth Cycle GNP	*Barometer*	*(+) Lead/(-) Lag (Quarters)*	
P	no	84.2	-	
T	no	84.3	-	
P	85.4	85.2	2	
T	no	85.4	-	
P	no	86.1	-	
T	87.3	87.1	2	
P	no	88.1	-	
T	no	88.1	-	
P	90.3	89.2	5	
T	no	91.2	-	
P	no	92.1	-	
T	94.2	93.1	5	
P	96.1	94.3	6	
T	96.4	96.3	1	
			Unweighted	Error-weighted[37]
Mean			3.5	1.5
P			4.3	1.9
T			2.7	1.1

Table 1.4 - Extra and Missing Growth Cycle Signals Given by the KOF/ETH-Barometer

	P	**T**	*Total*
Extra signals	4	4	8
Missed signals	0	0	0
Total	4	4	8

8 Conclusions and Outlook

This paper aims to evaluate, whether the use of the MS-models applied to business survey data improves the prediction of turning points. The results

[37] Missing and extra signals are penalized by a lead of zero.

of two quantitative and the balances of 13 qualitative questions derived from the quarterly Swiss industry survey were converted to a dichotomous signal by using Hamilton's Markov Switching Model. The derived series tends to coincide with phases of excess boom and the end of recessions respectively. It thus leads the turning points in the growth cycle. After determining the potential contributors to a leading indicator, the corresponding filtered series were combined into a single variable (H-Signal). The mean lead of the H-signal amounts to four quarters. Covering a period with ten turning points in GNP, four false signals occur. For comparison, the lead of the KOF/ETH-Barometer currently used is two quarters, and covering a period with six turning points, eight extra signals were detected. Because the variance of the lead of the barometer is smaller, it would be advisable to use the barometer as a confirmation indicator together with the longer leading and more accurate H-Signal.

A two step strategy seems to be reasonable: First the H-Signal could be used to indicate the risk of overheated economy and the probability of an end of recession. The signal is quite accurate, but the lead on the growth cycle turning points varies to some extent. The barometer could then be used to signal an acceleration or deceleration of the economy as a necessary but not sufficient condition for growth cycle turning-points. If both indicators agree that a turning point is detected, one can benefit from the accuracy of the H-signal and the stable lead of the barometer.

Future research should extend the application of the described methodology in several ways: Besides the application to other countires, the extension on surveys including service sectors should be considered. Furthermore, even though the used specification of the Markov Switching Model has proven to be appropriate, more elaborate[38] models could be used to test whether the constancy of the signal's lead can be improved. The same may also be achieved with a refinement of the 50%-rule which decides on the timing of turning points on the signal gained from the Markov-Switching-Filters.

---

[38] E.g. following Batchelor (1997) using time-varying transition probabilities or Layton (1997), who introduced a third regime.

References

Amstad, M. (2000), *Konjunkturelle Wendepunkte: Datierung und Prognose - Markov Switching Modelle mit Schweizer Umfragedaten*, Dissertation an der Universität St. Gallen.

Batchelor, R. (1997), *Confidence Indexes and the Macroeconomy: A Markov Switching Model*, Paper presented to the 23rd CIRET conference, Helsinki.

Béguelin, J.P. (1976), *Indicateurs statistiques de la conjuncture suisse. Essai sur la signification conjuncturelle des statistiques économiques suisses*, Genfer Dissertation, Bern: Haupt.

Bry, D. and C. Boschan (1971), *Cyclical Analysis of Time Series, Selected Procedures and Computer Programs*, NBER.

Hamilton, J.D. (1989), 'A New Approach to the Economic Analysis of Nonstationary Time Series and the Business Cycle', *Econometrica*, Vol. 57, pp. 357-384.

Hamilton, J.D. (1994a), *Time Series Analysis*, Princeton, Princeton University Press.

Hamilton, J.D. (1994b),'State Space Models', in: McFadden, R.F. and Engle D.L. (eds), *Handbook of Econometrics*, Volume IV.

Lahiri, Kajal, and Geoffrey H. Moore (eds) (1991), 'Introduction', *Leading economic indicators: new approaches and forecasting records*, Cambridge University Press.

Layton, A. P. (1997), *A further note on the three phases of the business cycle*, Paper presented to the 23rd CIRET conference, Helsinki.

Lindgren, Georg (1978), 'Markov Regime Models for Mixed Distributions and Switching Regressions', *Scandinavian Journal of Statistics*, Vol. 5, pp. 81-91.

Marty, Rudolf (1998), 'Revision des KOF/ETH-Konjunkturbarometers: Ziel, Methode, Ergebnisse', *Konjunktur, Monatsberichte der Konjunkturforschungsstelle der ETHZ*, 61(6).

McNees, S.K. (1991), 'Forecasting cyclical turning points: the record in the past three recessions', in: Lahiri K. and G. H. Moore (eds), *Leading Economic Indicators: New Approach and Forecasting Records*, Cambridge, Cambridge University Press.

Mills, T. (1991), 'Nonlinear Time Series Models in Economics', *Journal of Economic Surveys*, Vol. 5, No 3, pp. 215-242.

Mintz, Ilse (1969), *Dating Postwar Business Cycle: Methods and their Application to Western Germany, 1950-67*, Occasional Paper No. 107, NBER.

Neftçi, S. (1982), 'Optimal Prediction of Cyclical Downturns', *Journal of Dynamics and Control*, pp. 225-241.

Niemira, M. P. and P. A. Klein (1994), *Forecasting financial and economic cycles*, New York; Chichester and Toronto: Wiley.

OECD (1987), *OECD leading indicators and business cycles in member countries 1960-1985, Sources and Methods, No 39*, Paris: OECD.

Quandt, R. E. and J. B. Ramsey (1978), 'Estimating Mixtures of Normal Distributions and Switching Regressions: Rejoinder', *Journal of the American Statistical Association*, 73, pp. 751-752.

Robinson, P.M. (1978), 'Estimation of a nonlinear moving average process', *Journal of Stochastic Processes*, Vol. 3, pp. 135-156.

Spörndli, Erich and Catherine Bauer (1977), 'Indikatoren für die Konjunkturschwankungen der schweizerischen Volkswirtschaft seit dem zweiten Weltkrieg', *Konjunktur - Aus der Forschung*, edited by KOF/ETH.

Spörndli, Erich and Willy Roth (1978), 'Eine Vor- und Nachlaufhierarchie für Schweizerische Konjunkturindikatoren: Ergebnisse der Wendepunkt-Analyse und Überprüfung der vorlaufenden Indikatoren mittels Frequenzbereichs-Methoden', *Konjunktur - Aus der Forschung*, edited by KOF/ETH.

Stalder, Peter (1991), *Regime Transitions, Spillovers and Buffer Stocks: Analysing the Swiss Economy by Means of a Disequilibrium Model*, Lectures Notes in Econometrics and Mathematical Systems, Springer Verlag.

Tichy, G. (1994), *Konjunktur, stilisierte Fakten, Theorie, Prognose*, Springer Verlag.

Wecker, W.E. (1981), 'Asymmetric time series', *Journal of American Statistical Association*, Vol. 76, pp. 16-21.

Zimmermann, Klaus F. (1997), 'Analysis of Business Surveys', in: Pesaran M.H. and P. Schmidt, *Handbook of Applied Econometrics - Microeconometrics*.

2 The Lead Profile and other Non-parametric Tools to Evaluate Survey Series as Leading Indicators

ANIRVAN BANERJI

1 Testing for Cyclical Leads

The hallmark of a cyclical leading indicator is the property that its cyclical turning points lead cyclical turning points in the economy. However, there are no well-known methods to test whether these leads are statistically significant.

It has long been recognized that leading indicators can be a valuable forecasting tool for forecasting cyclical turning points. However, they have not always been properly evaluated. One method of evaluating leading indicators that has gained some popularity in recent years is the Granger causality test. It is thus interesting to note what Granger and Newbold (1986) have to say about the difficulty of evaluating the index of leading indicators (LEI):

> The index of leading indicators has become a widely quoted and generally trusted forecasting tool. However, it has been rather misinterpreted. The index is intended only to forecast the timing of turning points and not the size of the forthcoming downswing or upswing nor to be a general indicator of the economy at times other than near turning points. Because of this, evaluation of the (LEI) by standard statistical techniques is not easy.

This difficulty in evaluation has often led to flawed assessments of the performance of leading indicators, not necessarily based on their ability to anticipate turning points. Part of the problem has been a lack of familiarity with the standard methods of identifying turning points.

Yet, since leading indicators are meant primarily to forecast business cycle turning points, the identification of turning points in time series is a sine qua non for an appropriate evaluation of their forecasting performance. In fact, an objective algorithm for turning point identification, based on a systematic codification of the judgmental procedures used for decades at the NBER, was devised almost three decades ago (Bry and Boschan, 1971), shortly after the creation of the LEI. The Bry-Boschan procedure has certainly stood the test of time.

Geoffrey Moore, who helped create the LEI (Moore and Shiskin, 1967), used the Bry-Boschan procedure extensively in the decades following its creation (e.g., Klein and Moore, 1985). Other users have included King and Plosser (1989), who provide a description of the procedure. Watson (1994) points out that the Bry-Boschan procedure provides a good way to define turning points since it is based on objective criteria for determining cyclical peaks and troughs.

The objective (though not mathematically simple) definition of turning points given by Bry and Boschan's algorithmic formulation of the classical NBER procedure makes it possible to evaluate the performance of leading indicators in terms of an objective measure of the leads of leading indicators at turning points. In that sense, the Bry-Boschan procedure permits a more appropriate evaluation of the performance of leading indicators.

Given the cyclical turning points of a potential leading indicator, it is possible to measure the lead of that indicator at each business cycle turning point. However, many leading indicators cover only a small number of cycles. Thus the evaluation of leading indicators by parametric statistical methods is usually constrained by the limited number of cyclical turning points covered by the data. In addition, the need to make a heroic assumption that the probability distribution of the leads has a standard functional form also precludes the use of parametric tests of statistical significance.

This paper suggests simple nonparametric tests to evaluate the cyclical leads of leading indicators, and introduces lead profile charts that graphically depict these leads in probabilistic terms, to aid in the selection and evaluation of leading indicators.

2 The Problem

A number of considerations go into the evaluation of any time series as a cyclical leading indicator. There are at least two criteria on which survey series usually excel: One, unlike many other potential leading indicators, they are typically never revised; and two, they are very promptly available.

However, survey series must still be evaluated on the magnitude and variability of their leads compared with a reference cycle (such as the business cycle) at cyclical turns, as well as their leads compared with one another when two or more survey series are being compared. In all of these cases, the magnitude (and even the direction) of the lead may vary from one turn to the next. The issue, then, is the statistical significance of the leads, or of the difference in leads, as the case may be. Another major issue is the difference in the variability of the leads of two potential leading indicators that may have roughly the same magnitude of lead.

We have cited Granger and Newbold (1986) who suggest, in effect, that standard statistical approaches to the evaluation of leading indicators may be fraught with problems. The simpler classical approach of just measuring the mean and standard deviation of the leads does not result in tests of statistical significance without an assumption that the probability distribution of the leads has a standard functional form. Thus, no tests of significance can usually be performed. Under such circumstances, simple nonparametric tests may be the most appropriate solution.

3 Appropriate Non-parametric Test

Nonparametric tests are often called 'distribution-free' because they do not assume that the observations were drawn from a population distributed in a certain way, e.g., from a normally distributed population. These tests also do not require the large samples needed to reliably estimate parameters of distributions assumed in parametric tests. Such tests should therefore be uniquely suited to testing the significance of leads, which may be small in number, and for which the probability distribution function is quite unknown.

Since the leads in question are differences in timing at cyclical turns (between a pair of indicators, for example), the appropriate nonparametric tests are those applicable to matched pairs of samples. The most powerful tests in this class assume interval scaled data (like temperature in degrees Celsius) where equal intervals at any point in the scale imply equal differences. Leads measured in months or quarters are at least interval scaled, so such tests can be used with data on leads.

The most appropriate test to assess the significance of leads within this class is the Randomization test for matched pairs. This test has a power-efficiency of 100%, because it uses all the information in the sample (Siegel, 1956), but it does not lend itself to manual computation for sample sizes greater than about nine pairs. (For an example of a manual application and computational considerations see Appendix.) In such cases, a simple computer program can be used.

One alternative is the Wilcoxon matched-pairs signed-ranks test (Wilcoxon, 1945), which assumes that the data are at least ordinal, has a power-efficiency of 95% (Mood, 1954), and can be performed manually up to sample sizes of 25 pairs.

There is a much smaller choice of tests for the difference in the variability of leads. One appropriate test is the Moses test, which is based on the pooled ranks of the leads of the two leading indicators being compared.

4 The Randomization Test for Matched Pairs

The Randomization test (Fisher, 1935) is a simple and elegant way to test the significance of leads. It is easy to use manually for sample sizes under 10, and a simple computer program can be used for larger sample sizes, so a description of the procedure and rationale should be instructive.

The first step is to calculate the difference in timing at turns, that is, the leads of one indicator over another, or over the business cycle turning points. The null hypothesis, that these differences are not statistically significant, is to be tested against the alternative hypothesis that the leads are significant.

Now, some of the differences calculated in the first step may be positive, others negative. If the null hypothesis is true, the positive differences are just as likely to have been negative, and vice versa. So if there are N differences (from N pairs of observations), each difference is as likely to be positive as negative. Thus, the observed set of differences would be just one of 2^N equally likely outcomes under the null hypothesis.

Also, under the null hypothesis, the sum of the positive differences would, on average, equal the sum of the negative differences, so the expected sum of the positive and negative differences would be zero. If the alternative hypothesis were true, and the leads were positive and significant, the sum would very likely be positive.

The second step, therefore, is to sum the differences, assigning positive signs to each difference; then to switch the signs systematically, one by one, to generate all the outcomes which result in sums as high or higher than that observed. If there are R such outcomes, then the probability of the observed outcome (or a more extreme outcome) under the null hypothesis is $(R/2^N)$. In other words, the null hypothesis can be rejected at the $100(1-(R/2^N))\%$ confidence level.

5 Lead Profiles

So far, the discussion has focused on the confidence level at which the null hypothesis ('leads not significantly different from zero') can be rejected in favor of the alternative hypothesis ('leads significantly greater than zero months'). Now, even if it is established that the leads are significantly greater than zero months, it might be interesting to know how much greater than zero months the leads are likely to be – for example, whether the leads are also significantly greater than one month.

This is easy to determine. All one needs to do is to subtract one month from each of the differences in timing at turns (already calculated in the first step of the Randomization test). Then, as before, one finds the confidence level at which the null hypothesis is rejected in favor of the alternative hypothesis that the difference in timing at turns significantly exceeds one month.

In this way one can also determine the confidence levels for the hypotheses that the leads exceed 2,3,4, ... K months – simply by subtracting 2,3,4, ... K respectively from the original differences before performing the Randomization test. We call this full set of confidence levels a 'lead profile'.

Ordinarily, it would be rather tedious to calculate the lead profile for each indicator against business cycle turning points or against another indicator. But this happens to be the kind of computation ideally suited to a computer program, and our program typically computes a complete lead profile in a few seconds.

The lead profile can also be graphically represented in bar charts or 'lead profile charts'. Figure 2.1 is the lead profile chart for the lead of the University of Michigan's Consumer Expectations Index compared with the Conference Board's version at business cycle troughs. The question answered by this chart is whether the difference between the leads of the two indexes is statistically significant. The lead profile is a graphical depiction of the leads in strictly probabilistic terms, that aids meaningful comparisons between the indexes. It is clear from this chart that the difference between the leads is not statistically significant, since the confidence level that the Michigan index leads the Conference Board Index is only 20%.

Figure 2.2 depicts the lead profile of the National Association of Purchasing Management (NAPM) Index compared with U.S. business cycle turns. It shows that there is a 95% confidence level that the lead of this index at business cycle turns is at least seven months.

Similarly, Figure 2.3 shows the lead profile of the NAPM New Orders Diffusion Index against U.S. business cycle turns. It also shows that there is a 95% confidence level that the lead of this index at business cycle turns is at least seven months.

Figure 2.4 depicts the lead profile of the NAPM Production Diffusion Index against U.S. business cycle turns. It shows that there is a 95% confidence level that the lead of this index at business cycle turns is at least six months.

Figure 2.5 depicts the lead profile of the NAPM Inventory Diffusion Index against U.S. business cycle turns. It shows that there is a 95% confidence level that the lead of this index at business cycle turns is at least three months.

While these lead profiles show primarily the confidence level in different durations of lead, the rapidity of the decline also casts some light on the variability of the lead. For example, the lead profile of the overall NAPM Index (Figure 2.2) shows a drop of only 46% between six and 12 months. The corresponding number is 67% for the NAPM Production Diffusion Index (Figure 2.4), 71% for the NAPM Inventory Diffusion Index (Figure 2.5), and 80% for the NAPM New Orders Diffusion Index (Figure 2.3). In that sense, the leads of the latter indexes are clustered more closely than they are for the overall index.

However, the lead profile does not provide a formal statistical test of the difference in the variability of the leads of two indexes. An appropriate nonparametric test for that purpose is the Moses test.

6 The Moses Test

The Moses test (Moses, 1952) is designed for a situation when there may not be any significant difference in central tendency between two samples (e.g., the leads of two competing leading indicators), but the leads of one may be more spread out or variable than the other. Thus, even if the lead profile does not reveal any significant difference in the leads of two cyclical leading indicators, the leads of one indicator may be less variable than the leads of the other.

The Moses test focuses on the span or the spread of the leads with which the comparison is being made. Thus, if there are n_C such leads, and there are n_E leads of the 'experimental' leading indicator being compared to the reference series, the $n_E + n_C$ leads are arranged in order of increasing size. If the null hypothesis, that the leads of the two indicators come from the same population, is true, the Es and Cs should be well mixed in the ordered series.

Under the null hypothesis, therefore, the very long leads, the very short leads, as well as the moderate leads, should all contain a mixture of Es and Cs. Under the alternative hypothesis, most of the Es will be low, or most of the Es will be high, or most of the Es will be low or high with the Cs concentrated in the middle. Under these three conditions, the Cs will be concentrated at the high end, the low end, and the middle region, respectively. The Moses test determines whether the Cs are so closely compacted or congested relative to the $n_E + n_C$ leads as to call for a rejection of the null hypothesis that both Es and Cs come from the same population.

To perform the Moses test, the leads from the E and C indicators are combined and arranged in a single ordered series, retaining the identity of each lead as having come from the C indicator or the E indicator. Then the span of the C leads is determined by noting the lowest and highest C leads and counting the number of leads between them, including both extremes. Thus the span s' is defined as the smallest number of consecutive leads in an ordered series needed to include all the C leads. Since the sampling distribution of s' is known (Moses, 1952), it may be used for tests of significance.

Because s' is essentially the range of the C leads, and the range is known to be unstable, the modification suggested by Moses is to pick an arbitrary small number h, in advance of the analysis. A value such as 1 or 2 is typical. Then, the span s_h of the C leads is determined after dropping the h most extreme C ranks. Then,

$$g = s_h - (n_C - 2h) \tag{1}$$

The probability under the null hypothesis of observing the observed value of s_h or less is:

$$p\ (s_b \leq n_c - 2h + g) = \frac{\sum_{i=0}^{g} \binom{i + n_C - 2h - 2}{i} \binom{n_E + 2h + 1 - i}{n_E - i}}{\binom{n_C + n_E}{n_C}} \tag{2}$$

If p is smaller than or equal to the significance level, the null hypothesis is rejected in favor of the alternative hypothesis that the E leads are more spread out than the C leads.

As shown in part C of the Appendix, when the Moses test is conducted on the consumer expectations survey series produced by the University of Michigan and the Conference Board, respectively, it shows no significant difference in the spread of their leads at U.S. business cycle turning points. Specifically, the probability is 0.84 that the observed leads would have been observed given the null hypothesis that the spread of the leads of the two indicators is the same. In the case of a comparison between the NAPM Index and the NAPM New Orders Diffusion Index (calculations not shown), the comparable probability is less than 0.13. While this is not statistically significant, it is certainly very suggestive that the leads of the New Orders Index are less spread out than those of the overall index. Given that for both, the lead profiles show the confidence level for a lead of seven months (but no higher) to be above 95%, and both have a median lead of eight months at business cycle turns, the New Orders Index may be preferred as a leading indicator to the overall index. The Moses test allows such distinctions to be made on the basis of a formal statistical test.

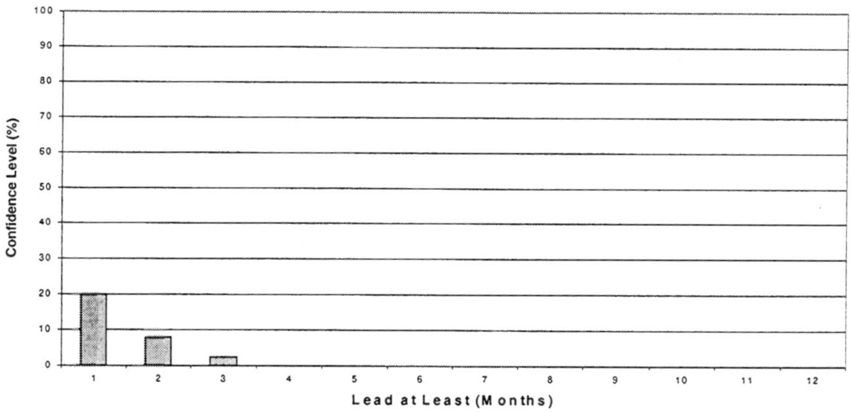

Figure 2.1 - Lead Profile: Lead of Univ. of Michigan Consumer Expectations Over Conference Board Consumer Expectations

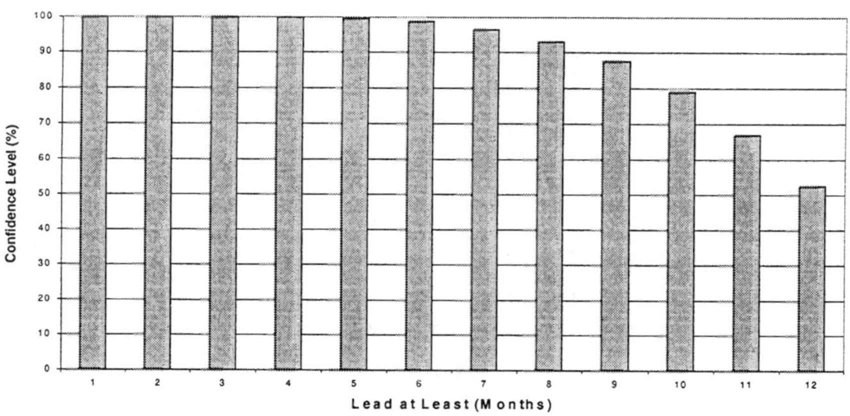

Figure 2.2 - Lead Profile of NAPM Index: Lead Over U.S. Business Cycle Turns

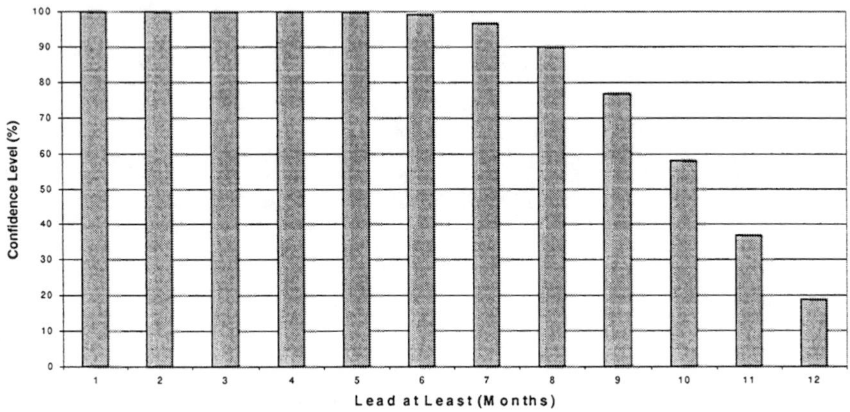

Figure 2.3 - NAPM New Orders Diffusion Index: Lead Over U.S. Business Cycle Turns

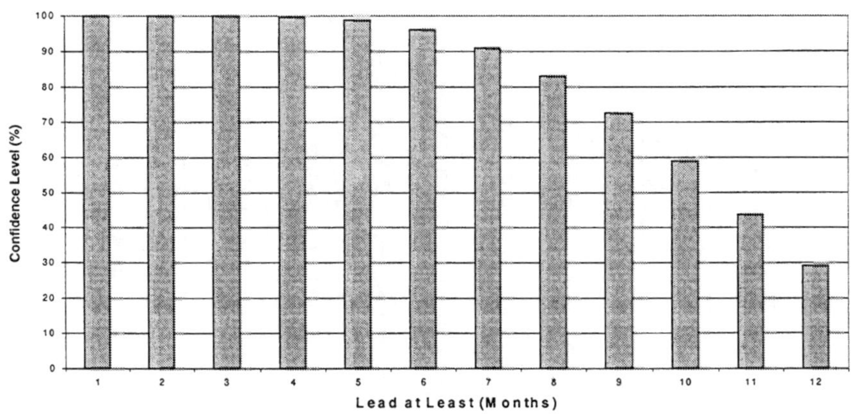

Figure 2.4 - Lead Profile of NAPM Production Diffusion Index: Lead Over U.S. Business Cycle Turns

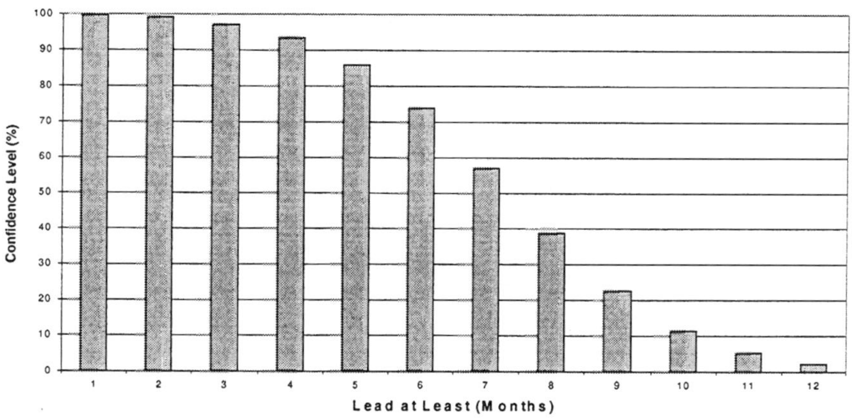

Figure 2.5 - Lead Profile of NAPM Inventory Diffusion Index: Lead Over U.S. Business Cycle Turns

7 Conclusions

Lead profile charts use as input just the information on the length of the leads at each turning point. However, by gleaning statistical inferences from the data rather than relying solely on averages, and by displaying the results graphically, they afford additional insights into the significance of leads.

The lead profile concentrates on the magnitude of leads, and can test whether the lead of one time series is significantly greater than another's. It cannot, however, tell whether there is a significant difference in the variability of the leads of two time series that do not have significantly different leads. The Moses test is well suited for that purpose, and can therefore supplement lead profiles in evaluating cyclical indicators.

Lead profile charts do not directly address the issue of extra cycles or missed turns, as they start with just the matched pairs of observations. However, in the case of missed turns, the exclusion of potential data points results in a smaller sample size, and a consequent reduction in the confidence level, which is appropriately conservative.

The major advantage of lead profiles lies in the explicit statistical inferences that can be made about the significance of leads without making any assumptions about the probability distribution of leads, or any restrictions on sample size. These inferences can be made about the leads of a given cyclical indicator over a reference cycle, such as a set of business cycle turning points. They can also be made about the leads of one cyclical indicator over another, to assess whether one has significantly longer leads than the other. Moreover, it is convenient to put lead profiles in the form of bar charts, for easy and effective visual appraisal of the significance of lengths of leads.

The magnitude and variability of the leads are perhaps the two most important factors in the evaluation of survey series as leading indicators. Given the ease of using these simple yet powerful statistical tools for evaluating cyclical leads, there is a strong case for using them routinely whenever the performance of a leading indicator needs to be assessed.

8 Appendix

A *Using the Randomization Test to Test the Significance of Leads of a Hypothetical Leading Indicator over Business Cycle*

The leads at troughs of this indicator compared to the business cycle troughs are 12, 4, 1, 0 and -27 months. The last figure represents a lag of 27 months. Although the convention is to use negative numbers for leads, and positive numbers for lags, it is simpler for the purpose of this exposition to think of leads as being positive, because we are, in general, concerned with the significance of leads, not lags.

The first step is to drop the zero-month lead from the analysis; keeping this observation would make no difference to the results, as is evident from the procedure for the Randomization test. Then N = 4, and the 4 observations are (12, 4, 1, -27), which add up to a sum of S = -10.

This sum S is now compared with the sums computed by starting with all positive numbers, and switching signs one by one so that the sums are in descending order until our sum of S = 10 is reached:

12	4	1	27	Sum = 44
12	4	-1	27	Sum = 42
12	-4	1	27	Sum = 36
12	-4	-1	27	Sum = 34
12	4	1	27	Sum = 20
12	4	-1	27	Sum = 18
12	-4	1	27	Sum = 12
12	-4	-1	27	Sum = 10
12	4	1	-27	Sum = -10 = S

Since R = 9 sums out of 24 (i.e. 16) possible combinations are greater than or equal to -10, the probability of such an outcome under the null hypothesis ('leads not significant') is 9/16 = 0.5625, so that the null hypothesis can be rejected only at the 100 (1-0.5625)% = 43.75% level of confidence. Hence, the null hypothesis is accepted for leads at troughs.

B Computational Considerations

The randomization test can be performed manually if the number of matched pairs is less than ten, as is often the case with turning points. For example, if the hypothesis needs to be tested at the 95% confidence level, the number of sums that need to be computed for nine matched pairs of observations is at most 5% of 29, that is 26, and possibly fewer. But the computational load increases with the lowering of the confidence level of the test, and increases exponentially with sample size. Also, the order in which signs are switched is important since the sums must be in descending order, and this complicates the procedure even further for large samples.

A computer program has therefore been prepared to calculate the confidence level at which the null hypothesis ('differences not significant') can be rejected, given a set of differences in the timing of turns of a pair of indicators.

If the sample size N is higher than 25 matched pairs, the normal approximation is appropriate, as long as the differences d_i are all about the same size, so that$(d_{max})^2/\Sigma(d_i)^2 = (5/2N)$ where d_{max} is the largest observed difference. In that case, Σd_i is approximately normally distributed with mean zero and standard deviation $\sqrt{\Sigma(d_i)^2}$, so that $Z= (\Sigma d_i - \mu)/\sigma = \Sigma d_i/(\sqrt{\Sigma(d_i)^2})$ is approximately normally distributed with zero mean and unit variance.

C An Application of the Moses Test

There are two popular measures of consumer expectations used in the U.S., one produced by the University of Michigan, and the other by the Conference Board. There is no significant difference between the magnitude of their leads against the business cycle, as shown by their lead profiles. Is there a significant difference between the variability of these leads?

The leads of the Michigan (m) index at business cycle turning points starting in 1969 are: 14, 9, 11, 5, 37, 2, 8, 8, 26 and 2 months. The corresponding leads of the Conference Board (c) index are: 10, 6, 15, 1, 38, 4, 2, 8, 18 and 5 months.

The m and c leads are now combined and arranged in a single ordered series, retaining the identity of each lead as having come from the m indicator or the c indicator:

38	37	26	18	15	14	11	10	9	8
c	m	m	c	c	m	m	c	m	m
8	8	6	5	5	4	2	2	2	1
m	c	c	m	c	c	m	m	c	c

Having chosen h=1 in advance, the span of ranks, after the most extreme-ranked m leads are dropped, comes to 15. The value of g, the amount by which this observed span exceeds $n_m - 2h$ is $(15 - (10 - 2)) = 7$. Using these values in equation 2 yields a probability of 0.84 that the observed leads would have been observed given the null hypothesis that the spread of the leads of the two indicators is the same. Thus the null hypothesis is accepted.

References

Bry, G. and C. Boschan (1971), *Cyclical Analysis of Time Series: Selected Procedures and Computer Programs.* Technical Paper 20. New York: Columbia University Press for NBER.

Fisher, R. A. (1935), *The design of experiments.* Edinburgh: Oliver and Boyd.

Granger, C. W. J. and P. Newbold (1986), *Forecasting Economic Time Series.* San Diego, CA: Academic Press.

King, R.G. and C.I. Plosser (1989), 'Real Business Cycles and the Test of the Adelmans.' Unpublished Manuscript, University of Rochester.

Klein, P. A. and G. H. Moore (1985), *Monitoring Growth Cycles in Market-Oriented Countries: Developing and Using International Economic Indicators.* Cambridge, Mass.: Ballinger for NBER.

Mood, A. M. (1954), 'On the Asymptotic Efficiency of Certain Non-parametric Two-sample Tests.' *Annals of Mathematical Statistics,* 25, pp. 514-522.

Moore, G. H. and J. Shiskin (1967), *Indicators of Business Expansions and Contractions.* New York: NBER.

Moses, L. E. (1952), 'A Two-sample Test.' *Psychometrica*, 17, pp. 239-247.

Siegel, S. (1956), *Nonparametric Statistics for the Behavioral Sciences.* New York: McGraw Hill.

Watson, M. W. (1994), 'Business Cycle Durations and Postwar Stabilization of the U.S. Economy.' *American Economic Review*, 84, pp. 24-46.

Wilcoxon, F. (1945), 'Individual Comparisons by Ranking Methods.' *Biometrics Bulletin*, 1, pp. 80-83.

3 Prediction of Business Cycle Turning Points: Using Two Types of Recession Probability Models for Japan

YASUYUKI KOMAKI*

1 Introduction

This paper presents some methods for predicting cyclical turning points during Japan's postwar period.

The main findings of this paper are: (1) Our method successfully signals turning points several months in advance. However, since the signals are not completely stable,[1] (2) we recommend the joint use of various methods and to combine real economic variables with monetary variables. (3) Our method seems to be more reliable than the government's current method based on diffusion indexes. Additionally the risk of generating erroneous signals seems to be smaller.

Section 2 looks at the problems of determination of business cycles in Japan. Section 3 describes the turning-point prediction method used in this paper. Section 4 presents estimation results using Japan's economic data, and Section 5 presents the conclusions.

---

* Yasuyuki Komaki is senior economist at the NLI Research Institute (ykomaki@nli-research.co.jp).
The author thanks Andras Vertes, Jens-Uwe G.Jungnickel, and anonymous referees for helpful comments and valuable suggestions.

1 Analysis of recent literature shows that no single model dominates in a predictive sense (see Filardo and Gordon(1995)).

2 Identification of Business Cycles

Until 1990, there was virtually no discussion of turning-point identification in Japan. The economy's persistently strong growth led people to believe that recessions were merely a slowdown in a positive growth environment. Interest in turning points awakened only after the economy began averaging below a 2% growth rate since 1990 and dipping into negative growth rates more recently. But a delay in identifying business cycles causes a number of problems. In particular, conflicting judgments often cause considerable confusion in the vicinity of turning points.

The observable divergent views can be attributed primarily to: (1) a long delay in releasing GDP statistics and other economic indicators compared to Europe and the U.S, and (2) the long delay of official announcements of turning points.

The confusion is sharpened by the fact that Japan currently has no clear criteria for determining turning points. Turning points are officially announced by the EPA's Advisory Board for Reference Dates, with a delay of approximately one year. The main reason for this delay, as Table 3.1 shows, is the delay in announcing economic data. Monthly data do not become available until the following month (bold data in Table 3.1). Another problem is the decision criteria. For example, the peak thought to have occurred in May 1997 was not officially recognized until data became fully available four months later and decision criteria were fulfilled another six months later. Thus the total lag between the occurrence and recognition of a turning point is almost one year.

A clear distinction needs to be made between an academically oriented approach to business cycle indexes, which uses relatively complete data and emphasizes accuracy and neutrality, and more practical approaches that emphasize promptness. For policy formulation purposes, the emphasis is decidedly on the latter.

Table 3.1 - Monthly Release Schedule for August 1998 to October 1998

Release Date	Indicator	Reference Period
August		
3	Nikkei Index of Commodity Prices(42)	July
3	Net Receipt & Payment of Treasury Account	July
3	Gold & Foreign Exchange Reserves	July
3	**Auto Sales**	**July**
3	Average Contracted Interest Rates	June
6	Public Works Starts	June
7	Machinery Orders Received	June
7	Service Industries Condition	June
11	Wholesale Price Indices	July
13	Balance of Payments(IMF Formula)	June
14	Operating Ratio & Production Capacity	June
14	Raw Materials Consumption,Inventory	June
15	Public Construction Order	July
17	EPA Survey on Business Conditions	Second Quarter
18	**Money Supply Outstanding**	**July**
20	**Industrial Demand for Electric Power**	**July**
20	**Foreign Trade**	**July**
20	Business Indicators	June
24	**Department Stores Sales**	**July**
24	Chain Stores Sales	July
24	Industrial Output/Input Price Index	July
27	Auto Production	July
27	Service Price for Business	July
28	**Consumer Price Indices**	**July**
28	**Labour situation(Wage,Unemployment)**	**July**
31	**Industrial Production**	**July**
31	**Sales Indices of Wholesaling & Retailing**	**July**
31	**Housing Starts,Construction orders**	**July**
September		
11	GDP	Second Quarter
October		
1	Short-Term Economic Survey(TANKAN)	Third Quarter

3 Prediction Method for Turning Points

A survey of recent literature on turning-point prediction shows that there are no completely reliable methods (for example, see Huh (1998)). Table 3.2 describes the strengths and weaknesses of different methods.

Table 3.2 - The Methods of Measurement of Turning Points

	strengths	weaknesses
Diffusion index composite index	Measurement easily Good in prediction of turning points	Arbitrary choice of variable Difficult maintenance for index because of revision of variables Unclear judgment for turning
Principal (Multivariate Time Series Variance Component	Abstraction of trend factor from Excel in prediction based on time series analysis	Arbitrary choice of model Difficult explanation of measured variables
Probit model	Judgment easily Clear explanation for mathematical statistics	Arbitrary choice of model Difficulty to remove trend factor from variables
Stock and Watson (State-space type model)	Clear explanation for mathematical Good in prediction based on probability function	Arbitrary choice of variable Arbitrary choice of model structure Difficult operation for model
(Beynsian) VAR	Clear explanation for mathematical Good in prediction based on probability function	Arbitrary choice of model
Neftci model (Regime switching model)	Clear explanation for mathematical Judgment easily	Arbitrary choice of model Difficulty to remove trend factor from variables

Because of their strengths concerning 'Judgment' and 'Explanation for mathematical statistics' we focus on two types of models designed to predict turning points: the probit type model and the Neftçi (1982) model. The probit model is a single regime model, the other one is a kind of regime switching model like a 'Markov switching model'. To signal turning points we are using the composite leading index (see Appendix).

3.1 Probit Model

A probit model is a statistical method of extracting qualitative characteristics (data) relating to cycles of economic variables and is based on probability modeling with a regression analysis approach. Specifically, economic variables are assumed to take one of two states, and turning points are converted into binary form such that contractions equal 1 and expansions equal 0. The method has a long history in the U.S.

The underlying idea of a probit model is quoted from G.S. Maddala (1992).

$$y_i^* = \beta_0 + \sum_{j=1}^{k} \beta_j x_{ij} + \mu_i \tag{1}$$

where y_i^* is an unobserved variable. We can observe only a process of time series. We measure a dummy variable,

$y_i = 1$ (contraction phase)
$y_i = 0$ (expansion phase)
Then,

$$P_i = \Pr ob(y_i = 1)\Pr ob\left[\mu_i > -\left(\beta_0 + \sum_{j=1}^{k}\beta_j x_{ij}\right)\right]$$
$$= 1 - F\left[-\left(\beta_0 + \sum_{j=1}^{k}\beta_j x_{ij}\right)\right] \tag{2}$$

where F is the cumulative distribution function of μ. Assuming μ_i is symmetrically distributed, since $1 - F(-Z) = F(Z)$, we obtain

$$P_i = F\left[\beta_0 + \sum_{J=1}^{k}\beta_j x_{ij}\right] \tag{3}$$

Since we assume μ_i to have a normal distribution,

$$F(Z_i) = \int_{-\infty}^{Z_i/\sigma} \frac{1}{\sqrt{2\pi}} \exp\left(\frac{-t^2}{2}\right) dt \tag{4}$$

Because the observed variable y_i is the realized value from the binomial distribution given by the probability in the above equation, its probability (which is dependent on x_{ij}) changes with each calculation. Thus the likelihood function can be written as follows:[2]

$$L = \prod_{y_i=1} P_i \prod_{y_i=0} (1 - P_i) \tag{5}$$

3.2 Neftçi Model

This approach uses changes in the Department of Commerce's index of leading indicators, as a signal of imminent change in business cycle phases.

---

[2] In this paper we calculate recession probabilities by TSP version 4.4.

Specifically, cyclical components are calculated using asymmetrical continuous probability distributions to obtain the predicted value of Z: (1) probability distributions are established for upturns and downturns, (2) prior probability distributions are derived, and (3) a recursive optimal posteriori probability formula is applied. Time series data are divided into upturn and downturn periods, such that the economic index X_t is

$$\begin{aligned} X_t &= \alpha^d + \varepsilon_t^d, 1 \le t \le Z \text{ (Downturn)} \\ X_t &= \alpha^u + \varepsilon_t^u, t \ge Z \text{ (Upturn)} \end{aligned} \tag{6}$$

Here, u and d denote cyclical upturns and downturns, α is a constant, ε is a mutually independent probability distribution for each cyclical phase (mean = 0, var = σ_u^2). We first obtain a probability density function for upturns and downturns. Next we define a conditional probability for change from the present phase as follows:

$$\begin{aligned} P_t^d &= p(X_t = x_t | Z > t) \\ P_t^u &= p(X_t = x_t | Z \le t) \end{aligned} \tag{7}$$

Meanwhile, ϕ, the prior probability of Z, is

$$\phi = P(Z = k | Z > k - 1) \tag{8}$$

Next, the probability of $Z \le t$ given observable data $\overline{x_t}$ at time t, that is, $P(Z \le t | \overline{x_t})$, is expressed as follows.

$$P(Z \le t | \overline{x_t}) = \frac{P(\overline{x_t} | Z \le t) \cdot P(Z \le t)}{P(\overline{x_t})} \tag{9}$$

Replacing $P(Z \le t | \overline{x_t})$ with π_t, we solve the following equation.

$$\pi_t = \frac{\left[\pi_{t-1} + \phi_t^u(1-\pi_{t-1})\right]P_t^d}{\left[\pi_{t-1} + \phi_t^u(1-\pi_{t-1})\right]P_t^d + (1-\pi_{t-1})P_t^u(1-\phi_t^u)} \tag{10}$$

4 Estimation Using Japan's Economic Data

4.1 Estimation of the Probit Model

Table 3.3 - Performance of Recession Probability Based on the Probit Model

Turning points		In sign of turning points	
Peaks/Troughs	date	Sign	lead/lag
Peaks	Jan 77	Oct 76	3
	Feb 80	Dec 79	2
	Jun 85	Oct 85	-4
	Feb 91	Jul 90	7
	Mar 97	Dec 96	3
Troughs	Mar 75	No sign	-
	Oct 77	Sep 77	1
	Feb 83	Feb 83	0
	Nov 86	Jul 86	4
	Oct 93	Mar 93	7
Peaks	**Average**		**2,2**
	Std.Dev.		**4,0**
Troughs	**Average**		**3,0**
	Std.Dev.		**3,2**
Total	**Average**		**2,6**
	Std.Dev.		**3,4**

Notes:

(1)The lead/lag shows periods against business cycle.
For example,'3' for the prediction of the January 1977 peak sh
lead signal using the threshold probability of 0.5.

(2)The turning points are determined by Economic Planning Age

We attempted to estimate a recession probability index with Japanese data[3] using a probit model. As for the performance of the probit model, the average lead time for past peaks and troughs is about three months.

[3] See Appendix.

However, the performance is not always consistent; the probit model signaled the October 1985 peak four months late, while the trough signal coincided with the February 1983 trough (see Table 3.3 and Figure 3.1).

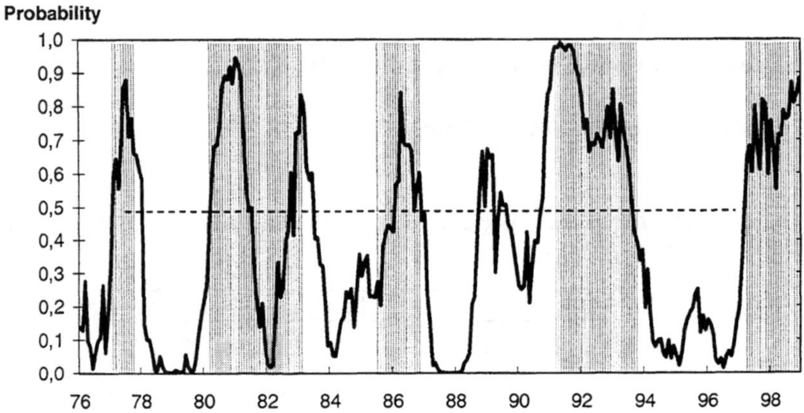

Notes:
(1)"The composite index" is composed of 7 indexes of the Japanese economy.
(2)The shaded areas designate the recessions determined by the Economic Planning Agency.
(3)The y-axis shows the probability of recessions.
(4)The probabilities of a recession are derived from sample simulations, based on the probit model.

Figure 3.1 - Predictive Power of the Composite Index

(1) Stability evaluation of the probit model

Research on turning points using the probit model is most advanced in the US. However, one commonly cited problem with this approach is the model's instability. We tested the model's predictive power by adjusting the ending point of the estimation period.

Table 3.4 - Estimation Stability of the Probit Model

Equation #	Estimation Period	lag	Composite Index	R-square	Fraction of Correct Prediction	Remarks (Figure No)
11	Dec 1971-Mar 1997	0	-12,873 *-7,968*	0,273	0,752	Figure 2.
12	Dec 1971-Oct 1993	0	-11,303 *-6,957*	0,235	0,705	-
13	Dec 1971-Feb 1991	0	-8,899 *-5,278*	0,148	0,686	-
14	Dec 1971-Nov 1986	0	-9,222 *-4,832*	0,151	0,671	-
1	Jan 1976-Mar 1997	0	-15,269 *-8,605*	0,344	0,803	Figure 1.

These results suggest that while the model's predictive power tends to decline as the estimation period is shortened, the overall results are good (see Table 3.4 and Figure 3.2).

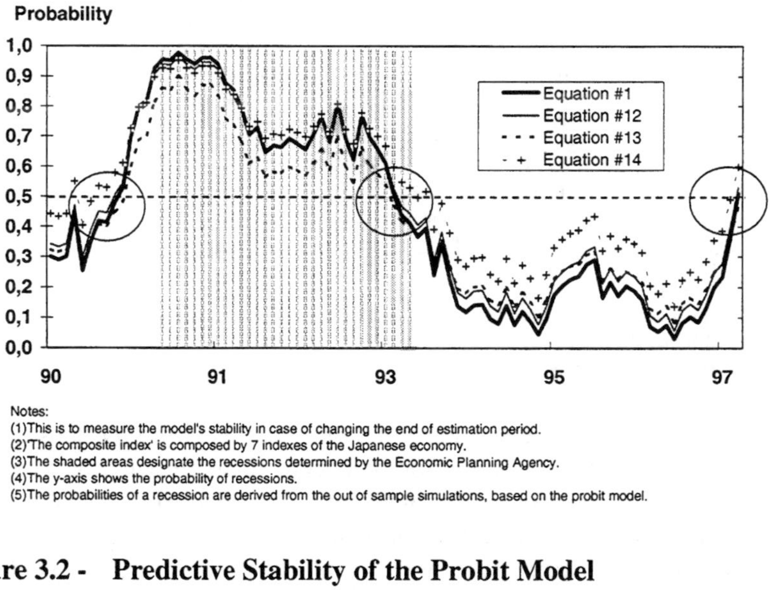

Notes:
(1)This is to measure the model's stability in case of changing the end of estimation period.
(2)The composite index' is composed by 7 indexes of the Japanese economy.
(3)The shaded areas designate the recessions determined by the Economic Planning Agency.
(4)The y-axis shows the probability of recessions.
(5)The probabilities of a recession are derived from the out of sample simulations, based on the probit model.

Figure 3.2 - Predictive Stability of the Probit Model

In addition, when extrapolations are made beyond the estimation periods, the model identifies historical turning points with fair accuracy. However, lead times for the cyclical turning points are inconsistent depending on the estimation period, leaving room for improvement.

(2) Stability test using monetary variables

The estimation results suggest that long-term interest rates have the best predictive power, and money supply the least. Moreover, with regard to the length of the lead time, the best fit for both stock prices and interest spreads is 3 to 4 months (see Table 3.5).

Table3.5 - Estimation Results Based on the Probit Model

Equation	lag	Composite Index	Yield Spread	Stock Price	Monetary Aggregates	R-square	Remarks (Figure No)
1	0	-15,269	(growth rate)	-	-	0,344	Figure 1.
		-8,605					
2	1	-4,648	(level)	-	-	0,111	-
		-5,757					
3	3	-	-0,368	-	-	0,157	Figure 5.
			-6,405				
4	5	-	-	-2,7114	-	0,121	Figure 3.
				-6,146			
5	0	-	-	-	-7,176	0,064	Figure 4.
					-4,655		
6	3	-8,318	-0,437	-1,051	-4,421	0,329	Figure 7.
		-4,059	*-3,295*	*-1,977*	*-1,493*		
7	2	-10,168	-0,361	-0,351	-5,399	0,340	-
		-4,806	*-2,839*	*-0,683*	*-1,794*		
8	4	-7,147	-0,467	-1,620	-3,009	0,321	-
		-3,587	*-3,491*	*-2,926*	*-1,037*		
9	5	-7,475	-0,401	-	-	0,257	-
		-4,588	*-3,602*				
10	4	-	-0,368	-1,399	-7,243	0,241	Figure 6.
			-6,035	*-2,857*	*-3,435*		

Notes:

(1) The dependent variable is a dummy taking 1 in recessions and 0 otherwise.

(2) Numbers in italics are t-statistics and they are all significant at the 5% level respectively.

(3) 'R-square' is MacFadden's R-square.

(4) Constant terms are not shown in the table.

In the early 1990s' recession following the bubble's collapse, stock prices were a leading indicator for both peaks and troughs. Nevertheless they had predicted earlier phases with less than adequate precision. Stock prices gave a false signal during the inventory adjustment phase in 1995. Thus, overall, stock prices are not a stable leading indicator (see Figure 3.3).

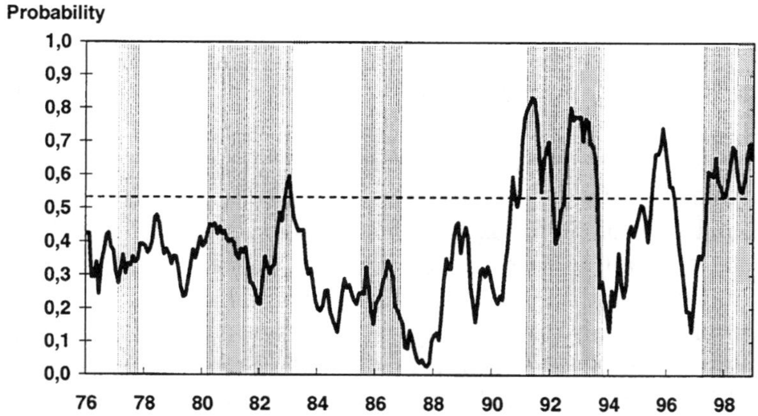

Notes:
(1)'Stock Price' is the change of the growth rate of 'Tokyo Stock Exchange Index'
(2)The shaded areas designate the recessions determined by the Economic Planning Agency.
(3)The y-axis shows the probability of recessions.
(4)The probabilities of a recession are derived from the out of sample simulations, based on the probit model.

Figure 3.3 - Predictive Power of the Stock Price

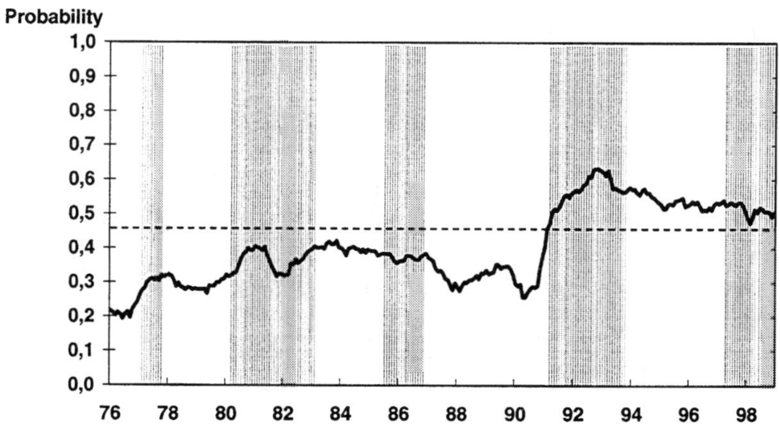

Notes:
(1)'Monetary Aggregates' is the change of the growth rate of 'Money Supply(M2+CD)'
(2)The shaded areas designate the recessions determined by the Economic Planning Agency.
(3)The y-axis shows the probability of recessions.
(4)The probabilities of a recession are derived from the out of sample simulations, based on the probit model.

Figure 3.4 - Predictive Power of the Monetary Aggregates

As for the money supply, except for the contraction phase following the bubble's collapse, it has not emitted a contraction signal up to the present.

Thus the money supply has practically no predictive power (see Figure 3.4).

The interest spread between long-term and short-term rates appears to have the best predictive power among monetary variables. It fell below zero just prior to and at the start of the contraction of the early 1990s. However, it does not emit a stable recovery signal, and recently failed to signal a turning point even after the present contraction phase began. In the US, a Stock-Watson model using short-term interest rate spreads also failed to predict the early 1990s contraction. Due to their unstable predictive power, monetary variables are being dropped from models.

However, greater overall stability can be achieved in predictive power by combining Yield Spread, Stock Price, and Monetary Aggregates (see Figure 3.6). Monetary variables such as interest rates and stock prices are theoretically supposed to contain information such as future economic growth rates and inflation rates.

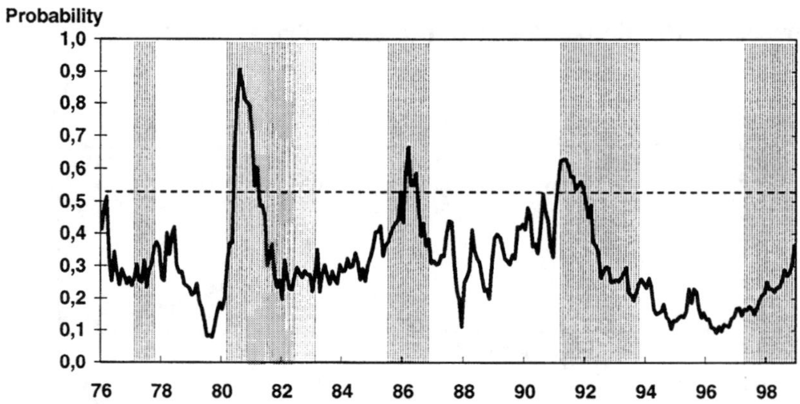

Notes:
(1)'Yield Spread' is the difference between the interest rates on 10-year JGB and the 3-month interest rates
(2)The shaded areas designate the recessions determined by the Economic Planning Agency.
(3)The y-axis shows the probability of recessions.
(4)The probabilities of a recession are derived from the out of sample simulations, based on the probit model.

Figure 3.5 - Predictive Power of the Yields Spread

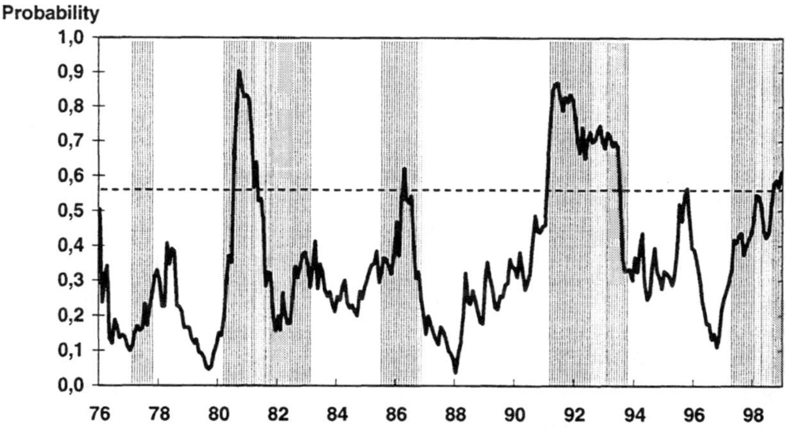

Notes:
(1)'The FINA Index' is composed of the Yield Spread, Stock Price and Monetary Aggregates.
(2)The shaded areas designate the recessions determined by the Economic Planning Agency.
(3)The y-axis shows the probability of recessions.
(4)The probabilities of a recession are derived from the out of sample simulations, based on the probit model.

Figure 3.6 - Predictive Power of the FINA Index

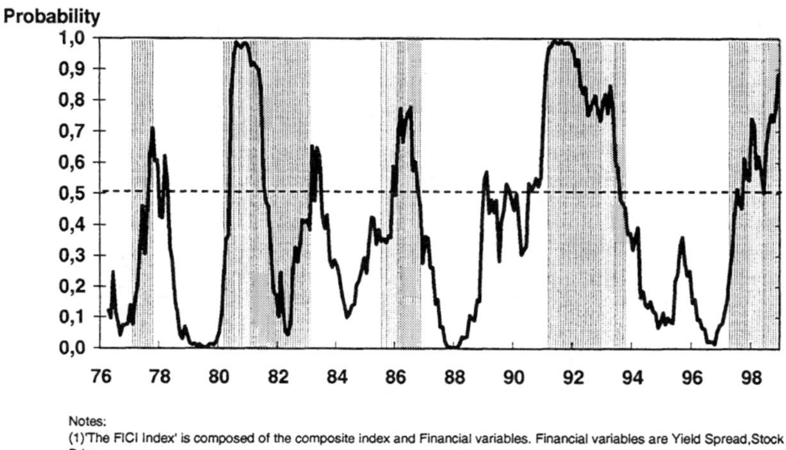

Notes:
(1)'The FICI Index' is composed of the composite index and Financial variables. Financial variables are Yield Spread,Stock Price
and Monetary Aggregates.
(2)The shaded areas designate the recessions determined by the Economic Planning Agency.
(3)The y-axis shows the probability of recessions.
(4)The probabilities of a recession are derived from the out of sample simulations, based on the probit model.

Figure 3.7 - Predictive Power of the FICI Index

Next, better overall stability can be achieved in predictive power by combining real economic variables with monetary variables (see Figure 3.7). However, the stability of their predictive power has yet to be empirically confirmed, in a large part because of the simplicity of prediction methods. The successful incorporation of monetary variables in models will be an issue for the future.

4.2 Estimation of the Neftçi Model

Next, we estimate the probability of recession using the Neftçi model. One strength of this model is that past average turning points can be used as prior probabilities, and be revised with the movement (changes) in recent monthly data. However, because the choice of prior probability can introduce more arbitrariness than any other factor, we decided to use the mean and variance from past business cycles (second cycle onward).

A problem with the Neftçi model is that of setting the probability of occurrence to eliminate false signals regarding turning point probability.

While most people would find 0.9 (10% probability of error) to be an adequate level for indicating a turning point, for this model we used 0.85 as the cutoff level because it would include almost all past turning points.

Table 3.6 - Performance of Recession Probability Based on the Neftci Model

Turning points		In sign of turning points(Threshold Probability)					
		0,50		0,70		0,85	
Peaks/Troughs	date	Sign	lead/lag	Sign	lead/lag	Sign	lead/lag
Peaks	Jan 77	Aug 76	5	No sign	-	No sign	-
	Feb 80	Jun 79	8	Sep 79	5	Dec 79	2
	Jun 85	Jun 84	12	Dec 84	6	May 85	1
	Feb 91	Jun 88	32	Sep 88	29	May 89	21
	March 97	Dec 95	15	Jun 96	9	Nov 96	4
Troughs	Oct 77	No sign	-	No sign	-	No sign	-
	Feb 83	Jun 81	20	Jan 82	13	Apr 82	10
	Nov 86	No sign	-	No sign	-	No sign	-
	Oct 93	Jul 92	15	Feb 93	8	Jul 93	3
Peaks	**Average**		**16,0**		**14,7**		**8,7**
	Std.Dev.		**11,5**		**12,5**		**10,8**
Troughs	**Average**		**17,5**		**10,5**		**6,5**
	Std.Dev.		**3,5**		**3,5**		**4,9**
Total	**Average**		**16,5**		**13,0**		**7,8**
	Std.Dev.		**9,0**		**9,3**		**8,1**

Notes:

(1)The lead/lag shows periods against business cycle.
For example,'5' for the prediction of the January 1977 peak shows the lead signal using the threshold probability of 0.5.

(2)The turning points are determined by Economic Planning Agency.

For the present cyclical phase, the model signaled a turning point in November 1996, indicating the possibility of a downturn sooner or later. For past phases, the model performed as a leading indicator with average lead times of 8.7 months for peaks and 6.5 months for troughs (see Table 3.6 and Figure 3.8 to 3.10).

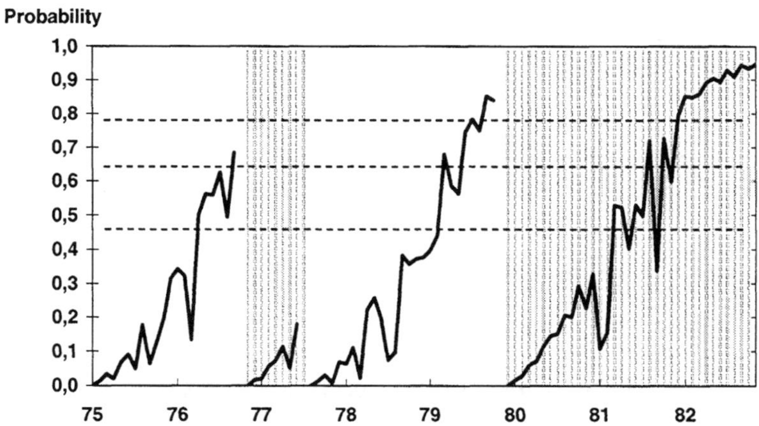

Notes:
(1)'The composite index' is composed of 7 indexes of the Japanese economy.
(2)The shaded areas designate the recessions determined by the Economic Planning Agency.
(3)The y-axis shows the probability of recessions.
(4)The probabilities of a recession are derived from the in-sample simulations, based on the Neftci model.

Figure 3.8 - Predictive Power of the Composite Index

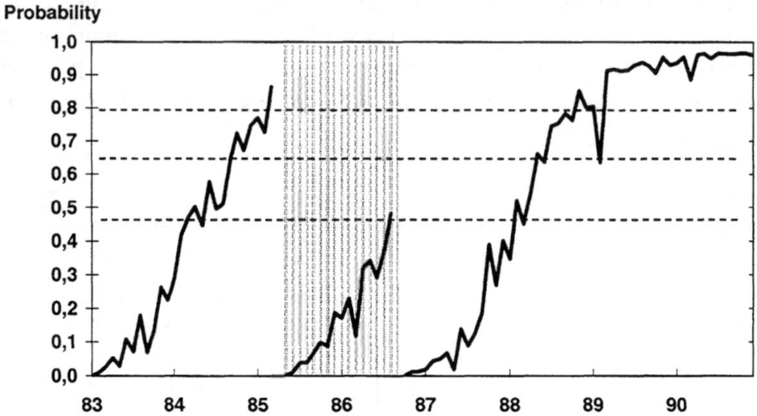

Notes:
(1)'The composite index' is composed of 7 indexes of the Japanese economy.
(2)The shaded areas designate the recessions determined by the Economic Planning Agency.
(3)The y-axis shows the probability of recessions.
(4)The probabilities of a recession are derived from the in-sample simulations, based on the Neftci model.

Figure 3.9 - Predictive Power of the Composite Index

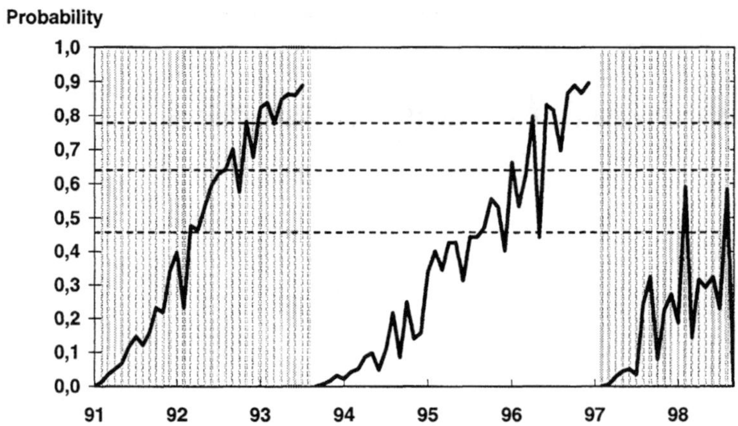

Notes:
(1)'The composite index' is composed of 7 indexes of the Japanese economy.
(2)The shaded areas designate the recessions determined by the Economic Planning Agency.
(3)The y-axis shows the probability of recessions.
(4)The probabilities of a recession are derived from the in-sample simulations, based on the Neftci model.

Figure 3.10 - Predictive Power of the Composite Index

Nevertheless, it failed to signal turning points for the peak in January 1977 and troughs in October 1977 and November 1986. This can be attributed to the considerably shorter duration compared to average phases in the past. (Thus the problem of how to set prior probability remains unresolved.)

5 Concluding Remarks

The two methods applied in this paper signaled a turning point in mid 1996, which (based on experience) indicated that the peak would occur around March to May 1997. In other words, when the tax hikes were implemented in April, the economy had probably already entered a recession. If the signal of the used models is correct and the economy had indeed peaked, the fiscal tightening was inappropriate to the point of overkill. This is a case in which delayed judgment of business conditions led to inappropriate policies that exacerbated the cyclical contraction. A more objective and quicker determination of turning points should help to reduce such fiscal policy lags.

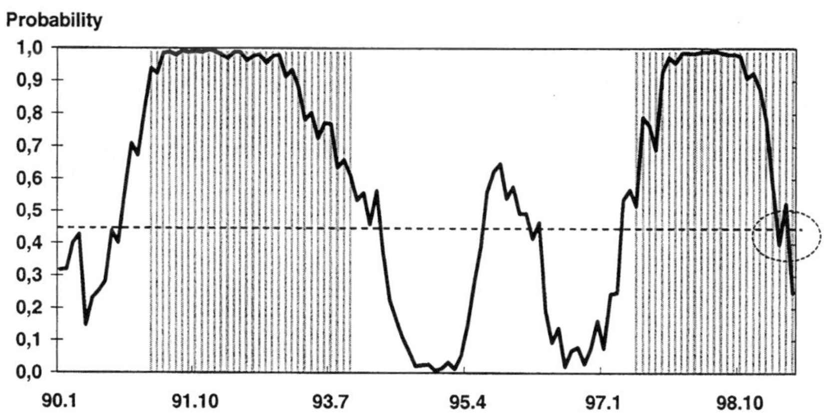

Notes:
(1)The shaded areas designate the recessions determined by the Economic Planning Agency.
(2)The y-axis shows the probability of recessions.
(3)The probabilities of a recession are derived from the out of sample simulations, based on the probit model.

Figure 3.11 - Current Signal Shows Turning Point in Japanese Economy

Our method successfully signals turning points several months in advance. However, since the signals are not stable we recommend the joint use of other methods and to combine real economic variables with monetary variables.

Recent signals of our models show that the Japanese economy is already recovering in April 1999 (see Figure 3.11).

6 Appendix: Data Supplement

A Composite Index

Data Processing: I composed 7 indexes of the Japanese economy using the NBER Composite Index method.
Original Data: These 7 indexes are (1) Auto Sales, (2) Money Supply Outstanding, (3) Inventory ratio for final Demand goods, (4) New job offers, (5) New construction starts of dwellings, (6) New building construction of dwellings, (7) Nikkei Index of Commodity Prices.
Source: Bank of Japan, *Economic Statistics Monthly.*

B Yield Spread

Data Processing: Yield spread is calculated as long-term interest rates minus short-term interest rates.
Original Data: Long-term interest rates ten-year interest-bearing Government bonds. Short-term interest rates: Call rates of collateralized.
Source: Bank of Japan, *Economic Statistics Monthly.*

C Stock Price

Data Processing: Original data converted into change from previous year.
Original Data: The Tokyo Stock Exchange 1st section price index.
Source: Bank of Japan, *Economic Statistics Monthly.*

D Monetary Aggregates

Data Processing: Original data converted into change from previous year.
Original Data: Money stock, average outstanding M2+CD.
Source: Bank of Japan, *Economic Statistics Monthly.*

References

Bernanke, Ben S. (1990), 'On The Predictive Power of Interest Rates and Interest Rate Spreads', Federal Reserve Bank of Boston, *New England Economic Review*, Nov. 1990.

Bry and C. Boschan (1971), 'Cyclical Analysis of Time Series: Selected Procedures and Computer Programs', NBER Technical Paper 20.

Kim, C. J. and C. R.Nelson (1998), 'Business Cycle Turning Points, A New Coincident Index, And Tests of Duration Dependence based on a dynamic factor model with regime switching', *The Review of Economic and Statistics.*

Diebold, F. X. and G. D. Rudebusch (1996), 'Measuring Business Cycles: A Modern Perspective', *The Review of Economic and Statistics.*

Dueker, Michael J. (1997), 'Strengthening the Case for Yield Curve as a Predictor of US Recession', Federal Reserve Bank of St. Louis, *Review*, March/April.

Estrella, A. and F. Mishkin (1995), 'Predicting US Recessions: Financial Variables as Leading Indicators', NBER Working Paper Series, December 1995, No. 5379.

Filardo, A. J. and S. F. Gordon (1995), 'Business Cycle Turning Points: Two Empirical Business Cycle Model Approaches', Federal Reserve Bank of Kansas City, working paper.

Huh, C. (1991), 'Recession Probability Indexes: A Survey', Federal Reserve Bank of San Francisco, *Economic Review*, Fall 1991, pp. 31-40.

Huh, C. (1998), 'Forecasting Industrial Production Using Models with Business Cycle Asymmetry', Federal Reserve Bank of San Francisco, *Economic Review*, Vol. 1.

Haubrich, J. G. and A. M. Dombrosky (1996), 'Predicting Real Growth Using the Yield Curve', Federal Reserve Bank of Cleveland, *Economic Review*, Vol. 32, No. 1.

Neftçi, S. (1982), 'Optimal Prediction of Cyclical Downturns', *Journal of Economic Dynamics and Control*, pp. 225-241.

Neftçi, S. (1984), 'Are Economic Time Series Asymmetric Over the Business Cycle?', *Journal of political economy*, pp. 307-328.

Komaki, Yasuyuki (1998), 'Using the New NLI Business Cycle Indexes (NBI) as a Policy Tool', NLI Research, No. 117.

Stock, J. and M. Watson (1989), 'New Indexes of Coincident and Leading Economic Indicators', *NBER Macroeconomics Annual 1989*, pp. 351-409.

Zarnowitz, V. and G. H. Moore (1982), 'Sequential Signals of Recession and Recovery', *Journal of Business*, Vol. 55, pp. 57-85.

4 New Composite Coincident and Leading Indexes for Poland

VICTOR ZARNOWITZ, MARIA DROZDOWICZ-BIEC,
PHILIP CHEN and PHOEBUS DHRYMES, JR.

1 Objective and Limitation

The new cooperative research project of the Foundation for International Business and Economic Research (FIBER) and The Conference Board (TCB) will extend the coverage of the composite indexes of coincident and leading indicators to a large number of countries around the globe. Poland was on our high-priority list because (1) it is a country that is well advanced in the transition from centrally planned to market economy when compared with other countries in the post-Soviet area of Central and Eastern Europe, and (2) it has already maintained for several years a high average rate of economic growth, which explains a substantial interest of international investors in the Polish economy.

Normally, the selection of component indicators and the estimation and evaluation of composite indexes requires large samples of observations; usually at least twenty years of monthly or quarterly data are required to cover from three to five complete cycles (Zarnowitz, 1992, 316-357, Lahiri and Moore, 1993, 57-61). However, for Poland it would seem inappropriate to extend the period of study back to the pre-1990 centrally planned economy. The construction of indicators depends on the existence of market relations, e.g., between price changes and excess demand (or excess supply), between demand (new appropriations, contracts, orders) for plant and equipment and the corresponding investment realizations (expenditures, output, shipments), and between sales, production and

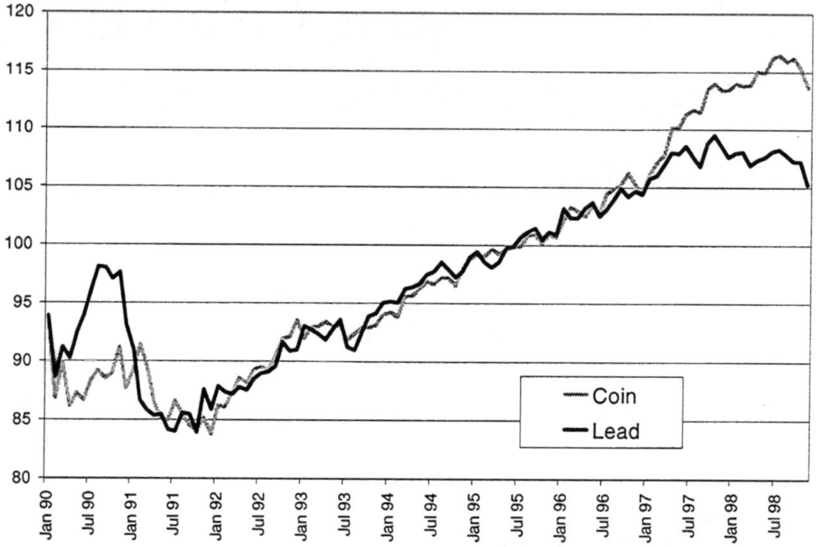

Figure 4.1 - Leading and Coincident Indexes

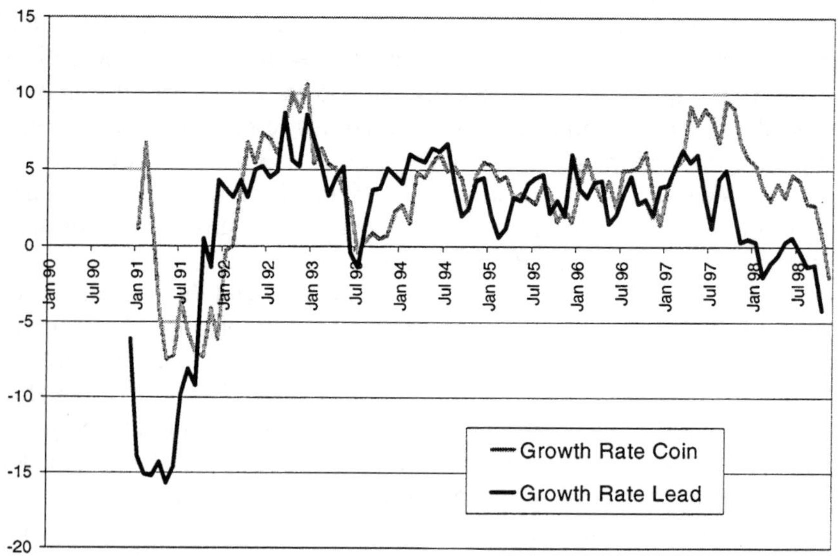

Figure 4.2 - Growth Rate of Leading and Coincident Indexes

employment for the economy as a whole and their diffusion among its major sectors. In the planned economy, these relationships did not apply as the logic of the system differed radically from that of free-markets. Secondly, statistical data for pre-1990 Poland, which served primarily the purpose of controlling production by the authorities of the time, are very deficient. Using such data for our purposes could easily do more harm than good. Therefore, we decided to base our research on data beginning in 1990. (Figures 4.1 and 4.2) (Note that in all figures which compare an index to another series, the index appears as the lighter colored series, and the other series appears as the darker.)

2 Selection of Coincident Indicators

Coincident indicators refer to the current state of the economy or, more precisely, because of the inevitable lags with which the data are collected and released, of the most recent state that can be estimated. (We shall attempt to make up for the information lags by extrapolations based on state-of-the-art time-series models.) The series included in the Composite Coincident Index for Poland are: industrial output (Figures 4.4 and 4.6), wages and salaries (Figure 4.3), income per capita (Figure 4.5) (all three in constant prices), employment (Figure 4.7) and rate of unemployment (Figure 4.8). For sources of these data, see Table 4.1.

Some of our series are not used for the entire period for which they are available. Let us now explain the reasons why this is the case.

The unemployment rate. Before 1990, the Polish economy featured effectively a high surplus of the labor force accompanied by very low productivity. There was, in fact, hidden unemployment. A constitutionally established 'right to work' and government policies aimed at maintaining 'full employment' regardless of the concomitant cost and waste. The transitional 1990-93 period brought a rapid rise of unemployment for at least three reasons. First, the rationalization of production process required drastic reduction of the swollen supply of unproductive excess workers. Second, freeing of prices caused enormous inflation, and the resulting drop in demand forced decrease of employment. Third, the methods for counting unemployment improved greatly. Hence, it is only after 1993 that we consider the unemployment data for Poland to be sufficiently representative to be included in our list of coincident indicators.

Table 4.1 - Characteristics of Coincident Index Components

No	Variable	Definition	Source	Period	Frequency	Raw data process
1.	Output	Index of production	Central Statistic. Office	1990/01 to 1998/11	Monthly (M)	Seasonally adjusted (S.A.)
2.	Income per capita	Average Monthly Income by Household per Capita	Central Statistic. Office	1994/01 to 1998/11	Quarterly (Q)	S.A. deflated
3.	Output	Output in Industry (balance)	Business survey. RIED	1990/01 to 1998/11	M	S.A.
4.	Employment	Industry Employment (balance)	Business survey. RIED	1990/01 to 1998/11	M	S.A.
5.	Unemploy-ment Rate		Central Statistical Office	1994/04 to 1998/11	M	S.A. inverted
6.	Wages and salaries	Industrial Net Monthly Average	Central Statistical Office	1990/01 to 1998/11	M	S.A. deflated

(Note: RIED stands for Research Institute for Economic Development)

The complement to these data is the information about the employment in industry coming from the business survey, available for the entire period.

Income per capita is used from 1994 on. These data come from the research on household budgets made by the Central Statistical Office. The decrease of income per capita observed in 1990-93 is much higher than other similar data such as pensions, wages and salaries or production. This may be because in 1993 the methodology of this research was changed and not all incomes of households were recorded before 1994. At this time, the income from a second or additional place of work as well from black market was probably not recorded (incomes from the black market had a considerable share in the Polish economy at this time). Because of this, the later data are more reliable.

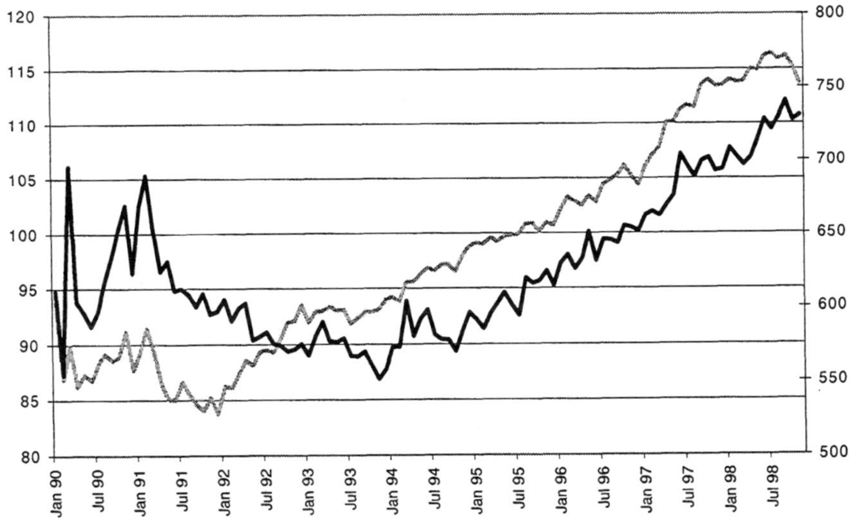

Figure 4.3 - Wages and Salaries versus Coincident Index

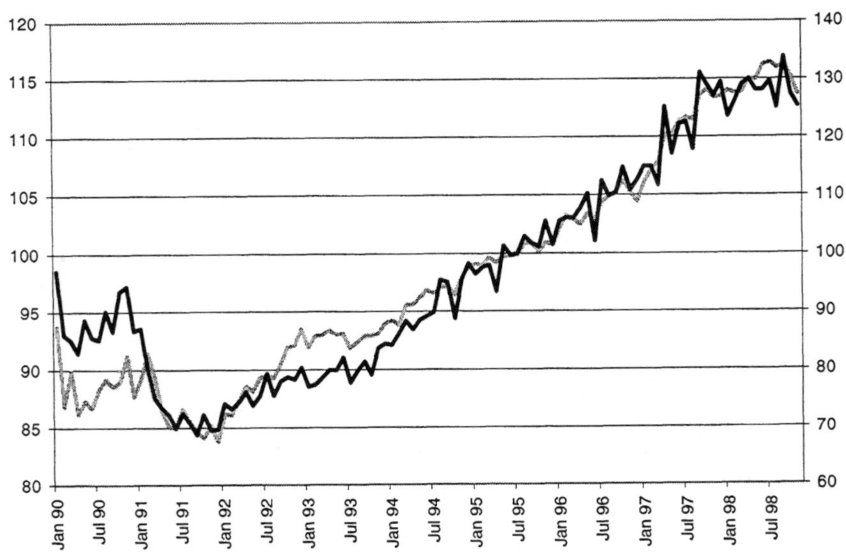

Figure 4.4 - Index of Production versus Coincident Index

Figure 4.5 - Income per Capita versus Coincident Index

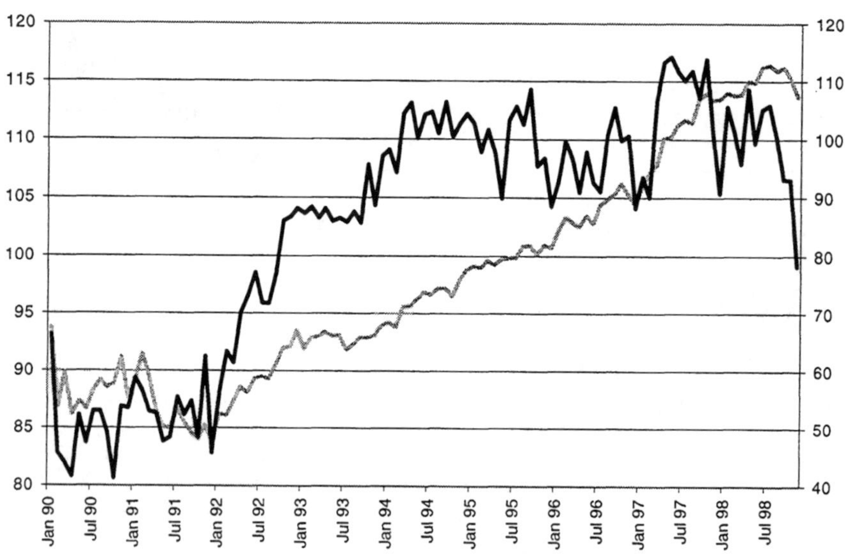

Figure 4.6 - Production: Balance versus Coincident Index

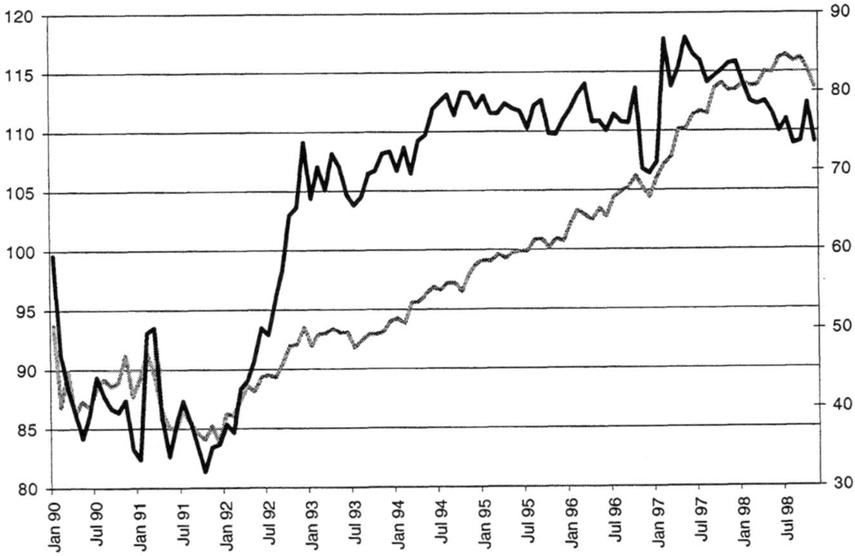

Figure 4.7 - Employment: Balance versus Coincident Index

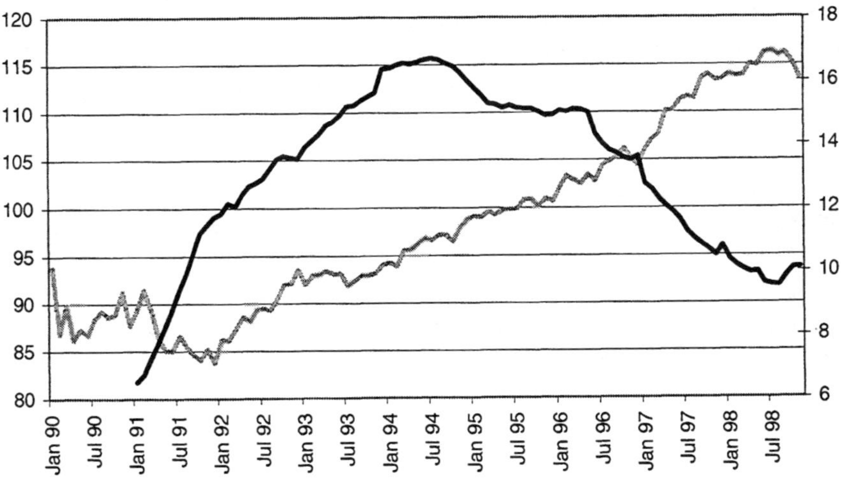

Figure 4.8 - Unemployment Rate versus Coincident Index

3 Selection of Leading Indicators

Leading indicators are time series that tend to move ahead of the coincident indicators in the sense of anticipating their major movements and turning points. For best results, the leads should be well observed and explained, at least in terms of the averages, though the dispersion of the individual timing measures around these averages may be high.

For Poland, the components of the Leading Index include: measure of indebtedness of households (Figure 4.15), productivity (Figure 4.10), money supply (Figure 4.9), interest rate (Figure 4.11), orders (Figure 4.14), inventories (Figure 4.13), financial situation of enterprises (Figure 4.16), stock price index (Figure 4.12) and the Consumer Confidence Index (Figure 4.17). For sources of these data, see Table 4.2. It is important to note that all these series have close counterparts in the composition of the leading indicators for the United States and several other countries.

As with our Coincident Index, not all series are used in our Leading Index for the entire period.

The Warsaw Stock Price Index is used in its deflated form; the deflation of stock exchange indexes is usually used for high inflation economies. In addition, this series was excluded in from 1993-94. During that period the stock price index rose about 5 times and then rapidly decreased to the previous level. At this time, the stock exchange was entirely novel to Poland. Initially, the exchange met only once a week and the number of company shares traded was very small (about 20). At first, profits coming from the stock exchange caused euphoria and heavy participation of individual investors. This caused rapid growth of the stock price index connected to the feelings rather than to the real economic situation. Therefore, it seems to be legitimate not to take this specific period in consideration.

Some of the data were issued or became available only sometime during the decade of the 1990s, and could not be included in the index at earlier dates.

Table 4.2 - Characteristics of Leading Components

No.	Variable	Definition	Source	Period	Fre-quency	Data raw process
1.	Money Supply	M2	Central Bank	1990/01 to 1990/11	Month-ly (M)	S.A. deflated
2.	Financial Situation of Enterprises, Balance	Business Survey	RIED	1990/01 to 1998/11	M	S.A.
3.	Credit Liabilities of Households	Monthly change in receivables from private persons	Central Bank	1991/01 to 1998/11	M	S.A. deflated
4.	Productivity	Output divided by employment in industry	Central Statistical Office	1990/01 to 1998/11	M	S.A. deflated
5.	Orders	New orders in industry balance	Business survey RIED	1991/04 to 1998/11	M	S.A. deflated
6.	Inventories	Stock of finished goods, balance	Business survey RIED	1991/04 to 1999/11	M	S.A.
7.	Real Interest Rate	Bill Rediscount in %	Central Bank	1996/01 to 1998/11	M	deflated
8.	Stock Price Index		Warsaw Stock Exchange	1991/04 to 1993/04, 1994/12 to 1998/11	Daily	Monthly average
9.	Consumer Confidence Index	Propensity to buy consumer goods	'Demoskop' private agency	1991/01 to 1998/11	M	

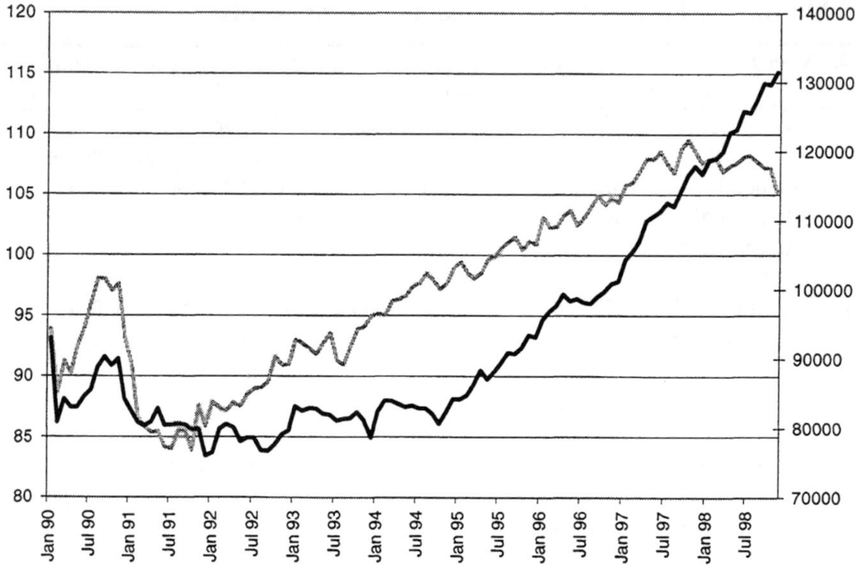

Figure 4.9 - Money Supply versus Leading Index

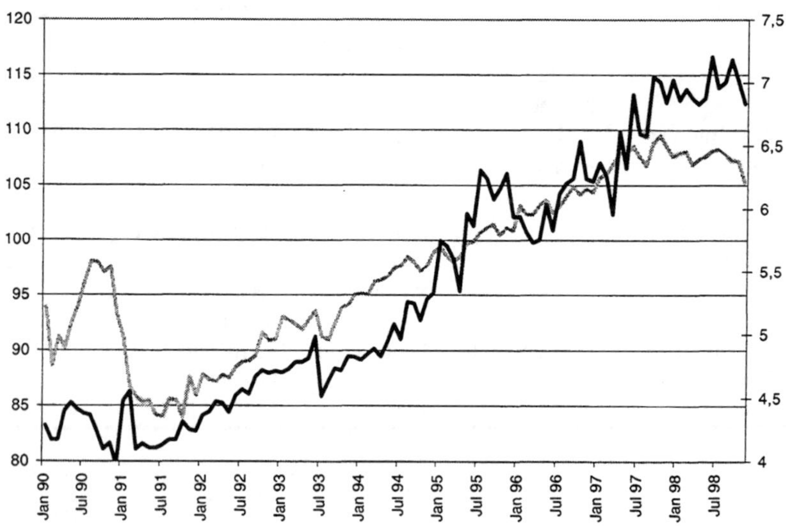

Figure 4.10 - Productivity versus Leading Index

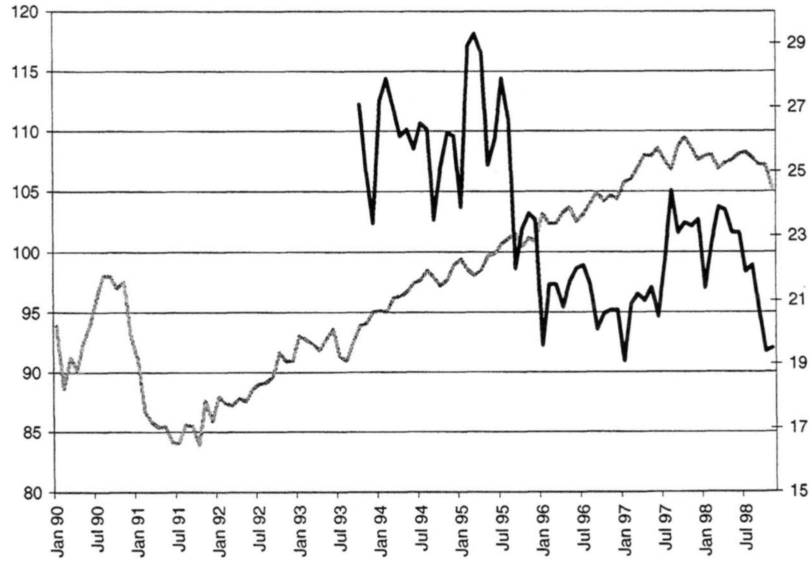

Figure 4.11 - Real Interest Rate versus Leading Index

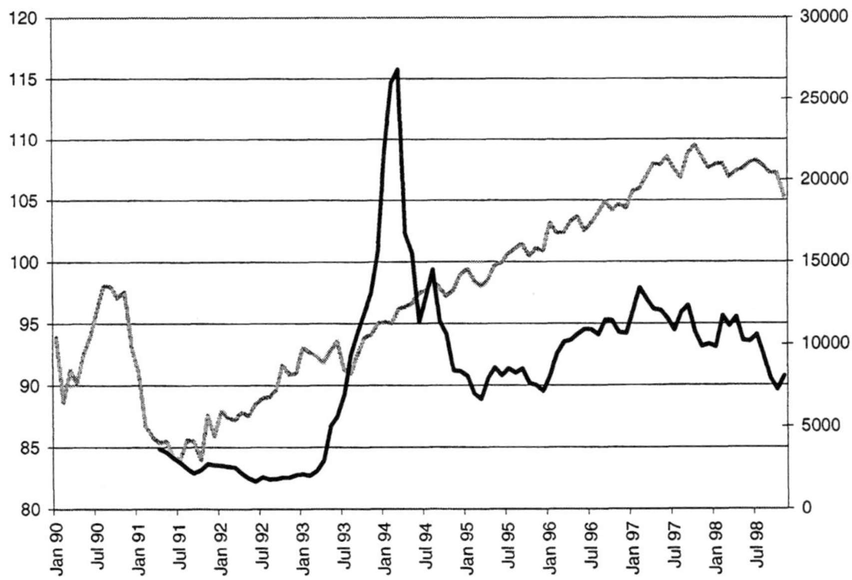

Figure 4.12 - Warsaw Stock Price Index versus Leading Index

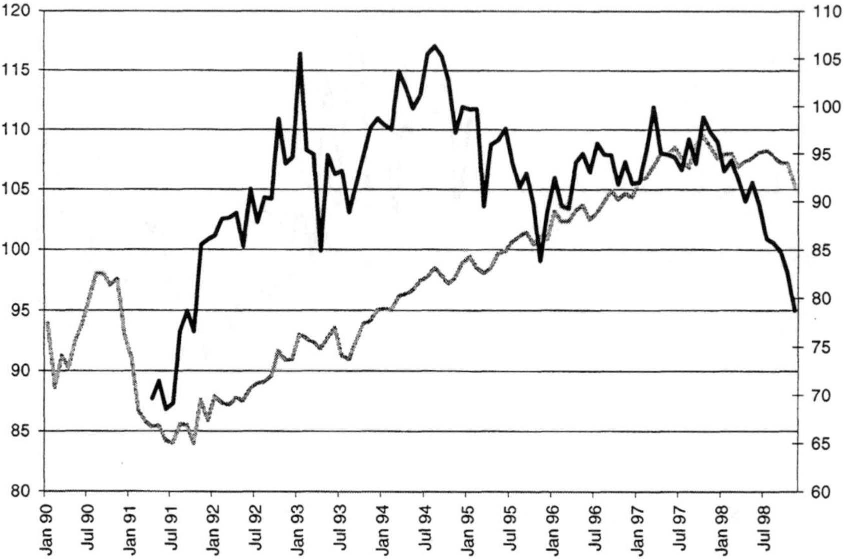

Figure 4.13 - Inventories versus Leading Index

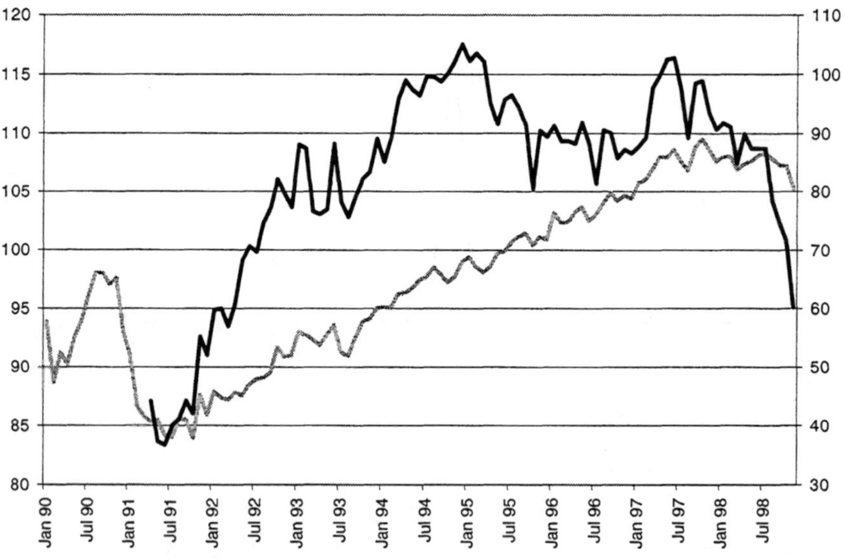

Figure 4.14 - Orders versus Leading Index

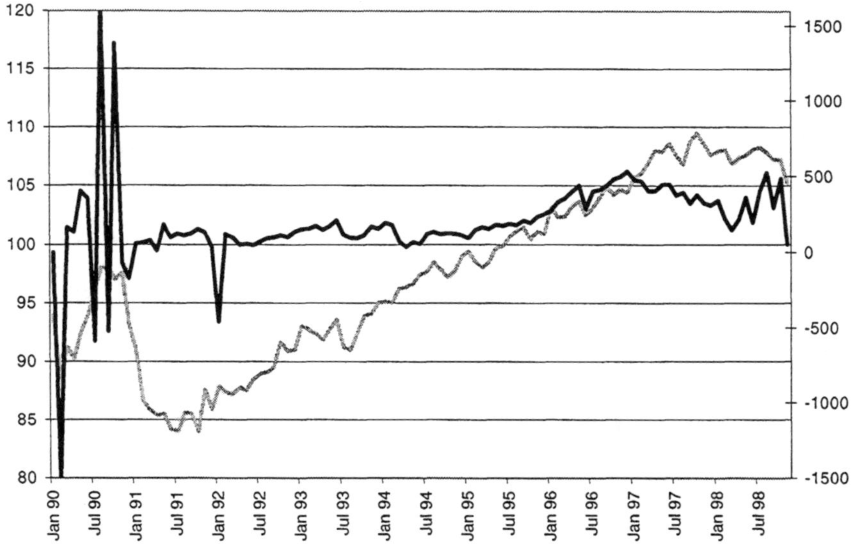

Figure 4.15 - Credit Liabilities of Households versus Leading Index

Figure 4.16 - Financial Situation of Enterprises versus Leading Index

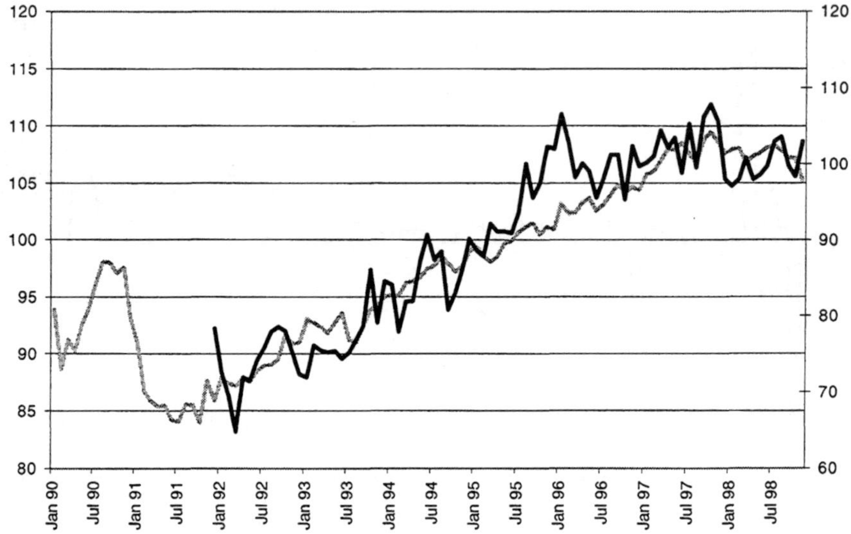

Figure 4.17 - Consumer Confidence Index versus Leading Index

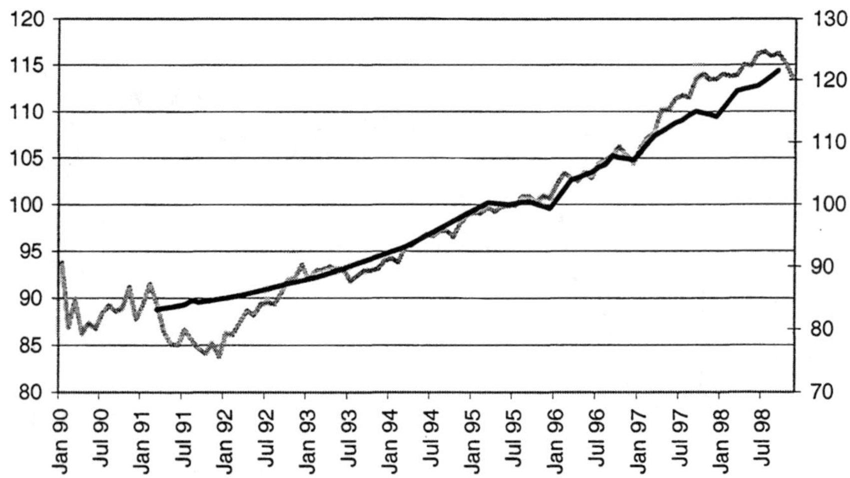

Figure 4.18 - GDP versus Coincident Index

4 Accuracy of Coincident and Leading Indicators

4.1 Accuracy of Coincident

The correlation between the Polish real GDP and our Coincident Index is as high as 0.98.

Unfortunately, quarterly economic data for Polish GDP is available only for the last three years. For previous periods there are only yearly data (See Figure 4.18 and Table 4.3).

Table 4.3 - GDP and Coincident Regression Statistics

No.	Y	X	Adjusted R-Square	Standard Error	No. of Observations
1.	GDP	Coincident	0.9832	1.4684	19

4.2 Accuracy of Coincident and Leading Indexes

It is important to know by how many months the Leading Index leads the Coincident Index. In addition, it is difficult to measure it correctly for such a short period as in the Polish case, when only one turning point occurred. The closest relationship between Coincident and Leading was found when the Leading Index is taken with a lead of 2 or 3 months. (-2, -3) (See Table 4.4). The Leading Index's one turning point (in 1991) also lead by 3 months.

It is interesting to note that the regression between the Coincident and Leading Indexes, for the period after 1994, gives the best result when the Leading Index is taken with 7 or 8 months lead time (See Table 4.5).

Probably, there are two main factors which have impacted such results. First, at the beginning of the 1990s the data did not reflect the condition of the economy properly because of weak methodology as well as volatility and rapid changes in the economy.

Table 4.4 - Coincident and Leading Regression Statistics for 1990/01 to 1998/11

No.	Y	X	Adjusted R-Square	Standard Error	No. of Observations
1.	Coincident	Lead	0.8906	2.4821	107
2.	Coincident	Lead -1 m.	0.8900	2.4870	106
3.	Coincident	Lead -2 m.	0.9021	2.3382	105
4.	Coincident	Lead -3 m.	0.8966	2.3936	104
5.	Coincident	Lead -4 m.	0.8888	2.4691	103
6.	Coincident	Lead -5 m.	0.8755	2.5961	102

Second, at the beginning of the 1990s the Polish economy was not a market economy in full and free market relations and did not work in the same manner as other economies. But, as transformations advanced (privatization, development of financial markets and institutions, opening of the economy), those free market rules started to work similarly to other market economies. This may have had a positive influence on the possibility to find some long leading indicators in the future.

Table 4.5 - Coincident and Leading Regression Statistics for 1994/01 to 1998/11

No.	Y	X	Adjusted R-Square	Standard Error	No. of Observations
1.	Coincident	Lead. -1 m.	0.9235	1.2202	59
2.	Coincident	Lead -2 m.	0.9279	1.2134	59
3.	Coincident	Lead -3 m.	0.9355	1.1738	59
4.	Coincident	Lead -4 m.	0.9375	1.1858	59
5.	Coincident	Lead -5 m.	0.9401	1.1975	59
6.	Coincident	Lead -6 m.	0.9446	1.1807	59
7.	Coincident	Lead -7 m.	0.9455	1.1812	59
8.	Coincident	Lead -8 m.	0.9467	1.1816	59
9.	Coincident	Lead -9 m.	0.9437	1.2330	59

5 Economic Outlook and Comments

It is desirable to summarize the 1989 economic situation prior to reviewing the coincident and leading indexes.

In mid-September 1989 when the first post-communist government was assuming its duties, the Polish economy was in a state of deep depression. The simplified picture of the Polish economy before 1990 can be characterized by:

- lack of equilibrium
- lack of competition
- lack of economic freedom.

Lack of Equilibrium. A very deep imbalance existed between supply and demand, which in practice meant lack of goods and long queue lines. Poland had a very large foreign debt, of 39 billion US$ in 1998 and a lack of hard currency reserves. Heavy industry and mining comprised a disproportionately large share of output. Poland's federal budget deficit was funded by the National Bank of Poland. Many goods and many producers were subsidized by the state. Service-Producing Industries made up only 38% of GDP. In 1989, the rate of inflation (CPI) was 640% from December to December. Currently, the yearly rate of inflation does not exceed 10%.

Lack of Competition. All prices were set by the state. Poland's economy saw a great deal of concentration of output and monopoly power by certain state enterprises; in practice, this meant that about 6,000 state enterprises made up almost 100% of total output. Most of the branches of these industries depended solely on the markets of the former Soviet Union. Employment in private industries made up only 10% of total employment. (Now, private industries make up over 60% of total employment.)

Lack of Economic Freedom. Only the state itself had the right to establish any business. Very few and very small private enterprises were in operation. Only certain state enterprises were permitted to trade abroad, and they were created solely for that purpose – the enterprises themselves did not produce any goods. There was no real and independent central bank in Poland at the time- only the central bank printed currency. There were no commercial banks, no stock market, and no other commercial financial institutions.

In early 1990 the government took steps designed mainly to equalize the overall demand and supply of money in the short run. In order to achieve this:

- A harsh discipline was introduced in equating budget income and administrating expenditure;
- Practically all forms of centrally administrated forms of distributing products and services were discarded;

- The scope of freely-set prices was expanded from 50 to some 90%, which meant that products and services were brought under market forces;
- The exchange rate was unified and stabilized, while Polish currency (Zloty) became internally convertible;
- The fundamental regulation of credit, the budget, and the banking system was imposed, removing such practices as financing the state budget deficit by the National Bank of Poland, which was the major source of inflation;
- A tangible liberalization of foreign trade was introduced by such moves as eliminating customs and foreign currency permits (M Biec, 1991).

The purpose of these steps was to achieve the most rapid possible transition through 'corrective' inflation and then reduction of it, which was fundamental to introducing any kind of systemic measures and to put the economy on its feet.

Using our Coincident and Leading Indexes, we can track five characteristic periods: one recession, one recovery, two slowdowns and one expansion.

Recession through December 1991. On the basis of our indicators, we can observe that the recession in the Polish economy persisted until December 1991. We can also observe that the recession ceased to deepen between June and December 1991. In this period, the value of production rapidly decreased. However, beginning in March 1991, the decreases were successively smaller. Employment cuts in enterprises increased. Until March 1991, monthly wages and salaries were alternately growing and dropping. These alternate increases and decreases can be explained by the Polish government's periodic 'revaluation' of wages and transfers (including wages of state employees and pensions). From April 1991, real wages in enterprises decreased systematically. The money supply also decreased, especially in 1991. The financial situation of enterprises worsened during this period. The rate of inflow of new orders also began to decrease, beginning in September 1991. Household debts substantially increased beginning in November 1990. This can be explained by extremely high interest rates (70-80%) during that period. In turn, these high interest rates can be seen as a result of introducing free market prices, which caused high levels of inflation. (Inflation in 1990 was 250% from December to December, and in 1991 60%.) The chaos that resulted from the abrupt change to the free market produced difficulties in linking market participants. An additional external factor that contributed to the deepening of this recession was the collapse of trade with the former COMECON. Enterprises needed to look for other markets to which they could export.

Recovery from January 1992 to December 1992. Many events during this period allow us to be certain that January 1992 indeed marked the beginning of this recovery. We can observe growth in production, an improvement in the financial situation of enterprises, as well slower employment decrease. The money supply was growing steadily. Orders were increasing in enterprises, as was productivity, and inventories. It is important to note that, during this period, the Polish National Bank devalued the Zloty on two occasions: the first was a devaluation of 17% in May 1991, and the second was a devaluation of 12% at the beginning of 1992. Together with the second devaluation, the new pegging mechanism of foreign exchange was established. Also during that time, the Polish government signed a special agreement concerning trade with the European Union. These undertakings made export easier for Polish producers. Additionally, in order to protect domestic producers, the Polish government established new frontier taxes and higher customs tariffs.

Short Slowdown from January 1993 to July 1993. During this period, various economic aggregates slowed and/or leveled off in their rate of growth. However, none of these indicators actually decreased. These slowdowns in growth can be observed in money supply, new orders, and, in consequence, production. The growth of wages and profits was also slower than it was earlier. Several factors impacted this slowdown, the major factor being the government's increases in prices of energy and oil, and higher income taxes for enterprises. The combination of these two factors created higher costs of production. Lastly, the economic activity in European Union countries began to slow.

Stable High Growth from August 1993 to September 1997. These four years of high and stable growth began and finished with a period of very rapid growth (October 93 to June 94; and January 96 to September 1997). The ratio of growth between these periods was also high but more stable. Almost all components of our Coincident and Leading Indicators improved during this period. Additionally, the first period of rapid growth (October 93 to June 94) was caused, in part, by growing activity in European countries (especially in Germany – Poland's largest partner in foreign trade) and third devaluation of Polish currency (Zloty) by 8% in the second half of 1993.

During this period, inflation dropped from 35% in 1993 to 14% in 1997; the unemployment rate dropped from 16% in 1994 to 10% in 1997; private enterprise's share in GDP grew from 52% in 1993 to 65-70% in 1997; the privatization was continuing and the financial market was developing.

Slowdown from October 1997. The first signals of slowdown in 1997 are observed in some of the components of the Leading Index. Real changes in credit liabilities of households dropped from the beginning of 1997, the deflated stock price index and inventories dropped from August 1997, as did orders. Inventories in industry were dropping beginning in September 1997. From November 1997, the financial situation in industry worsened. Only money supply and productivity were growing at rates similar to those in the past (productivity's rate was a little lower).

It is important to notice that in August 1997 the interest rate was increased by the National Bank of Poland. The rate of growth of the Leading Index slowed down beginning in May 1997.

6 Conclusion

This is one of the first attempts to construct the Coincident and Leading Indexes for an economy in Eastern and Central Europe. Some of our findings may be useful in creating similar indexes for other countries in the region.

The major problems are:

- The lack of some data, such as: average workweek, vendor performance, building permits, and interest rate spread.
- The lack of quality of the data (especially at the beginning of transition period).
- The lack of other official (private) independent sources of data available for more than the last 3 years, monthly or quarterly.

We also came up against other problems typical to the transformation process, such as rapid growth in unemployment at the beginning of the transformation, or 'emotional boom' on the stock exchange at the beginning of its operation.

The above-described experience proves that the concepts of Coincident and Leading Indicators are useful analytical tools when applied to the post-communist economies.

References

Drozdowicz-Biec, M. (1992), Stabilization Programme of the Polish Economy in the Light of Economic Situation Surveys. *CIRET Studien No. 42*, New Development of Business Surveys in the Transition Process in Central and Eastern European Countries, CIRET, Munich, pp. 87-106.

Lahiri, K. and G. Moore (1993), *Leading Economic Indicators. New approaches and forecasting records*. Cambridge University Press, Cambridge.

Niemira, M.P. and Ph. A. Klein (1994), *Forecasting Financial and Economic Cycles*. J. Wiley and Sons, Inc., New York.

Rogers, R.M. (1994), *Handbook of Key Economic Indicators*. Mc Graw-Hill, New York.

Sherman, H.J. (1991), *The Business Cycle Growth and Crisis under Capitalism*. Princeton University Press, Princeton.

Zarnowitz, V. (1992), *Business Cycles: Theory, History, Indicators and Forecasting*. Univ. of Chicago Press, Chicago.

Zarnowitz, V. (1998), *Cyclical Indicators and National Account. International Economic Indicators*, Vol. 22, Nos. 9-10.

Part II

Classification of Business Cycles

5 Multivariate Analysis for the Measurement of Economic Growth Cycles

PIERRE BEZIZ[1]

Cyclical analysis is based on the view that market-oriented economies experience repetitive and non-periodic fluctuations of their activity. The OECD developed its system of leading indicators and business cycle analysis to provide economic analysts with early signals of turning points in economic activity (see Beziz (OECD)). This is important information for economists, businessmen and policy makers to enable correct analysis of the current economic situation and for the anticipation of economic developments. In particular, it provides key information about when adjustments in economic policy should be implemented.

The OECD system of cyclical analysis has been in place since the middle of the 1980s. Since then, new statistical methods have emerged. Such developments have been facilitated by progress in information technology, which makes it possible to perform quickly complex statistical operations on large quantities of data. Thus, it may be worth reviewing the methodology of the OECD system. In parallel with my work at the OECD, I am carrying out research work on 'Statistical Tools for Cyclical Analysis'. The first objective of this research is to undertake a detailed review, comparison and assessment of different statistical techniques. Following this analysis, it may be possible to propose improvements in the methodology of the OECD system of business cycle analysis.

Results presented in this paper show that multivariate analysis is a useful tool for cyclical analysis. In particular, it provides reliable estimates for the end of the period. This is the weak point of the majority of the methods

---

[1] The author may be contacted at the following email address: pierre.beziz@oecd.org

commonly used. Multivariate analysis has been used for one country and could easily be generalised to a group of countries. It seems particularly suitable for calculating synthetic indicators for geographical zone aggregates, using data derived from the same type of surveys. These include, for example, business tendency surveys which are conducted in different sectors of the economy (manufacturing, construction, retail trade and services) and consumer surveys. Synthetic indicators for zone aggregates would give timely and pertinent information about the most recent developments of the economy. This would complement ideally the monthly information provided by the OECD Composite Leading Indicators.

1 Introduction

In order to develop models and indicators that give early signals of turning points, it is first necessary to measure the economic cycles. The objective of this paper is to present a technique based on Multivariate Analysis (MVA) for the measurement of economic cycles and then compare these results with the Phase Average Trend method (PAT) currently used at the OECD (see Section 2). The MVA technique extracts global cyclical information directly from a given set of time series. Hence, the cyclical information reflects a general phenomenon. Work presented in this paper was carried out on data for the Mexican economy. This is a continuation of a number of studies recently conducted on that country at the OECD. In particular, detailed simulations of the 1994 economic crisis were carried out (see Beziz, Petit (OECD, 1997)).

Timely recognition of economic turning points, peaks and troughs which mark the changes between expansion and recession phases, is a key element in quickly adapting to economic changes. This is of prime importance for economic policy since such policy can be tied to the stage of the cycle (recession and expansion). For instance, investment or fiscal policy can differ between a recessionary and an expansionary period. In a similar way, a large public debt can be considered viable during a recession, while adequate economic reforms should be implemented to reduce the amount of the debt during an expansion.

Two different types of economic cycles are commonly considered: business and growth cycles. The approach adopted at the OECD, which is also used in this paper, is based on the growth cycle definition.[2] Growth cycles measure the deviation from long-term trend, while business cycles correspond to the sequence of absolute growth and absolute decline in economic activity. Growth cycles will then show the sequence of periods of fast growth and periods of slower growth (i.e. a recession does not necessarily mean that there has been an absolute decline in the period). An increasing trend in a time series may make the detection of small cyclical movements more difficult. Thus, the growth cycle approach (deviation from long-term trend) is particularly relevant in cyclical analysis.[3] Also, it is important to mention that growth cycles encompass and appear more frequently than business cycles. Growth cycle turning points lead those of business cycles.

Different methods and statistical techniques are commonly used by National Statistical Offices, research institutes or International Organisations to measure economic cycles. These methods generally use univariate analysis (cycles are extracted separately for each individual time series). This is the case for instance at the OECD where trend and cycles are estimated individually for each time series. The MVA technique proposed in this paper is based on multivariate analysis. A common trend is estimated directly from a set of economic variables, hence, it is possible to estimate the turning points of each individual time series. Economic cycles are the result of the interaction of developments observed in the different sectors of the economy. Hence, the MVA method is a suitable way of taking into account global phenomenon in the economy.

Methods frequently used for the measurement of economic cycles are presented in Section 2. MVA results for Mexico and comparisons with PAT (one of the univariate methods described in the paper) are presented. Also advantages and drawbacks of the MVA method are analysed. This is done in Section 3. Further developments of the MVA to extract information for geographical zone aggregates are then presented in Section 4. Some details on the mathematical theory behind the MVA, as well as additional graphs and tables are presented in the Annexes. Finally, a bibliography listing the principal methodological references and details of the computer programs is provided.

---

2 Growth cycle definition was proposed by W. Mitchell from the National Bureau of Economic Research (NBER) in 1947.

3 Growth cycles are particularly useful for determining fluctuation in business activity of economies dominated by trend. This is particularly the case for Japan after the Second World War.

2 Univariate Methods for the Measurement of Economic Cycles

This section gives details of the methods most widely used to extract cyclical behaviour from time series. A methodological reference is indicated for each of these methods.

In time series analysis, a given macroeconomic time series X(t) can be decomposed into:

$$X(t) = C(t) + T(t) + S(t) + I(t) \qquad (2.1)$$

where C(t): cycle
T(t): trend
S(t): seasonal
I(t): irregular

The above components are not directly observable. Time series analysis provides tools to identify and estimate these components.

2.1 Moving Averages

Moving averages are very simple operations that can be used for cyclical analysis. In order to remove the trend in time series, it is possible to apply a moving average to the data. The length of the moving average is equal to the average length of the cycles observed in the historical data. The length is determined empirically or on theoretical grounds. Cycles in the time series are then extracted using equation 2.1.

This method has the advantage of simplicity. However, it has many disadvantages. In particular, the length of the moving average (n months) has to be kept fixed over the whole series, although lengths of cycles are changing. The moving average will perfectly estimate cycles of length n months. However, it will under-estimate longer cycles and over-estimate shorter cycles. It is also important to mention that end of period data are lost when moving averages are used. Thus, crucial information at the end of time series has to be estimated using extrapolation methods (a Henderson weight is the method most widely used).[4]

2.2 Annual Growth Rates

Cyclical components can be approximated using the annual percentage changes in time series. This method is one of the most frequently used.

[4] For more details see Harvey, 1992.

This is in part because it is very easy to implement. It also presents a clear economic interpretation. However, important drawbacks can be formulated: the method induces a phase shift in the original time series. Therefore it is not possible to precisely date the turning points.[5]

2.3 PAT Method

At the OECD, long-term trends in time series are estimated using a modified version of the Phase Average Trend method (PAT) developed by the US National Bureau of Economic Research. The trend is estimated by splitting the series into cyclical phases using a preliminary estimation of peaks and troughs (Bry-Boschan routine).[6] Averages of the data over each phase (phase averages) are calculated and a three-month moving average of the phase averages is computed. The values obtained are located at the midpoint of the three-phase period, called 'triplets'. A second approximation of the trend is calculated by connecting midpoints of the triplets. The level of the final trend is then adjusted to match the level of the original data. The trend is extrapolated to the end of the series by using the slope between the last two triplet mid-points. Finally, the level of the trend of the last segment is adjusted to match the level of the original data and cycles are calculated from the trend estimate using equation 2.1.

End of period data, lost with the PAT method, have to be estimated using linear extrapolation. In practice, the end of period trend estimate may be substantially revised. It has also been found that cycles calculated by the Bry-Boschan routine tend to be too flexible. This is because there is no control over the amplitude of the cycles. Minor fluctuations are selected in the routine and are given the same weight as more important cycles.[7]

---

[5] For more details see Harvey, 1992 and Niemira/Klein, 1994.

[6] The PAT procedure requires an initial list of turning points which define the cyclical phases. Initial turning point estimates are calculated using the Bry-Boschan routine (see [4]). The process for deriving the initial list using this procedure entails calculation of an estimated trend for the preliminary identification of peaks and troughs (using a 75-month moving-average). The procedure then executes a series of tests on the deviation from the estimated trend in order to eliminate extreme values. It also specifies a minimum duration of each phase (five months) and the minimum duration for a cycle (15 months). Finally, an OECD expert validates the list of turning points to be used as input to the PAT program. This is mainly to validate each turning point from an economic point of view and to make the distinction between major and minor cycles (only major cycles are taken into account for PAT trend calculation).

[7] For more details see OECD, 1987.

2.4 Hodrick Prescott Filter

The HP filter represents a simple method for the estimation of cycles in time series. The HP filter has become very popular and is widely used in applied economics (in particular by the OECD Economics Department).

The HP filter must be applied to seasonally adjusted time series. The HP filter is the solution of the following minimisation problem:

$$\text{Min}\,[\sum (X(t)\text{-}T(t))^2 + \lambda \sum [(X(t+1) - X(t)) - (X(t) - X(t\text{-}1))]^2] \tag{2.2}$$

The smoothing coefficient λ has to be chosen *a priori*. A different value for λ will give a different trend estimate. The lower/higher is λ the less/more flexible is the trend. Cycles are then derived using equation 2.1.

The HP filter method is relatively intuitive and is very easy to implement (see Hodrick, Prescott, 1980). Empirical results are in general close to those obtained from other methods. However, a number of criticisms can be formulated. The smoothing coefficient λ has to be set *a priori* and will govern the final trend estimate. A value of λ=1600 for quarterly series and λ=6400 for monthly series has become the standard (see Univ. of Auckland, 1996). It has also been noticed in practice, that the end of period trend estimates may be substantially revised.

2.5 Kalman Filter

This method sets a specific model for the trend and cycles. For a time series X(t) equation 2.1 can be written under a form called the state space model:

$$\begin{cases} E(t) = F\,E(t-1) + Ga(t) \\ X(t) = H\,E(t) + a(t) \end{cases} \quad \text{a(t) matrix white noise} \tag{2.3}$$

with

$$F(t)=\begin{bmatrix}1 & 0 & 0 & .... & 0\\ 0 & a & 0 & .... & 0\\ 0 & 0 & -1 & -1.. & 0\\ 0 & 0 & 0 & 1..0 & 0\\ 0 & 0 & 0 & .. .. & 1\end{bmatrix},\ E(t)=\begin{bmatrix}Tt\\ Ct\\ St\\ .\\ .\\ St-10\\ St-11\end{bmatrix},\ G=\begin{bmatrix}1\\ 1\\ 1\\ 0\\ .\\ .\\ 0\end{bmatrix}, \qquad (2.4)$$

$$H(t)=[1 \quad 1 \quad 1 \quad 0 \quad .. \quad 0]$$

and components are modelled according to:

$$\begin{aligned} &T(t)=T(t-1)+\varepsilon(t) && \varepsilon(t) \text{ white noise}\\ &S(t)=-S(t-1)-...-S(t-11)+\gamma(t) && \gamma(t) \text{ white noise} \qquad (2.5)\\ &C(t)=aC(t)+\beta(t) && \beta(t) \text{ white noise}\end{aligned}$$

It is possible to estimate each of the unobserved components of the state space model using the iterative algorithm of the Kalman filter. The resulting filter is the estimator that minimises the mean square error of X(t). The Kalman filter represents a powerful tool for the modelling and estimation of components in the domain of time series. In particular, this technique seems to present a solution for reliable estimates for the end of the period. State space model specification is large enough to be generalised. In particular, Kalman filter technique is very often used to jointly model several time series taking into account their relation (multivariate analysis). This method is being used by an increasing number of institutes.[8]

2.6 Probabilistic Methods

This method specifies a probabilistic model for the trend. For each time period t,

$$\begin{cases} X(t)=C(t)+T(t) \\ T(t)=T(t-1)+M(t)+\varepsilon(t) \qquad \varepsilon\ (t) \text{ white noise}\end{cases} \qquad (2.6)$$

[8] For more details see Harvey, 1992.

Where M(t) is a random walk. That is, Mt comprises two different states: 1 and 0, respectively for increase and decrease. A probability is attached to the transition between the two different states. Therefore, there are four probabilities for the transition from states: 1 to 0; 0 to 1; 1 to 1; 0 to 0.

First, it is necessary to estimate an empirical probability rule for Mt given the historical figures in the original time series. Then, it is possible to estimate the trend and cycles of the original time series. Hamilton proposed this method. The results for the turning points of the US economy were close to those of National Bureau of Economic Research. Given its relative theoretical complexity, this method is not easy to implement in practice for a regular estimation of the turning points.[9]

3 Multivariate Methods for the Measurement of Economic Growth Cycles

As mentioned in the introduction to this paper, the multivariate technique (MVA) can be used to estimate the cyclical behaviour of macroeconomic time series. This section describes how the MVA has been implemented in the case of Mexico. In particular, this section includes:

- selected macroeconomic indicators.
- theory and description of the MVA technique.
- results and comparisons with the PAT method.
- advantages and drawbacks of the MVA method.
- See Annex 1 for mathematical details.

3.1 Macroeconomic Indicators for the Mexican Economy

In order to run the MVA method, it is first necessary to select a set of key macroeconomic indicators. For the example presented in this article, 31 macroeconomic indicators have been selected for Mexico. These indicators cover the key sectors of the national economy, in particular: industrial production, business tendency surveys,[10] foreign trade, prices, monetary and financial indicators, employment and wages. Selected indicators are compiled on a monthly basis and historical data cover the period from January 1986 to May 1998 (137 observations). These indicators are

---

[9] For more details see Hamilton, 1989.

[10] Business tendency surveys collect qualitative information about the current and future states of the economy. Results are generally expressed as the percentage of positive over negative replies.

available on a regular basis in the monthly *Main Economic Indicators* publication. See Annex 2 for a detailed list of indicators.

Time series are usually viewed in the *time* domain, i.e., they are considered as observations for successive time period (t=1..T). In that case, the basic decomposition of time series is given by equation 2.1 (see Section 2). It is also possible to analyse a time series in the *frequency* domain where interest is centred on the contributions made by the various periodic components of the series. Here, the basic assumption is the decomposition of time series as a finite sum of sine and cosine functions of different frequencies. It is possible to represent the relative importance of each frequency. This representation is called the periodogram. Frequency domain analysis represents a powerful tool for identifying the cyclical movements in time series.

The MVA method can be used on either time or frequency data. The initial set of 31 indicators was observed on 137 time observations. It is possible to directly analyse this set of data (time domain). For an analysis in the frequency domain, time series first need to be converted to periodograms. Time series with 137 observations will generate periodograms with 68 frequencies. Hence, the set of data analysed in this case is composed of 31 variables (periodograms) and 68 observations (frequencies). MVA has been applied to seasonally adjusted time series.

In order to facilitate the reading of this article, only the results for the frequency domain are presented in detail. The main differences with the results in the time domain are briefly discussed. Detailed results of the analysis in the time domain are available upon request.

3.2 *Theory and Description of the MVA*

The MVA extracts cyclical movements directly from a set of indicators using the statistical technique known as Principal Component Analysis (PCA). For a given set of data, the PCA calculates a new set of variables (principal axes) which explain the variance of the initial data. Axes are usually arranged in descending order according to the share of variance they explain (the inertia). That is, the first axis explains more variance than the second axis, etc.

PCA axes synthesise the characteristics of a set of data. For macroeconomic indicators, the main variance (i.e. the first PCA axis) is *generally* explained by the trend. It is possible using the PCA technique, to reconstruct the initial set of variables omitting one or several axes. For example, when axes characterising the trend are omitted, the resulting set of variables is corrected for the trend and then shows the cyclical behaviour.

The main operations that were carried out to apply MVA on the frequency domain are:

- convert the 31 time series to periodograms.
- carry out PCA analysis of the set of 31 variables and 68 observations.
- reconstruction of the periodograms without trend (axis characterising the trend is omitted).
- calculation back to time of the detrended series from the reconstructed periodograms.[11, 12]

The methodology adopted for the analysis in the time domain is the same. Obviously, the first and last bullet points above, which refer to the conversion between time and frequency, are not relevant.

3.3 *Results of the MVA Analysis*

The inertia explained by the first three PCA axes represents 96% of the total inertia of the initial set of data. In particular, the first axis represents 86% of the total inertia. After the third axis, the percent of inertia declines quickly and becomes insignificant (see Table 5.1 for details). In practice, this means that the initial set of 31 variables can be summarised using three synthetic variables. It is possible to give an interpretation for each PCA axis (see Annex 1). The first axis clearly represents the *global trend* of the Mexican economy. Interpretation of axis 2 and axis 3 is not so clear. There is a mix of cyclical components and irregular components.

Therefore, a reconstruction of the initial set of data without the first axis will show detrended time series and focus on the cyclical behaviour. It is important to emphasise that each series is corrected for the global trend of the economy. Each indicator however, has a different contribution (thus, a specific representation) to the first axis. Consequently, the implicit trend is specific to each indicator. Peaks and troughs of the cycles are finally determined by graphical inspection of the reconstructed indicators. A generic rule is applied:

- time span between peaks and troughs (phases) should be longer than 4 months.

---

[11] For details see Annex 1.

[12] The calculation back to time is based on the average of the time series. Given the manipulation on the data, the average of the detrended series to be reconstructed is unknown. Thus, only n-1 observations over the n of the original time series can be generated.

- time span between two peaks or two troughs (cycles) should be longer than 14 months.

The cyclical behaviour of a selected number of economic indicators is detailed below. These key indicators of the Mexican economy refer to total industrial production, consumer prices, share prices, level of stock of finished goods (from business tendency surveys) and total imports. The chronology of turning points has been compared with that of PAT. Table 5.2 gives details of the turning points detected by both methods as well as the difference in the number of months between each turning point. See Annex 2 for the detailed list of turning points detected using the MVA method.

Table 5.1 - Percent of Inertia - PCA Axis

Axis	Percent inertia	Cumulated inertia
1	86%	86%
2	6%	92%
3	4%	96%
4	2%	98%
5	1%	99%

MVA results are consistent with those obtained using the PAT method for all historical data. Timing of turning points is in general very close, except for one cycle of total industrial production. There is only one extra/missing cycle between PAT and MVA (for total imports). It should be mentioned, however, that given their amplitude these are minor cycles.

In particular, MVA picks up very well the cyclical behaviour of the series Finished goods stocks: level, which is very irregular. MVA and PAT give a close chronology of turning points. However, MVA picks up the general behaviour and the amplitude of the different cycles more effectively (in fact, PAT cycles are irregular and the method gives poor information about the real amplitudes). This should not be surprising as trend and irregular components correspond to opposite frequency bands in the periodogram. They can easily be disassociated using analysis in the frequency domain.

Table 5.2 - Chronology of Turning Points Selected Indicators

	Total industrial production			Finished goods stocks level			Consumer price index		
Turning points	MVA	PAT[13]	diff.[14]	MVA	PAT	diff.	MVA	PAT	diff.
Peak	9/87	9/87	0	3/87	1/87	+2	-	-	-
Trough	7/89	7/88	+12	3/89	4/89	-1	-	-	-
Peak	8/90	8/90	0	7/90	8/90	-1	1/89	3/88	+9
Trough	5/91	1/92	-7	1/92	1/92	0	12/94	12/94	0
Peak	6/92	7/92	-1	2/93	1/93	+1	1/97	2/97	-1
Trough	10/93	6/93	+4	3/94	2/94	+1	-	-	-
Peak	5/94	8/94	-3	3/95	2/95	+1	-	-	-
Trough	5/95	5/95	0	11/96	12/96	-1	-	-	-
Peak	-	-	-	-	-	-	-	-	-

	Share price index			Total imports		
Turning points	MVA	PAT	diff.	MVA	PAT	diff.
Peak	9/87	9/87	0	-	-	-
Trough	6/88	2/89	-8	-	2/87	-
Peak	7/89	9/89	-2	-	8/88	-
Trough	4/90	9/90	-5	1/90	4/90	-3
Peak	2/92	2/92	0	92/7	1/91	+18
Trough	9/92	5/93	-8	10/93	11/93	-1
Peak	11/93	1/94	-2	5/94	11/94	-6
Trough	2/95	2/95	0	4/95	4/95	0
Peak	11/97	9/97	+2	-	-	-

As mentioned previously, MVA has also been applied on the time domain for the complete set of indicators. Results are consistent with those in the frequency domain. It appears however, that the distinction between irregular and trend in the time domain, appears less clearly than in the frequency domain, which gives far better cyclical estimates for irregular series. Thus, the MVA method in the frequency domain provides a useful tool to separate irregular components from trend. It better estimates the cyclical behaviour, and thus facilitates the interpretation of most recent data. The advantage however, of the analysis in the time domain is that no

[13] All turning points detected by PAT (major and minor cycles).

[14] Number of months. A positive (resp. negative) sign indicates that the turning point appears before with PAT (resp. MVA).

data are lost at the end of the period (one observation is lost when MVA is applied in the frequency domain).

3.4 Advantages and Drawbacks of the MVA Method

The MVA method is a useful tool to estimate the cyclical behaviour of a set of time series. In particular, it is possible to use this technique to mix different types of indicators. In the example described above, the initial set of data is composed of quantitative indicators (indices of industrial production, wages, etc.) as well as qualitative indicators (from business tendency surveys).

This multivariate method clearly presents some advantages compared to other methods, but also some drawbacks (see below). Given the short experience using this method, this list is not necessarily exhaustive.

- Advantages
  - no data are lost at the beginning and end of period, as is the case with methods derived from moving averages (including PAT). It is not necessary to extrapolate data. Thus, MVA provides reliable data for the end of the period.
  - it is possible to estimate the cyclical behaviour of a set of data composed of quantitative indicators and qualitative indicators from business tendency surveys at the same time (see footnote 4, page 4).
  - the general trend of the economy is estimated from a large set of indicators. Thus, it reflects a global phenomenon.
  - the MVA in the frequency domain clearly separates irregular behaviour from trend, as these are associated to opposite frequency bands in the periodogram. In particular, it gives very good cyclical estimates for irregular series.
  - it is possible to further develop the MVA. For instance, it would be possible to classify indicators according to their cyclical behaviour.
  - it is possible to estimate cycles of a very large set of time series concurrently (1000 indicators or more). The computing time does not exceed 10 minutes to perform the operations presented in this paper.
- Drawbacks
  - MVA directly extracts the cycles from the original series (cycles are not derived from the trend estimate). Thus, it is not possible to assess directly how 'correct' the cyclical estimates are.

- all time series should have the same length of historical data (same start and end dates). Series should be compiled on the same frequency (monthly, quarterly, etc.).
- the initial set of indicators is chosen a priori. A different set of indicators will give different results. In practice however, the method is quite robust. MVA was applied to a slightly different set of indicators and key results were the same.
- MVA may give spurious results if initial indicators have very little in common.
- the mathematical theory is rather complex and the method may be not intuitive for a non-expert.

4 MVA for Geographical Zone Aggregates

MVA proposes a convenient tool for extracting the main information from a set of data. In this article, it has been implemented to estimate the general trend of the economy and then the cycles in time series for Mexico. It seems natural to further develop the method. In particular, MVA could be used to estimate the main cyclical behaviour of geographical zone aggregates (including OECD-Total, OECD-Europe, North America, etc.).

Given the advantages and drawbacks presented above, MVA seems particularly well adapted to extracting information from a set of series from the same type of surveys. In such a case, indicators generally show close cyclical behaviour. Harmonised business tendency surveys for instance, are conducted in the majority of OECD Member countries in different sectors of the economy (construction, trade, manufacturing, etc.). Business tendency surveys are considered a timely and convenient tool providing accurate information for the analysis of the economic situation. Indicators derived from these surveys are characterised by strong cyclical behaviour (data are calculated as the percent balance of positive over negative replies, thus in general do not show trend). Therefore, MVA seems particularly well adapted to synthesising the general cyclical behaviour from this set of time series (PCA axis). Such synthetic indicators would give timely and reliable information about the current state of different sectors of the economy.

In addition to the strengths and weaknesses mentioned in the previous Section, MVA presents, for the calculation of zone aggregates, a number of advantages compared to other methods. These include:

- it is possible to use a large number of indicators to estimate the cyclical behaviour of the zone. This will give more reliable information. In particular, it is not necessary to select a set of indicators according to specific criteria as is currently the case in the OECD system (this operation is particularly time consuming).
- MVA provides an implicit weight for the aggregation. The weight of each indicator reflects its contribution towards the general cyclical behaviour. This approach gives increased flexibility compared to other systems where each country has received a given weight (consequently all indicators for a country have the same weight).[15]
- an analysis of the contribution to the general behaviour gives useful information on which are the key economic indicators (for example the level of Order books export for Germany).

Finally, it is worth mentioning that when using MVA all indicators should have the same length of historical data and should be compiled with the same frequency. Zone aggregates include data for different countries. So, it may be necessary to convert all series to the same frequency. In order to ensure the most timely data, one should convert all figures to monthly data using a linear interpolation.

5 Conclusion

This paper has shown that multivariate techniques can be successfully applied to estimate cyclical behaviour from a set of economic indicators. In general, the results of the MVA technique for Mexico are close to those from the PAT method. The main advantage of the MVA method is that it is not necessary to extrapolate end of period figures[16] as is the case with methods derived from moving averages (for instance, 37 end of period data points have to be extrapolated with PAT). Hence, MVA provides more reliable data at the end of the period. This is a key point for a correct analysis of the current economic situation and for the anticipation of future developments. In addition, the analysis in the frequency domain (rather than in the time domain) allows one to separate irregular components and thus, gives a better estimate of the cyclical behaviour.

---

[15] In addition, it is also possible to weight (or score) each indicator according to their timeliness, economic significance, etc. before running MVA (weighted MVA). There is no difficulty from the theoretical point of view. The difficulty is practical and refers to the method and criteria used to calculate these scores.

[16] Except in the frequency domain: one observation is lost at the end of the period.

Work presented in this paper could be improved in a number of ways. These include:

- quantifying the stability and robustness of the method, the reliability of end of period data. Comparing this with other methods described in this article.
- classifying indicators according to their common cyclical behaviour, etc.
- calculating composite indicators (leading, lagging, coincident) to give signals of turning points in the economy.
- generalising the MVA to more than one country and measuring economic cycles for geographical zone aggregates.

The use of multivariate techniques is still relatively recent. It is particularly appropriate to cyclical analysis and it would be worth further elaborating this method. In particular, given the advantages and drawbacks mentioned above, the MVA seems particularly adapted to estimate for one country, the underlying cyclical behaviour of a set of indicators issued from the same survey. In that case, indicators generally present close cyclical pattern, are compiled with the same frequency, and historical data cover the same period. For example, the use of MVA to extract information from a large set of business tendency survey indicators seems particularly appropriate.

OECD could conduct further investigation and assessment of the MVA method to elaborate the extraction of cyclical behaviour for geographical zone aggregates, using results from consumer and business tendency surveys. This timely and easily available information, compiled for different key sectors of the economy, would complement information obtained from the monthly composite leading indicators.

6 Appendix

A Annex 1 - Mathematical Details

The main mathematical points used in MVA are presented briefly below:

The Frequency Domain. A time series can be examined either in the time domain or in the frequency domain. The later is based on the decomposition of time series as the sum of sine components with different frequencies and amplitudes. Frequency is defined as the inverse of cycle length and amplitude is the range between peaks and troughs. Analysis in the frequency domain provides a useful tool for estimating the main cyclical behaviour in time series. The decomposition is known as a Fourier series transform:

$$X(t) = X + 2 \sum \ [Aj\cos(2\pi\, j^*(t\text{-}1)/N) + Bj\sin(2\pi\, j^*(t\text{-}1)/N)] \qquad (A.1)$$

With t=1..N, j=1..N/2 if N is odd, j=1..N-1/2 is N is even, Aj and Bj are the Fourier coefficients, X is the average of Xt over all observations. The relative importance of each frequency in the time series is defined as:

$$Pj = Aj^2 + Bj^2. \qquad (A.2)$$

The *periodogram* is the representation of Pj against each frequency. Peaks in the periodogram are interpreted as the cyclical dominance in the time series. See next page for an example.

Finally, it is important to mention that using the above equation A.1, it is possible to reconstruct series in the time domain from data in the frequency domain, using the Fourier coefficients. For more details see bibliography [3].

Principal Component Analysis. Principal Component Analysis (PCA) provides a useful tool for extracting information from large tables of data (observations and variables). PCA calculates a new set of variables in order to obtain a synthetic representation of the original set of data. These new variables are the PCA axes. They are associated with the eigenvalues of the correlation matrix of the set of data. PCA axes have some characteristic properties: they are not correlated and the information explained by all the axes together is equal to the variance of the initial set of data. Axes are classified in decreasing order according to the share of total information they provide (inertia). Each PCA axis represents a characteristic of the data set and thus, can be interpreted. This is done by displaying graphically the co-ordinates of all observations on the axis (principal components).

It is possible in PCA to reconstruct the set of data omitting one or several axes. This is done projecting each variable on the selected axis (using the reconstruction formula). The new set of data therefore does not include the characteristics of the omitted axes.

The calculation from frequency back to time is done using the Fourier coefficients after reconstruction of the set of data omitting the first axis. To do this, the initial Fourier coefficients are included in the PCA as additional variables. These variables are not used for the calculation of the PCA axes, but it is always possible to calculate their co-ordinates on the new system of PCA axes (correlation with the axis). The new set of Fourier coefficients is calculated omitting the first PCA axis. Time series calculated from these new coefficients are obviously corrected for the trend.[17]

B Annex 2 - MVA Results

Detailed MVA results on the Mexican economy are shown in this Annex.

Interpreting PCA Axis. It is possible to interpret the first PCA axis from the graphical representation of the first principal components. Figure 5.1 below suggests that the first PCA axis be characterised by a spectral peak at a 137-month cycle. The length of the cycle is equal to the total length of historical data. Thus, it corresponds to the global trend observed on all the indicators of the Mexican economy.

Turning Points of the Key Indicators of the Mexican Economy.[18] The cyclical behaviour of selected key indicators are presented below (see Figures 5.2-5.6).

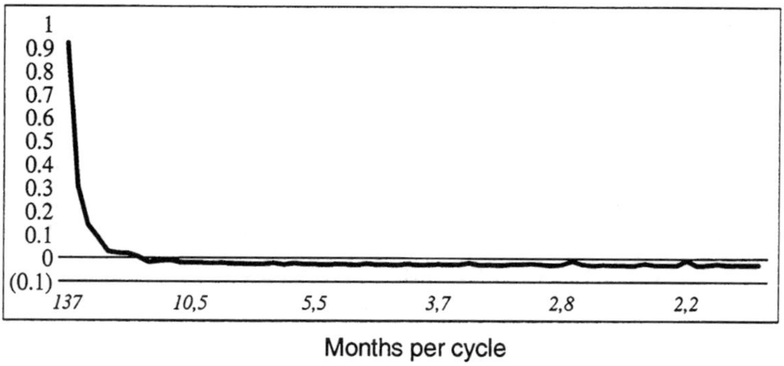

Figure 5.1 - First PCA Axis - Frequency Domain

[17] For more details on PCA see Jackson, 1991.

[18] P: Peak; T: Trough.

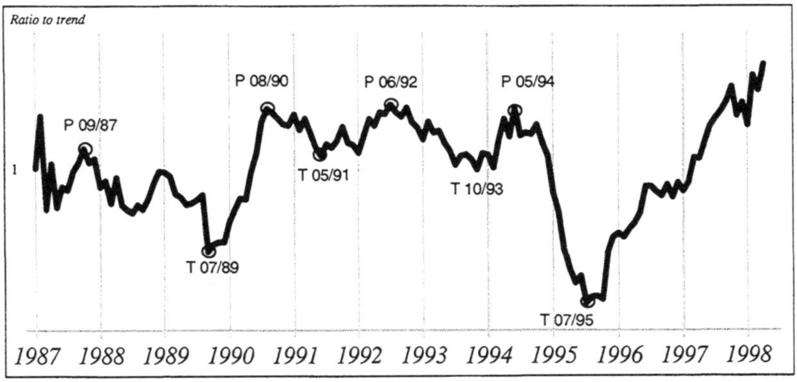

Figure 5.2 - Industrial Production - Total

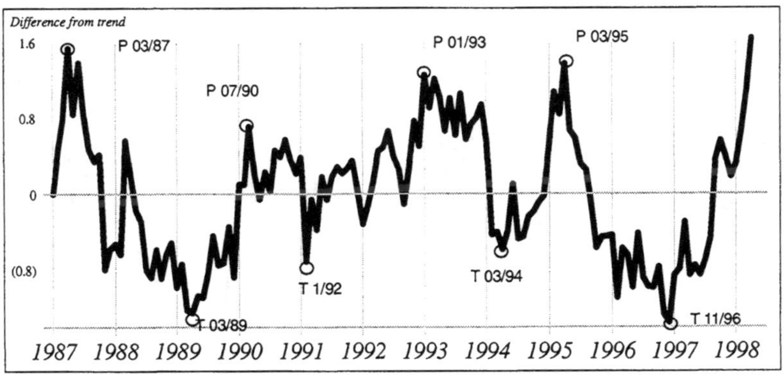

Figure 5.3 - Finished Goods Stocks: Level

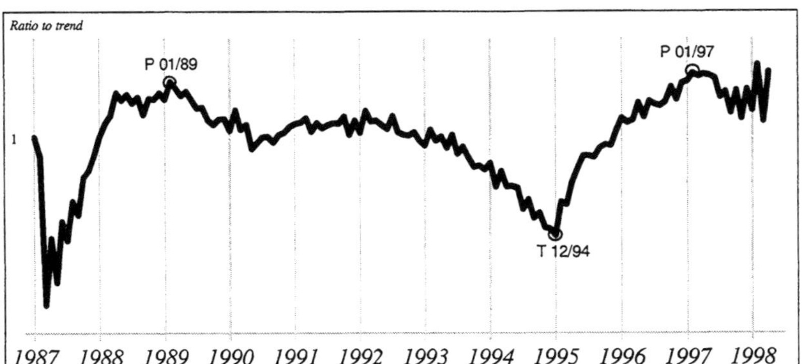

Figure 5.4 - Consumer Prices - All Items

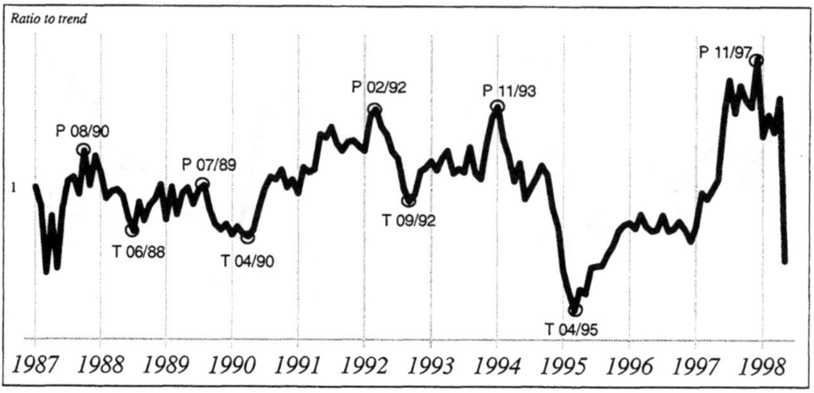

Figure 5.5 - Share Prices

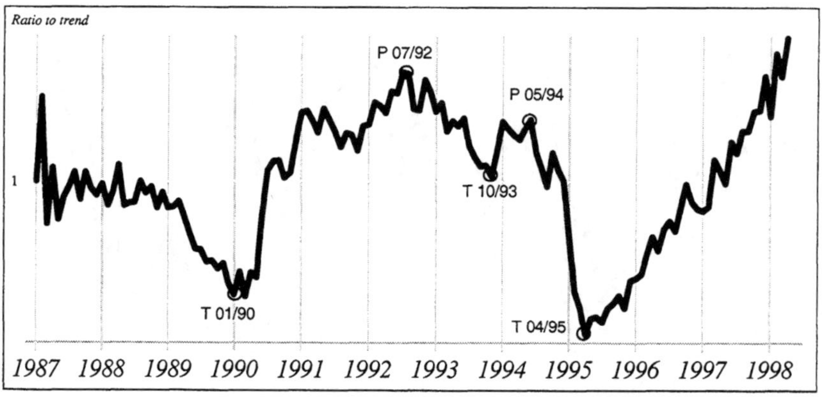

Figure 5.6 - Total Imports

Table 5.3 below includes the complete list of indicators used in MVA as well as all detected turning points.

Table 5.3 - Chronology of MVA Turning Points - All Indicators

Industrial production - total	P 9/87	T 7/89	P 8/90	T 5/91	P 6/92	T 10/93	P 5/94	T 5/95	
Industrial production - manufacturing	P 9/87	T 6/88	P 11/88	T 11/89	P 7/90	T 5/93	P 9/94	T 7/95	
Industrial production - mining	P 12/87	T 9/89	P 5/94	T 9/95					
Industrial production - elect, gas water	P 6/90	T 7/91	P 9/92	T 10/93	P 11/94	T 9/95	P 8/97		
Industrial production - construction	T 8/89	P 4/95	T 8/95						
Crude petroleum	P 2/91	T 9/95							
BTS Production: tendency	T 4/95	P 10/95							
BTS Finished goods stocks: level	P 3/87	T 3/89	P 7/90	T 1/92	P 2/93	T 3/94	P 3/95	T 11/96	
BTS Sales: tendency	No evident cyclical behaviour								
BTS Employment: tendency	T 8/87	P 3/88	T 1/89	P 5/93	P 9/94	T 1/95	P 2/96		
BTS Stocks related to sales	No evident cyclical behaviour								
Cost of construction	P 3/88	T 12/94	P 3/97						
Wholesale trade	P 6/92	T 7/93	P 9/94	T 7/95					
Retail trade	T 1/88	P 9/92	T 10/93	P 8/94	T 10/95				
Employment - manufacturing	T 11/89	P 8/92	T 10/93	P 10/94	T 8/95				
Insured workers	T 8/88	P 10/91	T 8/95						
Unemployment rate	P 10/88	T 8/92	P 7/95	T 9/97					
Hours of work - manufacturing	T 1/90	P 9/92	T 4/95	P 9/97					
Total wages - manufacturing	T 3/90	P 11/94	T 3/96						
Producer prices - total	P 2/89	T 11/94	P 12/96						
Producer prices - agricultural products	P 10/88	T 11/89	P 5/92	T 12/94	P 9/96				
Consumer prices - all items	P 1/89	T 12/94	P 1/97						
Money supply M1	T 12/89	P 1/92	T 4/95						
Money supply M3	T 3/87	P 8/91	T 5/95						
3-month interest rate (CETES)	P 12/87	T 9/88	P 2/95						
Share prices	P 9/87	T 6/88	P 7/89	T 4/90	P 2/92	T 9/92	P 11/93	T 2/95	P 11/97
Real effective exchange rate	T 2/88	P 7/94	T 4/97						
Official reserves	P 3/88	T 5/89	P 12/93	T 12/94					
Imports - total	T 1/90	P 7/92	T10/93	P 5/94	T 4/95				
Exports - total	P 2/89	T 4/90	P 1/91	T 8/94					
Net trade	T 8/94	P 7/95	T 12/97						

Note. BTS: business tendency survey

References

Beziz, Pierre (OECD), 'OECD Composite Leading Indicators: A Tool for Short-term Analysis' available on the OECD web-site: http://www.oecd.org.std/li1.htm.

Beziz, Pierre and Gérald Petit (OECD, 1997), 'The 1994 Mexican Crisis: Were Signals Inadequate?', Paper published in the *Cambridge Review of International Affairs*, Vol XI, No. 1.

Harvey, Andrew C. (1992), '*Time series models, second edition*', Philip Alan, Oxford UK.

Hodrick R.J. and Edward Prescott (1980), 'Post-War U.S. Business Cycles: An Empirical Investigation', Discussion paper, Carnegie-Mellon University.

National Bureau of Economic Research (1971), 'Programmed Turning Point Determination', Gerhard Bry and Charlotte Boschan, Paper published in *Cyclical Analysis of Time Series: selected procedures and computed programmes*.

OECD (1987), 'OECD Leading Indicators and Business Cycles in Member Countries', *Sources and Methods 1960-1985*, No. 39.

University of Auckland (1996), 'The Hodrick Prescott filter, a Generalisation, and a New Procedure for Extracting an Empirical Cycle from a Series', Working Paper No. 160.

Hamilton, James D. (1989), 'A New Approach to the Economic Analysis of Non-stationary Time Series and the Business Cycle', paper published in *Econometrica*, Vol. 57 No. 2, pp. 357-384.

Jackson, J. Edward (1991), '*A User's Guide to Principal Components*', Wiley, New York.

The main reference for cyclical analysis is:

Niemira, Michael P. and Philip A. Klein (1994), '*Forecasting Financial and Economic Cycles*', Wiley, New York.

Computer programmes

- Calculations of the periodograms, Fourier coefficients, and PCA were performed using SAS software.
- Calculations from the frequency domain back to time (Fourier inverse) were programmed in FAME.
- Additional calculations (including multiplication of matrix, etc.) were carried out in Excel 97.

All data, complete results and computer programmes are available upon request (pierre.beziz@oecd.org).

6 Quantitative and Qualitative Leading Indicators: Evaluating Performance in Long and Average Expansions

LORENE HIRIS and PHILIP A. KLEIN[1]

The current U.S. economic expansion, which began in March 1991, exhibited an unusually weak and long recovery period. As of March 1999, it is 96 months old and is the second longest expansion to be officially recorded in U.S. history thus far. It has overtaken the 1982-1990 expansion, which lasted 92 months and is within striking distance of overtaking the 1961-1969 longest U.S. expansion of 106 months duration. In the post World War II period, the average length of all expansions, including the current one, thus far has been 55 months, while the mean of the three longest expansions (1961-1969, 1982-1990, 1990-present) is 98 months as of now.

The focus of this study is to compare the performance of qualitative versus quantitative leading indicators over long expansions as contrasted with expansions of more traditional length in order to ascertain whether the behavior of the qualitative leading indicators is distinctive and subsequently more useful than the quantitative leading indicators.

[1] We wish to thank Jean Maltz, Michele Ha, and Nancy Cole for assistance in preparing this paper.

1 Timing at Business Cycle Peaks

Table 6.1 presents the timing of 18 quantitative leading indicators at the nine business cycle peaks since 1948. Table 6.2 shows a similar analysis for seven qualitative leading indicators. Turning points of all series were determined by the computerized algorithm (Bry and Boschan, 1971), based on the systematic codification of judgmental procedures used for decades at the National Bureau of Economic Research (NBER). The Bry-Boschan procedure provides a good way to define turning points since it is based on objective criteria for determining cyclical peaks and troughs. (It is also notable that the U. S. Bureau of Labor Statistics is currently recording the Bry-Boschan program as part of its plans for having all its important computer systems year 2000 compliant (Hiles, 1998).)

Table 6.1 shows that the average lead of the 18 quantitative series is 12 months at the seven traditional expansion peaks and 13 months for the two long expansion peaks. Table 6.2, reporting results for the qualitative indicators, presents similar results. The mean lead before the peaks ending the two long expansions (1961-1969, 1982-1990) is 12 months, although the lead before the peak ending the first long expansion is nine months, while that before the peak ending the second long expansion is 17 months. Table 6.1 reveals that variability in the leads exists for the qualitative indicators and also exists for the quantitative indicators. However, the differences in average timing between the two types of indicators before the peaks ending the two types of expansions seem negligible and are well within the margins that can be explained by rounding.

During the 50 years covered in this study, all the indicators, both quantitative and qualitative, lead by 12 months at all the peaks on average. As the terminal month for the current long expansion is not as yet known, we have eliminated this expansion from these calculations. This portion of our study also reaffirms the conclusions that have been stated in previous papers that qualitative indicators are useful primarily as supplements to the quantitative indicators, or substitutes when the latter are not available, and that their major temporal advantage lies in the promptness with which the data become available.

Table 6.1 - Timing, Eighteen Quantitative Indicators at Business Cycle Peaks; in Months, Lead (-) or Lag (+)

Quantitative Indicators ↓ / → Peaks	Seven Average Expansions								Two Long Expansions			Avg. at All Expansions
	Nov 48	Jul 53	Aug 57	Apr 60	Nov 73	Jan 80	Jul 81	Average	Dez 69	Jul 90	Average	
Money Supply (M2)	NTC	NTC	-19	NTC	-10	-24	NTC	-18	-11	-7	-9	-14
M2+ Household Long-term Mutual Funds	NTC	NTC	NTC	NTC	-10	-25	NTC	-18	-12	-7	-10	-14
Yield Spread	NTC	NTC	-6	-4	-3	NTC	-7	-5	-4	-13	-8	-6
Risk Differential	NTC	-3	-24	-10	4	-15	2	-8	-25	-3	-14	-9
Price to Unit Labor Cost	2	-30	-25	-17	-25	-27	3	-17	-17	-9	-13	-16
Labor Productivity,Manufacturing,Growth Rate	NTC	-8	-6	-17	-11	-17	0	-10	-20	3	-9	-10
CPI for Services,Growth Rate	NTC	NTC	NTC	NTC	-9	-37	NTC	-23	-25	-40	-33	-28
Housing Permits	NTC	-8	-30	-17	-11	-29	-10	-18	-10	-21	-16	-17
Average Work Week,Manufacturing	-18	-3	-21	-11	-7	-10	-7	-11	-14	-15	-15	-12
New Orders,Consumer Goods	-5	-3	-29	-13	0	-15	-3	-10	-11	-18	-15	-11
New Orders,Consumer Goods,Manufacturing	-5	-3	-25	-13	0	-13	-9	-10	-3	-19	-11	-10
Contracts for Plant & Equipment	NTC	-26	-21	-13	-1	-15	-6	-14	-11	-18	-15	-14
Average Weekly Overtime,Manufacturing	NTC	NTC	NTC	-10	-7	-10	-6	-8	-13	-15	-14	-10
Initial Claims,Unemployment Insurance	-13	-10	-23	-12	-9	-21	-4	-13	-11	-21	-16	-14
Real Estate Loans, Growth Rate	NTC	NTC	NTC	NTC	NTC	-17	8	-5	NTC	-9	-9	-6
JOC Index, Growth Rate	NTC	NTC	-23	-17	1	-10	NTC	-12	-9	-15	-12	-12
S&P 500 Index	NTC	-6	-13	-9	-10	NTC	-8	-9	-12	-1	-7	-8
S&P Industrial Index	-5	-6	-13	-9	-10	NTC	-8	-9	-12	0	-6	-8
Average	-7	-10	-20	-12	-7	-19	-4	-12	-13	-13	-13	-12

* NTC : No Timing Comparison

Table 6.2 - Timing, Eighteen Qualitative Indicators at Business Cycle Peaks; in Months, Lead (-) or Lag (+)

Qualitative Indicators ↓ → Peaks	Seven Average Expansions								Two Long Expansions			Avg. at All Expansions
	Nov 48	Jul 53	Aug 57	Apr 60	Nov 73	Jan 80	Jul 81	**Average**	Dez 69	Jul 90	**Average**	
Conference Board, Consumer Expectations	NTC	NTC	NTC	NTC	-11	-37	-8	**-19**	-14	-26	**-20**	**-19**
University of Michigan, Consumer Expectations	NTC	NTC	-9	-2	-15	-38	-2	**-13**	-10	-18	**-14**	**-13**
Average Consumer Expectations of C.B. and U of Michigan	NTC	NTC	-9	-2	-14	-38	-2	**-13**	-10	-26	**-18**	**-14**
NAPM, Buying Price Index	NTC	-4	-17	-18	0	-6	NTC	**-9**	-2	3	**1**	**-6**
D&B, Business Optimism Index	NTC	NTC	NTC	-11	-3	-17	1	**-8**	-7	-32	**-20**	**-12**
NAPM, Vendor Performance	NTC	-29	-28	NTC	0	-9	-3	**-14**	-4	1	**-2**	**-10**
NAPM, Inventory Change	-5	-4	-26	-10	-1	-18	-1	**-9**	-17	-24	**-21**	**-12**
Average	**-5**	**-17**	**-18**	**-5**	**-7**	**-26**	**-3**	**-12**	**-9**	**-17**	**-13**	**-12**

* NTC : No Timing Comparison

2 Extra Cycles

Indicators, whether quantitative or qualitative, often exhibit extra cycles. The greater the degree of volatility in a series, the greater the number of extra cycles a series is likely to produce and the less certain one can be that a downturn in a leading series represents a genuine phase change. The value of leads for forecasting business cycle turning points is thereby reduced.

Consider the evidence presented in Table 6.3. It provides the documentation concerning the prevalence with which the six qualitative indicators exhibit extra cycles as compared to six quantitative leading indicators. The six quantitative indicators were selected because they have a long successful history. They were included in the original leading index, created by Geoffrey H. Moore for the Department of Commerce and are currently among the components included in the Long Range and Short Range Gauges developed at the Economic Cycle Research Institute (ECRI). In other words, they are the only quantitative leading indicators about whose superior performance there is a consensus. Figures 6.1 and 6.2 present the performance of the quantitative and qualitative indicators with respect to the business cycle.

Among the quantitative indicators, we find that 5 of the 6 exhibit one extra cycle during the 5 expansions of traditional length analyzed over the 50 years covered. None has more than one. Further, the average frequency with which one may encounter extra cycles from the quantitative indicators is no more than 2 during the three long expansions. For the six qualitative indicators we also find that extra cycles are generally no more frequent during the traditional expansions than was the case for the quantitative indicators (there is one exception). However, during the long expansions, the picture is radically and consistently different. Extra cycles are far more prominent among the qualitative indicators over long expansions. In fact, they average four times as frequent. One might attribute greater volatility to the fact that qualitative indicators are sensitive to the changing psychological perceptions of economic agents. The findings in this study are widespread and cover too long a period to be due to random factors.

Table 6.3 - Number of Extra Cycles in Three Long Expansions and in Seven Average Expansions, Quantitative and Qualitative Indicators

Six Quantitative Leading Indicators	Number Of Extra Cycles (1948 - 1998)		
	7 Average Expansions	3 Long Expansions	All Expansions
1. Average Work Week, Manufacturing	1	2	3
2. Initial Claims, Unemployment Insurance	1	1	2
3. New Orders, Consumer Goods, Manufacturing	1	0	1
4. Contracts for Plant & Equipment	0	0	0
5. Housing Permits	1	2	3
6. S&P 500 Index	1	2	3
Average	**1**	**1**	**2**
Median	**1**	**2**	**3**
Six Qualitative Leading Indicators	**Number Of Extra Cycles (1948 - 1998)**		
	7 Average Expansions	3 Long Expansions	All Expansions
1. NAPM, Buying Price Index	1	5	6
2. NAPM, Vendor Performance	0	3	3
3. NAPM, Inventory Change	2	4	6
4. D&B, Business Optimism Index	0	3	3
5. Conference Board, Consumer Expectations	0	3	3
6. University of Michigan, Consumer Expectations	0	5	5
Average	**1**	**4**	**4**
Median	**0**	**4**	**4**

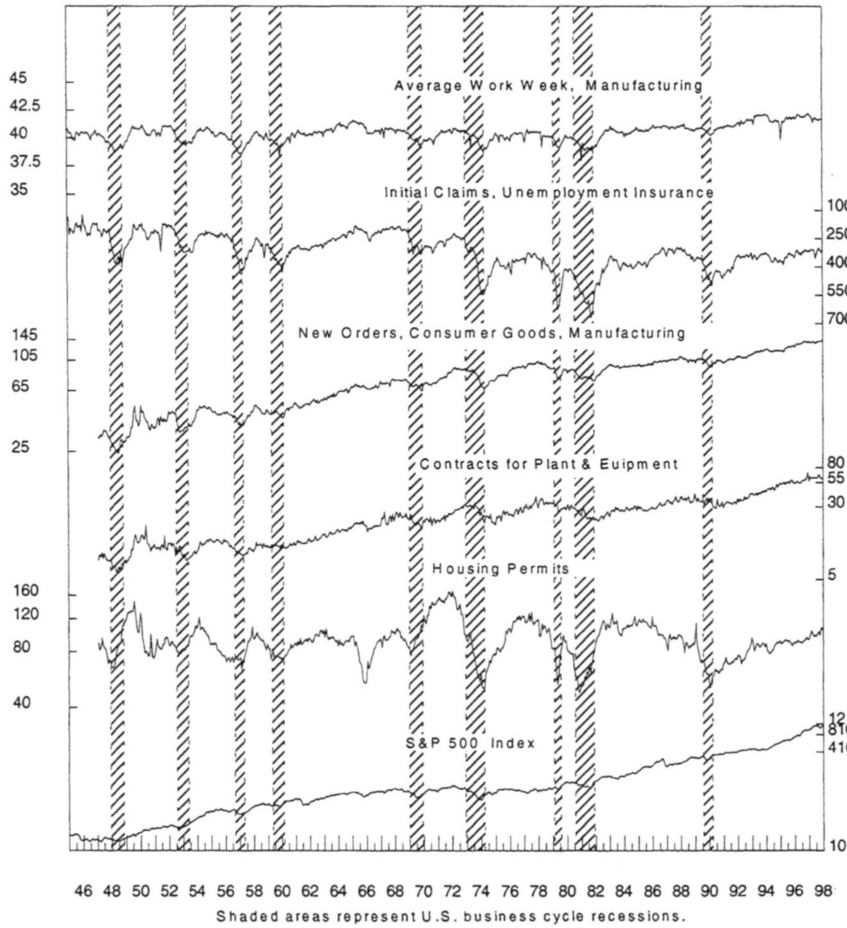

Figure 6.1 - Quantitative Leading Indicators (Levels of Economic Activity)

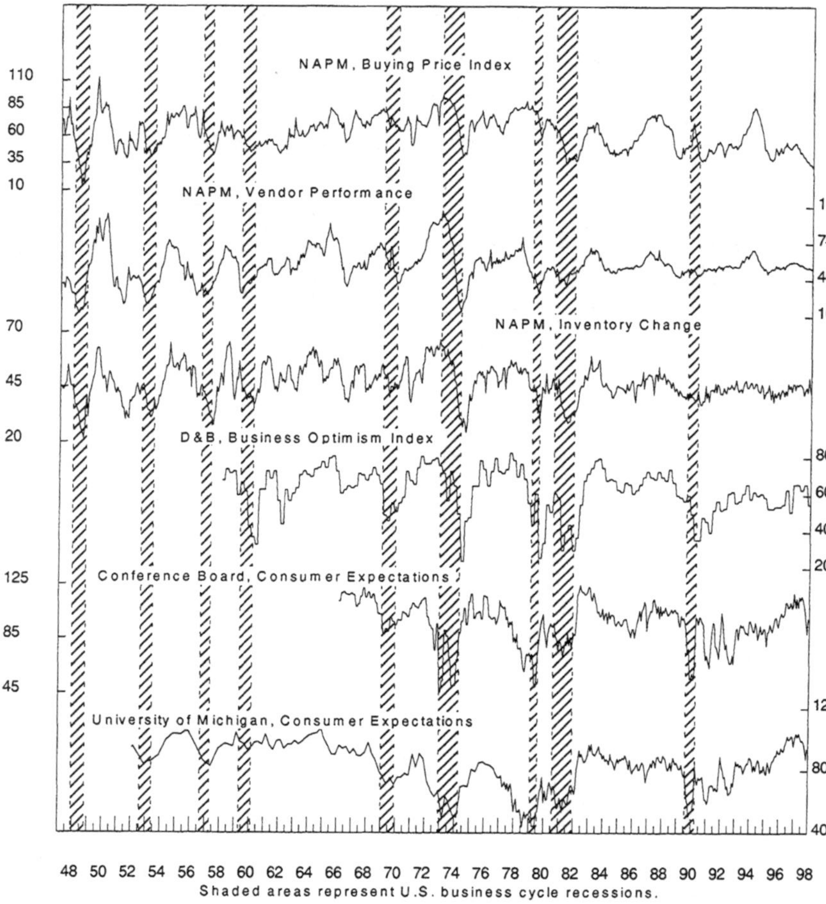

Figure 6.2 - Qualitative Leading Indicators (Levels of Economic Activity)

3 Qualitative Indicators and Growth Rate Cycles

Leading indicators were originally designed to anticipate classical recessions or sustained periods of absolute decline in economic activity. In the 1960s, however, recessions were few and far between and the cycle manifested itself as a period of faster growth interrupted by bouts of slower growth. Such cyclical behavior became known as 'growth cycles' as opposed to 'classical cycles'. Subsequently, there was a move among business cycle students in many countries to study the growth cycle. The international economic indicators (IEI) project (Klein and Moore, 1985) started at the NBER in the 1970s. The move was precipitated by Ilse Mintz's pioneering study of post-war German cycles (Mintz, 1969), in which she demonstrated the usefulness of growth cycle analysis, based on deviations from trend in economic activity. (Today the OECD, among others, monitors growth cycles for member countries.) We underscore that the calculation of the underlying trend is critical, particularly for the recent past, which is critical for forecasting. These trends, however, are difficult to measure accurately on a real-time basis (Boschan and Banerji, 1990) and are subject to revision (Cullity and Banerji, 1996). They are, therefore, especially suspect when used in forecasting which depends critically on deviations from the most suspect part of the trend - the recent past. To solve this problem, Moore began to use growth rate cycles for the measurement of series which manifested few actual cyclical declines, but did show cyclical slowdowns (Layton and Moore, 1988). Moore's 'six month smoothed growth rate' concept eliminated the need for extrapolation of the past trend in growth cycle analysis. We now call cycles calculated by this method growth rate cycles. For monthly data, the calculation is based on the ratio of the current value of the series to its average during the previous 12 months, expressed as an annual rate by raising to the 12/6.5 power. (For quarterly series, the calculation is the ratio of the current quarter to the average of the proceeding four quarters raised to the 4/2.5 power.) These rates are much smoother than those based on monthly or quarterly changes. Growth rate cycles are episodes in which the overall amplitude of the phase percent change is 'large'. But the comparison is in terms of smoothed growth rates and so is relative to all the phase amplitudinal changes being examined without any necessity to achieve an arbitrary threshold amplitude change such as the underlying trend as one needs to do in growth cycle analysis. In his extensive study of Swedish business cycles, Klein demonstrated that the growth rate cycle is another effective way to monitor slowdowns (Klein 1998). It has the advantage that peaks in growth rate cycles occur before business cycle peaks—that is, economic activity slows down before it turns down and therefore aids in forecasting potential business cycle developments.

It has previously been noted in Table 6.3 that qualitative series exhibit an average of four times as many extra cycles as quantitative series over long business cycle expansions. Attention is invited to Table 6.4 showing business and growth rate cycle expansions. The long expansions of 1961-1969, 1982-1990, and the current long expansion, which began in March

1991, have exhibited at least two growth rate cycle expansions. Further analysis reveals that the qualitative series track growth rate cycle expansions more closely than do the quantitative indicators. Table 6.5 and Figures 6.3 and 6.4 show the average lead at thirteen growth rate cycle peaks for each of the components of both indexes. The quantitative indicators have slightly longer leads on average but also greater variability as shown in the standard deviations. In the end the greater length of the lead in the quantitative indicators on average would be balanced out by the greater promptness with which the qualitative indicators become available. This is, of course, an old story.

Table 6.4 - United States Business Cycle and Growth Rate Cycle Expansions* (October 1949 - March 1999)

Business Cycle Expansions (1)	Growth Rate Cycle Expansions (2)	Number of Months in Business Cycle Expansions	Number of Months in Growth Rate Cycle Expansions
10/49 - 7/53	10/49 - 8/50 7/52 - 3/53	45	10 8
5/54 - 8/57	1/54 - 5/55	39	16
4/58 - 4/60	4/58 - 5/59	24	13
2/61 - 12/69	12/60 - 11/61 12/62 - 1/66 5/67 - 7/68	106	11 37 14
11/70 - 11/73	11/70 - 1/73	36	26
3/75 - 1/80	3/75 - 2/76	46	11
7/80 - 7/81	6/80 - 1/81	12	7
11/82 - 7/90	7/82 - 1/84 1/87 - 12/87	92	18 11
3/91 -	2/91 - 5/94 1/96 -	96**	39 38**
Average		55	19

* Expansions in bold are considered long expansions.
** As of March 1999.

(1) Source : National Bureau of Economic Research
(2) Source : Economic Cycle Research Institute

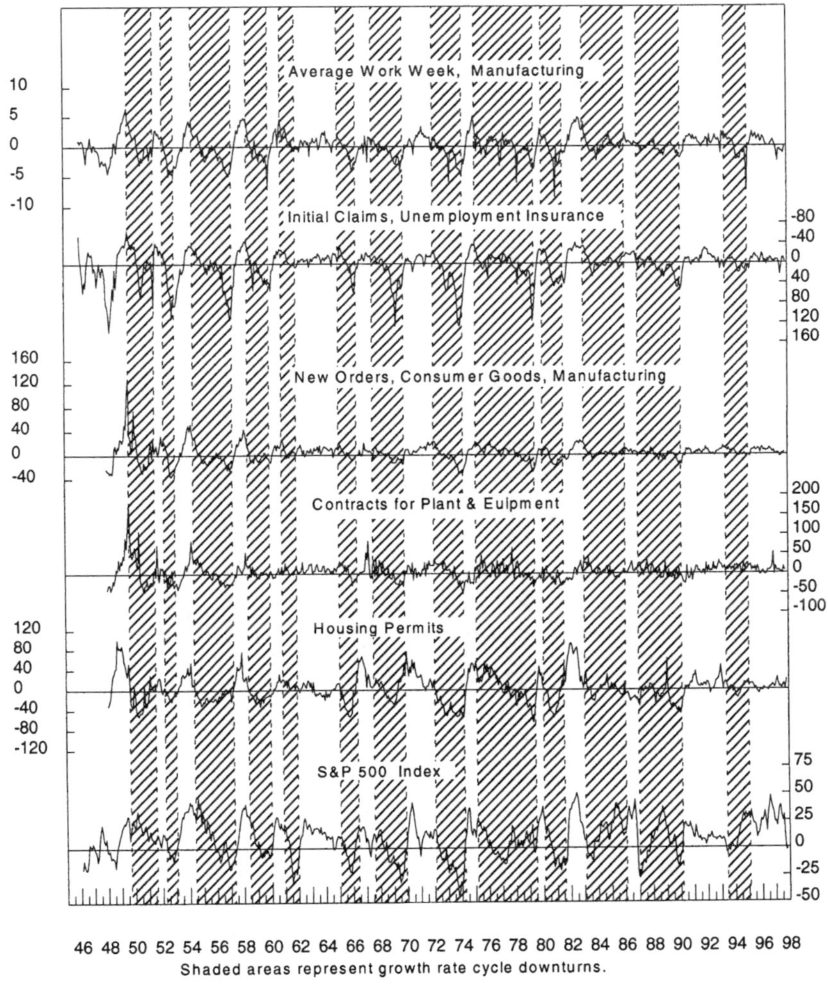

Figure 6.3 - Quantitative Leading Indicators (Rates of Change)

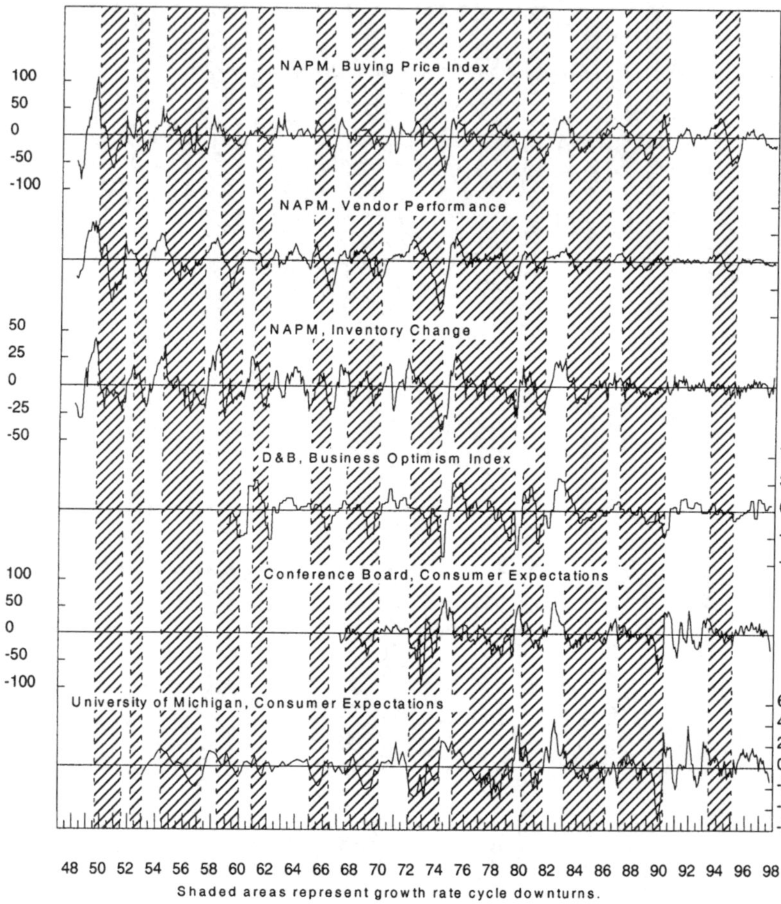

Figure 6.4 - Qualitative Leading Indicators (Rates of Change)

Table 6.5 - Average Lead (-) or Lag (+) of Growth Rates of Quantitative and Qualitative Indicators at 13 Growth Rate Cycle Expansions (Months)

Six Quantitative Leading Indicators	Mean	Median
1. Average Work Week, Manufacturing	-3	-2
2. Initial Claims, Unemployment Insurance	-3	-1
3. New Orders, Consumer Goods, Manufacturing	-3	-2
4. Contracts for Plant & Equipment	0	0
5. Housing Permits	-7	-5
6. S&P 500 Index	-5	-5
Overall Average	-4	-3
Standard Deviation	2,3	2,1
Six Qualitative Leading Indicators	**Mean**	**Median**
1. NAPM, Buying Price Index	-2	-2
2. NAPM, Vendor Performance	-1	-1
3. NAPM, Inventory Change	-3	-2
4. D&B, Business Optimism Index	0	2
5. Conference Board, Consumer Expectations	-4	-3
6. University of Michigan, Consumer Expectations	-3	-4
Overall Average	-2	-2
Standard Deviation	1,5	2,1

4 U. S. Quantitative vs. Qualitative Leading Indexes

At the Economic Cycle Research Institute, we have constructed two experimental leading indexes from the components listed on Table 6.3—one consisting exclusively of the six quantitative indicators and the other comprising the six qualitative indicators. As shown on Figure 6.5 and Table 6.6, both the Quantitative Leading Index and the Qualitative Leading Index are excellent leading indexes of business cycles in their own rights.

It is interesting to note (Figure 6.5) that the U. S. Qualitative Leading Index exhibits an extra cycle in both the 1982-1990 business cycle expansion and in the 1991 to date (March 1999) ongoing current U. S. expansion that are not observed in the U.S. Quantitative Leading Index.

This may suggest that the Quantitative Leading Index is more reliable—at least in recent years—in forecasting business cycle downturns than is the Qualitative Leading Index. Table 6.6 surveys the results and suggests that while the qualitative index has a slightly longer average lead than the quantitative index (ten months against nine month) the quantitative index leads a larger percentage of the time. It also has a slightly larger variability. In the end the two indexes are probably about equal in their reliability.

When the performance of the quantitative and qualitative leading indicators are compared against the growth rate cycle chronology as viewed in Figure 6.6 and Table 6.7 the quantitative index has a longer average lead than the qualitative index (six months on average versus four months on average). This time again the quantitative index leads more consistently as well. In the end the two indexes perform with similar degrees of usefulness and reliability.

Tables 6.8 and 6.9 focus on the cyclical timing of the individual quantitative and qualitative indicators at the three most recent growth rate cycle peaks. There are two instances in which the quantitative indicators miss a growth rate cycle peak while the qualitative indicators miss one peak. The difference is not significant. The average lead for all the quantitative indicators is seven months against four for the qualitative indicators. While this difference is the largest we have seen, it does not really change the fundamental finding which is that the two types of indicators have reasonably similar leading patterns.

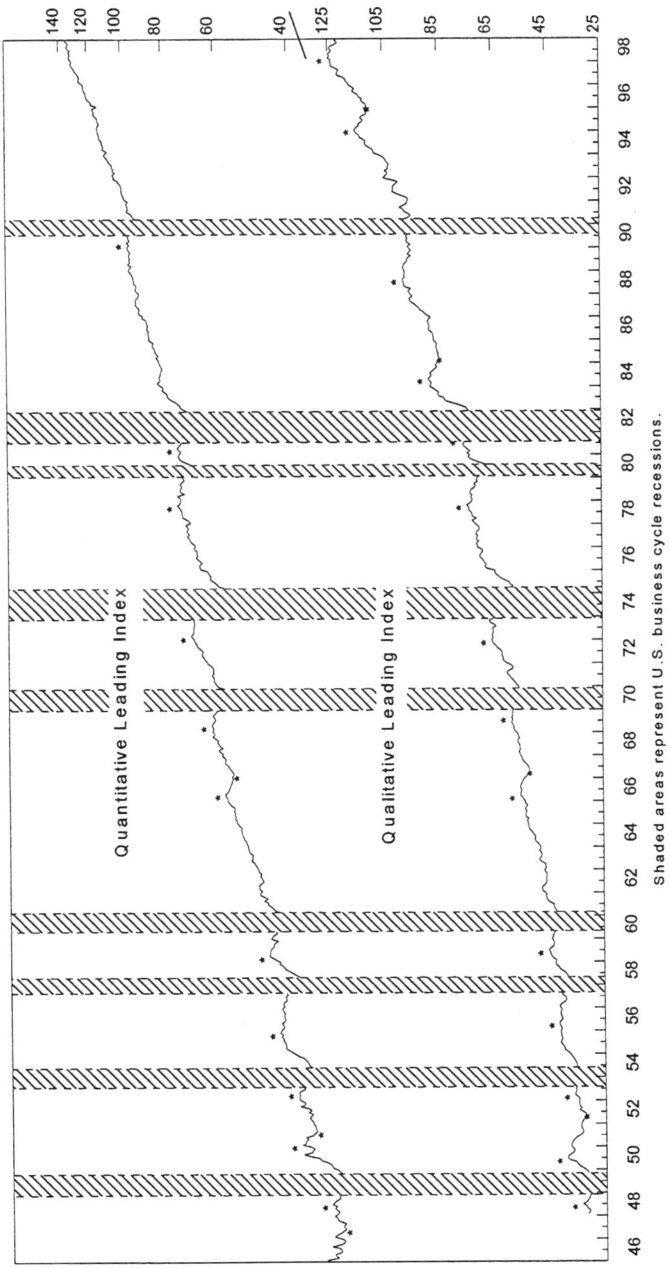

Figure 6.5 - US Quantitative vs. Qualitative Leading Indexes

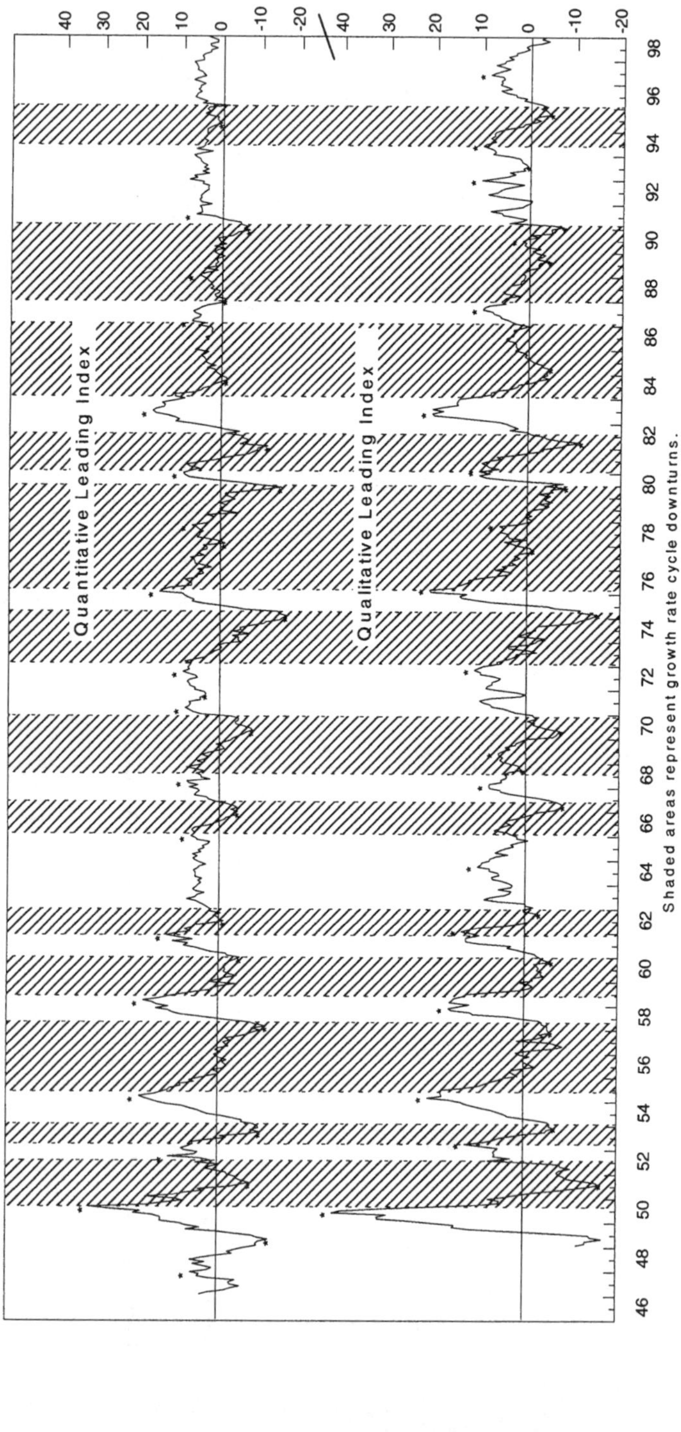

Figure 6.6 - US Quantitative vs. Qualitative Leading Indexes, Growth Rates

Table 6.6 - Cyclical Performance in Months of US Quantitative and US Qualitative Indexes at Business Cycle Peaks

	Quantitative Leading Index	Qualitative Leading Index
Average Lead	-9	-10
Median Lead	-8	-10
Percent Lead	100%	89% *
Standard Deviation	8,2	7,5

* A one-month lag at the July 1981 business cycle peak resulted in 89% rather than 100% cyclical leads.

Table 6.7 - Cyclical Performance in Months of US Quantitative and US Qualitative Indexes Growth Rate at US Growth Rate Cycle Peaks

	Quantitative Leading Index Growth Rate	Qualitative Leading Index Growth Rate
Average Lead	-6	-4
Median Lead	-2	-3
Percent Lead	92%	77%
Standard Deviation	9,1	4,7

Table 6.8 - Timing Six Quantitative Index Components, Growth Rates, at US Growth Rate Cycle Peaks (1984-1994); In Months. Lead (-) or Lag (+)

Quantitative Index Components ↓ → Peaks	Jan 84	Dez 87	Mai 94	Average at Growth Rate Cycle Expansions
Average Work Week, Manufacturing	-4	miss	-2	**-3**
Initial Claims,Unemployment Insurance	-6	-2	-17	**-8**
New Orders, Consumer Goods, Mfg.	-3	-10	-2	**-5**
Contracts for Plant & Equipment	4	-5	-6	**-2**
Housing Permits	-12	miss	-5	**-9**
S&P 500 Index	-8	-20	-14	**-14**
Average	**-5**	**-9**	**-8**	**-7**
Standard Deviation	**-**	**-**	**-**	**4**

Table 6.9 - Timing Six Qualitative Index Components, Growth Rates, at US Growth Rate Cycle Peaks (1984-1994); In Months. Lead (-) or Lag (+)

Qualitative Index Components ↓ / → Peaks	Jan 84	Dez 87	Mai 94	Average at Growth Rate Cycle Expansions
NAPM, Buying Price Index	-5	-4	5	**-1**
NAPM, Vendor Performance	-2	-1	5	**1**
NAPM, Inventory Change	-6	-6	-24	**-12**
D&B, Business Optimism Index	-4	0	-20	**-8**
Conference Board, Consumer Expectations	-8	-3	-1	**-4**
University of Michigan, Consumer Expectations	-8	9	miss	**1**
Average	**-4**	**-4**	**-5**	**-4**
Standard Deviation	**-**	**-**	**-**	**7**

5 Conclusions

For followers of both quantitative and qualitative indicators there is both good and bad news in our findings. The difference in timing at post-war business cycle peaks, as well as at growth rate cycle peaks, for both quantitative and qualitative indicators has been on average similar both at peaks ending long expansions and those ending average expansions. The differences which show up are slight and involve things like the average length of the lead, the percent of the peaks which exhibit leads, and the variability in the length of the lead. In the end, certainly for the composite indexes based on the qualitative indicators and the quantitative indicators respectively we judge the results essentially alike.

A major finding is that qualitative indicators reveal more extra cycles during long expansions than do the quantitative indicators, even though both average the same number of extra cycles during traditional expansions. This finding, should it be substantiated by similar results for other countries, suggests that the advantage that qualitative indicators have displayed in terms of greater promptness of publication may be at least partially vitiated by greater uncertainty surrounding the reliability of the business cycle peak signal.

References

Banerji, Anirvan and Charlotte Boschan (1989), 'Constructing a Time-Consistent Composite Index: An Eclectic Approach', CIBCR Working Paper, Center for International Business Cycle Research, Columbia University, New York.

Boschan, Charlotte and Walter W. Ebanks (1978), 'The Phase-Average Trend: A New Way of Measuring Economic Growth', *Proceedings of the Business and Economics Statistics Section*, American Statistical Association.

Bry, Gerhard and Charlotte Boschan (1971), *Cyclical Analysis of Time Series: Selected Procedures and Computer Programs*. Technical Paper 20. New York: National Bureau of Economic Research.

Hiles, David (1998), *Personal Communication*, Washington D.C.: Bureau of Labor Statistics.

Klein, Philip A. (1998), *Swedish Business Cycles-Assessing the Recent Record*. Stockholm: Federation of Swedish Industries, Working Paper No. 21.

Klein, Philip A. and Geoffrey H. Moore (1985), *Monitoring Growth Cycles in Market Oriented Countries: Developing and Using International Economic Indicators*. NBER Studies in Business Cycles No. 26. Cambridge, Mass.: Ballinger.

Layton, Allan P. and Geoffrey H. Moore (1989), *Leading Indicators For The Service Sector. Journal of Business and Economic Statistics*, Vol. 6(3), pp. 379-386.

Mintz, Ilse (1969), *Dating Postwar Business Cycles, Methods and Their Application to Western Germany, 1950-67*. Occasional Paper 107. New York: National Bureau of Economic Research.

Moore, G. H., Philip A. Klein and Lorene Hiris (1994), 'The Role of Surveys in Developing Promptly Available Indexes for Forecasting.'

Paper presented at 21st CIRET Conference, Stellenbosch, South Africa, 1993, in *The Explanatory Power of Business Surveys*, K.H. Oppenländer and G. Poser (eds), Aldershot, England, Avebury Press, pp. 217-239.

OECD Department of Economics and Statistics (1987), *OECD Leading Indicators and Business Cycles in Member Countries 1960-85. Sources and Methods* 39. Paris: OECD.

7 The Use of Survey Data in Economic Barometers for Poland

ZBIGNIEW MATKOWSKI

1 Introduction

The usefulness of survey data in monitoring systems designed to detect changes in economic activity has been evidenced by many theoretical and empirical studies. It has been proved that certain qualitative indicators, reflecting the opinion of economic agents (enterpreneurs, consumers, etc.) on their own situation and on the tendency of business in general, may be a valuable source of information on the actual course of business. On a theoretical plane, the concept of rational expectations explains the link between real economic developments and their reflection in people's attitudes and judgements. On an empirical plane, the analysis of leads and lags between micro- and macroeconomic variables provides strong proof in favour of monitoring and forecasting properties of such qualitative indicators as investment plans, order-books and capacity utilization rates of enterprises, or major purchase intentions of the consumers. Therefore, survey data are widely used in macroeconomic assessments and forecasts.

Several institutions in Poland are continuously testing public opinion about the course of business, collecting qualitative data on different aspects of economic activity in individual sectors of the economy and compiling various composite indicators to indicate the general tendency of business. The most important sources include the surveys conducted by the Research Institute of Economic Development at the Warsaw School of Economics (RIED) and by the Central Statistical Office (CSO).

The RIED surveys now cover the following sectors:

(a) industry: since 1986, monthly;

(b) agriculture: since 1992, bimonthly;
(c) construction, since 1993, quarterly;
(d) trade (retail and wholesale): since 1993, quarterly;
(e) households: since 1990, quarterly.

The CSO surveys cover three sectors:
(a) manufacturing industry: since 1992, monthly and quarterly;
(b) construction: since 1993, monthly and quarterly;
(c) retail trade: since 1993, monthly and quarterly.

These business surveys are supplemented by the consumer survey carried out since 1991 on a monthly basis by DEMOSKOP, a private polling company.

Qualitative data as well as composite indicators compiled by the above institutions have been continuously used, with more or less success, to depict current business tendencies in relevant sectors. Less attention was devoted to utilize the information rendered by those sources in macroeconomic estimates of the general condition and prospects of national economy.

The aim of this paper is to show the applicability of survey data in macroeconomic appraisals and forecasts pertaining to the general course of business in the national economy of Poland. Section 2 describes the application of certain survey data to a composite leading indicator (CLI), based on quantitative and qualitative data. Section 3 presents alternative variants of an economic sentiment indicator (ESI) for the Polish economy, based exclusively (or predominantly) on survey data. Section 4 brings some conclusions.

2 The Use of Survey Data in Composite Leading Indicators

The research on the development of a composite leading indicator for the Polish economy was initiated by I. Kudrycka and R. Nilsson in 1993 and continued in the next three years (I. Kudrycka, R. Nilsson, 1993, 1995, 1996). In 1994, this author began to develop his own set of composite leading indicators for Poland, based on quantitative and qualitative data, using the OECD methods and procedures. As a reference indicator, the author used a composite quantitative indicator called GCI (general coincident index), based on the output data of five major sectors of economy: industry, construction, agriculture, transport, and trade. Sectoral indicators of production volume entering the general index are weighted by the yearly shares of the respective sectors in GDP. The GCI index, compiled on a monthly basis for the period starting in January 1975, has been used to reconstruct growth cycles seen in the development of the Polish economy over the last 25 years.

The first presentation of the reference cycle indicator and of the two experimental versions of a short-lead CLI appeared in a paper published in the Polish economic journal 'Ekonomista' and in another paper presented at the OECD meeting on leading indicators in Paris in 1996 (Z. Matkowski, 1996). A revised and more comprehensive set of short- and long-lead CLIs was presented at the 23. CIRET Conference in Helsinki in August 1997 (Z. Matkowski, 1997). The newest 1998 edition of our CLIs was published in the book 'Composite Indicators of Business Activity for Poland based on EU and OECD Standards' (RIED Papers and Proceedings, vol. 61). The full account of methods and procedures employed in compiling our CLIs is contained in the volume 'Synthetic Indicators of Business Activity for the Polish Economy' (RIED Papers and Proceedings, vol. 51), published in 1997.

Looking for the candidates to our CLIs, we have analyzed, apart from quantitative variables, the dynamic properties of ca. 20 qualitative indicators taken from business surveys. Some of them have been found acceptable for CLI purposes in the light of the common criteria.

The newest edition of our CLIs contains 7 experimental formulas of a general leading indicator for Poland's economy. The alternative CLI versions are composed of 13-17 individual variables, including 5 indicators taken from business surveys (BS). These are:

(a) industrial production tendency (RIED),
(b) industrial production appraisal (RIED),
(c) economic prospects (RIED),
(d) consumer sentiments (DEMOSKOP),
(e) economic prospects (DEMOSKOP).

Indicators taken from the RIED surveys are originally expressed as net balances of positive and negative answers whereas indicators from DEMOSKOP are scaled from 0 to 200. For the aims of our analysis, all the indicators have been rescaled and transformed into indices based on 1992 = 100 as to assure their comparability.

The CSO surveys data could not be included since the available time series are too short for X12 ARIMA and OECD PAT procedures applied to discriminate cyclical components.

Statistical properties of the time series taken from the RIED and DEMOSKOP surveys are shown in Table 7.1. The code indicates the variable number in our database and the manner of detrending. Letters A and C stand for the PAT automatic routines for moving trend substraction while letter R denotes linear trend removal.

F-test for seasonality excludes any identifiable seasonality except of the RIED's series on the industrial production tendency. All indicators taken from the RIED industrial survey are good in terms of the limited amount of irregular and seasonal movements. Consumer attitudes adopted from the DEMOSKOP survey also display very moderate seasonality but they are quite erratic as regards irregular movements. Most indicators yield ARIMA 12-month forecasts of acceptable reliability.

Table 7.1 - Statistical Properties of some Leading Indicators from Business Surveys

Code	Indicator	Relative contribution to stationary variance			F-test for seasonality			Arima forecast
		I	S	TC	Stable	moving	combined	
A060	Ind. Prod. Tendency (RIED)	0.6	2.9	90.9	8.7*	0.9	present	no
A061	Ind. Prod. Appraisal (RIED)	5.0	7.7	83.5	11.7*	5.4	rather not	yes
C062	Future Ind. Prod. (RIED)	4.4	5.0	82.7	6.4*	2.9	not present	yes
A069A	Economic Prospects (RIED)	6.0	1.3	88.8	1.5	3.8	not present	no
DR02	Economic Prospects (DEMO)	29.2	7.0	56.1	0.5	1.0	not present	yes
DR05	Consumer Sentiments (DEMO)	25.5	6.2	62.6	0.3	0.6	not present	yes

* Seasonality present at the 0.1% level.

Table 7.2 shows important performance characteristics of qualitative indicators entering our CLIs. The quality control statistics (QCS) is acceptable for the first three indicators but rather poor for the three other. All the indicators have acceptable MCD length, ranging from 1 to 4 months.

Table 7.2 - Performance Characteristics of Leading Indicators

Code	Indicator	Start date	QCS	MCD	Cross - correlation against reference series	
					lead (-)	R
	Selected Leading Indicators					
A060	Ind. Prod. Tendency (RIED)	01.1987	0.76	1	-3	0.915
A061	Ind. Prod. Appraisal (RIED)	01.1987	0.94	4	-5	0.905
C062	Future Ind. Prod. (RIED)	01.1987	0.85	3	-3	0.770
A069A	Economic Prospects (RIED)	01.1987	1.50	4	-6	0.846
DR02	Economic Prospects (DEMO)	12.1991	1.61	4	-17	0.693
DR05	Consumer Sentiments (DEMO)	12.1991	1.66	4	-16	0.672
	Composite Leading Indicators					
L115	13 series including A060, 069A	01.1975	.	.	0	0.951
L115C	15 series including A060, A061, C062, A069A, DR02, DR05	01.1975	.	.	0	0.944
L115D	16 series including A060, A061, C062, A069A, DR02, DR05	01.1975	.	.	0	0.942
L116	15 series including A060, A061, C062, A069A	01.1975	.	.	0	0.943
L117	17 series including A060, A061, 90C062, A069A	01.1975	.	.	0	0.928
	Reference Series					
X091	GCI2D	01.1975	0.62	5	x	x

Table 7.3 - Performance of the Selected Leading Indicators at Turning Points

Code	Indicator	Start date	Extra (x) or missing (n) Cycles	Leads (-) or lags (+) at reference turning points		
				P03/89	T10/91	P04/97
A060	Ind. Prod. Tendency (RIED)	01.1987	1x	-28	-23	-36
A061	Ind. Prod. Appraisal (RIED)	01.1987	1x	-8	-22	-37
C062	Future Ind. Prod. (RIED)	01.1987	1x	-30	-22	+3
A069A	Economic Prospects (RIED)	01.1987	1x	-18	+4	-36
DR02	Economic Prospects (DEMO)	12.1991	0	+4	-14	-15
DR05	Consumer Sentiments (DEMO)	12.1991	0	+4	-14	-14

Cross-correlation results indicate that the four qualitative indicators taken from the RIED industrial survey are well correlated with the reference cycle at 3-6 month lead which makes them useful for a short-lead CLI. The two indicators taken from the DEMOSKOP consumer survey are not so closely correlated with the reference cycle and they display a longer, 16-17 month-lead which makes them more suitable for a long-lead CLI. However, some of these indicators display quite flat correlograms meaning that the established leads may not be very stable.

The period covered by the available survey data is too short for assessing their performance at reference cycle turning points. As Table 7.3 shows, most indicators revealed quite long-leads at both the peak of 1989 and the trough of 1991 and at the new apparent peak of 1997. This seams to indicate that some of the qualitative indicators may signal the changes ensuing in general economic activity well in advance.

The evolution of cyclical components of the qualitative leading indicators over time against the reference cycle is also illustrated by the graphs. Figure 7.1 shows the six survey indicators and the reference series in the form of seasonally adjusted, MCD-smoothed and detrended data. Noteworthy is the fact that the current slowdown in economic growth was signalled by some of the indicators two or three years earlier.

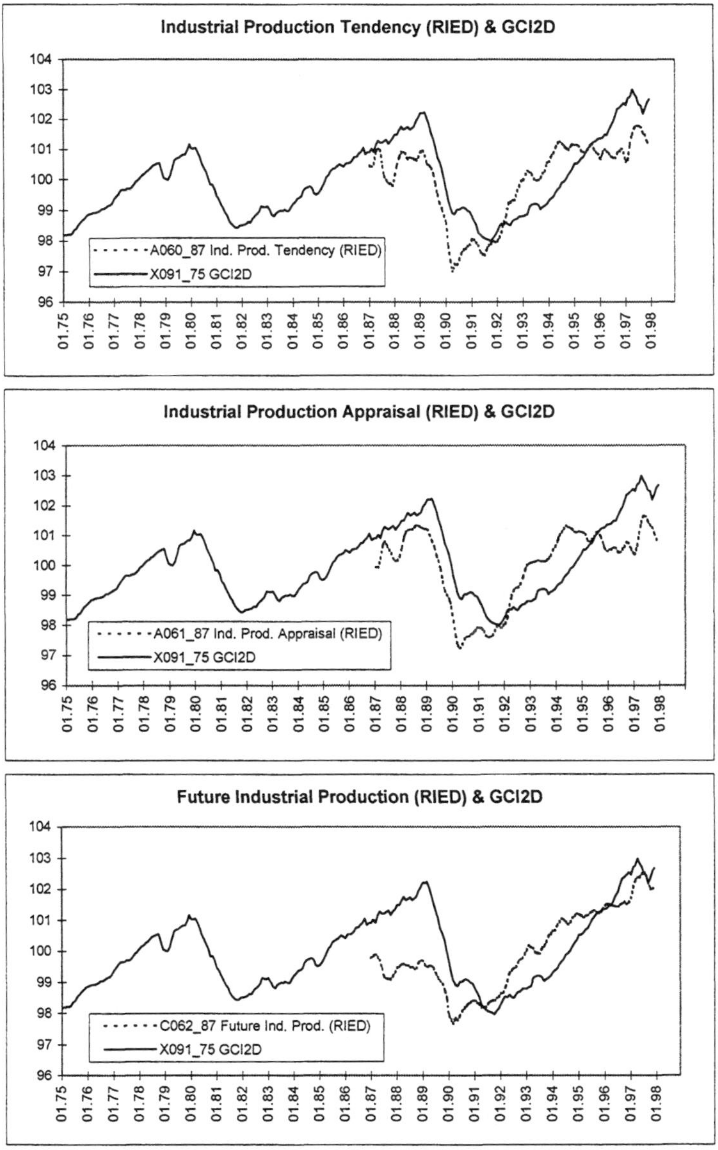

Figure 7.1 - Leading Indicators from Business Surveys and the Reference Cycle

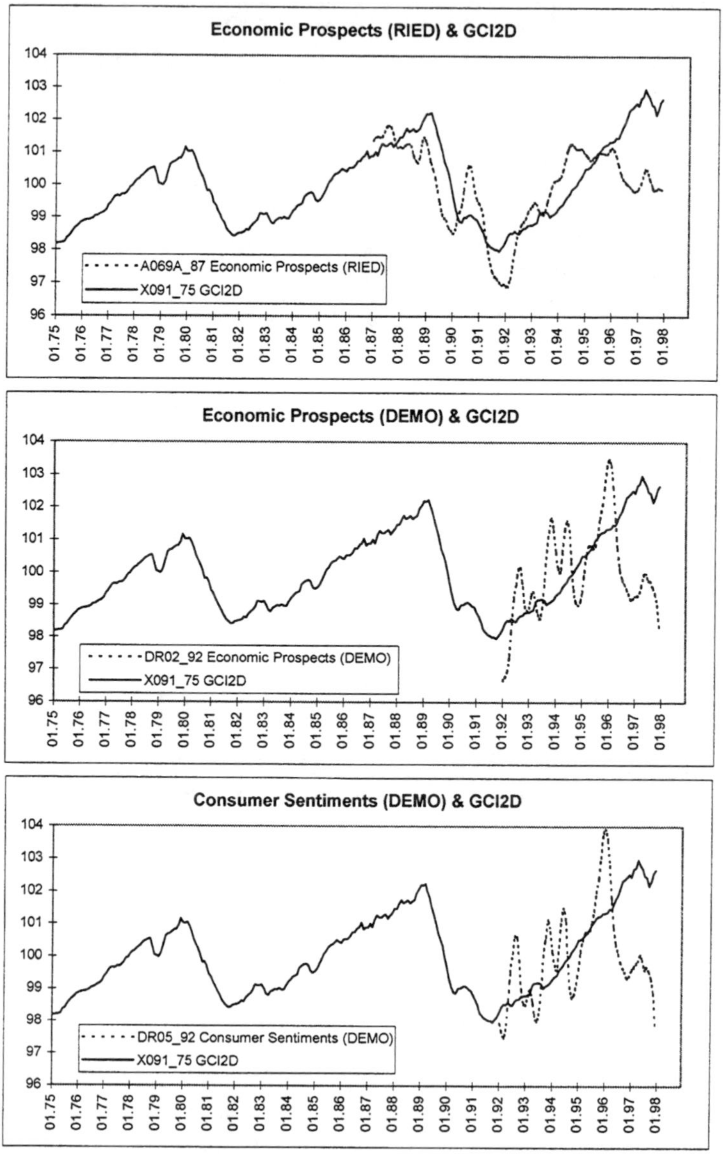

Figure 7.1 (continued) - Leading Indicators from Business Surveys and the Reference Cycle

All the six indicators have been included in the last edition of our CLIs. The RIED survey indicators for industry, along with 13 quantitative indicators, entered the CLI variants denoted as L115, L116 and L117. Consumer judgements from DEMOSKOP entered the auxiliary variants 115A through 115D.

Figure 7.2 shows three versions of our CLI denoted L115A, L115C and L117, composed of 13-17 individual leading indicators, including the above mentioned qualitative indicators. The CLIs are presented in the form of amplitude adjusted and MCD-smoothed R/T series against the reference index. All the CLIs are very well correlated with the reference index (R = 0.94 or 0.95), but in the last updating they have almost entirely lost their short lead properties displayed before. This is because of the new peak which appeared in the cyclical movement of the reference index in early 1997 but has not yet been reflected in the cyclical development of most component leaders. Presumably, the leading properties of our CLIs will be restored with the next updating.

Our barometer is not yet fully operational and it calls for further testing and improvement. Nonetheless, some of the CLI constructions, rapeatedly tested and modified in the successive editions of our barometer, seem to be useful for monitoring purposes, helping us to detect changes in general economic activity in the country. Noteworthy, our barometer correctly detected the current slowdown in economic growth as early as in the begining of 1997, or roughly one year earlier than most other sources did. Our estimate of the GDP growth rate in 1997, based on a GCI projection, was conservative in comparison with most other forecasts, yet it proved very precise and has been recently confirmed by the official statistical data.

3 General Indicators of Economic Activity Based on Survey Data

Another part of our research aims at developing and testing various experimental formulas of a general indicator of economic activity for Poland based exclusively (or predominantly) on qualitative data taken from business surveys. The basic idea behind these attempts is to combine composite indicators of business activity in individual sectors of economy, compiled from survey data, into a single synthetic indicator reflecting the general condition of the national economy. This kind of a macroeconomic index resembles the EU concept of the economic sentiment indicator, though some of the tested formulas have different coverage and weights.

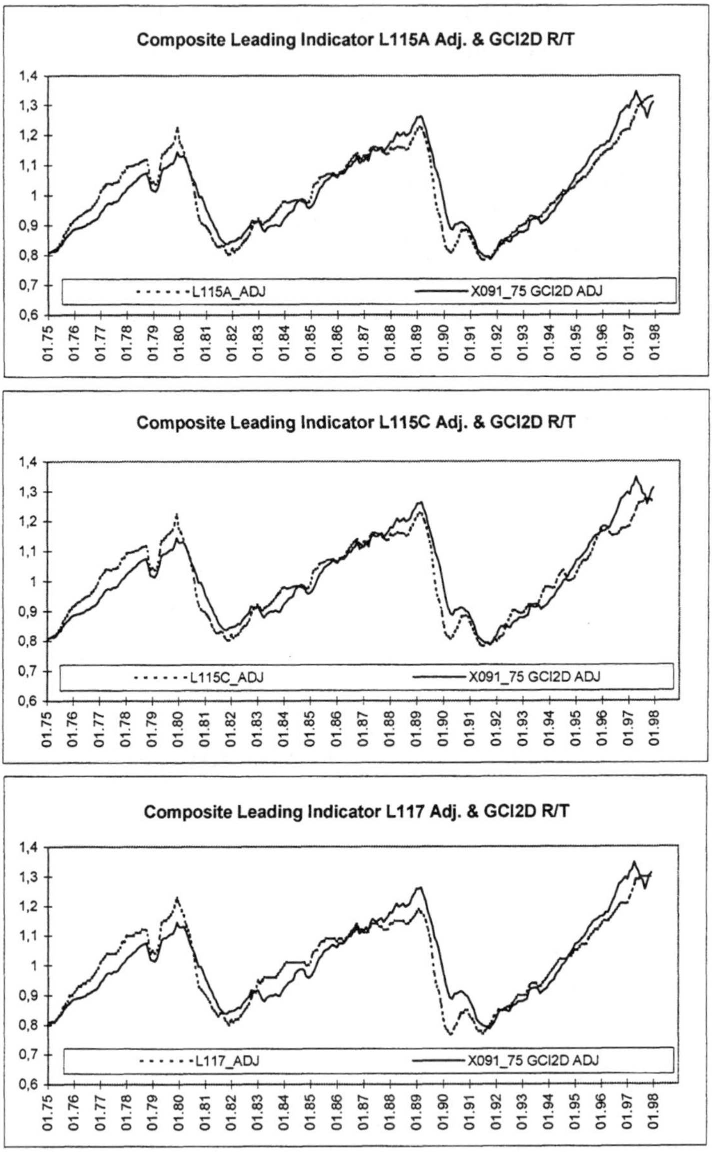

Figure 7.2 - Composite Leading Indicators and the Reference Cycle

The first attempts to construct a general indicator of business activity for Poland based on survey data were made in 1993 independently by two researchers using the RIED survey data (K. Stanek, 1993; Z. Matkowski,

1993). Both of them calculated a general indicator inspired by the EU ESI concept, but different in coverage. Since 1994, K.Stanek continues to compile two versions of his synthetic indicator covering industry, agriculture, households, construction and trade (since 1997, also transport), using his own system of constant weights and two different concepts of sectoral composite indicators. The first is called 'RIED formula', and the second one is denoted 'EU formula', though the latter differs from the harmonized ESI concept both in coverage and weigths.

In 1998, this author developed several alternative formulas of a general indicator of economic activity for Poland based on survey data and filled them with the RIED and CSO survey data, supplemented by the consumer sentiment indicator provided by DEMOSKOP. The analysis, aimed at evaluation of different formulas of the indicator and the selection of the best operational formula, covered the period from November 1993 till January 1998, for which the original data were available at the time of study (March 1998).

The full presentation of the results appeared in two papers included in the book published by the author in 1998 (Z. Matkowski, 1998). Here we wish to present some of the variants compiled from the RIED survey data.

Table 7.4 includes the list of component indicators entering the general index based on the RIED data. Most of them are in fact composite indices composed of 2-5 single time series to represent the general tendency of business in the given sector. Some of the component variables have been calculated by the author according to his own (ZM) or harmonized (EU) formulas. Two supplementary series describing consumer attitudes and the Warsaw Stock Exchange Index were also included in some of the tested variants.

The alternative formulas of the general indicator based on the RIED data have been denoted ZHG1 to ZHG5 while similar formulas of the indicator filled with the CSO survey data are recorded as ZGG1 to ZGG5. Here we present four variants (variant 1, 3, 4 and 5) of the indicator based on the RIED data.

Table 7.4 - Component Variables Entering the General Indicators of Business Activity Based on the RIED Survey Data

Code	Indicator / Formula	Start date	Compiled as:
ZH01	Business Indicator - Ind. (RIED)	10.1993	Avg. of ind.prod. appraisal and forecast - 2 months
ZH03A	Ind. Activity Tendency (ZM)	10.1993	Avg. of ind. prod. appraisal and forecast
ZH05A	Ind. Confidence Indicator (EU)	10.1993	Future ind. prod., change in stocks and order book
ZH11A	Constr. Activity Tendency (ZM)	10.1993	Avg. of constr. prod. appraisal and forecast
ZH09	Constr. Confidence Indicator (EU)	10.1993	Order book and expected change in employment
ZH17	Business Indicator - Trade (RIED)	10.1993	Future sale tendency, anticipated change in supplies, commodity stocks
ZH20A	Trade Sale Tendency (ZM)	10.1993	Avg. of sale appraisal and forecast
ZH25	Business Indicator - Agr. (RIED)	10.1993	Current and future revenue tendency, adjusted for anticipated economic condition of the farm
ZH28	Consumer Conf. Indicator (RIED)	10.1993	Change in income and savings, modified by an anticipation factor; since 1995 - EU formula
ZD05	Consumer Conf. Indicator (DEMO)	10.1993	EU formula
ZW01	Warsaw Share Price Index	10.1993	Not detrended
ZWR01	Warsaw Share Price Index R/T	10.1993	Detrended

Variant 1 is deemed as the closest implementation of the harmonized EU ESI concept. It was calculated according to the formula:

ZHG1 = 1/3 Industry + 1/3 Households + 1/6 Construction + 1/6 Share Prices (1)

The entry variables here are: the industrial confidence indicator, consumer sentiment indicator, construction confidence indicator (all compiled according to the EU harmonized standards), and the detrended share price index of Warsaw Exchange.

Variant 3 refers to the RIED concept of the synthetic business indicator, denoted RIED-EU. It applies the EU concept of confidence indicators for industry and construction, and a compromise RIED-EU concept of consumer sentiments, but it also includes agriculture and trade, with confidence indicators compiled specifically. Unlike the original EU ESI concept, this indicator does not include the share price index. Industry and households are given weights twice as high as each of the remaining sectors. The resulting general indicator was calculated according to the algorithm:

ZHG3 = 2/7 *Industry* + 2/7 *Households* + 1/7 *Construction* + 1/7 *Trade* + 1/7 *Agriculture* (2)

Variant 4 includes four productive sectors: industry, construction, agriculture, and trade, which directly contribute to the creation of GDP. Composite indicators reflecting the business tendency in each sector are calculated according to EU concepts except for agriculture where businesss tendency is determined according to the RIED's own formula. Unlike in the preceding variants, component indicators reflecting the activity in individual sectors are combined using no arbitrary constant weights, but weights that represent their actual share in the GDP (more precisely, in gross value added). The weights are changed each year, according to the changing structure of the economy. For the period covered by the analysis, the average shares were: industry - 32.8%, construction - 6.4%, agriculture - 7.1%, trade - 16.3%. Since the above sectors do not cover the whole economy (amounting to slightly less than 2/3 of GDP), the sum total of the weighted indices must be divided by the sum of weights. The resulting algorithm is:

$$\text{ZHG4} = \frac{a_1 \times Industry + a_2 \times Construction + a_3 \times Trade + a_4 \times Agriculture}{a_1 + a_2 + a_3 + a_4} \tag{3}$$

where weights a_1, a_2, a_3, a_4 reflect the contribution of individual sectors to the creation of GDP in the given year.

Variant 5 has the same coverage and the same weighting system as variant 4, but it is filled with standardized component indicators reflecting the business tendency in individual sectors. Instead of different concepts of business tendency for different sectors (a practice adopted in RIED and recommended by EU harmonized standards), this variant employs a uniform concept of business tendency for each sector, namely the average of the production (sales) appraisal and forecast (except of agriculture where the available survey data do not provide the relevant information). The algorithm here used is the same as in variant 4:

$$\text{ZHG5} = \frac{a_1 \times Industry + a_2 \times Construction + a_3 \times Trade + a_4 \times Agriculture}{a_1 + a_2 + a_3 + a_4} \tag{4}$$

The general indicators of economic activity calculated according to the above formulas have been filled with survey data of the period from November 1993 till January 1998 which were available at the time of analysis (March 1998). Quarterly data were transformed into monthly series by interpolation. All the component series entering the combined indicator have been smoothed with 3-month moving average and standardized using the following formula (OECD, 1987):

$$\left[(x - \bar{x}) : \frac{\sum |x - \bar{x}|}{n} \right] + 100 \tag{5}$$

where x denotes numerical values of the given variable, $\bar{x}$ - arithmetic mean of the time series values, n - number of observations (months). Standardized component series and the composite general indicators derived thereof usually range between 95 and 105.

It should be noted that the resulting general indicators express relative deviations of the values observed from their long run average (= 100), so they should not be mistaken for simple dynamic indices. Anyway, numerical values of indicator higher than 100 mean that current level of business activity is assessed positively (above the average) while values lower than 100 indicate that current condition of the economy is perceived as rather poor (below the long-run trend). An increase of the indicator suggests a rising (favourable) tendency of economic activity whereas its decrease is tantamount to a slowdown.

Four alternative variants of the general indicator calculated from the RIED data are shown in Figure 7.3. The general tendency of economic development in Poland during the last 4-5 years, in the light of these indicators, is somewhat uncertain and differently depicted by different variants of the indicator. ZHG1 and ZHG3 show a rising tendency with some signs of slowdown towards the end of the period. ZHG4 displays massive seasonal fluctuations, reinforced by the changing yearly weights, with no distinct trend. ZHG5 indicates a levelling of the boom between 1994 and 1996, and a sharp slowdown since 1997. In fact, the Polish economy developed quite rapidly during the five years 1992-1997, but the last year brought about a marked slowdown in economic growth, with a decrease of the GDP growth rate from 6-7% a year to less than 5%. Macroeconomic forecasts suggest a further slackening of economic growth in 1999.

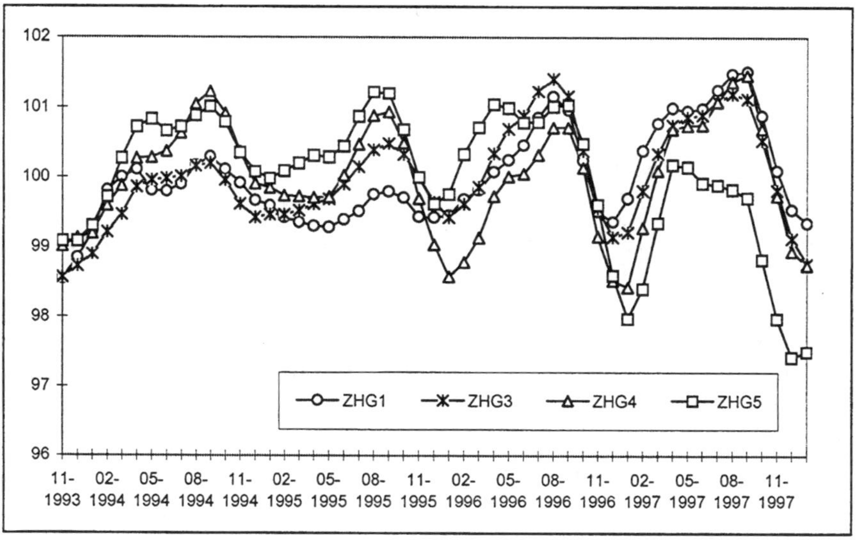

Figure 7.3 - General Indicator of Economic Activity Based on the RIED Survey Data

The author has also compiled a parallel set of general indicators of business activity based on the CSO survey data, supplemented by the DEMOSKOP consumer survey. The formulas here used were analogous with those applied to RIED survey data except for the modified weights due to a narrower coverage (CSO surveys do not cover agriculture). For the lack of space, we cannot discuss the peculiarities of the synthetic indices derived from this source. Table 7.5 lists the component time series included in the aggregate index. Four alternative CSO-founded indicators, based on similar formulas to those employed to RIED data, are presented in Figure 7.4.

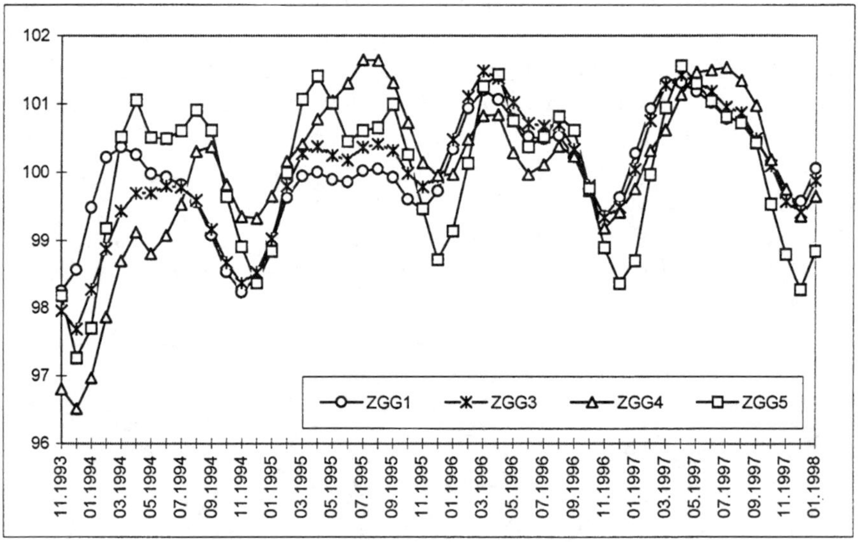

Figure 7.4 - General Indicator of Economic Activity Based on the CSO Survey Data

Comparing the RIED- and CSO-based general indicators of economic activity, we see that the latter display a more pronounced seasonal pattern which can be removed during the next updating, when the time series reach the suitable length. At the same time, the general trend indicated by the CSO indices is a little more encouraging than the tendency implied by the RIED data - a finding not surprising since CSO surveys do not include agriculture, the sector most severely affected by the transformation process. Nevertheless, the CSO-based sythetic indicators also reveal a slowdown of the economic boom towards the end of period.

Table 7.5 - Component Variables Entering the General Indicators of Business Activity Based on the CSO Survey Data

Code	Indicator / Formula	Start date	Compiled as:
ZG01	Industrial Climate (CSO)	10.1993	Avg. of ind. enterprise situation and prospect
ZG03A	Ind. Activity Tendency (ZM)	10.1993	Avg. of ind. prod. appraisal and forecast
ZG05A	Ind. Confidence Indicator (EU)	10.1993	Future ind. prod., change in stocks and order book
ZG08	Constr. Climate (CSO)	10.1993	Avg. of constr. prod. appraisal and forecast
ZG08A	Constr. Activity Tendency (ZM)	10.1993	Avg. of constr. prod. appraisal and forecast
ZG10A	Constr. Confidence Indicator (EU)	10.1993	Order book and expected change in employment
ZG13	Retail Trade Climate (CSO)	10.1993	Avg. of trade enterprise situation and prospect
ZG15A	Retail Sale Tendency (ZM)	10.1993	Avg. of sale appraisal and forecast
ZD05	Consumer Conf. Indicator (DEMO)	10.1993	EU formula
ZW01	Warsaw Share Price Index	10.1993	Not detrended
ZWR01	Warsaw Share Price Index R/T	10.1993	Detrended

The most adequate formula of the general indicator of business activity derived from survey data will be chosen by comparing the evolution of alternative indicators over a longer period with the actual development of the economy, as reflected by the GDP growth rates and other objective statistical measures, including our monthly reference index GCI. A more comprehensive and thorough analysis of the informative value of our indicators will be undertaken in March 1999, when the available time series reach the 5-year length required for the X12-ARIMA routine.

4 Conclusion

1. Several qualitative indicators from business and consumer surveys have been used in composite leading indicators for the Polish economy and they have proved helpful in macroeconomic forecasts.

2. Alternative formulas of a general indicator of economic activity for Poland filled with business survey data have been developed and tested in order to find the most adequate formula.
3. The research on economic barometers for the Polish economy justifies the conclusion that survey data may efficiently be used in macroeconomic assessments and forecasts, increasing their accuracy.
4. The author believes that the experience gained in our work on economic barometers for Poland may also be of interest for the analysts engaged in developing similar monitoring systems for other economies in transition.

References

Kudrycka, I. and R. Nilsson (1993), 'Business Cycles in the Period of Transition', *Z Prac Zakładu Badań Statystycznych GUS i PAN*, No. 216, GUS: Warszawa.

Kudrycka, I. and R. Nilsson (1995), 'Business Cycles in Poland', *Z Prac Zakładu Badań Statystycznych GUS i PAN*, No. 227, GUS: Warszawa.

Kudrycka, I. and R. Nilsson (1996), 'Cyclical Indicators in Poland', *Cyclical Indicators in Poland and Hungary*, OECD, Paris.

Matkowski, Z. (1993), 'In Search for an Economic Sentiment Indicator for Poland: The RIED Approach and Preliminary Results', Workshop on Business Surveys in Transition Countries, Poznań.

Matkowski, Z. (1996), 'Ogólny wskaźnik koniunktury dla gospodarki polskiej' (General Indicator of Business Activity for Poland), *Ekonomista*, No. 1.

Matkowski, Z. (1996), 'Composite Leading Indicators for Poland and the Concept of the Reference Cycle', A contributed paper prepared for the meeting on OECD Leading Indicators: Paris, 17-18th October 1996.

Matkowski, Z. (1997), 'Business Cycles in Poland', in: Oppenländer, K.H., Poser, G. (eds), *Social and Structural Change - Consequences for Business Cycle Surveys (Selected Papers presented at the 23rd Ciret conference)*, Helsinki, pp. 407-428.

Matkowski, Z. (ed) (1997), *Z prac nad syntetycznymi wskaźnikami koniunktury dla gospodarki polskiej* (Synthetic Indicators of Business Activity for the Polish Economy), Prace i Materiały Instytutu Rozwoju Gospodarczego, Vol. 51, Szkoła Główna Handlowa: Warszawa.

Matkowski, Z. (1997), 'Cykle w rozwoju gospodarki polskiej' (Cycles in the Development of the Polish Economy), *Ekonomista*, No. 5-6.

Matkowski, Z. (ed) (1998), *Złożone wskaźniki koniunktury dla gospodarki polskiej oparte na standardach UE i OECD* (Composite Indicators of Business Activity for Poland based on EU and OECD Standards), Prace i Materiały Instytutu Rozwoju Gospodarczego, Vol. 61, Szkoła Główna Handlowa, Warszawa.

OECD (1987), 'Leading Indicators and Business Cycles in Member Countries 1960-1985', *Main Economic Indicators. Sources and Methods*, No. 39.

Stanek, K. (1993), 'Koncepcja barometru gospodarczego koniunktury' (The Concept of an Economic Barometer), *Badania koniunktury gospodarki Polski*, Szkoła Główna Handlowa, Warszawa.

Stanek, K. (1994), 'Syntetyczny wskaźnik koniunktury IRG SGH' (Synthetic Business Indicator by RIED), *Zeszyty koniunktury w gospodarce polskiej*, No. 6, Szkoła Główna Handlowa, Warszawa.

Part III

Survey Data and Policy Decisions

8 Mobilization of Household Savings: Background for Policy Recommendations

ELENA BELYANOVA and SERGUEI NIKOLAENKO[1]

The paper analyses the dilemma faced by Russian consumers: to hold cash or to use financial intermediaries for money transactions, savings and investments. Russian households have accumulated substantial amounts of cash both in roubles and in hard currency. The issue now is how to use this money to finance economic recovery, i.e. how to turn savings into investments.

The paper studies evidence from consumer surveys aiming to find out the rationale behind the fact that consumers avoid financial intermediaries, discusses the immediate consequences of the August-98 financial crisis and comments on government policies towards financial intermediaries and consumers.

1 Introductory Notes

1.1 Survey Data, Sample and Characteristics of Observation Period

The survey data used in this paper are those of VCIOM, the largest RF polling agency which has been conducting nation-wide surveys of consumers on a regular basis since 1988. The bulk of the information used relates to special surveys, which in addition to regular VCIOM survey questions comprised a set of special questions on savers' behavior and

[1] This research was undertaken with support from the European Union's Tacis ACE Programme 1995.

motivations. These surveys covered 1,600 respondents. Data from regular VCIOM surveys are also used here where relevant. Normally they cover about 2,400 respondents.

The sample covered represents a wide rage of consumer categories excluding, however, the poorest and the wealthiest groups of population. This does not substantially affect the relevancy of the results of the analysis, since both these categories are not the main target for financial intermediaries, at least, not in the current situation in Russia. The poor will not use financial intermediaries anyway, and the rich are focused on making direct investments in Russia and/or on investing/saving outside Russia.

The first special survey was conducted in June 1998, just before the outbreak of the August crisis. Judging by the responses given, the respondents did not anticipate the crisis. Rather, the survey presents a picture of consumers' attitudes and behavioral patterns which formed in a year and a half prior to the survey, i.e. beginning from late 1996. In terms of financial shocks affecting consumers, this period was less eventful than previous years of transition, when consumers suffered from depreciation of deposits (January 1992), the collapse of 'financial pyramids' (summer-autumn 1994), and commercial bank failures (August 1995).

The second special survey was conducted in December 1998 and hence reflected changes in saving performance triggered by the August financial crisis.

1.2 Sources of Official Data and Estimation Method

The paper also uses official reports of the Central Bank of Russia and State Statistical Committee. This data were used to produce the estimates of hard currency holdings by households by applying the methodology developed by one of the authors (see Nikolayenko (1998)).

2 Economic and Financial Background

In the former Soviet Union the choice of financial instruments that households could use to accumulate wealth was limited to government bonds, deposits in the State Saving Bank (Sberbank) and domestic currency. Up until late 1950, investments in government bonds were 'forced', but later, when they were no longer mandatory, these low-yielding bonds failed to become popular among households. Until the beginning of the transition period the bulk of savings was concentrated in the State Saving Bank. Holdings of domestic currency accommodated primarily the transactions demand for money.

With the reform of the financial sector which started in late 1980s, the situation changed in many respects. The State Saving Bank (Sberbank) was transformed into a stockholding company; apart from accumulation of household funds, which had been its only activity under the Soviet financial system, Sberbank started to perform various other activities similar to those of an ordinary commercial bank. Meanwhile it remained heavily controlled by the state having the Central Bank of Russia (CBR) as its largest shareholder.

The state banks that previously serviced institutional clients were, with very few exceptions, privatised and became private commercial banks. New commercial banks, the ones that started from scratch, emerged. Some of former state and new commercial banks offered current and time deposits for private individuals. Another type of financial institutions that entered the scene early in the transition period and became popular among households were stylised quasi-banks that built financial pyramids.

As a result of privatization of state property, many private citizens became holders of corporate shares; most of these shares, however, did not have any market value. The government in its turn introduced saving bonds with market interest rates. Investment and private contractual saving institutions started to develop since late 1980s, but the role of these in the accumulation of household savings remains quite modest until this day.

Apart from the increased diversity of financial institutions and financial instruments available to them, there was another innovation that strongly affected households' financial strategy, that is, the circulation of hard currency, primarily, US dollars. Transactions in hard currency became one of the most profitable activities of commercial banks and Sberbank. Households could easily buy and sell hard currency in numerous offices of Sberbank and other commercial banks, and at least in urban areas whenever there were any problems with changing money at the banks, there was always street trade in hard currency. Making payments for goods and services with hard currency was officially prohibited. However, such practices abound, especially in personal services.

Since the beginning of transition period in early 1992, one can identify five distinct periods with regard to household financial performance and motivations (see Table 8.1; Figures 8.1 and 8.2):

I. January 1992 – late 1992. Sharp depreciation of savings; huge forced ruble cash holdings for transaction purpose

II. Late 1992 - 1994. Low attractiveness of savings; predominance of ruble cash holdings and diversification of the rest of savings
III. 1995 - late 1996. Low attractiveness of savings; saving opportunities narrow down
IV. Late 1996 - July 1998. Attractiveness of saving increases; role of institutional savings first shrinks but then recovers by the end of the period August 1998 - date. Dissaving.

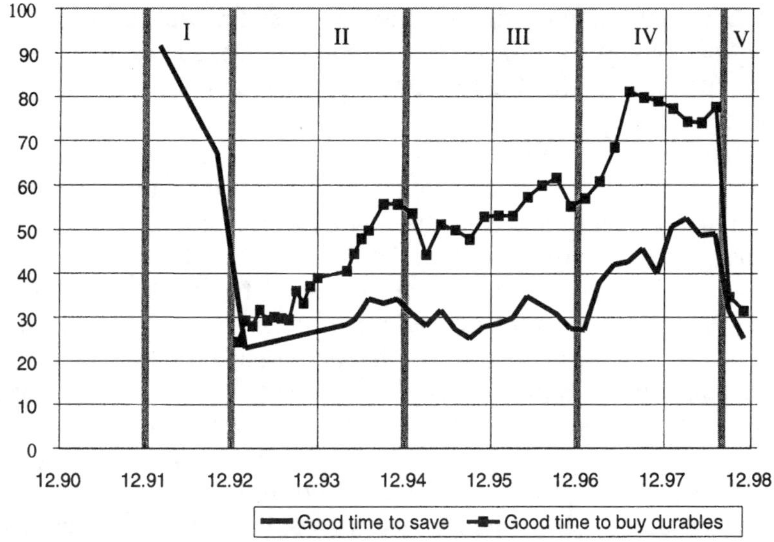

Figure 8.1 - Attitudes Toward Purchases of Durable Goods and Savings[2]

[2] Note: Indices are computed as a difference between positive and negative responses plus 100.

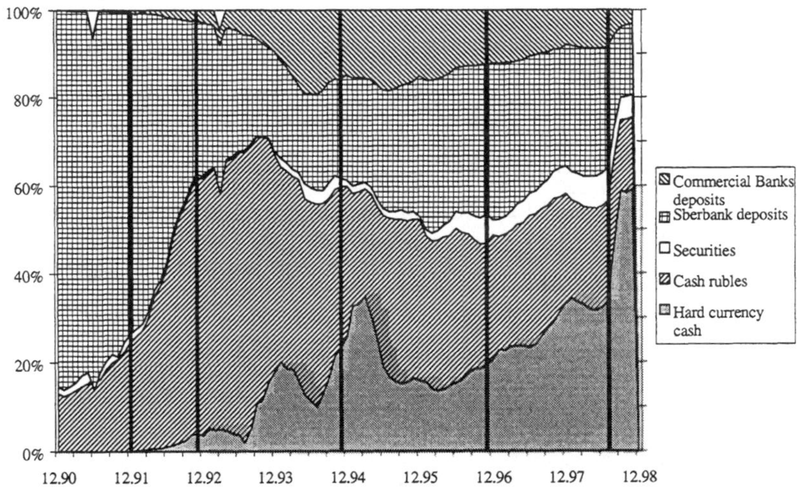

Source: Time series were constructed by S. Nikolayenko from Goskomstat data.

Figure 8.2 - Changes in the Composition of Household Financial Assets[3]

[3] Note: Data on the stock of securities were available since 1997. For earlier period only flow data were available and the stock series were reconstructed from flow series. In June 1991 and March 1993, when securities stock estimates were negative, totals do not make 100% on this graph.

Table 8.1 - Household Finance and Underlying Economic Factors

Period	HH finance: main features	Macro-economic background of HH behavior	Main factors affecting HH finance
I. Jan-1992 - late 1992	Sharp depreciation of savings; huge forced ruble cash holdings for transaction purpose	Price liberalization	• Hyperinflation • Sharp reduction in real PI • Increased income disparities • No guaranties that HH deposits in Sberbank shall be safe
II. Late 1992 - 1994	Low attractiveness of saving; predominance of ruble cash holdings and diversification of the rest of savings	Stagflation	• High inflation • Increase in real PI • Growth of spending moods • Strengthening of the $ • Expansion of com. banks and fin. pyramids • Collapse of fin.pyramids (mid-94)
III. 1995 - late 1996	Low attractiveness of saving; savings opportunities narrow down	Tight monetary policy and financial stabilization	• Slowing down of inflation • Real PI income drops • Exchange rate corridor (May 95) • $ attractiveness weakens • First com.banks crisis • Sberbank strengthens
IV. Late 1996 - Aug- 1998	Attractiveness of saving increases; role of institutional savings shrinks, But recovers by the end of the period	Temporary stabilization in the real sector*	• Moderate inflation • Relative stability of exchange rate • Growth of real PI (till Jan-98) • No negative consequences of ruble denomination (Jan-98) contrary to expectations • Strong position of Sberbank • No major visible shocks in the commercial banking sector
V. Aug-1998 - date	Dissaving	Financial crisis	• Bank runs • Failure of a number of major com.banks • Payments frozen by other commercial banks • Worsening of liquidity position of Sberbank • Sharp depreciation of the ruble

* The recovery in the real sector started in late 1996, the first major drop in industrial production index since 1996 took place in May 1998.

PI - Personal Income, HH - households.

3 Households' Financial Performance Before the August Crisis

3.1 Composition of Households' Financial Assets in mid-1998

In mid 1998, the composition of households' financial assets was as follows:

Table 8.2 - Financial Assets of Households as of 1 August 1998, Billion RUR

Description	Billion RUR	As a share of total cash holdings, %
Total financial assets	490	193%
of which:		
Total cash holdings	254	100%
Rubles	101	40%
Hard currency	153	60%
Total organized savings	236	93%
Total bank deposits	202	79%
RUR deposits at Sberbank	124	49%
RUR deposits at commercial banks	38	15%
Hard currency deposits total SB/CB	41	16%
Securities and other assets	35	14%
For reference: Real sector investments in fixed capital (without investments into social infrastructure) in 1997	263	104%

Source: Central Bank of Russia, Nikolayenko 1998 [6].

Notes: Item 'securities and other assets' is the least reliable piece of data in household financial statistics, because it is a balancing item. Insurance assets are not included in statistics of personal savings for two reasons: (1) state insurance is mandatory and therefore is not governed by personal saving decisions; (2) private insurance sector is weak and data are either unavailable or unreliable.

As Table 8.2 shows cash holdings both in rubles and in hard currency was by far the most important financial asset held by households in mid 1998. The total of domestic and foreign currency holdings exceeded the amount of bank deposits and investments in securities taken together, and almost equaled total investments in the real sector in 1997. Therefore, almost a decade since the beginning of reforms in the financial sector of the Russian economy, any effective intermediation of savings was still lacking.

Among financial instruments other than currency, deposits in Sberbank had the largest share. Deposits in commercial banks and investments in securities came a distant third and forth respectively.

3.2 Households' Transactions Demand for Money

One of the reasons behind the preference for holding domestic currency is the underdeveloped state of the banking sector as a whole and banking technologies, in particular, as the weakness of technologies makes it difficult for the banks to mediate household transactions. Checking accounts were introduced only recently and only by a small number of banks. As of mid-1998, only a very limited number of customers availed themselves of this service. Checking accounts could be used only in selected jurisdictions and within such jurisdiction only in up-scale restaurants, supermarkets and department stores. Apart from the underdeveloped state of banking technologies, the lack of appropriate technologies in retail trade also hindered the progress. Another difficulty had to do with the availability of a large shadow economy. The share of street trade in total retail turnover is as high as 40%, and the 'over-the-counter' trade in services is almost 80% of total sales of personal services. This situation suits both parties: consumers gain from cheaper prices, and retailers gain by avoiding taxes.

The consumer survey of June 1998 revealed that 68% of households did not have bank accounts. And among one third of those who had at least one bank account, only 3% used bank transfers to pay for goods and services (Table 8.3). In other words, banks recorded retail transactions performed by less than 1% of the Russian population.

It is unlikely that this situation will change soon. Required technological and organizational innovations both inside and outside banking system will take time. The same is true in respect of overall changes in the economic environment that are required to combat the shadow economy.

Therefore, in the nearest future banks can not count on household transaction money even if the financial environment is stable and public confidence in banks is restored. In the mean time, the potential customer base of banks shall remain limited to only those private customers who manage to make savings in spite of the crisis.

Table 8.3 - Purpose for Having a Bank Account (% of Respondents Who do Have a Bank Account), June 1998 Survey

Purpose:	%
- to save money	39
- to earn interest	23
- to receive salary	23
- to receive pension	15
- to pay for purchases	3
- other	14
- don't know	7

Note: The respondents were asked to mark all the right answers.

3.3 Savers' Attitudes Towards Banks vs. Foreign and Domestic Currency Cash Holdings

The June-1998 survey showed that in Russia the population of savers is much smaller than the population of consumers. Only one third of respondents reported that their family has savings. The survey also showed the ambiguity of savers' attitude towards banks. The question in the survey was: 'In what form would you prefer to hold your savings in the current situation?; it was permitted to select three best-fitting responses. In the savers' group, it was hard currency that got the highest rank (Table 8.4). Sberbank deposits came second, having been marked by just under 50% of respondents in the savers' group. Ruble cash holdings came third, and other assets - including deposits in commercial banks - stayed far behind. Therefore, the survey evidenced that after more than a year of relative tranquility in the banking sector savers still preferred hard currency cash holdings to Sberbank deposits, and the number of savers who preferred to hold their money in cash - be it domestic or foreign - was significantly greater of those who chose to save their money by depositing it to commercial banks.

Given such saving preferences, it is not surprising that 36% of respondents-savers reported that they do not have a bank account either in Sberbank or in any commercial bank. Thus, more than one third of savers kept their savings outside the banking system -- in all likelihood these savers do not trust banks at all. We shall refer to this category of savers as *Bank Avoiders (BA).*

Table 8.4 - Q: 'In what form would you prefer to hold your savings in the current situation?': Responses Given by Those Who Have Savings, June 1998 Survey

Form of saving:	% of answers
Cash holding: hard currency	51
Deposits in Sberbank	46
Cash holding: rubles	34
Precious metals, antiquities	13
Deposits in commercial banks	8
Corporate securities	7
Government securities	3
Insurance	0.2
Other	5
Don't know	0

Note: Respondents could choose up to three items.

What about attitudes of the rest of savers towards banks? Out of the respondents that reported they have savings 64% also reported they have at least one bank account and the majority reported they trusted banks with their money in order to save or gain income, or both. We shall call this group of savers *Bank Users (BU)*. However, Bank Users do not have 100% trust in banks. When asked about their saving preferences in terms of bank deposits vs currency holdings, less than half of Bank Users responded that they would deposit the bulk of their money in a bank, and roughly an equal number of respondents said they would put only half of their money in a bank, and keep the other half as cash, and some respondents said they would rather keep most of their money in cash form (Table 8.5).

One of the main reasons for the negative attitude towards banks on the part of Bank Avoiders and the reserved attitude on the part of Bank Users is that many depositors had their own negative experience with banks, including Sberbank, since early 1992, and the relatively stable period in the second half of 1990s did not last long enough to restore their confidence in the banking system.

Table 8.5 - Q: 'What would you prefer: To deposit most of your money savings in banks, to keep them as cash-on-hand or to use both forms of saving in approximately equal amounts?', % of Bank Users, June 1998 Survey

Preferences:	% of answers
Bank deposits	40
Cash holdings	14
Both in equal amounts	39
Don't know	7
Total	100

Both groups, Bank Avoiders and Bank Users include households that suffered losses from depreciation of their savings in Sberbank, collapse of 'financial pyramids' and failures of commercial banks (Table 8.6).

Table 8.6 - Percentage of Bank Avoiders (BA) and Bank Users (BU) Who Had Losses, June 1998 Survey

Cause of loss:	BA	BU
Depreciation of deposits at Sberbank in 1992	51	67
Collapse of 'financial pyramids'	24	21
Failures of commercial banks	11	15

As seen from the Table 8.6, in mid-98 both groups had their negative experiences with banks, and on a comparable scale. However, in the case of Bank Avoiders this experience resulted in complete distrust and aversion, while in the case of Bank Users it resulted in a more cautious attitude towards banks. The difference between these two groups may be due to differences in individual propensity to take risk. It seems that the BA group has just a strong concentration of risk avoiders in it. At least, our comparison of the two groups showed that in terms of such properties as years of education, level of income and also age, there were no significant differences between them.

When asked to assess the general public's attitude towards banks, Bank Avoiders gave a rather negative assessment: the number of those who thought that the general public would be reluctant to keep its money in banks was almost the double of the number of those who thought that people in general would prefer keeping their money in banks (Table 8.7).

Bank Users gave a more positive assessment but still quite a large number of them thought that people in general are reluctant to use bank services.

Table 8.7 - Q: 'Do you agree with the statement that the general public is reluctant to keep money in banks?' Percentage of Respondents in Each Group, June 1998 Survey

Suggested answers:	BA	BU
1. I agree	59	41
2. I disagree	30	46
3. Do not know	11	14
4. Agree-Disagree (1-2)	+ 29	-5

In order to determine the reasons behind the negative attitude towards banks on the part of the general public, the respondents who assessed the attitude of the general public as negative (in the Table above) were asked to provide the rationale, i.e. to mark three most fitting reasons (Table 8.8).

Table 8.8 - Reasons Why General Public is Reluctant to Keep Money in Banks, % of Respondents in Each Group Out of Total Number of Respondents Who Disagreed With the Previous Statement (Table 8.7), June 1998 Survey

Reasons	BA	BU
Don't trust banks	81	71
Low interest rates	47	52
People hide their income	17	10
Low quality of bank services	10	6
Banks do not guarantee confidentiality	4	8
No bank office nearby	1	0
Don't know	13	18

Note: Respondents could select up to three answers.

In answering this question, the BA and the BU produced very similar percentage distributions, and the reasons were almost the same. The two most important reasons are *lack of confidence* and *low interest on deposits.*

Lack of confidence in banks. It should be stressed, that respondents' assessments refer to the banking system as a whole, i.e. including the Sberbank which is controlled by the state. This suggests that behind low confidence in banks *per se* stands low confidence in the government and CBR policy towards the banking sector. In other words, given their experience gained during the transition years, savers do not believe that the state will protect their interests if things in the financial sector and in the economy change for worse. At the same time, many respondents thought that unfavorable changes are quite probable (Table 8.9). (Again, the predominance of pessimistic assessments does not mean that there was an anticipation of a financial crisis - on the average, the responses given were more optimistic than, say, a year before this survey.)

Table 8.9 - Q: 'In what way do you think the economic situation in the country will change within one year? Within 5 years?', % of Sample. June 1998.

	Within a year	Within 5 years
For the better	8	11
Neither for better, nor for worse	21	19
For the worse	49	26
Don't know	22	44
For better - For worse	-41	-15

If one compares the attitude towards banks and attitude towards hard currency holdings as revealed in responses to different questions of the survey, it would seem that hard currency is regarded by a large share of the population as a less risky option that Sberbank deposits. This also testifies to the low rating of government policies in respect of ensuring safety of organized savings. However, people still do believe that their hard currency cash holdings would not be adversely affected by government policies. For instance, a large share of respondents thought that foreign exchange policy will not effect ruble convertibility (Table 8.10).

Low interest on deposits. This reason for not keeping money in banks was indicated by almost half of BA and more than half of BU. This is a direct evidence of savings sensitivity to the rate of return on assets. According to survey results, should deposit rates be higher, Bank Avoiders would have deposited some of their currency holdings, and Bank Users would have raised their deposits-to-currency holdings ratio. In other words, from the point of view of savers, the interest rates offered by banks were not sufficiently high to cover liquidity and default risks.

Table 8.10 - Q: 'How high is the likelihood that changing rubles into hard currency and back will be banned?', % of Answers

Degrees of likelihood	Total sample	BA	BU
1. High	10	8	10
2. Rather high	13	13	14
3. Rather low	27	35	27
4. Zero	20	24	20
5. Don't know	30	20	29
Balance: (1+2) - (3+4)	-24	-38	-23

Presented above traditional and survey statistics as of mid 1998 register very low capability of the banking sector to mobilise household savings and a highly cautious attitude of households towards banks. However, during 6 months that preceded the survey, there were signs of improvement in the general public attitude towards banks. In December 1997 when answering the question 'In what form would you prefer to hold your savings in the current circumstances?', only 3% of all the respondents said they would deposit money in commercial banks, and 37% said they would deposit their money in Sberbank. In June 1998, the shares of these answer groups were already 6% and 40% respectively. According to official figures, since the end of December 1997 to the end of June 1998, household deposits not only in Sberbank and but also in commercial banks grew at a higher pace than household financial assets on average. Total share of household bank deposits in financial assets increased from 40% to 42%.

These positive changes may be explained by the fact that since 1995 the banking sector did not produce any shocks that could have badly affected depositors. Ironically the slight improvement in household attitudes towards banks in the first half of 1998 took place against the background of deterioration of financial position of the banking sector (RET 98 [5]). In the first half of 1998 the core group of the largest commercial banks servicing households experienced solvency problems. However, these problems were not visible to the general public, and the Central Bank did not render the information on the troubled banks public due to notorious 'too big to fail' approach.

4 Household Financial Performance During 1998 Financial Crisis

The August-98 crisis started with the government default on debts and the collapse of the market of government securities with dire consequences for many Russian banks, including Sberbank, that did a lot of trading and investments in government securities. The crisis stroke a hard blow on household savings, ruined the tenuous confidence in the banking system that the public had, and once more confirmed the role of hard currency as the safest and the most profitable financial asset from among those available to households in Russia.

With the devaluation of the ruble and sharp increase in consumer prices, the purchasing power of ruble savings dropped by at least 60% in the first three months of the crisis. Depositors demanded to redeem bank debt for cash. This involved both commercial banks and Sberbank, and both ruble and dollar deposits. Bank runs were the result of increased risks of depreciation of ruble deposits, liquidity risks and default risks. According to November 1998 survey, since the beginning of the crisis, 47% of respondents made attempts to withdraw their money from banks; as a result 25% succeeded, 10% got only part of the claimed amount, and 12% received nothing.

Several largest commercial banks that have their headquarters in Moscow and branches in different regions of Russia suspended payments. In early September, the Central Bank made public the list of six insolvent commercial banks, and these were the ones where the bulk of household deposits was concentrated (outside the Sberbank). The CBR suggested that the customers of these commercial banks transfer their ruble and hard currency savings to Sberbank. Under this CBR regulation, hard currency deposits were to be transferred to Sberbank ruble accounts at the exchange rate as of the end of August. The deadline of the transfer was fixed on mid-November 1998.

Sberbank in its turn was experiencing liquidity problems. When withdrawing money from Sberbank, depositors had to meet daily withdrawal limits and had to visit Sberbank offices several times (each time waiting in long queues) to withdraw the full amount.

According to the Central Bank data, ruble deposits of households in commercial banks dropped by 40% in three months since August. Deposits in Sberbank shrank by 12% in the first two months, but then the trend was reversed and by the beginning of December their volume reached 95% of the pre-crisis level. The growth of deposits in Sberbank is explained by transfers of deposits from bankrupt banks to Sberbank, pursuant to the Central Bank regulation, rather than by restoration of the public trust.

The comparison of December 1998 survey data with June survey clearly demonstrates changes in the attitudes of households towards banks as a result of the crisis (Table 8.11).

Hence the survey evidences that as a result of the crisis people just do not want to deal with commercial banks. Their trust in Sberbank has also dropped substantially. The majority of respondents showed lack of confidence in the banking sector as a whole and unwillingness to use its services. On the other hand the attractiveness of hard currency went up substantially.

5 Conclusions and Reflections on Policy Issues

The main factors behind the propensity to save money in cash form and reluctance to deposit money in any bank, including Sberbank, is a combination of mistrusts:

- lack of trust in banks
- lack of trust in state policies towards banks
- lack of trust in sustainable economic recovery
- lack of trust in political stability.

Looking behind, one comes to a conclusion that prior to the crisis households were insufficiently cautious and took excessive risk. Bank Avoiders showed the most prudent behaviour. Moreover those who saved money in hard currency benefited from the crisis.

Before the crisis, the CBR and the government failed to create the economic, legal and institutional environment that could have helped build up public confidence in banks. There was no system of deposit insurance; a law on instituting such a system was drafted more than two years ago but has not yet passed the parliament. The CBR supervision over commercial banks was ineffective. Sberbank which held the bulk of household deposits was allowed to take excessive risks, being one of the main players in the government securities market. Moreover, government policies towards this market, the escalation of government debt and high interest rates undermined the financial system as a whole and triggered the financial crisis.

Table 8.11 - Households' Attitudes Towards Banks: Before and After the Crisis, in Percentage of Total Sample, June and December 1998 Surveys

Questions	June-98	Dec-98	Change (Dec-June)
'In what form would you prefer to hold your savings in the current situation?'	%	%	percentage points
Cash holdings: hard currency	44	50	+6
Sberbank deposits	40	28	-12
Cash holdings: roubles	38	37	-1
Commercial banks deposits	6	1	-5
'What would you prefer: to deposit most of money savings in banks, to keep them as cash-on-hand or to use both forms of saving in approximately equal amounts?'			
In banks	23	15	-8
In cash	35	48	+13
Equal amounts	29	22	-7
Don't know	13	15	+2
'Do you agree that today the general public is reluctant to keep money in banks?'			
Yes	58	72	+14
No	27	15	-12
Don't know	15	13	-2
'Why do you think people are reluctant to keep their money in banks?' *(in percent of those who answered Yes to the previous question)*			
Lack of confidence in banks	77	86	+9
Low interest rates	44	30	-14
Threat of disclosure of income and savings	10	7	-3

Restoration of confidence at least to the its pre-crisis level is highly problematic. Apart from political, economic and financial stabilization, this requires overall restructuring of the banking system. However, today, five months after the banking crisis broke out, the government still has not come up with a clear strategy for reforms. Various options are being discussed: from nationalization of financial institutions that would work with individual clients, to encouraging foreign banks to serve resident households, which has been prohibited so far. The last option seems to be the only viable one in the short and medium term (provided that foreign banks are willing to take the risk and expand their operations in Russia in spite of the current political and economic uncertainties). Building a sound private banking system by restructuring domestic banks would apparently take much longer. Judging by households attitudes towards Sberbank, nationalization could hardly become an effective remedy. Mistrust in state policy towards banks and lack of trust in the effectiveness of consumer protection measures will still keep a huge part of savers outside the banking system. Besides, state banks are also prone to liquidity and solvency problems, and if their well-being is ensured only by money emission, this would eventually lead to a new depreciation of savings. In any case, radical improvements in bank supervision and regulation and in consumer protection should be the kernel of any restructuring strategy.

References

Belyanova E. and S. Nikolayenko (1997), Personal savings as a source of investments, *Russian Economic Trends*, No. 3.

Gregory P., M. Mokhtari and W. Schrettl (May 1997), Do the Russians really save that much? Alternative estimates from the *'Russian Longitudinal Monitoring Survey'*.

Николаенко С.А. (1998), Личные сбережения населения, Экономический журнал ВШЭ , Том 2, No. 4, (Nikolayenko S., Household Saving, *HSE Economic Journal,* Vol. 2, No. 4, 1998).

Kriuchkova P. (1997), *Household Deposits and Financial Intermediation in Russia,* RECEP, Working paper No. 3.

Personal saving and income (1997), *Russian Economic Trends,* No. 1.

Resolving the Banking Crisis (November 1998), *Russian Economic Trends,* Monthly update.

Римашевская Н.М., Сбережения населения и внутренние источники экономического роста в России: результаты экспериментальных исследований, Экономика и математические методы, Том 34, вып. 3. (Rimashevskya N. M., Household saving and internal source of economic growth in Russia, *Economics and Mathematical methods,* Vol. 34, No. 3).

Сбережения населения (сентябрь 1998), Мониторинг общественного мнения No. 6(38) (Savings of the Population (September 1998), *The Russian Public Opinion Monitor,* No. 6(38), 1998).

9 Employment Expectations in the European Union: An Empirical Assessment Based on Qualitative Survey Data

MARCELLA CORSI and FRANZ-JOSEF KLEIN

The Community shall have as its task, by establishing a common market and an economic and monetary union and by implementing common policies or activities [..] to promote throughout the Community a harmonious, balanced and sustainable development of economic activities, a high level of employment and of social protection, equality between men and women, sustainable and non-inflationary growth, a high degree of competitiveness and convergence of economic performance, a high level of protection and improvement of the quality of the environment, the raising of the standard of living and quality of life, and economic and social cohesion and solidarity among Member States. [Amsterdam Treaty on the European Union, Article 2]

1 Introduction

The most dominant feature of the European Union, in the stability-oriented framework of EMU, is the *mediocrity of its employment growth and level* with respect not only to what the Union was able to sustain during the 1960s but also compared with the United States and Japan.

According to Eurostat's standardised unemployment definition, the number of unemployed persons in the Union amounted to approximately 18 million in 1997, representing 10.9% of the civilian labour force. Furthermore, the weak employment performance of the Union since the mid-1970s has not only led to a five-fold increase in the unemployment rate but has also resulted in a very low ratio of effectively employed persons with respect to the working-age population. This ratio, the employment rate, fell from 67% in 1961 (a level reached even before the considerable expansion of the female labour force) to about 60% at present, whereas it exceeds 74% in the USA and Japan. Such a large fall goes beyond the impact of unemployment alone since activity rates tend to fall when unemployment goes up ('discouraged worker' effect).

The future employment rate will depend on economic and social conditions that may strongly differ from previous periods. However, in the medium to long term, if sufficient jobs are created, the EU employment rate could easily return to a level at least as high as in the early 1960s (67%). In fact, if the female employment rate remains unchanged at the level reached in 1997 and if the male employment rate returns to its high level of the 1960s, then the overall employment rate for the EU could even be 70%. Besides, a further (and likely) increase in female participation would bring the EU employment rate to 72% or even close to the US and Japanese figures.

However, in the short run, the present degree of non-employment is undoubtedly a weakness and the source of a large social cost in terms of both private and public consumption.

The aim of this paper is to concentrate on the EU short-term employment perspectives mainly using simple and composite indicators stemming from the EU-harmonised qualitative surveys results. As is known, harmonised surveys do present many advantages as sources of economic information, because they allow to study aggregate behaviour on the basis of micro-founded data (at firm and household levels) plus they provide a rapid mean of compiling simple statistics, with the results available before those obtained with traditional statistical methods. Moreover, business surveys provide information in areas not covered by quantitative statistics and therefore may be considered as complementary to official statistical sources.

The layout of the paper is as follows. Section 2 highlights the main characteristics of the European labour market both in terms of productivity and employment. Section 3 draws attention both on entrepreneurs' and consumers' employment expectations at EU level. Section 4 draws some conclusions.

2 The Employment Challenge

To achieve a high employment rate in the EU, which is a requirement of the Amsterdam Treaty (Article 2), it will be crucial to generate, over an extended period of time, economic growth well above the rate coming from increases in labour productivity in the overall economy, whatever the pace of the latter might be.

Over the last two decades, overall labour productivity has increased at a stable rate of 2% per year on average in the Union.[1] This has resulted, in more or less equal proportion, from the incorporation of technological and organisational progress (total factor productivity) and a substitution of labour by capital at the macroeconomic level.[2]

Since technological progress is the main source of wealth and improvement in the quality of living standards over the long run, policies should be directed at maintaining, and even accelerating, the pace of technological change. This is also necessary in order to safeguard the Union's competitiveness in an ever closely integrated world economy. Furthermore, there are powerful forces at work, such as globalisation, the competition of the internal market and the move towards a knowledge-based economy, which are expected to sustain the trend of total factor productivity but also of labour to capital substitution in the Union in the future.

On the other hand, with respect to substitution of capital for labour at the macroeconomic level, the Union's economy has traditionally been characterised by a comparatively strong degree of substitution, implying a stronger increase in the capital intensity of its production process than, for instance, in the United States. However, the analysis of the 1986-90 data shows that the combination of wage moderation (hence, profitability increases) combined with good demand prospects and strong growth in capacity-expanding investment may reduce significantly the rate of labour to capital substitution. Thus, if the evolution of wages continues to be appropriate, a further slowing-down of this substitution process is to be expected. Simultaneously, through increased profitability, it reinforces the

---

1 With the productivity trend stable at 2% per year, a growth of real GDP of 2% per year will simply keep employment constant. Furthermore, since labour supply is surely likely to grow by about 0.4 to 0.5% per year in the medium term, a real GDP growth rate higher than 2.5% is needed to reduce unemployment.

2 For a detailed analysis, cf. European Commission (1997).

Table 9.1 - Labour Market Situation (EU, D, F, I, UK)

	D	*F*	*I*	*UK*	*EU*
a) Non activity rate, as % of population 15-64 years (a=100-b)					
1985	*32.0*	*31.0*	*41.9*	*25.3*	*33.6*
1990	*30.8*	*30.9*	*40.9*	*22.2*	*32.2*
1993	*30.5*	*31.6*	*41.2*	*23.6*	*32.3*
1996	*31.3*	*31.2*	*41.6*	*24.0*	*32.3*
b) Activity rate, as % of population 15-64 years (b=c+d)					
1985	*68.0*	*69.0*	*58.1*	*74.7*	*66.4*
1990	*69.2*	*69.1*	*59.1*	*77.8*	*67.8*
1993	*69.5*	*68.4*	*58.8*	*76.4*	*67.7*
1996	*68.7*	*68.8*	*58.4*	*76.0*	*67.7*
c) Employment rate, benchmark series, % of population 15-64 years					
1985	*63.1*	*62.0*	*53.1*	*66.2*	*59.8*
1990	*66.3*	*62.9*	*53.7*	*72.4*	*62.6*
1993	*64.0*	*60.4*	*52.7*	*68.5*	*60.4*
1996	*62.6*	*60.3*	*51.4*	*69.8*	*60.3*
d) Unemployment rate , as % of population 15-64 years (d=b-c)					
1985	*4.9*	*7.0*	*5.0*	*8.5*	*6.6*
1990	*2.9*	*6.2*	*5.4*	*5.4*	*5.2*
1993	*5.5*	*8.0*	*6.1*	*7.9*	*7.2*
1996	*6.1*	*8.5*	*7.0*	*6.2*	*7.4*
e) Unemployment rate , as % of civilian labour force (1)					
1985	*7.2*	*10.1*	*8.5*	*11.5*	*10.0*
1990	*4.8*	*8.9*	*9.1*	*7.0*	*7.7*
1993	*6.0*	*11.7*	*10.3*	*10.4*	*10.7*
1996	*8.8*	*12.4*	*12.0*	*8.2*	*10.9*

Source: European Commission Services
Note: Variables c and e are original input. Other variables are derived from these.
(1) Definition Eurostat.

Table 9.2 - Growth, Employment and Productivity Trends (EU, USA, Japan)

	1961-73	1974-96	1974-85	1986-90	1991-99
			Real GDP growth		
EU	4.7	2.1	2.0	3.2	1.9
USA	4.4	2.6	2.6	2.9	3.0
Japan	9.7	3.2	3.4	4.6	0.8
			Labour supply		
EU	0.4	0.2	0.7	0.9	0.1
USA	1.9	1.7	2.1	1.7	1.2
Japan	1.2	1.0	0.9	1.4	0.9
			Employment		
EU	0.3	0.2	0.0	1.3	0.0
USA	1.9	1.8	1.8	2.1	1.7
Japan	1.3	0.8	0.7	1.0	0.2
			Labour productivity (2)		
EU	4.4	1.9	2.0	1.9	1.9
USA	2.4	0.8	0.8	0.7	1.2
Japan	8.2	2.5	2.7	3.6	0.5
			Total factor productivity (3)		
EU	2.9	1.1	1.0	1.5	1.1
USA	1.9	0.5	0.5	0.6	0.9
Japan	6.3	1.1	1.1	2.3	-0.5
			Labour to capital substitution (4)		
EU	1.5	0.8	1.0	0.4	0.8
USA	0.5	0.3	0.3	0.1	0.3
Japan	1.9	1.4	1.6	1.3	1.0

Source: European Commission Services

(2) Real GDP per employed person.

(3) Average of capital and labour productivity, weighted by factor income shares in GDP.

(4) Discrepancy between labour productivity and total factor productivity.

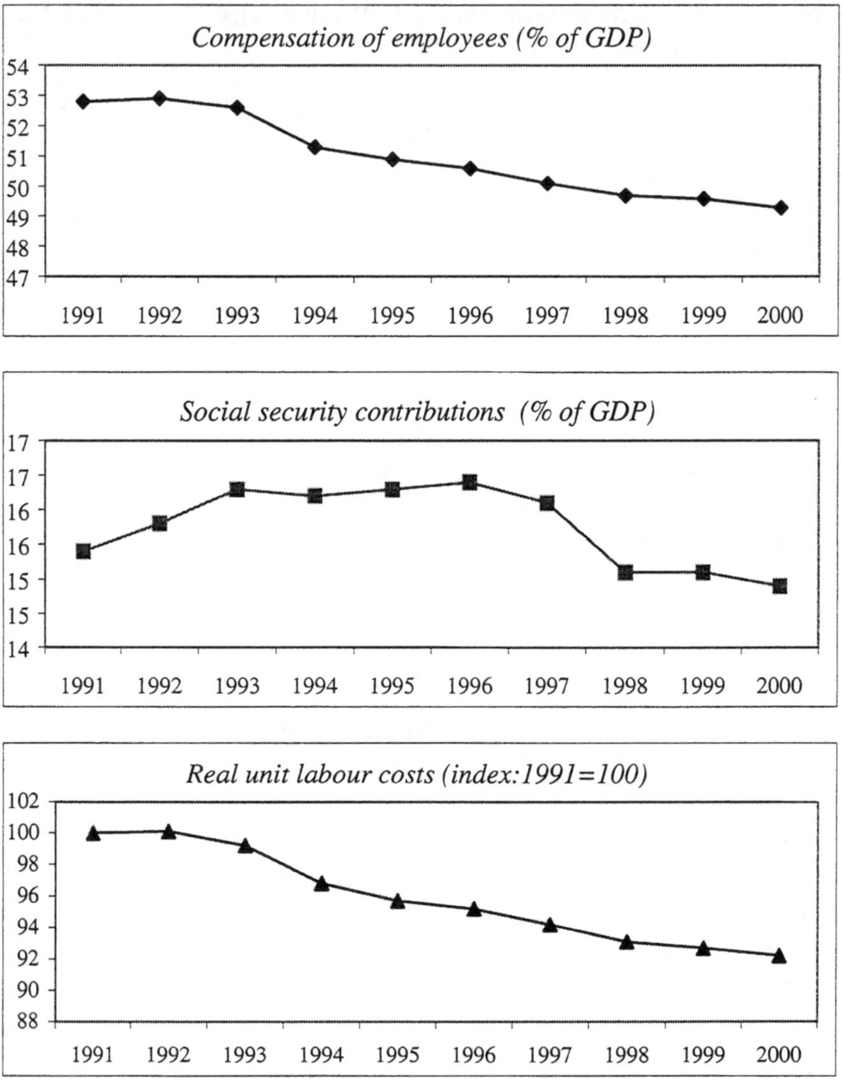

Source: European Commission services

Figure 9.1 - EU – Wages and Non-wage Labour Costs

foundations for higher, investment-supported, economic growth as demand prospects brighten. By incorporating new technologies, the new investment will contribute to sustaining total factor productivity growth and, to the extent that it is capacity widening, slow down the substitution process.[3]

3 Employment Expectations at Firm and Consumer Levels

The EU-harmonised qualitative surveys offer a variety of indicators suitable to track employment expectations in the Union.

As is known, the EU-harmonised system includes five different surveys: the industry survey, the investment survey, the construction survey, the retail trade survey and the consumer survey. Four of the five surveys provide information concerning employment either at firm or consumer level:

- *Industry Survey*: Employment expectations (quarterly);
- *Construction Survey*: Employment expectations (monthly);
- *Retail Trade Survey*: Employment expectations (quarterly);
- *Consumer Survey*: Unemployment expectations (monthly).

The individual qualitative survey data can be aggregated to provide composite information concerning employment expectations in the Union (Figure 9.2).

---

[3] The experience of Ireland seems to bear this out in an even clearer way. In Ireland, macroeconomic wage moderation since the mid-1980s has been much stronger than in the Union on average (e.g. over the period 1991-97, in Ireland real wages grew by 1.5 percentage points less than the labour productivity trend of 4% p.a. whereas in the EU they rose by 1.1 percentage points less than the labour productivity trend of 2% p.a.). This has resulted in a significant slowing down of capital-labour substitution, but the growth of labour productivity has been maintained, helped by higher capacity-widening investment which incorporated technical progress. Simultaneously, in Ireland, economy activity and employment grew at a strong pace (average annual rate of growth of 6.5 and 2.5%, respectively). On the other hand, in the Netherlands wage moderation in combination with labour market reforms (especially part-time work) since 1983 has led to a slowdown in capital-labour substitution but also in apparent labour productivity growth. Cf. European Commission (1998).

Source: European Commission services

Figure 9.2 - EU – Employment Composite Indicator

Indeed, the employment composite indicator seems to track reasonably well the cyclical behaviour of EU employment figures: the correlation between the overall employment growth figures and the composite survey indicator is more than 80% over the period 1992-1998 (Figure 9.3). Alike overall employment growth, the survey composite indicator first accelerated between 1987 and 1990, and then slowed down in the early 1990s. Recovery started in 1994, but growth rates remained much below the ones reached in the preceding expansion.

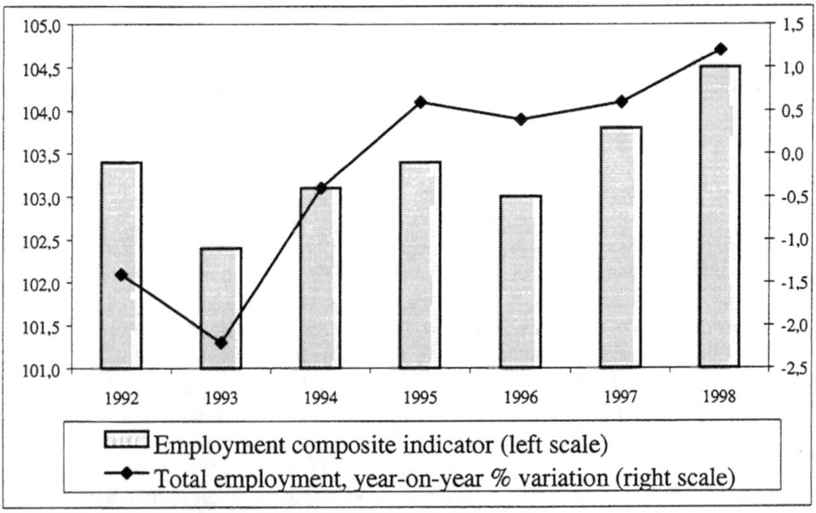

Source: European Commission services

Figure 9.3 - EU – Employment figures

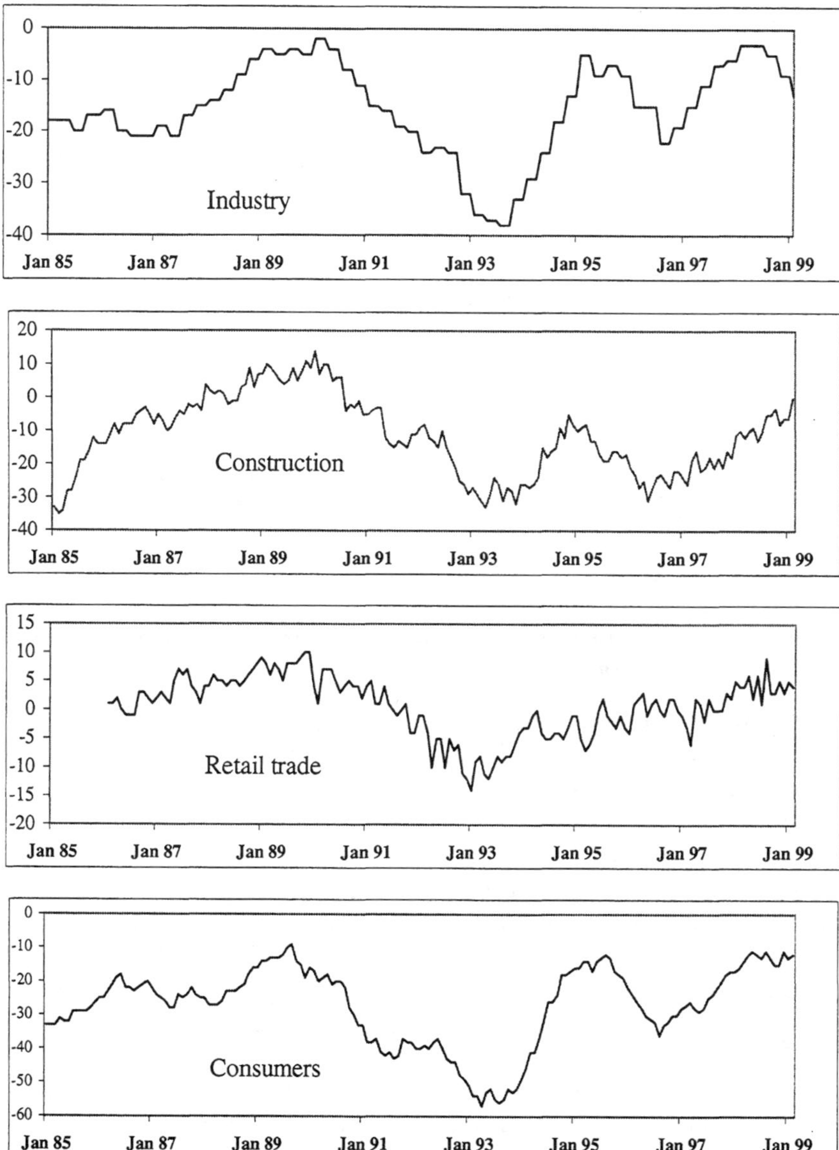

Source: European Commission services
(*) Consumer survey: unemployment expectations (inverted sign)

Figure 9.4 - EU – Employment Expectations (*)

Recent survey data show a weakening of employment expectations at EU level, which could imply a deceleration of employment growth in 1999. Such a deterioration of overall expectations is mainly due to the worsening of the industrialists' opinion, which has steadily deteriorated from a peak at –3 in the second quarter of 1998 down to –11 in the first quarter of 1999 (Figure 9.4).

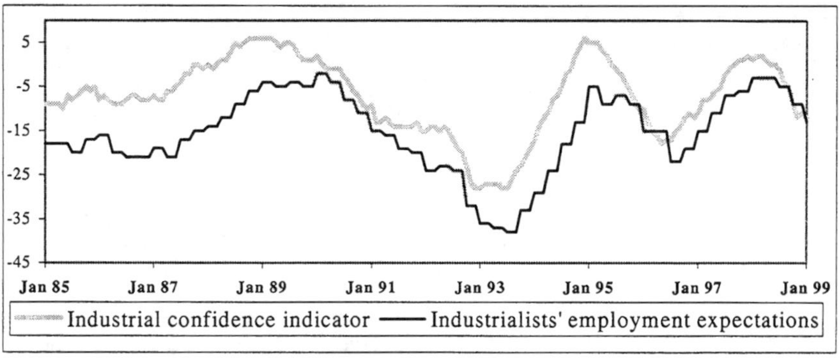

Source: European Commission services

Figure 9.5 - EU – Business Confidence and Employment Expectations in Industry

However, since last summer, labour market trends have eased only marginally when compared with the sharp downturn in industrial business confidence. This is particularly unusual as historical data show that a change in the business confidence used to cause a quick and similar reaction of employment expectations in the past (Figure 9.5). This time, after having peaked simultaneously in the first months of 1998 the industrial confidence indicator dropped back to its long term average (-8 over the period 1988-1998) whereas the balance of employment expectations fell to a level still significantly higher than the long term average (-15 over the same reference period). Thus, survey data suggest that the EU labour market is at least partially unscathed by the recent drop in industrial production which is behind the worsening of business confidence and much less reactive to the industrial downturn than it has been in the previous cycles.

Moreover, the degree of the worsening of EU employment prospects as reflected in the industry survey is almost exclusively due to the deterioration of the German situation. On average, the industrialists' opinion on future employment in the European Union excluding Germany has remained broadly stable, with the index hovering between 2 and 3 since the end of 1997. In most EU economies, employment is therefore still largely immune from the downturn in industrial activity which explains why consumers' optimism continued to improve until recently and reached an historic high in latest months. By contrast, in Germany the indicator of employment expectations in industry has lost 14 percentage points since its peak in the second quarter of 1998 and it is now at its long term average value.[4]

4 Conclusions

The labour reserve associated with EU non-employment represents a very important growth potential which should be properly seized. Indeed, the utilisation of this potential would greatly alleviate Member States' public finances and social security systems,[5] facilitating the safeguarding and development of common European social values, as well as the reduction of tax pressure both on companies and on individuals.

To exploit the huge labour reserve, two conditions must be met: firstly, the existing workforce must be *employable* and secondly must meet the changing skill requirements of the economy.

In the context of this paper, attention has been paid only to the issue of *employability* - namely the availability of working posts in the near future - taking into account employment expectations both at firm and consumer level.

Indeed, the effects of globalisation and the permanent introduction of new technologies are raising the skill requirements for jobs. That is why,

---

4 Cf. Goldman Sachs, *European Daily Comment*, 17/2/1999. Two factors seem to explain the larger deterioration in Germany. First, German industrial labour costs are the highest in Europe, one reason why job creation lagged that of other countries after the 1996-97 upturn. Second, current uncertainty surrounding the new government's policy targets (e.g., fiscal reform, wage policy) has probably triggered cautious behaviour from industrialists.

5 The ratio of people aged 65 and over to those in the active age groups (the so-called *grey pressure*) will increase by about one third between 1995 and 2020. If the employment rate, i.e. the share of those financing pay-as-you-go pension schemes, remains as low as it is now and unemployment remains above 10% of the labour force, social contributions likewise will have to be increased by 33% if one wants to maintain the present ratio of pensions to earned income. On the other band, if the employment rate could be raised to the present US or Japanese levels (74%) with a return to (nearly) full employment, the increase in contributors would nearly match the increase in pensioners. Furthermore, the increase in contribution rates required to maintain the same relative pension levels would be negligible. For more details, cf. European Commission (1994).

training policies (broadly defined) should provide the environment needed for the improvement in human capital which remains a major economic and social goal.

However, it should be kept in mind that in order to produce their full return, training policies must go together with a strong creation of working posts in the economy so that people going through these retraining efforts do actually find a job afterwards. If this is not the case, the full potential of these costly efforts cannot be realised.

It should be appreciated, at the present time, that both cyclical (about 2% of the labour force) and nearly one half of the non-cyclical part of unemployment (i.e. about 4%) is composed of persons still in the normal turnover of the labour market, in the sense that they could easily return to work, with some (limited) retraining, provided that new working posts are created for them. This means that from the present 10.7% of the labour force which is unemployed, about 6% could re-enter the job market fairly fast if and when jobs are offered to them.[6] Thus, despite some bottlenecks in a few specific sectors, there is no evidence that the skills offered by a sizeable share of the workforce are basically outdated or insufficient to ensure employability. The true immediate bottleneck is located at the level of net job creation in the economy.

References

European Commission (1994), Annual Economic Report for 1994 - Analytical Study No. 5, *European Economy, No. 56.*

European Commission (1997), Annual Economic Report for 1997, *European Economy, No. 63.*

European Commission (1998), Growth and Employment in the Stability-Oriented Framework of EMU, *European Economy, No. 65.*

Klein, F.-J. and G. Nerb (1985), Performance of the EC Composite Leading Indicator and its Components, 17th CIRET Conference, Vienna (mimeo).

[6] In a longer term perspective, even part of the structural unemployment *strictu sensu* (about 5% of the labour force) could be reintegrated into employment by active labour market policies and other structural measures if the economy creates the required working posts. Cf. European Commission (1998).

Brand, D., F.-J. Klein, G. Nerb and K. Stock (1990), Construction and Performance of a World Economy Leading Indicator, in K. H. Oppenländer and G. Poser (eds) *Business Cycle Surveys with Special Reference to Pacific Basin Economies*, Aldershot, pp. 249-290.

10 Household Incomes, Professional Status and Inflation in Italy in the 1990s: Evidence from the ISAE Consumer Survey

ENRICO D'ELIA and BIANCA MARIA MARTELLI

Abstract

This paper describes the income distribution changes in Italy over the 1990s as well as the existing income inequalities between the main professional categories. The analysis is based on a VAR model applied to income data stemming from the ISAE[1] consumer survey and price data allowing to identify the mechanism underlying the slowdown in the households' incomes and propensity to save.

1 Introduction

In the present paper, income data stemming from the ISAE consumer survey are used to investigate the behaviour of the Italian households during a rather critical period, namely the 1990s, when the Italian economy has been facing a sharp recession and several economic policy changes.

---

[1] ISAE, Istituto di Studi e Analisi Economica (Institute for Studies and Economic Analyses), Rome, was founded in 1998 by merging ISCO, National Institute for the Studies of the Economic Situation, and ISPE, Institute of Studies for Economic Planning.

Following upon a long expansion lasting ever since 1983, in 1992 Italy faced one of the harshest recessions of the post-war period with a high public debt and the lira leaving the EMS in September and undergoing a strong depreciation. However, the recession, as well as the introduction of a restrictive budgetary policy aimed at honouring the European agreements, and indeed a new incomes policy, succeeded in curbing the inflation dynamics. The awareness of getting through a period of social and economic emergency paved the way for a deep reform of wage agreements to control wage dynamics (bound to macroeconomic variables and excluding automatic indexation) which started in July 1992 and was completed in July 1993. This led to a major wage differentiation and to lesser sensitivity of wages to price variations and indirect taxation. Indeed, during the further period of monetary instability affecting the Italian economy in 1994-95 at the beginning of the recovery, neither prices nor nominal wages showed significant increases. The persisting restrictive budgetary and fiscal policies brought Italy into the first phase of the European Union in late 1998, though it still suffered from a feeble economic growth and a high and persistent unemployment rate.

The aim of this paper is to investigate the effects of such shocks on household income dynamics. The paper is organised as follows: section 2 describes the basic qualitative data collected by ISAE and their main features. Section 3 deals with the method used to quantify income data, while section 4 introduces the VAR model and section 5 describes the main results of generalised impulse response function analysis. Conclusions follow.

2 The ISAE Survey on Consumers' Income

Some main characteristics of the survey are worth noticing (for details see Martelli, 1998). Within the framework of the European Commission (EC) harmonised project, ISAE has carrying out since 1982 a monthly survey on Italian consumers. The survey is carried out on the basis of a stratified random sample of about 2000 consumers proportional to the consumers' universe. Besides the fifteen qualitative requested by the EC, the households are requested to indicate their actual income, and 'normal standard of living' as well, selecting them from predefined 22 income categories.

The first question is related to the households net disposable income (this question belongs to the EC five categorical questions) comprehensive of all families' net revenues (wages, salaries, self-employment income, pensions, transfers, net property income, etc.). The monthly series on disposable income represent a useful source of information on a phenomenon on which quantitative statistics are scarce (national account estimates concerns only overall income) and diffused with significant delay (on annual basis).

The second question, specifically posed by ISAE, relates to the 'normal standard of living income'. The proper wording of the question is as follows: 'which amount of money would a household like yours require to cover all your needs without luxury?'. This piece of information is very interesting as it reveals the degree of economic balance (or imbalance) of the household's budget.

The ratio between the two can be seen as a 'capability' indicator according to Sen (1982), namely the amount of money that households are allowed to assign to consumption or saving after they have satisfied their standard needs (dependent on general economic conditions, culture, interpersonal comparison, etc.). This ratio could be also interpreted as the excess income or 'supernumerary' expenditure referenced in the literature about demand systems (see Pollak and Wales, 1992, for a survey), that is the expenditure which exceeds 'subsistence' consumption. Carnazza and Oneto (1996) utilised this ratio as an indicator of private consumption dynamics, assuming implicitly a stable saving propensity. In this paper capability is simply regarded as the maximum amount of income disposable for saving or non-basic consumption.

This paper focuses the attention on the breakdown of incomes by professional status of breadwinners, thanks to the related question posed within the survey. No official estimates of such series are available at the moment.

Given the long life of the consumer survey, some structural breaks have been brought about by the sample design updating. Since 1982 the sample was built in three stages (municipalities, voting sections, households), stratified in the first one by 6 geographical areas and 7 sectors according to the demographic width of the Italian municipalities. Since 1995, following the requests of the EC to change the statistical unit (from the household to the consumer), the sample has been build with four stages (adding the selection of a consumer inside the household) and has been changed the collection techniques (up to 1994 face-to-face, from 1995 telephonic). Since 1998, due to the new data-gathering technique, the stages have been reduced to two (telephone address, consumer), thus increasing the sample efficiency. Those breaks are to be considered when analysing data. EC (1997) recognises that telephone interviewing tends to underestimate the personal situation, whereas the general situation could be biased by optimism. This effect is evident in the series concerning the 'standard of living income'. Quite the reverse, the change of the statistical unit (from household to consumer), however, does not seem to have significant influence in our case, because the questions on income are still referred to the household.

3 Quantifying Household Income from Tendency Surveys Results

There are at least two ways to evaluate income dynamics from these surveys: the former tends to estimate the average of income distribution, the latter is based on the use of location indexes, such as median and mid-mean.

Where the discrete N class distribution of incomes is observed in place of the continuous one, the approximation of sample mean

$$\hat{y}_t = K_t + \tfrac{1}{2}(y_{1,t} + y_{0,t})f_{1,t} + \tfrac{1}{2}(y_{N,t} + y_{N-1,t})f_{N,t} \qquad (1)$$

can be computed; where $K_t = \tfrac{1}{2}\sum_{i=1}^{N-1}(y_{i,t} + y_{i-1,t})f_{i,t}$; $f_{i,t}$ are the observed frequencies; $y_{i,t}$, for i=2,N-1, are the known limits of income classes, while the extrema $y_{0,t}$ and $y_{N,t}$ are generally unknown. The approximated formula (1) relies on Couchy's mid-point theorem, thus the estimate $\hat{y}_t$ can be biased if the frequency distribution of incomes is not linear between each specified couple of class bounds. However, this bias should be negligible if the classes are narrow enough and non-linearity tends to compensate on the classes as a whole. The latter assumption is quite reasonable for a frequency distribution alternating peaks and throats, so that the function is not allowed to be concave or convex anywhere, apart from several aberrant cases (i.e.: an income distribution heavily concentrated toward the lowest or highest incomes).

It is crucial that the estimate $\hat{y}_t$ turns out to depend on two unknown parameters, namely $y_{0,t}$ and $y_{N,t}$. The simplest hypothesis is that $y_{0,t}$ and $y_{N,t}$ are fixed over time or, more realistically, that they vary with price level p_t. The latter solution has the advantage to be very simple, but it implies a strong assumption about the neutrality of inflation on highest incomes. Quite the reverse, the economic theory states that highest incomes are more volatile compared to others, because richest people revenues mainly depend on capital incomes and profits. Thus, every cyclical variation in productivity and mark-up affects the highest incomes more than prices. On the other hand, poorest people usually earn revenues that are under-indexed with respect to the price index (including pensions and social benefits). As a result, an index based on the previous hypothesis tends to smooth the actual dynamics of income; namely it overestimates lower incomes and underestimates richest people earnings.

Provided that some independent evaluation of y_t is available (for instance from annual or quarterly national accounts), say Y_t, it is possible to obtain an estimation of $y_{0,0}$ and $y_{N,0}$ regressing Y_t on a constant and the terms: $(K_t + ½\ y_{1,t}f_{1,t} + ½\ y_{N-1,t}f_{N,t})$, $p_tf_{1,t}$ and $p_tf_{N,t}$. The estimated first term coefficient is a scalar factor, those of the last two regressors are proportional to the unknown parameters $y_{0,0}$ and $y_{N,0}$. This method generalises the Pesaran (1984) procedure for the quantification of tendency survey results.

Another way to get an estimate of the crucial parameter $y_{N,t}$ relies on the assumption that the frequency of incomes in the right tail of the frequency distribution shall decrease with the level of income. It is also possible to interpolate the known part of the distribution by means of some theoretical function and using the parameters of the latter to compute the mean of the N-th class of incomes. Visco (1984) provides an example for the estimation of price expectations from a tendency survey that are supposed normally distributed. Many other assumption can be made with reference to the right tail of income distribution. Brandolini (1993) provides the results of a test on the Italian data and suggests the use of inflation-corrected bounds.

An alternative approach to the estimation of income dynamics is based on the use of order statistics (see Hoaglin, Mosteller and Tukey, 1983, for an extensive survey). As matter of fact, sample mean can be regarded as only one of the possible summary statistics providing an estimate of the location of the data distribution centre. Many other location estimators are available, such as median, modal value, trimmed means, etc. For symmetric distribution those estimators coincide with the mean, but income distribution is generally asymmetric. In which case, the proper location index strongly depends on the distribution shape (see Johnson and Kotz, 1970, for an exhaustive survey of distribution functions and related location indexes). Thus no general and 'natural' estimator for location index is available.

However, in the income analysis at least two alternative estimators make sense: the former is the median, that is the upper income level of the poorest half of population (or, conversely, the lower income bound of the richest half of population). The latter is α-trimmed mean, that is the average income of (1 - 2α)% intermediate group of population ordered by income level. It excludes both poorest and richest classes.

The median $\hat{y}^M_t$ of the income distribution can be easily computed by assuming that the income distribution inside the M-th class for which $F = \sum_{i=1}^{M-1} f_{i,t} < 0.5$ and $F + f_{M,t} > 0.5$ is flat. In that case

$$\hat{y}^M_t = y_{M,t} + (y_{M+1,t} - y_{M,t})\,(0.5 - F)\,/\,f_{M+1,t} \tag{2}$$

A graphical demonstration of equation (2) is provided in Figure 10.1. Given that the cumulative frequency of income less than or equal to $y_{M,t}$ is $F < 0.5$, by hypothesis, than the frequency of income included in the interval $[y_{M,t}\,,\,\hat{y}^M_t]$ is (0.5-F). If the income distribution in the M+1 th class is rectangular, hence the income density function inside that class is $h = f_{M+1,t} / (y_{M+1,t} - y_{M,t})$. Thus the value d for which dh = (0.5-F) is given by $d = (y_{M+1,t} - y_{M,t})\,(0.5\text{-}F) / f_{M+1,t}$. Equation (2) follows.

By adopting a similar hypothesis it is easy to get other L-estimators, based on quantile estimation, such as mid-summaries and trimmed mean (see Hoaglin, Mosteller and Tukey, 1983, chapter 10). L-estimators have the general form

$$L = \sum_{i=1}^{N} a_i y_i \tag{3}$$

where the observation on the variable y are rearranged in increasing (or decreasing) order, and a_i are weights such as $\sum_{i=1}^{N} a_i = 1$, that generate different L-estimators. For instance, if $a_i = 1/N$, for i = 1, N, then L coincides with sample mean. Where N is odd, $a_i = 1$ for $i = N/2$ and $a_i = 0$ otherwise, then L is the median. If $a_i = 1/(N-2\alpha N)$ for $\alpha < i/N < (1 - \alpha)$ and for $a_i = 0$ otherwise, then L is the so called α-trimmed mean. The 25%-trimmed mean is also called mid-mean. It excludes extreme values and is often used to deal with samples including outliers. Whereas we regard as outliers the missing observations on bounds of the open classes of distribution, α-trimmed mean can possibly solve the problem of income quantification.

L-estimators have the advantage that they do not depend on the estimation of income bounds and could turn out to be more robust than the average based methods whereas the income distribution is multimodal, as it is usually the case. The conjecture about the income distribution inside the median or quartile class is usually not very binding, and any other assumption requires strong (and hard to be verified) hypothesis about the distribution of incomes.

A drawback of quantile based procedures is that equation (2) implies a discontinuity in the neighbourhood of each class bound. Therefore, if the estimated median (or a quartile) falls near one of these bounds, a slight variation of frequencies observed might produce a large index variation. In addition, the quantiles computation may be only estimated from closed classes, for which the parameter h is easily evaluated. Thus, if a frequency exceeding 50% (or 25% for mid-mean) is attached to one of the extreme classes, some artifact is needed. For instance h should be estimated from the nearest class. This constraint is quite unimportant for median estimation, but could be very binding for mid-mean computed on few income classes. This is not the case for our data, which are disaggregated in 22 classes.

In order to discriminate among the various quantification procedures, Brandolini (1993) regressed several quantified income indexes against overall households' disposable income estimated according to national accounts system (see CEC, 1993, chapter 8, for details), and selected the quantification method which ensured the higher possible correlation with reference data. Of course, this test procedure is suitable only for overall income, and it is based on the hypothesis that overall income declared by households is an unbiased estimate of related national account data. In addition, it is generally acknowledged that there is no optimal quantification procedure, overwhelming all the others, specially when the dynamics of variables is concerned, rather than their absolute level.

In this paper the behaviour of several categories of breadwinners is analysed, for which no national-accounts-style estimates are available, thus the previous comparison is not possible. Indeed, we preferred to specify and estimate a set of VAR models (see section below) by utilising different indexes, so as to choose the quantification procedure that ensured the best fitting. As matter of fact, differences among the models turned out to be quite negligible, but the use of mid-mean was found to ensure best performances in terms of standard errors and residuals 'whiteness'.

Figure 10.2 and 10.3 show the dynamics of series quantified by utilising the mid-mean method.

4 A VAR Model of Real Incomes, 'Normal Standard of Living' and Prices

The dynamics of the time series of (logs of) consumer price index (P), real households' income (Y), and capability (C), were found to be conveniently represented by means of a VAR (vector autoregressive model). Such class of models explains the dynamics of the relevant time series $\mathbf{x'}_t = (x_{1,t}, \ldots, x_{N,t})$ as linear functions of their own past. VAR models are 'reduced' forms of structural models, and were found very useful in analysing and forecasting economic time series, since the appraisal of Sims (1980), because they do not include any *a priori* hypothesis on the true structure of the economic system, in contrast with standard econometric models.

The structure of each equation of the VAR model we utilised is:

$$Z_t = a_Z + a_{ZP}(L)\,P_t + a_{ZC_E}(L)\,C_{E,t} + a_{ZC_S}(L)\,C_{S,t} + a_{ZC_N}(L)\,C_{N,t} + \\ + a_{ZY_E}(L)\,Y_{E,t} + a_{ZY_S}(L)\,Y_{S,t} + a_{ZY_N}(L)\,Y_{N,t} + \varepsilon_{Z,t} \qquad (4)$$

where Z_t is a generic variable; the subscript to C and Y indicate the professional breadwinner status: E stays for employees (white and blue collars), S for self-employed (entrepreneurs, professionals, shopkeepers, etc.) and N for non active people (unemployed, retired, housekeepers, etc.); a_Z is a constant term; $a_{ZW}(L)$ is a polynomial in the lag operator *L*, with $L\,Z_t = Z_{t-1}$; $\varepsilon_{Z,t}$ is an univariate white noise. In addition, seasonal and impulse dummies were included in every equation, along with a level dummy accounting for the major structural break in survey methodology (occurred since 1995).

As no constraints are imposed on the parameters, model (4) can be consistently and efficiently estimated by means of ordinary least squares (see Lüktepohl, 1991, chapter 11). Model (4) was estimated by utilising monthly data, from January 1991 to December 1998, on household income and 'normal standard of living' estimated from the Isae survey. Preference was given to the formulation in terms of capability C, rather than in terms of 'normal standard of living', because it proved to be more parsimonious, compared to the latter. A standard specification procedure (based on Akaike, 1973, Hannan and Quinn, 1979, and Schwarz, 1978) was utilised to identify the structure of lag polynomials.

Table 10.1 reports statistics computed on models including from 1 to 15 lags of each variable. It turned out that the dynamic structure of the more parsimonious model is very simple: the location of the minimum according to Hannan and Schwarz criteria suggests that one lag for each explicative variable generally enables us to describe the time series dynamics. Akaike criterion would urge us to adopt a more complicated model, but it is well known that this criterion tends to overestimate the true VAR order (see Lütkepohl, 1991, chapter 4.3). In addition, residuals from the VAR(1) model turned out to show no relevant sign of autocorrelation, as the Ljung and Box (1978) tests reported in table 10.1 suggest. However, in the final model, Y_N and C_S two months lagged and P 6 months lagged were included in every equation in order to 'whitening' residuals.

Main statistics on the estimated model are summarised in tables 10.2 and 10.3. Standard errors of residuals range from 0.01% for prices to 4% for variables concerning self-employed. Those results reflect the high price forecastability and the strong volatility of self-employed income: residuals standard errors for other incomes are about one half of the latter. Ljung and Box (1978) tests against serial correlation in the residuals are quite satisfying: in 4 cases out of 7, the statistics did not allow us to reject the null hypothesis that residuals are white noises at a significance level of 40% ore more. Only for the residuals of Y_E, C_E and C_S the null hypothesis is rejected at 15-20% confidence level.

Table 10.3 shows the F-tests on the overall significance of the explicative variables in each equation. These results could be interpreted as Granger-causality tests (see Geweke, 1984). The structure of dynamic relations among the variables turns out to be quite simple. The autoregressive component of each model (associated with the lagged values parameters of the dependent variables) plays a major role, but not for variables concerning self-employed and for C_N. Again, this result can be explained by the high volatility of self-employed income. In addition, non-active people are hardly capable to smooth the dynamics of their excess income, thus the oscillations of C_N turn out to be less inertial.

Capability of households with an employee as breadwinner is linked to that of other class of breadwinners, possibly because these households include also members earning different revenues. Quite the reverse, the capability of self-employed is linked essentially to that of employees, while non-active breadwinners' excess income is affected by the one of self-employed, possibly owing to secondary incomes of members of the same households.

Real incomes are likely to Granger-cause capabilities, but no significant feedback exists from capabilities to incomes. As matter of fact, actual self-employed revenues are linked to the dynamics of real wages more directly than to the past trend of profits, net operating results, etc. Self-employed people are likely to follow a mark-up rule, implying a virtual revenue indexation to revenues of their employees. Real labour income, in turn, seems to be also linked to self-employed revenues, the values of which are probably implicit targets for employees.

Prices essentially affect C_E, C_N, real self-employed incomes and themselves. The latter result is trivial: price series are very 'inertial' and tend to incorporate permanently any exogenous shock. In addition, in the shortest run inflation reduces real wages and pensions, which are fixed in nominal terms, but not self-employed revenues, that are potentially allowed to vary following general prices dynamics. On their turn, prices are Granger-caused by real income of employees, albeit we shall see below that there is a negative relation between those two variables.

5 The Analysis of Generalised Impulse Response Functions

Direct inspection of single VAR parameters estimates is quite cumbersome, and might be misleading. Several alternative techniques were developed to analyse the dynamic relations among variables accounted for by the model. One of the most widespread is the analysis of impulse response function, that points out the impact on the relevant variables of a shock affecting the system.

Assume

$$x_t = \sum_{i=1}^{p} B_i x_{t-i} + \varepsilon_t \qquad (5)$$

be the finite (p -order) VAR representation of the relevant time series; where $\mathbf{A}_i$ are parameters' matrices and $\varepsilon'_t = (\varepsilon_{1,t}, \ldots, \varepsilon_{N,t})$ is a vector of multivariate white noises with mean zero and non-singular variance matrix Σ_{ε}. If $\mathbf{x}_t$ is stationary, model (5) can be 'inverted' in the multivariate Wold VMA (vector moving average) representation

$$\mathbf{x}_t = \sum_{i=0}^{\infty} \mathbf{A}_i \varepsilon_{t-i} \qquad (6)$$

where the recursive relation

$$\mathbf{A}_s = \sum_{i=1}^{s} \mathbf{A}_{s-i} \mathbf{B}_i \qquad (7)$$

holds, and $\mathbf{A}_0 = \mathbf{I}_N$ by definition (see Lutekepohl, 1991, chapter 11). If $\mathbf{x}_t$ is stationary, hence $\mathbf{A}_s \to \mathbf{0}$ as $s \to \infty$. According to (6), the response of $\mathbf{x}_t$ to the arbitrary shock $\varepsilon_t = \delta$ after h periods is given by $\mathbf{A}_h$. Thus the sequence $\{\mathbf{A}_i\ \delta\}$ is commonly called impulse response function of the model (5).

Notice that (7) makes sense for no-stationary series too, even though, in this case, condition $\mathbf{A}_s \to \mathbf{0}$ as $s \to \infty$ does not necessarily hold, that is the shock effect does not necessarily vanish in the long run. However, the latter condition holds if variables included in the model are linked by a long-run equilibrium relation, such as those implied by the hypothesis of cointegration (see Engle and Granger, 1987, and Johansen, 1995) or those concerning the transitory nature of non-structural shocks (see Blanchard and Quah, 1989).

Each element of the impulse response function $\mathbf{F}_h$ can be viewed as the difference between two conditional forecasts on $\mathbf{x}_t$: provided that the shock $\varepsilon_t = \delta$ occurred in the former case, and under the baseline hypothesis that $\varepsilon_t = 0$. That is

$$F(\delta)_h = E(\mathbf{x}_{t+h} | \varepsilon_t = \delta) - E(\mathbf{x}_{t+h} | \varepsilon_t = 0) \tag{8}$$

Of course, in a multivariate framework, where $N>1$, the choice of δ turns out to be crucial. Given that ε_t has generally a non-diagonal variance matrix, its elements are not mutually independent. Therefore, it could be cumbersome to analyse the effect of a shock on a *single* equation, given that no shock occurred on the others. This problem is traditionally coped with by analysing the effect of a set of mutually incorrelated shocks that are linear combination of the original ones. More specifically, the impulse response function is redefined over η_t, provided that $\Sigma_\eta = E(\eta_t \eta'_t)$ is a diagonal (definite positive) matrix and

$$\eta_t = \mathbf{U}\, \varepsilon_t \tag{9}$$

The implied condition $\Sigma_\eta = \mathbf{U}\, \Sigma_\varepsilon \mathbf{U}'$ can be satisfied by an infinite set of matrices $\mathbf{U}$, thus some normalisation on Σ_η and $\mathbf{U}$ is needed in order to identify η_t. The most traditional approach (see Bernanke, 1986), suggests to fix the diagonal elements of Σ_η (that are the variances of η_t) equal to the corresponding original shocks ε_t, and to impose a lower triangular structure to $\mathbf{U}$, by means of the so-called Cholesky decomposition of Σ_ε.

Unfortunately, this decomposition is not unique and depends on the variables ordering in the model. As matter of fact, owing to the triangular structure of $\mathbf{U}$, only the first element of the transformed shock vector η_t has an unique and direct economic interpretation, because it turns out to coincide with the original first element of ε_t. The *i*-th transformed shock is a linear combination of the original shocks hitting the equation that precede the *i*-th variable. Thus, each reshuffling of the equations provides a different set of impulse response functions. In addition, each equation ordering implies a different hypothesis on the causal relations existing among shocks: that is, the *i*-th shock causes that affecting the variables from *(i+1)*-th to *N*-th and is caused, in turn, by the others.

Of course, other normalisations of (9) are possible, but all of them imply some kind of structural interpretation of the VAR model (see Watson, 1994). A way out of this and of other difficulties of the standard impulse response analysis was recently proposed by Koop, Pesaran and Potter

(1996). It comes directly from the interpretation of impulse response functions in terms of conditional forecasts on $\mathbf{x}_t$ (8). If one conditioned the forecasts on the past history Ω_t of the variables included in the model, then the shock $\varepsilon_t = \delta$ itself can be viewed as a realisation of the same stochastic process generating $\mathbf{x}_t$. Thus δ has to exhibit the same covariance structure Σ_ε characterising ε_t.

As a consequence, a unitary shock hitting the i-th equation is necessarily associated with shocks hitting all the other variables, whose size is

$$\delta_{j,t} = \frac{\sigma_{i,j}}{\sigma_{i,i}}, \qquad (10)$$

where $\sigma_{i,j}$ are elements of the covariance matrix Σ_ε. In that case, Koop, Pesaran and Potter (1996) demonstrate that a generalised impulse response function $G(\delta)_h$ can be defined, and in a linear multivariate model it is simply

$$G(\delta)_h = E(\mathbf{x}_{t+h} | \varepsilon_t = \delta, \Omega_t) - E(\mathbf{x}_{t+h} | \varepsilon_t = 0, \Omega_t) = F(\delta^*)_h \qquad (11)$$

where the elements of δ^* are defined by (10). It can be easily verified that $G(\delta)_h = F(\delta)_h$ when the innovation in the model (5) are mutually incorrelated; that is, in such a case the traditional impulse response function coincides with the generalised one.

Expression (11) has several advantages compared to traditional formulations. First of all, the generalised impulse function does not depend on the ordering of the VAR model variables and implies no causal structure among the innovations. In addition, the shock to which the system reacts is allowed to be easily interpreted in economic terms: it is the 'typical' innovation that used to hit variables in the past, normalised for a scalar factor. On the other hand, at least in linear models, $G(\delta)_h$ turns out to be as easy to be computed as $F(\delta)_h$.

The variance matrix of innovation in VAR model turns out to be crucial in evaluating generalised impulse response functions. Contemporary correlation among residuals of model (5) is shown in table 10.4. As expected, correlation among residuals of incomes and capabilities were found to be positive, while residuals of prices show a weak negative correlation with those of real variables. As a consequence, it may be argued that the possible substitution effect between different kinds of revenues is weak, and price shocks have an adverse impact on real incomes and capability.

Strongest links between innovation were found among incomes and corresponding capabilities. This indicates that positive shocks affecting real revenues also widen excess income, rather than pushing for a fast change in 'normal standard of living'. Hence, for a given standard of living, households consider any positive shock on real incomes as an unexpected increase in potential saving. As far as unplanned capability goes into consumption, a positive shock on real incomes tends to push down the saving ratio. Since shocks on capability are not independent from those on actual income, 'normal' income changes less than actual one. This effect is stronger for self-employed, but is significant also for the other categories of breadwinners.

Positive correlation among the innovations on different kind of incomes is generally weak, but not the correlation between employees' revenues residuals, on the one hand, and other innovations on incomes, on the other. It could be argued that shocks affecting real wages also hit other revenues, while innovations on self employed revenues are generally independent from those on non-active revenues. In addition, households where the breadwinner is an employee or a self-employed are likely to include people earning other kinds of revenues (specially retired and self-employed). Thus, overall income of those households is strongly correlated with incomes of breadwinners belonging to the other two categories. Quite the reverse, households where breadwinners are unemployed or retired hardly include working people.

The contemporary correlation among innovations can be strengthened or weakened by dynamic relations among the variables. Figures 10.4-10.11 show the response of the system to unitary shocks hitting incomes and prices. Following the philosophy of generalised impulse response, these shocks must be regarded as 'typical' innovations normalised with respect to reference variables, but embodying non-null shocks on the other variables. For instance, according to standard errors and covariance matrix of residuals shown in tables 10.2 and 10.4, a unitary shock hitting of employees income also implies the following perturbations on the other variables: 0.484 on C_E, 0.195 on C_S, 0.251 on C_N, 0.723 on Y_S, 0.472 on Y_N and –0.005 on P.

First of all, it is worth noticing that different incomes have different inertia too. Labour income seems to react very inertially to an initial shock (see figure 10.4). It takes about 6 months in order to absorb 75% of initial impulse. In addition, self-employed revenues are likely to catch up innovations on real wages. This could be explained by the mark-up component of self-employed revenues and by the positive demand effect of an increase in real wages. On the other hand, innovations affecting wages and salaries slightly hit pensions and other non-active allowances. The initial impact is mainly due to the instantaneous correlation among real incomes. Moreover, no catch up effect is evident for non-active breadwinners.

Shocks on real incomes of self employed breadwinners seem to be quite 'insulated' (see figure 10.5). They do not tend to carry over as time goes on, signalling the volatility (non-persistence) of typical shocks hitting real revenues of entrepreneurs, professionals, craftsmen and shopkeepers. Most of their revenues are not determined by long-term contracts (as wages are), but depend on idiosyncratic shocks on demand and prices that are transitory in nature. In addition, those shocks are market-specific and thus hardly spill over on other kinds of incomes. Only the instantaneous correlation structure of 'typical' shocks determines a weak covariance among the three income categories. Hence, in the mid-long run volatility of self-employed incomes does not influence other revenues too much.

Non active real incomes (mainly pensions) respond to an initial shock in a way similar to self-employed incomes (see figure 10.6). The inertial effect is quite weak (but a slightly stronger than in the case of self-employed), and the effect on other incomes is negligible. As a matter of fact, pensions and other benefits are hit by idiosyncratic shocks, mainly depending on legal clauses, rather than on the past history of those revenues. The inertia of this kind of incomes might be explained by some form of staggering in pensions indexation (pensions and other allowances are often paid only every two or three months). In addition, a possibly demand effect on other revenues is very weak, even though incomes of households with an employee breadwinner (and possibly including some retired member) seem to react positively to a shock on revenues of non-active people for few months.

When a shock hits capabilities, it has minor effects on the dynamics of corresponding revenues (see figure 10.7). Of course, this kind of shocks is (as noted beforehand) instantaneously correlated with movements in the same direction of actual real incomes. However, those shocks do not transfer 1 to 1 on actual incomes, because they affect the 'normal standard of living' at the same time. Only self-employed breadwinners seem to react to the shock on their capability by adjusting their revenues to restore the initial excess income during the first month. That reaction, if any, only absorbs 10% of the initial shock. Employees' income, in turn, carry over the initial shock on capability during few months, owing to the inherent inertia of this kind of revenues (see figure 10.4).

A shock on incomes has a weak effect on capability, apart from the 'mechanical' instantaneous impact (see figure 10.8). Only self-employed breadwinners succeed in partially adjusting their excess income to the planed level: an adverse initial shock on their income is followed by a slight recovery of capability after 2 months. Conversely, non active people seem to adequate their capability to the real disposable income dynamics, carrying over for few months the initial shock on capability caused by each revenue innovation. The latter effect seems to be long lasting for employees, who almost permanently bear the effect of every fluctuation in capability induced by revenue shocks. This implies a higher inertia in their standard of living, compared to other breadwinners.

In the short run, a 1% increase in prices reduces real incomes by an amount ranging from 1-1.5% for employees to 1.5-1.8% for other breadwinners (see figure 10.9). Thus inflation is likely to over-affect real revenues, reducing both consumption and saving capability of each household. However, this negative effect becomes negligible after 18 – 24 months, even though in the long run self-employed breadwinners witness a reduction in their real income, while non-active succeed in recovering a small fraction of the initial loss (10%), probably owing to the indexation of pensions and other benefits. Inflation seems to be almost for employees neutral in the long run. As a consequence, during the 1990s, inflation brought about paradoxical long lasting effects on income distribution: it hit non-contractualised incomes and improved the relative position of pensioners and other non active people (protected by escalation mechanisms). This is a consequence of the peculiarity of the Italian labour market, where most self-employed keep the weakest position on the market, playing the role of sub-contractors and temporary or unskilled workers (see Rossi, 1996).

Inflation is non-neutral for capability (see figure 10.10). A 1% increase in prices reduces the employees' excess income by 2% instantaneously and in the following 4-5 months. With regard to the other households, capability is only reduced after one month. However, in the short run non active people suffer from a shortage in their capability similar to employees, while self-employed witness a reduction by 0.6-1%. It could be argued that, at least in the first 6 months, entrepreneurs and shopkeepers partially adjust (reduce) their normal standard of living in order to preserve the desired saving level. Indeed, other breadwinners have to face both a reduction of real income and a corresponding increase in their 'normal standard of living' that double the effect of a price increase. Nevertheless, in the long run inflation cuts each household's consumption/saving capability by a similar amount (30-40% of the initial shock on prices).

In turn, the real income dynamics affects price dynamics (see figure 10.11). More specifically, given that monetary policy stance is very restrictive, as it was actually during the 1990s (see Signorini and Visco, 1997), real income is allowed to increase if and only if prices decrease, in compliance with the Fisher's equation $\dot{y} = \dot{m} - \dot{p}$, when the money growth rate ($\dot{m}$) is exogenous and does not accommodate to the tendency of inflation rate ($\dot{p}$) and real income growth ($\dot{y}$). Therefore, it is not surprising that a shock hitting real revenues ends up with an adverse effect on prices in the long run. In the model this effect overwhelms the standard short run positive relation between wages and prices: as a matter of fact a 1% increase in employees' real income pushes down permanently prices by 0.1%. This is a likely result of a successful income policy (see Fabiani *et al.,* 1998). Nevertheless, such a policy was unable to force other real incomes in order to grow along a non-inflationary path. For instance, according to the model, a shock on pensions and other social benefits turns out to be independent from prices, and a 1% increase in self-employed revenues only produces a 0.03% long run decrease in prices.

6 Concluding Remarks

The analysis based on a VAR model allows us to sketch a representation of the mechanisms underlying the slowdown in households' incomes and in their propensity to save over the past few years. According to the evidence shown in Figures 10.4-10.11, a typical shock on prices reduces real income by a comparable amount (see Figure 10.9) and shrinks the households' excess income, particularly that of employees and non-active people (see Figure 10.10). The first impact on incomes tends to persist in the employees' revenues (see Figure 10.4), while it vanishes within few months for other households (see Figure 10.5 and 10.6). Capability for consumption and saving is partly recovered by the self-employed, but not by employees and non-active breadwinners (see Figure 10.8). As the overall real income dynamics slows down, the 'normal standard of living' dynamics of the self-employed falls below that of other breadwinners. Hence, the overall saving ratio decreases, but, at the same time, the saving distribution changes in favour of households with a self-employed breadwinner. The overall effect on aggregate demand is an increasing contribution of consumption to the GDP growth, which contrasts with the slowdown in the households' disposable income. On the other hand, saving is more and more conditioned by the self-employed revenue dynamics, which is also very volatile (see Figure 10.5). This eventually decreases the investment growth, increasing its variance as well. In the long run, inflation reduces the self-employed purchasing power and preserves employees' (via income policies) and non-active (via indexation clauses) real incomes (see Figure 10.9). This distributive effect of inflation is slightly reinforced by the negative long run impact on prices of employees' real incomes (see Figure 10.11), which tends to carry over onto prices the initial shock.

Finally it is worth noticing that the (sample and qualitative) data used conform both theory and other empirical evidences stemming out from more extensive analysis carried out utilising National Account estimates and household budget survey.

7 Appendix - Tables and Figures

Table 10.1 – Model Selection Criteria

VAR order	Criteria			Significance level of Ljung-Box tests against residuals autocorrelation (24 lags)						
				Capability			Real income			*Prices*
	Akaike	*Hannan-Quinn*	Schwarz	Employees	*Self employed*	Non active	Employees	*Self employed*	Non active	
1	-57.388	-56.920	-56.237	0.197	0.062	0.399	0.106	0.438	0.795	0.360
2	-57.697	-56.758	-55.383	0.997	0.584	0.926	0.059	0.685	0.925	0.493
3	-57.602	-56.186	-54.113	0.999	0.919	0.918	0.142	0.711	0.976	0.083
4	-57.681	-55.782	-53.003	0.998	0.951	0.833	0.085	0.690	0.984	0.328
5	-58.007	-55.620	-52.126	0.988	0.706	0.754	0.105	0.351	0.948	0.853
6	-58.660	-55.780	-51.564	0.999	0.458	0.286	0.254	0.446	0.772	0.829
7	-59.087	-55.710	-50.762	0.946	0.579	0.517	0.158	0.255	0.128	0.648
8	-59.621	-55.739	-50.052	0.504	0.146	0.326	0.318	0.633	0.167	0.151
9	-60.618	-56.227	-49.792	0.015	0.080	0.003	0.046	0.238	0.000	0.590
10	-60.655	-55.740	-48.534	0.061	0.054	0.000	0.024	0.000	0.019	0.094
11	-60.692	-55.253	-47.276	0.067	0.008	0.099	0.019	0.210	0.000	0.000
12	-54.406	-48.438	-39.683	0.402	0.483	0.000	0.000	0.000	0.000	0.000
13	-60.765	-54.278	-44.759	0.000	0.000	0.000	0.000	0.000	0.000	0.000
14	-44.298	-37.269	-26.950	0.000	0.001	0.004	0.000	0.000	0.000	0.000
15	-27.830	-20.259	-9.141	0.000	0.000	0.011	0.000	0.000	0.000	0.000

Table 10.2 – Overall Statistics on Model Fitting

Depend variables	**Standard error of residuals**	$\bar{R}^2$	**Ljung-Box tests against residuals autocorrelation**		**Tests against autoregressive residuals heteroschedasticity**	
			Q(24)	*Rejection level*	ARCH(24)	*Rejection level*
Capability						
Employees	0.021	0.784	30.86	*0.158*	1.129	*0.350*
Self employed	0.034	0.402	29.12	*0.216*	0.605	*0.831*
Non active	0.026	0.820	24.47	*0.435*	1.084	*0.386*
Real income						
Employees	0.019	0.538	28.74	*0.230*	0.746	*0.702*
Self employed	0.037	0.702	18.32	*0.787*	0.937	*0.516*
Non active	0.027	0.595	20.04	*0.694*	0.714	*0.733*
Prices	0.001	1.000	25.33	*0.388*	1.305	*0.233*

Table 10.3 – Significance of Explicative Variables (F-tests)

Dependent variables	**Explicative variables**						
	Capability			*Real income*			*Prices*
	Employees	*Self employed*	*Non active*	*Employees*	*Self employed*	*Non active*	
Capability							
Employees	42.438	3.219	4.115	2.233	1.059	3.475	5.585
	(0.000)	*(0.046)*	*(0.046)*	*(0.139)*	*(0.307)*	*(0.036)*	*(0.006)*
Self employed	9.099	0.260	1.025	2.746	3.666	2.960	0.613
	(0.003)	*(0.772)*	*(0.315)*	*(0.102)*	*(0.059)*	*(0.058)*	*(0.544)*
Non active	0.652	2.633	0.494	5.574	3.370	4.461	5.912
	(0.422)	*(0.079)*	*(0.484)*	*(0.021)*	*(0.070)*	*(0.015)*	*(0.004)*
Real income							
Employees	0.026	1.989	1.950	10.785	4.375	1.177	0.271
	(0.871)	*(0.144)*	*(0.167)*	*(0.002)*	*(0.040)*	*(0.314)*	*(0.763)*
Self employed	0.376	1.320	0.589	8.755	0.407	0.416	2.844
	(0.542)	*(0.273)*	*(0.445)*	*(0.004)*	*(0.525)*	*(0.661)*	*(0.064)*
Non active	0.747	2.280	5.407	1.316	0.107	9.431	1.071
	(0.390)	*(0.109)*	*(0.023)*	*(0.255)*	*(0.745)*	*(0.000)*	*(0.348)*
Prices	0.906	0.178	0.431	11.238	0.947	2.185	27587.3
	(0.344)	*(0.837)*	*(0.514)*	*(0.001)*	*(0.334)*	*(0.119)*	*(0.000)*

Note: Rejection levels of the null hypothesis that explicative variables are not significant are shown in parentheses below F-tests.

Table 10.4 – Correlation Matrix of Residuals

	Capability			*Real income*			*Prices*
	Employees	*Self employed*	*Non active*	*Employees*	*Self employed*	*Non active*	
Capability							
Employees	1.000						
Self employed	0.361	1.000					
Non active	0.402	0.365	1.000				
Real income							
Employees	0.409	0.107	0.203	1.000			
Self employed	0.089	0.530	0.327	0.359	1.000		
Non active	0.274	0.122	0.412	0.354	0.174	1.000	
Prices	-0.107	0.003	-0.028	-0.073	-0.056	-0.085	1.000

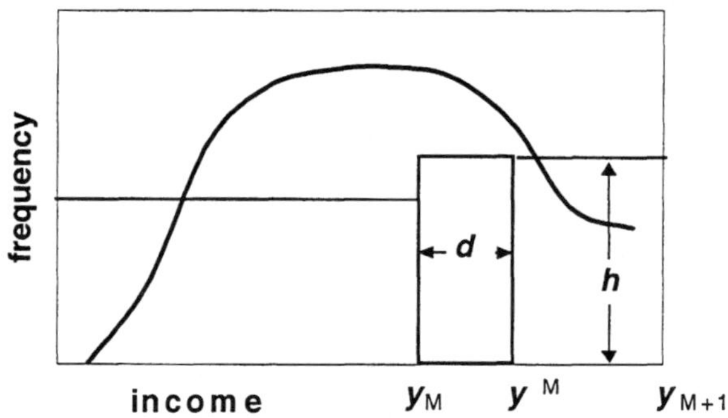

Figure 10.1 - The Estimation of the Median

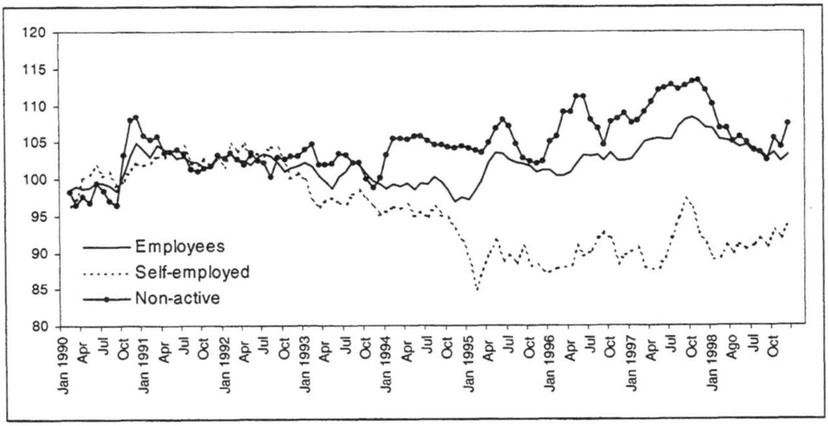

Figure 10.2 – Real Income Indexes (Base 1990=100) (3 Month Moving Averages)

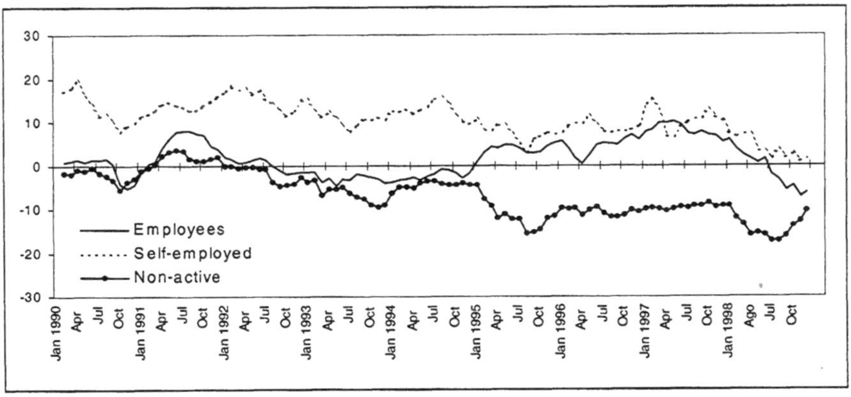

Figure 10.3 – Capabilities (Percentage of Actual Income) (3 Month Moving Averages)

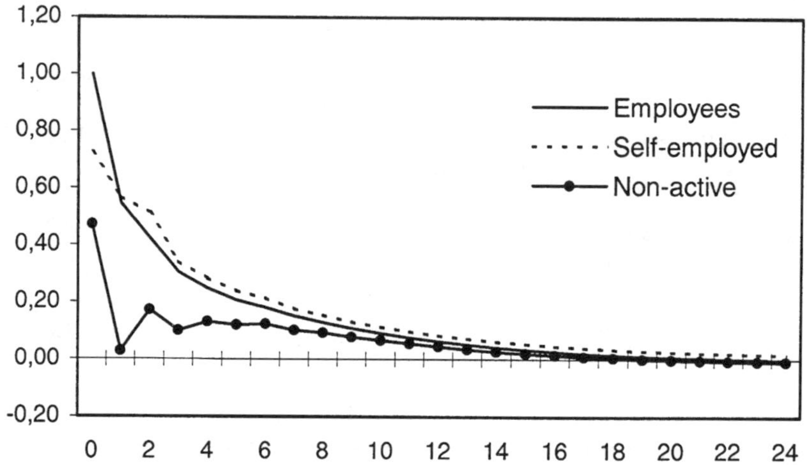

Figure 10.4 - Response to a Shock on Employees Income

Figure 10.5 - Response to a Shock on Self-employed Income

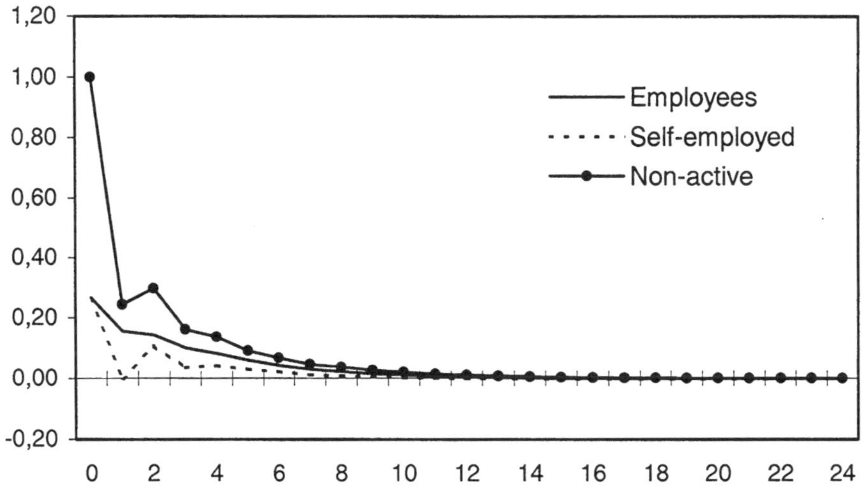

Figure 10.6 - Response to a Shock on Non-active Income

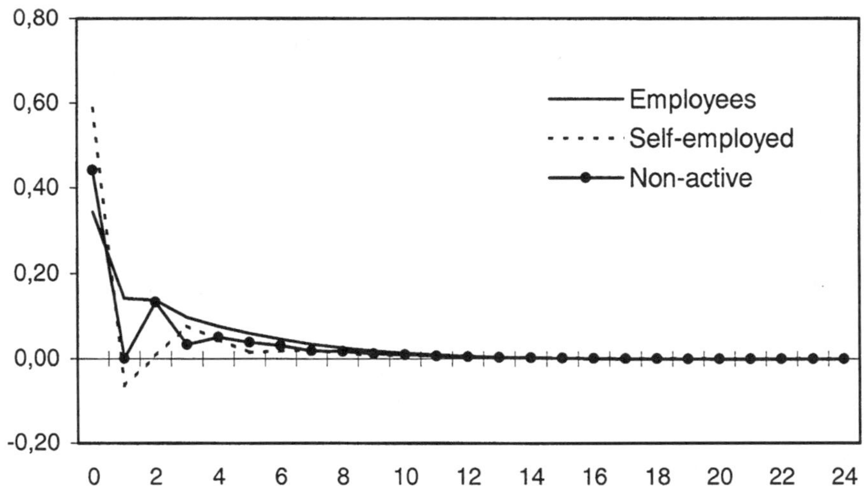

Figure 10.7 - Response of Incomes to a Shock on Capabilities

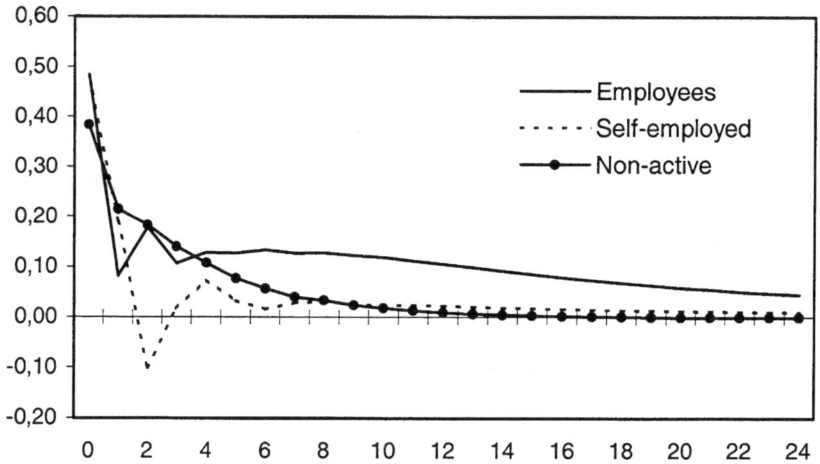

Figure 10.8 - Response of Capabilities to a Shock on Incomes

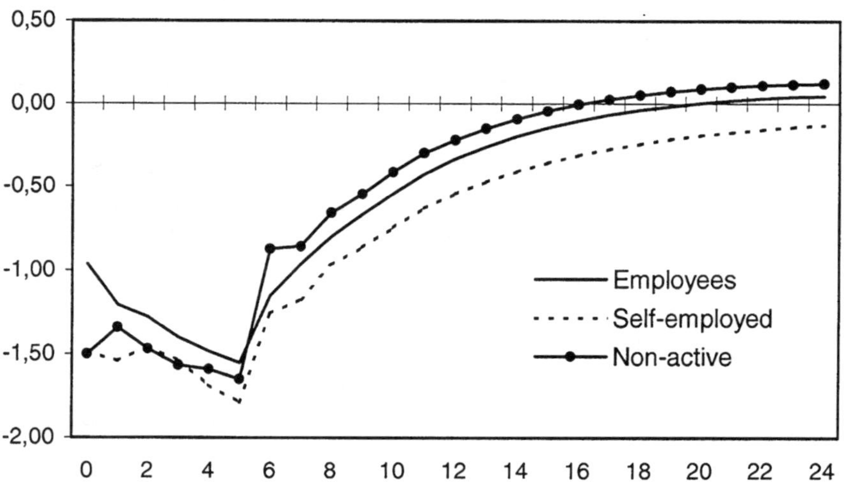

Figure 10.9 - Response of Incomes to a Shock on Prices

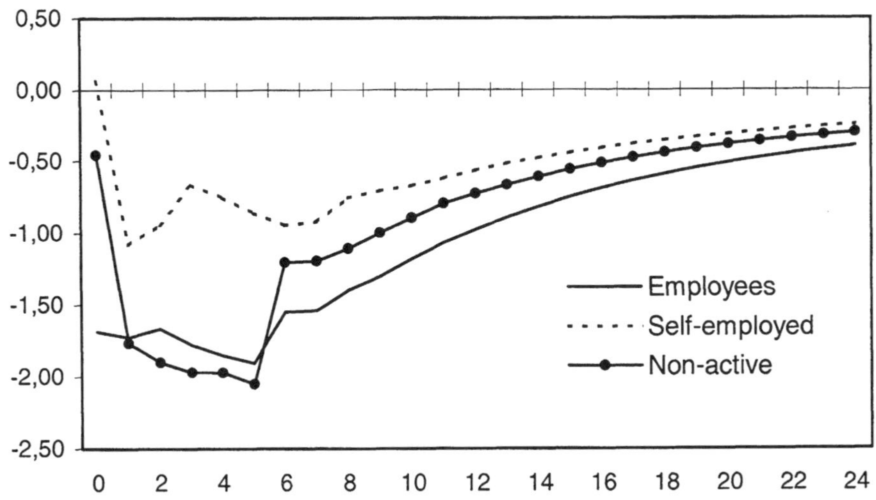

Figure 10.10 - Response of Capabilities to a Shock on Prices

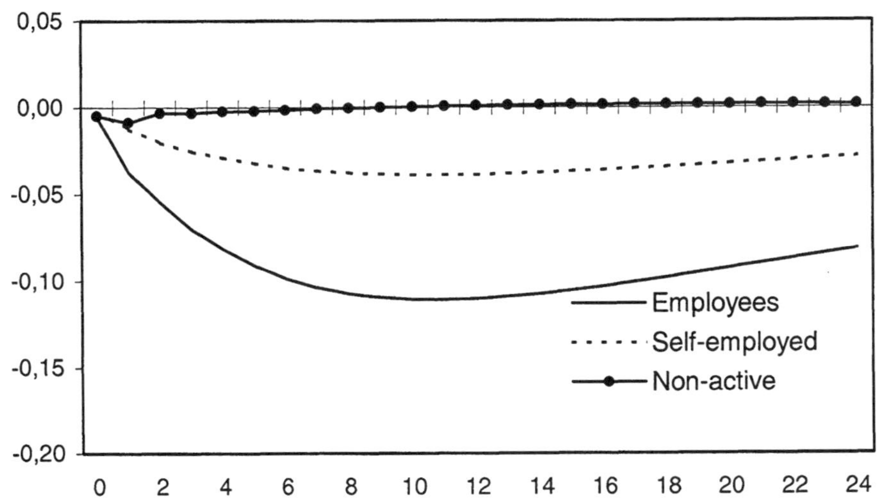

Figure 10.11 - Response of Prices to a Shock on Incomes

References

Akaike, H. (1973), 'A New Look at the Statistical Model Identification', *IEEE Transactions on Automatic Control*, AC-19, pp. 716-723.

Bernanke, B. (1986), 'Alternative Explanations of the Money-Income Correlation', *Carnegie-Rochester Conference Series on Public Policy*, 25, pp. 49-99.

Blanchard, O. and D. Quah (1989), 'The Dynamic Effects of Aggregate Demand and Supply Disturbances', *American Economic Review*, 79, pp. 655-673.

Brandolini, A. (1993), 'Il reddito disponibile delle famiglie e la sua distribuzione: una stima derivata dall'inchiesta mensile dell'Isco', mimeo, Banca d'Italia.

Carnazza, P. and G. Oneto (1996), 'Searching for a Leading Indicators of Household Consumption in the Italian Economy', in Oppenländer K.H. and G. Poser (eds), *Business Cycle Survey. Forecasting Issues and Methodological Aspects*, Avebury.

CEC (1993), *System of National Accounts 1993*, Commission of the European Communities, Brussels.

EC (1997), 'The joint Harmonised EU Programme of Business and Consumer Surveys', *European Economy*, No. 6.

Engle, R. F. (1982), 'Autoregressive Conditional Heteroscedasticity with Estimates of the Variance of United Kingdom Inflation', *Econometrica*, 50, pp. 987-1007.

Engle, R.F. and C.W.J. Granger (1987), 'Co-Integration and Error Correction: Representation, Estimation and Testing', *Econometrica*, 55, pp. 251-276.

Fabiani, S., A. Locarno, G. Oneto and P. Sestito (1998), 'Risultati e problemi di un quinquennio di politica dei redditi: una prima valutazione quantitativa', *Temi di discussione*, Banca d'Italia, Rome.

Geweke, J. F. (1984), 'Inference and Causality in Economic Time Series Models', in Griliches, Z. and M. D. Intriligator, (eds) *Handbook of Econometrics*, Vol. II, North Holland, Amsterdam, pp. 1102-1144.

Hannan, E.J. and B.G. Quinn (1979), 'The Determination of the Order of an Autoregression', *Journal of the Royal Statistical Society*, B 41, pp. 190-195.

Hoaglin, D. C., F. Mosteller and J. W. Tukey (1983), *Understanding Robust and Exploratory Data Analysis*, (eds) John Wiley and Sons, New York.

Johansen, S. (1995), *Likelihood Based Inference in Cointegrated Vector Autoregressive Models*, Oxford University Press, Oxford.

Johnson, N. L. and S. Kotz (1970), *Continuous Univariate Distribution*, John Wiley and Sons, New York.

Koop, G., H. M. Pesaran and S. M. Potter (1996), 'Impulse Response Analysis in Nonlinear Multivariate Models', *Journal of Econometrics*, Vol. 74, No. 1, pp. 119-147.

Ljung, G. M. and G. E. P. Box (1978), 'On a Measure of Lack of Fit in Times Series Models', *Biometrika*, 67, pp. 297-303.

Lüktepohl, H. (1991), *Introduction to Multiple Time Series Analysis*, Springer-Verlag, Berlin.

Martelli, B.M. (1998), 'Le inchieste congiunturali dell'ISCO: aspetti metodologici', Rassegna di Lavori dell'ISCO, AnnoXV, No.3.

Pesaran, M. H. (1984), 'Expectations formation and macroeconomic modelling', in *Contemporary macroeconomic modelling*, P. Malgrange and P.A. Muet (eds), Blackwell, Oxford.

Pollak, R. A. and T. J. Wales (1992), *Demand System Specification and Estimation*, Oxford University Press, Oxford.

Rossi, N. (1996), *III Rapporto CNEL sulla distribuzione e la redistribuzione del reddito in Italia*, (ed) Il Mulino, Bologna.

Schwarz, G. (1978), 'Estimating the Dimension of a Model', *Annals of Statistics*, 6, pp. 461-464.

Sen, A. (1982), *Choice, Welfare and Measurement*, MIT Press, Cambridge.

Signorini, L. F.and I. Visco (1997), *L'economia italiana*, Il Mulino, Bologna.

Sims, C.A. (1980), 'Macroeconomics and Reality', *Econometrica*, 48, pp. 1-48.

Visco, I. (1984), *Price Expectations in Rising Inflation*, North-Holland, Amsterdam.

Watson, M.W. (1994), 'Vector Autoregressions and Cointegration', in: Engle R.F. and D.L. McFadden (eds), *Handbook of Econometrics*, Vol. IV, Elsevier, New York, pp. 2843-2915.

11 The Predictability of Currency Crises: The Case of Turkey

BENGI KIBRITCIOGLU, BÜLENT KOSE and GAMZE UGUR[1]

Abstract

Currency crises experiences in the past (ERM 1992-93, Latin America 1994-95 and Asia 1997-98) have always had broad reflections on the theory of economics. In order to explain the triggering factors of the crises many models had been developed by economists following the seminal paper of Krugman (1979). In this paper, we firstly presented a summary of the different generations of these models in connection with the case studies mentioned above. Then, we analyzed the 1994 financial crisis in Turkey, including its determinants and policy implications for the future. The main purpose of this paper is to investigate and discuss the predictability of possible currency crises in Turkey by using the leading economic indicators approach.

1 Introduction

Financial crises, in general, may be attributed to the need for sudden and sharp changes in prices and/or quantities in financial markets for bonds, equities and foreign exchanges. The delay in the adjustment process

---

[1] The authors, listed in alphabetical order above, thank Özhan Üzümcüoglu, Aykut Kibritcioglu and Fatih Ozatay for their useful comments and suggestions. The opinions expressed in the paper are those of the authors and should not be interpreted as representing the views of the organization with which they are affiliated.

increases the sharpness of the change, and hence, the degree of the crisis. In that respect, a currency crisis may be expected to occur when a speculative attack on a specific currency results in a devaluation (or a sharp depreciation) or forces the authorities to defend the exchange rate by depleting large volumes of international reserves or by sharply raising interest rates.

In the last decade of the 20th century, several crises in financial and foreign exchange markets in Europe (1992-93), Latin America (Mexico, 1994-95) and Southeast Asia (1997-98) led economists to focus on the causes and timing of these crises. They tried to explain different experiences of countries with their differing economic structures and historical backgrounds by using different models, since there is no unique reason of crises. Traditional models regarding the balance of payments and currency crisis in the late 1970s and the first half of the 1980s suggest that the determinants of crises can be explained by looking at economic fundamentals, while more recent models link currency crises to self-fulfilling behaviors or contagion effects with moral hazard problem and herding behavior. Recent literature also concentrates on (the determination of the indicators and) the predictability of currency crises by developing statistical methods like leading economic indicators or early warning systems (e. g. Kaminsky et al. 1998).

The paper is organized as follows. In Section 2, we shortly summarize the theoretical background of the crisis models in the literature. In Section 3, we analyze the origins of crises in the European Exchange-Rate-Mechanism countries (1992-93),[2] Turkey (1994),[3] Mexico (1994-95)[4] and Southeast Asian countries (1997-98)[5] in order to investigate the suitability of theoretical crisis models and to show whether there is any common cause of these crises. In Section 4, we summarize the empirical literature on the predictability of currency crises and then, examine the predictability of potential crises for the case of Turkey using the leading economic indicator methodology which was first proposed by Burns and Mitchell (1946). And finally, in Section 5, we present some concluding remarks.

---

2 Eichengreen et al. (1994) deal with the ERM crisis in Europe in 1992.

3 Ertugrul and Zaim (1996), Ozatay (1996) and Celasun (1998) focus on the 1994 financial crisis in Turkey.

4 The Mexican peso crisis is analyzed mainly by Lustig (1995), Calvo and Mendoza (1996), Edwards (1996), Sachs et al. (1996) and Gil-Diaz (1998).

5 Krugman (1997), Moreno et al. (1998) and Corsetti et al. (1998a and 1998b) try to illuminate the theoretical origins and (international) effects of the Asian crisis in 1997-98.

2 Theoretical Models

The theoretical models on currency crises can be classified into two generations.[6] The first-generation models (Krugman 1979, and Flood and Garber 1984) accounted well for many of the currency crises in the 1970s and also for the 1982 developing-country debt crisis, but they failed to explain crises such as in Chile (1982), Europe (1992-93), Mexico (1994-95) and Asia (1997-98). Second-generation models (Obstfeld 1994) differ from the former one because of being multiple-equilibria models. They consider an interaction between private sector and government behavior that gives rise to several possible solutions, i.e. the economy's equilibrium can jump from one solution to another.

2.1 First-generation Models

In his seminal paper, Krugman (1979) stressed the role of the weak fundamentals as a triggering factor of currency crises. He assumed that the government budget deficits were at the root of speculative attacks on pegged exchange rates.

These models argue that the currency crises are preceded by the macroeconomic imbalances in the economy that are inconsistent with the maintenance of fixed exchange rates. According to Krugman (1979), under a fixed exchange rate regime, monetization of fiscal deficits, which creates domestic inflation, leads to an appreciation in the real exchange rate. The deteriorating effect of increasing domestic prices on the current account balance causes a gradual loss of reserves and ultimately, a speculative attack against the currency. When the authorities are no longer able to defend the pegged exchange rate, they are forced to abandon the parity. The foresighted speculators would reallocate their portfolios by selling domestic currency for foreign currency before the exhaustion of reserves since they would notice that the price of foreign exchange would begin rising. By doing so, they accelerate the period that ends with the abandonment of the fixed exchange rate. In that respect, these models combine a linear behavior rule by the private sector (the money demand function) with linear government behavior (domestic credit growth).

---

[6] For theoretical models see Agenor et al. (1992), Kaminsky et al. (1998), Kruger et al. (1998) and Flood et al.(1998).

2.2 *Second-generation Models*

The second-generation crisis models do not reject the role of the fundamentals in the economy. However, financial crises are not always necessarily determined by the weak fundamentals. That means that not all speculative attacks may be warranted by the weaknesses of fundamentals.

The second-generation models (Obstfeld, 1984, 1986, 1994) consider nonlinear behavior rules by one or more agents. Therefore, these nonlinearities can lead to multiple solutions. For example, a multiple equilibria exists in the foreign exchange market because of the contingent nature of the policy makers' and governments' objective function. According to these models, maintenance of the pegged exchange rates depends on the government's decision. The authorities might abandon a peg, if it were concerned that economic policies necessary to maintain the exchange rate might have adverse effects on other macroeconomic variables. In this context, these models stress the trade-offs between the benefits of a credible exchange rate peg and the costs in terms of higher interest rates, higher unemployment or lower growth of defending peg (Reisen 1998).

The recent studies of Paul Krugman (1998) and others in the aftermath of the structural financial crisis in Asia can be viewed as 'third generation' of currency crisis models. These new models consider some disputed issues such as (1) moral hazard or asymmetric information problem that lead to an underpricing of the risks associated with investing in emerging markets, (2) herding behavior of bankers and portfolio managers and (3) international contagion effects appearing by some transmission channels such as trade and financial linkages between countries.

3 Country Experiences

In this section, we briefly survey selected four financial crises in the 1990s in order to demonstrate both the similarities and differences between the causes and consequences of the crises. This will help us in determining the indicators of currency crises, and hence, in constructing and implementing the leading economic indicator method for Turkey in the sixth section of our study.

3.1 The European Exchange-Rate-Mechanism Crises of 1992-93

In the fall of 1992, foreign exchange markets in Europe were experienced a succession of crises. The dynamics of the exchange-rate-mechanism (ERM) crises were different from those of the crises explained by the first generation models since it could not explained by weak fundamentals. For the period of ERM crisis, Eichengreen et al. (1994) found evidence against the fundamentals-based models of speculative attacks. In the ERM countries, governments had no need to monetize their budget deficits, and they were not suffering from any limitation on foreign exchange reserves. They had low and stable inflation rates both before and after the crisis. So, what caused the ERM crises?

According to the ERM of the European Monetary System, all participating countries pegged their currencies to the German mark in a narrow range. In the aftermath of the fall of the Berlin wall and reunification of Germany in October 1990, capital inflows were directed to the country because of the new opportunities for investors. On the other hand, the reunification of Germany caused heavy expenditures. This expansionary fiscal policy increased aggregate demand. National production expanded rapidly in 1990 and 1991. However, the economy began to overheat as demand exceeded production capabilities, so that inflation rate increased. In order to slow down inflation, the German Bundesbank implemented tight monetary policy and interest rates rose.

The capital inflows with tight monetary policy of the Bundesbank led to the appreciation of German mark against the US dollar. In order to maintain fixed exchange rates, other European countries pegging their currencies to the German mark found themselves forced to match the tight monetary policy without fiscal expansion. This caused a slow down in economic growth and created unemployment. Many speculators, especially George Soros, foresaw that members of the ERM would devalue their currencies. At the final stage, the ongoing process led some countries to exit from the ERM. Britain exited from the mechanism by devaluing the pound by about 25%. Then, Spain and Italy devalued their currencies. These devaluations had spillover effects on some other EU countries like Republic of Ireland and Portugal due to the trade links (Eichengreen et al. 1996).

In the light of these events, the case of the ERM crisis can be explained by the second-generation models, since the government had multiple objectives some of which conflicting the fixed exchange rate target. In the countries concerned, the decision to abandon the pegged exchange rate seems related to the cost of defending a peg by raising interest rates. Because of the high unemployment rising interest rates might worsen the unemployment problem. Therefore, the authorities were less willing to defend their currencies. In that respect, it seems that the decision to leave the ERM was to some extent an optimizing decision in terms of the second-generation models.

3.2 The Mexican Peso Crisis (1994-95)

During the period of 1987-93, Mexico successfully pursued major structural reforms. They were designed to liberalize foreign trade, reduce the public sector's role in the economy and eliminate the macroeconomic imbalances. Mexico's 18 commercial banks and many important public enterprises were privatized. A major tax reform was realized. Credit controls were removed and interest rates were determined freely.

These policies led to economic recovery in the economy. Inflation was brought down from around 160% at the end of 1987 to under 10% in 1993. Primary fiscal deficit of 6% of GDP was shifted to surplus exceeding 7% of GDP. These achievements coupled with the North American Free Trade Agreement (NAFTA) led to substantial capital inflows into the country. The Mexican peso was overvalued and the country had a very large current account deficit.[7]

Although the structural reforms were successful in bringing down the inflation, the use of the nominal exchange rate-based stabilization measures resulted in a real appreciation of the peso. The fact lying behind this appreciation was the differential between the domestic and foreign inflation rates. The actual inflation rate was still above the target level. On the other hand, there was a huge capital inflow to the country because of the economic recovery and the fall of the interest rates in the US. These factors also caused the currency overvaluation by attracting the foreign capital. The real appreciation of the currency resulted in a growing disequilibrium in the current account balance in Mexico. However, it did not seem unsustainable to the government, because they thought that this growing deficit was temporary. Furthermore, it was financed by massive capital inflows.

Rising interest rates in the US and the assassination of presidential candidate Donaldo Colosio (in March 1994) had an undesirable impact on the Mexican economy. In the aftermath of this assassination, the risk

---

[7] According to Sachs et al. (1996), the widening current account deficit was the result of excess investment over savings.

premium demanded by foreign investors increased, the capital outflows began and the first sharp fall in reserves occurred. The Mexican government issued more *tesobonos*[8] in order to attract investors by covering them against the risk of devaluation.

However, the huge change in the amount of tesobonos was a signal for many investors for the unsustainability of the existing exchange rate policy. This time, the Mexican monetary authorities decided to sterilize the fall in reserves by expanding domestic credit. This led to a fall in the interest rates while the interest rates in the US were high. The expansion of domestic credit increased the pressures on the peso. Because of these factors the Mexican economy became more vulnerable. The first devaluation was announced on December 20, investors panicked and ran from the Mexican peso. On December 22, the authorities switched their exchange rate policy to the floating one. The devaluation was resulted in a financial crisis with significant spillover effects on other countries in Latin America.

In the light of these events we can say that self-fulfilling expectations arising from the misperceptions about the development of economic fundamentals or political uncertainties were at the root of the Mexican peso crisis. The spill over effect of this crisis might be interpreted as a reflection of investor pessimism. Investors who believed that other emerging market economies might experience similar difficulties ran on other currencies even though fundamentals were unchanged. In their paper, Calvo et al. (1996) explain that countries with weak fundamentals had more affected from the self-fulfilling investor panic than those with strong fundamentals.

3.3 1994 Financial Crisis in Turkey

Turkey experienced a severe currency crisis in early 1994. This crisis was different from those in European countries, Mexico and Southeast Asian Countries due to the fact that the exchange rate system was a managed float rather than being fixed.

In the first half of the 1990s, there were imbalances in the macro economic variables such as increasing and high public sector deficits, inadequate private savings to finance these deficits and as a result of these two deficits growing external deficit. This disequilibrium and the efforts to sustain it by inappropriate policies had some reflections to the relative prices. Some developments precipitating the crisis were observed in the foreign exchange markets.

---

[8] Tesobonos are short-term dollar-denominated government debts.

After the financial liberalization in 1989, Turkey had attracted capital inflows due to the high real interest rates. This led to an overvaluation of the Turkish Lira (TL). The appreciation of the currency and also the tariff reductions in 1989 caused current account deficits. The pressures on the exchange rate and the interest rates, and the open position of the banking system, which was about 5 billion dollars, increased the demand for dollars.

There was a run from the TL. The banks rushed to foreign exchange market to close their position in foreign exchange. The Central Bank intervened the foreign exchange market in order to defend the exchange rate. As a result the Central Bank lost half of its reserves and overnight interest rates reached a record level. The open position of commercial banks declined to 1.1 billion dollars in June 1994. Finally, these developments had an impact on the parity. It was about 15000 TL/US$ in January 1994, but jumped to 38000 TL/US$ by the first days of April 1994.

In the first quarter of 1994, the Turkish lira (TL) depreciated by more than 50% against the US dollar, real output contracted by about 6%, annual inflation rate jumped to three digit levels (see Table 8.1). At the end of 1993, public sector debt and deficits as a percentage of GDP reached record levels and interest payments became an increasing burden. The government attempted not to impede growth prior to local elections of March 1994 and it was pressured to control the interest rates.[9] So, there was a policy shift from bond-finance to money-finance in the last months of 1993. Several Treasury bill auctions were cancelled and the Treasury started to rely on short-term advances from Central Bank. Therefore, a substantial real increase was observed in Central Bank's domestic credits from the beginning of the September 1993. The real return of Treasury bills that turned to negative at the end of 1993 and the cancellation of auctions increased the uncertainty in the financial markets and shook the confidence of investors. Finally the Treasury lost its borrowing ability.

Özatay (1996) argues that the 1994 currency crisis of Turkey started due to public debt mismanagement. At a time of large and rising PSBR and declining maturity of debt stock, interventions to decrease the interest rate and cancellations of auctions was a poor idea (Celasun 1998).

The 1994 crisis was not an unexpected event due to the fact that many economic indicators were giving warning signals. There were deteriorated fiscal fundamentals financing by domestic credit expansion, increased

---

9 Ozatay (1996) and Celasun (1998) argue that instead of trying to correct the fundamental imbalances, which cause interest rates to be so high, to control the interest rate was a policy error.

demand for foreign currency and loss of reserves. With these characteristics, it can be said that the Turkish currency crisis fits the first-generation models (Celasun 1998). On the other hand, the 1994 currency crisis had some features of the second-generation models. Because of the forthcoming elections, the government was reluctant to increase the interest rates in order to avoid the devaluation of the TL. In that respect, the 1994 currency crisis of Turkey might be explained by the second-generation models because of the government's objective function.

3.4 Asian Crisis of 1997-98

The case of the Asian crisis does not fit the Krugman's model since the Asian currency crisis was neither driven by huge fiscal deficits nor by excessive domestic credit expansion. Actually, before the crisis, most of the significant economic indicators were quite strong.

The inflation rate was relatively moderate in the affected countries like Thailand, Indonesia, Korea, Malaysia and the Philippines. Fiscal indicators were sound. They had rapid growth and did not suffer from any substantial unemployment. However, there were few macroeconomic vulnerabilities such as high and growing current account deficits, especially in Malaysia and Thailand.

The main factors underlying behind the large current account deficits were as follows: (1) The devaluation of Chinese currency in 1994 which had a negative impact on the competitiveness of region countries. (2) The appreciation of dollar after mid 1995 which led to the appreciation of the region currencies.[10] (3) In 1996 a sharp decline in the demand for semi-conductors had an adverse effect on export growth. (4) The long period of stagnation in Japan led to significant decrease in export growth in region countries.[11]

Financial liberalization in many Asian countries in 1990s in conjunction with the strong macroeconomic fundamentals attracted investors looking for higher returns and caused a very rapid growth of net capital inflows into these countries. The growing current account deficit was financed by this large amount of foreign capital inflows. On the other hand, huge capital flows (mainly through international lending of banks) into the region countries caused an expansion of aggregate demand and considerable increase in stock and real estate prices.

---

[10] By the July 1997, the region currencies were mainly pegged to the US dollar.

[11] Japan was the second important export market for the region countries with a share of 30%.

Table 11.1 - Selected Macroeconomic Indicators of Turkey (in percent, 1987-1997)

Indicator	1987	1988	1989	1990	1991	1992	1993	1994	1995	1996	1997
Consumer Price Inflation	38.9	75.4	63.3	60.3	66.0	70.1	66.0	106.3	88.1	80.3	85.7
Real GDP Growth	9.8	1.5	1.6	9.4	0.4	6.4	8.1	-6.1	8.0	7.1	8.3
Current Account Balance to GNP	-0.9	1.8	0.9	-1.7	0.2	-0.6	-3.5	2.0	-1.4	-1.3	-1.4
Average Change in TL/$ Rate	27.8	66.0	49.3	23.0	59.9	65.2	59.5	170.8	54.0	77.4	86.6
Gross Total International Reserves (Average) *	4773	5465	7251	10571	10923	13089	16342	14964	21925	24499	25446
Change in FX Reserves of the Central Bank		27.1	70.6	84.2		4.1	42.3	-22.4	148.7	18.4	10.8
Treasury Average Auction Rate	47.5	62.9	58.8		80.0	86.5	87.5	193.2	121.8	130.1	108.5
Public Sector Borrowing Requirement / GNP	6.1	4.8	5.3	7.4	10.2	10.6	12.0	7.9	5.2	8.8	7.6
Public Foreign Debt Stock / GNP	36.1	36.2	31.7	24.8	25.8	24.8	23.6	45.4	29.2	26.6	
	23.0	22.0	18.2	14.4	14.8	17.6	17.9	20.0	17.3	21.0	21.4
Foreign Exchange Deposits / M2Y	16.8	22.9	19.7	19.3	24.8	35.2	42.5	49.4	46.9	49.4	46.9
Foreign Direct Investment (Net)*	106	354	663	700	783	779	622	559	772	612	554
Foreign Portfolio Investment (Net) *		1178		547	623	2411	3917	1158		570	1634
Other Short-Term Capital Inflow (Net) *	50	-2281	-584	3000	-3020	1396	3054	-5127	3713	5945	1761

Source: Undersecretariat of Treasury, Ankara.
* In million US$.

The region countries were developed without a well-functioning and robust financial system. The weaknesses in the financial system led to serious adverse selection and risky lending.[12] A large share of their lending were used in markets for real estate, which incurred a 'bubble' element. As much of the capital inflows were short term, the banks were borrowing from international markets in short term and lending in domestic markets in long term (Asian Development Bank 1998). There was a mismatch in the maturities of banks' assets and liabilities.

Relying on the government's guarantee both depositors and lenders (international and domestic banks) led to *moral hazard problem*. As lenders have less information than borrowers there was an asymmetric information between the market participants and hence, a moral hazard problem on the investors' parts (see Asian Development Outlook 1998). Depositors had no incentive to monitor the soundness of the banks because of the implicit or explicit deposit insurance. The lack of monitoring created moral hazard for bank managers. Another type of moral hazard problem occurred on the part of financial institutions, which had undertook high-risk lending activities by ignoring the costs of these investment projects. Financial institutions did not hedge their funds to currency and interest rate movements. On the contrary, they believed the future bailout and took even more risk. Large amounts of borrowing from abroad to finance rapid expansion made companies highly leveraged.

All these complicated set of structural and economic factors made region countries quite vulnerable to financial crises and led to markets concern about the prevailing exchange rates. Drop of the real estate and stock prices and the bankruptcy of the companies were observed. Rapid reversals of capital inflows led to investors panic. As a result, in July 1997, Thailand abandoned the fixed rate of the baht against the US dollar by causing competitive devaluations in some of the other region countries with similar structural weaknesses.

The Asian crisis invoked further theoretical and empirical research on causes, timing and effects of currency crises worldwide. It is neither fully completed in affected Asian countries nor prevented from spilling over to countries like Russia and Brazil. Therefore, it is difficult to evaluate entirely the relevance of this new generation of models presented by Krugman (1998) and others.

[12] However, they were hidden by rapid growth, high savings and strong fiscal positions.

4 The Empirical Literature

Currency crises that occurred and still occurring in various developing and developed countries over the world directed a great deal of empirical research to this area. They were being done to find 'early warning signals' of these crises, where the predictability of crises is still being discussed. Although most of the time the results vary across countries, it has almost been common to work with a class of crisis indicators.

Before 1990s, currency crises were mainly condensed under standard first generation models, where they were thought to have significant predictable component. The underlying reason of speculative attacks was a fiscal deficit financed by domestic credit creation (Flood and Marion 1998) as mentioned above. Empirical work using structural models on these crises focused on a particular country in a specific time period, so the results were far from being general. Some examples to such models are Blanco and Garber (1986) which used a version of Krugman-Flood-Garber model to predict the timing of devaluations realized as a result of attacks on Mexican peso. They calculated the probability of pursuing rates exceeding the fixed rate in the next quarter.

The non-structural models used in late 1980s confirmed the role of traditional factors in predicting crisis. Edwards (1989) examined the behavior of various indicators before the devaluations and compared their patterns with those of the control group that pursued fixed exchange rate regime during the working period. Klein and Marion (1994) performed a panel data analysis for devaluation periods in Latin American countries. They calculated the monthly probability of abandoning a pegged exchange rate increased with real overvaluation and declined with the level of foreign assets.

Frankel and Rose (1996) identified currency crises as substantial nominal currency devaluation. As pointed out this criterion would exclude instances where a currency came under severe pressure but the authorities successfully defended it by intervening heavily in the foreign exchange market, or by raising interest rates sharply, or by other means. Alternatively, an index of speculative pressure that takes into account not only exchange rate changes, but also movements in international reserves or interest rates that absorb pressure and moderate the exchange rate changes. This definition includes both significant currency depreciations and the actions by the authorities averted a large devaluation or the abandonment of an exchange rate peg.

Most crises occurred after 1990s did not support the idea of fiscal and monetary deterioration preceding crisis. This caused researchers to work with a wide variety of indicators. In most of the empirical studies aiming to predict the currency crises non-parametric tests based on the observation of the behavior of the individual series for the periods of prior to crises and tranquility were employed. To our knowledge, most comprehensive study on empirical survey of currency crises is Kaminsky, Lizondo and Reinhart (1998) (KLR). They had employed the so-called 'signal approach' based on monitoring the behavior of a number of indicators to observe the warning signals about the potential currency crises. They found exports, real exchange rate, international reserves, output, domestic credit, inflation, fiscal deficit and equity prices as useful indicators in predicting currency crises for a sample of 15 developing and 5 industrial countries during 1970-1995.

Uçer, Rijkeghem and Yolalan (1998) (URY), using the same methodology for Turkey, had found that short- term external debt to GNP, ratio of exports to imports, short-term advances to Treasury over GNP and M2Y plus government domestic debt to GNP have strong predictive power for the 1994 crisis in Turkey rather than the indicators which take place in the study of KLR.

Eichengreen, Rose and Wyplosz (1994) applied an empirical analysis based on monitoring the behavior of macroeconomic variables for 22 countries (mostly OECD countries) for the period of 1967-1992. They found significant differences among the behavior of some variables like budget deficits, inflation, export/import ratios between the periods of speculative pressures and tranquility for the non-ERM sub-sample. However, they did not find any noticeably differences for the ERM sub-sample between periods of speculative attack and tranquility. Moreno (1995) stressed in his study covering the economies in the Asia-Pacific Basin that if no difference is found then episodes of speculative pressure might be the result of arbitrary shifts in expectations.

5 Data Description and Sources

In this study, we used monthly data for the period of 1986-1998 taken from IMF's International Financial Statistics (IFS) CD-ROM version, The Undersecretariat of Treasury and electronic data distribution system of Central Bank of the Republic of Turkey (CBRT) (http://www.tcmb.gov.tr).

The variables used in our study are as follows (see table 11.2): Broad-money (M2), M2Y (M2 plus foreign exchange deposits), domestic credits of deposit banks, nominal exchange rate (TL/$), gross international reserves, manufacturing industry price index (1987=100), manufacturing industry production index (1992=100), short-term capital flows, current account balance, budget balance, wholesale price index (general and sub-items, State Institute of Statistics (SIS), 1987=100), consumer price index (SIS, 1987=100), deposit money banks credits to private sector, net domestic assets of Central Bank, reserve money, interbank overnight interest rates, foreign assets of Central Bank, foreign exchange deposits, export and import price indexes, market determined exchange rates (for the period of 1986-93 from World Currency Yearbook and for 1994-98 from Daily Newspaper Milliyet), business survey data (Central Bank Tendency Surveys) were obtained from CBRT. Equity price index was taken from Istanbul Stock Exchange, the average auction rates from the Undersecretariat of Treasury and exports (line70d), imports (line 71d), Treasury bill rate of US (line 60c) from IFS CD-ROM version. Because of the non-availability of monthly GNP figures, monthly manufacturing industry production index was multiplied by manufacturing industry price index in order to derive a proxy of nominal GNP.

We define currency crises, obeying the trend in literature, as being an abnormal behavior of index of exchange rate market pressure. The currency crisis index (CCI) was constructed as a weighted average of monthly exchange rate changes, the negative of monthly international reserve changes and the difference between the domestic interest rates (average auction rates of Treasury) and foreign interest rates (Treasury bill rate of US). The weights are chosen so as to equalize the variance of the three components in order to avoid any of the component's dominating the index. When the value of this index exceeds the threshold value (means that when the domestic currency depreciates, international reserves decline and the interest rate increase) which is 1.5 times the pooled standard deviation of the calculated index plus the pooled mean, there is an indication of currency crises (see Figure 11.1).

Table 11.2 - List of Variables

CCI	Crisis Index (Growth of nominal exchange rates, growth of Central Bank international reserves and id-if)
A1	Growth of M2 (%)
A2	Growth of Domestic Credits of Deposit Banks(%)
A3	M2/Gross International Reserves
A4	Growth of Exports (%)
A5	Growth of Imports (%)
A6	Exports/ Imports
A7	Short-Term Capital Flows/ Nominal Industrial Production
A8	Current Account Balance/ Nominal Industrial Production
A9	Budget balance/ Nominal Industrial Production
A10	Average Auction Rates (%)
A11	Public Sector WPI Inflation(%)
A12	Private Sector WPI Inflation(%)
A13	Total WPI Inflation(%)
A14	Growth of Private Sector Manufacturing Industry Price Index (1987=100)
A15	Growth of Total Manufacturing Industry Price Index (1987=100)
A16	Growth of Equity Price Index (%)
A17	CPI Inflation (%)
A18	Growth of Deposit Money Banks Credits to Private sector (%)
A19	Net Domestic Assets/Reserve Money (%)
A20	Terms of Trade (Export Prices/Import Prices) (%)
A21	Interbank Overnight Interest Rates (%)
A22	M2Y/Central Bank Foreign Assets (%)
A23	M2Y/International Reserves minus gold (%)
A24	M2Y/Foreign Assets of Monetary Authorities (%)
A25	Total Industrial Production Index (1992=100)
A26	Growth of Industrial Production Index (%)
A27	FX Deposits / M2Y (%)
A28	Domestic Credits of Deposit Banks/ Total Credits (%)
A29	Your Opinion about the General Course of Business in Your Industry, Compared to Previous Month: A-C
A30	Over the Next Three Months, Opinion about the Export Possibilities Compared to Previous Month: A-C
A31	Total Amount of Orders Received in this Month: A-C
A32	Amount of Monthly Export Orders Received: A-C
A33	Total Amount of Employment: A-C (Trend of Last 3 Months)
A34	Total Amount of Employment: A-C (Trend of Next 3 Months)
A35	The Amount of New Orders Received from the Domestic Market: A-C (Trend of Last 3 Months)
A36	The Amount of New Orders Received from the Domestic Market: A-C (Trend of Next 3 Months)
A37	The Amount of New Orders Received from the Exports Market: A-C (Trend of Last 3 Months)
A38	The Amount of New Orders Received from the Exports Market: A-C (Trend of Next 3 Months)
A39	The Volume of Output: A-C (Trend of Last 3 Months)

Table 11.2 - List of variables (continued)

A40	The Volume of Output: A-C (Trend of Next 3 Months)
A41	The Volume of Raw Material Stocks: A-C (Trend of Last 3 Months)
A42	The Volume of Raw Material Stocks: A-C (Trend of Next 3 Months)
A43	The Volume of Finished Goods: A-C (Trend of Last 3 Months)
A44	The Volume of Finished Goods: A-C (Trend of Next 3 Months)
A45	Average Unit Cost: A-C (Trend of Last 3 Months)
A46	Average Unit Cost: A-C (Trend of Next 3 Months)
A47	Average Price for the New Orders Received from the Domestic Market: A-C (Trend of Last 3 Months)
A48	Average Price for the New Orders Received from the Domestic Market: A-C (Trend of Next 3 Months)
A49	Average Price for the New Orders Received from the Export Market: A-C (Trend of Last 3 Months)
A50	Average Price for the New Orders Received from the Export Market: A-C (Trend of Next 3 Months)
A51	Market Determined Exchange Rate/ Official Exchange Rate

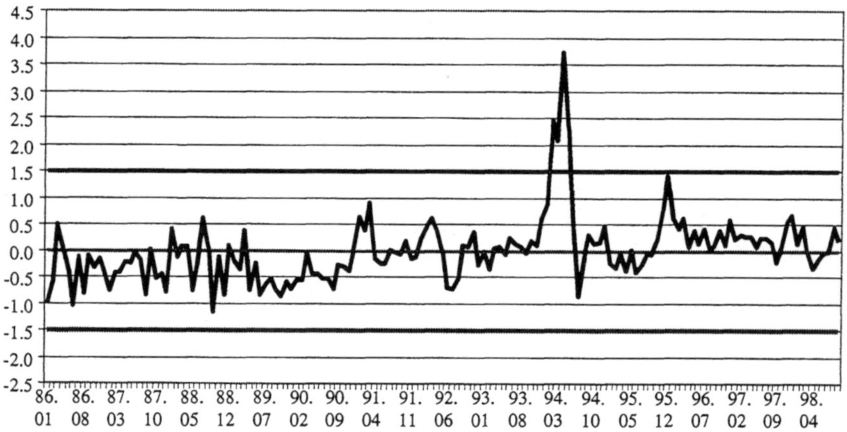

Figure 11.1 - The Index of Foreign Exchange Market Pressure of Turkey

6 Leading Economic Indicators Approach: The Case of Turkey

Leading economic indicators (LEI) method is a non-structural time series technique, which was first proposed by Burns and Mitchell (1946). It is being widely used to predict the turning points of various economic aggregates, besides econometric and structural time series models. This approach exploits the phenomenon that the cyclical movements in some variables systematically pre-date those in the other variables for sound economic reasons. Cyclical patterns are an abstract concept and cannot be observed in any direct way. Each time series might be expressed as Y=C+S+T+I, where C is the cyclical component, S is the seasonal component, T is the trend component, and I is the irregular component. In order to obtain cyclical component, we first deseasonalized the series, which have seasonal component by using X11-Census filter founded by the Bureau of Census of the US Commerce Department. For the series having trend component, detrending was performed by Hodrick-Prescott (λ=14400; default for monthly data) filtering which was introduced by Kydland and Prescott (1990). In another step, we also de-trended and de-seasonalized all the series to keep a standard. As a result, we reached almost the same conclusions. Defining the cyclical movements in both the 'reference series' and the other variables is the first step in constituting the leading indicators system. Reference series is an economic variable or a composite index of coincident economic variables that the forecaster wishes to explain its turning points. We considered foreign exchange market pressure index as reference series and tried to find out the indicators signaling the crises systematically. To forecast the reference series a composite index including the leading indicators might be used via least square models. After determining the cyclical patterns of the series, the relationship between the reference series and the potential indicators are investigated. Cross-correlogram analysis is the method that compares two series not only at the turning points but also all through the sample. The cycle of a leading series exhibit a turning points before that the reference series. In order to observe the cycles clearly some analysts prefers smoothing although this method leads to loss of information and possible shifts of the turning points.

Majority of the empirical work deals with multi-country analysis. In this study, like in few numbers of papers we tried to determine the facts that cause or indicate currency crises through utilizing single country, Turkey. To our knowledge, the methodology used here was distinct from those used up to now.

We compared the behavior of a number of indicators' with that of the foreign exchange market pressure by using the LEI approach. As a result, we found terms of trade (A20), market determined exchange rate over official exchange rate (A51) and some of survey data (A37 and A38) listed in Table 11.3, as leading indicators of the currency crisis index (see Figure 11.2). Parallel with the results of Sachs et al. (1996), Kaminsky et al. (1998),

Kruger et al. (1998), and Frankel and Rose (1996) the ratios budget deficit and current account balance to GDP were found to be insignificant.

Table 11.3 - The Results of LEI Approach

	Crisis Index	number of months	cross correlation
A1	lag	3	0,43
A2	no relation	-	-
A3	no relation	-	-
A4	no relation	-	-
A5	no relation	-	-
A6	lag	3	0,45
A7	no relation	-	-
A8	no relation	-	-
A9	no relation	-	-
A10	lag	1	0,65
A11	coincident	0	0,43
A12	coincident	0	0,51
A13	coincident	0	0,53
A14	coincident	0	0,64
A15	coincident	0	0,56
A16	coincident	0	-0,31
A17	coincident	0	0,49
A18	lag	1	-0,28
A19	coincident	0	0,38
A20	**lead**	**9**	**0,22**
A21	coincident	0	0,7
A22	lag	1	0,35
A23	coincident	0	0,47
A24	coincident	0	0,36
A27	coincident	0	0,5
A28	coincident	0	-0,39
A30	**lead**	**2**	**-0,35**
A31	lag	2	-0,57
A32	lag	1	-0,22
A33	lag	2	-0,59
A34	lag	1	-0,65
A35	lag	2	-0,62
A36	lag	1	-0,63
A37	**lead**	**1**	**-0,34**
A38	**lead**	**1**	**-0,34**
A51	**lead**	**1**	**0,34**

One has to notice that an indicator exhibiting abnormal behavior in the pre-crises period is not always a perfect evidence for a crisis. Nevertheless, following the patterns of critical indicators might help the policy makers for adapting their decisions accordingly.

As a result, one can conclude that such time series techniques might be useful in determining the direction of the cycles that we want to forecast. However, observing that some important vulnerability indicators like M2 over gross international reserves gives (A3) no significant relation and some indicators like short term capital flows over industrial production (A7) or current account balance over industrial production (A8) did not give the expected results, it can be said that relying solely on these methodologies will not be sufficient to predict the future financial crises.

7 Concluding Remarks

Since the causes of crises are different for each country, mechanical econometric models are always subject to serious criticisms. Cross-sectional models are also criticized as providing concurrent information rather than leading.[13] These efforts are found to be helpful in understanding past crises but they are weak in predicting crises. Although, models relying on time series techniques are also found to be weak in predicting crises, the leading indicators approach might be useful in constituting an early warning system. At least they might provide valuable information to the authorities to take measures in order to avoid from crises.

Nevertheless, for crises arising from pure contagion effects or speculative attacks, early warning systems may not be available because these crises arise from unpredictable market reactions.[14] For recent crisis experiences in Mexico (1994-95) and Asia (1997-98), it is difficult to predict crises solely looking at indicators because prior to crisis these countries had sound macroeconomic fundamentals. However, they had weak financial system characterized by inadequate supervision and regulation and they incurred policy shocks.

The present study could be made more powerful by including indicators related to political circumstances. One shortcoming of the LEI method is the systematic relationships among the indicators and crises index being

---

[13] Eichengreen and Rose (1998) and Flood and Marion (1998).

[14] See IMF Staff (1998).

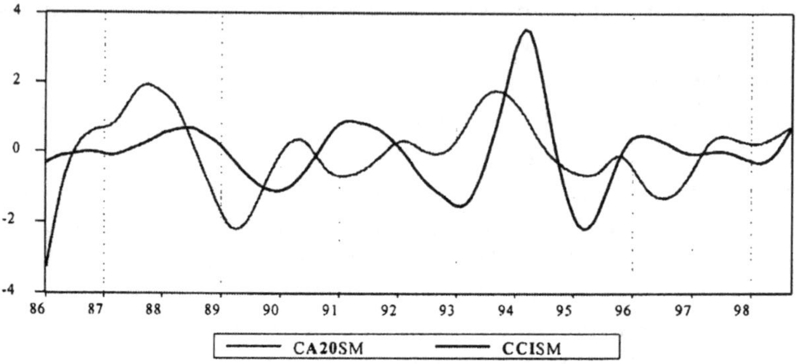

A20: Terms of Trade C: Cycle SM: Smoothed CCI: Currency Crisis Index

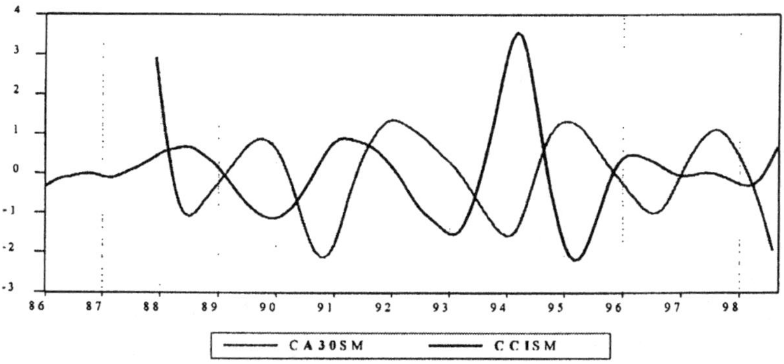

A30: Over the next three months, opinion about the export possibilities compared to previous month

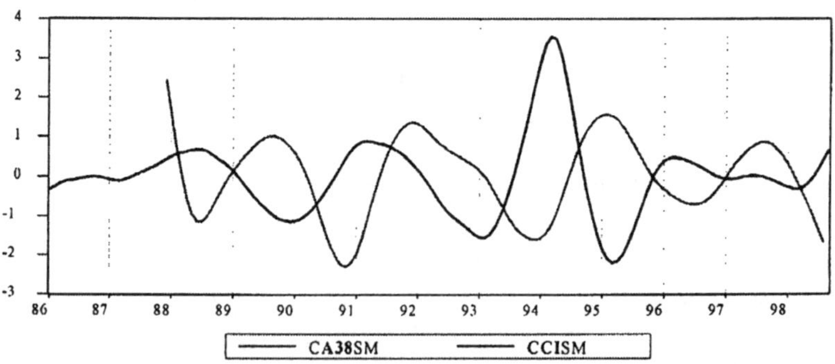

A38: The amount of new orders received from the export market, A-C (Trend of next three months)

Figure 11.2 - Selected Relations Between the Smoothed (SM) Cycles (C) of Currency Crises Index and Leading Indicators

very sensitive to structural breaks, such as policy changes. Taking this fact into account, one has to check the significance relationships between the indicators frequently.

As a result we may conclude that if the weak fundamentals (first-generation models) are at the root of the currency crises, it might be possible to predict this type of crises. However, if the crises occur because of the self-fulfilling attacks (second-generation) the prediction of this type of crises become impossible. Furthermore, one indicator that gives a signal for one country, might not be work for another country.

In the light of the financial crises especially in emerging markets it can be said that it is necessary to put in place institutions and policies to manage and reduce the macroeconomic financial risks in countries removed restrictions on capital account movements (IMF 1998b). These countries should implement appropriate macroeconomic, exchange rate and financial policies with measures towards building a more prudent and transparent financial system. Otherwise, it should not be a surprise that they find themselves in the center of new financial and currency crises.

References

Agenor, P.-R., J. S. Bhandari and R. P. Flood (1992), 'Speculative Attacks and Models of Balance of Payments Crises', *IMF Staff Papers, 39/2*: pp. 357-394.

Asian Development Bank (1998), Asian Development Outlook 1998. ADB.

Blanco, H. and P. M. Garber (1986), 'Recurrent Devaluation and Speculative Attacks on the Mexican Peso', *Journal of Political Economy, 94/1*: pp. 148-166.

Burns, A. F. and W. C. Mitchell (1946), *Measuring Business Cycles,* New York: NBER.

Calvo, G. A. and E.G. Mendoza (1996), Mexico's Balance of Payments Crisis: A Chronicle of a Death Foretold. Board of Governors of the Federal Reserve System, Washington D.C., *International Finance Discussion Papers, No. 545.*

Celasun, O. (1998), 'The 1994 Currency Crisis in Turkey'. *Policy Research Working Paper, No. 1913.*

Corsetti, G., P. Pesenti and N. Roubini (1998a), 'Paper Tigers? A Model of the Asian Crisis', Mimeo (http://www.stern.nyu.edu/~nroubini/asia/AsiaHomepage.html).

Corsetti, G., P. Pesenti and N. Roubini (1998b), 'What caused the Asian Currency and Financial Crisis', Mimeo (http://www.stern.nyu.edu/~nroubini/asia/AsiaHomepage.html).

Edwards, S. (1989), *Real Exchange Rates, Devaluation and Adjustment: Exchange Rate Policy in Developing Countries*, Cambridge, Mass.: MIT Press.

Edwards, S. (1996), 'A Tale of Two Crises: Chile and Mexico', NBER *Working Paper, No. 5794.*

Eichengreen, B., A. K. Rose and C. Wyplosz (1994), 'Speculative Attacks on Pegged Exchange Rates: An Empirical Exploration with Special Reference to the European Monetary System', NBER *Working Papers, No. 4898.*

Eichengreen, B., A. K. Rose and C. Wyplosz (1995), 'Exchange Market Mayhem: The Antecedents and Aftermath of Speculative Attacks', *Economic Policy, 21*: pp. 249-312.

Eichengreen, B., A. K. Rose and C. Wyplosz (1996), 'Contagious Currency Crises', NBER *Working Papers, No. 5681.*

Eichengreen, B. and A. K. Rose (1998), 'The Empirics of Currency and Banking Crises', Mimeo (http://haas.berkeley.edu/~arose).

Ertugrul A. and O. Zaim (1996), *The Efficiency of the Turkish Banking System* (in Turkish), Ankara.

Flood, R. P. and N. P. Marion (1998), 'Perspectives on the Recent Currency Crisis Literature', *IMF Working Paper*, No. 98/130

Frankel, J. A. and A. K. Rose (1996), 'Currency Crashes in Emerging Markets: Empirical Indicators', NBER *Working Papers, No. 5437.*

Gil-Diaz, F. (1998), 'The Origins of Mexico's 1994 Financial Crisis', *The Cato Journal, 17/3.*

IMF (1998a), 'Currency and Banking Crisis: Characteristics and Indicators of Vulnerability', *World Economic Outlook, Chapter IV*, pp. 74-97, May 1998, Washington D.C.: IMF.

IMF (1998b), International Capital Markets: *Developments, Prospects and Key Policy Issues,* September 1998, Washington D.C.: IMF.

IMF Staff (1998), 'The Asian Crisis', *Finance and Development, 35/2*, pp. 18-21.

Kaminsky, G., S. Lizondo and C. M. Reinhart (1998), 'Leading Indicators of Currency Crises', *IMF Staff Papers*, forthcoming.

Klein, M. and N. P. Marion (1994), 'Explaining the Duration of Exchange-Rate Pegs', NBER *Working Papers, No. 4651.*

Kruger, M., P.N. Osakwe and J. Page (1998), 'Fundamentals, Contagion and Currency Crises: An Empirical Analysis', *Bank of Canada Working Papers, No. 98/10.*

Krugman, P. (1979), 'A Model of Balance-of-Payments Crises', *Journal of Money, Credit and Banking, 11/3*: pp. 311-325.

Krugman, P. (1997), 'Are Currency Crises Self-Fulfilling?', NBER Macroeconomics Annual, Cambridge: MIT Press.

Krugman, P. (1998), *Bubble, Boom, Crash: Theoretical Notes on Asia's Crisis*, Cambridge Massachusetts MIT Press, forthcoming.

Kydland, F. E. and E. C. Prescott (1990), *Business Cycles: Real Facts and a Monetary Myth,* Federal Reserve Bank of Mineapolis.

Lustig, N. (1995), *The Mexican Peso Crisis: The Foreseeable and the Surprise,* Mimeo, Washington D.C., Brookings Institution.

Moreno, R. (1995), 'Macroeconomic Behavior During Periods of Speculative Pressure or Realignment: Evidence from Pacific Basin Economics', *Federal Reserve Bank of San Francisco Economic Review, No:3.*

Moreno, R., G. Pasadilla and E. Remolona. (1998), 'Asia's Financial Crisis: Lessons and Policy Responses', *Federal Reserve Bank of San Francisco, Pacific Basin Working Paper Series, PB98/02.*

Obstfeld, M. (1984), 'Balance-of-Payments Crises and Devaluation'. *Journal of Money, Credit, and Banking, 16*, pp. 208-217.

Obstfeld, M. (1986), 'Rational and Self-Fulfilling Balance-of-Payments Crises', *The American Economic Review,76/1*: pp. 72-81.

Obstfeld, M. (1994), 'The Logic of Currency Crises', NBER *Working Papers, No. 4640.*

Obstfeld, M. (1995), 'International Currency Experience: New Lessons and Lessons Relearned', *Brookings Papers on Economic Activity, 1*: pp. 119-220.

Ozatay, F. (1996), 'The Lessons from the 1994 Crisis in Turkey: Public Debt (Mis)Management and Confidence Crisis', *Yapı Kredi Economic Review, 7/1*: pp. 21-37.

Reisen, H. (1998), 'Domestic causes of Currency Crises: Policy Lessons for Crisis Avoidance', *OECD Development Center, No. 136.*

Sachs J., A. Tornell and A. Velasco (1996), 'Financial Crises in Emerging Markets: The Lessons from 1995', *Brookings Papers on Economic Activity,1*: pp. 147-215.

Sachs J., A. Tornell and A. Velasco (1996), 'The Collapse of the Mexican Peso: What Have We Learned', *Economic Policy, 22*: pp. 15-63.

Ucer, E. M., C.V. Rijkeghem and O.R. Yolalan (1998), 'Leading Indicators of Currency Crises :The Case of Turkey', *Yapı Kredi Bank Research Department Discussion Paper Series, No:98-03.*

Wyplosz, C. (1998), 'Speculative Attacks and Capital Mobility'. Revised version of the paper presented at the Fourth Dubrovnik Conference on June 24-26, 1998.

12 National Identity and Economic Expectations Determining Attitude towards the Euro

W. FRED VAN RAAIJ and YVONNE M. VAN EVERDINGEN[1]

Abstract

National identity, national pride, macro and micro economic expectations affect the attitude towards the single currency, the euro. In a cross-national study in the fifteen member nations of the European Union, data were collected on the attitude towards the euro and the factors explaining this attitude. Consumers in EU countries differ in their feelings of nationalism, national and European patriotism, national pride, and their expectations towards the euro. These factors largely explain the attitude towards the euro. Significant differences exist between the northern and southern European countries. People in the southern countries expect a lower inflation, lower unemployment and economic growth due to the euro. People in the northern countries expect less favourable economic developments, due to the euro.

1 Introduction

The establishment of the European Monetary Union (EMU) and the introduction of the euro, the European currency in eleven EMU nations, are topics with high political, economic and social impact, both for consumers

[1] Acknowledgement: We thank the European Commission for financing part of the study.

and businesses (Van Everdingen, 1995). Many consumers did not yet form a balanced opinion about the new currency, although it will strongly affect their financial wellbeing, both for their day-to-day purchases (short-tern) and for the value of their pensions and savings (long-term). It is remarkable that European citizens, who have to give up one of their national symbols, i.e., their domestic currencies, have rarely been asked about their opinions towards the introduction of a single European currency. The consumer attitude is an important determinant of the trust in the single currency and acceptance of the euro in 2002.

On the one hand, a strong national identity and national pride may lead to a negative attitude towards the euro, because the euro will replace the national currency. An attitude based on national identity is expected to be negative, and rather holistic and unstructured. On the other hand, the attitude towards the euro may be based on economic expectations, the perception of advantages and disadvantages or costs and benefits of the euro. Citizens taking these aspects into account have a more analytical attitude towards the euro. The impact of national identity, national pride and economic expectations on the attitudes will be tested with data collected in the EU nations during the summer of 1997, in the context of a cross-national study (Müller-Peters et al, 1998; Van Everdingen and Van Raaij, 1998). With the cross-national data, comparisons can be made between the EU nations that will adopt the euro or not.

The European Union uses the *Eurobarometer*, a continuous opinion poll on European matters. In the *Eurobarometer*, a question is included on the euro. We included this question in our measurement of the attitude towards the euro. The difference between this study and the *Eurobarometer* is that this study is not just an opinion poll, but a study in which the demographic and psychological factors are assessed that explain the attitude towards the euro.

The *outline* of this paper is as follows. In the next two sections, the theoretical evidence will be discussed on the relationship of national identity, national pride, economic expectations and attitude towards the euro. Further, we discuss the results of the analyses of the cross-national study, and provide directions for future research.

2 National Identity and National Pride

In discussions about the single European currency, national identity and national pride play important roles. People are proud of their country, culture, language, history, political and economic achievements. It is expected that national identity and pride are negatively related to the attitude towards the euro and the acceptance of the euro.

2.1 National Identity

National identity is a type of social identity, a self-definition including the reference group one belongs to. In each country, national identity may arouse commitment, emotional attachment, feelings of nationalism and patriotism, and even self-sacrifice (Brewer, 1991). National identity manifests itself in history, culture, collective values and symbols, such as the currency (Müller-Peters, 1998). Three dimensions of national identity can be distinguished:

1. Nationalism: the differentiation of one's own country from other countries, and feelings of superiority of one's own country.
2. National patriotism: attachment and affinity to one's own country.
3. European patriotism: attachment to and involvement with Europe.

Social and national identity depend on the context and level considered (Brewer, 1991). In this study, the context of national identity is at Europe and its countries, i.e., the difference between one's own country and national currency, on the one hand, and the EU and the euro, on the other hand. At a supranational level, the difference may be between the EU/Europe versus North America, Japan and Australia/New Zealand. At the supranational level, 'European identity' may play a role and in this context we may consider ourselves to be 'Europeans'.

Papadopoulos et al. (1990) and Usunier (1993) discuss the concept of consumer patriotism, i.e., the preference for products of one's own country. Papadopoulos et al. (1990) conclude that consumers in countries where feelings of national identity are strong, compared to less patriotistic consumers, are more likely to prefer domestic to foreign products. Usunier (1993) states that consumers in developed countries prefer domestic to foreign products, whereas consumers from developing countries often prefer foreign products to their own products. Here we may draw a parallel with the euro. Citizens of countries with strong currencies, such as Germany and The Netherlands, may show a higher level of patriotism regarding their own currency, compared with citizens of countries with weaker currencies, such as Italy and Portugal.

The results of a preliminary study in Germany (Peters, 1996) show that people fear that loss of their national currency would threaten their national identity. Although lay people do not use the concept 'national identity' when expressing this idea, some people stated that their currency represents their country. They consider their currency as a national symbol they do not like to trade in for the euro. Consequently, we expect that feelings of national identity are negatively related to the attitude towards the euro.

2.2 *National Pride*

Countries differ in their national pride. Germans may consider the German mark as a symbol of the *Wirtschaftswunder* (economic miracle), and almost a self-definition of their country. The British, living on an island 'between' the US and Europe, prefer having their own way of doing things without interference of 'Brussels.' They think about the European Union in terms 'us and them' and are attached to their sovereignty and the pound sterling. Losing the pound is perceived as losing power. The French may consider their culture to be superior to other cultures. The French franc is part of the French culture. In the same way, people of other nationalities have their national pride and national symbols. The sources of national pride include pride of economic and political achievements, history and culture. The national symbols include the queen, king or president, and the national currency itself.

Two national-pride factors emerge all across Europe (Müller-Peters, 1998, table 12.2):

1. Economic and political performance (EPP), including economic power, political influence, welfare system, public safety, national currency, and the head of the state.
2. Cultural and historical past (CHP), including traditions, customs, language and history.

3 Economic Expectations

The euro is a financial product that may be considered an innovation (Rogers, 1995). However, it is a forced innovation, in the sense that once the national currencies are replaced by the euro, the national currencies are no legal tender anymore, and citizens are forced to adopt the euro for their financial transactions. Only in Denmark and France, consumers were consulted through national referendums about the euro. In the other nations, people's opinions were never asked. They are forced to adopt the giral euro in 1999 and the chartal euro (coins and banknotes) in 2002. Forced innovations are not rare. New service procedures and new computer protocols are often introduced as 'improvements' over the former procedures, and thus forced innovations.

If the euro is considered to be an innovation, albeit a forced innovation, expected consequences of using it are hypothesised to influence the attitude toward it (Gatignon and Robertson, 1985; Rogers, 1995). In this case, the expected consequences are especially related to long-term economic consequences. Katona (1951) distinguishes macro- and micro-level economic expectations. Macro and micro economic expectations are components of the Index of Consumer Sentiment, an indicator of consumer optimism/pessimism and a predictor of financial behaviour such as spending, saving and borrowing (Katona, 1975; Van Raaij and Gianotten, 1990). Both types of long-term expectations are expected to be important determinants of the attitude towards the euro. Short-term expectations relate to the introduction problems and solutions of the euro, such as the ease of adaptation. In this paper, only long-term expectations are included.

3.1 Macro-economic Consequences

The economic consequences for the nation as a whole constitute the 'macro-level' expectations. The post-war macro-economic developments in European countries suggest that countries with high inflation rates have higher levels of unemployment and lower income levels per head than low-inflation countries (OECD, 1989). Since price stability and a low inflation rate are the main objectives of the EMU (Crawford, 1993), one may expect an increase in the employment rate and income level in the EMU countries.

Countries differ in their economic expectations. People in the southern European EMU member countries expect more favourable developments for their nation and for themselves due to the euro than people in the northern countries. People in the southern countries expect more benefits of the single currency (less inflation, less unemployment, and a better economic development) than people in the northern countries. People in the southern countries even tend to favour the central control and discipline of the European Bank (in Frankfurt) over their national bank.

Within countries, people differ with regard to their economic expectations (Van Raaij and Gianotten, 1990). Consequently, not all citizens of a country will expect these positive developments to happen. People that expect these positive consequences of the single currency, such as high employment, low inflation, and economic growth, will have a more favourable attitude towards the euro than people that do not expect these or other positive consequences.

3.2 Micro-economic Consequences

People will try to understand and anticipate the consequences of the new currency for themselves. People may expect positive consequences for their personal situation. It is often assumed that the introduction of a common currency will improve the allocative efficiency of the price mechanism, lead to lower consumer prices. This will increase the welfare in Europe (De Grauwe, 1992). If one indeed expects an increase in the level of welfare, it may lead to more positive expectations about one's future financial situation, and consequently to a more favourable attitude towards the euro. Other expected benefits of the euro are the ease of using the same currency when travelling and avoiding changing money.

One may also harbour fears concerning one's personal economic future: job security, personal income and savings. Historical experiences may be important. In Germany, for example, the monetary reform of 1948 resulted in a large devaluation of savings. If individuals take this historical event as a point of reference, negative expectations of the personal economic situation due to the single currency may be aroused.

People within the EMU countries may differ in their expectations. Generally, for several segments of society, the expectations will be more favourable in the southern countries, although differences between segments may be expected.

3.3 From Macro to Micro Expectations

Macro- and micro-level economic expectations are related. Katona (1951, 1975) obtained evidence for a direct influence of macro- on micro-level economic expectations. If one is optimistic about the economic developments of the nation as a whole, it is likely that one is also optimistic about one's own economic future. The results of a study among Dutch people by Van Raaij and Gianotten (1990) showed that the macro-economic expectations were a leading indicator of micro-economic expectations, which, in turn, affect economic behaviour such as spending and saving. Based on these studies, we conclude that optimistic expectations about the economy of the nation under the EMU will positively affect peoples' expectations about their own economic situation. Macro expectations are likely to affect micro expectations.

However, macro and micro economic expectations are not always correlated nor at the same level of favourability. Although macro and micro economic expectations were correlated, Van Raaij and Gianotten (1990) found that during the 1970s in The Netherlands, micro expectations were more favourable than macro expectations. In the 1970s, people seemed to think that their own household was still running strong, but that the national economy was in trouble. During the 1980s, however, macro expectations became more favourable than micro expectations. In the 1980s, people seemed to think that their personal finances were affected, but that the national economy was still OK.

4 Data Collection

Table 12.1 - Overview of Data-collection Methods and Sampling

Country	*Response rate (%)*	*Sample size*	*Sampling*	*Data collection*
Austria	56	534	Quota sample	Mail survey
Belgium	60	721	Random municipality lists	Personal delivery
Denmark	70	1167	Panel	Mail survey
Finland	87	1079	Panel + quota sample	Mail survey
France	26	526	Quota sample	Mail survey
Germany	80	1046	Quota sample	Personal delivery
Greece	58	644	Snowball sample	Mail survey
Ireland	-	396	Quota sample	Personal delivery
Italy	-	5220	Nielsen panel	Computer
Luxembourg	60	301	Random municipality lists	Personal delivery
The Netherlands	25	762	Random sample	Mail survey
Portugal	52	504	Stratified random sample	Interviews
Spain	6	410	Quota sample	Mail survey
Sweden	46	1152	Random sample	Mail survey
United Kingdom	40	1140	Random sample	Mail survey

Data were collected in the fifteen EU nations during the summer of 1997, before the political decision which nations will be allowed to the EMU and the introduction of the giral euro. See Müller-Peters *et al.* (1998) for details about the cross-national survey and the questionnaire. In the reference to the cross-national study the names of the participating researchers are given. In table 12.1, the methods of data collection, sample sizes and response rates are given. Most countries used a mail survey, but in Denmark and Italy a panel was used, while in Portugal personal interviews were carried out. In Belgium, Germany, Ireland and Luxembourg, a system with personal delivery and collection of questionnaires was used. Most countries used quota sampling, based on gender, age, education level, geography, and/or income level. In other countries a random sampling procedure was used, based on municipality lists (Belgium and

Luxembourg), telephone directories (The Netherlands) or a survey-agency list (Sweden). In total, more than 15,000 persons participated in this cross-national study.

5 Indicators

Attitudes, national identity, national pride and expectations are latent variables that are not directly observable. However, a number of indicators can be used to represent these latent variables. Based on the theories of Tajfel and Turner (1979), Papadopoulos et al. (1990), and Usunier (1993), national identity contains some aspects or dimensions that will be measured separately. Macro and micro economic expectations may be distinguished. Macro expectations relate to the economy as a whole, whereas micro expectations relate to individuals and households.

5.1 Expected Results

National identity and national pride will not only affect the attitude, but it may also influence the extent to which people evaluate the euro based on beliefs and expectations that people have about the euro. According to Papadopoulos et al. '... feelings of national pride may result in an overall assessment of the country's economic strength or vulnerability' (1990, p. 285). We expect the following results of the data analysis:

1) Persons with a high level of national identity, will have a negative attitude towards the euro.
2) Persons with a high level of European identity, will have a positive attitude towards the euro.
3) Persons with a high level of national pride, will have a negative attitude towards the euro.
4) Persons with positive macro expectations, will have a positive attitude towards the euro.
5) Persons with positive micro expectations, will have a positive attitude towards the euro.

5.2 Attitude towards the Euro

The attitude towards the euro is measured with six bipolar scales and one *Eurobarometer* question. The six bipolar scales are:

A single European currency is:

ATT1: unreasonable (=1), ..., reasonable (=5)

ATT2: bad (=1), …, good (=5)
ATT3: insecure (=1), ..., secure (=5)
ATT4: uncontrollable (=1), …, controllable (=5)

When thinking about a single European currency I feel:

ATT5: worried (=1), ..., calm (=5)
ATT6: tense (=1), …, relaxed (=5)

The *Eurobarometer* question is:

Are you for or against the European Union having one European currency in all member states, including (X)? That is, replacing (X's currency) by the European currency?

ATT7: very much for (=1), …, very much against (≙5).

These seven questions were asked at the beginning and at the end of the questionnaire to test their reliability and stability. The reliabilities were high in all countries with α's ranging from 0.85 to 0.96. The correlations between the measures at the beginning and at the end of the questionnaire, indicating the stability of the attitude measure, were high, ranging from 0.75 to 0.93, except for Italy (0.62). The means for each country are shown in table 12.2; higher scores meaning a more positive attitude.

Table 12.2 - Attitudes towards the Euro Across Nations

Country	*Mean attitude*	*SD attitude*	*Cronbach α*
Spain	3.77	0.98	0.90
Italy	3.71	0.86	0.92
Ireland	3.66	1.06	0.92
Belgium	3.47	0.97	0.90
France	3.42	1.10	0.93
Portugal	3.37	0.91	0.88
Luxembourg	3.33	1.01	0.90
Greece	3.29	1.03	0.85
EU-15	3.19	1.16	0.93
Austria	3.15	1.20	0.93
Finland	3.03	1.17	0.94
The Netherlands	2.98	1.13	0.95
Denmark	2.77	1.35	0.96
Germany	2.74	1.14	0.94
Sweden	2.64	1.25	0.95
UK	2.55	1.22	0.95

Eight, mainly southern, European countries are above the European attitude average (EU-15): Spain, Italy, Ireland, Belgium, France, Portugal, Luxembourg and Greece. People in these countries favour the euro. Note that Greece did not qualify for the euro criteria. Seven northern European countries are below the EU-15 average: UK, Sweden, Germany, Denmark, The Netherlands, Finland and Austria. These people have a rather unfavourable attitude towards the euro. Three of these countries decided not to participate in the single currency: UK, Sweden and Denmark. The standard deviations (SD) of the attitude scores are higher in the negative group (below EU-15). This means that within the 'negative countries' there is less agreement on the attitude towards the euro than in the 'positive countries'.

5.3 National Identity

National identity refers to the degree to which people are committed and attached to their country (X). The impact of national identity is measured as the degree to which a person is attached to and wants to maintain the national character of his/her country. The following survey questions are used:

NI1: A country that does not have its own currency is not a true country (1=strongly disagree, ..., 5=strongly agree).

NI2: In many respects (people of X) are superior to people from other countries
(1=strongly disagree, ..., 5=strongly agree).

NI3: (X) should maintain its national character and differentiate itself from other countries
(1=strongly disagree, ..., 5=strongly agree).

NI4: If I had the chance to set up home in another country, I would leave (X) straightaway
(1=strongly disagree, ..., 5=strongly agree).

NI5: I feel attached to (X) and its people
(1=strongly disagree, ..., 5=strongly agree).

NI6: I feel more involved with matters relating to other European countries than to countries outside Europe.
(1=strongly disagree, ..., 5=strongly agree).

NI7: I feel attached to Europe and its people
(1=strongly disagree, ..., 5=strongly agree).

Questions NI1, NI2 and NI3 are indicators of *nationalism*. Questions NI4 (reversed) and NI5 are indicators of *national patriotism*. Questions NI6 and NI7 are indicators of *European patriotism*. Principal-components analysis (Müller-Peters, 1998, table 12.1) confirms the validity of this categorization. In table 12.3, the scores on nationalism, national patriotism and European patriotism are given.

Table 12.3 - Nationalism, National Patriotism and European Patriotism

Country	*Nationalism*		*National patriotism*		*European patriotism*	
	Score	Correlation with attitude towards the euro	Score	Correlation with attitude towards the euro	Score	Correlation with attitude towards the euro
Greece	3.37	-.23	3.95	-.09	3.02	.42
Portugal	3.37	-.18	3.84	-.02	3.53	.34
Germany	3.25	-.37	3.60	.09	3.32	.45
Austria	3.15	-.57	4.05	.03	3.37	.44
UK	3.15	-.62	3.81	-.21	2.78	.61
Finland	3.07	-.45	4.00	-.11	3.26	.57
Denmark	3.03	-.53	4.36	-.11	3.11	.44
Ireland	2.99	-.29	4.04	-.09	3.24	.26
EU-15	2.97	-	3.87	-	3.20	-
Luxembourg	2.83	-.43	3.52	.18	3.21	.43
The Netherlands	2.79	-.51	3.81	-.05	2.96	.40
Belgium	2.78	-.40	3.45	.12	3.26	.36
Spain	2.76	-.27	4.11	.00	3.46	.47
Italy	2.75	-.22	3.73	.09	3.17	.44
Sweden	2.71	-.47	4.00	-.17	3.04	.54
France	2.62	-.45	3.71	.00	3.28	.50

Nationalism is high in Greece, Portugal, Germany, Austria and the UK, and low in France, Sweden, Italy and Spain. National patriotism is especially high in Denmark and low in Belgium and Luxembourg. For all countries, nationalism scores are lower than national patriotism scores. For all countries, nationalism is negatively correlated with the attitude towards the euro. The largest negative correlations are found for the U.K., Austria, Denmark and The Netherlands.

In all countries, people score higher on national than on European patriotism. The European Union is not yet an entity for which a European patriotism and European affinity exits that is higher than for one's own country. European patriotism is especially high in Portugal and Spain, but low in the UK and The Netherlands. National patriotism is neither positively nor negatively correlated with the attitude towards the euro.

Correlations range between -.21 (UK) and .18 (Luxembourg). For all countries, European patriotism is positively correlated with the attitude towards the euro. European patriotism and attitude towards the euro coincide for the pro-Europe respondents in all countries.

5.4 National Pride

National pride is a concept related to national identity. Two national-pride factors are obtained after principal-components analysis (Müller-Peters, 1998, table 12.2):

1. Economic and political performance (EPP), including economic power, political influence, welfare system, public safety, national currency, and the head of the state.
2. Cultural and historical past (CHP), including traditions, customs, language and history.

Table 12.4 provides the scores of the European nations on the EPP and CHP factors. There are high EEP scores for Denmark, Austria, Finland, Ireland, The Netherlands and Germany. These countries experienced economic growth in recent years. There are low EEP scores for Greece, Italy, Portugal, Spain and Belgium. Many countries with low EEP scores have high CHP scores. These countries are obviously proud of their glorious past, especially Greece, Portugal and Spain. Low CHP scores are obtained by Germany, The Netherlands, Belgium, Luxembourg, Sweden and Austria. These countries seem to be less proud of their cultural past.

The correlations of EPP and CHP with the attitude towards the euro are generally low, and mainly negative for CHP. The EEP factor also contains items on pride in the currency and in the head of state. These items are more related to EEP than to CHP. This means that the currency is perceived in the context of economic and political pride rather than in the context of cultural and historical pride.

Table 12.4 - Economic and Political Pride (EPP) and Cultural and Historical Pride (CHP) Across Nations

Country	*Economic and political pride (EPP)*		*Cultural and historical pride (CHP)*	
	Score	Correlation with attitude towards the euro	Score	Correlation with attitude towards the euro
Denmark	3.58	.04	3.97	-.18
Austria	3.49	.08	3.86	-.15
Finland	3.37	.00	4.00	-.12
Ireland	3.36	.02	4.06	.02
The Netherlands	3.30	.07	3.49	-.10
Germany	3.28	.13	3.40	-.03
Luxembourg	3.18	.16	3.59	.19
UK	3.16	-.17	3.98	-.33
Sweden	3.16	-.04	3.75	-.19
France	3.15	.15	3.85	-.07
EU-15	3.10	-	3.89	-
Belgium	2.89	.17	3.51	.14
Spain	2.86	.23	4.10	.06
Portugal	2.62	.17	4.20	-.04
Italy	2.56	.09	4.01	.13
Greece	2.48	-.02	4.55	-.04

5.5 Economic Expectations

Micro and macro economic expectations refer to the expected consequences of the introduction of the euro. The indicators for the macro expectations are the following survey questions:
What effect do you think the introduction of a single European currency would have on each of the following? (1=strongly increase, ..., 5=strongly decrease)

MA1: Level of unemployment in (X)
MA2: Rate of inflation in (X)
MA3: Economic growth in (X) (reverse scale).

In table 12.5, the macro expectations across countries are given. This measure is a scale based on the macro questions on unemployment, inflation and economic growth. The southern countries and Ireland have most positive expectations about the macro effects of the single currency, whereas the northern countries, including Austria, expect less positive effects. The southern countries and Ireland have much to gain from the euro for their economic growth, employment level and inflation control.

Table 12.5 - Macro Economic Expectations Across Countries

Country	*Macro economic expectations*	*Correlation with attitude towards the euro*
Spain	3.25	0.51
Italy	3.20	0.45
Ireland	3.09	0.32
Portugal	3.06	0.41
Greece	3.01	0.51
Denmark	3.00	0.44
France	2.98	0.51
EU-15	2.90	0.49
Sweden	2.90	0.60
Luxembourg	2.90	0.21
Belgium	2.89	0.41
Finland	2.87	0.60
The Netherlands	2.75	0.56
Austria	2.64	0.63
UK	2.63	0.63
Germany	2.49	0.52

The indicators for the micro economic expectations are the following survey questions:

What impact do you expect a single European currency to have on each of the following?

(1=strongly decrease, ..., 5=strongly increase)

MI1: the value of your savings

MI2: your job security

MI3: your personal income.

In table 12.6, the micro economic expectations across countries are given. This measure is a scale based on the micro questions on value of personal savings, job security and personal income. The southern countries, Ireland and Denmark have most positive expectations about the micro effects of the single currency, whereas the northern countries, including Austria, expect less positive effects. Consumers in the southern countries, in Denmark and in Ireland expect much to gain from the euro for their personal income, savings and job security.

Table 12.6 - Micro Economic Expectations Across Countries

Country	*Micro economic expectations*	*Correlation with attitude towards the euro*
Italy	3.02	0.36
Portugal	2.99	0.47
Ireland	2.91	0.50
Denmark	2.89	0.51
France	2.86	0.41
Spain	2.85	0.60
Belgium	2.82	0.43
Finland	2.81	0.56
Luxembourg	2.79	0.45
Greece	2.79	0.44
EU-15	2.77	0.52
Sweden	2.73	0.60
The Netherlands	2.69	0.52
Germany	2.58	0.54
Austria	2.55	0.71
UK	2.50	0.65

6 Clustering of Countries

The EU countries may be clustered into groups with similar characteristics. Pepermans and Verleye (1998) obtained five clusters of countries based on the dimensions (1) national economic pride and satisfaction, (2) self-confident open-mindedness, and (3) progressive non-nationalistic attitude. Ireland and the UK could not be clustered, and thus remain separate entities. The first dimension explains most variance (table 12.7).

Table 12.7 - Clustering of EU Nations (Pepermans and Verleye, 1998)

	Countries	Dimension 1	Dimension 2	Dimension 3	Attitude towards the euro
1	*Northern-central*: Germany, The Netherlands	+1.7	+1.0	-0.1	2.86
2	*Pseudo-Scandinavian*: Austria, Denmark, Finland, Sweden	+1.1	-0.5	+0.1	2.90
3	*Central region*: Belgium, France, Luxembourg	-0.3	+1.2	+0.1	3.41
4	*Latin-south*: Italy, Spain	-1.5	-0.3	+1.0	3.74
5	*Deep-south*: Greece, Portugal	-1.7	-0.4	-1.2	3.33
6	UK	+0.4	-1.0	-1.1	2.55
7	Ireland	-0.6	-1.9	+1.0	3.66

1. The northern-central region consists of two countries (Germany and The Netherlands) with high levels of economic pride and satisfaction, self-confident open-mindedness and progressive non-nationalistic attitudes. These countries have a rather negative attitude towards the euro (2.86).
2. The pseudo-Scandinavian region largely consists of new member countries. These countries have a moderately high level of economic pride and satisfaction, but neutral levels of self-confident open-mindedness and progressive non-nationalistic attitudes. Denmark and Sweden have negative attitudes toward the euro (2.70), whereas Austria and Finland have moderately positive attitudes (3.09).
3. The central region, including Belgium, France and Luxembourg, is neutral in economic pride and satisfaction, high on self-confident open-mindedness and neutral on progressive non-nationalistic attitudes. People have a positive attitude towards the euro (3.41).
4. The Latin-south region (Italy and Spain) is negative on economic pride and satisfaction, neutral on self-confident open-mindedness, but positive on progressive non-nationalistic attitudes. People have a very positive attitude towards the euro (3.75).

5. The deep-south region (Greece and Portugal) is negative on economic pride and satisfaction, neutral on self-confident open-mindedness, but negative on progressive non-nationalistic attitudes. People have a moderately positive attitude towards the euro (3.33).
6. The UK is neutral on economic pride and satisfaction, negative on self-confident open-mindedness, negative on progressive non-nationalistic attitudes. The British have a negative attitude towards the euro (2.55).
7. Ireland is negative on economic pride and satisfaction, negative on self-confident open-minded-ness, positive on progressive non-nationalistic attitudes. The Irish have a positive attitude towards the euro (3.66).

7 Policy Implications

Policy recommendations based on this study can be summarized in six points, as given below. The attitude towards the euro is a major determinant of the trust in the new currency and the acceptance of the euro.

1. Large differences exist between countries in the attitude towards the euro and the determinants of this attitude, especially a north-south difference. A global European information campaign to increase the acceptance of the euro is likely to be less effective, because it does not take these cross-national differences into account. Information campaigns should be country-specific, providing different arguments depending on the national identity and economic expectations of the people in each EU/EMU country. This study provides information on these cross-national differences, arguments and starting points for information campaigns.
2. Large differences exist within countries in the attitude towards the euro and the determinants of this attitude, especially differences in national identity, national pride and economic expectations. These differences are related to age, gender, education and income. These within-country differences are not reported in this paper. A national information campaign is likely to be less effective, because it does not take these differences into account. Information campaigns should be targeted, providing different arguments for different target groups in the EU/EMU countries. This study provides information on these within-country differences, arguments and starting points for information campaigns.

3. European patriotism is positively related to the attitude towards the euro. Creating and strengthening European patriotism is likely to have positive effects on the attitude towards the euro. European patriotism may be strengthened by economic and political achievements of the European Commission and parliament. Unfortunately, frequent negative news on the European parliament and Commissioners reaches the press and thus affects public opinion. Efforts should be made to increase the affinity, trust and attachment of people to the EU, EMU and other European institutions.
4. National pride has a low correlation with the attitude towards the euro. For some countries there is a moderate positive correlation between these concepts. If national pride can be integrated into a European context, it may have some positive consequences on the attitude, trust and acceptance of the euro. The dimensions of national pride are certainly not a main determinant of the attitude towards the euro. Campaigns based on national pride have no high priority.
5. Long-term economic expectations, both micro and macro expectations, are the major determinants of the attitude towards the euro. Long-term macro expectations, such as the expected effects of the euro on inflation, unemployment and economic growth, are of major concern to people. Long-term micro expectations, such as the expected effects of the euro on personal income, savings and job security, are also of major concern. Where possible, information should be provided to the publics on the positive impact of the euro on these macro and micro economic developments.
6. Short-term expectations, such as the ease of adaptation to the new currency and ease of travelling, are not reported in this paper. In information campaigns, these factors may also play a role, especially at the introduction of the euro. Short-term expectations are related to the conversion, both at the macro and at the micro level. In present information campaigns in many countries, these factors play a dominant role. The long-term effects should, however, not be overlooked, because these factors are, in the end, more important for people to accept the euro.

8 Future Research

Future research on the determinants of the attitude towards the euro could take several directions. In this section, we suggest the following four research topics.

1. An obvious extension of this study is the analysis of the combined effects of national identity, national pride and economic expectations on the attitude towards the euro. This is not a simple linear-additive effect, because national identity has a direct effect on attitude towards the euro and an indirect effect through economic expectations. This can be modeled with multiple regression including interactions, or with a structural-equations model (LISREL). A LISREL model has been tested with the Dutch data (Van Everdingen and Van Raaij, 1998). This could also be applied to the data of other EU member countries.
2. In 1998 it was agreed that eleven of the fifteen EU member countries would introduce the single currency during the period 1999-2002. Our data were collected before this decision was made. A replication study could reveal how attitudes of consumers change depending on whether the country participates in the EMU or not. It may be expected that consumers in participating countries (Austria, Benelux, Finland, France, Germany, Ireland, Italy, Portugal and Spain) develop a more positive attitude towards the euro than consumers in countries that do not participate in the EMU (Denmark, Greece, Sweden, and the UK). A hypothesis is that consumers in non-participating countries develop a negative attitude in accordance with the reality in their country ('sour grapes'). For these consumers, this is a form of reduction of cognitive dissonance.
3. Another extension of this study is the hypothesis that many consumers are still undecided, but will develop a more pronounced attitude as the introduction of the chartal euro comes nearer. The polarization hypothesis states that undecided persons need only small incentives or reasons to develop an attitude in one direction or another. Economic 'incidents' and 'news' related to the euro and the EU may lead to negative causal attributions (correct or not) and trigger more extreme negative attitudes (De Raaf and Van Raaij, 1999). For politicians and media it is extremely important to explain whether the euro may be correctly considered as a cause of particular economic developments and incidents.

4. A fourth possible study is as follows. People in countries that expect a lot of the new currency, may have too positive expectations. They may become disappointed if the favourable developments they expect do not take place. In a similar way, people in Eastern Europe expected a lot after the end of communist power in 1989. They became disappointed when the expected improvements did not come as soon as they expected. A replication study after the introduction in 2002 may reveal disconfirmed expectations for the high-expectations countries such as Ireland, Italy and Spain.

9 Conclusions

In a cross-national study in the fifteen member nations of the European Union, data were collected on the attitude towards the euro and the factors explaining this attitude. Consumers in EU countries differ in their feelings of nationalism, national and European patriotism, national pride, and their expectations towards the euro. These factors largely explain the attitude towards the euro. Consumers are not homogeneous in their attitudes towards the euro and its determinants. Within and between countries large differences exist. Information extension on the euro should incorporate these differences in their approach to segment markets and to select target groups for information extension.

Significant differences exist between the northern and southern European countries. People in the southern countries, with less stable currencies, expect a lower inflation, lower unemployment and economic growth due to the euro. People in the northern countries, with stable currencies such as the German mark and the Dutch guilder, expect less favourable economic developments, even a slight economic downturn, due to the euro. Nevertheless these consumer seem to accept the euro for the sake of the European Union and its economic integration.

References

Brewer, M. B. (1991), 'The social self: On being the same and different at the same time', *Personality and Social Psychology Bulletin* 17(5), pp. 475-482.

Crawford, M. (1993), *One Money for Europe? The Economics and Politics of Maastric,* Chippenham, Wilts, U.K.: Macmillan Press.

De Grauwe, P. (1992), *The Economics of Monetary Integration,* New York: Oxford University Press.

De Raaf, D. I. and W. F. Van Raaij (1999), *The formation and adjustment of corporate image and reputation.* Corporate Reputation Review 2.

Gatignon, H. and T. S. Robertson (1985), 'A propositional inventory for new diffusion research', *Journal of Consumer Research 11* (March), pp. 849-867.

Katona, G. (1951), *Psychological Analysis of Economic Behavior,* New York: McGraw-Hill.

Katona, G. (1975), *Psychological Economics,* New York: Elsevier.

Müller-Peters, A. (1998), 'The significance of national pride and national identity to the attitude toward the single European currency: A Europe-wide comparison', *Journal of Economic Psychology 19(6), pp.* 701-719.

Müller-Peters, A., R. Pepermans, G. Kiell, N. Battaglia, S. Beckmann, C. Burgoyne, Y. M. van Everdingen, M. Farhangmehr, G. Guzman, E. Kirchler, C. Koenen, F. Kokkinaki, M. Lambkin, D. Lassarre, F. Lenoir, R. Luna-Arocas, A. Marell, K. Meier, J. Moisander, G. Ortona, C. Pinho, I. Quintanilla, W. F. van Raaij, D. Routh, F. Scacciati, C. Simões, and R. Wahlund (1998), 'Explaining attitudes towards the euro. Design of a cross-national study', *Journal of Economic Psychology 19(6), pp.* 663-680.

OECD (1989), *Regional Policy Developments in OECD Countries,* Paris: OECD.

Papadopoulos, N., L. A. Heslop and G. Bamossy (1990), 'A comparative image analysis of domestic versus imported products', *International Journal of Research in Marketing 7(4), pp.* 283-294.

Pepermans, R. and G. Verleye (1998), 'A unified Europe? How euro attitudes relate to psychological differences between countries', *Journal of Economic Psychology 19(6), pp.* 681-699.

Peters, A. (1996), *Psychology of the European Monetary Union. A cross-national comparison of attitudes in France, Great Britain and Germany.* Paper presented at the 21st IAREP Conference, Paris.

Rogers, E. M. (1995), *Diffusion of Innovations.* New York: The Free Press. Fourth edition.

Tajfel, H. and J. C.Turner (1979), 'An integrative theory of intergroup conflict', in: Austin, W.G. and S. Worchel (eds). *The Social Psychology of Intergroup Relations,* Monterey CA: Brooks/ Cole, pp. 33-57.

Usunier, J-C. (1993), *International Marketing. A Cultural Approach,* New York: Prentice Hall.

Van Everdingen, Y. M. (1995), *Adoption and Diffusion of the European Currency Unit.* An Empirical Study among European Companies, Amsterdam: Thesis Publishers.

Van Everdingen, Y. M. and W. F. van Raaij (1998), 'The Dutch people and the euro: A structural equations analysis relating national identity and economic expectations to attitude towards the euro', *Journal of Economic Psychology 19(6), pp.* 721-740.

Van Raaij, W.F. and H. J. Gianotten (1990), 'Consumer confidence, expenditure, saving, and credit', *Journal of Economic Psychology 11(2), pp.* 269-290.

13 The Indicator Monitoring Taiwan's Business Conditions

THOMAS M. F. YEH

1 Introduction

The Business Conditions Monitoring Indicator of Taiwan, compiled by the Council for Economic Planning and Development (CEPD), has been in existence since 1975. The purpose is to furnish guidance to the government in making timely and appropriate economic policy decisions. The entrepreneurs can also use it to adjust their expansion plans.

Employing five signal lights to represent current economic conditions, the monitoring indicators serve as a 'warning' system to the government and entrepreneurs.

- The green light signal indicates a satisfactory and stable state of the economy, with appropriate monetary and fiscal policies under implementation.
- The red light signal shows overheating of the economy to such an extent that the cooling-off effect of a contractionary policy is called for.
- The blue light signal indicates a falling into recession and the need for an expansionary policy to stimulate the economy.
- Both the yellow-red and yellow-blue light signals indicate that the potential changes in business conditions should be closely watched, with the government remaining on the alert to respond to undesirable changes by taking remedial measures.

2 Method of Compilation

There are three stages in compiling this monitoring indicator:

2.1 Selection of Component Series

As the monitoring indicator should deliver warning signals to the government to make economic policy, the contents should include series that are closely related to the policy goal of the country. If the external equilibrium is emphasized, there should be more statistical series related to the balance-of-payments account. If the domestic equilibrium is emphasized, more series related to the price level, the domestic supply and demand should be considered. Besides that, the seven criteria–economic significance, statistical adequacy, conformity, consistency of timing, smoothness, prompt availability and revision–are also considered in choosing a proper series. That is, the series should be understood well in economic significance, be conformed to the business cycles, be consistent in leading (or coincident with) the reference turning points, be smooth so that a cyclical turn can be detected, be available promptly and without frequent revision.

Since stable growth and balancing of the financial sector and the real sector are major goals of the economic policy now in Taiwan, four indicators from the financial sector and five indicators from the real goods-sector are included in the system:

- Annual change rate of money supply M1B
- Annual change rate of loans and discounts of monetary institutions extended to private enterprises
- Annual change rate of real bank clearings
- Annual change rate of the stock price index
- Annual change rate of the manufacturing new orders index (deflated by output WPI of manufacturing industry)
- Annual change rate of exports (deflated by export price index)
- Annual change rate of the industrial production index
- Manufacturing inventory ratio (inverted)
- Annual change rate of non-agricultural employment.

2.2 Determination of Checkpoints

The checkpoints are the critical levels of the individual seasonal-adjusted series adopted in the monitoring indicator. When the level of the series exceeds one critical level, a predefined signal will be assigned to indicate that the series is coming into another phase. This critical level is called the check point. By four checkpoints, each series is divided into five phases and a signal is assigned to each phase:

Phase	Signal
recession	blue light signal
phase between recession and stable condition	yellow-blue light signal
stable condition	green light signal
phase between stable condition and overheated condition	yellow-red light signal
overheated condition	red light signal

The determination of checkpoints should take the following factors into account:

A. The experience of domestic business cycles and economic development.
B. The economic and social goals of the country and the targets of economic plans for the future.
C. The time points when the economy aproached recession or overheated condition, the dates when the government adopted contractionary or expansionary policies, and the time lags of these policy effects during the past.

In other words, we assume that the levels of individual series during some selected periods that showed greater stability and fair growth in the past two decades are 'normal levels'. Then the upper and lower limits of these 'normal levels' are considered as the upper and lower checkpoints of the green light. For those indicators which are related to production, exports or money supply, the upper and lower limits of their 'normal levels' are modified by considering the necessary levels needed to achieve the target rate of economic growth. The average level of each series in the periods 4 to 5 months prior to the peak of business cycles is taken to be the checkpoint between yellow-red and red lights; the average level of each series in the periods 4 to 5 months prior to 'the trough' to be the checkpoint between yellow-blue and blue lights.

In addition to the above factors, we consider the probability for each signal to be assigned. In order to prevent false forecasts and keep the system stable, we predefine the probability of assigning the green signal to be around 25%, while the other signals have the even chance to be assigned. The checkpoints for individual series are showed in table 13.2.

2.3 Compiling the Monitoring Indicator

After each series has been assigned a score ranging from 1 to 5, that is 1 for blue light, 2 for yellow-blue light, 3 for green light, 4 for yellow-red light, 5 for red light, we add them up to obtain the total score of the monitoring indicator. If all the nine series are blue lights, the indicator reaches its minimum, 9; if all are red lights, it reaches the maximum, 45. The joint signal is determined by ranging total scores as follows:

Total Score	Joint Signal
9 to 16	blue light
17 to 22	yellow-blue light
23 to 31	green light
32 to 37	yellow-red light
38 to 45	red light

Because the monitoring indicator should meet the policy goals in every stage of economic development for a country, it should be adjusted according to the change in policy goals. The individual series contained in this system has to be constantly observed, be compared with reference cycles of business conditions, and the checkpoints should be revised if necessary.

3 Historical Review and Evaluation

3.1 History of Revision

Since its first compilation in 1975, the Business Conditions Monitoring Indicator of Taiwan had been revised four times to reflect the changes in economic conditions. The major revisions are the following:

A. Content of lights: When the monitoring indicator was established in 1975, we focused on preventing the overheating of the economy. There were also 5 lights in the system, but 3 lights above the green light, and 1 light below it, namely the double-red light, red light, yellow light, green light, and blue light. After the second oil crisis, we applied symmetric signals in order to monitor the overheating as well as the recession of the economy.

Table 13.1 - Content of Revision (1975-1998)

Date of Publication	Date of Application	Number of Components (checkpoints)	Component Series	Background
0. Original 1975	1968	12(51,43,36,23)	wholesale price index, consumer price index, money supply M1', loans and discounts, bank clearings, ratio of dishonored bills, stock price, export exchange settlement, exports by customs clearance statistics, industrial production, manufacturing production, time and savings deposits	-
1. Oct. 1981	1978	12(51,44,30,23)	-Add new order and inventory ratio -delete 2 price indexes -deflate 2 exports indicators	-stagflation occurred after the second oil crisis
2. June. and Aug. 1987	1984	9(38,32,23,17)	-delete dishonored bills and savings deposits -replace M1' with M1B -delete export exchange settlement	-policy goals changed toward liberalization -financial indicators changed pattern
3. April 1990	1989	9(38,32,23,17)	-delete manufacturing production -add nonagricultural employment -deflate new order	-service industry weight increased
4. Nov. 1995	1994	9(38,32,23,17)	-	-emergence of a mature economy

Table 13.2 - Content of Checkpoints

		Original	1st Revision	2nd Revision	3rd Revision	4th Revision
PRICE	Wholesale Price[1]	12,8,4,0	-	-	-	-
	Consumer Price[1]	12,8,5,2	-	-	-	-
FINANCIAL	Money Supply M1B[2]	25,22,18,10[3]	25,20,14,10[3]	20,16,10,7	18,15,9,6	15,12,7,5
	Loans and Discounts[2]	40,22,18,10[1]	30,25,18,12	23,19,13,10	23,20,14,11	23,20,14,11
	Bank Clearings[2]	56,40,32,12[1]	45,32,18,12	38,29,17,10	38,31,16,9	25,17,6,0
	Stock Price[2]	45,30,20,15	40,20,5,-10	35,20,5,-5	41,28,5,-10	36,21,0,-10
	Ratio Of Dishonored Bills (‰)	1.7,2.0,2.5,3.5	2.0,2.2,3.2,3.5	-	-	-
	Time and Savings Deposits	12,15,18,30[1]	12,18,25,30[2]	-	-	-
REAL	MFGs' New Orders[2]		35,28,18,10	28,22,12,6	20,15,5,1 [d]	12,9,3,0 [d]
	Export Exchange Settlement	35,30,20,10[1]	25,20,12,7[2d]	-	-	-
	Exports By Customs Clearance[2]	35,30,20,10[1]	25,20,12,7[d]	20,16,8,5 [d]	14,9,3,1 [d]	15,10,3,0 [d]
	Industrial Production[2]	27,22,12,5	22,16,10,6	16,12,6,3	13,9,4,2	12,9,3,0
	Manufacturing Production[2]	27,22,12,5	22,16,10,6	17,14,7,4	-	-
	MFGs' Inventory Ratio (%)	-	54,59,67,72	54,60,72,78	52,58,70,75	52,56,67,72
	Nonagricultural Employment[2]	-	-	-	5,4,2,1	4.0,3.2,1.6,0.8
Monitoring Indicator		51,43,36,23	51,44,30,23	38,32,23,17	38,32,23,17	38,32,23,17
		◉, ●, ⊗, ○, ▽	●, ◒, ○, ◓, ▽	●, ◒, ○, ◓, ▽	●, ◒, ○, ◓, ▽	●, ◒, ○, ◓, ▽

Note: ◉: double-red light, ●: red light, ⊗: yellow light, ○: green light, ▽: blue light, ◒: yellow-red light

◓: yellow-blue light

Note: 1. 6 month percentage change at annual rate. 2. 12 month percentage change. 3. M1' d: deflated

B. Content of components: There were 12 components included in the system in 1975: the wholesale price index, the consumer price index, the money supply M1'(including M1 and the time and savings deposits by private enterprises), loans and discounts, bank clearings, ratio of dishonored bills, stock price, export exchange settlement, exports by customs clearance statistics, industrial production, manufacturing production, time and savings deposits.

As the stagflation occurred after the second oil crisis, we dropped two price indicators and added new orders of manufacturing industry, and the ratio of goods inventories to sales in manufacturing industry in 1981. At the same time we deflated the two export indicators.

Following to the mid-1980s, Taiwan's industrial structure, as well as the changing policy goals toward liberalization, internationalization and systemization, led Taiwan's economy from rapid growth to the more mature stage. The financial indicators in the monitoring signals experienced quite different patterns than before. In June 1987, we removed indicators of the dishonored bills and savings deposits, replaced M1' with M1B. Two months later, when the scope of the statistics of export exchange settlement changed, we deleted that indicator.

When the output of service industry accounted for nearly half of the gross domestic product in late 1980s, we deleted the manufacturing production indicator to weight down industrial production. Meanwhile we added nonagricultural employment, and deflated the new order indicator. (see Table 13.1)

C. Content of checkpoints: As stated above, the checkpoints should be modified along with the changes in policy objectives and the long-term trend and the distributions of individual series. When the second oil crisis occurred, we adjusted the checkpoints for each component series in expectation to meet the 8% target rate of economic growth. As Taiwan's economy tended to be mature, we set the limits for green light in accordance with the target economic growth rate as 7% in the second and the third revisions, and 6.5% in the fourth revision (see Table 13.2).

3.2 Evaluation

Table 13.3 presents the correlation coefficients between the total score of the monitoring indicator and the growth rate of real GDP and with the annual change rate of the coincident indicator of business conditions. (We compare the quarterly average of the monthly total scores with quarterly data of GDP.) We can see that, after 1994, the monitoring indicator is highly correlated with the economic growth rate with correlation coefficient of 0.88 and with the annual growth rate of Taiwan's composite index of business conditions coincident indicators with 0.80. This shows that the monitoring indicator provides valuable information on the economic activity.

Table 13.3 - Correlation Coefficients Between Monitoring Score and Other Indicators

	Economic Growth Rate	Annual Change Rate of Coincident Indicator
1971~1998	0.74	0.71
1984~1998	0.82	0.70
1994~1998	0.88	0.80

As we mentioned before, the content of the monitoring indicator needs to be revised regularly to comply with the changes of the economy. When the Asia financial crisis occurred in the second half of 1997, it triggered Taiwan's economy stopping expansion. The economy was recovering since March, 1996 then it slowed down after the fourth quarter of 1997. The economic growth rate declined from 7.1% in the fourth quarter of 1997 to under 6% in 1998. Table 13.4 presents the probability distributions of the components of the monitoring indicator from January 1996 to November 1998. Most of them showed skewed distributions, biased to the blue light. The total score did not show any red light or yellow-red light after January 1996. As we see into it, we find out that the probabilities of the blue light for the three indicators of the financial sector were extremely high, especially the loans and discounts of monetary institutions to private enterprises. As for the five indicators of the real sector, the probabilities of the red and yellow-red lights were zero for the manufacturing inventory ratio and the non-agricultural employment. The only exception was the manufacturing new orders index, which did not show any blue light in these three years.

The central tendencies of the components showed that the medians of 4 financial indicators and the inventory indicator were equal to or lower than their arithmetic means. Their means fell below the lower limit of the green light, except the stock price indicator. The spreads of the probability distribution of individual series showed that the interquartile ranges and standard deviations for the series of bank clearings, stock prices, and exports recorded a relative big value. As the differences of checkpoints between the lower limit of red light and the upper limit of blue light for money supply were smaller than its interquartile range, this might cause the probability of lights of red and blue to flash more frequently.

Table 13.4 - Probability Distribution of Monitoring Indicator From January 1996 to November 1998

		Financial Sector				Real Sector					Total Score
		M1B	Loan	Bank Clearing	Stock Prices	New Order	Export	Ind. Prod.	Inven-tory	Em-ployment	
Red	in percentage	8.6	0	2.9	31.4	31.4	11.4	0	0	0	0
R-Y		17.1	0	5.7	11.4	28.6	14.3	8.6	0	0	0
Green		17.1	0	37.1	28.6	34.3	34.3	57.1	34.3	60.0	51.4
Y-B		11.4	14.3	17.1	5.7	5.7	11.4	25.7	57.1	17.1	40.0
Blue		45.7	85.7	37.1	22.9	0	28.6	8.6	8.6	22.9	8.6
Mean	in original unit	6.9	6.4	4.0	16.0	10.3	5.3	4.3	68.1	1.56	22.7
Median		5.2	6.3	4.0	15.5	10.6	5.5	4.7	68.8	1.7	23.0
s.d.		5.7	3.5	9.8	27.2	4.8	7.0	3.4	4.3	0.89	4.8
Range		19.7	13.4	41.5	94.4	20.2	30.5	16.1	21.1	3.5	18
Q3-Q1		10.2	6.3	13.4	44.6	6.3	10.2	4.5	6.1	1.15	7.5
CR-CB		10	12	25	46	12	15	12	20	3.2	21

Note: Q3-Q1 stands for the interquartile range.
CR-CB stands for the difference between the checkpoints of red light and blue light.

4 Measures Taken by Government

In the past forty-some years, our government has taken many measures to maintain stable growth. With the monitoring indicator providing information about the tendency of the economic development, our government is able to take actions at the right time. When the economy goes down and the monitoring indicator turns from green lights to yellow-blue lights, the government takes expansionary measures to stimulate the economy. When there is a sign of over-heating, the government takes up a contractionary policy to cool off the situation.

When the total score dropped 16 points in seven months from 39 (red light) in November 1994 to 23 (lower limit of green light) in July 1995, the Central Bank of China lowered the rediscount rates immediately on July 25, 1995 and cut the required reserve ratios of deposits three times in the following three months. After the first blue light flashed in October, Executive Yuan started to execute the 'Policy for Stimulating Current Economy' in November 1995. These measures included an increase of the money supply, the clearing of obstacles for investment (December 1995), a stabilization of the stock market through a stock stabilization fund (February 12, 1996) in order to ease the effect of Mainland China's military manoeuvres near Taiwan, an extrication of the construction industry by appropriating more postal savings to the banks for housing loans (March 11,1996), solving small and medium enterprises' problems in investing and finance, speeding up the public investment and labor policies (August 1996). Under those efforts, Taiwan's economy regained momentum. The monitoring indicator came off the blue light in June 1996, and signaled green light three months later.

After the Asia financial crisis outburst in July 1997, the total score of the monitoring indicator started to drop down in October 1997. In April 1998, it flashed the first yellow-blue light after seventeen consecutive green lights. The government implemented such measures as the 'Export Promotion Scheme' (March 1998) and the 'Domestic Demand Stimulus Plan' in August 1998. Till the end of 1998, Taiwan's financial markets were among the least affected compared with other East Asia economies. Taiwan's economic growth rate in 1998 is estimated to be the highest among the Four Tigers.

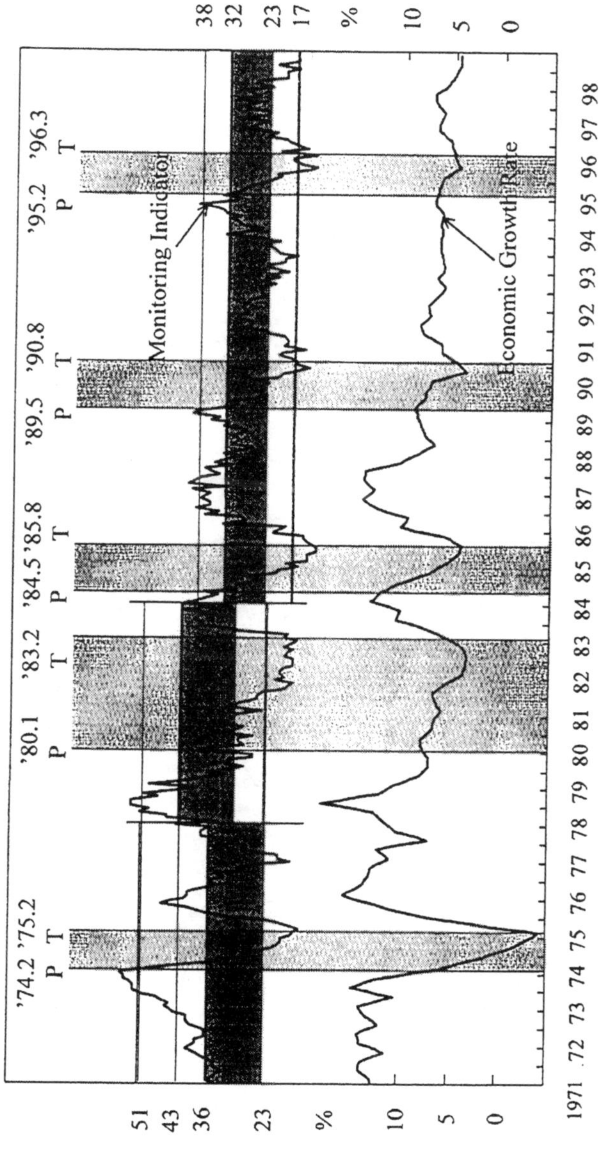

Figure 13.1 - Monitoring Indicator and Economic Growth Rate

Note: The vertically shaded area stands for the recession period.

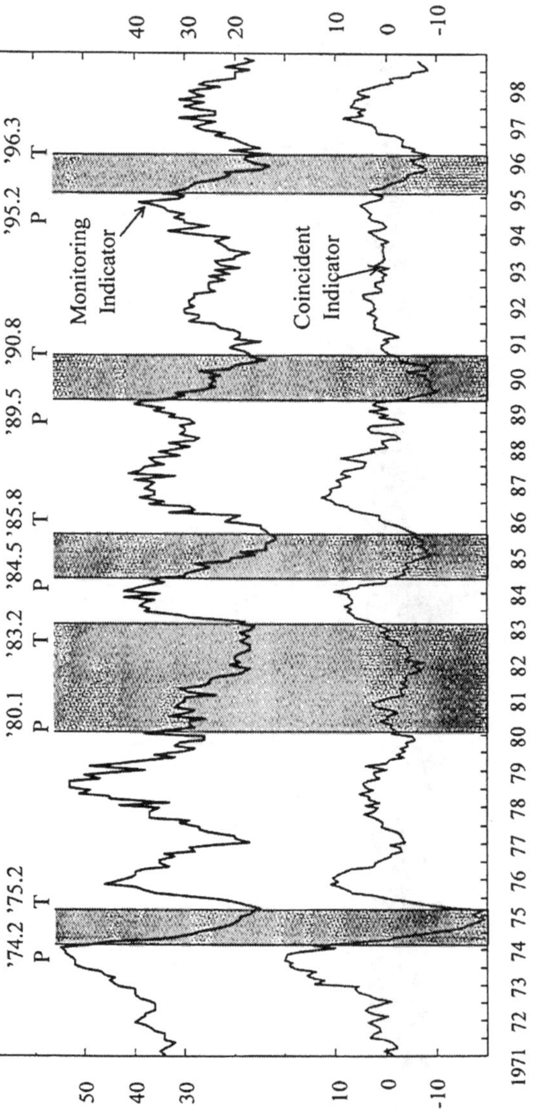

Figure 13.2 - Monitoring Indicator and Coincident Indicator*

* the annual growth rate of composite index of coincident indicator.

Note: Vertically shaded areas indicate periods of recession

5 Concluding Remarks

Since its first development, the monitoring indicator has been playing an important role in describing Taiwan's business conditions and gone through four revisions. In Taiwan, it has been used extensively by the government and enterprises as well as investors.

Although the time series of the monitoring indicator consists of information from different components and ranges, it is quite correlated with the economic growth rate and the coincident indicator. While the economic growth rate has never exceeded 7.1%, it did not signal any red light in the current cycle and three financial components showed too many blue lights as well. Is this simply caused by the Asia financial crisis or has Taiwan's economy changed its pattern? It will be our task to find out the practical checkpoints for these series and introduce more suitable series into this system.

Part IV

Attitudes and Behaviour of Firms

14 Menu Costs, Firm Size and Price Rigidity: Evidence from Business Survey Data

ROBERT A. BUCKLE and JOHN A. CARLSON

Abstract

If menu costs of changing price have a non-negligible lump-sum component and with larger firms having greater benefits from price adjustments, then larger firms will change price more frequently than smaller firms. Data from an extensive survey of firms in New Zealand support this hypothesis. Ordered probit analysis indicates that the effect comes primarily from larger firms being more likely than smaller firms to raise price in response to a demand or cost increase and not from a greater likelihood of lowering price in response to a demand or cost decrease.

1 Introduction

In recent years 'menu costs' of price adjustment have become a popular explanation for price stickiness in markets characterised by monopolistic competition. Ball and Mankiw (1994a), for instance, have remarked that 'menu costs are a convenient formalization that captures the fact that prices are not adjusted continuously, and that they tend to adjust more quickly to large than to small shocks' (pp. 142 - 143).

Menu costs include the administrative, technical and informational costs of deciding on and implementing a price change. They are generally assumed to be lump-sum costs so that a significant component of menu costs may be independent of firm size. For example, an important cost of price adjustment is the time and attention required by managers to gather the relevant information to make and implement pricing decisions. The scale of this problem is likely to be similar for firms producing similar products and operating in similar markets, irrespective of the size of the firm. Hence, the information costs involved in pricing decisions are likely to involve a common lump-sum component. Similarly, although the total cost of changing price lists, price tags, price catalogues and advertising price changes may vary with firm size (for instance, firms with a large volume of output and sales may need to distribute new price catalogues to a larger number of distribution outlets than firms with a small volume of output and sales), there will nevertheless be lump-sum set-up costs which are likely to be similar across firms irrespective of their size.

When there are fixed costs of price adjustment, a firm's decision to change its nominal price in response to a shock to its desired price is not automatic. That decision will depend on whether the benefits of price adjustment are perceived to outweigh the menu costs of price adjustment. Rigorous analysis of the implications of menu costs of price adjustment for microeconomic pricing behaviour were initially provided in the seminal paper by Barro (1972) while Sheshinski and Weiss (1977, 1983) considered the implications of constant and stochastic inflation. These latter papers show that, in the presence of menu costs, it is optimal for a firm to let its real price fall to some lower bound s before adjusting nominal price. When a firm does increase its nominal price it is optimal for the firm to raise its real price to an upper bound S. These optimal trigger points S and s, and therefore the range of shocks over which firms do not change price, are evidently increasing functions of the cost of price adjustment.

The Sheshinski and Weiss models are one-sided S,s pricing models in which prices change in only one direction. However it appears that the implications of menu costs found for one-sided S,s pricing models, when there is general inflation, may also carry over to circumstances in which firms may increase or decrease price. For instance, it can be shown that under certain assumptions concerning either the process by which optimal price is determined over time (Benassi, Chirco and Colombo, 1994, Chapter 7) or by assuming firms adopt a combination of time-dependent and state-dependent pricing rules (Ball and Mankiw, 1994b), the range of shocks over which firms do not adjust price is an increasing function of the per unit menu cost of price adjustment.

These models all imply that, for a given distribution of shocks to optimal real price, the probability of a price change decreases as the cost of price adjustment increases. This paper considers a simple extension to that result. If menu costs of price adjustment involve a common lump-sum or fixed cost component, the cost of price adjustment per unit of output will vary systematically with the volume of output and therefore with firm size. The unit cost of price adjustment for large firms will be smaller than for small firms. It follows therefore that if, in response to shocks to desired price, firms only adjust the price of a unit of output when the benefits of adjustment exceed the menu costs per unit of output, price stickiness will vary systematically with firm size. Accordingly, the presence of lump-sum menu costs of price adjustment implies, other things equal, that small firms will tend to exhibit greater price stickiness than large firms.

This paper provides evidence showing that price stickiness does in fact vary systematically with firm size. We estimate price stickiness in two ways: (i) by an estimate of the duration of prices, defined as the average length of time between successive price changes, and (ii) by price responsiveness of firms to cost and demand changes.

These measures of price stickiness are estimated for firms of different sizes using information about changes to individual firm prices, costs and demand obtained from a quarterly survey of New Zealand manufacturing and building firms.

The remainder of the paper is structured as follows. Section II specifies a menu-cost model of price change in which larger firms will tend to change prices more frequently. Section III discusses the data and section IV presents tests of our hypotheses about the effects of firm size on price stickiness. Section V examines evidence that frequency of cost changes also varies with firm size. Section VI concludes.

2 Hypotheses about the Effects of Firm Size on Frequency of Price Changes

This section specifies a simple model of price change which incorporates fixed menu costs of price adjustment and identifies the conditions that must hold before a firm will adjust actual price in the presence of cost and demand shocks.

Consider a simplified version of an optimal Ss rule for a price setting monopolist specified by Blanchard and Fischer (1989, pp. 402-405). Assume the following linear demand and cost functions:

$$Y = \alpha - \beta P + u \tag{1}$$

$$C = (b + v)\, Y \tag{2}$$

The firm's profit maximizing price and quantity can be readily shown to be

$$P^* = [(\alpha + u) + (b + v)\beta]/2\beta \tag{3}$$

$$Y^* = [(\alpha + u) - (b + v)\beta]/2 \tag{4}$$

If the larger firms have more of a customer base, then quantity demanded will be more responsive to a price change. This means a larger value for β. At the same time, for a given price, if larger firms have a larger quantity demanded, then the coefficient α should be larger. Finally, we assume that any outside factors that shift the demand function will have a greater effect on larger firms. This implies larger values for u. Thus, we assume that larger firms tend to have proportionately higher values α, β and u.

By contrast the cost function should not be significantly different for different sizes of firms. If the marginal cost of supplying output is roughly the same for all firms, then the coefficients b and v are not systematically related to firm size.

These considerations lead to the observations that in equation (3) the optimal price is not affected by size whereas in equation (4) output varies directly with the extent to which the customer base varies, as reflected in the magnitudes of the α, β and u parameters.

Now suppose price has been set to maximize profits when u = 0 and v = 0. As u and v change over time, the firm could increase profits by changing its price but may not do so when there are menu costs of making a price change. When u and/or v are non zero, the difference between profits with an optimal price and profits with no change in price can be shown to be:

$$B(u,v) = \frac{u^2}{4\beta} + \frac{\beta v^2}{4} + \frac{uv}{2} \tag{5}$$

Call this benefit from changing price the opportunity cost of not changing price. Blanchard and Fischer postulate that the firm will change price whenever this opportunity cost exceeds the cost of making a price change. At that point, price is reset optimally, the α and b parameters are redefined to include the u and v changes that have occurred since the prior price change, and the process is repeated.

We have assumed that larger firms have a larger demand. More explicitly, in this model a larger firm has larger values of both β and u. However, any upward shift in costs will tend to be the same across firms of different size. As a result, a term-by-term examination of equation (5) reveals that B(u,v), the opportunity cost of not changing price, rises in direct proportion to firm size.

If the cost of changing price has a non-negligible lump-sum component or rises less than proportionately to the increase in the size of the firm, then smaller firms will tend to change price less frequently than larger firms. Consider, for example, a distribution of cost changes. Larger firms, with larger values for β, will have a more dispersed distribution of B(u,v). As a result a higher proportion of larger firms with cost increases will decide to raise price and a higher proportion of larger firms with cost decrease will decide to lower price compared to smaller firms. A similar prediction holds for demand changes if larger firms tend to have a more dispersed distribution of demand shifts.

If, as suggested by the foregoing argument, larger firms change prices more frequently than smaller firms do, then we predict that a measure of price duration, the average time between price changes, will be longer for smaller firms.

These hypotheses will be tested with survey data from New Zealand.

3 Data

Information about firm price, cost and demand changes and firm size was obtained from the New Zealand Institute of Economic Research's *Quarterly Survey of Business Opinion*. The NZIER survey involves the distribution to business executives of a standard questionnaire that identifies the firm, its principal activity, location, size, and a series of questions asking about the firm's operating environment. It also contains a standard question asking executives to report their perceptions of the actual change during the immediate past three months by reporting 'Up' (which is coded 1) or 'Same' (coded 2) or 'Down' (coded 3) or 'N/A' (coded 4) for several activity variables. Firms do not indicate the magnitude of change, only the direction of change.

The proportion of firms reporting changes to their prices, changes to their costs and changes to their demand were obtained from responses to the following questions:

What has been your firm's experience during the past three months in respect of :

	Up	*Same*	*Down*	*N/A*
Average selling prices ?	-	-	-	-
Average costs ?	-	-	-	-
All new forward orders received?	-	-	-	-

Firms that did not respond to these questions were dropped from the sample of observations for that particular quarter, and we re-coded the remaining firms responses to 'Up' = 1, 'Same' = 0 and 'Down' = -1.

Firms were allocated to one of six size categories according to their response to the following question:

How many employees are covered by this return?

The six size categories are:

1: Employees ≤ 20
2: 20 < Employees ≤ 50
3: 50 < Employees ≤ 100
4: 100 < Employees ≤ 200
5: 200 < Employees ≤ 500
6: 500 < Employees

Firms that did not respond to this question were also dropped from the sample of observations for that particular quarter. Our sample commences in 1984:3 because prior to that date extensive regulations applied to price and wage setting in New Zealand (See Evans, Grimes and Wilkinson, 1996).

4 Tests

4.1 Duration of Prices

A procedure for obtaining statistics for price duration from qualitative data has been suggested by Buckle and Carlson (1996). Let p^u = percent of firms reporting price increases in the last n months and p^d = percent of firms reporting price decreases in the last n months. An average time T in months between price changes is then given by the following:

$$T = n/(p^u + p^d) \qquad (6)$$

For example, if in a quarterly survey 75% of the firms report they did not make a price change in the last 3 months and 25% did, then a representative firm will go 3/0.25 = 12 months before changing price. There are potential biases in this measure. On the one hand, if firms tend to change prices on only some items during the quarter but their average prices are up or down, then $(p^u + p^d)$ overestimates the extent of price changing activity and T is biased downward. On the other hand, if firms change prices more frequently than once a quarter, then T overestimates the average duration between price changes.

Table 14.1 - Duration in Months of Prices, Costs and Demand by Firm Size (Quarterly Surveys: 1984:3 – 1996:1)

Firm size:	1	2	3	4	5	6	All Firms	Spearman's ρ
Prices	8.1	7.6	6.6	6.4	6.2	5.1	6.7 (1.03)	Prices and Size: -1.00 [0.00] Prices and Costs: 0.83 [0.04] Prices and Demand: 0.70 [0.12]
Costs	6.5	5.6	5.4	5.1	5.4	4.8	5.5 (0.57)	Costs and Size: -0.83 [0.04] Costs and Demand: -0.82 [0.05]
Demand	4.8	4.7	4.6	4.4	4.6	4.6	4.6 (0.11)	Demand and Size: -0.70 [0.12]

Notes: Standard errors in ( ) brackets; p-values in [ ] brackets.

Table 14.1 shows duration estimates for New Zealand manufacturing and building firms by firm size using this procedure. Our concern at this point is with the estimates for price duration. The data on costs and demand in this table will be considered below. From Table 14.1 it is clear that the length of time firms hold prices constant does in fact vary by firm size. The smallest firms in our sample changed prices on average every 8.1 months during our $11^1/_2$-year sample period. This is more than 50% longer than the average 5.1 months duration of prices for the largest firms. There is also a perfect rank-order correlation between firm size and the average frequency of price changes. These results strongly support our hypothesis that large firms change price more frequently than small firms.

4.2 Price Responsiveness to Cost and Demand Changes

We next look more specifically at the effect of firm size on price responsiveness to cost and demand changes. To do that, we use ordered probit regressions to estimate the influence of changes in costs and demand on the probability of a change in price separately for small firms (categories 1 and 2) and large firms (categories 5 and 6).

The idea of an ordered probit analysis is to assign a value v to each price change observation. According to expression (5) the probability of a price change will be influenced by changes in costs, changes in demand and the interaction of changes in costs and demand. In our particular application, for firm j at time t, let

$$v_{jt} = \gamma_1 c_{jt} + \gamma_2 d_{jt} + \gamma_3 c_{jt} * d_{jt} \tag{7}$$

where c = change in costs (c = 1 if costs = 'Up', c = 0 if costs = 'Same', c = -1 if costs = 'Down') and where d = change in demand (d = 1 if demand = 'Up', d = 0 if demand = 'Same', d = -1 if demand = 'Down') and where c*d is the interaction of changes in costs and demand experienced by firm j in quarter t. Let u be a standard normal variable (with zero mean and variance of one) and define three price change probabilities:

$$\Pr[p=-1 \mid c,d] = \Pr[v + u < k_1] = \Pr[u < k_1 - v] \tag{8}$$

$$\Pr[p= 0 \mid c,d] = \Pr[k_1 < v + u < k_2] = \Pr[k_1 - v < u < k_2 - v] \tag{9}$$

$$\Pr[p= 1 \mid c,d] = \Pr[k_2 < v + u] = \Pr[k_2 - v < u] \tag{10}$$

An ordered probit regression procedure estimates the coefficients γ_1, γ_2 and γ_3 and two additional 'cut-point' parameters k_1 and k_2 that maximize the likelihood of observing the actual sample of reported price changes. For more details about the ordered probit procedure, see Greene (1993) and Stata Corporation (1995).

Table 14.2 reports the results of ordered probit estimates of the coefficients γ_1 and γ_2 and the parameters k_1 and k_2 for small and large New Zealand manufacturing and building firms. The coefficient γ_3 was insignificant for both small and large firms and therefore the interactive variable c*d was dropped from the model estimation. The coefficients on cost and demand changes are highly significant for both small and large firms.

Table 14.2 - Ordered Probit Estimates of Influences of Cost and Demand Changes on Price Changes (Quarterly Observations: 1984:3 – 1996:1) ($v_{jt} = \gamma_1 c_{jt} + \gamma_2 d_{jt}$)

	Small Firms	**Large Firms**
No. Observations	2549	2646
γ_1	0.78 (19.10)*	0.59 (18.14)*
γ_2	0.37 (12.24)*	0.20 (7.33)*
k_1	- 0.95	- 0.85
k_2	1.05	0.60

Notes: z ratios are in parenthesis; * denotes significant at 1% level.

While the γ coefficients are much smaller for large firms than for small firms, the range of the cut points is also smaller. To assess the relative responsiveness of large and small firms to cost and demand changes, we need to convert these estimates into probabilities of price changes in response to specific cost and demand changes. For example, for small firms that report a cost increase (c=1) and no demand change (d=0), the probability of a price increase is given by the Pr $[0.78 + u > 1.05] = \Pr[u > 0.27] = 0.39$ where the last equality comes from a table of standard normal variables. These probabilities for small and large firms are shown in Table 14.3.

Table 14.3 - Conditional Probabilities of Price Changes
($\Pr[p= 1 \mid c,d] = \Pr[k_2 - v < u]$, $\Pr[p=-1 \mid c,d] = \Pr[u < k_1 - v]$)

	Small Firms	**Large Firms**
Pr[p=1| c=1, d=0]	0.39	0.50
Pr[p=1| c=0, d=1]	0.25	0.35
Pr[p=-1| c=-1, d=0]	0.43	0.40
Pr[p=-1| c=0, d=-1]	0.28	0.26

Notes; $v_{jt} = \gamma_1 c_{jt} + \gamma_2 d_{jt}$. Probabilities are based on estimates of the γ and k coefficients reported in Table 14.2.

In response to a cost increase, large firms have a 50% probability of raising price whereas small firms have only a 39% probability. In the case of a demand increase, large firms have a 35% probability of raising price and small firms 25%. Thus, as predicted, large firms are more likely to increase price in response to a cost increase or to a demand increase than small firms.

When there are cost or demand decreases, there is not much difference in the probabilities that large firms will lower price than small firms. In fact, small firms are slightly more likely to decrease price in response to a cost decrease or to a demand decrease than large firms. We had not expected that result. The shorter price duration for larger firms appears to be primarily because larger firms are quicker to respond to cost and demand increases than are smaller firms.

5 Frequency of Cost Changes and Firm Size

Larger firms may have more frequent price changes because they tend to have more frequent demand or cost changes than smaller firms. As can be seen in Table 14.1, there does not appear to be any notable differences in the frequency with which larger and smaller firms report demand changes, so this evidently does not contribute to the fact that larger firms change price more frequently than smaller firms.

The frequency of cost changes, however, does tend to increase as firm size increases. As shown in Table 14.1, the duration of costs, i.e., the average time in months between reported cost changes, is longer for smaller firms than for larger firms. The rank correlation is not perfect but the association is unlikely to have occurred by chance.

Does this mean that menu costs may be irrelevant and small firms change price less frequently because their costs change less frequently? While the frequency of relative cost changes may be part of the story about the frequency of relative price changes, the evidence indicates that it is a partial explanation at best. For one thing, cost changes occur more frequently than price changes for all sizes of firms. Furthermore, price duration relative to cost duration is much larger for small firms than for large firms. This is consistent with our menu cost hypothesis.

There is of course a question of why larger firms tend to report more frequent cost changes. Possible explanations include monopsony power and costs of negotiating input prices. The presence of monopsony power implies that changes in a firm's demand for production inputs will influence the price of those inputs and hence the firm's costs. If the degree of monopsony power increases with firm size we should expect to find, other things equal, that the sensitivity of input prices (and therefore a firm's costs) to changes in a firm's demand for production inputs will rise as the size of the firm increases.

Monopsony power implies that a firm has some discretion over the price it pays for production inputs. However there are likely to be costs to renegotiating input prices, for reasons similar to those that generate menu costs of output price adjustment. Firms that pay efficiency wages for example, will incur managerial decision and negotiation costs and will incur administration costs associated with introducing changes to wage rates and other agreed changes to the labour contract. If a significant component of total negotiation costs involve lump-sum costs, then negotiation costs per unit of output will fall as firm size increases. The way that negotiation costs influence input price rigidity and the duration of a firm's costs will be similar to the way menu costs influence the rigidity and duration of output prices.

Since we do not have a good test of this possibility, we leave it for now as a conjecture.

6 Conclusions

We have argued that if menu costs of changing prices have a sizeable lump-sum component, then costs of changing prices are smaller relative to the benefits of changing prices for larger firms. We therefore expect to find that larger firms make more frequent price changes. Evidence from surveys conducted by the New Zealand Institute of Economic Research support this prediction. In six different size categories, the average time between price changes falls monotonically as one moves from smaller to larger categories of firms.

An ordered probit analysis of price responsiveness to demand and cost changes shows that this shorter duration arises primarily because larger firms are more likely to raise price when costs are higher or when demand is higher than are smaller firms. It is not the case, however, that larger firms are more likely to lower price when reported costs or demand has fallen.

The frequency of reported demand changes is not systematically related to firm size so this cannot be a reason for the different price durations by firm size.

Larger firms do tend to report more frequent cost changes than smaller firms. This may be a partial explanation for the evidence that larger firms change prices more frequently. However, cost changes are more frequent than price changes for all sizes of firms, and smaller firms change price notably less frequently relative to the frequency of cost changes than do larger firms. This is consistent with our menu-cost argument.

References

Ball, Laurence and N. Gregory Mankiw (1994a), 'A sticky-price manifesto', *Carnegie-Rochester Conference Series on Public Policy*, 41, pp. 127-151.

Ball, Laurence and N. Gregory Mankiw (1994b), 'Asymmetric price adjustment and economic fluctuations', *Economic Journal*, 104, pp. 247-261.

Barro, Robert J. (1972), 'A theory of monopolistic price adjustment', *Review of Economic Studies*, 34, pp. 17-26.

Benassi, Corrado, Alessandra Chirco and Caterina Colombo (1994), *The New Keynesian Economics*, Oxford, Blackwell, pp. 458.

Blanchard, Olivier J. and Stanley Fischer (1989), *Lectures on Macroeconomics*, Cambridge, MIT Press, pp. 650.

Buckle, Robert A. and John A. Carlson (1996), 'Price duration with two-sided pricing rules', in Karl Heinrich Oppenländer and Günter Poser (eds), *Business cycle surveys: forecasting issues and methodological aspects*, Avebury, Aldershot, pp. 99-118.

Evans, Lewis, Arthur Grimes and Bryce Wilkinson with David Teece (1996), 'Economic Reform in New Zealand 1984 - 1995: The Pursuit of Efficiency', *Journal of Economic Literature*, 34, pp. 1856-1902.

Greene, William H (1993), *Econometric Analysis*, Second edition, New York, MacMillan.

Sheshinski, Eytan and Yoram Weiss (1977), 'Inflation and costs of price adjustment', *Review of Economic Studies*, 44, pp. 287-303.

Sheshinski, Eytan and Yoram Weiss (1983), 'Optimal pricing under stochastic inflation', *Review of Economic Studies*, 50, pp. 513-529.

Stata Corporation (1995), *Stata Statistical Software: Release 4.0*, College Station, Texas.

15 What Determines Firm Investment Intentions? Micro and Macro Analyses using Business Survey Data

ROBERT A. BUCKLE, DAVID HAUGH and PAUL RODWAY

Abstract

This paper investigates the forecast value and determinants of firm investment intentions collected by NZIER's business survey. Contemporaneous investment intentions data significantly improve the performance of autoregressive models of investment. Lagged intentions were not significant. Nevertheless, their short publication lag means they are a valuable leading indicator of investment. Estimates of 'micro' (using firm-level data and estimated by ordered probit) and 'macro' (using aggregate data and estimated by generalised least squares) models of investment intentions suggest Tobin's q, conditioned by a firm's financial situation, explains a large proportion of investment intentions. Some difference between large and small firms was detected.

1 Introduction

Investment spending is typically the most volatile component of aggregate demand in modern economies (Backus and Kehoe, 1992, Table 3, page 875). New Zealand is no exception (see Kim, Buckle and Hall, 1994, Table 1, page 60) and the latest business cycle has been a sharp reminder of this fact. A potentially valuable indicator of future investment spending is the NZ Institute of Economic Research's (NZIER) survey of business investment intentions. Each quarter the survey asks the same sample of firms the following question:

> *Do you expect the amount of new investment approved for your firm during the next twelve months to be greater / same / less than that approved during the past twelve months?*

The survey asks for responses under two categories: 'Buildings' (IIB) and 'Fixtures and fittings, plant and equipment' (IIP). Firms do not indicate the magnitude of change, only the direction of change.

Early research by Modigliani and Weingartner (1958), and subsequent studies by Lund, Martin and Bennett (1980) and Driver and Dowrick (1995) for example, have shown that anticipatory survey data can provide valuable information about future investment. However, apart from the early work of O'Dea (1980) and Ashley-Jones (1982), the value of survey data on investment intentions is relatively unexplored in the New Zealand context. The purpose of this paper is to partially fill that gap.

The first part of the paper evaluates whether investment intentions contain significant information about investment additional to the information contained in the past history of investment. This test is undertaken by first estimating an autoregressive model of investment and then evaluating whether the addition of investment intentions data improves the performance of this model. The results are presented in Section 2.

In the second part of the paper, having established there is some information value in investment intentions data, we evaluate whether the Tobin's q model, extended to capture the effect of a firm's internal financial position on desired investment, can explain investment intentions. The q model was chosen because of its theoretical attractiveness (Romer, 1996) and, while generally it has had mixed success in explaining investment behaviour, it has been found to work well as an explanation of aggregate New Zealand business investment in the years since financial deregulation (Murphy, 1998). Furthermore, when combined with firm balance-sheet information, the q model has also recently been successful in explaining business investment in the UK (Devereux and Schiantarelli, 1990), Australia (Mills, Morling and Tease, 1994) and the US (Kaplan and Zingales, 1997).

Two models of investment intentions are estimated: an ordered-probit ('micro') model using the micro firm data on investment intentions and indicators of their financial circumstances, and a generalised least squares ('macro') model using an aggregate measure of firm investment intentions and their financial circumstances. For the macro model, the Theil balance statistic (Theil, 1952) is used to aggregate firm responses.[1] The results are presented in Section 3. While methods used to aggregate survey data can affect the statistical properties of the resulting aggregate series (Batchelor, 1986), we nevertheless find that variables used to capture the finance-constrained q model are significant in both the micro and macro models. Section 4 contains concluding comments.

2 Do Investment Intentions Help to Explain Investment?

2.1 Investment Categories

In this section we evaluate whether firm investment intentions provide valuable information about future investment. The first step in this exercise requires an appropriate matching of the survey data with New Zealand System of National Accounts (SNA) investment data. Quarterly SNA private investment data are available only from 1982:2 and in six categories: residential buildings (RB), non-residential buildings (NRB), other construction (OC), land improvements (LI), transport equipment (T) and plant, machinery and equipment (PM). Table 15.1 shows summary statistics for these categories of private investment.

The NZIER survey respondents include manufacturers, builders, retailers, wholesalers and firms in the services sector. The survey does not cover government investment and there are some private sector categories not covered by the survey, notably households and agricultural producers. The survey is therefore unlikely to provide adequate coverage of residential buildings and land improvements investments. Also, other construction investment behaves very differently from buildings investment intentions, suggesting the survey does not adequately cover this category.

The survey provides better coverage of non-residential buildings, transport equipment and plant, machinery and equipment which sum to 65% of average total private investment. Figure 15.1 compares real non-residential buildings (NRB) with the survey-based Buildings investment intentions (IIB) and plant, machinery and equipment plus transport

[1] Suppose firms can respond to a survey question by marking one of the following: Up, Same, Down, N/A. The Theil balance statistic is derived by measuring the proportion of firms that mark each of these categories then deriving a net proportion as follows: [(%Up – %Down)/ (100 – %N/A)]*100.

equipment (PT) with the survey-based Fixtures and Fittings, Plant and Equipment investment intentions (IIP).

The survey question implies that the annual percentage change in investment is the appropriate measure to compare with the Theil balance statistic for investment intentions. It does not make clear whether respondents are expected to answer in terms of nominal or real investment. However, differences in the contemporaneous correlation coefficients between investment intentions balance statistics and the nominal and real series for the respective investment series are not significant. The contemporaneous correlation coefficients between the Theil balance statistics for intentions and annual percentage change in real investment for these two groups are 0.60 and 0.65 respectively.[2]

It is evident from Figure 15.1 that in general the Theil balance statistics for investment intentions follow very similar patterns to those exhibited by annual percentage changes in the respective investment series. There are nevertheless periods where they diverge substantially. The survey reported a fall in IIB in early 1987, whereas annual growth in NRB did not decline until mid 1988. Similarly, IIP declined sharply in December 1987 (after the sharemarket crash), and yet PT continued to grow until mid 1988. A similar divergence appears to have emerged during late 1997 and early 1998 when intentions continued to decline but this is not apparent in the investment series. In contrast, intentions remained high for several quarters after investment growth had started to decline in mid-1993. Furthermore, the sharp spike in PT growth during 1989 is not evident in the IIP series.

2.2 *Autoregressive Models of Investment*

A Granger causality procedure is used to determine whether investment intentions data contain significant information in addition to that which is contained in the past history of non-residential buildings (NRB) and plant, machinery and transport equipment (PT) investment. Autoregressive (AR) models are estimated for NRB and PT using SHAZAM (1993). Investment intentions data are then added to these initial models where the appropriate

---

2 This preliminary analysis involved a comparison of the change in the contemporaneous correlation coefficient between investment intentions and the annual percentage change in investment as the categories of investment were aggregated. The correlation coefficient between IIB and non-residential investment fell as the categories land improvements and other construction were added to non-residential investment. The correlation coefficient between IIP and plant and machinery investment growth increased when transport equipment was added to this category of investment.

lag length for investment intentions is chosen on the basis of the Akaike Information Criterion. The Granger test, an F test of the null hypothesis that the coefficients on the intentions series (and its lags if they are introduced) are zero in the second regression, is then performed to determine whether intentions contained significant additional information.

The AR model for NRB is a generalised least squares model estimated using the Cochrane-Orcutt procedure. For this model the 1st, 4th and 5th lags of NRB were significant. Diagnostic tests reveal no significant problems apart from evidence of heteroscedasticity. However the tests for heteroscedasticity are likely to be of low power because of the relatively small sample. The Granger test rejects the null hypothesis that the coefficient on buildings investment intentions (IIB) is zero and the model continues to satisfy the diagnostic tests after the inclusion of investment intentions data, apart from the tests for heteroscedasticity.

PT investment appears to follow an AR(1) process. The initial model fails the Ramsey Reset test at R(3) and R(4) and the B-P-G (Breusch-Pagan-Godfrey) test, but other diagnostic tests reveal no other significant problems. The addition of investment intentions (IIP) to the model results in the Ramsey Reset and the B-P-G[3] tests being satisfied and the Granger test rejects the null hypothesis that investment intentions have no influence on PT investment. The Jarque-Bera statistic testing for normally distributed residuals however now exceeds the 5% critical value.

These results are summarised in Table 15.2. The presence of a first-order lag in both the NRB and PT models is not surprising in view of the time-to-build that occurs with investment decisions. The presence of the 4th and 5th order lags in the model for NRB suggests seasonal effects. On the basis of the Granger test, investment intentions are found to contain significant information about investment. Although only contemporaneous intentions are significant and not their lags, they are typically published at least two months ahead of the SNA investment data and therefore have some value as a leading indicator of investment.

3 The possibility of heteroscedasticity was detected in the initial model which was then re-estimated using White's heteroscedasticity-corrected variances.

3 Modelling Investment Intentions

3.1 Tobin's q, Financial Constraints and Firm Investment

This section investigates possible determinants of investment intentions. Tobin's q theory of investment is the basic model used for this investigation. A key assumption of the Tobin's (marginal) q model is that firms face costs of adjusting their capital stock so there can exist a gap between the market value of the firm and the replacement cost of the capital of the firm. Tobin's q is a measure of this gap. A firm increases its capital stock if the market value of capital exceeds what it costs to acquire it and decreases its capital stock if the market value of the capital is less than what it costs to replace it.

Because marginal q is more difficult to observe than average q, Hayashi (1982) identified a set of necessary and sufficient conditions for marginal q to be equal to average q. These revolve around requiring linear homogeneity in the production function and in the capital installation function. Under these conditions, the q model can be expressed as follows:

$$I_{i,t}/K_{i,t-1} = \alpha_i + \beta q_{i,t} + \varepsilon_{i,t}; \beta > 0 \quad (1)$$

where i denotes the firm and t the time period; I and K represent investment and the capital stock, respectively; q is the tax-adjusted value of Tobin's (average) q; α_i is a firm specific constant representing the long-run normal value of the investment-capital ratio; and ε is an error term. The value of the coefficient β is inversely related to the marginal cost of adjusting the capital stock.

Despite its theoretical attractiveness, the q theory of investment has had a generally disappointing empirical performance. For example, Hayashi uses annual US data from 1953-76 to regress the ratio of investment to capital stock (I/K) on a linear function of (tax-adjusted) q. This regression explains about half the variation in I/K and has high positive serial correlation. Other researchers have tried hybrid specifications incorporating accelerator-type current income variables or lagged I/K along with the q term. For example, using quarterly Australian data, McKibbin and Siegloff (1988) use a specification where a portion of business investment is explainable by q theory and the reminder by firms basing their investment decision on current output (accelerator).

A potential reason for the disappointing performance of the q theory is that firms' balance-sheet positions may limit their ability to realise their preferred capital-stock positions. In the absence of asymmetric information between firms and external capital markets, all available information to guide a firm's investment decision is summarized in q which shows how an additional dollar of capital affects the present value of profits. A firm's balance sheet and internal cash positions should have no incremental influence over q. In the presence of capital-market imperfections, however, expression (1) should be modified to capture the additional effect of a firm's internal financial position as follows (see Devereux and Schiantarelli, 1990):

$$I_{i,t}/K_{i,t-1} = \alpha_i + \beta q_{i,t} + \gamma_1(C_{i,t}/K_{i,t-1}) + \gamma_2(L_{i,t}/K_{i,t-1}) + \gamma_3(B_{i,t}/K_{i,t-1}) + \varepsilon_{i,t};$$
$$\beta > 0;\ \gamma_1,\ \gamma_2 > 0;\ \gamma_3 < 0 \qquad (2)$$

where $C_{i,t}$ is the cash flow, $L_{i,t}$ the stock of liquid assets and $B_{i,t}$ the stock of debt for firm i in period t.

The sensitivity of investment to a firm's financial position can be explained by the fact that, in the presence of asymmetric information, external funds are more costly than internal funds. This wedge between internal and external funds may be caused by hidden information problems, as in Myers and Majluf (1984) or Greenwald, Stiglitz and Weiss (1984); or agency problems, as in Jensen and Meckling (1976), Grossman and Hart (1982), Jensen (1986), and Hart and Moore (1995).

Following Kaplan and Zingales (1997), we assume that for all firms the total cost of raising external funds increases in the amount of funds raised and in the extent of the agency or information problems. This strategy avoids the need to form an *a priori* view about which firms are likely to be finance-constrained. The possible effects of agency or information costs on investment are instead captured by including information about the internal financial position of firms. This strategy is similar to the panel-data studies by Devereux and Schiantarelli (1990), Mills, Morling and Tease (1994) and Kaplan and Zingales (1997). In contrast to these studies, however, we use qualitative business survey data to obtain indicators of firms' internal financial circumstances.

3.2 Estimation of Micro and Macro Models of Investment Intentions

Based on these ideas, the following model of investment intentions was estimated:

$$II_{i,t} = \alpha_i + \beta q_{i,t} + \gamma'_1 Plsfg_{i,t} + \gamma'_2 Odd_{i,t} + \gamma'_3 Dnz_{i,t} + u_{i,t};$$
$$\beta > 0,\ \gamma'_1 < 0,\ \gamma'_2 < 0,\ \gamma'_3 > 0 \qquad (3)$$

where II is the change in a firm's investment intentions and Plsfg, Odd and Dnz are indicators of the change in a firm's financial position. These data are all from the NZIER's business survey. q is a measure of Tobin's q; u is a random error term.

We do not have observations for the level of each firm's capital stock (K in expressions (1) and (2)). The use of investment intentions data is a way to overcome this problem because a rise/fall in investment intentions implies a rise/fall in the $I_{i,t}/K_{i,t-1}$ ratio.[4]

Ideally, q would be derived for each firm in our sample based on appropriate micro firm financial data such as that used by Devereux and Schiantarelli (1990), Mills, Morling and Tease (1994) and Kaplan and Zingales (1997). However, at this point we do not have access to data suitable for this purpose. Instead, we use a measure of Tobin's average q derived from the New Zealand Model 1998 (NZM98), a macroeconomic model of the New Zealand economy developed by Murphy (1998).

In NZM98, Tobin's (average) q is derived as the ratio of capitalised future returns, net of variable costs, to the cost of building a unit of capital. Tobin's q is expressed in difference form so that equilibrium occurs when the actual rate of return equals the required rate of return (i.e. $q = 0$). A value of $q > 0$ will raise investment spending and a value of $q < 0$ will lower investment spending. The actual rate of return is the nominal value of model-determined output less the value of production inputs scaled by the nominal value of the capital stock. The required rate of return depends on the real interest rate (the 10-year bond rate less expected inflation), the depreciation rate and a risk premium for holding equity over bonds. This measure of q is therefore an aggregate measure based on the NZM98 model data which are ultimately derived from the aggregate SNA data. It does not reflect firm-specific differences for the sample of firms covered by the NZIER survey.

Similarly, we do not have direct observations of each firm's cash flow, stock of liquid assets and stock of debt (variables C, L and B in expression (2)). Instead, a firm's responses to the following questions in the NZIER's survey are used to indicate the change in their financial position:

---

4 Note $I_t / K_{t-1} = (K_t - K_{t-1}) / K_{t-1} = (K_t / K_{t-1}) - 1$. Now $II_t > II_{t-1} \Rightarrow K_t > K_{t-1} \Rightarrow I_t / K_{t-1}$ increases, provided II is an accurate indicator of the change in net investment spending.

What has been your firm's experience during the past three months ... in respect of the following:

Deliveries in New Zealand: Up / Same / Down / N/A

Overdue debtors: Up / Same / Down / N/A

Do you consider your present level of stock of finished goods to be: Too high / Satisfactory / Too low / N/A

In expression (3), Dnz denotes Deliveries in New Zealand, Odd, Overdue debtors, while Plsfg denotes the Present level of stocks of finished goods. These variables are more likely to indicate the change in a firm's cash flow and stock of liquid assets rather than the change in their stock of debt. Responses of 'Too low' to the question on Plsfg, 'Down' to Odd and 'Up' to Dnz are each interpreted as an improvement in the firm's cash flow and liquid asset positions. The converse interpretation holds for firms responding 'Too high' to the question on Plsfg, 'Up' to Odd and 'Down' to Dnz.

The impact on investment intentions is interpreted as follows. Firms responding 'Too low' to Plsfg are expected to have a higher probability of an increase in investment intentions, for a given value for q, than firms responding 'Too high' to the Plsfg question. Similar interpretations apply for the corresponding responses to Odd and Dnz.

As in the case with responses to the investment intentions question, firms do not indicate the magnitude of change, only the direction of change. The responses to these questions are coded 'Up' and 'Too high' = 1, 'Same' and 'Satisfactory' = 0, and 'Down' and 'Too low' = -1. Firms that did not respond to these questions and the investment intentions question were dropped from the sample.

Table 15.3 presents the results of ordered probit and generalised least squares (GLS) estimates of expression (3). The ordered probit model is estimated using the individual firm survey responses to investment intentions (II), Plsfg, Odd and Dnz. The ordered probit procedure estimates the coefficients β, γ'_1, γ'_2, and γ'_3, and two additional 'cut-point' parameters k_1 and k_2 that maximize the likelihood of observing the actual sample of reported investment intentions. The programme used for this purpose was Stata Corporation (1995). The GLS model is estimated using quarterly Theil balance statistics for these variables. The programme used for this purpose was SHAZAM (1993). The models are estimated using the NZM98-based measure of Tobin's q. Both models are estimated for the same sample of manufacturing and building firms surveyed by the NZIER and for the post-deregulation period 1985:4 to 1998:2.

From Table 15.3, it is clear that our aggregate measure of Tobin's q has a significant influence on investment intentions. This conclusion holds for both the ordered probit model and the GLS model. Furthermore, in the ordered probit model the coefficients on all the indicators of a firm's internal financial position are significant and have the expected sign. In the GLS model, Dnz and Odd are also significant and have the expected sign. However, Plsfg is not significant (and has the wrong sign for IIP).

3.3 Large and Small Firms

A research strategy common in the literature is to divide a sample of firms according to an *a priori* measure of financing constraints (e.g. dividend-payout ratios as used by Fazzari, Hubbard and Petersen, 1988 or membership in a *keiretsu*, or large industrial group, as used by Hoshi, Kashyap and Scharfstein, 1991), and then compare the investment-cash flow sensitivities of the different sub-samples. However, while it can be shown that investment by constrained firms should be sensitive to internal cash flow, Kaplan and Zingales (1997) point out that it is not necessarily true that the magnitude of the sensitivity increases with the degree of financing constraint.

Nevertheless, Devereux and Schiantarelli (1990) and Mills, Morling and Tease (1994) provide evidence that firm size may affect investment behaviour. Gertler and Gilchrist (1994) find that small firms account for a significantly disproportionate share of the decline in manufacturing sales and inventory demand in the US that follows a shift to tight monetary conditions. They attribute this finding to differences between the access of small and large firms to capital markets. Differences between small and large firms are not as clear in a similar study of Canadian firms by Kuszczak and Orcheson (1994).

The idea that size affects a firm's access to capital markets and its reliance on internally generated funds suggests that the behaviour of investment intentions may vary by firm size. In particular, if this hypothesis is true, we should find that investment intentions for large firms are less responsive than for small firms to changes in their internal financial position.

Our preliminary investigation of this idea involved first selecting large and small firms from the NZIER survey based on their responses to the following question:

How many employees are covered by this return?

Firms with more than 200 employees were classified as large, and those with fewer than 51 employees classified as small. Expression (3) was then estimated using the ordered-probit procedure and an interactive dummy variable (Dum = 1 for large firms, Dum = 0 for small firms) was introduced to evaluate whether there is a significant difference in the response of investment intentions to the variables q, Plsfg, Odd and Dnz.

The results of the ordered probit estimates comparing the responsiveness of investment intentions for large and small firms are presented in Table 15.4. There is evidence to suggest that investment intentions of large firms are less sensitive than small firms to inventories departing from the preferred levels (Plsfg*Dum). This is consistent with the idea that investment intentions of larger firms are less sensitive to the firm's internal financial position. But there is no evidence of a significant difference in the way investment intentions of larger firms respond to the other variables. The coefficients on the shift dummy variable Dum and the interactive dummy variables for q, Odd and Dnz are not significant.

4 Conclusions

Using a Granger procedure, we find that firm's investment intentions data collected by the NZIER survey contain significant information about investment. However, only contemporaneous intentions and not their lags are significant. Nevertheless, the intentions data have a shorter publication lag than the SNA investment data which means they are a valuable leading indicator of investment.

Our preliminary investigation suggests that the Tobin's q model, perhaps also conditioned by a firm's internal financial position and access to external capital markets, successfully explains investment intentions. Tobin's q was found to be highly significant in the micro model estimated using individual firm data on investment intentions and the macro model estimated using an aggregate measure of intentions. The variables used to approximate the internal financial position of a firm were significant in most cases. There is also evidence to suggest that compared to smaller firms, investment intentions of larger firms are less sensitive to their internal financial circumstances.

Our test of the Tobin's q hypothesis and the effects of financial conditions is limited by the availability of suitable financial data about the firms in our sample. The measure of Tobin's q used in this study is an aggregate measure derived from the NZM98 model of the New Zealand economy. While this may be a satisfactory measure of q for estimating of our macro model, it is not ideal for estimating the micro model. Furthermore, although the indicators of a firm's financial conditions used in this study are the responses by firms in our sample to the NZIER survey, they are not direct measures of changes in a firm's cash flow and stock of liquid assets.

Despite considerable theoretical and empirical research in recent years showing that balance-sheet variables significantly influence firm behaviour and the business cycle, there remains a paucity of suitable firm-level information about firms' balance sheets. This is an area where suitably designed business surveys could make a significant contribution by generating timely indicators of firms' financial conditions and by providing a stronger foundation for economic research about firm behaviour.

5 Appendix - Tables and Figures

Table 15.1 - New Zealand SNA Investment Categories (1982:2 – 1998:2)

Investment Category	Residential Buildings	Non-Residential Buildings	Other Construc-tion	Land Improve-ments	Transport Equipment	Plant, Machinery and Equipment	Total
Mean ($m)	817	417	148	42	391	1,062	2,877
Share of total private investment (%)	28.4	14.5	5.1	1.5	13.6	36.9	100
Standard deviation ($m)	151.2	123.4	52.6	16.8	108.6	389.4	693.2
Coefficient of variation (%)	18.5	29.6	35.5	40.3	27.8	36.7	24.1

Table 15.2 - Autoregressive Models of Investment

Investment Category :		Non- Residential Buildings (NRB) (1984:3 - 1998:2)		Plant, Machinery And Transport (PT) Equipment 1998:2) (1983:3 -	
AR Model :		AR	AR + IIB	AR	AR + IIP
Constant		0.70 (0.47)	8.53* (3.71)	2.69 (1.97)	4.38* (2.79)
NRB_{t-1}		0.98* (12.70)	0.83* (10.80)	-	-
NRB_{t-4}		-0.55* (-4.26)	-0.58* (-5.16)	-	-
NRB_{t-5}		0.44* (3.76)	0.50* (4.85)	-	-
PT_{t-1}		-	-	0.66* (5.69)	0.44* (4.20)
IIB_t		-	0.42* (4.12)	-	-
IIP_t		-	-	-	0.34* (3.73)
Observations		56	56	60	60
Diagnostic tests:	Null hypothesis (5% critical value)				
Adjusted R^2		0.59	0.68	0.45	0.55
F statistic	4.08	-	16.10*	-	13.94*
Durbin h	No 1st order AC (+/-1.96)	0.75	-0.03	0.02	-0.22
LM (8)	No higher order AC (χ^2=15.5)	9.81	6.36	7.20	7.40
Jarque-Bera	Residuals normal (χ^2=5.99)	3.52	2.85	4.59	8.64
Ramsey Reset	No mis-specification				
R(2)	(F=4.0)	0.24	0.22	3.23	1.95
R(3)	(F=3.15)	0.34	0.14	5.25	1.03
R(4)	(F=2.76)	0.41	0.10	4.55	0.72
ARCH	No ARCH (χ^2=3.84)	5.97	5.18	0.58	0.00
B-P-G	Homoscedasticity (in brackets)	15.63 (7.81)	15.63 (9.49)	5.18 (3.84)	3.95 (5.99)

* Significant at 5% level and t statistics in parenthesis.

Table 15.3 - Ordered Probit and GLS Models of Investment Intentions (1985:4 – 1998:2)

Ordered Probit Generalised Least Squares					
Explanatory variables:		IIB	IIP	IIB	IIP
q_t		18.20* (3.00)	23.07* (2.99)	7.75* (2.52)	9.50* (2.29)
$Plsfg_t$		-0.12* (-0.03)	-0.13* (-0.03)	-0.05 (-0.35)	0.12 (0.71)
Odd_t		-0.05* (-0.02)	-0.14* (-0.02)	-0.17** (-1.68)	-0.24** (-1.72)
Dnz_t		0.25* (0.02)	0.31* (0.02)	0.32* (4.27)	0.57* (5.86)
Constant		-	-	-0.29* (-4.83)	-0.15* (-1.86)
ρ		-	-	0.48* (3.88)	0.48* (3.93)
k_2 / k_2		-0.05 / 1.23	-0.13 / 0.84	-	-
Observations		5707	5707	51	51
Diagnostic tests:	Null hypothesis (5% critical value)				
Log likelihood		-5676.05	-6020.54	-	-
χ^2 (4)		268.70	427.81	-	-
Adjusted R^2		-	-	0.80	0.84
Durbin h	No 1st order AC (+/-1.96)	-	-	0.38	1.35
LM (8)	No higher order AC (χ^2=15.5)	-	-	8.50	13.00
Jarque-Bera	Residuals normal (χ^2=5.99)	-	-	0.69	0.67
Ramsey Reset	No mis-specification				
R (2)	(F=4.0)	-	-	0.20	0.26
R(3)	(F=3.15)	-	-	0.06	0.14
R(4)	(F=2.76)	-	-	0.21	0.16
ARCH	No ARCH (χ^2=3.84)	-	-	0.14	2.13
B-P-G	Homoscedasticity (χ^2=9.49)	-	-	4.65	10.27

Notes: The table reports the ordered probit and generalised least squares estimates of the coefficients and z values (for the ordered probit estimates) and t values (for the GLS estimates), where * denotes the coefficient is significant at 5% level and ** at the 10% level.

Table 15.4 - Ordered Probit Comparison of Large and Small Firms

(1985:4 – 1998:2)

Explanatory variables:	**IIB**	**IIP**
Q_t	20.83* (3.82)	26.99* (4.94)
$Plsfg_t$	-0.13* (-2.47)	-0.19* (-3.75)
Odd_t	-0.05 (-1.30)	-0.11* (-2.56)
Dnz_t	0.32* (8.10)	0.37* (9.41)
Dum	-0.10 (-0.85)	0.02 (0.13)
Q_t*Dum*	-2.14 (-0.29)	-1.41 (-0.19)
$Plsfg_t$*Dum*	0.00 (0.05)	0.12** (1.83)
Odd_t*Dum*	0.02 (0.30)	-0.01 (-0.12)
Dnz_t*Dum*	-0.05 (-0.91)	-0.07 (-1.30)
Observations	3831	3831
K_1 / k_2	-0.08 / 1.20	-0.08 / 0.93
Log likelihood	-3788.59	-4015.87
χ^2 (9)	233.53	324.74

Notes: The table reports the ordered probit estimates of the coefficients and z values (in parenthesis) where * denotes the coefficient is significant at 5% level and ** at the 10% level. Dum = 1 if firms are large (employees > 200), Dum = 0 if firms are small (employees < 51).

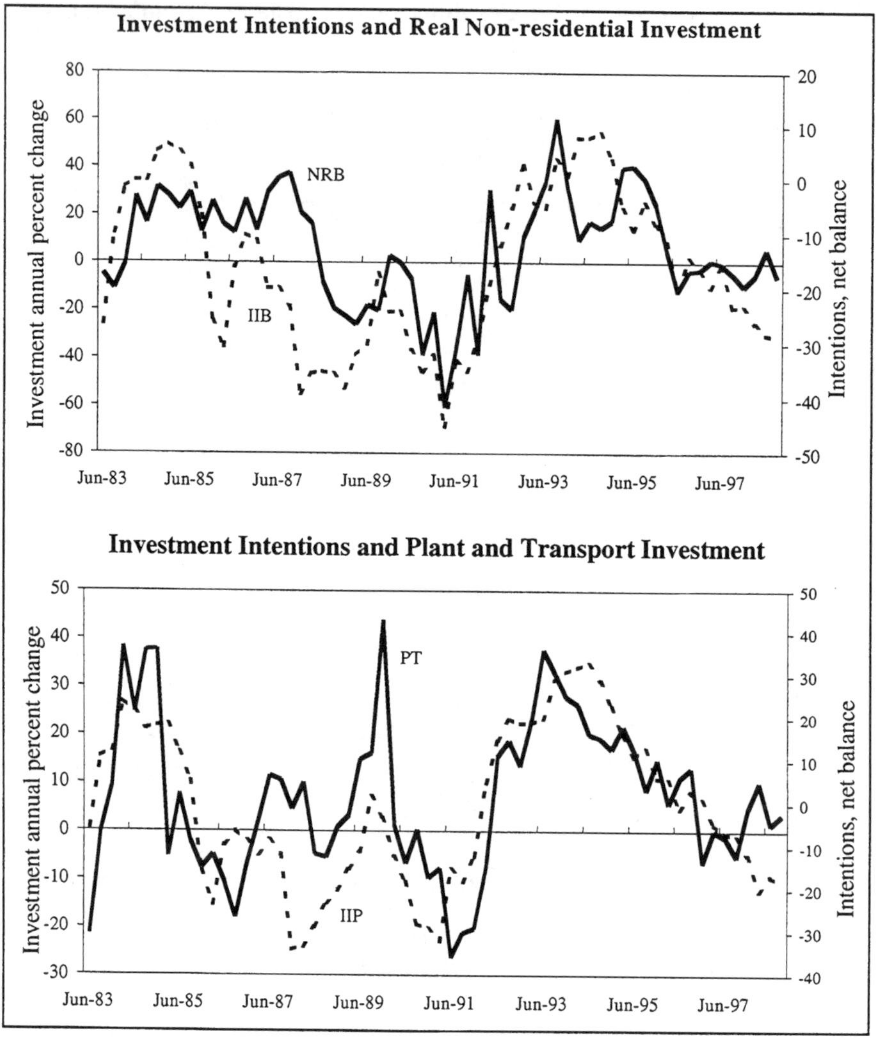

Figure 15.1 - Comparison of Investment Intentions and Investment

References

Ashley-Jones, C. (1982), 'Using business opinion: Investment intentions', *Quarterly Survey of Business Opinion*, No. 86, September, pp. 2–5.

Backus, D. K. and P. J. Kehoe (1992), 'International evidence on the historical properties of business cycles', *American Economic Review*, 82, pp. 864–888.

Batchelor, R. A. (1986), 'Quantitative v. qualitative measures of inflation expectations', *Oxford Bulletin of Economics and Statistics*, 48, pp. 99-120.

Devereux, M. and F. Schiantarelli (1990), 'Investment, financial factors and cash flow: Evidence from U.K. panel data', Chapter 11 in R. Glenn Hubbard (ed), *Asymmetric information, corporate finance and investment*, NBER Project Report, Chicago, University of Chicago press, pp. 281–306.

Driver, C. and S. Dowrick (1995), 'Investment intentions and investment realisations in Australian manufacturing', Centre for Economic Policy Research Discussion Paper No 326, May, pp. 18.

Fazzari, S. R., R. G. Hubbard and B. Petersen (1988), 'Financing constraints and corporate investment', *Brookings Papers on Economic Activity*, pp. 141-195.

Gertler, M. and S. Gilchrist (1994), 'Monetary policy, business cycles, and the behaviour of small and large firms', *Quarterly Journal of Economics*, 109, pp. 309-340.

Greenwald, B., J. Stiglitz and A. Weiss (1984), 'Information imperfections and macroeconomic fluctuations', *American Economic Review*, 74, pp. 194-199.

Grossman, S. and O. Hart. (1982), 'Corporate financial structure and managerial incentives', in J. J. McCall (ed), *The Economics of Information and Uncertainty*, Chicago, University of Chicago Press.

Hart, O. and J. Moore (1995), 'Debt and seniority: An analysis of the role of hard claims in constraining management', *American Economic Review*, 85, pp. 567–585.

Hayashi, F. (1982), 'Tobin's marginal 'q' and average 'q': A neoclassical interpretation', *Econometrica*, 50, pp. 213-224.

Hoshi, T., A. Kashyap and D. Scharfstein (1991), 'Corporate structure, liquidity and investment: Evidence from Japanese panel data', *Quarterly Journal of Economics*, 104, pp. 33-60.

Jensen, M. (1986), 'Agency costs of free cash flow, corporate finance and takeovers', *American Economic Review*, 76, pp. 323–329.

Jensen, M. and W. Meckling (1976), 'The theory of the firm: Managerial behaviour, agency costs and ownership structure', *Journal of Financial Economics,* 3, pp. 305–360.

Kaplan, S. N. and L. Zingales (1997), 'Do investment-cash flow sensitivities provide useful measures of financing constraints?', *Quarterly Journal of Economics*, 110, pp. 169-215.

Kim, K. H, R. A. Buckle and V. B. Hall (1994), 'Key features of New Zealand business cycles', *The Economic Record*, 70, pp. 56–72.

Kuszczak, J. and P. Orcheson (1994), 'Does business asset size matter? Evidence from Canadian data', in *Credit, interest rates spreads and the monetary policy transmission mechanism*, Proceedings of a Conference held at the Bank of Canada, Ottawa, Bank of Canada, November, pp. 115–147.

Lund, P. J., W. E. Martin and A. Bennett (1980), 'Price expectations and their role in the analysis of the UK Department of Industry's investment intentions inquiries', *Journal of Industrial Economics*, March, pp. 225–239.

McKibbin, W. J. and E. S. Siegloff (1988), 'A note on aggregate investment in Australia', *Economic Record,* 64, September, pp. 209–215.

Mills, K., S. Morling and W. Tease (1994), 'The influence of financial factors on corporate investment', Reserve Bank of Australia Discussion Paper 9402, May, pp. 24.

Modigliani, I. and H. M. Weingartner (1958), 'Forecasting uses of anticipatory data for investment and sales', *Quarterly Journal of Economics*, 72, pp. 23-54.

Murphy, C. (1998), *New Zealand Model 1998 (NZM98)*, Report Commissioned by the New Zealand Treasury, June, pp. 52.

Myers, S. and N. Majluf (1984), 'Corporate financing and investment decisions when firms have information that investors do not have', *Journal of Financial Economics*, 13, pp. 187-221.

O'Dea, D. (1980), 'Business expectations and investment intentions', *Quarterly Predictions,* June, pp. 35–40.

Romer, D. (1996), *Advanced Macroeconomics*, New York, McGraw-Hill, pp. 540.

SHAZAM (1993), *User's Reference Manual Version 7,* New York, McGraw-Hill.

Stata Corporation (1995), *Stata Statistical Software: Release 4.0*, College Station, Texas.

Theil, H. (1952), 'On the time shape of economic microvariables and the Munich Business Test', *Review of the International Statistical Institute*, 20, pp. 105–120.

16 Irreversibility and Uncertainty: An Empirical Analysis on Italian Firms' Investment Decisions

PAOLO CARNAZZA and GIUSEPPE TRAVAGLINI

Abstract

The aim of this paper is to analyse the problems caused by the co-existence of different degrees of capital irreversibility, which may characterize firms' investment activity. In Spring 1998, ISAE carried out a specific survey on a panel of about 1,200 Italian manufacturing firms within its traditional bi-annual investment survey.

The study develops on both a theoretical and an empirical ground. Specifically, in the first part, after a discussion on the 'real option theory' of investment, the main factors affecting selling decisions of capital goods on the secondary market are investigated. The influence of the uncertainty-irreversibility mix on the future economic activity is then examined and its effects on investment projects are taken into account. In its last part, the analysis focuses on some industrial policy measures which might increase flexibility in capital goods secondary markets.

1 Introduction

A great part of recent literature has emphasized the role of capital irreversibility in influencing firms' investment decisions. The main result stemming from those contributions is that, in the presence of uncertainty and irreversibility,[1] entrepreneurs would rather postpone new investment projects. Indeed, if investment is a sunk-cost, investing at present may imply an opportunity cost, as it takes away the *option* of investing in the future, when more information about the plan profitability can be gained. However, no definitive answers have been found so far on empirical ground for the effects of uncertainty on firms' investment decisions;[2] moreover no convincing empirical analysis has yet been developed on the causes and consequences of irreversibility.

The aim of this paper is to provide empirical evidence to evaluate the effects of the uncertainty-irreversibility combination on firms' investment. To this end, we use the statistical information drawn from a specific survey ISAE carried out in its 1998 spring bi-annual investment survey.[3] The resort to a specific survey confirms the importance of business surveys while dealing not only with short-term economic analyses but also with structural phenomena.

The paper is organized as follows. In the next section the recent theoretical problems caused by irreversibility and uncertainty are summarized (Section 2). In the third section the survey's structure is examined (Section 3) while in the fourth section the main results are discussed (Section 4). In order to extrapolate relevant information, different kinds of reading are employed: sectorial classification; the Pavitt taxonomy; dimensional features and, finally, aggregation by geographical area.

The results focus on the different degrees of capital irreversibility according to firms' opinions on 'irreversibility'. Furthermore, the influence of the uncertainty-irreversibility combination on the future economic activity is examined and its effects on the current evaluation of investment projects are taken into account. Finally, an attempt to measure the degree of predictability of the main economic variables affecting firms' strategic decisions is carried out (Section 5). In the final part of the paper some possible measures of economic policy aimed at reducing the degree of

---

1 Irreversibility denotes the degree of availability of firms to disposing of installed capital assets.

2 A first contribution is a recent survey by Guiso and Parigi (1996) carried out among italian firms.

3 The survey was elaborated by ISCO; at the beginning of 1999, a new Institute (Istituto di Studi e Analisi Economica – Institute for Studies and Economic Analyses, ISAE) was created from the merging of two existing research Institutes (ISCO and ISPE). It is worth noting, however, that most functions carried out by ISCO (mainly consumer and business surveys developed within the European harmonization scheme) have been and will be continued by ISAE.

capital goods irreversibility are suggested (Section 6). These measures might encourage private investment with further positive effects on employment and growth.

2 Uncertainty and Irreversibility

The agreement on both the nature and the sign of the investment-uncertainty correlation is scarce, depending on a great number of factors, such as the degree of market competitiveness, their completeness, and, among other features, the nature of the capital stock, i.e. whether it is a commitment or a flexible factor for production (Hartman 1972, Abel 1983, Bertola 1988).

On theoretical grounds, the question is relative to the property of the investment-uncertainty correlation to be a positive or a negative relation. In the Keynesian world, this relation is certainly negative. In turn, in Jorgenson's model - which is the basis of the neoclassical investment theory - a positive correlation is assumed.[4] Certainly, this latest statement may appear bizarre while looking at the statistical report of the macroeconomic time series, which generally labels as 'stylized fact' the tendency of the aggregate flow of investment to slow down in presence of rising uncertainty: periods of high variability in real and financial markets are hardly perceived as good times.

In this perspective, the previous statement must be qualified saying that perfect, complete and competitive markets are required in order to assure a positive relation between investment and uncertainty. Furthermore, the completeness and efficiency of markets imply the reversibility of any investment decisions, hence the property of the capital stock – once acquired - to be easily re-sold, without losses. Indeed, irreversibility may be an essential element in many capital accumulation decisions and firms' choices might be constrained when capital stock is mostly irreversible. For example, in an uncertain world with emerging information, the firm may rather postpone its investment decisions, adopting a flexible position and waiting before taking the final choice. When irreversible investment can be postponed, it is customary to say that the firm holds a real *option* on the

4 In Jorgenson's model, the profit function is a convex function of stochastic variables. More precisely, if profits' volatility depends on the random behavior of prices, the expected profit is an increasing function of variance. This property follows solely from the assumption of profit maximization, and it means that, if the expected cash stream increases with volatility, then a rising economic instability might be desirable for firms.

investment plan.[5] Such an *option* is the value of the flexibility for taking decisions about real irreversible investments at some future date (Bernanke 1983, McDonald-Siegel 1986, Pindyck 1991).

2.1 The Investment Strategies

Traditionally, any investment strategy is considered in isolation. The firm faces a binary investment problem, whose set of feasible actions is *invest in the project immediately* if the net present value (NPV) is positive or *renounce the investment* for ever whenever the NPV is negative. Unlike this one-shot game, if the firm can defer the immediate choice, any irreversible project can actually be seen as a chain of subsequent investment choices. The set of strategies encompasses a sequence of tactical investment plans providing alternative net present values, depending on the date when the real *option* is abandoned in favour of the stock. Clearly, the value of this flexible property affects the current global value and the risk of any time-dependent investment. Hence, the expected profitability of any prospect is determined by the trade-off between the cost of waiting, that is renouncing to gain the current profit, and the cost of irreversibility, i.e. the potential loss suffered from wrong early commitment. As a consequence, the firm may find it convenient to quit the flexible position only when the present value of the contingent project overcomes the global cost given by the direct cost of investment plus the *option* value.

One aspect worth stressing is that the uncertainty-irreversibility mix introduces a further temporal element in the investment decision problem, notably the moment chosen to make a new investment or to expand the existing activity. Since the intertemporal investment profile changes dramatically because of the *option* property, the aim of this paper is to evaluate to what extent firms' investment decisions are affected by irreversibility, and which policies can make real investment more flexible. The main point here is that factors' flexibility may induce a higher investment ratio and, consequently, a higher growth rate of the real activity as a whole.

---

[5] This term derives from the fact that, in the presence of irreversibility, any investment opportunity is like a financial call option on a dividend-paying asset.

2.2 *Causes of Irreversibility*

Before presenting our results, it is worth pointing out the main factors causing capital to be irreversible.

For capital-specific firms, the real asset is a sunk-cost because, once new capital units are installed, they cannot be re-sold to any other industry or firm. This is the case of productive sectors with capital-intensive technology. This difficulty may also arise in the presence of imperfect information on the quality of second-hand capital goods and/or about the number of firms which are adopting the same technology. More precisely, with asymmetric information, the quality of second-hand goods is not perfectly mirrored in prices, and the average selling price on the secondary market may be so low, that agents can find it convenient to take back the high quality assets from the market. When this happens, the market becomes very 'thin' and the capital good behaves like an irreversible factor.

Traditionally, the degree of irreversibility is considered an exogenous element. Obviously, this is a simplified assumption, since the value of any real asset can be strictly related to the different phases of the economic cycle. From this perspective, the reversible characteristics of any real investment can change with the pattern of macroeconomic activity and a capital good which is reversible now may become irreversible in periods of recession and depression. In fact, in bad times the opportunity cost to renew the capital equipment can be very high because the depressed demand in the secondary market may cause old capital prices to be low and unfair. Consequently, with endogenous irreversible projects, the role of uncertainty can be amplified since firms suffer unexpected losses from the foregoing commitment.[6]

Furthermore, the degree of competitiveness may affect the *option* value of any investment strategy. Indeed, when potential competitors can act, the non-investing choice might give entrants the chance to take the opportunity. Hence, the implicit advantage to defer investment is counterbalanced by the risk to loose the market. Moreover, under imperfect competition, the decision to implement the investment has preemptive effects, implying that immediate investment may discourage competitors. Thus, the essential idea is that imperfect competition cuts down the *option* value without affecting the current investment dynamics.

---

6 For a more detailed analysis on the main causes of irreversibility, see Travaglini (1996). Some of the causes will be examined in this paper basing on empirical grounds.

3 The Survey's Structure

The analysis is based on ISAE data on Italian industrial firms. More precisely, the evidence is drawn from an *ad hoc* survey carried out within the 1998 spring bi-annual investment survey, through a questionnaire mailed to almost 4,000 firms.[7] There were almost 1,200 firms participating with a total of almost 300,000 employees. Most firms interviewed (70%) have less than 100 employees; 23% concerns a number of employees between 100 and 499; the remainder is related to large firms. The percentage of respondents to the specific survey on irreversibility and uncertainty has been quite high (almost 85%).

The replies' aggregation has been obtained by adopting as weights the number of employees and the percentage of sectoral value added. Results related to firms' size and geographical area have been computed by weighting only the number of employees.

The questionnaire contains a vast array of questions, mainly of qualitative nature, aimed at deepening some aspects related to firms' investment decisions, with the aim of clarifying, on empirical grounds, some disputed aspects of the economic theory. The questionnaire is divided into three sections.

In the first section, firms are asked to give detailed information on their degree of capital irreversibility.[8] Three modalities have been provided indicating a decreasing order of flexibility: i) capital goods can be easily re-sold without incurring significant losses; ii) machines can be re-sold with some difficulties due to not very remunerative prices and/or to excessively long waiting time; iii) capital goods do not have a secondary market at all. In the same section, there are questions referring to the main causes

[7] The survey is carried out in spring and in autumn of each year within the European harmonization programme and contains questions on the predicted investment programmes; the main investment destinations; factors influencing investment decisions, etc.

[8] More specifically, the degree of irreversibility refers to the various capital goods: machinery, equipment and means of transportation, utilized in the productive process. Among these three different types of capital goods, the means of transportation should be characterized by the highest degree of reversibility. Including means of transportation should not significantly affect the survey's qualitative result, since its relative importance is limited. Indeed, on the basis of the National Institute of Statistics (ISTAT) estimations, the percentage of investments of this kind on the total investments for machinery made by Italian industrial firms most recently in the most recent period has been equal to less than 6%.

explaining the difficulty and/or impossibility of firms to re-sell capital goods on a secondary market.[9]

The second section regards the influence of uncertainty 'on the evolution of economic activity' in the next three years and the impact of uncertainty on current investment programmes.[10] Firms have been asked to assign different values (from one to eight) to a chosen set of variables in order to 'capture' the relative degree of predictability.[11] Through that ranking the relative importance of factors driving the 'uncertain world' where firms operate is analysed.

A third section (whose results are not followed in this paper) contains two different types of questions: in the former one, each firm has been asked to assign weights (summing up to 100) to a set of intervals for the rate of demand growth in the next three years assuming constant product prices;[12] in the latter question type, each firm has to indicate the net desired profit whereby it shall implement its investment programme under the opposite hypotheses of reversible or irreversible capital goods.

4 The Degree and Causes of Irreversibility: The Main Results

A modest percentage (17%) of respondents have declared to be able to sell capital goods 'quite easily' on the secondary market, implying that above 80% of firms judge their capital stock to be only partially reversible or not reversible (Figure 16.1).[13] It is worth noticing some interesting cases:

---

9 There may be many reasons leading firms to sell capital goods on the secondary market: they may have the need to renew their capital goods due to technological reasons, and/or to a significant and unexpected fall of demand of final product; they may decide to cease their activity or are obliged to sell their machines after an insolvency.

10 As pointed out, the effects of uncertainty on investment decisions are not well defined either on theoretical or on empirical grounds. In this section, we wonder about the expected demand evolution, the expected pattern of goods' selling prices; the expected investment cost; the level of profit; the interest rate; the exchange rate; the strategic behaviour of competing firms and the fiscal policy measures.

11 The different values indicate the increasing degree of predictability, where one indicates the easiest and eight the most difficult variable to predict. In the paper we have elaborated from each variable a synthetic indicator of predictability (which can be considered as a proxy of uncertainty) as the weighted average of different replies given by firms considering the values (from one to eight) as weights.

12 Through these questions it is possible to elaborate an indicator of uncertainty (a similar attempt has already been developed in Guiso-Parigi, 1996).

13 The various Figures and Tables are contained in Appendix 1.

(i) in some sectors (textiles; pulp, paper and paper products; machinery and equipment) the percentage of firms declaring to be able to sell easily used machines is quite high (almost 30%);
(ii) in turn, sectors like electrical machinery and machine tools seem to be characterized by a high degree of irreversibility;
(iii) in other transport equipment, the replies are equally distributed among the three different modalities.[14]

On the basis of the Pavitt classification,[15] it is worth pointing out the relevant percentage of firms in the high-technology sector characterized by a high degree of capital goods irreversibility (Figure 16.1); on the basis of dimensional features, there emerges a quite significant proportion of large firms, declaring that they have quite easily reversible machines (Figure 16.1).

The analysis of factors making it difficult or impossible to sell capital goods on secondary market does reveal that two of them play a relevant role: notably the limited number of firms adopting the same technology and the technological specificity of capital goods (Table 16.1).[16] Conversely, the factor related to imperfect information about the quality of goods has not been considered by firms (with the exception of two sectors: notably machinery and equipment and precision and optical instruments).

The sectoral cyclical phase seems to be quite relevant for firms mainly operating in the traditional sector (Table 16.1). Moreover, significant differences emerge among firms on the basis of their size: the importance of technological specificity increases with the dimension, while large firms appear to be less 'cycle dependent' in comparison to small and medium-sized firms (Table 16.1).

A further set of information can be gathered through the screening of replies based on geographical aggregation. The sample has been divided into four areas, following the standard ISTAT classification:[17] the degree of capital equipment irreversibility seems to be very high in the Southern area

---

14 The results based on sectoral classification are available on request by the paper's authors.

15 This classification distinguishes four macrosectors: traditional; high-technology; specialized supplier; scale-intensive. For the aim of this paper we have tried to put into evidence possible differences regarding the degree of reversibility of capital of these four macrosectors characterized by a different technological profile (Pavitt, 1984).

16 Firms have been invited to answer more than one question.

17 We refer to the North-West area which indicates the regions of Piemonte, Val D'Aosta, Lombardia, Liguria; the North-East area (Veneto, Trentino, Emilia Romagna, Friuli Venezia Giulia); the Central area (Toscana, Lazio, Marche, Umbria); the Southern area (Campania, Abruzzo, Molise, Puglia, Basilicata, Calabria, Sicilia, Sardegna).

of Italy and quite high in the North-East area; it is a less important factor in the two remaining areas. Specifically, in the North-East area, a high percentage (32%) of firms declare their capability to re-sell machines on the secondary market (Figure 16.1). This is probably due to the dominance of sectors - such as manufacturing of textiles, metal products, machinery and equipment - characterized by a high number of firms with easily reversible capital goods. However, it is firms' opinion that irreversibility marks the majority of new investments: summing up the replies to the questions 'easily reversible' and 'reversibility quite difficult', an average value of 80% replies was obtained, with peaks of 89% in the North-West area. This is impressive evidence illustrating that the degree of irreversibility might be an essential element in many capital accumulation processes.

How can these replies be interpreted? Analysing the productive structure which mainly characterizes the different areas, it is worth noting that, while in the Central and Southern areas traditional productive sectors (like clothing industry, leather products, wood products, paper and paper products, manufacturing of construction material, glass, ceramics) prevail, in the other areas there is a relevant presence of innovative and scale-intensive industries, like machinery and equipment, and metal products. Thus, it appears that irreversibility of capital equipment can be determined not only by the previously examined factors, but also by other causes such as, for instance, the industrial structure characteristics. More specifically, where a rich and complex industrial structure prevails, like in the Northern area, the role of irreversibility in influencing investment sseems to be less important than in other geographical areas (the South), which indeed are characterized by a very modest industrial and economic structures.

What are the sources for that irreversibility in the different areas? On the basis of the survey's results, the limited number of firms adopting the same technology and the technological specificity seem to be still prevalent among firms localized in different areas. The cyclical phase plays quite an important role only in the Central and Southern areas, while the technological specificity of capital goods is less relevant – in comparison with other geographical areas – among firms localized in the central area (Table 16.1).

5 The Role of Uncertainty in Influencing Investment Decisions

An important aspect explored by the economic literature refers to the influence of uncertainty on investment programmes. The uncertainty 'on the future evolution of economic activity' may appear at first sight a 'black hole'. What do firms mean by uncertainty? Is uncertainty relevant only with regard to the evolution of prices and product demand (as the majority of economic theories suggest), or do other factors characterize the uncertain world where firms operate?[18]

To begin with, note that quite a high percentage of firms (59%) have declared that uncertainty 'on the future evolution of economic activity' will influence their investment decisions in the next three years (Table 16.2). On the basis of the Pavitt classification and of the employment dimension, it is worth stressing, respectively, the modest percentage of firms operating in the scale-intensive sector affected by uncertainty (48%) and, conversely, the relevant influence of uncertainty on large firms' investment decisions. At geographical level, this influence plays a relevant role particularly among firms localized in the Southern area (Table 16.2).

We attempted to provide a comprehensive explanation to the above questions by asking each firm which economic variables are supposed to be the most relevant in their investment decisions. Some interesting (and not always intuitive) results emerge: according to the total manufacturing industry, the most difficult 'variables' to predict are fiscal policy measures, the future profit evolution and demand (Table 16.3). These same variables (with a slight change in the relative position, demand being considered the most difficult to predict) have been indicated by small and medium-sized firms. In the meanwhile, large firms attribute a greater uncertainty to the future profit evolution, to product prices and to competitors' strategies (Table 16.3). Notice that the evolution of interest rates and exchange rates is easily predicted by firms; it can be attributed, at least partially, to the 'Euro-effects'. In fact, firms seem to have just incorporated the macroeconomic effects of Italy's participation in the European Union, which should lead to a stabilization of interest rates and exchange rates.

Finally, the effects of uncertainty on investment programmes - which have not reached a definite assessment on theoretical and empirical grounds - find a definite answer on the basis of the survey's results: the majority of firms declare that uncertainty leads to a delay in their investment

[18] Uncertainty should refer to a lot of different variables interacting one with the other (for an attempt to build a global indicator of uncertainty see Carnazza, 1998).

programmes, while only 12% have declared to renounce them definitely (Table 16.4).This last percentage appears to be slightly higher among firms operating in the traditional sector, among small firms and among firms localized in the North-Western area of the country (Table 16.4).

These results are consistent with the real *option* theory: in implementing their investment decisions, firms evaluate the uncertainty-irreversibility combination to choose the starting time of their capital expenditure. If investment were completely reversible, the best choice should be to invest immediately to gain immediate profit. Then, if in the next period the negative state of nature is realized, the firm could easily re-sell the real estate on the secondary market taking back the residual value. But, with irreversible stock, that opportunity is cancelled (the capital stock being a commitment with zero residual price) and uncertainty can negatively influence firms' decisions (through a delay or a definite abandonment of their investment).

6 Some Economic Policy Implications

Which policy implications can be drawn from this survey? Can our data suggest a way to make the capital stock more reversible? If aggregate investment is the engine of growth, the more flexible is technology and the more reversible are investment choices, the more firms shall be inclined to sustain new and innovative investment plans. From this viewpoint, the first step to make (to remove the stickiness of the secondary markets) should be the creation of agencies operating to enlarge the 'potentiality' of secondary markets for capital goods. More specifically, these agencies should create a data-set aimed at picking up the various information (on the demand and supply side) regarding the technological features of capital goods; their average life; the relative degree of obsolescence; etc. Through this data-set, the information problem (referring mainly to the existence of a limited number of firms adopting the same technology) should be, at least partially, reduced.

Besides, the introduction of incentives to facilitate firms offering second-hand capital goods, or of fiscal discounts to acquire used machines can help reducing the degree of capital irreversibility in the short run. The goal should be widening the dimensions of the existing second-hand capital markets.[19]

Finally, the irreversibility of capital can also be attributed to cyclical phases which may characterize the sector where firms operate: a negative phase, generally accompanied by a strong and unexpected fall of demand, may lead firms (mainly of small dimension, operating in the traditional sector and localized in the central and Southern area) to revise their investment strategies, renewing their capital stock.[20] But, firms can encounter difficulties in selling used machines due to the negative economic evolution of the whole sector. Consequently, policy makers should devote more attention to the sectors appearing more 'cycle sensitive', through some specific countercyclical measures of industrial policy.

To summarize, the irreversibility characteristics of capital goods seem to be considered very carefully by entrepreneurs in evaluating their investment decisions. More specifically, a high degree of irreversibility, accompanied by high uncertainty about the future macroeconomic scenario, may induce firms to postpone the realization of investment projects; they may prefer to renounce present profit to get more information useful to choose the 'right' time for investment. Thus, the reduction in the degree of capital stock irreversibility may induce firms to invest more, since they can find their choices more flexible, in case of wrong decision.

Investment decisions should be significantly affected by these measures, while – as some recent contributions have shown (e.g. Ingersoll-Ross, 1992) – an expansive monetary policy reducing the yield curve may have little impact on the current investment, because firms might interpret it as the beginning of a phase of decreasing interest rates. Against this background, firms might find it worth 'wait and see'. This can help understand some puzzling 'stylized facts' described by the macroeconomic data for the Italian economy: the existence of a negative correlation from 1988 to 1997 between the growth rate of investment and real long term

---

[19] Quantitative information on used capital goods, in Italy, are not much diffused. A recent study developed by the Italian association of machine-tools builders (UCIMU, 1995) has shown some interesting quantitative and qualitative results on the used machine-tools market. In 1993, this market accounted for 20% of the new machine-tools market. Fourty percent of the demand for used machines was satisfied by imports (especially from Germany) given the structural lack of supply of specific machines existing in Italy.

[20] According to the bi-annual survey on investments, in the nineties small firms have devoted the greatest share of their investments to machines renewal. This feature is consistent with the 'opportunity cost' theory of growth.

interest rates. This evidence seems to confirm the importance of capital goods' irreversibility on the accumulation process.

7 Concluding Remarks

In this paper we have analysed, on empirical grounds, to what extent Italian manufacturing firms perceive their investment decisions may be affected by capital stock irreversibility and the uncertainty about the future pattern of economic activity. The aim was to fill some 'black holes' not sufficiently explored by economic literature. In particular, the investigation was about the degree and the meaning of irreversibility, and on the main factors which can explain the difficulties met by firms in re-selling capital goods on the secondary market.

Some interesting results have been reached. The majority of interviewed firms (65%) have declared to find difficulties in selling machines, while 18% have indicated to have no secondary market at all. These difficulties have been mainly attributed to the technological specificity of capital and to the existence of a limited number of firms which utilize the same technology. The cyclical economic phase seems to negatively influence small firms and those operating in the traditional sector mainly localized in the central and Southern area.

Further interesting considerations stem from the question of the influence of uncertainty on investment decisions: the uncertainty-irreversibility combination seems to be a quite relevant element in leading firms to postpone their investment programmes. All these features confirm that the irreversibility-uncertainty mix plays a crucial role on the accumulation process, and that specific economic policy measures aimed at reducing the degree of capital irreversibility may help increasing private investments and, consequently, the growth rate of the whole economy.

Appendix - Figures and Tables

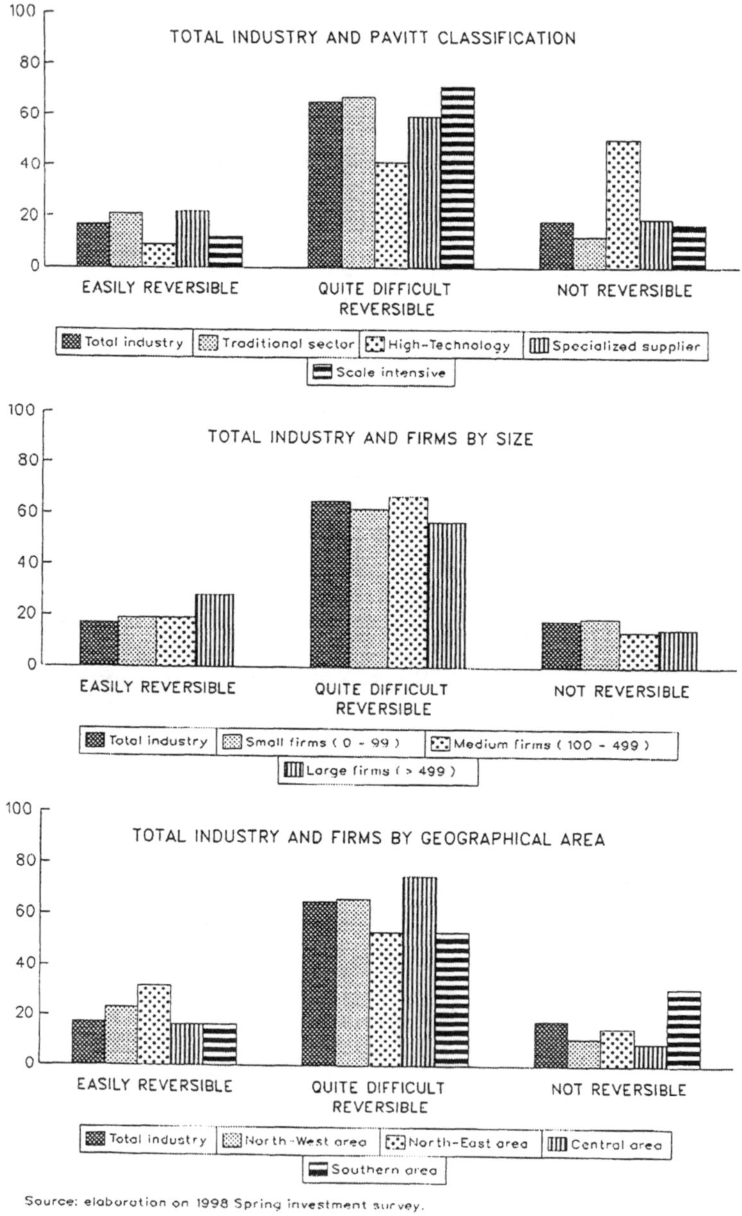

Figure 16.1 - Degree of Reversibility of Capital Goods

Table 16.1 - Factors Which Can Explain the Difficulty or Impossibility to Sell Capital Goods in Secondary Market (% of Multiple Replies)

MACROSECTOR/FACTORS	LIMITED NUMBER OF FIRMS WHICH ADOPT THE SAME TECHNOLOGY	TECHNOLOGICAL SPECIFICITY OF CAPITAL GOOD TO BE RE-SOLD	SPECIFIC ECONOMIC PHASE WHICH CHARACTERIZES THE SECTOR WHERE FIRM OPERATES	LIMITED INFORMATION ON THE QUALITY OF CAPITAL GOOD TO BE- RESOLD
Total manufacturing industry	52	65	22	6
Traditional	50	50	33	4
High-tecnology	68	69	12	15
Specialized supplier	47	75	12	20
Scale intesive	56	79	13	3
DIMENSION/FACTORS	LIMITED NUMBER OF FIRMS WHICH ADOPT THE SAME TECHNOLOGY	TECHNOLOGICAL SPECIFICITY OF CAPITAL GOOD TO BE RE-SOLD	SPECIFIC ECONOMIC PHASE WHICH CHARACTERIZES THE SECTOR WHERE FIRM OPERATES	LIMITED INFORMATION ON THE QUALITY OF CAPITAL GOOD TO BE- RESOLD
0 - 99	47	50	31	7
100 - 499	62	65	16	2
>=500	42	90	11	12
TOTAL MANUFACTURING BY GEOGRAPHICAL AREA/FACTORS	LIMITED NUMBER OF FIRMS WHICH ADOPT THE SAME TECHNOLOGY	TECHNOLOGICAL SPECIFICITY OF CAPITAL GOOD TO BE RE-SOLD	SPECIFIC ECONOMIC PHASE WHICH CHARACTERIZES THE SECTOR WHERE FIRM OPERATES	LIMITED INFORMATION ON THE QUALITY OF CAPITAL GOOD TO BE- RESOLD
North-West area	65	75	11	4
North-East area	39	81	12	16
Central area	38	65	25	8
Southern area	50	85	18	1

Source: elaboration on April 1998 Investment survey.

Table 16.2 - Effects of Uncertainty on Investment Decisions in the Next Three Years

MACROSECTOR/EFFECTS	EFFECTS	NO EFFECTS
Total manufacturing industry	59	41
Traditional	65	35
High-technology	67	33
Specilized supplier	61	39
Scale intensive	48	52

DIMENSION/EFFECTS	EFFECTS	NO EFFECTS
0-99	64	36
100-499	48	52
>= 500	74	26

TOTAL MANUFACTURING BY GEO(AREA/EFFECTS	EFFECTS	NO EFFECTS
North-West area	65	35
North-East area	67	33
Central area	63	37
Southern area	71	29

Source: elaboration on April 1998 Investment survey.

Table 16.3 - Degree of Predictability of Different Variables Affecting Firms' Strategic Decisions (*)

Variables/Dimension	0-99	100-499	> = 500	Total manufacturing industry
Demand of firm's products	11,3	11,6	9,8	10,1
Price of firm's products	8,6	8,9	11,1	8,8
Investment cost	8,4	8,4	7,9	8,6
Profit	10,1	10,8	11,8	10,8
Interest rates	6,9	6,8	7,2	6,9
Exchange rates	3,9	4,7	7,3	4,6
Strategies of competing firms	7,9	9,7	11,1	9,0
Meausures of fiscal policy	11,1	10,6	10,6	10,9

(*) Each firm has been asked to assign to each variable a value from 1 (very easy to predict) to 8 (difficult to predict)
The degree of predictability - as a synthetic indicator - has been derived as a weighted average of different replies given by firms cosidering the values from 1 to 8 as weights.
Higher is this indicator, more difficult to predict is the variable under observation.

Source: elaboration on April 1998 Investment survey.

Table 16.4 - Effects of Uncertainty on Investment Projects

MACROSECTOR/EFFECTS	DELAY	DEFINITIVE ABANDONMENT	ANTICIPATION
TOTAL MANUFACTURING INDUSTRY	84	12	4
TRADITIONAL	83	16	1
HIGH-TECHNOLOGY	97	0	3
SPECIALIZED SUPPLIER	86	11	2
SCALE INTENSIVE	84	8	8

DIMENSION/EFFECTS	DELAY	DEFINITIVE ABANDONMENT	ANTICIPATION
0-99	80	17	3
100-499	88	9	3
> = 500	91	6	3

TOTAL MANUFACTURING BY GEOGRAPHICAL AREA/EFFECTS	DELAY	DEFINITIVE ABANDONMENT	ANTICIPATION
North-West area	82	18	0
North-East area	96	4	0
Central area	80	6	14
Southern area	94	4	2

Source: elaboration on April 1998 Investment survey.

References

Abel, A. B. (1983), 'Optimal Investment Under Uncertainty', *American Economic Review, No. 73*, pp. 228-233.

Bernanke, B. S. (1983), 'Irreversibility, Uncertainty and Cyclical Investment', *The Quarterly Journal of Economics, No. 98*, pp. 85-106.

Bertola, G. (1988), 'Irreversible Investment', Research in Economics, No. 52, pp.3-37.

Carnazza, P. (1998), 'A Leading Indicator of Equipment Investment Demand in the Italian Economy', Social and Structural Change – Consequences for Business Cycle Surveys, Selected Papers presented at the 23rd Ciret Conference, Helsinki 1997, Ashgate.

Guiso, L. and G. Parigi (1996), *'Investment and Demand Uncertainty', Temi di discussione del Servizio Studi Banca d'Italia, No. 289*, November.

Ingersoll, J. E.and S. A. Ross (1992), 'Waiting to Invest: Investment and Uncertainty', *Journal of Business, No. 65*, January, pp.1-29.

Pavitt, K. (1984), 'Sectoral Patterns of Technical Change: Towards a Taxonomy and a Theory', *Research Policy, No. 13*.

Hartman, R. (1972), 'The Effect of Price and Cost Uncertainty On Investment', *Journal of Economic Theory, No. 5*, pp. 258-266.

Jorgenson, D. (1963), 'Capital Theory and Investment Behaviour', *American Economic Review*, May, pp. 247-259.

Pindyck, R. (1991), 'Irreversibility, Uncertainty and Investment', *Journal of Economic Literature, XXIX*, pp. 11-148.

Travaglini, G. (1996), 'The Relationship Between Investment and Demand with Uncertainty and Irreversible Capital', *Giornale degli Economisti ed Annali di Economia, No. 4*, pp. 549-566.

UCIMU - Centro Studi (1995), 'Il mercato delle macchine utensili usate in Italia', Discussion Paper, February.

17 Lumpy and Irreversible Investment in Italy: An Empirical Test Based on Investment Survey Data*

MARCELLA CORSI and ASSUNTA DRAICCHIO

1 Introduction

The 1990s have witnessed a revival in economist's interest and hope of explaining aggregate and microeconomic demand behaviour.

On the investment side, a large theoretical debate has arisen on lumpiness and irreversibility.[1] As is known, in standard neo-classical models of investment, assumptions, such as convex adjustment costs and reversibility, dictate that firms continuously and smoothly adjust their capital stock over time.[2] By contrast, a growing number of studies has suggested that capital adjustment may occur in lumpy episodes: firms occasionally adjust their capital in discrete bursts when the capital stock falls (rises) below (above) a threshold level.

In spite of the abundance of theoretical work concerning non-convexities in the cost of capital adjustment, the supporting empirical research is more limited mainly because 'smoothness' and 'lumpiness' seem to depend upon the level of aggregation and frequency of investment data, and by the

---

* Financial support from the Ministero dell' Università e della Recerca Scientifica Tecnologica (MURST) (project 'Domestic demand and economic growth', by Marcella Corsi) is gratefully acknowledged.

1 Cf. Caballero (1997).

2 While theoretically tractable, these models generally fail to adequately explain investment fluctuations. Cf. Abel – Blanchard (1986).

motivation of investment expenditure (expansion, replacement or rationalisation of plants).

This paper aims to test to what extent is investment lumpy by documenting the distribution of investment for a sample of Italian industrial plants taking part to the EU-harmonised investment survey carried out by ISCO over the period 1989-1998.

The layout of the paper is as follows. Section 2 clarifies the theoretical framework for the empirical analysis and describes the EU-harmonised investment survey. Section 3 concentrates on lumpiness of Italian investment at microeconomic level. Section 4 draws some conclusions.

2 Theoretical and Empirical Framework

2.1 The Investment Function

The theory of aggregate demand has been enriched in the 1990s by new interesting insights concerning both investment and consumption.

On the investment side, the traditional *accelerator*-like model, linking investment to the desired level of capital (i.e., to the level of output and the cost of capital) has been partly abandoned because of a change in emphasis from aggregate to microeconomic investment behaviour. Theories of lumpy and irreversible investment have drawn attention on the *path* leading capital stock to its desired level, highlighting the existence of obstacles to investment at the firm level. In brief, such a vast literature on microeconomic investment behaviour stresses that

- investment occurs when the marginal profitability of capital is substantially above the cost of capital (this is the famous 'reluctance to invest' result);
- a considerable fraction of a firm's investment is bunched into infrequent and lumpy episodes;[3]

---

[3] Cf. Doms - Dunne (1994). Doms and Dunne documented investment patterns of a balanced panel of 13,702 plants in US manufacturing over the period 1972-1988. For each establishment they constructed a series of the proportion of the total equipment investment (over the 17-year period) made in each year. They found that on average the largest investment episode accounts for about 25% of the 17-year investment of an establishment and that the highest capital growth rate is close to 50% in a single year. They also noted that the second largest investment spike often came next to the largest investment spike (right before or after) suggesting that both spikes correspond to a single investment episode. As evidence of the macroeconomic relevance of microeconomic lumpiness, Doms and Dunne documented - using data on about 360,000 establishments

- aggregate investment is heavily influenced by the degree of synchronisation of microeconomic investment spikes.[4]

Moreover, there is now a large body of evidence supporting the view that credit constraints have substantial effects on firm level investment; in other terms, the cumulative evidence seems overwhelmingly in favour of the claim that investment is more easily financed with internal than external funds.[5]

In accordance with the recent developments in the theory of investment, the most suitable specification of an investment function is as follows:

$$I = f(U, G, E(G), L, \sigma) \tag{1}$$

G = current profits; L = liquidity constraint;
U = capacity utilisation; σ = uncertainty on future income.[6]

The investment function states that firms' investment behaviour depends on their own financial means, depending on current profits, and by their possibilities of drawing on bank credit, again influenced by current profits. If current profits determine the possibility of financing investment, the inducement to invest is given by expected profits. Moreover, demand is relevant for firm's investment behaviour insofar as it determines the degree

---

for Census years 1977 and 1987 - that about 18% of aggregate investment is accounted for by the top 100 projects; as a metric, only 6% of employment is in the top 100 employers, and less than 10% of production occurs in the top 100 producers.

4 Cf. Gale (1996). Informational problems play an important role in the synchronisation mechanism, causing episodes of gradualism during which industry investment can occur at an excessively slow pace, or even collapse altogether. As a matter of fact, information seldom arrives uniformly and comprehensively to every potential investor. Each investor probably holds part of a truth which would be more easily seen if all investors could (or would) pool their information. Actions by others are a partial substitute for information pooling, for they reveal the information of those who have taken actions. Indeed, if investment is irreversible, it may pay to wait for others to act and reveal their information before investing. However, if lumpiness leads to periods of no or little action, information may remain trapped for extended periods of time, and when agents finally act, an avalanche may occur because accumulated private information is suddenly aggregated. These issues are the focus of the literature on 'social learning'.

5 Cf. Bernanke *et al.* (1996).

6 Uncertainty may play a role in the determination of firm's investment, but the sign and intensity of the investment-uncertainty (on demand) relationship cannot be settled on a purely theoretical ground. Depending on assumptions about the production technology, competition in product markets, the shape of adjustment costs and management attitudes toward risk, increases in uncertainty over the demand for the firm's product and over input costs may have opposite effects on demand. That is why such a link is ignored in this paper and is left as an empirical problem. Cf. Guiso - Parigi (1996) and references.

of utilisation of their production capacity: this seems the most appropriate expression of that variant of the accelerator principle known as the capital-stock adjustment principle.

2.2 *The Characteristics of the EU-harmonised Investment Survey*

The EU-harmonised system of qualitative surveys offers a variety of indicators suitable to track investment in accordance with the theoretical framework described above.

As is known, the EU-harmonised system includes five different surveys: the industry survey, the investment survey, the construction survey, the retail trade survey and the consumer survey. Each of the former three surveys provides information concerning some aspects of investment activity.[7] In particular, the Investment Survey collects important information on managers' investment decisions, on the purposes of investment and on the factors influencing investment. Nowadays it is conducted twice a year in all EU member countries: in March/April (Spring survey) and in October/November (Autumn survey). Questionnaires are answered by managers – not by accountants - due to the important role of expectations in defining investment decisions.

Since it is difficult to allocate a firm's investment to its various activities, industries are classified in only seven groups: energy and water related industries, intermediate goods, motor vehicles, investment goods, durable consumer goods, food and beverages, non durable consumer goods (Appendix).[8]

Questionnaires are sent by post to a sample which generally consists of the firms questioned in the monthly business survey in industry. However, the number of firms surveyed in the investment sample is somewhat larger for some sectors than in the sample of industry in order to eliminate, as far as possible, the wider fluctuations that are apt to occur with the movement in the investment variable. These variations arise due to the sharp variation in the growth of investment between two successive years and because of cyclical fluctuations which are very pronounced and sharper than those of production.

---

[7] Cf. Corsi (1998).

[8] This classification has been used since autumn 1997. In the past, firms were classified into six categories: basic materials, metal working, equipment goods, processing, extraction and food. Cf. European Commission (1997).

Box 17.1 - EU-harmonised Investment Survey – Observable Variables

Investment decisions

Investment decisions are asked as the change in the firm's investment expenditure at current prices

- Spring survey:

1. percentage change in investment last year compared with investment two years ago.
2. percentage change in investment this year compared with investment last year.

- Autumn survey:

1. percentage change in investment this year compared with investment last year.
2. percentage change in investment next year compared with investment this year.

Investment purposes

The autumn survey includes a question relating to the purposes of investment, the aim being to assess the impact of investment on the change in production capacity and on productivity. The suggested motives are:

(a) replacement of worn-out capacity;
(b) investment aimed at extending production capacity:

- with an unchanged product range;
- so as to extend the product range;

(c) investment specifically designed to improve operating efficiency:

- automation or mechanisation of existing manufacturing processes;
- introduction of new production techniques;

(d) other investment objectives (pollution control, safety, etc.).

The questionnaire normally cannot refer to a specific product. It must cover the overall activity of the firm since investment cannot be broken down and related to each item manufactured in the firm. Therefore, the investment surveys are conducted on a basis of selected units of production. Purpose selection and stratified selection are the two sampling methods used by the institutes. The stratification criteria used are size and activity sector.

Results are weighted by a system similar to the one used in the monthly business survey in industry. Individual replies are weighted according to the size of the firms involved.

Box 17.1 - EU-harmonised Investment Survey – Observable Variables (continued)

Factors influencing investment

The aim of this question is to help economic policy makers to decide on the best way to promote investment. Firms are requested to state whether each of the following factors has a very stimulating effect, a stimulating effect, no effect, a limiting effect or a very limiting effect on investment:

(a) demand: this relates to the capacity utilisation rate and the sales prospects;

(b) anticipated financial resources or expected profits: this covers the availability of resources for investment (and their cost) together with the return on investment and the lack of opportunities for the company to use its resources more profitably than by investment (notably by purely financial operations);

(c) technical factors: the main ones are technological developments, the availability of labour and its attitude towards the new technologies, and lastly the technical conditions set by public authorities before they grant the investment permit;

(d) other factors: these may include the policy of the public authorities, notably with regard to taxation, and whether or not production can be transferred abroad.

3 Lumpiness of Italian Investment

3.1 The ISCO Investment Panel

The EU-harmonised investment survey carried out by ISCO over the period 1989-1998 has questioned on average 1,200 Italian firms at plant level, biannually. This set of industrial plants gives rise to a longitudinal panel that may be used to test investment lumpiness by documenting the distribution of investment within the panel and by focusing on observable plant characteristics such as size and activity sector.

Plants must meet two requirements to be included in the panel: first, they must have replied to a minimum of eleven over twenty questionnaires sent by ISCO in the reference period; second, their replies must allow to calculate a minimum of ten years of continuous investment data. Plants satisfying only the first requirement form the reference sample: it contains 442 plants and is biased towards large establishments.[9] Table 17.1 presents the number and the average size of plants by length of time in the reference sample: in brief, 43% of the selected plants have life-spans of 9 years or less, and 57% span the entire period. Thus, plants fitting both requirements to be included in the panel amount to 252, and employed on average 715 workers in 1990.

Table 17.1 - Reference Sample Characteristics

Life-span	*Number of plants*	*Percent of plants*	*Average size (1990)*
< 8 years	28	6.3	2,268
8 years	67	15.2	306
9 years	95	21.5	790
10 years	252	57.0	715

Source: ISCO Investment Survey

Table 17.2 - Sample and Panel Structure (%)

	Sample	*Panel*
Kind of activity		
Motor vehicles	4	4
Intermediate goods	47	46
Investment goods	16	17
Consumer goods	33	33
Size		
< 50 employees	29	29
50-249 employees	49	51
250-499 employees	8	7
≥ 500 employees	14	13
Total	100	100

Source: ISCO Investment Survey

9 The average plant in the reference sample employs 768 workers in 1990.

As table 17.2 shows, the longitudinal panel and the reference sample have similar structural characteristics in terms of both size and activity sector.

Selected plants mostly belong to the intermediate goods sector, although also consumer goods industry plays an important role, both in the panel and in the reference sample. In terms of size, almost 80% of firms are characterised by a small-medium size; the weight of medium-sized plants is only slightly higher in the panel than in the reference sample.

3.2 *Investment growth rates*

It is possible to calculate investment growth rates by taking into account firms' replies to the quantitative question about the percentage change in firms' current investment expenditure compared with the previous year.

Investment expenditure holds capital growth and depreciation costs

$$I_{i,t} = K_{i,t} - K_{i,t-1} + \delta\, K_{i,t-1} \tag{2}$$

where $I_{i,t}$ represents period t (one year) current investment of plant i, $K_{i,t}$ represents period t capital stock of plant i, and δ represents the depreciation rate. $I_{i,t}$ cannot be nil on account of plant's persistent needs to change part of its capital stock at any rate.[10]

Survey data refer to investment growth rates, GI_t defined as

$$GI_t = \frac{I_t - I_{t-1}}{I_{t-1}} \tag{3}$$

Figure 17.1 presents the density distribution of GI_t for all plants included in the panel.[11] The distribution appears largely asymmetrical taking into account positive and negative values of GI_t. On the one hand, firms seem to adjust their capital in discrete bursts especially when the investment rises above a threshold level: 17% of plant year observations present positive investment growth rates higher than 100%, while only 1.8% are

[10] Survey data do not discriminate current investments from retirement or opening expenditures.

[11] In figure 17.5 some outliers (26 firms) have been removed from the panel. The exclusion of such firms does not modify the structural characteristics of the panel in any important direction. Outliers concentrate in consumer and intermediate goods sectors and mostly present a small size.

characterised by correspondingly high negative growth rates. On the other hand, firms appear very cautious in decreasing their investment expenditure abruptly: about 40% of plant year observations show relatively low values of negative investment growth rates, between –20% and –50%.

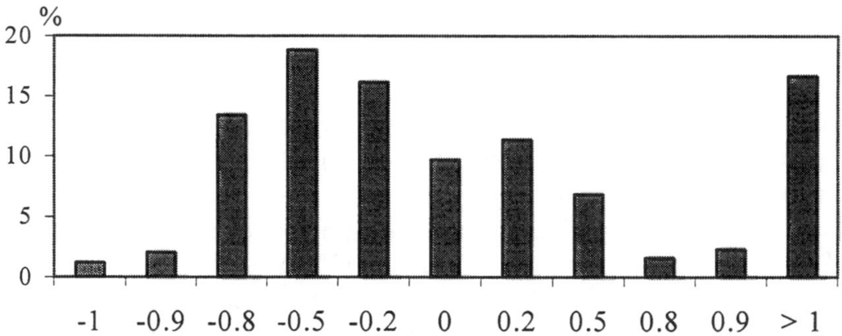

Source: ISCO Investment Survey

Figure 17.1 - Investment Growth Rate Distribution

To examine the patterns of plant-level investment focusing especially on those periods when firms undergo large changes to their capital stocks, it is necessary to rank GI_t from highest to lowest, so that the maximum growth rate is rank 1 and the lowest growth rate is rank 9; the rank 1 investment growth rates can be denoted by MAXGI.

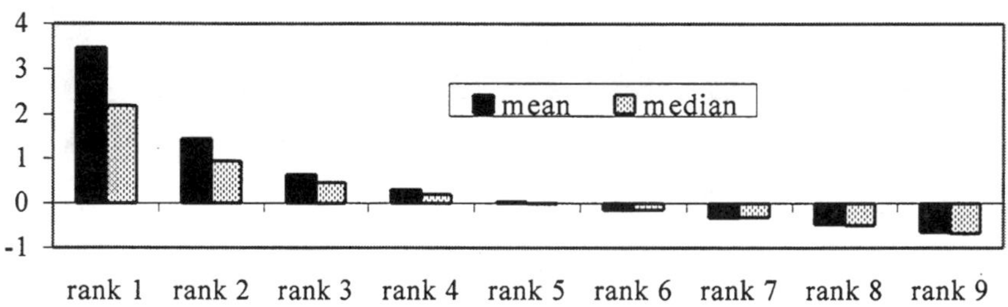

Source: ISCO Investment Survey

Figure 17.2 - Mean and Median of Investment Growth Rates by Rank

Figure 17.2 presents the means and medians of these ranked growth rates, so the first set of bars shows the mean and median MAXGI; the next set of bars shows the mean and median of the secondary largest growth rates, and so on. These bars indicate that the mean MAXGI exceeds 300%, while the median is slightly above 200%. The means and medians drop off significantly after rank 1; thus plants included in the panel seem to experience, on average, a few periods of intense investment and many periods of relatively small capital adjustment: of the 9 investment growth rates ranks, 7 possess means and medians between –70% and +70%.

Besides the growth rate of investment, it is important to consider those episodes of investment that account for a large share of the individual plant's investment expenditure over time. Figure 17.3 plots the mean proportion of total 10 year investment that occurs in each year, in decreasing order; for instance the left most bar represents that the average (median) plant experiences a one-year investment episode that accounts for 15% of its total real investment spending over the reference period (1988-1998). The secondary episode accounts for 12%, the third highest for 11%, and so on. This implies that about half of the average plant's total investment over the reference period is performed in four annual episodes; moreover, it shows that while a significant portion of investment occurs in lumpy episodes, plants still spread investment over time.

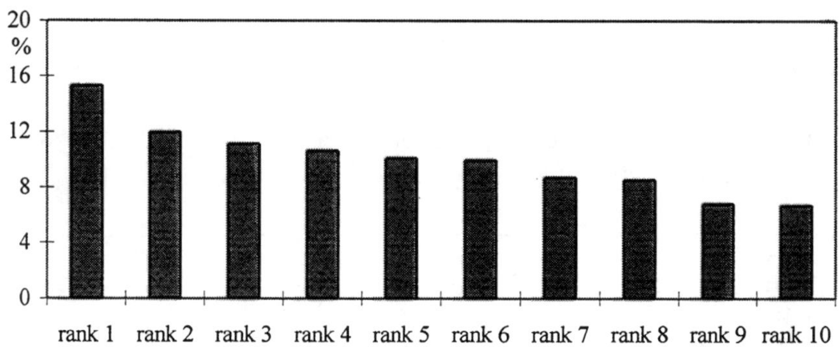

Source: ISCO Investment Survey

Figure 17.3 - Investment Share by Rank

The main results concerning the whole panel apply also to different activity sectors and firms' sizes represented within the panel (Appendix B).

With respect to investment growth rate distribution by rank, intermediate goods and consumer goods have mean MAXGI in excess of 300% while motor vehicles and investment goods show lower maximum growth rates (Figure 17.1). In terms of investment shares, investment and consumer goods have particularly large investment spikes, reaching 50% of total 10 year investment in only three annual episodes (Figure 17.3).

Taking into account differences by size, the important result is that smaller plants have higher maximum growth rates (Figure 17.2) and larger maximum investment shares (Figure 17.4) than the largest plants. That is, as plant size increases, investment expenditures become smoother.[12]

4 Conclusive Remarks

A growing number of theoretical studies have suggested, in recent years, that investment may occur in lumpy episodes, implying non-convex adjustment costs and irreversibility in the revised *accelerator*-like model.

However, the empirical research supporting the hypothesis of lumpiness and irreversibility of investment has been quite limited.[13] This paper aims to give an empirical contribution by documenting the distribution of investment for a panel of plants drawn from the sample used by ISCO to carry out the EU-harmonised investment survey during the period 1989-1998. Selected plants mostly belong to the intermediate goods (46%) and consumer goods (33%) sectors, while, in terms of size, they are largely characterised by a small-medium size (80%).

In brief, panel data show that:

- firms seem to adjust their capital in discrete bursts especially when the investment rises above a threshold level: 17% of plant year observations present positive investment growth rates higher than 100%, while only 1.8% are characterised by correspondingly high negative growth rates;
- selected plants seem to experience, on average, a few periods of intense investment and many periods of relatively small capital adjustment: about half of the average plant's total investment over the reference period is performed in 4 annual episodes.
- with respect to plant characteristics, the degree of lumpiness does not vary considerably across activity sectors. By contrast, smaller plants show lumpier investment patterns; in other words, as plant size increases, investment expenditures seem to become smoother.

---

[12] The same result is present in Doms-Dunne (1994). Models of plant growth predict there should be plant-level heterogeneity in growth within an industry. A basic result of this line of research is that plant growth varies by identifiable plant-level characteristics, in particular, plant size and age. Cf. Jovanovic (1982), Dunne *et al.* (1989).

[13] Cf. Doms-Dunne (1994). Some studies have focused on specific kinds of investment, e.g. replacement investment. Examples include Rust (1988) with bus engines and Cooper - Haltiwanger (1993) with automobile assembly plant retoolings.

These results certainly raise the question of whether traditional representative agent models, based on convexity and reversibility, are adequate enough to examine the dynamics of investment and capital accumulation. Moreover, show a new way of exploiting the large informational content of the EU-harmonised investment survey, indicating a very promising direction for further research.

5 Appendix

Table 17.1 - EU-harmonised Investment Survey - Sector Classification to be Used Since Autumn 1997

Code in DGII database	Description	Code in recommendation*
ENWA	energy and water	R02
INTM	**intermediate goods**	**R03**
34	motor vehicles	R04
INVE	**investment goods**	**R05**
CDUR	durable consumer goods	R06
FOBE	food and beverages	R07
CNDU	Non-durables	R08
CONS	**Consumer goods**	**R06 up to R08**
TOTI	**Total industry**	**R02 up to R08**

(*) OJL 38, 16/2/1996

Table 17.2 - EU-harmonised Investment Survey - Classification by Size of Firms**

SIZE1	firms with less than 50 employees
SIZE2	firms with 50-249 employees
SIZE3	firms with 250-499 employees
SIZE4	firms with 500 employees and more
SIZE5	firms with less than 250 employees
SIZE6	firms with 250 employees and more

(**) According to recommendation OJL 107, 30/4/1996

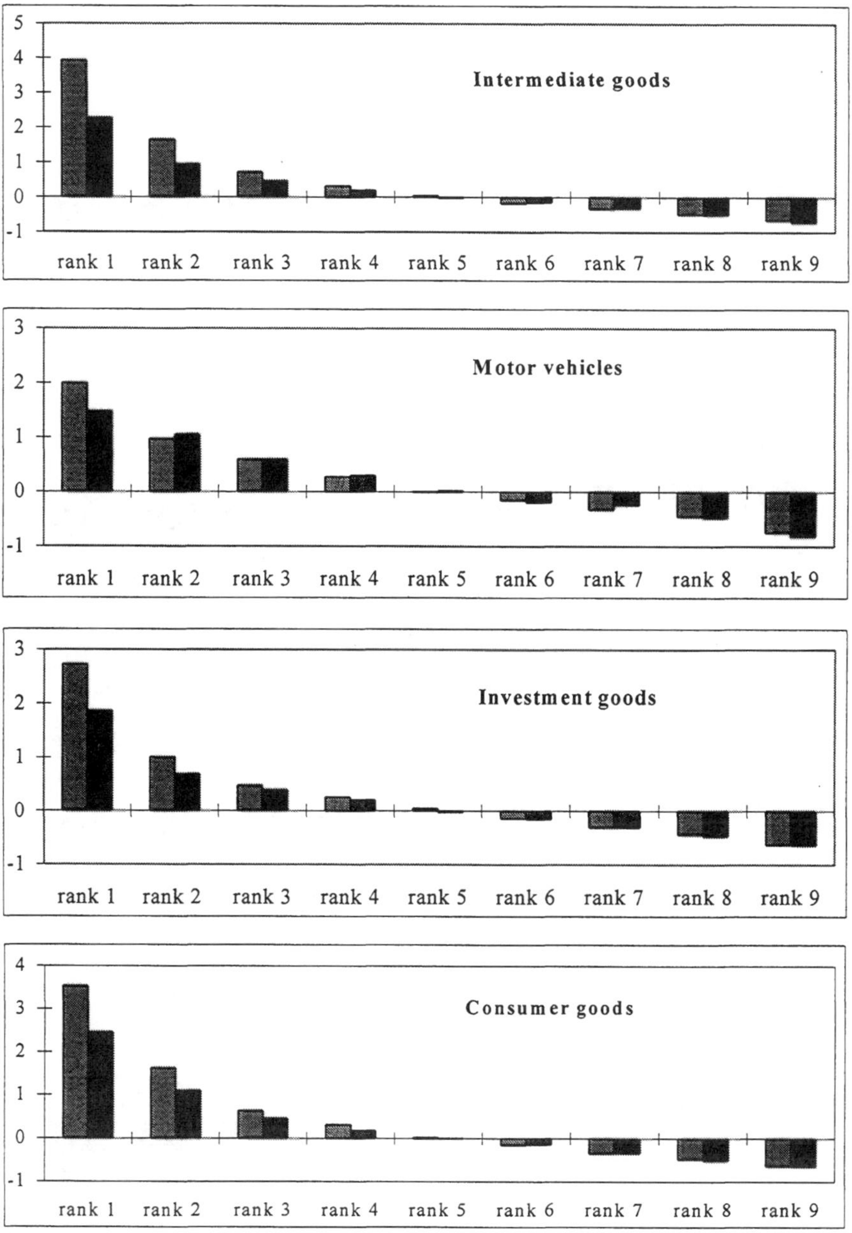

Source: ISCO Investment Survey

Figure 17.1 - Mean and Median of Investment Growth Rates by Rank and Activity Sector

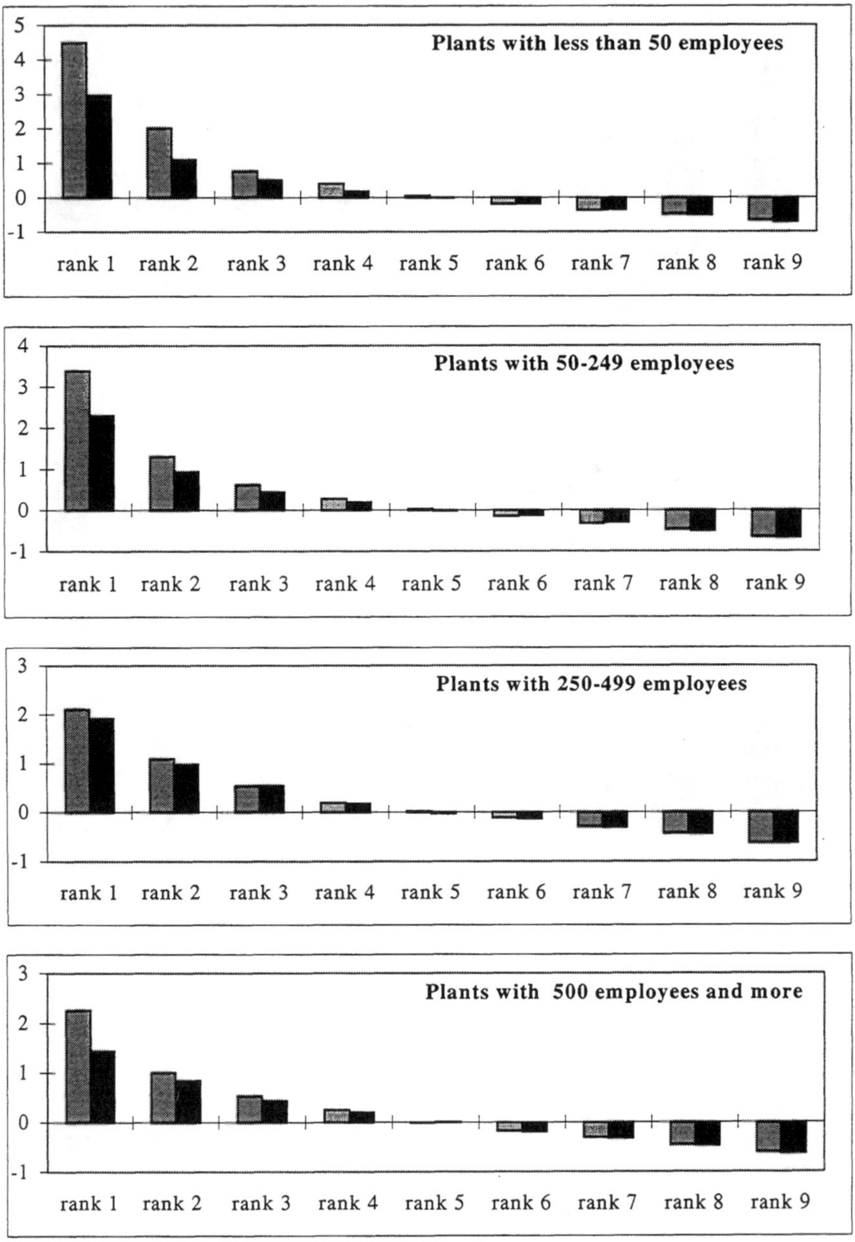

Source: ISCO Investment Survey

Figure 17.2 - Mean and Median of Investment Growth Rates by Rank and Size

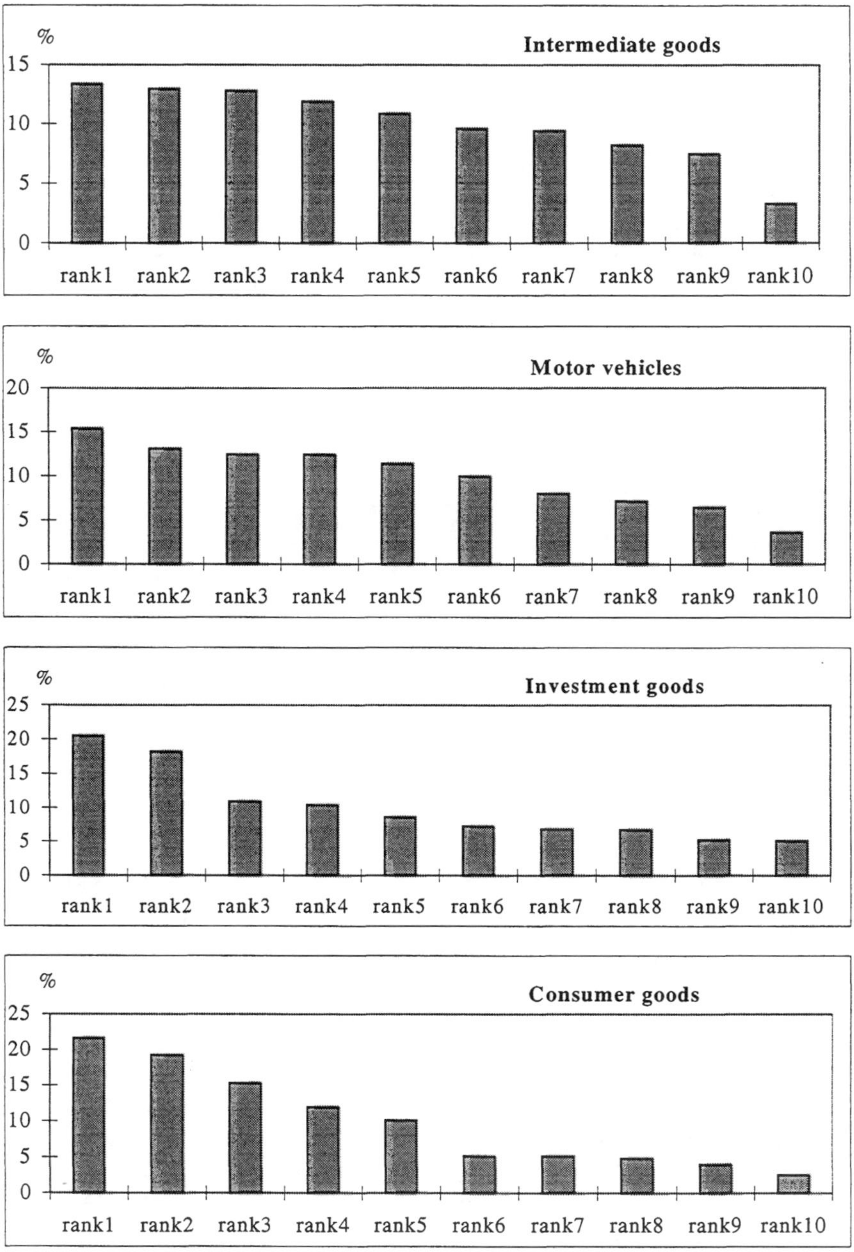

Source: ISCO Investment Survey

Figure 17.3 - Investment Share by Rank and Activity Sector

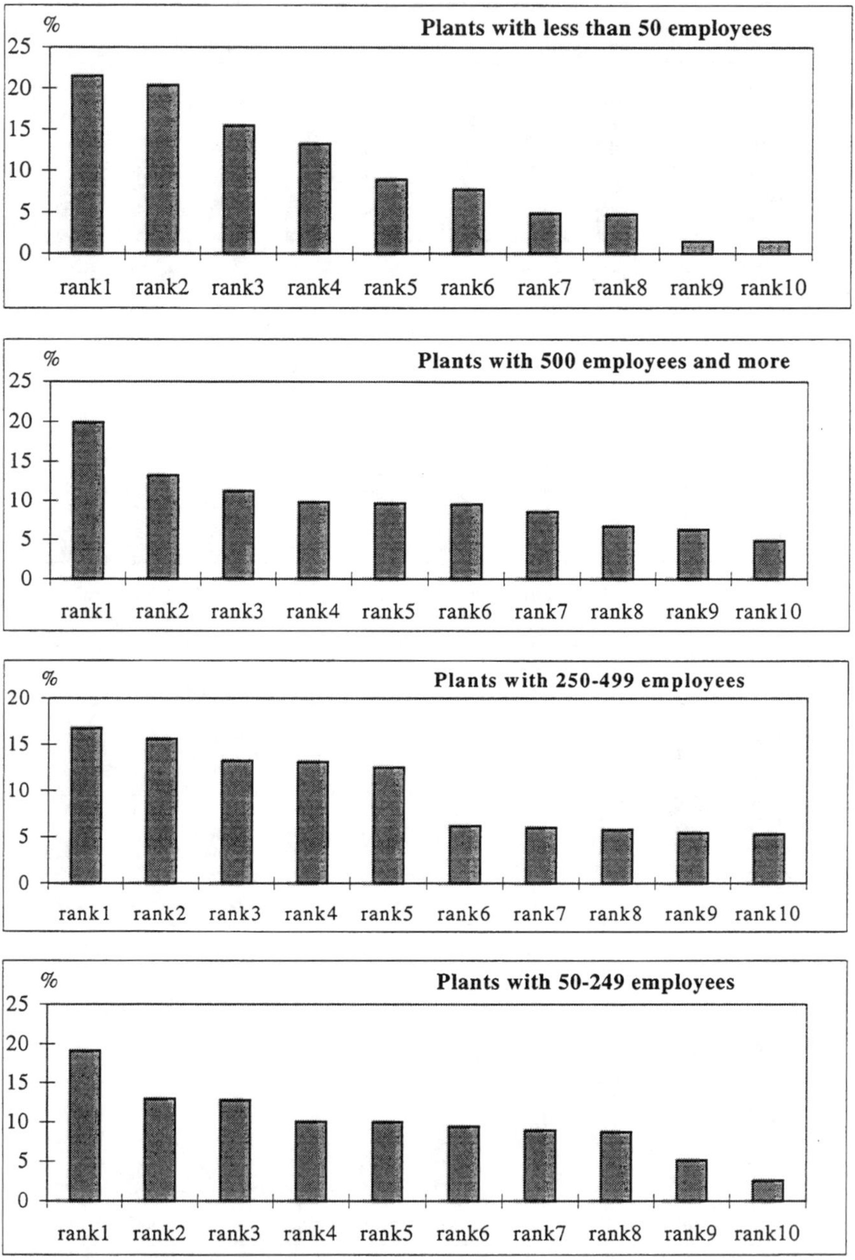

Source: ISCO Investment Survey

Figure 17.4 - Investment Share by Rank and Size

References

Abel, A. and O. Blanchard (1986), 'The Present Value of Profits and Cyclical Movements in Investment', *Econometrica*, Vol. 54, pp. 249-273.

Bernanke, B. *et al.* (1996), 'The Financial Accelerator and the Flight to Quality', *Review of Economics and Statistics*, Vol. 78, pp. 1-15.

Caballero, R. (1997), 'Aggregate Investment: A 90's View', mimeo; forthcoming in Taylor, J. and Woodford, M. (eds), *Handbook of Macroeconomics*.

Cooper, R. and J. Haltiwanger (1993), 'The Aggregate Implications of Machine Replacement: Theory and Evidence', *American Economic Review*, Vol. 83, pp. 360-382.

Corsi, M. (1998), 'Aggregate Demand and Economic Growth' in Oppenländer, K.H. and G. Poser (eds), *Social and Structural Change: Consequences for Business Cycle Surveys*, Ashgate, Aldershot.

Doms, M. and T. Dunne (1994), 'Capital Adjustment Patterns in Manufacturing Plants', CES 94-11, U.S. Census Bureau.

Dunne, T. *et al.* (1989), 'Patterns of Firm Entry and Exit in U.S. Manufacturing Industries', *Rand Journal of Economics*, Vol. 19, pp. 495-515.

European Commission (1997), 'The Joint Harmonised EU Programme of Business and Consumer Surveys, *European Economy – Reports and Studies*, No. 6.

Gale, D. (1996), 'Delay and Cycles', *Review of Economic Studies*, Vol. 63, pp. 169-198.

Guiso, L. and G. Parigi (1996), 'Investment and Demand Uncertainty', *Temi di Discussione*, Banca d'Italia, No. 289.

Jovanovic, B. (1982), 'Selection and Evolution of Industry', *Econometrica*, Vol. 50, pp. 649-670.

Rust, J. (1987), 'Optimal Replacement of GMC Bus Engines: An Empirical Model of Harold Zurcher', *Econometrica*, Vol. 55, pp. 999-1034.

18 Investment Surveys Analysing Innovations in Hungary

MIKLÓS HEGEDÜS, GÁBOR PAPANEK and RAYMUND PETZ

In 1998, on request of the OECD, GKI Economic Research Co. analysed the Hungarian Innovation System. Beside the new research topic the techniques of GKI's traditional surveys could also be used in this research project. In our paper we will present the methodological experiences of this experiment.

1 Methods of Research

The research we would like to present was based on the theoretical foundations of OECD elaborated recently. During our work, we accepted the definition of the so-called Frascati Manual: 'Innovation is the transformation of a concept into either an introduced, new or modernised product, or into a new or improved operation in trade or industry, or a new approach to a social service' (p. 19). Based on the generally used grouping of J. Schumpeter, we distinguished the following types of innovation: 'introduction of a new product and production method, opening of a new market, acquisition of new resources or raw materials, new organisation of labour'. Accepting the recommendations of the so-called Oslo Manual, we counted on that 'R&D is only one of the innovation activities... The list of innovation activities beyond the scope of R&D (without aiming at completeness) is the following: planning, installation and engineering, start of production, marketing of new products' (p. 29-30).

During our research we also widely used the so-called National Innovation System (NIS) concept that was elaborated also in the framework of OECD works (with S. Metcalfe, B.A. Lundvall, etc.). Therefore, we judged 'knowledge' flow (flow of information, experts) that is necessary for competitive production as one of the fundamental elements of innovation. Systematic investigation that concentrates on the main functions and relations of institutions which participate in the 'birth and diffusion of innovation' (in other words: which participate in knowledge flows) was considered to be of outstanding importance (OECD 1998b).

Information needed for analyses was gathered with the help of the traditional investment surveys of GKI (in order to supplement the inadequate statistics). As it is known,[1] GKI launches postal surveys twice a year on the mid-term (1-2 year) expectations of Hungarian enterprises. These surveys are well-known among experts, have 30 years of tradition and were first done by adopting the IFO (Munich) surveys. In the last decade the methodology was improved along EU recommendations. The target population is the group of active enterprises (legal entities) employing more than 20 people, which group covers about 40-50 thousand companies. An 8000 member random sample was taken place from this population stratified by the sectors of the national economy. The examined sectors exclude the monetary sphere as examining this sphere needs a different questionnaire from GKI. Administration, the obligatory social security, healthcare and social care, education were also left out because production of these fields is not realised by legal entity businesses. Sectoral, size and regional distributions of the responding firms do not differ from the national proportions.

In the 1998 Spring enterprise survey that was also used for the 'innovation' research, we put more questions than the usual for the innovation practice of the firm and we also attached a separate questionnaire that dealt with the special characteristics of the innovation system exclusively. The 'regular' questionnaire was sent back by 664 firms (the occasionally also quoted traditional Autumn questionnaire by 754 firms), and the supplementary 'innovation' questionnaire was posted back by 295 companies. The 9-10% response rate of the 'traditional' questionnaires is about in accordance with the Hungarian practice. The responding companies cover about 9% (Spring) and 14% (Autumn) of the business sphere (calculated on the number of employees). The samples provide a reliable representation of the 'population' (the processing

---

1 See for instance: Csernenszky, L., Papanek, G., Pető, M. (1992), Papanek, G., Petz, R., Vértes, A. (1997).

industry and small firms in general are slightly under-, the transportation-telecommunication sector is slightly over-represented).

'Innovation' questionnaires were filled in and sent back by companies who had something to say and who had experience in the subject. As a rough judgement, we can say that the additional questionnaire was filled in by those firms, which consider themselves as innovative (understanding freely the concept of 'innovative'). The internal proportions of this given group also slightly differ from the structure of the Hungarian economy. In industry 57% described their activity (above average), in trade, construction, and transportation-telecommunication responding was below average. Concerning small and medium size enterprises less than the half, concerning large companies more than the half responded. Finally, it has to be mentioned (as it is opposing the general tendencies) that regarding our subject we received more information from foreign-owned companies. The reason may well be that foreign and mixed ownership enterprises are more actively participating in innovation processes than the Hungarian owned firms (especially the state-owned companies).

As GKI surveys are as representative as they can be, the data received on innovative Hungarian companies, on their characteristics and on the innovation processes (which mostly means the distribution of answers) can be judged as reliable concerning Hungarian ratios and tendencies. However, information from the innovation questionnaire is occasionally a bit too optimistic.

The questionnaire, which was used for investigating the innovation processes, included questions about the following main factors:

- In the 1997 sales of the enterprises, what was the share of products/services that could compete with the products of developed countries; which had only a little competitiveness lag; and which had not been competitive (yet).
- In the last three years, did the firm develop or introduce new products, technologies?
- Number of R&D employees, the directions for R&D workforce mobility,
- The significant obstacles to innovative behaviour and to innovations.

The questions raised were in accordance with traditional survey techniques. The responders had to answer closed questions.

2 Modernisation Processes, Innovative Companies

The last decades already saw a few questions regarding innovation in the Hungarian investment surveys. Therefore during the last 40 years the international competitiveness of the majority of Hungarian products was known to be poor due to the 'historical' heritage on the one hand and to the economic policy forcing extensive development and the conserving nature of COMECON relations on the other. Though there were some Hungarian goods with obvious export potential, but in order to achieve world market success, there was a need for modernisation at more than one-third of the products, and about half of the production could not be sold on the market of developed countries (see Z. Román 1973 for instance). In the last years, however, on this field there were significant changes and in many sectors of the economy significant modernisations took place according to our 1998 innovation surveys. The ratio of competitive products rigorously went up to one-third of the production while the same figure for non-exportable products shrank markedly to about one-fourth. The facts concluded from the survey were confirmed by the statistics, also (rigorous export growth, and the slowly started GDP growth since 1993).

In the framework of the innovation surveys, we also tried to investigate the explanatory factors for the improving competitiveness. First of all (putting the standard OECD question) we can state that the share of innovative companies in the Hungarian economy is as shown in the following table 18.1.

The table shows that although innovative Hungarian firms are low in number in international comparison,[2] they are spreading and now they are estimated to 10-20 thousand. Large firms are not much more innovative than the small ones. It also gives an explanation for an important reason of the recent modernisation that the group of foreign owned companies contains more innovative firms. From some other data we can also see that in each larger sector and region one can already find innovative companies.

The detailed case studies, which were elaborated within the framework of the research, also supported the quoted results of our surveys. The case studies also stated that at many firms, especially at some companies that were purchased by foreigners, many significant modernisation efforts were undertaken.

---

[2] According to IFO surveys, in the West German provinces 3/4 of the firms introduce new products every 2-3 years.

Table 18.1 - Share of Firms Undertaking Significant Development Between 1995-1997*(%)

Development type	Firms employing -50 people	Firms employing 51-300 people	Firms employing 301- people	State owned companies	Hungarian private owned companies	Foreign owned companies	Total
Development of a markedly new product/service or technology** (new in Hungary)	8 (10)	9 (11)	15 (19)	6 (16)	8 (9)	23 (19)	10 (12)
Entering the market with a markedly new product/technology**	14 (28)	20 (32)	28 (42)	13 (36)	18 (32)	30 (37)	20 (33)
Starting the use of a markedly new technology in production**	7 (13)	12 (21)	18 (17)	3 (16)	11 (17)	20 (19)	11 (17)
Conquering a new market***							
- in Hungary	35 (35)	24 (42)	18 (43)	22 (42)	25 (42)	38 (31)	27 (40)
- abroad	13 (21)	23 (27)	29 (43)	3 (41)	20 (23)	40 (35)	21 (28)
Investment/turnover							
- mean (%)****	12	10	8	8	8	10	9
- median (%)	9	5	6	7	6	7	6

* Figures without brackets are for developments that brought about significant economic result, figures in brackets are the ratios for development that have not brought result (yet)

** Figures of the 1998 Autumn survey

*** Figures of the 1998 Spring survey (and as they are based on only the answers of firms that declared themselves innovative, they reflect an optimistic view)

**** Means weighted with the number of staff

Source: GKI's surveys

As the subjects of the first three lines of the table were asked in both the 1998 Spring and Autumn questionnniare, measurement of the optimistic nature of the answers received in the Spring 'innovation' survey was possible. The reason is that the frequencies of the positive answers received from the Spring 'innovative' firms were significantly higher than those of the Autumn (nationwide representative) sample. The Spring frequency totals

- of firms recording markedly new innovation in Hungary were 15% (20%),
- of firms introducing new products on the market were 23 (34)% and
- of firms starting the use of a markedly new technology in production were 19 (19)%.

Our surveys also justify that generally the business activity of innovative firms is better than the average. The innovative firms are strongly market oriented, an ambitious market strategy and market success are much more frequent among them than at the average firm. In this company group market perspectives are also more favourable than in the average (Table 18.2).

Case studies justify the survey results also in this field. They support that in the recent years at many Hungarian (and especially at many foreign-owned) companies significant innovation efforts were undertaken. Within the framework of these efforts often rigorous 'technological' innovations took place together with applying modern management practices in order to overcome the lag especially on the field of marketing (that proved to be successful in the developed countries).

Furthermore, survey data support the idea that in the Hungarian economy the chance for success is greater in the group of innovative firms than in the group of conservative enterprises (Table 18.3).

Realistic judgement of the relationship between innovation efforts and profit making capability (which can be read from the table) is not easy. We have to consider that among the both innovative and lucrative Hungarian companies there are many foreign owned firms. All this does not mean however, that in any case we should expect the improvement of the business from giving a company to a foreign owner. The reason is that the explored correlation originates from the fact that foreign capital in Hungary aimed at acquiring the good-quality i.e. innovative and lucrative enterprises.

Table 18.2 - Market Position of Innovative Firms as of Spring 1998 (Figures of the Innovation Survey)

Figures	Developers of	Introducers of		Hungarian	Foreign	Firms doing R&D	Mean of population
	new product/ service		new technology	market conquerors			
% of firms undertaking expanding market strategy	56,8	61,4	64,4	60,6	68,9	63,6	28,1
Weight of export in sales, %**	38	36	27	30	58	28	19
% of							
- EU	76	72	62	58	93	61	(49)
- Eastern European	54	47	38	38	49	34	(28)
- USA	24	14	16	11	22	23	(10)
- Far Eastern	11	7	4	3	11	5	(4)
relations in export-import							
Sales turnover forecast (1997=100 %)**							
- domestic sales	117,5	118,4	114,8	120,9	121,8	126,4	117,3
- sales abroad	112,7	123,0	120,6	126,1	129,3	132,9	121,0
- together	115,6	118,2	116,5	122,0	127,6	130,8	117,6
Producer price increase for 1998** (1997 = 100)							
- domestic	113,8	113,7	111,2	111,9	112,3	109,7	113,3
- foreign sales	120,5	119,8	121,0	112,5	114,8	112,5	113,7

* Figures of responders to the 'traditional' questionnaire (except for those in brackets, which are at our disposal only from the innovation questionnaire)

** Means weighted with average staff number

Source: GKI's surveys

Table 18.3 - Some Figures of Efficiency at Innovative Companies as of Spring 1999 (Figures of the Innovation Survey)

Figures	Developers of	Introducers of		Hungarian	Foreign	Firms doing R&D	Mean of population
	new product/ service		new technology	market conquerors			
Average* share of products competitive on the world market, %	36	34	39	55	57	50	(35)
% share of firms increasing their staff in 1998	58	53	48	53	59	49	27
Gross wage expected for 1998*(1997=100)	116,4	116,6	116,4	116,5	117,5	118,4	115,3
% share of profit making firms in 1997	87	91	96	87	87	80	78
% share of firms in a favourable liquidity position	65	58	58	45	51	52	49

* Figures of responders to the 'traditional' questionnaire (except for those in brackets, which are at our disposal only from the innovation questionnaire)

** Means weighted with average staff number

Source: GKI's surveys

3 R&D and Technology Transfer

Types of innovation activities planned by the companies are also traditional subjects of GKI surveys. The 1998 Autumn data are presented in table 18.4 (basically reflecting unchanging ratios for years):

Based on the data in the table, though the number of companies planning innovation is significant, it is still much smaller than in developed economies. Among the examined companies those aiming at acquiring the basic 'knowledge' for innovation (by own research and development or by purchase of patent, licence, know-how) are notably low in number especially if we take into consideration the technological gap featuring the Hungarian economy.

Table 18.4 - Share of Firms Planning Innovation in the Near Future as of Autumn 1998 (%)

Innovation type	Basic	Significant	Negligible	No innovation planned	Total
	Action is planned				
Research and Development	13	23	19	45	100
Purchase of patent, licence, know-how	1	7	19	73	100
Large investment*	16	40	25	19	100
Market research	28	45	15	12	100
Development of sales network	19	38	20	23	100
Advertisement, PR	11	40	30	19	100
Improvement of after sales service	12	34	23	31	100

* The majority of investment has a supplementary role. As a result of such investment, 'only' 32% of the firms expect modern, more competitive products, 23% expect modernisation of its technology.

Source: GKI's surveys

Unfavourable statistics[3] about the expenditures on R&D also support the weakness of Hungarian efforts to acquire 'knowledge'. For international comparison, R&D expenditures are at about 0.7% of the GDP and the per capita R&D expenditures are at US$ 50 (declining until 1996). In developed countries however, the respective figures are 2-2.5% and US$ 400-450; even in Spain they reach 1% and US$ 130 respectively.

Due to the lack of statistics regarding the 'purchase' of knowledge, especially regarding technology transfer, our survey's information on the subject is supported 'only' by the experiences gained during case studies (see: Lakatos, B. –Papanek, G.1994).

[3] Though we would not like to debate the rightness of statements drawn from the statistics (which will also be shown here), we would like to make a comment. The Hungarian statistics measured R&D activities of only 220 (larger) companies. However, according to our surveys several thousand smaller Hungarian companies also have their own R&D.

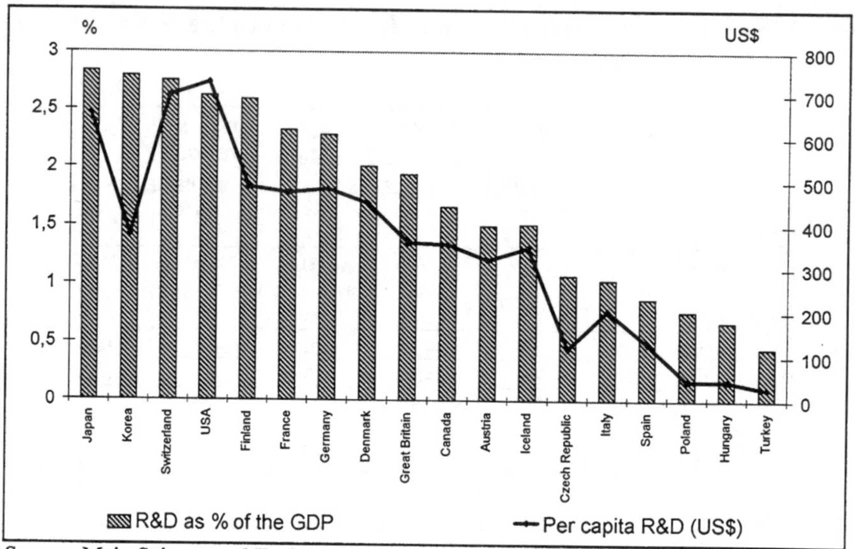

Source: Main Science and Technology Indicators, OECD 1998/1

Figure 18.1 – R&D Expenditures, 1996

Our research showed: the so-called bridging institutions that should 'intermediate' innovation information flows are weak in the Hungarian economy, which fact is more unfavourable than the above mentioned. Undoubtedly, such institutions are gaining in number rapidly in recent years, based on the available information. Beside the earlier knowledge transferring organisations (e.g.: libraries, specialised R&D institutions) many new non-profit companies and enterprises undertook the role of helping enterprise innovation processes. The Hungarian Enterprise Development Fund (based on the British example financed from abroad and by the state) established a network to support enterprises. Chambers, professional associations started a similar type of activity. Many foundations, consulting institutions operating on an enterprise basis and incubator houses, industrial parks came to existence. Researches that started in this field however, show that the enterprises, which utilise innovations, are dissatisfied with the efficiency of this network.

Based on the data, direct relationships between enterprises and independent R&D institutions (universities or specialised research institutes) are unfortunately rare in the Hungarian economy. The Patent Office information on new technological results is not used either. Also the (mainly new) documentary, information providing, advisory institutions could not (yet) find the necessary connections to the majority of today's innovative firms.

Table 18.5 - Breakdown of Firms (that Participated in the Research) in Judging the Importance of Support Received for Innovation* (%)

Institution providing support	Significant, frequent	Occasional	No	Total
	Help			
Hungarian documentary, information, advisory organisation	10	22	68	100
Patent Office	3	15	82	100
Universities, colleges	9	28	62	100
R&D institutions	5	17	78	100
Hungarian enterprises	11	23	66	100
Foreign mother company	13	13	74	100
Other foreign organisations	13	14	73	100

* Figures from the innovation questionnaire. Obviously 'optimistic' this time as well.
Source: GKI's surveys

At the same time on the field of supporting innovation, foreign relations were the most frequent according to the data, which firmly supports the earlier mentioned great importance of technology transfer in the case of Hungary. Certainly, Hungarian and foreign companies differ a lot in this respect. Out of the latter 26% denoted that relations with the mother company are of basic importance, 14% said them to be significant, 24% mentioned that occasionally they receive some help in given matters (moreover, their cooperation links with other foreign companies are also stronger than with Hungarian enterprises). For the majority of the companies, however, this source of innovation information does not exist.

4 Successes and Problems in the Diffusion of Innovations

To give a general view on the result of Hungarian innovation efforts is rather difficult. As first attempt at national level studies, one can examine the per capita GDP, its sectoral and export breakdown, which describe the developed (competitive) nature of an economy in the broadest way. Statistics on patents, scientific publications etc. are more detailed but partial sources of information. One has to understand however, that on the efficiency of Hungarian R&D expenditures, we can give only approximate and contradictory pictures in spite of all the information base at our disposal.

GDP figures are the most reliable elements of evaluation. As it is known, Hungarian per capita GDP was US$ 4.405 in 1996 (calculated with official exchange rates). The PPP GDP was slightly above US$ 7.000. This level is rather low in international comparison. A more favourable judgement of the economy can be traced in the production structure: industry, especially machinery and services provide for high proportions in the Hungarian GDP. The mentioned favourable view is supported by the high export content of the output especially by the high export figures to the developed countries (that grew markedly in the last 4-5 years) and by the significant export of machinery as well.

To judge the results of Hungarian R&D is not easy either. According to the 1996 patent statistics for instance, 188 Hungarian patents were registered in Hungary, and 273 abroad (CSO 1997), much less than in earlier years. Moreover, calculations of recent months showed explicitly a negative (though weak) correlation between the sectoral R&D expenditures and sectoral export, i.e. the recent improvement of competitiveness was not a consequence of domestic R&D. From these figures and trends however, the efficiency or changes of Hungarian R&D cannot be judged clearly. (We can only see the more frequent foreign registration of enterprise patents than patents of other organisations, which refers to different utility of academic and enterprise patents.) Nonetheless, the patent statistics published below by the OECD draw a favourable picture on the results of Hungarian R&D. The cited Hungarian indices for 'inventiveness', 'dependency' and 'autosufficiency' are of good medium level value in international comparison, and 'only' the diffusion rate is slow.

Table 18.6 - Patent Applications

No.		1992	1993	1994	1995
1.	National patent applications, total	10.925	12.772	17.005	20.882
2.	of which: - resident patent appl.	1.500	1.144	1.164	1.112
3.	- non-resident patent applications	9.425	11.628	15.841	19.770
4.	External patent applications	2.006	3.364	3.668	3.953
	Inventiveness coefficient (resident patent appl. per 1000 inhabitant)	1,5	1,1	1,1	1,1
3/2	Dependency ratio	6,28	10,16	13,63	17,78
2/1	Autosufficiency ratio	0,14	0,09	0,07	0,05
4/2	Rate of diffusion	..	2,24	3,21	3,40

Source: OECD (1998a), page 49-52

During our surveys, we always received important information from our traditional questions put on the obstacles to innovation processes.

Table 18.7 - Share of Firms Recording the Given Obstacle to Innovation as of Autumn 1998 (%)

Obstacle	Firms employing			State	Hungarian private	Foreign	Total
	-50	51-300	301-	owned companies			
		people					
Lack of capital	45	43	53	49	50	26	45
Lack of information	14	17	13	11	18	12	16
Limited own R&D capacities	27	37	49	39	36	32	36
Poor chance of return	41	41	46	39	45	34	41

Source: GKI's surveys

Table 18.7 has a dramatic 'message'. In the Hungarian economy besides capital shortage, the poor chance of return on innovation is the greatest obstacle to modernisation. According to more detailed investigations, the problems of return are explained by the high costs of innovation (dubbed by significant tax and other contribution burdens) and by the limited possibilities of asserting 'intellectual property rights', i.e. rights to brands, trademarks, patents.

5 Some Concluding Remarks

The presented research justified that the enterprise investment survey can provide us with many useful pieces of information on the National Innovation System and on the innovative companies. This information can hardly be obtained by other methods. The advantages of the applied methodology are the following:

- Hungarian innovation statistics are rare and cover a small range of companies so they are not reliable enough. Therefore, information on the innovations of the business sphere is very valuable.
- The applied survey method provided us with a fast and relatively cheap source of information regarding innovations as well. A further advantage is that the received data was easy to process and to evaluate.
- The survey results and the conclusions could be verified from other information sources, databases and they proved to be in accordance with the result of other researches.[4]

We cannot deny however, that the applied method has drawbacks as well:

- The response ratio is smaller than usual in case of the innovation questionnaire. This is especially true for small and medium sized enterprises.
- As there were closed questions, what happened was primarily verification of the research team's hypotheses because the enterprise was limited in giving information. Further case studies, interviews, 'brainstorming' type of workshops with participating managers and researchers are needed to overcome this problem.
- Regarding certain other important questions with respect to innovation, we still could not get information even with the presented survey. It seems for instance, that the methods for investigating innovation beyond the scope of R&D (such as technology transfer) have still not been elaborated. We also found the techniques that meant to explore the efficiency of innovation to be rather inadequate.

---

[4] We would quote the results of the enterprise survey by Chikán (1997), which concluded that the following factors were the most important obstacles to enterprise innovation: lack of financing funds, 'over'-taxation, no capacity to innovate, lack of market feedback, high costs of innovation. This list of factor groups differs from our results only in the wording of the questions and answers.

References

Chikán, A. (1997), *Versenyben a világgal* (Competing the World), Budapest University of Economic Sciences, Department of Corporate Economics.

Csernenszky, L., Papanek, G. and M. Pető.(1992), 'Business Surveys and Forecasts in Hungary', in: Oppenländer, K.H., G. Poser, and G. Nerb, (eds): *New Development of Business Surveys in Central and Eastern Europe*. CIRET Studien No.42.

Habuda, J. (1998), Financing R&D in Germany, Manuscript.

KSH (1997), Tudományos kutatás és kísérleti fejlesztés. (CSO-Scientific research and experimental development).

Lakatos, B. and G. Papanek (1994), Motivations of FDI in Hungary. GKI Co's. *Economic Trends and Research Summaries, No.3.*

Lundvall, B. (1988), 'Innovation as an Interactive Process: From User-producer Interaction to National Systems of Innovation,' in: Dosi, G. et al (eds): *Technical Change and Economic Theory,* Pinter, London.

Metcalfe, S. (1995), 'The Economic Foundations of Technology Policy', in: Stoneman, P. (ed): *Handbook of the Economics of Innovation and Technical Change*, Blackwell, London.

OECD (1993), *Frascati Manual*, Paris, in Hungarian: OMFB, 1996.

OECD (1994), *Oslo Manual*, Paris, in Hungarian: Miniszterelnöki Hivatal, 1996.

OECD (1998a), *Main Science and Technology Indicators, No. 1.*

OECD (1998b), *National Innovation Systems, Analytical Findings.*

OECD Proceedings (1998), *The Competitiveness of Transition Economies.*

Papanek, G., R. Petz and A. Vértes (1997), *EU Harmonized Enterprise Surveys,* in Hungarian: Special English edition of the Statisztikai Szemle.

Román, Z. (1973), *Termelékenységünk az iparban,* KJK.

Schumpeter, J. (1934), *The Theory of Economic Development,* Harward U.P. Cambridge, Mass., in Hungarian: A gazdasági fejlődés elmélete. KJK 1980.

19 Human Capital and Growth

ALEX SUNDAKOV and DOUG STEEL

1 Introduction

The measurement of quality of the labour input is one of the most difficult aspects of growth accounting. Using the Cobb-Douglas form, the traditional production function appears as:

$$Y_t = A\,K_t^{\alpha}\,L_t^{1-\alpha} \tag{1}$$

Thus, economic growth can be represented as:

$$\Delta\,Y = A\,(K_t^{\alpha}\,L_t^{1-\alpha} - K_{t-1}^{\alpha}\,L_{t-1}^{1-\alpha}) \tag{2}$$

New Zealand data indicate that both K and L (measured as hours worked) have been increasing in recent years, hence the productivity puzzle - economic growth appears to be largely explained by the increased quantity of inputs, rather than by their better use. This seems inconsistent with the extent of economic reforms undertaken in New Zealand. The New Zealand puzzle is the reverse of the more usual problem of growth accounting, where increase in the volume of inputs leaves a large unexplained residual in the above equation.

However, the traditional production function is really no more than an *ad hoc* representation, with little theoretical grounding. It would be more appropriate to write a generic production function in terms of human capital:

$$\Delta\,Y = A\,(K_t^{\alpha}\,H_t^{1-\alpha} - K_{t-1}^{\alpha}\,H_{t-1}^{1-\alpha}) \tag{3}$$

In this form, there is no *a priori* reason why the value of human capital should have been on a rising trend in New Zealand in recent years. In fact, there are some theoretical reasons, which are discussed below, to suggest the value of human capital could have fallen during the period of reforms.

Our research program looks at various ways to proxy the value of human capital available for production in New Zealand. The hypothesis we wish to test is that the value of human capital may indeed have declined during the reform period, and that this decline may explain some or all of the productivity puzzle. What is more, we are particularly interested in using data from the business opinion surveys to test that proposition.

2 The Value of Human Capital

New Zealand's human capital can be thought of as the sum total of all skills possessed by the New Zealand labour force which are relevant to economic activity. Each individual adds to these skills through education and training, as well as through life experience. The greater the investment, the higher the level of human capital is likely to be. However, human capital can also be devalued as old knowledge and skills become outdated with changing market conditions. For the society as a whole, human capital can also depreciate as age cohorts move through and pass into retirement. Consequently, measured gross investment in human capital cannot be equated with a net increase in that capital. Given market volatility, in particular, a nation's human capital is just as likely to go up as down in the short term.

During the periods of significant structural change, such as experienced by New Zealand during the late 1980s and early 1990s, the types of skills and knowledge demanded in the labour market are likely to change very rapidly. Past training, especially firm-specific and industry-specific training, is likely to lose its value. During such periods, new training may not keep pace with the depreciation of the previously accumulated human capital, so that the total level of human capital may well decline.

From the point of view of growth accounting, the problem is that standard techniques for measuring the quality of labour tend to include new human capital investment (such as years of education), but ignore human capital depreciation.

3 Labour Force Characteristics

The conventional approach is to adjust the volume of labour input by the level of education, the age distribution of those employed and the occupational structure of the employed. This information is available from the Household Labour Force Survey, although there are a number of problems which will need to be resolved. First, the time series for the occupational breakdown in HLFS only goes back to 1985. Second, HLFS measures the number of employees rather than the hours worked. To account for the quantity of the labour input properly, we will need to reconcile the HLFS measure with the hours worked information in the Quarterly Employment Survey.

While the data of this kind are unable to capture the important depreciation effects discussed above, they are a useful starting point for the analysis. The creative challenge is to construct a labour quality index which incorporates the relevant information. Alternatively, the index components can be used separately and the significance of each can be tested. We will commence the investigation by testing the consistency of the survey data. For example, if the proportion of employees in professional occupations is increasing, we would expect to find that the level of educational attainment on average is also increasing. If the data do not appear to be consistent, we will need to consider possible explanations.

A quality index can be constructed from unit record data as follows:

$$Q_i = f(AGE_i, QUAL_i, OCCUP_i) \qquad (4)$$

where for each individual (i) in the survey, AGE_i is self explanatory, $QUAL_i$ is their highest level of qualification, and $OCCUP_i$ represents their occupational group. A quality rating will need to be allocated to each survey category. For example, the survey classifies respondents as having no qualifications, school and post school qualifications. These categories could be allocated ratings of 1 to 3 respectively. It will be more difficult to rate the occupational and age categories. The age ratings will show a skewed inverted parabola reflecting the experience of the labour units. Income distributions across age bands may be used as an indication to the likely parameters for the parabola. We will explore the human capital literature for guidance.

The human capital measure will be constructed as:

$$H_t = \Sigma^t_i Q_i \qquad (5)$$

We will analyse this human capital measure by estimating an equation of the type:

$$\log Y=\alpha+\beta_1\log K+\beta_2\log H+\beta_3\log L \quad (6)$$

The full equation:

$$\log Y=\alpha+\beta_1\log K+\beta_2\log L+\beta_3\log AGE+\beta_4\log QUAL +\beta_5\log OCCUP \quad (7)$$

will be used to see if the human capital factors enter the model as separate explanatory variables. Econometrically this approach is more widely accepted as it avoids restricting the coefficients on the individual components of the labour quality index. Approaching the problem this way will indicate the weights that should be applied in the labour quality index. The actual form of the estimation equation may, however, differ from the above to avoid econometric problems such as multicollinearity, which may arise due to correlation between the QUAL and OCCUP variables. Also, other variables will be examined. For example, a health proxy, life expectancy will be included and examined.

In addition, the quality of the labour input may also depend on the relative proportion of full-time and part-time employees. We will examine whether inclusion of an employment status variable affects the measure of human capital.

4 Quarterly Survey of Business Opinion

An alternative data source is the NZIER *Quarterly Survey of Business Opinion*, which asks respondents to report whether it has become more or less easy to find skilled and unskilled labour (see Figure 19.1).

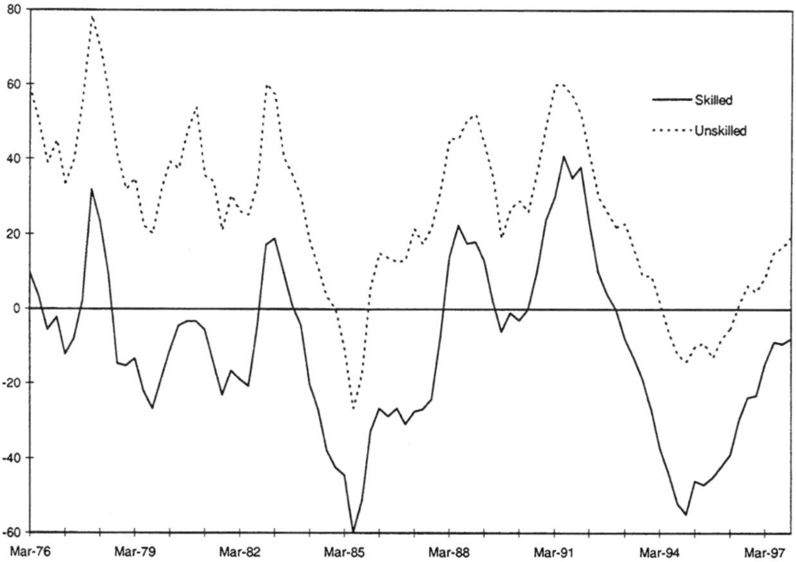

Source: NZIER

Figure 19.1 - QSBO: Ease of Finding Labour (Net Percent of Respondents)

For any given level of employment, greater reported difficulty in finding skilled labour could be interpreted as a deterioration in the level of human capital in New Zealand. If, after adjusting for the level of economic activity, employers find it harder to recruit skilled staff, then it can be said that the pool of skills available in New Zealand has become less valuable relative to requirements.

An important advantage of using the QSBO data is that the survey questions allows respondents to change their definition of skill over time. For example, if ability to speak Maori becomes a valued skill, compared to the past, then the new requirement will be reflected in the reported perception of the difficulty. Consequently, these data, unlike the measure of qualifications, are more likely to capture the depreciation of the human capital stock.

The difficulty with using these data is that it is not immediately obvious how changes in other factors can be disentangled from changes in the value of the human capital stock. A particular problem is that responses related to both skilled and unskilled workers tend to move in tandem.

One way to deal with this issue is to estimate an equation of the type:

$$S = \alpha + \beta U + \varepsilon \tag{8}$$

where S represents perceptions about the difficulty of hiring skilled labour, U refers to unskilled labour. In particular, we will examine whether S and U should be estimated using levels or differences. In theory, they are already change variables because the QSBO question asks about difficulty relative to the previous period. However, our analysis of the survey suggests that respondents may in fact treat this as a levels variable. We will examine the residual from this equation to see if it can be interpreted as a short fall in human capital. If so, we will adjust hours worked to account for this short fall. We will also try alternative specifications of the equation.

5 Initial Investigation

A visual examination of the *QSBO* data reveals that the relative difficulty of finding skilled labour compared to unskilled labour varies over time. We believe this variability in the difference may contain significant information. When the difference (defined as ease of finding unskilled labour – ease of finding skilled labour) increases, it is likely to indicate that there is relatively less human capital in the country. This is because a widening gap between the ease of finding unskilled and skilled labour signals a relative shortage of skill in the economy. A decline in the difference means that the relative difficulty of finding skilled labour compared to unskilled also declines. These differences are represented in charts 5.1.2 and 5.2.2 (for the economy as a whole and for the manufacturing sector only). On these charts, an upward movement in the difference curve can be interpreted as an increase in the abundance of human capital, while a downward movement indicates a decrease in human capital. Another way of thinking about this is that an upward movement in the curve signals that the human capital constraint on economic growth is relaxing, while a downward movement suggests it is tightening.

We believe it is possible to argue that by focusing on the difference between the skilled and unskilled series, we are able to take out the influence of cyclical macroeconomic factors. This is because both series are cyclical, but there is no reason to expect that the difference would be cyclical.

We examine the effects of these changes on productivity in figures 19.4, 19.5 and 19.8, 19.9. The productivity numbers are standard measures of average labour productivity obtained by dividing GDP by the hours worked. It is instructive to look at the manufacturing sector separately from the economy as a whole, because for the economy-wide measure, services may bias labour productivity. However, we do not find any fundamental differences.

5.1 Economy Wide Charts

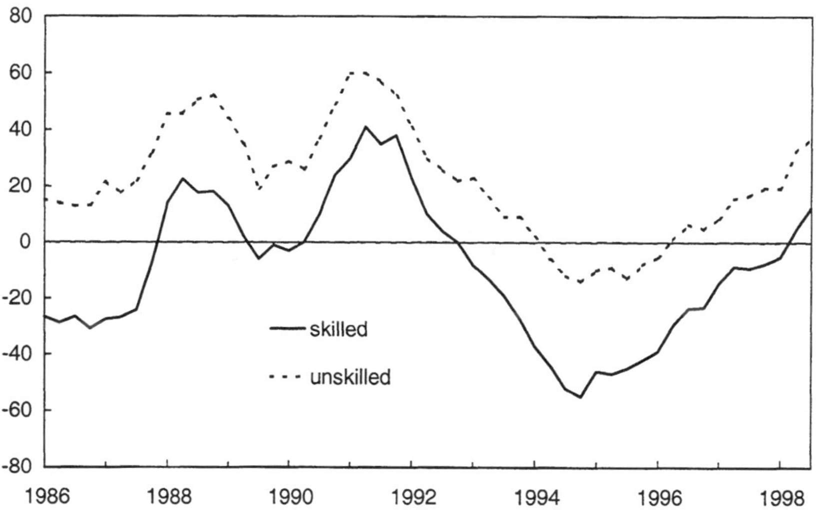

Figure 19.2 - Underlying Economy-wide QSBO Data (Ease of Finding Skilled and Unskilled Labour)

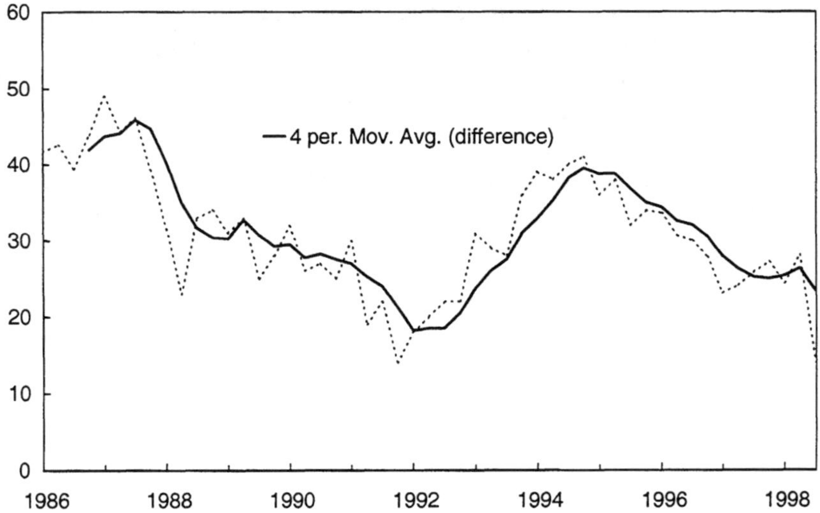

Figure 19.3 - Difference Between the Skilled and Unskilled Series (Actual and 4 Quarter Moving Average)

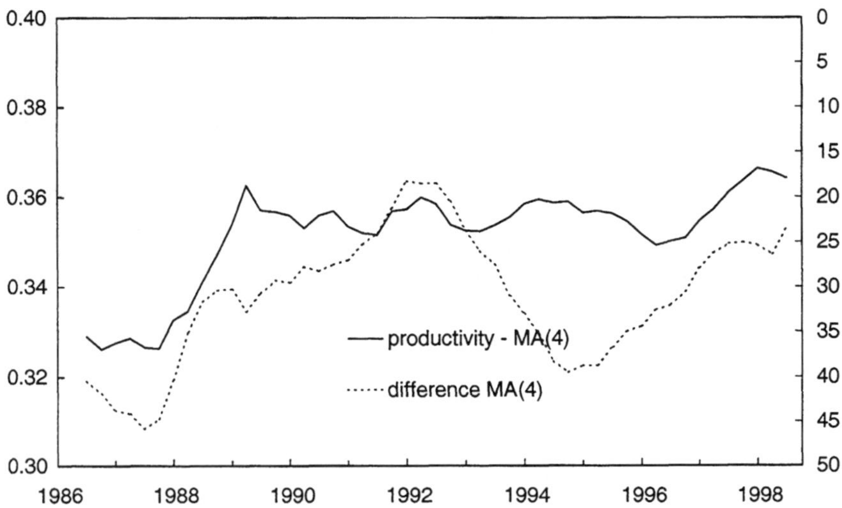

Figure 19.4 - Economy-wide Labour Productivity and Human Capital (4 Quarter Moving Averages, Contemporaneous)

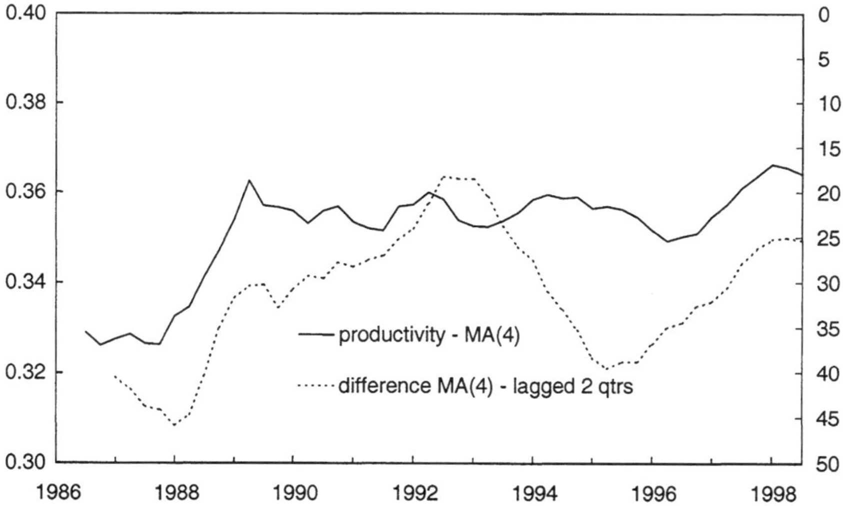

Figure 19.5 - Economy-wide Labour Productivity and Human Capital (4 Quarter Moving Averages, Human Capital Lagged 2 Quarters)

5.2 *Manufacturing Charts*

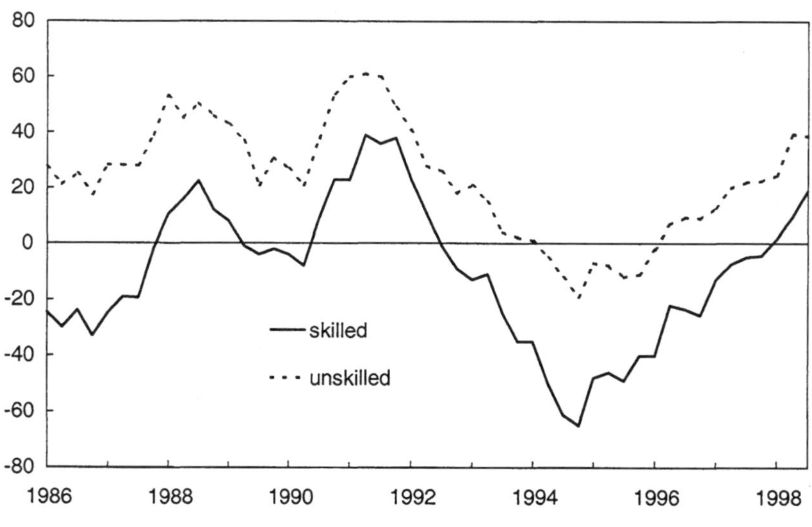

Figure 19.6 - Underlying Manufacturing Sector QSBO Data (Ease of Finding Skilled and Unskilled Labour)

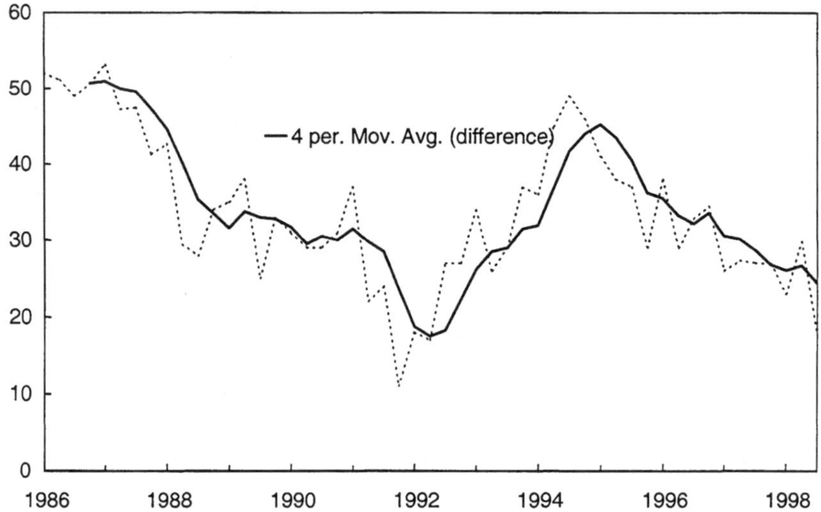

Figure 19.7 - Difference Between the Skilled and Unskilled Series (Manufacturing Sector)

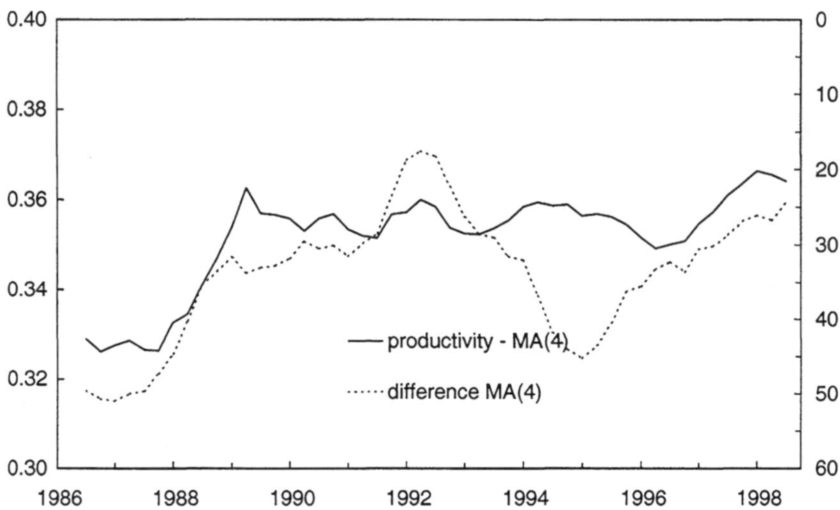

Figure 19.8 - Manufacturing Productivity and Human Capital (4 Quarter Moving Averages, Contemporaneous)

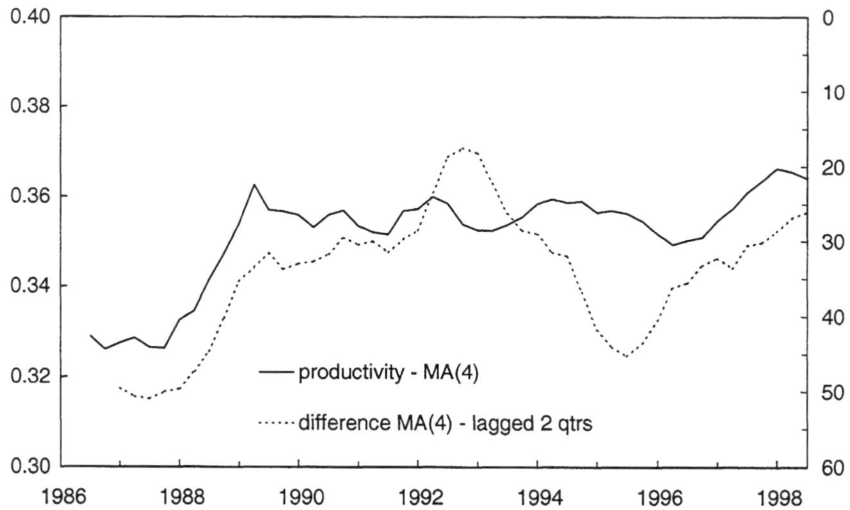

Fugure 9 - Manufacturing Productivity and Human Capital (4 Quarter Moving Averages, Human Capital Lagged 2 Quarter)

6 Conclusion

This work in progress incorporates both conventional and speculative approaches. Inclusion of labour force characteristics into growth equations follows international literature, although adjusted for the specific properties of New Zealand data bases. The QSBO approach does not follow an established procedure. However, we believe an approach of this kind is most likely to shed new light on the value of human capital available in New Zealand.

Our initial investigation suggests that with the exception of a short period in 1995, there seems to be a strong correlation between improvement in productivity and an increase in human capital as measured by our construct from the *QSBO* series. The change in human capital indicated by the series, however, is counterintuitive. It shows human capital rising from 1986 to 1992, which is precisely the period of very rapid reforms when we would have expected higher than usual depreciation of human capital in New Zealand. This puzzle is the next step in our on-going work.

20 Role of Firm-Specific Factors and Lending Relationships in Availability of Bank Credit: Firm-Level Evidence from Finnish Survey Data

JUKKA TOPI*

Abstract

The Bank of Finland has been involved in conducting a semi-annual survey on Finnish service-sector firms' views on their financing since autumn 1994. The survey has charted the firms' acquisition, availability, terms and servicing of credit as well as their growth and profitability prospects. Descriptive analysis on the survey indicates that the Finnish firms have been successful in their activities during 1994 – 1998. However, the decrease in the firms' credit availability problems has been even more substantial than the decrease in the firms' profitability problems. Results from an econometric analysis based on the survey data show that both firm-specific factors and lender-borrower relationships affect the probability of credit availability problems. Moreover, the analysis indicates that the economic condition of the banking sector has an impact on credit availability.

* The views in the paper are those of the author and do not necessarily correspond to the views of the Bank of Finland.

1 Introduction

The Bank of Finland (BOF) has been involved in conducting a semi-annual survey on Finnish service sector firms' views on their financing since autumn 1994.[1] The survey has charted the firms' acquisition, availability, terms and servicing of credit as well as their growth and profitability prospects. This paper offers a short presentation of the survey and presents some econometric evidence based on the survey data. The survey provides an extensive data set for the years 1994 - 1998, and the results can best serve as an example for the future research. The paper has its origins in the work of Kuussaari and Vesala (1995) who carried out logistic estimations using the data from the survey in autumn 1994.

In the first part of the study, we present some descriptive statistics from the survey and examine the sampling process employed in the survey. Results from the descriptive analysis indicate that the Finnish firms have been successful in their activities, and the profitability problems of the firms have decreased during years 1994 - 1998. The firms' growth and profitability prospects have also been positive. Firms have been able to follow their debt servicing plans well, and the number of deviations from the plans has decreased during the period.

The results concerning firms' economic activity fit well the general picture of the Finnish economy. In the early 1990s, the Finnish economy experienced a severe depression and a banking crisis. The GDP contracted from the beginning of the 1990s until the growth turned positive in 1994. In the latter part of the 1990s, the economy has been recovering from the depression. The conditions of the banking sector have also improved since mid-1990s while the banking sector has experienced drastic structural changes through mergers and take-overs.

While the signs of firms' success measured by the real economy factors have been positive in the late 1990s, the improvement in firms' access to finance has been even more substantial according to our descriptive analysis. The share of firms with credit availability problems has approached zero from 16% in autumn 1994. Irrespective of the credit availability problems, the firms' demand for funding has remained quite stable during the years 1994 - 1995.

---

[1] A parallel survey on manufacturing firms' financing has been conducted from 1993 by the Confederation of Finnish Industry and Employers (TT). In 1997, the surveys were integrated and are now conducted jointly by the BOF, the TT, and the Ministry of Trade and Industry. In this study, the emphasis is on the firms from service sector industries.

In the second part of the study, we take a closer look at the explanations for credit availability problems with firm-level data, which is also motivated by the descriptive analysis on aggregate data. In the literature, credit availability problems have been explained by the relationship between the lender and the borrower and by various firm-specific factors that have an impact on the borrower's reputation. Attention has also been paid to the factors associated with lenders and their economic condition. Our econometric work supports the view that both firm-specific factors and the type of lender-borrower relationship affect the probability of credit availability problems. We also find evidence on the significant role of the banking sector condition in credit availability problems. This evidence underlines the importance of a sound and stable banking sector to ensure sufficient financing for the firms.

The paper is outlined as follows. In section 2, the contents of the survey are introduced. In section 3, we construct a simple empirical framework for explaining the credit availability problems of firms. In section 4, we review the data and the econometric method, and present some estimation results. Finally, conclusions are drawn in section 5.

2 Description of the Survey

In total, the survey on Finnish service-sector firms' financing issues has been conducted nine times since autumn 1994. Statistics Finland has composed the samples for the survey and collected the basic data set through firm interviews. Other bodies involved[2] have contributed to further analyses and published the results of the survey. In this section, we shortly examine the sampling process and review the developments in some of the core variables from 1994 to 1998.

Statistics Finland composed the sample for the first survey in autumn 1994 on the basis of its Register of Enterprises. The initial target population included 11,500 service-sector firms. The smallest firms and enterprises with non-corporate status were excluded. The sample of the initial survey was targeted to include about one thousand firms from Finnish service sector industries representing firms of various sizes and locations.

Various sampling schemes were used in combination to achieve as representative a sample as possible. Since the firms in the target population are unevenly distributed across various industries, stratified sampling was

2 See footnote 1.

used. However, the 350 largest firms in the target population were automatically included into the sample. The rest of the target population was divided into four sub-populations by their employment size and industry. Trade was separated from other industries since it accounted for more than a half of the whole firm population. Stratification was done to ensure that firms even from small industries were appropriately represented in the sample. Altogether, 1,004 firms were included in the initial sample in autumn 1994. Accepted responses were obtained from 810 firms.

In spring 1995, the sample consisted of 783 firms from the initial sample. Others were excluded, mainly because they had not replied or they had announced their reluctance to attend subsequent waves of the survey. A new set of 150 firms was added to improve the representativeness of the sample. After these changes, the sample of surveyed firms included 938 observations. The number of accepted responses was 823 in spring 1995.

The number of firms in the sample and the number of accepted responses during the years 1994 - 1998 are presented in Table 20.1. After spring 1995, additional firms have not been included in the sample. In contrast, firms have been excluded from the sample over time mainly because of refusal to reply. Moreover, firms have been excluded due to bankruptcy, insolvency or other corporate developments.

Table 20.1 - Number of Firms in Sample and Number of Accepted Responses 1994 – 1998

	Number of firms in sample	Number of accepted responses
1/1994	1.004	810
1/1995	938	823
2/1995	788	735
1/1996	727	662
2/1996	666	620
1/1997	619	537
2/1997	589	529
1/1998	552	495
2/1998	526	473
Total	6.409	5.684

Because of the changes in the sample composition, one must be cautious while drawing conclusions from the data set extracted from the survey. Analyses based on firm-specific comparisons between various points of time should be made only after careful harmonisation of data sets.

Moreover, the observations may be missing due to some factors correlated with observed data, especially with profitability problems and credit availability problems. Finally, the target population has probably changed from the time of composing the initial sample.

2.1 Descriptive Analysis of Core Variables

The survey provides a large variety of firm-level data on financing issues of high relevance. The questions posed consistently since autumn 1994 can be divided into four categories. The first category incorporates questions on the background information of the firm to categorise the scope and the scale of its activities. The second category includes questions assessing the financing conditions and problems of the firm. The third category puts questions covering the financing plans of the firm. The fourth category incorporates questions on the firm's prospects both concerning its own activities and its business environment. As from the beginning of 1995, questions on the banking relations of the firm were gradually added to the survey as a fifth category. In addition to the questions presented in the survey on a permanent basis, additional topics have been touched from time to time. These digressions do not provide, however, a basis for a systematic analysis.

Here, we concentrate on a few interesting variables from the data set and discuss their developments on an aggregate level by a descriptive analysis. The data set consisting of all 5.672 observations during 1994 – 1998 is used for the descriptive analysis. We examine distributions of six variables covering the firms' size and profitability as well as their credit availability, credit servicing ability and future plans to acquire credit. By the descriptive analysis, we get insights into the aggregate developments and interaction of the core variables.

In Figure 20.1, the distribution of turnover across three categories (small: < FIM 50 million, medium: > FIM 50 million and < FIM 300 million, large: > FIM 300 million) is presented. The distribution remains basically the same throughout the period of investigation. As one can notice, the share of small firms has been gradually diminishing. However, the distribution of turnover highlights the small average size of the Finnish service sector firms.

In Figure 20.2, the distribution of reported current profitability across three categories (good, fair, poor) is presented. Throughout the period, a clear majority of the firms have reported their profitability to be good or fair. A remarkable decrease in the profitability problems can be noticed.

One could expect that the exclusion of firms from the sample (see Table 20.1) to be the reason for the decrease in the profitability problems. However, according to our calculations, the distribution of profitability follows almost the same pattern in the sample of 402 firms for which we have replies throughout the years 1995 - 1998.

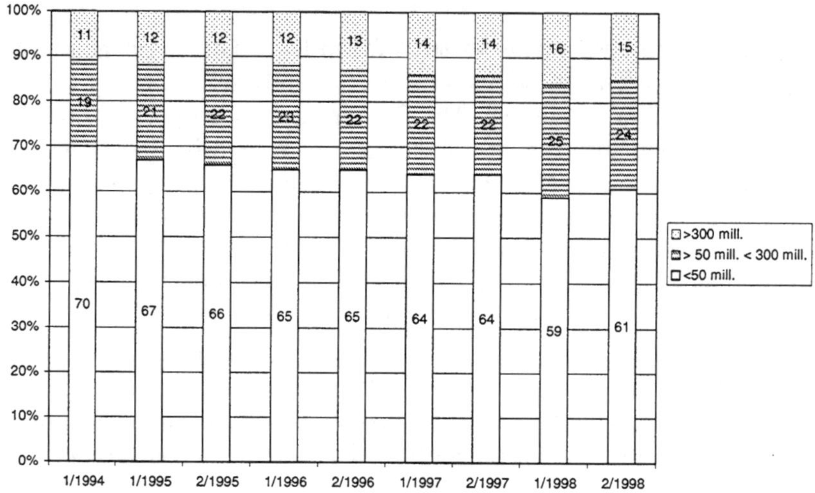

Figure 20.1 - Turnover Distribution (% of Total)

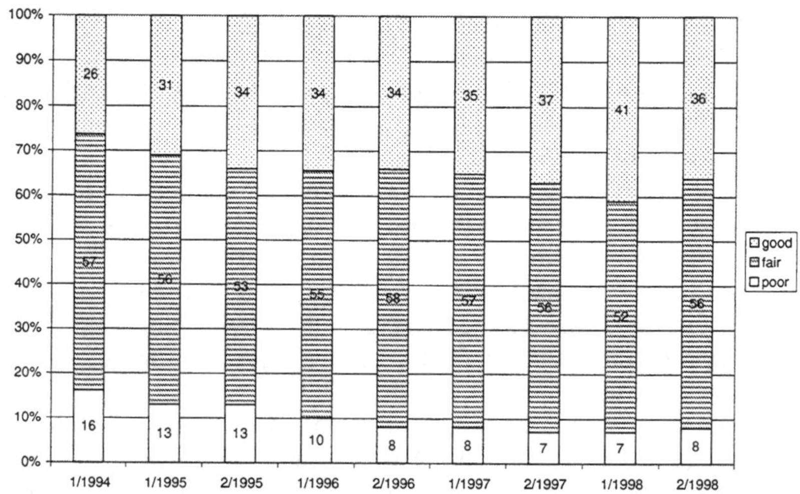

Figure 20.2 - Profitability Distribution (% of Total)

In Figure 20.3, profitability prospects of the firms in sample are reviewed. The large number of firms reporting an improvement in their profitability outlook in 1994 - 1995 reflects the general positive atmosphere experienced in Finland after the depression in the early 1990s. Towards the end of the decade, deceleration of expected profitability increase can be observed, but the general trend of profits is still clearly upwards.

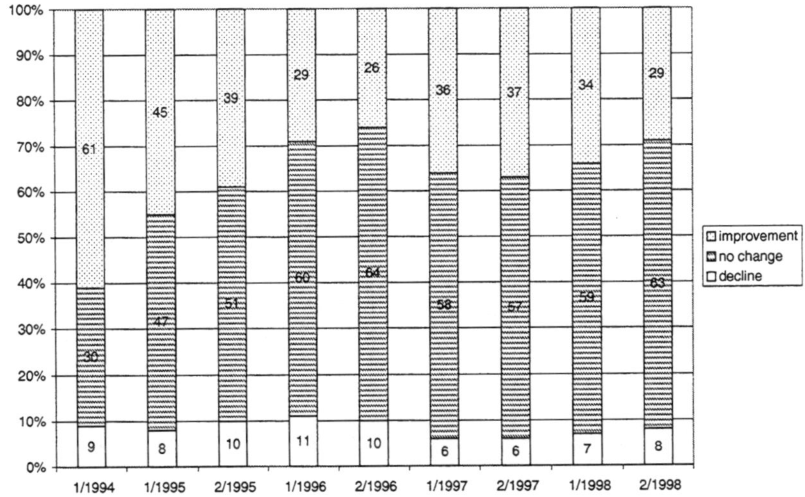

Figure 20.3 - Assessment on Changes in Profitability (% of Total)

The share of firms that deviated from their debt servicing plans is shown in Figure 20.4. There is a decrease in the number of debt servicing problems although the share of problem loans still remains noticeable until 1998. On the basis of a descriptive analysis, the firms' debt servicing problems have reduced at a slower pace than their profitability problems.

In Figure 20.5, the changes in the number of reported funding problems are shown. As shown in Figure 20.1, the sample mainly consists of relatively small firms. Small firms are commonly assumed to acquire funding mostly from the banking sector or other financial intermediaries. This allows us to interpret the firms' funding problems as credit availability problem in the context of this study. The main finding drawn from the survey is in this respect that the problems due to poor access to funding, or credit have diminished remarkably. Especially, comparing Figure 20.5 with Figures 20.2 and 20.4 reveals that the share of the firms with credit availability problems has decreased more rapidly than the share of firms violating their debt servicing plans or facing profitability problems. This observation increases the relevance of examining the explanations for the credit availability problems with firm-level data, which is our topic in subsequent sections.

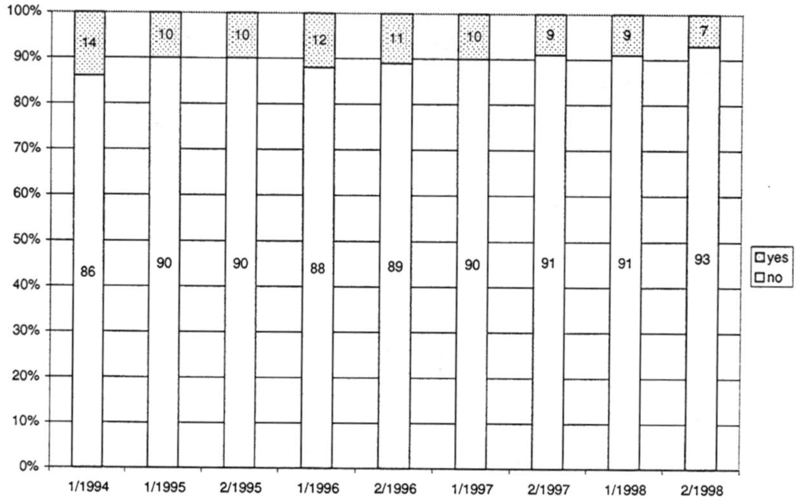

Figure 20.4 - Deviations From Debt Servicing Plan (% of Total)

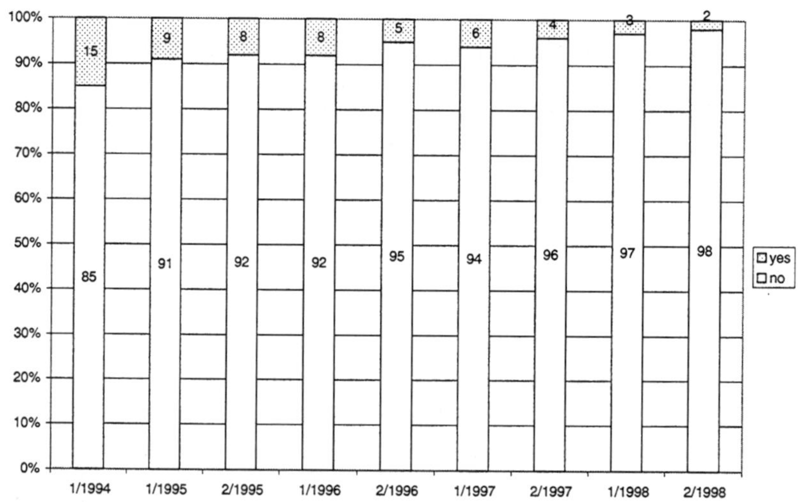

Figure 20.5 - Problems Due to Poor Availability of Credit (% of Total)

Figure 20.6 describes the firms' plans to acquire new funding within the following 6 months from the survey. The share of firms with plans to acquire funding remains fairly stable during the period despite a clear tendency of firms to increase their investments in fixed assets throughout the period.[3] Even the reported adequate access to credit has not been reflected in plans to acquire new funding. In part, the firms may have increasingly relied on internal financing thanks to their improved profitability.

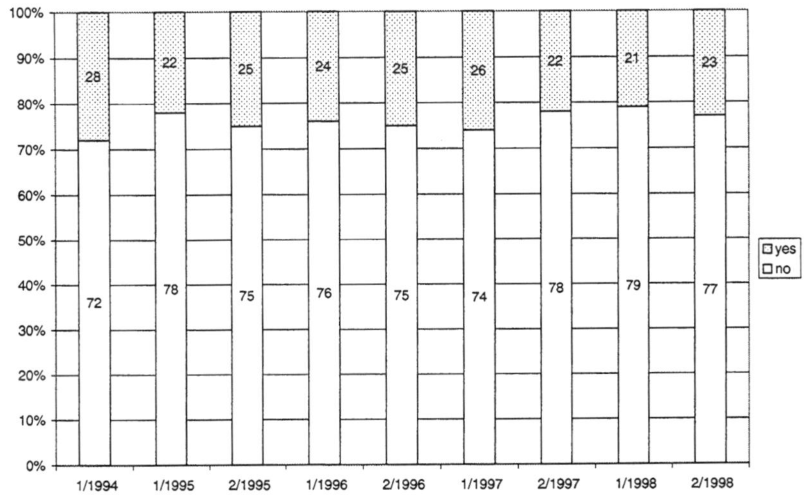

Figure 20.6 - Plans to Acquire Funding in the Following 6 Months (% of Total)

3 An Empirical Analysis of Credit Availability Problems

In this section, we review the potential reasons for firms' problems in inadequate access to funding and construct a framework for empirical analysis. As we have stated above, the small size of the firms in our firm population allows us to use funding as a proxy for bank lending which has constituted a major part of small business finance in Finland until now.

[3] The pattern of investment behaviour is not described here in detail, but 25-30% of the firms reported an increase in their investments in fixed assets throughout the period.

First, we discuss the possible explanations for the problems in credit availability. Then we construct an empirical model using available variables from the data set extracted from the survey.

3.1 Explanations for Credit Availability Problems

Availability of credit has been widely explained by firm-specific factors and borrower-lender relationships between the firm and its potential creditor. The influence of relationships on the availability of credit has been analysed by Cole (1998), Berger and Udell (1995), Petersen and Rajan (1994), among many others. In addition to the factors determining the relationship between firms and their potential lenders, these studies consider firm-specific factors as explanations for credit availability.

The relationship literature is derived from the literature of financial intermediation that points out that there exist informational asymmetries between firms and investors (e.g. Diamond 1984, 1991). Financial intermediaries, especially banks, are proposed to have economies of scale or other comparative advantages in monitoring firms to mitigate the problem of asymmetric information. A pre-existing relationship with the firms is understood to help the bank to obtain private information on the financial prospects of the firm.

The influence of relationship between firm and its potential lender on credit availability can be analysed from at least two different points of view. On the one hand, the pure pre-existence of a business relationship with a bank may be seen as a factor relieving a firm's credit availability problems. On the other hand, the strength of the relationship between a firm and its bank can also affect the probability of credit availability problems. Relationship characteristics have been measured by e.g. length of relationship; firm age; dummies for having accounts with the current lender; purchasing informationally intensive or non-informational financial services from the potential lenders; number of banks from which firm borrows (see, e.g. Petersen and Rajan, 1994). Linked with relationship literature, recent analyses have suggested that bank mergers and acquisitions may have adverse effects on small business lending (see, e.g. Berger et.al., 1997).

Various firm-specific factors disclose information on the riskiness of the firm. Thus, these factors affect the probability that the lender extends a credit to the firm with agreeable terms. Measures of firm-specific risks include leverage, profitability, and debt servicing problems. Concerning the measures of riskiness, it is commonly assumed that high profitability of firm signal low levels of risk while high leverage and debt-servicing problems indicate high risks (see e.g. Cole, 1998). Moreover, other firm-specific characteristics, like the industrial classification, the organisational form and the size, may contain information on the probability of credit availability problems. Among other things, the firm's size may also tell about its relationship with the potential source of credit.

Some aggregate level studies have also considered the effects on credit decisions of the conditions of the banking sector (e.g. Hancock and Wilcox, 1998). However, analyses with firm-level data on the role of banking conditions in credit availability have been rare.

Poor economic conditions of the lender may weaken its ability to grant credit to good customers whose firm-specific characteristics and relationship with the lender would allow extending a credit. The economic conditions of the lender may appear as profitability problems inducing the lender to more prudent behaviour, or as capital constraints limiting the amount of credit supply. The economic conditions of the banking sector have experienced especially drastic changes in Finland during 1990s. After a period of extraordinary rapid extension of credit (with inadequate pricing of credit risk) the Finnish banking system ran into severe profitability problems in the early 1990s due to mounting credit losses. It took until 1996 for banks' operating results to recover from the crisis into positive figures. Therefore, one could expect signs of the banking sector recovery in the firms' access to credit.

Based on the overall infrequency of the financing problems observed in the section 2, one can expect that the problems should not in the first place be linked with the financial conditions of the lenders, or banking sector. Rather, the firm-specific problems or relationship-based problems would seem to be natural candidates to explain the problems. However, a distinct reduction in the number of credit availability problems takes place from the beginning of 1995 up to the end of 1998. This trend could reflect either an improvement in the conditions of the firms or in the conditions of the banking sector.

3.2 Construction of Model Variables

On the basis of the analysis above, we formulate equations to estimate the explanations for credit availability problems using the data set from the survey described above. First, we construct a conventional model with variables indicating firm-specific factors and pre-existence of relationship between the firm and its potential lender. Then, we extend the model to test the effects of economic conditions of the banking sector on the credit availability.

The selection of the endogenous variable has proved to be difficult in the earlier literature (see e.g. Petersen and Rajan, 1994). Fortunately, our data set includes a variable that indicates whether the firm has reported problems due to inadequate access to funding. Based on the small size of the firms in the sample, this variable (ACCESDEB) seems a natural proxy for credit availability problems. We define that variable ACCESDEB equals one if the firm has reported problems due to inadequate access to credit during the six months before the survey has been conducted. Otherwise, ACCESDEB equals zero. Since ACCESDEB is a dichotomous variable, we must estimate the models using binary choice models. The econometric specification will be reviewed in section 4.

The survey also offers another candidate for an endogenous variable that reports the firms' notifications on any kind of financing problems. The variable relates to a wider range of problems than ACCESDEB, all of which are not necessarily linked with credit availability. Therefore, we only use ACCESDEB in our econometric analysis.

First, we follow the practice of relationship lending literature and incorporate variables on firm-specific factors and the relationship between the firm and the lender. Our initial formulation to model ACCESDEB is

$$\text{ACCESDEB} = f(\underset{(-)}{\text{PFOFITAB}}, \underset{(-)}{\text{DEVPROF}}, \underset{(-)}{\text{TURNOVER}}, \underset{(-)}{\text{DEVTUOP}}, \underset{(+)}{\text{DEBT}}, \underset{(+)}{\text{DEBTSERVI}}, \underset{(+)}{\text{LENDERCH}}) \qquad (1)$$

At this stage, we employ firm-specific variables that characterise the risks involved in the firm. These include the firm's current profitability (PROFITAB), the firm's profitability prospects during the following 12 months (DEVPROF), the firm's current leverage measured by the ratio of debts to turnover (DEBT), and a dummy for debt servicing problems during the preceding 6 months (DEBTSERVI). Other firm-specific variables include the firm's current size measured by its turnover (TURNOVER) and the firm's growth prospects in the following 12 months (DEVTUOP). PROFITAB and DEVPROF are assessments given in a three-grade scale. TURNOVER is reported in FIM millions and DEVTUOP in percentage points.

The relationship characteristics are represented by a dummy variable for a change of the firm's main lender during the current or previous year (LENDERCH).[4] This variable reflects an adverse change or even termination of a pre-existing relationship between the firm and its principal lender. The change in the main lender may also result from a bank merger or acquisition.

In equation (1), the expected signs of the coefficient are presented in parentheses below the variables. Current and future profitability are expected to decrease the risk level of the firm and reduce the probability of credit availability problems, accordingly. On the contrary, high leverage and problems in debt servicing indicate high risks and increased probability of credit availability problems. High turnover is expected to indicate a positive size effect on the probability to obtain credit without problems. Positive growth prospects mirror the expected increase in the firm's cash flow in the future. Disturbances in the lender-borrower relationship are expected to intensify the problems of asymmetric information and also credit availability problems.

We also reformulated the equation as follows to test whether the economic condition of the banking sector affects the probability of credit availability problems in a model including firm-specific and relationship-related variables:

$$\text{ACCESDEB} = f(X, \underset{(-)}{\text{PROFBASE}}) \tag{2}$$

In equation (2), X refers to the vector of exogenous variables in equation (1).

The variable characterising the conditions of the banking sector is a semi-annual profitability index for the Finnish banks describing their relative aggregate profits on ordinary operations. The average of the index is zero for the whole period from 1995 to 1998. Since it is an aggregate variable, PROFBASE is equal for all observations pertaining to a certain point in time. We have constructed the index on the basis of public balance sheet information of the banking sector.

Poor profitability affects banks' credit decisions and increases the value of prudence in their behaviour. Thereby, an improvement in the bank

---

4 Exceptionally, the observation for spring 1995 refers to a change in the firm's main creditor in years 1993-1994.

profitability is expected to decrease the probability of credit availability problems as indicated in the parentheses below the variable.

In addition to profitability, various capital and solvency figures could be used as proxies for the state of the banking sector. In the same manner, the use of bank-specific data in the estimations could help explaining credit availability problems of firms. This is, however, left for future work.

4 Econometric Work

4.1 Data

The data set we use in estimation consists of replies of Finnish service-sector firms in 1995 - 1998. The observations from autumn 1994 were excluded because their data contents were not totally coherent with data obtained in later stages. Altogether, the survey includes 4.874 observations from years 1995 - 1998. After having discarded the incomplete observations with partially missing data, we used a sample of 4.770 observations in estimations introduced in the following section.

Due to data processing problems, we were able to establish a panel data set for only 402 firms with complete data throughout the sample period. At this stage, we used also this balanced sub-panel for some tentative estimations where the longitudinal nature of the data set was exploited. As our balanced sub-panel includes eight semi-annual observations for each firm, the total number of observations is 3.216.

In addition to the data from the survey, we have composed a single variable using other data sources. The semi-annual profitability index of the Finnish banking sector has been constructed on the basis of the balance sheet information of major Finnish banking groups. The profitability index value for autumn 1998 was created on the basis of profitability figures of the third quarter of the year.

4.2 Econometric Method

Since the firms report their credit availability problems as discrete phenomena, we have to use qualitative response models for their econometric analysis. More specifically, binary choice models are applied, as the replies of the firms on their problems are dichotomous.

In the binary choice models, regressors are used to explain the probability of the two possible outcomes of the endogenous variable. In other words, with y being the endogenous variable, x a vector of regressors and β a vector of parameters, we have Prob(y = 1) = F(β'x) and Prob(y = 0) = 1 - F(β'x) where F is an appropriate distribution function. Alternatively, we can write a binary choice model as y* $= \beta' x + \varepsilon$, and y = 1 if y* > 0 and y = 0 if y* ≤ 0, where ε is an idiosyncratic error term which follows an appropriate distribution.

The most commonly used distributions in the binary choice models are the standard normal distribution and the logistic distribution, giving rise to the probit and the logit model, respectively. Thus, the probabilities of incident y = 1 in the probit model is

$$\text{Prob (y = 1)} = \int_{-\infty}^{\beta' x} \phi(t)\ dt \tag{3}$$

where ϕ is the notation for a probability density function of the standard normal distribution. Correspondingly, the probability of incident y = 1 in the logit model is

$$\text{Prob (y = 1)} = \frac{e^{\beta' x}}{1 + e^{\beta' x}} \tag{4}$$

On theoretical grounds, it is problematic to choose between the probit and the logit model (see e.g. Greene, 1997). The tails of the logistic distribution are heavier than those of the normal distribution, but otherwise they are similar. In our analysis, we use both distributions. Estimation of both probit and logit models is based on the method of maximum likelihood. The log-likelihood of a basic form for both models can be written

$$\ln \text{L} = \sum_{i=1}^{n} \ln F((2y_i - 1)\beta' x_i) \tag{5}$$

where F is the associated cumulative distribution function, n is the number of observations, y_i is the *i*th observation. The Newton's method is used to estimate both basic probit and logit models, and the covariance matrix for the coefficients is estimated with the second derivatives of the log-likelihood function.

By using the panel nature of the data set, heterogeneity across individual firms could be better distinguished. Some factors represented by omitted variables tend to affect the observations in a constant manner over time. In a panel data set, firm-specific effects can summarize these factors, which allows a more advanced analysis of the intertemporal effects on the endogenous variables. We made some preliminary work employing random effects treatment on probit models following the specification developed by Butler and Moffit (1982). For technical details, see Greene (1997), or LIMDEP (1995).

4.3 Estimation Results

Estimation results for equation (1) are presented in columns 1 and 2 of Table 20.2. Results for probit and logit models and random effects treatment on probit model are shown, pointing out the robustness of the results irrespective of the econometric specification. It should be noticed that the coefficients reported are not the marginal effects of the endogenous variables as would be the case with a linear model.

The estimated parameters are largely in accordance with our expectations. High turnover and high profitability clearly tend to reduce the probability of credit availability problems. They are also highly statistically significant and quite robust irrespective of the econometric specification. High leverage and violations of debt servicing plans seem to increase the probability of credit availability problems as expected. The significance of the debt-servicing problem is especially high, and leverage is also statistically significant at the 1% level, irrespective of the specification. The variable for growth prospects of the firm is not statistically significant in any of the specifications although the sign of the coefficient is negative as expected. This suggests that growth prospect signals are of limited significance in credit decisions.

At first sight, the estimation result for the profitability outlook is a confusing one. Irrespective of the econometric specification, the coefficient on the variable is positive, suggesting that a firm's positive profitability views increase its probability to face credit availability problems. The coefficient is also statistically significant. Possible reasons for the result lie in the relatively high negative correlation between current profitability and profitability prospects (-0,1691) which hints to biased reporting by the firms. Profitable firms may be too cautious in their future prospects while the attitudes of non-profitable firms to the future may be too optimistic.

The dummy variable for a recent change of the firm's main lender has an expected sign. That is, a new lender-borrower relationship increases the probability of credit availability problems. The variable is also statistically significant irrespective of the specification.

Table 20.2 - Probit and Logit Regression Results for Endogenous Variable ACCESDEB

Variable	(1) Probit: Coeff.	(2) Logit: Coeff.	(3) Probit: Coeff.	(4) Logit: Coeff.
Constant	-1,087* (-5,753)	-1,997* (-5,196)	-1,167* (-6,115)	-2,134* (-5,531)
PROFITAB	-0,5416* (-9,725)	-1,069* (-9,577)	-0,5242* (-9,360)	-1,033* (-9,212)
DEVPROF	0,2012* (3,469)	0,4517* (3,800)	0,2009* (3,448)	0,4399* (3,706)
DEVTUOP	-0,2198 (-0,956)	-0,5195 (-1,140)	-0,2164 (-0,947)	-0,5045 (-1,123)
DEBT	0,07599* (3,321)	0,1357* (3,325)	0,07576* (3,239)	0,1333* (3,128)
DEBTSERV	1,0078* (13,141)	1,9107* (13,558)	1,013* (13,129)	1,923* (13,558)
TURNOVER	-1,037* (-4,307)	-2,434* (-3,925)	-1,060* (-4,306)	-2,414* (-3,914)
LENDERCH	0,3848* (3,019)	0,7725* (3,736)	0,3655* (3,327)	0,7349* (3,558)
PROFBASE	-	-	-0,1928* (-4,166)	-0,3720* (-3,973)
LogL	-850,4978	-850,3875	-841,6280	-842,2602

Restricted Log-L = -1071,046, n = 4770

Note: * denotes coefficient significant at 1% level (t-statistics in parentheses).

Columns three and four of Table 20.2 show the estimation results for equation (2) including the profitability index of the banking sector as a regressor. As expected, an increase in the banking sector profitability reduces the probability of credit availability problems. The variable is significant at the 1% level in both models. This evidence supports the view that the economic condition of the banking sector has an independent impact on the efficiency of the financial intermediation. The results for firm-specific factors and the pre-existence of a lending relationship are not affected by the inclusion of PROFBASE.

We also made preliminary estimations on a balanced sub-panel data set with complete observations for 402 firms over the years 1995 – 1998. We employed a random effects specification of a probit model. The results did not show any significant deviations from the results presented in Table 20.2 It can be noted that the random effects treatment improves the significance of PROFBASE in comparison with the results from cross-sectional probit and logit models with an equivalent sample.

5 Conclusions

As the various results of this paper are scrutinized, at least two concerns should be kept in mind. First, as we indicated in section 2, the results may suffer from biases in the sample. Second, the overall economic development in Finland has been rather exceptional over the period of analysis in this study. The results should thus be interpreted in a context of a rapid recovery of the economy from a deep recession.

The positive economic development experienced by the firms can clearly be seen in the results of the descriptive analysis. The number of firms with profitability problems has collapsed over the years 1994 - 1998 according to the results. Good news about the firms' economic condition has also been reflected in their ability to service their financial obligations. This can be seen in the reduction in the number of debt servicing problems. The descriptive analysis shows that improvements in the firms' access to finance have been especially intense. Aggregate data even suggest that the recovery of the firms does not alone explain the substantial fall in the cases of credit availability problems.

Three classes of explanations for credit availability problems were discussed and tested using simple analyses on the basis of firm-level data set from the survey in 1995 - 1998. The proposed explanations include firm-specific factors, pre-existence of relationship between the firm and its potential source of credit, and the economic conditions of the banking sector. Our results confirm the common view that firm-specific factors and pre-existing relationships affect the probability of credit availability problems. We also find evidence that the economic condition of the banking sector has effects on the firms' credit availability. However, there remains a need for further research on the influence of lenders' conditions on credit availability using firm-level data. Especially, using lender-specific variables as explanations for credit availability is a challenge for future work. On the other hand, other conditions in the overall economy should be controlled in estimations.

References

Berger, A. N. and G. F. Udell (1995), 'Relationship Lending and Lines of Credit in Small Firm Finance', *Journal of Business,* 68, 3, pp. 351–381.

Berger, A. N., A. Saunders, J. M. Scalise and G. F. Udell (1997), *The Effects of Bank Mergers and Acquisitions on Small Business Lending, Finance and economics discussion series,* 28, Federal Reserve Board, Washington, D.C.

Butler, J. S. and R. Moffit (1982), 'A Computationally Efficient Quadrature Procedure for the One-Factor Multinomial Probit Model', *Econometrica,* Vol. 50, No. 3, pp. 761–764.

Cole, R. A. (1998), 'The importance of relationships to the availability of credit', *Journal of Banking and Finance,* 22, pp. 959-977.

Diamond, D. W. (1984), 'Financial Intermediation and Delegated Monitoring', *Review of Economic Studies,* LI (3), pp. 393-414.

Diamond, D. W. (1991), 'Monitoring and Reputation: The Choice between Bank Loans and Directly Placed Debt', *Journal of Political Economy,* 99, 4, pp. 689-721.

Greene, W. H. (1997),:*Econometric Analysis.* International Edition (3rd edition) Prentice Hall Inc.

Hancock, D. and J. A. Wilcox (1998), 'The 'credit crunch' and the availability of credit to small business', *Journal of Banking and Finance* 22, pp. 983–1014.

Kuussaari, H. and J. Vesala (1995), *Teollisuus- palveluyritysten rahoitustilanne ja näkymät syksyllä 1994* (in Finnish). Bank of Finland Financial Markets Department. Working Paper 1/95.

LIMDEP (1997), *Limdep Version 7.0 User's manual.* Econometric Software, Inc. New York.

Petersen, M. A. and R. G. Rajan (1994), 'The Benefits of Lending Relationships: Evidence from Small Business Data', *Journal of Finance,* XLIX, 1, pp. 3–37.

21 Formation of Production Plans and Demand Expectations of Russian Industrial Enterprises in the Course of Market Reforms

SERGEY TSUKHLO[1]

1 Introduction

This paper investigates models and factors, which determine the formation of production plans and demand expectations under the conditions of large scale market reforms. We believe that the estimation of the mechanism and degree of demand influence on output can be a good indicator for the firms' evolution from a plan to a market economy. At the same time I am sure that such problems and analysis are extremely unusual for a 'western' economy and for western researchers.

In the planned soviet economy demand was not the main determinant of production and price policy. Shortages allowed the production of any goods, enterprises did not take into account demand constraints and volumes of output and the price level were set by the plan. Even when enterprises had the right to set their goals themselves, demand was not taken into account. Controlled prices and shortages allowed to produce as many goods as enterprises thought possible.

[1] The presentation of this paper at the 24th CIRET Conference was partially funded by a grant from the US Agency for International Development (USAID) and partially by a grant from the International Association for the promotion of co-operation with scientists from the New Independent States of the former Soviet Union (INTAS).

From the beginning of market reforms the situation has changed very much. Price liberalisation and absence of price setting have showed the importance of demand. But many enterprises continued to produce as before. The production of overstocks started. Only when the stocks of finished goods increased up to incredible sizes enterprises decided to change their behaviour. They understood that demand could be the limiting factor for production. But it was not easy for former soviet directors to take into account this constraint.

In this paper we are going

- to formulate models of output plan and demand expectation formations in the New Independent States (NIS),
- to show the potential of the models as indicators of market reforms on the microlevel,
- to test the models on the basis of Russian manufacturing business surveys,
- to estimate the evolution of enterprises plan (expectation) formation during market reforms in Russia.

We intend to check the following hypotheses:

- During effective market reforms enterprises do not stick to output plans on the basis of the 'reached level'-principle.
- During effective market reforms enterprises start to take into account effective demand.
- During effective market reforms enterprises start to take into account deviations of output from effective demand and to use such deviations for corrections in their output plans.

During effective market reforms first type models of plan (expectation) formation have to be substituted by models of a second and third type.

Expectations play a crucial role in western economic theory. Models of output and price expectation formation were investigated frequently. The hypothesis of rational expectations was tested frequently, too, whereas hypotheses of expectation formation (adaptive, extrapolative, error-learning) were tested rarely. Such models are presented in the work of Nerlove (1956, 1958, 1981, 1983). He includes not only direct variables from business surveys (expectations and realisations) but also derivatives: 1) the difference between expectations and realisations and 2) the change of variables between two surveys. The adaptive expectations model relates the change of the expected variable (in survey at time t) to the differences between the realised variable (in survey at time t) and the last period's expectation (in survey at time t-1). The error-learning model relates the change of an expected variable between two surveys (t and t-1) to the difference between expectations (in t-1) and realisations (in t). In the extrapolative model current expectations are related to the two preceding realisations.

In our paper the expectation formation models will be used to investigate the influence of demand on the output plan formation of Russian manufacturing enterprises. We will also show the evolution of such influence.

2 The Data

To test the model, we use the results of Russian manufacturing business surveys. The Institute for the Economy in Transition (IET) has conducted business surveys on the basis of the European harmonized program since 1992. This activity of IET has been supported by the Confederation of British Industry, the European Community, EUROSTAT and the Organisation for Economic Co-operation and Development. The IET's results were recognised to meet the European standards and have been published in the quarterly journal 'Short-Term Economic Indicators: Transition Economies- Paris- OECD' since 1995.

The IET's surveys cover the whole territory of the Russian Federation. The surveys are conducted monthly including 900-1000 replies. The panel consists of 1400 top-managers of manufacturing enterprises (among them 41% - directors, 35% - vice directors, 18% - heads of economic departments). The panel is biased to the biggest firms in each sector. Out of all sectors we picked 50 achieving a response rate of about 70%.

The questionnaire designed for the business survey includes questions about actual and expected trends in production and demand (see Appendix). The usual trichotomous scale is used for the answers: up - same - down.

The following variables from business surveys will be included in our models:

Q_t - actual change of output in the survey (period) t;
D_t - actual change of demand in the survey (period) t;
Q_t^* - expectation in survey t for the output in period t+3;
D_t^* - expectation in survey t for the demand in period t+3.

Two derivative variables will be included in the models:

1) precision of the forecast and
2) change of a variable between two surveys.

Precision of the forecast $\Phi(X_t,X^*_{t-3})$ is defined from the contingency table for expectations X^*_{t-3} and the realisations X_t to which they refer. This variable is trichotomous and has the following values: (+) - the realisations are more optimistic than previous expectations; (=) - the realisations are equal to the previous expectations; (-) the realisations are more pessimistic than previous expectations.

Change of a variable between two surveys $\Delta(X_t,X_{t-3})$ is defined from the contingency table for the variable in survey t-3 and for the same variable in survey t. This variable is trichotomous and has the following values: (+) - the variable improved; (=) - the variable did not change; (-) the variable worsened.

3 Models

We suggest to formulate and investigate three models of enterprise behaviour. In times of the planned economy enterprises preferred to form their production plans 'from the reached level'. This is the first model. In the course of market reforms enterprises started to take into account effective demand when forming production plans. This is the second model. Mistakes are inevitable and probably considerable. The enterprises have to reveal mistakes and to take them into account when correcting their production plans. This is the third model.

For checking our hypotheses we are going to investigate adaptive, error-learning and extrapolative models of plan expectation formations.

1. *The adaptive expectations model* relates the expectations X^*_t of the variable X_t in the survey period t to the precision of the forecast $\Phi(X_t,X^*_{t-3})$ in survey t-3. We suppose to test the following adaptive models of output plans formations:
   - 1.1. $(Q^*_t|\Phi(Q_t,Q^*_{t-3}))$ - production plans in period t are defined by the precision of the output plans registered in survey t-3;
   - 1.2. $(Q^*_t|\Phi(D_t,D^*_{t-3}))$ - production plans in period t are defined by the precision of the demand forecasts registered in survey t-3;
   - 1.3. $(Q^*_t|\Phi(D_t,Q^*_{t-3}))$ - production plans in period t are defined by the precision of the output plans registered in survey t-3 with respect to actual demand change in period t;
   - 1.4. Also the adaptive model of demand expectations formations will be investigated:

$(D^*_t|\Phi(D_t,D^*_{t-3}))$ - demand expectations in period t are defined by the precision of the demand expectations registered in survey t-3;

2. *The error-learning model* relates a change of expected variables between two surveys (t and t-3) to the precision of the forecast $\Phi(X_t,X^*_{t-3})$ in survey t-3: $(\Delta(X^*_t,X^*_{t-3})|\Phi(X_t,X^*_{t-3}))$. We suppose to test the following error-learning models of output plans formations:
   2.1. $(\Delta(Q^*t,Q^*t-3)|\Phi(Qt,Q^*t-3))$ - change of production plans in period t is defined by the precision of the output plans registered in survey t-3;
   2.2. $(\Delta(Q^*t,Q^*t-3)|\Phi(Dt,D^*t-3))$ - change of production plans in period t is defined by the precision of the demand expectations registered in survey t-3;
   2.3. $(\Delta(Q^*t,Q^*t-3)|\Phi(Dt,Q^*t-3))$ - change of production plans in period t is defined by the precision of the output plans registered in survey t-3 with respect to actual demand change in period t;
   2.4. Also the error-learning model of demand expectations formations will be investigated: $(\Delta(D^*_t,D^*_{t-3})|\Phi(D_t,D^*_{t-3}))$ - change of the demand expectations in period t is defined by the precision of the demand expectations registered in survey t-3;
3. *The extrapolative expectations model* relates the expectations of the variable in survey (period) t to the two preceding realisations. We suppose to test the following extrapolative models of output plans formations:
   3.1. $(Q^*_t \mid Q_t)$ - production plans in period t are defined by actual production changes in period t;
   3.2. $(Q^*_t \mid D_t)$ - production plans in period t are defined by actual demand changes in period t;
   3.3. Also the extrapolative model of demand expectations formations will be investigated: $(D^*_t \mid D_t)$ - demand expectations in period t are defined by actual demand changes in period t.

Models 1.1, 2.1 and 3.1 can be regarded as models of the first type. In the course of effective economic reforms these models will have to be replaced by second and third type models. Models 1.2, 2.2, 3.2 and 3.3 can be regarded as models of the second type. Models 1.3, 1.4, 2.3 and 2.4 can be regarded as models of the third type.

4 Results

We use the Goodman-Kruskal gamma coefficient as the most simple way to check the results. All estimations are based on quarterly data (1993 until 1998).

In table 21.1 and figure 21.1 our results are presented for the adaptive expectations models. It is obvious that the adaptive expectations hypothesis is not supported at all. All types of adaptive interaction of output and demand in the Russian industry have not yet occurred.

The results for the error-learning model for output and demand are presented in table 21.2 and figure 21.2. Our results show strong, significant and positive signs of applicability of this model. We may conclude that the error-learning model is strongly supported by Russian data.

The results for the extrapolative model are demonstrated in table 21.3 and figure 21.3. The estimates show reasonably stable positive correlation for the whole period. The correlation is stronger than for the adaptive model but weaker than for the error-learning model.

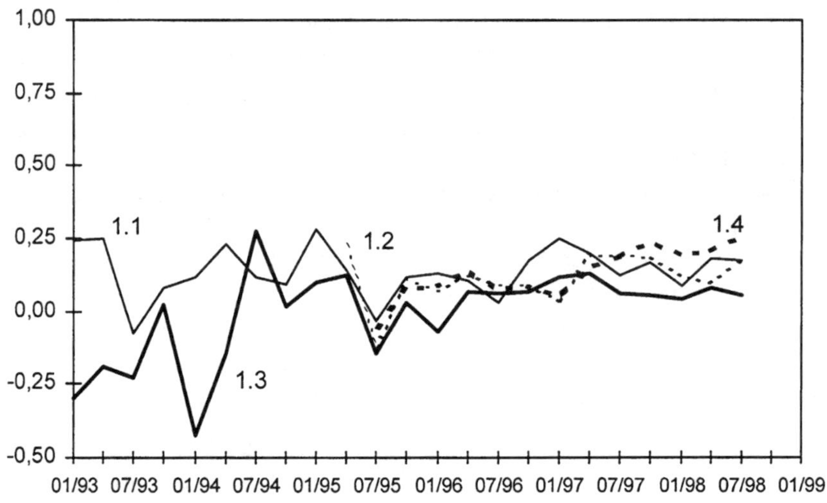

Figure 21.1 - Goodman-Kruskal Gamma Coefficient for Adaptive Expectations Models

Table 21.1 - Sample Size, Chi-square Test Against Independence and Goodman-Kruskal Gamma Coefficient for Adaptive Expectations Models

Period	Sample size	Models							
		1.1. $(Q^*_t\|\Phi(Q_t,Q^*_{t-3}))$		1.2. $(Q^*_t\|\Phi(D_t,D^*_{t-3}))$		1.3. $(Q^*_t\|\Phi(D_t,Q^*_{t-3}))$		1.4. $(D^*_t\|\Phi(D_t,D^*_{t-3}))$	
		X^2	Gamma	X^2	Gamma	X^2	Gamma	X^2	Gamma
01/93	313	288	0,245	-	-	105	-0,297	-	-
04/93	286	405	0,250	-	-	296	-0,190	-	-
07/93	279	738	-0,076	-	-	88	-0,226	-	-
10/93	281	90	0,079	-	-	1263	0,024	-	-
01/94	324	355	0,120	-	-	252	-0,427	-	-
04/94	356	433	0,228	-	-	329	-0,147	-	-
07/94	460	433	0,116	-	-	264	0,273	-	-
10/94	491	386	0,094	-	-	228	0,014	-	-
01/95	548	1558	0,280	-	-	1048	0,100	-	-
04/95	660	971	0,144	556	0,226	874	0,121	-	-
07/95	733	604	-0,036	241	-0,130	502	-0,144	310	-0,050
10/95	1088	3072	0,116	871	0,109	985	0,032	2332	0,071
01/96	1466	1521	0,128	394	0,071	695	-0,072	1340	0,083
04/96	1439	1508	0,103	870	0,121	1367	0,068	1444	0,145
07/96	1474	880	0,030	421	0,091	1454	0,060	1515	0,074
10/96	1652	2267	0,175	1923	0,094	1931	0,070	4055	0,084
01/97	1719	10839	0,250	802	0,037	7445	0,117	2662	0,047
04/97	1775	6748	0,200	3457	0,196	6874	0,129	3322	0,152
07/97	1775	8657	0,122	3173	0,194	6538	0,062	4410	0,188
10/97	2062	4795	0,171	6088	0,189	7282	0,054	7819	0,238
01/98	2212	2115	0,083	1144	0,121	1311	0,039	3920	0,196
04/98	2150	4888	0,180	1583	0,099	2977	0,081	3470	0,209
07/98	2079	1547	0,174	1666	0,172	1969	0,057	2939	0,257
10/98	-	-	-	-	-	-	-	-	-

Table 21.2 - Sample Size, Chi-square Test Against Independence and Goodman-Kruskal Gamma Coefficient for Error-learning Models

Period	Sample size	Models							
		2.1. Δ(Q*t,Q*t-3)| Φ(Qt,Q*t-3)		2.2. Δ(Q*t,Q*t-3)| Φ(Dt,D*t-3)		2.3. Δ(Q*t,Q*t-3)| Φ(Dt,Q*t-3)		2.4. Δ(D*t,D*t-3)| Φ(Dt,D*t-3)	
		X^2	Gamma	X^2	Gamma	X^2	Gamma	X^2	Gamma
01/93	313	4598	0,811	-	-	1831	0,737	-	-
04/93	286	4090	0,888	-	-	1382	0,771	-	-
07/93	279	1780	0,556	-	-	436	0,294	-	-
10/93	281	1554	0,700	-	-	1476	0,784	-	-
01/94	324	4142	0,783	-	-	740	0,803	-	-
04/94	356	3840	0,783	-	-	653	0,703	-	-
07/94	460	6710	0,740	-	-	1592	0,745	-	-
10/94	491	6518	0,737	-	-	2659	0,792	-	-
01/95	548	8669	0,814	-	-	5210	0,734	-	-
04/95	660	8205	0,667	1366	0,475	8035	0,732	3649	0,817
07/95	733	5628	0,647	1859	0,573	3702	0,634	2952	0,659
10/95	1088	13611	0,705	4398	0,509	8009	0,720	10561	0,708
01/96	1466	16502	0,775	5957	0,558	12406	0,793	15962	0,804
04/96	1439	14719	0,703	7319	0,575	13281	0,767	15668	0,759
07/96	1474	14545	0,594	8577	0,565	15156	0,720	16539	0,767
10/96	1652	15139	0,672	6878	0,505	13522	0,726	19846	0,757
01/97	1719	30941	0,722	6591	0,460	23965	0,753	19949	0,695
04/97	1775	26590	0,690	7981	0,456	23688	0,734	25613	0,739
07/97	1775	32946	0,707	11314	0,524	28590	0,748	30671	0,768
10/97	2062	29427	0,650	17997	0,621	27228	0,699	32516	0,715
01/98	2212	38685	0,668	13889	0,471	29116	0,755	36197	0,795
04/98	2150	22142	0,601	13862	0,552	17126	0,642	29119	0,709
07/98	2079	38749	0,799	11300	0,443	32067	0,779	38439	0,816
10/98	-	-	-	-	-	-	-	-	-

Table 21.3 - Sample Size, Chi-square Test Against Independence and Goodman-Kruskal Gamma Coefficient for Extrapolative Expectations Models

Period	Sample size	Models					
		3.1. (Q*t I Qt)		3.2. (Q*t I Dt)		3.3. (D*t I Dt)	
		X^2	Gamma	X^2	Gamma	X^2	Gamma
01/93	-	-	-	-	-	-	-
04/93	520	3299	0,667	1086	0,639	-	-
07/93	498	2886	0,609	1471	0,585	-	-
10/93	510	2499	0,591	196	0,283	-	-
01/94	548	2344	0,593	953	0,707	-	-
04/94	635	5004	0,682	2677	0,684	-	-
07/94	726	2466	0,486	1295	0,312	-	-
10/94	796	1776	0,453	764	0,466	-	-
01/95	877	1854	0,428	460	0,406	-	-
04/95	1030	2565	0,507	2151	0,437	884	0,494
07/95	1123	3529	0,453	1501	0,374	1055	0,388
10/95	1482	4758	0,487	2555	0,389	3824	0,460
01/96	2136	7349	0,393	2615	0,438	3240	0,461
04/96	2242	6072	0,518	3186	0,416	4597	0,445
07/96	2125	8621	0,412	5102	0,459	7568	0,494
10/96	2306	7275	0,422	6448	0,534	6604	0,518
01/97	2436	7006	0,391	4176	0,395	8633	0,417
04/97	2600	11375	0,446	5442	0,365	9614	0,477
07/97	2467	9598	0,311	4071	0,344	7757	0,336
10/97	2767	15405	0,440	7775	0,486	10328	0,452
01/98	2976	11897	0,365	9061	0,336	16446	0,424
04/98	3022	13691	0,401	6848	0,438	17498	0,560
07/98	2874	18271	0,391	7569	0,372	15366	0,441
10/98	2996	12313	0,438	6985	0,421	17816	0,607

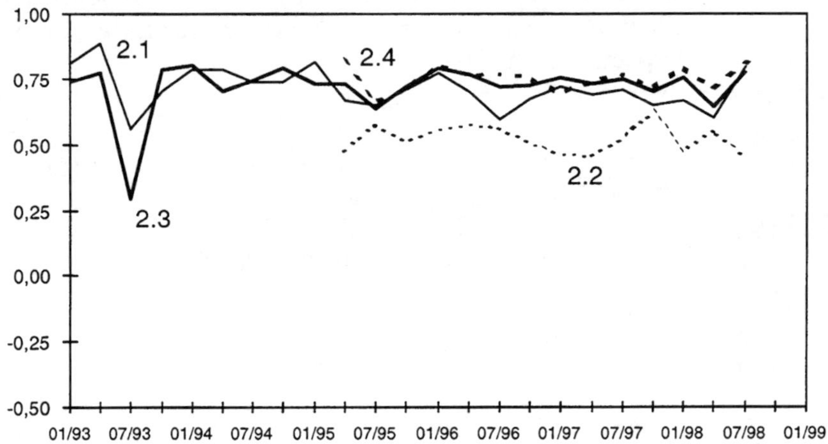

Figure 21.2 - Goodman-Kruskal Gamma Coefficient for Error-learning Models

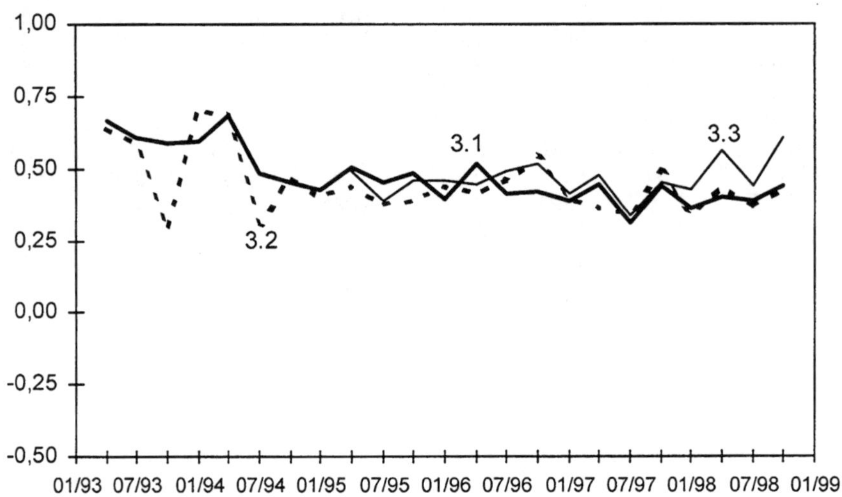

Figure 21.3 - Goodman-Kruskal Gamma Coefficient for Extrapolative Expectations Models

5 Conclusion

The results from business surveys in Russia are important and interesting for the investigation of enterprise behavior in the course of market reforms. They are aimed to check the change of behavior. A traditional set of expectation formation models could be used for the description of enterprise behavior and provide new results regarding to economies in transition. For a brief presentation of the results the average values of the Goodman-Kruskal gamma coefficient were calculated for three types of models (Figure 21.4).

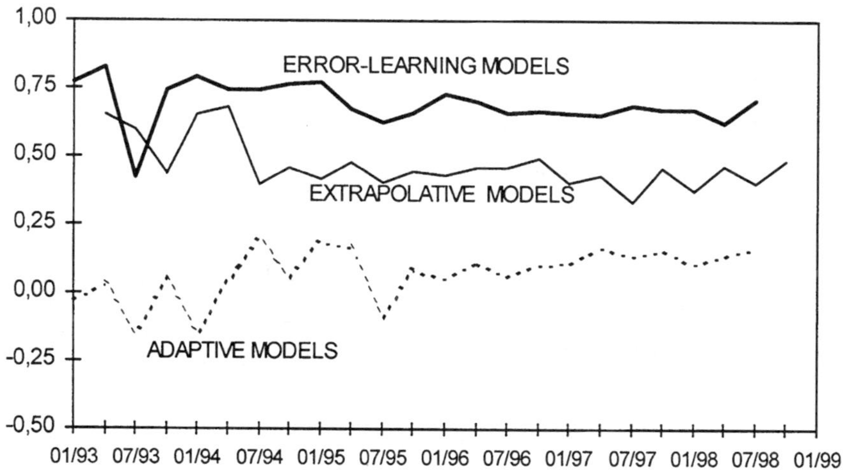

Figure 21.4 - The Average Value of Goodman-Kruskal Gamma Coefficient

Our conclusions are:

1. Russian enterprises correct their expectations/plans taking into account previous realizations. The most important model 2.3 shows strong and stable estimations for the whole period. This means that enterprises control the demand and change their production plans in accordance with the demand trend.

2. Demand does not solely have influence on output expectations. Output expectations are formed under influence of both output and demand.

6 Appendix

IET's Business Surveys Inquire

103918 MOSCOW, GAZETNY PER, 5, IET BUSINESS SURVEYS PHONE: (095) 229-93-91 FAX: (095) 203-88-16	Institute for the Economy in Transition MONTHLY INDUSTRIAL TRENDS SURVEY N 79 DECEMBER 1998

Please tick and return immediately after receiving!

Please tick appropriate answers.
If question not applicable, tick N/A.

What is the current trend of:	Up	Same	Down	N/A
1. volume of your output				
2. average prices for your products				
3. volume of effective demand for your products				
4. volume of barter demand for your products				
Do you consider that in volume terms:	Above normal	Normal	Below normal	N/A
5. your present total output is				
6. your present total order book is				
7. your present export order book is				
8. your present stocks of finished goods are				
What is the expected trend over the next 2-3 months with regard to:	Up	Same	Down	N/A
9. volume of your output				
10. average prices for your products				
11. volume of effective demand for your products				
12. volume of barter demand for your products				

How many employees are there at your firm:

1-50	51-200	201-500	501-1000	1001-2000	2001-5000	5001-10000	10001-20000	>20000
1	2	3	4	5	6	7	8	9

Please enter the code number or the name of the main manufacturing activity:

If you wish your reply to remain anonymous, please detach this slip and return it under separate cover!

Name ______________________________

Position Title ______________________________

Telephone ______________________________ Fax ______________________________

Company ______________________________

Address ______________________________

References

Aiginger, K. (1981), '*Empirical evidence on the rational expectations using reported expectations*', Empirica, 1, pp. 25-72.

Buckle, R. A., E. W. Assendeleft and L. F. Jackson (1990), 'Manufacturers' expectations of price and quantities: New Zealand experience, 1964-1987', *Applied Economics,* 22, pp. 579-598.

Figlewski, S. and P. Wachtel (1981), 'The formation of inflationary expectations', *Review of Economics and Statistics,* 63, pp. 1-10.

Horvath, B., M. Nerlove, M. and D. Willson (1992), *Direct test of forecast rationality using categorical business survey data: Some new results,* Concordia University, Montreal.

Kawasaki, S. and K. F. Zimmermann (1986), 'Testing the Rationality of Price Expectations for Manufacturing Firms', *Applied Economics,* 18, pp. 1335-1347.

Konig, H. M., M. Nerlove and G. Oudiz (1981), 'On the formation of price expectations: An analysis of business test data by log-linear probability models', *European Economic Review,* 16, pp. 103-138.

de Leuuw, F. and M. J. McKelvey (1981), 'Price expectations of business firms', *Brookings Papers on Economic Activity,* pp. 299-314.

Marty, R. (1995), *Survey evidence of the rationality of expectations*. Paper presented at the 22 CIRET Conference, Singapore.

Nerlove, M. (1956), 'Estimates of the elasticities of supply of selected agricultural commodities', *Journal of Farm Economics* 38, pp. 496-509.

Nerlove, M. (1958), *The Dynamics of supply: Estimation of farmers' response to price, Baltimore,* The Johns Hopkins Press, 1958.

Nerlove, M. (1983), 'Expectations, Plans, and Realisations in Theory and Practice', *Econometrica,* 51, pp. 1251-1279.

Noble, N. R. and T. Fields (1982), 'Testing the rationality of inflation expectations derived from survey data: a structure-based approach', *Southern Economic Review,* 49, pp. 361-373.

OECD, *Short-Term Economic Indicators: Transition Economies*, Paris.

Stalhammar, N. (1988), 'Price and Demand Expectations in the Swedish Manufacturing Industry', *Scandinavian Journal of Economics,* 90, pp. 233-243.

Theil, H. (1966), *Applied economic forecasting,* North-Holland, Amsterdam.

Tompkinson, P. and M. Common, (1983), 'Evidence on the rationality of expectations in the British manufacturing sector', *Applied Economics,* 15, pp. 425-436.

Part V

Capacity Utilisation

22 The Degree of Utilisation of Production Capacity in the Belgian Manufacturing Industry

JEAN-JACQUES VANHAELEN and LUC DRESSE

The National Bank of Belgium holds a quarterly survey on the utilisation of production capacities in the manufacturing industry. The latest observations exhibit unprecedentedly high levels for the degree of utilisation of production capacity in the manufacturing industry as a whole. What seems to be a jump in the series could possibly be explained by short-term economic developments, by technical considerations in the way the degree of utilisation is calculated, or by structural changes in the replies given by entrepreneurs participating in the survey.

Since the degree of capacity utilisation is used as a rapidly available, coincident indicator of the growth rate of manufacturing production, it is important to assess what the actual importance of these various possible causes has been.

The National Bank of Belgium is particularly interested in this question, since the institution is at the same time in charge of the organisation of the business surveys, is responsible for the national accounts statistics, and has to carry out economic analyses for the Belgian economy, including macroeconomic forecasts.

This paper is organised as follows. The first part gives a short description of the quarterly survey on production capacity held by the National Bank of Belgium. In the second part, the facts supporting the assumption of a structural increase in the level of the degree of utilisation of capacity production are presented. The different reasons which could possibly explain such a movement, namely the economic context, the changes in the statistical treatment of replies and the evolution by sectors, are analysed in parts 3 to 5 of the analysis. The last part considers the factors that should be taken into account when examining how the degree of utilisation of production capacity can be used as a business cycle indicator.

1 Brief Description of the Survey on Production Capacity

Since October 1962, the National Bank of Belgium has organised, on behalf of the Federation of Belgian Companies, a survey on the utilisation of production capacity in the manufacturing industry. The survey, which was harmonised by the European Commission and which has been carried out on a quarterly basis since September 1978, is chiefly aimed at determining the limits to production potential. It includes a quantitative question on capacity utilisation as a percentage of total capacity.

In the typology of measures of capacity utilisation presented by Christiano (1981), the series produced by the National Bank of Belgium may be characterised as a type 1 survey-based method. The entrepreneurs are asked to give their assessment, expressed as a percentage, of the rate of utilisation of the production capacity during the month under review. Additional, qualitative, questions cover the entrepreneur's judgement about the present production capacity in view of the present and future level of demand, as well as his judgement on possible bottlenecks in production capacity.

Even if the questions about the possible bottlenecks suggest that all kinds of production factors - manpower, equipment and stocks - should be considered, there is no precise definition of capacity attached to the questionnaire. The aggregate figure of the rate of utilisation results from the combination of individual replies based on different concepts. However, if all entrepreneurs consistently use over time the same definition of capacity, whatever that may be, the aggregate results will be consistent over time too.

From experience, it seems that, like the monthly synthetic curve,[1] the rate of utilisation can be used as a coincident indicator of the growth in production: high (resp. low) levels of the rate of utilisation indicate high (resp. low) growth rates of production. Due to the considerable volatility characterising seasonally adjusted quarterly data on value added in the

[1] The synthetic curve summarises the results of the qualitative monthly survey held by the National Bank, according to EC prescriptions, within a panel of enterprises in the manufacturing industry.

manufacturing sector and on quarterly GDP as well, the correlation coefficient is higher when the degree of capacity utilisation is compared to the year-on-year growth rate, than to the growth rate with respect to the previous quarter.

2 Is the Degree of Utilisation of Production Capacity Increasing?

In the description of the economic and financial developments for the Belgian economy presented in the 1997 Annual Report of the National Bank of Belgium, it has been pointed out that the rate of utilisation of production capacity reached an unprecedentedly high level in the course of 1997. The question was raised as to whether these results were the consequence of a particularly buoyant economic situation at that time, or if they were driven by structural forces, such as, for instance, a more efficient use of the stock of capital.

The purpose of this paper is to offer a discussion of certain factors which provides an answer to this question. The first step is to look into the results of the series of capacity utilisation, in order to establish the movement of the series in a medium- to long-term perspective.

As a benchmark, Table 22.1 gives the descriptive statistics for the rate of utilisation of production capacity in the manufacturing industry as a whole, for the period 8OQ1 to 98Q3.

Table 22.1 - Rate of Utilisation of Production Capacity in the Manufacturing Industry (Percentages)

Sample 1980: 1 1998: 3	
Observations 75	
Mean	78.0
Median	77.8
Maximum	83.0
Minimum	73.9
Std. Dev.	2.46
Skewness	0.233
Kurtosis	2.05

Source : National Bank of Belgium

As explained in the previous section, undue attention should not be paid to the level of the mean value of the degree of utilisation, since it is the average of individual replies based on different implicit definitions of production capacity. Only the movements around the mean value are important.

Up to the end of 1995, the rate of utilisation of production capacity only on two occasions exceeded the mean by more than once the standard deviation: during the four quarters of 1989, when the growth rates of value added in industry were more than 5%, and during the first semester of 1995 (Figure 22.1).

From 96Q2 onwards, the rate of utilisation was continuously above this level, by more than 2 points between 97Q2 to 98Q3. The absolute maximum level, of 83%, was reached in 98Q2.

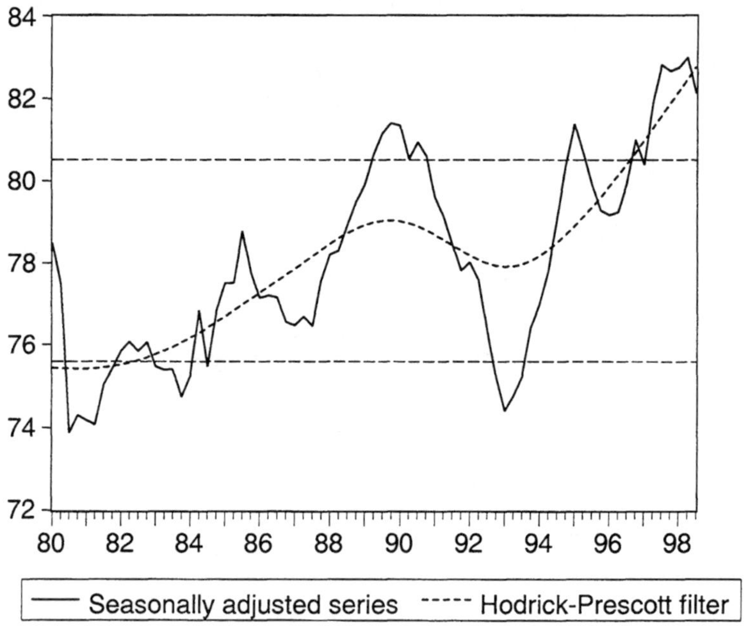

Source : National Bank of Belgium

Figure 22.1 - Degree of Utilisation of Production Capacity in the Manufacturing Industry (percentages)

The trend line obtained by the application of a Hodrick-Prescott filter on the series over the entire period has a positive slope. Even if, given the method used to draw the tendency, the results at both ends should be considered with caution, the slope is at its steepest during the last four years. The Augmented Dickey-Fuller (ADF) test does not reject the zero hypothesis of unit root even at the 10% critical value, meaning that the hypothesis of non-stationarity may not be rejected either.

From this brief univariate analysis of the series, it seems that if the degree of utilisation of capacity production in the manufacturing industry has been higher in 1997 and 1998 than ever before, it is more because it is driven by an increasing tendency than because of a jump in the results.

3 Economic Context

As fluctuations in the degree of capacity utilisation of the production potential are designated as economic fluctuations (Oppenländer 1997 p.7), it is obvious that economic conditions should be taken into account when assessing the level of the degree of capacity utilisation. On the one hand, high figures for the rate of utilisation for a short period of time could be the consequence of an upturn in the business cycle. On the other hand, the long-term growth path of the economy ought not to lead to a steady rise in the rate of utilisation of production capacity, but to an increase in the production potential, by the accumulation of manpower, capital stock, natural resources and knowledge. The degree of utilisation of production capacity should be stable across the business cycle.

In order to establish if the position in the business cycle could have contributed to the high level of the rate of utilisation since 1996, we will successively examine four indicators.

a) Growth rates of the value added in the manufacturing industry

For the period from 81Q1 to 98Q3, the year-on-year growth rate of the value added in the manufacturing industry, which is presented in the first panel of Figure 22.2 (a), as well as the growth rate with respect to the previous quarter, seem to be stationary series. For both, the ADF-test rejects the hypothesis of unit root, at the 5% critical value for the year-on-year growth, and at the 1% critical value for the growth with respect to the previous quarter.

However, the growth rate has been relatively high in the most recent quarters. From 96Q4 onwards, the year-on-year growth rate has continuously exceeded the mean and the median value for the whole period. Nevertheless, similar or even higher growth rates have been observed on several occasions in the past.

b) Synthetic curve of the business survey

The profile of the synthetic curve in the manufacturing industry drawn from the replies to the monthly business survey is reasonably similar to the growth rate's path. Here too, the outcomes for the last quarters, from 96Q4 to 98Q2, suggest that business climate was favourable; however, similar figures were obtained in the past, for example during the period 1989-90 and for the year 1995. Unlike the series of growth rates, the ADF-test does not reject the hypothesis of unit root, and the synthetic curve may not be stationary.

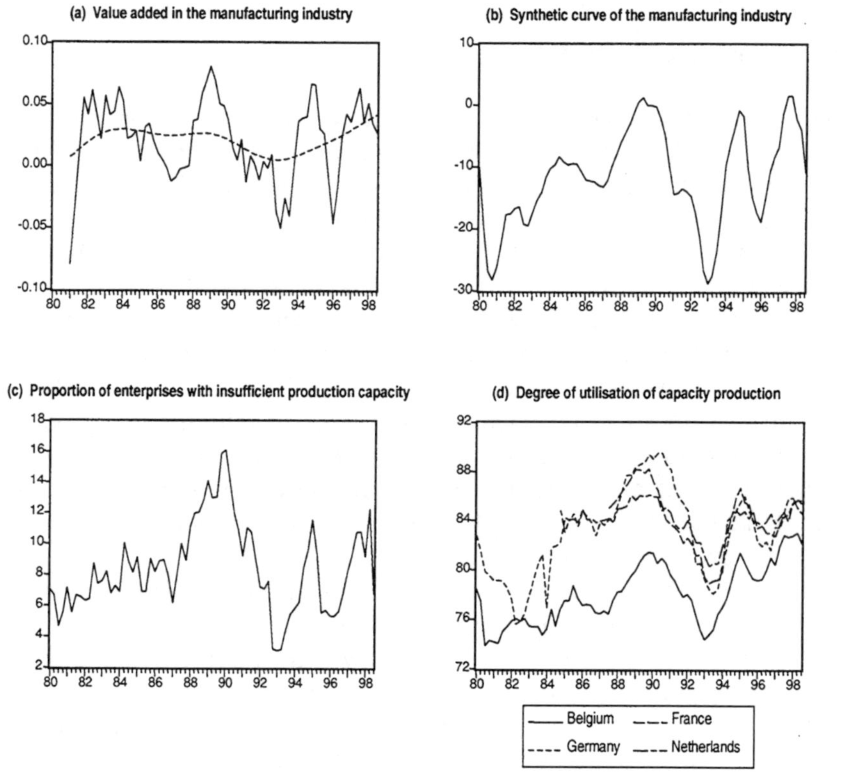

Sources: Panel a: National Account Institute; panels b and c: National Bank of Belgium, panel d: European Commission

Figure 22.2 - Economic Context

c) Qualitative assessment of the production capacity

Apart from posing the question on the rate of utilisation of production capacity, the National Bank's quarterly survey also includes a qualitative question concerning the entrepreneurs' judgement about how the present production capacity can meet the demand, in view of the current level of demand and of sales expectations for the following 12 months.

Figure 22.2 (c) illustrates the proportion of entrepreneurs answering a current production capacity insufficient to meet demand. Higher levels for the degree of utilisation should lead to a higher proportion of enterprises with unsatisfactory production capacity. This relation seems to hold for the period 80Q1 to 93Q3. The correlation between the two series then reaches 0.84. This is less the case subsequently. The correlation falls to 0.61 when the period is extended to 98Q3. Over the past 2 years, from 1996 to 1998, the proportion of enterprises with unsatisfactory production capacity was considerable, but did not reach an exceptional level. The proportion was significantly higher during the years 1988 and 1989, while the degree of utilisation was lower. In contrast to this last series, the ADF-test for unit test does not reject the hypothesis of stability for the proportion of enterprises with unsatisfactory production capacity.

d) Degree of utilisation in the neighbouring countries

As a small open economy, the business cycle of the Belgian economy depends for a large part upon the situation in the neighbouring countries. The rate of utilisation of production capacity should follow a similar evolution.

As for the assessment on production capacity, the parallelism is reasonably good up to the end of 1995. Table 22.2 shows that the correlation coefficients between Belgium and Germany, France or The Netherlands are close to, or exceed, 0.85. When the period of observation is extended to 98Q3, the correlation coefficients for Belgium decrease to around 0.65 with respect to Germany and France, and to 0.80 with respect to The Netherlands.

Table 22.2 - Correlation Coefficients Between the Degrees of Capacity Utilisation in Belgium and in the Neighbouring Countries

Sample 87:3 98:3 (Sample 87:3 95:4)				
	Germany	France	Netherlands	Belgium
Germany	1			
France	0.85 (0.86)	1		
Netherlands	0.87 (0.93)	0.91 (0.94)	1	
Belgium	0.63 (0.89)	0.67 (0.83)	0.80 (0.87)	1

Source : European Commission

The decrease since 1996 of the correlation coefficients for the rate for production capacity utilisation in Belgium with respect to those in Germany and in France can be illustrated by the fact that, in these countries, the degree of utilisation achieved a maximum value in 1990, and not during the most recent period. It cannot be explained by differences in the movements of production : the correlation for the growth rate of the value added in the manufacturing industry in Belgium and in Germany and France is the same for the period up to the end of 1995 or up to the end of 1998.

From the comparison between the evolution of the degree of utilisation of the production capacity in Belgium presented in point 2, and the evolution of four reference indicators, it would appear that the position in the business cycle can explain high values for the degree of utilisation during 1997 and the beginning of 1998. However, according to these reference indicators, there are no reasons why the degree of utilisation should be higher now than in other periods of rapid growth in the past, or why the degree of utilisation should have a rising tendency.

At the same time, a recent study carried out by National Bank on the investment function in Belgium has shown that the volume of investments by enterprises during the period 1988 to 1998 has been in line with the evolution of its determinants, namely production and relative factor costs, even if capital is only one of the factors to be taken into account in production capacity.

These results may not help to explain the divergence between the evolution of the degree of utilisation and the economic situation.

4 Changes in the Statistical Treatment of the Replies

Structural movements in the degree of utilisation could result from changes in the statistical treatment of the replies. First, for two particular sectors, the processing of the individual replies has recently been transferred from the sectors' federation to the National Bank of Belgium. It would be useful to analyse whether this has caused any change in the outcome. Second, the aggregation of individual replies into global results depends on weighting systems. These systems have to be updated if they are to continue reflecting the structure of the population.

4.1 Specific Sectors

The statistical process used to aggregate individual replies into sectorial results is identical for most of the sectors, and has been left unchanged throughout the period of observations. This has not been the case, however, for two sectors, chemicals and non-ferrous metals. Up to the end of 1994, individual results from enterprises of these two sectors were collected and treated by the sectors' federations. The National Bank of Belgium only received aggregate results for these two sectors, which were used to calculate the degree of utilisation for the manufacturing industry as a whole. From the first quarter of 1995 onwards, the treatment of the individual replies has been assumed by the National Bank of Belgium, as for all other sectors. At the same time, the panel's size has been increased in the chemical sector.

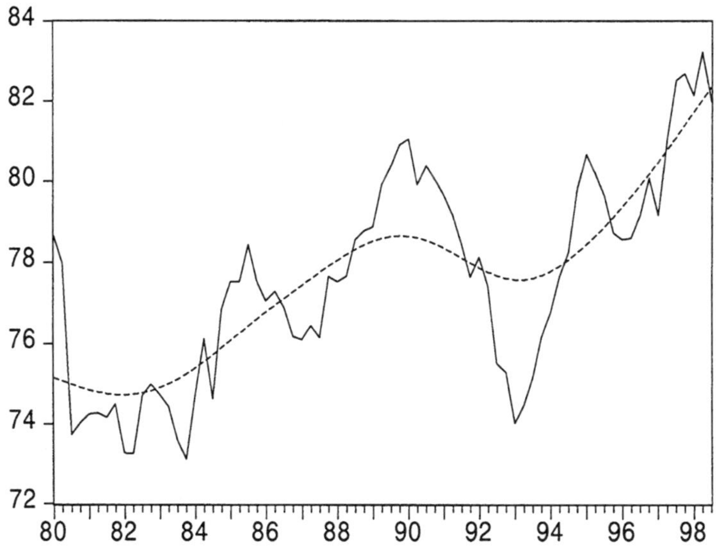

Source : National Bank of Belgium

Figure 22.3 - Degree of Utilisation of Production Capacity in the Manufacturing Industry, Excluding Chemicals and Non-ferrous Metals

It seems that the effects of this transition are limited, since the degree of utilisation calculated by aggregating all sectors of the manufacturing industry except chemicals and non-ferrous metals is very close to the unrestricted results (Figure 22.3). The correlation between the two series reaches 0.98.

4.2 Weightings

To compute the rate of utilisation of the manufacturing industry as a whole, different aggregation steps are necessary. At each step, an appropriate system of weightings is used. First, turnover figures, communicated once a year by the participating entrepreneurs, are used to aggregate individual replies into *product results*. Second, by grouping together products of the same nature, detailed value added statistics are used to calculate *sector results*. Third, more aggregate value added data are used to obtain results for the *manufacturing industry as a whole*.

Data necessary to establish the second weighting system are very specific; they are extracted from the input-output matrix of the Belgian economy. For quite some time, the most recent estimates of the input-output matrix available were for the year 1985. New estimates, for the year 1995, have recently been made available, but they have not yet been used in the weighting of the products' results for the degree of utilisation.

4.2.1 Weightings of the Sectors Within the framework of the Belgian survey on production capacity, the results of twelve sectors are aggregated to calculate the degree of utilisation of the production capacity in the manufacturing industry as a whole. The weightings applied to each sector are deduced from the national account statistics on value added. However, even if these data are available on an annual basis, the weights used are modified only occasionally: this occurred most recently in November 1996. To avoid discontinuity in the results, the changes are introduced gradually, month after month, over one year.

The introduction of a new system of weightings for the sectors could affect - and in our case, augment - the level of the degree of utilisation in the manufacturing industry, if sectors which become relatively more important within the manufacturing industry also exhibit higher than average degrees of utilisation.

Table 22.3 shows that as a consequence of the changes, the relative weightings within the manufacturing industry have increased for sectors with for which the rate of utilisation is usually higher than on average (such as the publishing industry), as well as for those sectors with a low rate of utilisation (such as the food industry). By contrast, the relative weight has decreased for sectors with a high as well as low rate of utilisation.

Table 22.3 - Weightings of the Sectors

	Weights up to 96Q3	Weights from 97Q4	Differen-ces in weights	Average degree of utilisation	
				Average 80Q1 to 98 Q3	Average 95Q1 to 98 Q3
Textiles and clothing	10.3	7.8	-2.5	77.6	78.0
Footwear and leather	0.6	0.2	-0.4	76.7	79.2
Food, beverages	8.8	13.0	4.2	75.5	75.5
Iron and steel	6.7	5.7	-1.1	72.6	85.3
Non-ferrous metals	2.1	3.1	1.0	83.4	88.2
Metal-working industry	39.0	33.6	-5.4	77.2	81.2
Paper	2.7	2.6	-0.1	83.4	83.6
Publishing industry	0.0	4.0	4.0	82.1	83
Wood and furniture	2.7	4.5	-2.2	82.2	80.3
Non-metallic minerals	6.6	5.4	-1.0	81.0	84.0
Plastic	2.7	3.2	0.5	80.4	80.5
Chemicals	14.1	16.9	2.8	79.4	82.9
TOTAL	100.0	100.0		78.1	81.1

Source : National Bank of Belgium

All in all, the results for the rate of capacity utilisation in the manufacturing industry have only been marginally influenced, in a downward direction, by the changes in the weightings introduced at the end of 1996. These changes do not help in any way to explain the higher results observed in 1997 and 1998: calculated on the basis of the old weightings per sectors, the degree of utilisation in the manufacturing industry as a whole over the period 96Q1 to 98Q3 would have reached 81.5%, which is slightly more than with the new weightings (81.4%).

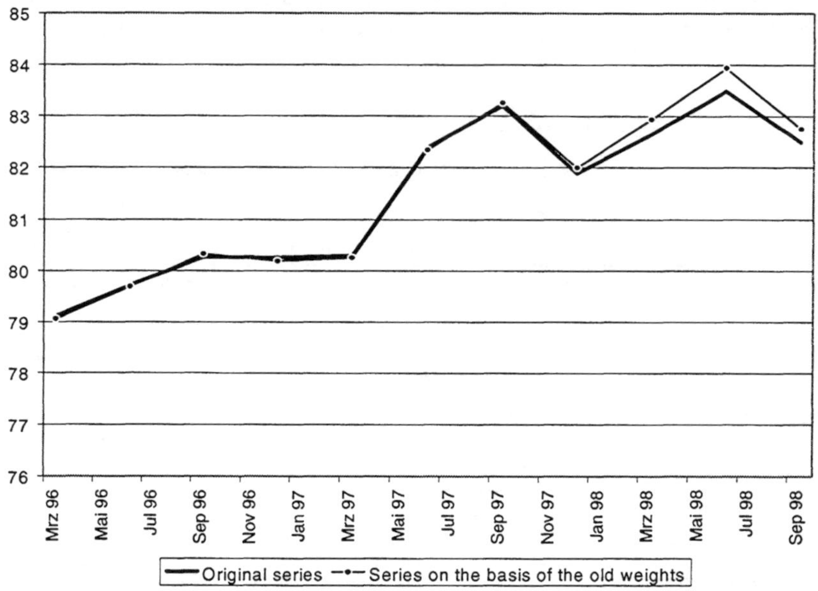

Source : National Bank of Belgium

Figure 22.4 - Influence of the Changes in the Sectors' Weightings on the Degree of Utilisation of the Manufacturing Industry

4.2.2 Individual Weightings As a first step in the aggregation process, individual replies are summed up into product results, using turnover figures as weightings. These weightings are obtained once a year from the respondents. Again, as for the changes in the sectors' weights, the new individual weights are introduced progressively to avoid breaks in the series. Nevertheless, changes in the weights could induce changes in the degree of utilisation of the production capacity for a product, and therefore for a sector and for the manufacturing industry as a whole. This will happen if :

- the replies are significantly different between small and large enterprises, in terms of average level of the rate of utilisation or in terms of the evolution rate of utilisation, and,
- the relative importance of small and large enterprises within the panel changes over time.

These two effects can be combined by comparing the aggregate rate where the turnover figures of the enterprises are used as weightings for the individual replies, with the aggregate rate where all replies are given the same weight, whatever the importance of the enterprise. In the second case, more importance is given to small enterprises, while the influence of the replies given by large enterprises is dramatically reduced. As no individual replies are available before 1995 for chemicals and non-ferrous metals, these two sectors are excluded from the comparison. For the other sectors, individual replies are available from the beginning of 1988.

Table 22.4 - Comparison Between Weighted and Non-weighted Individual Replies (Percentages)

Sample:	1988: 1 1998: 3	
Observations:	43	
	Weighted	Non-weighted
Mean	79.4	75.7
Median	79.5	75.5
Maximum	83.2	78.9
Minimum	75.6	71.3
Std. Deviation	1.75	2.05
Correlation	0.74	

Source : National Bank of Belgium

The descriptive statistics for the two series show that, on average for all enterprises together except those of the sectors chemicals and non-ferrous metals, the degree of utilisation of the production capacity is some 4 points higher when obtained from weighted replies than from non-weighted replies. Large firms' entrepreneurs report on average a significantly higher rate of utilisation than small firms.

The second panel of Figure 22.5 indicates that the difference between the two serices has not remained constant during the complete period of observation. From 1988 to the end of 1990, the ratio of the degree of utilisation based on weighted replies with respect to that based on non-weighted replies fluctuated between 1 and 1.02. This ratio increased progressively up to 1994, and then stabilised around 1.06. In fact, the degree of utilisation observed during 1997 and 1998 represents a top level only on the basis of weighted replies. Calculated on the basis of non-weighted replies, the level of the degree of utilisation level is close, but still lower than the maximum recorded in 1990.

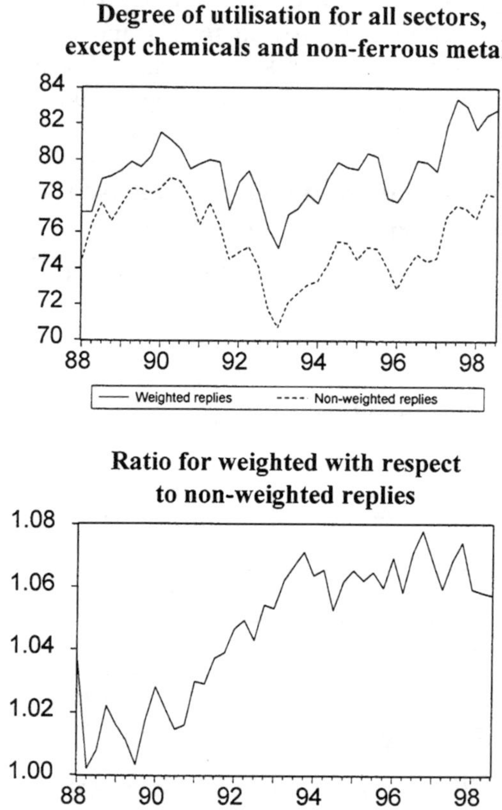

Source : National Bank of Belgium

Figure 22.5 - Influence of the Weighting of Individual Replies

The increasing difference between weighted and non-weighted results makes it necessary to treat the weighting system for individuals replies with caution. It does not yet prove that the results for the degree of utilisation of production capacity are biased by some inadequate treatment. It could be that the replies of large firms and small firms are more divergent in the second half of the 1990s than at the end of the 1980s. It is also possible that the relative importance of large firms has increased. Certainly, further investigation is required in this respect.

5 Evolution by Sector

As a first step towards a more in-depth investigation, Figure 22.6 presents the evolution of the degree of utilisation in the different sectors which constitute the manufacturing industry. The sectors are ranked according to their relative importance.

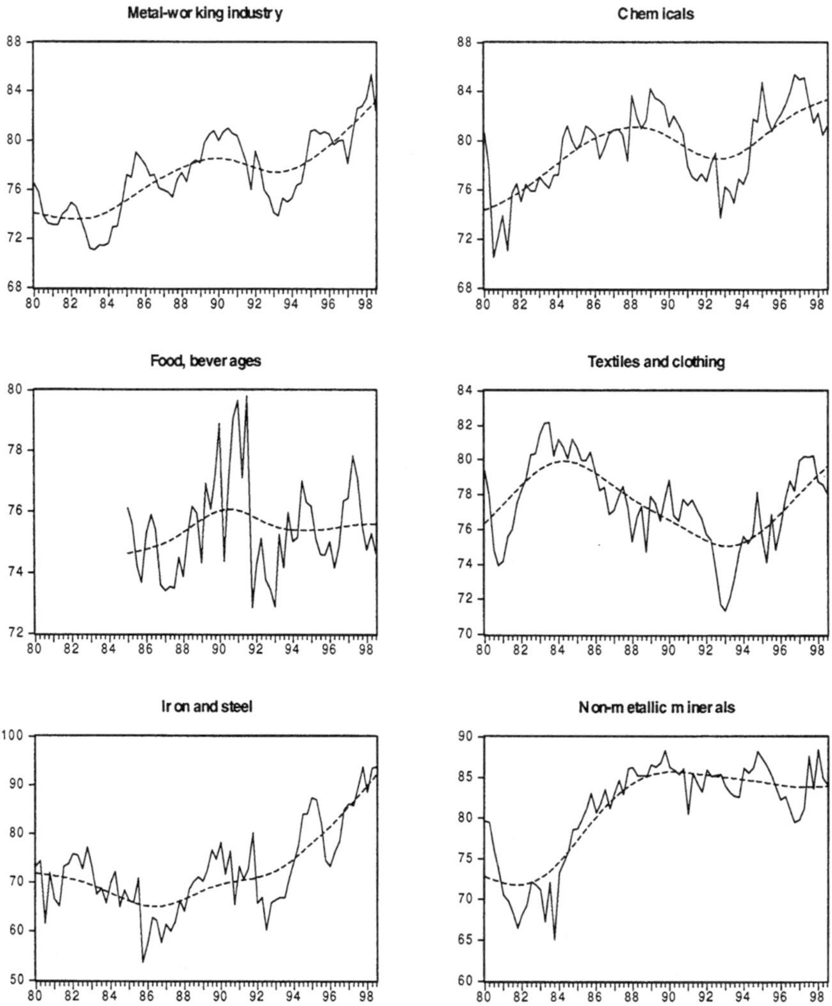

Figure 22.6a - Degree of Utilisation of the Production Capacity in Certain Sectors (Percentages)

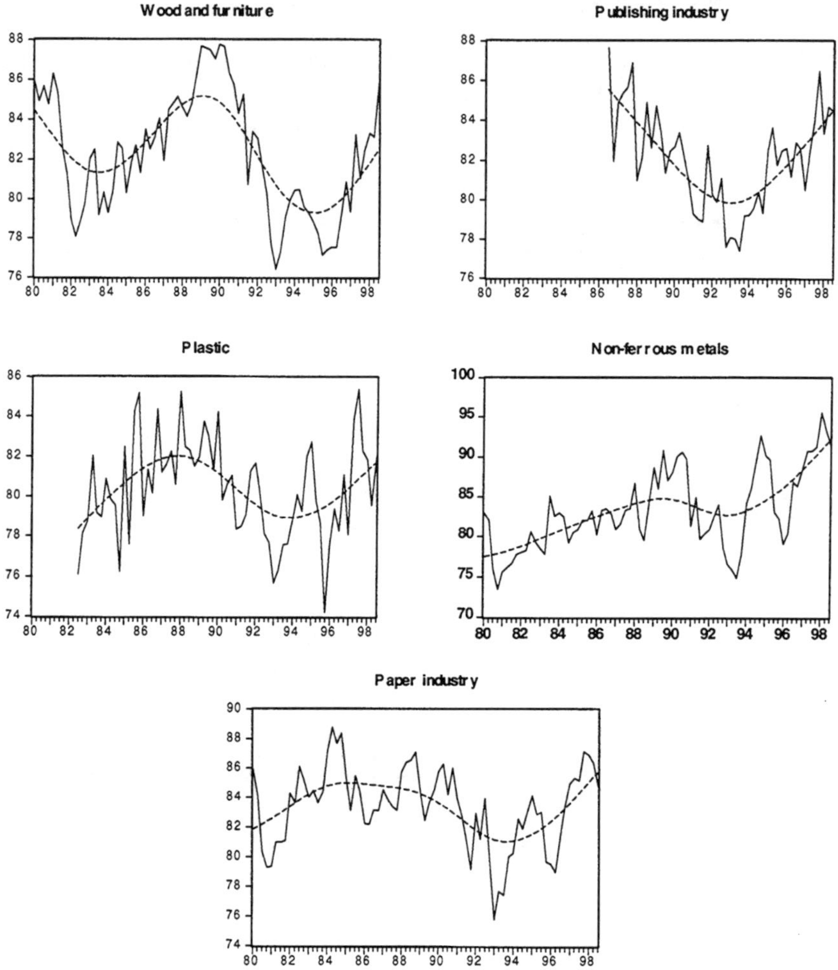

Source : National Bank of Belgium

Figure 22.6b - Degree of Utilisation of the Production Capacity in Certain Sectors (Percentages)

The general profile of the evolution of the utilisation rate varies greatly from sector to sector. The Hodrick-Prescott filters exhibits a continuously positive slope for the metal-working and the chemical industries, the two biggest sectors of the manufacturing industry, but also for iron and steel and non-ferrous metals. For other sectors, the fundamental evolution of the degree of utilisation has been quite stable, or has gone through multiple turning points. However, for most sectors, the degree of utilisation increased during the last quarters of the period of observation, certainly from the beginning of 1996.

Among the different sectors for which individual replies are available for a sufficiently long period of time, the overall movement in the ratio between results based on weighted or non-weighted replies presented in the previous section is also visible in the metal-working industry. This ratio has systematically increased between 1989 and 1994 in this sector, while it does not show any clear tendency in the other sectors (Figure 22.7).

6 Conclusions

According to the results of the quarterly survey held by the National Bank of Belgium, the degree of utilisation of production capacity for the manufacturing industry reached unprecedentedly high levels in 1997 and 1998. This is partially due to the position in the business cycle, characterised by accelerating growth rates of production. However, in the past, similar economic contexts have been observed that were accompanied by lower levels of capacity utilisation.

In addition to the short-term effects arising out of the general economic situation, the evolution of the utilisation rate in the manufacturing industry seems to have been driven by structural forces, which introduced a rising tendency. These result neither from the transfer of the treatment of individual replies in the chemical and non-ferrous metals from the sectors' federations to the National Bank, nor from the adaptation of the sectors' weights to compute aggregate results for the manufacturing industry.

The comparison between the degree of utilisation obtained on the basis of weighted individual replies, on the one hand, and non-weighted individual replies, on the other, indicates that the upward tendency is present only in the first. Large enterprises report on average a higher degree of utilisation, and their contribution to the aggregate result has increased, particularly in the metal-working industry. Possible causes for this phenomenon are:

- a structural modification in the composition of the population of enterprises, with more concentration on production, resulting in a higher average degree of utilisation;
- a structural change in the replies;

- an inappropriate composition of the panel, with the large enterprises being more and more over-represented in the panel in comparison with their actual importance in the population of enterprises.

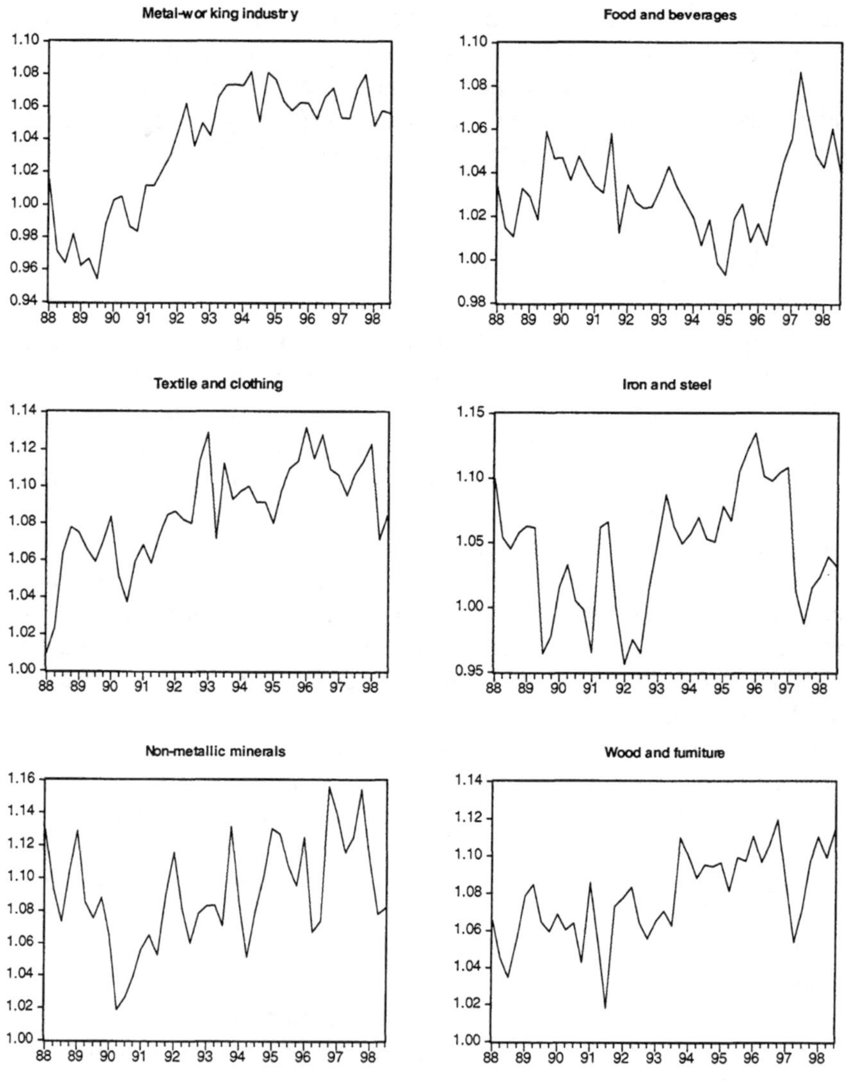

Source : National Bank of Belgium

Figure 22.7 - Ratio of Degrees of Utilisation Based on Weighted w.r.t Non-weighted Replies

Structural changes could have occurred through a larger concentration of the enterprises leading on average to a higher degree of utilisation of production capacity, or by higher figures being reported by the individual respondents. They should be reflected in the average degree of utilisation: better use of production induces more efficiency for the economy, due to progress in the organisation of the enterprises or due to the fact that, by enlarging their size, more enterprises reach the high degree of utilisation observed for large enterprises. However this structural development should be explicitly taken into account in the use of degree of production capacity as an indicator for economic growth, or as a determinant for the enterprises' investments.

An inappropriate composition of the panel should be rectified, in order to obtain results which are representative for the economy. Individual data from the Central Balance Sheet Office, also located in the National Bank, could help to verify, and if need be to improve, the representativity of the panel with respect to the size of the enterprises. As a first test, gross information based on the value added as reported by the enterprises in their balance sheets does not indicate that the importance of large firms in the metal-working industry has increased between 1985 and 1993.

References

Christiano, L. J. (1981), 'A survey of Measures of capacity utilisation', *IMF-Staff papers*, Vol. 28, No. 1, March 1991, pp. 144-198.

National Bank of Belgium, Annual Report 1997.

National Bank of Belgium (1998), 'Les investissements des entreprises', unpublished paper.

Oppenländer, K. H. (1997), 'The phenomenon of business cycles', in *Business Cycle Indicators*, K. M. Oppenländer (ed) Avebury, pp. 3-23.

Vanhaelen, J.-J. and H. De Doncker (1993), 'The use of the capacity survey to explain the behaviour of entrepreneurs', in Oppenländer, K. H. and G. Poser (ed), *The Exploratory Power of Business Cycle Surveys*, (papers presented at the 21st CIRET Conference, Stellenbosch, 1993, Avebury), pp. 133-158.

23 Investment Forecast and Capacity Utilisation: A Panel Data Analysis

MICHEL HOUDEBINE

1 Introduction

Investment business surveys in industry ask firm managers to give evaluations of their investment : they are supposed to give investment forecasts and realisations on a period of three consecutive years. This survey system thus gives the opportunity to measure how firms evaluate and re-evaluate their investment. The evolution of the answers of the firms could be significant: at least in two occasions (in January 1995 and January 1998) firms had given a very different figure than three months earlier (in October survey). This study wants to investigate how firms are forming their investment forecasts and how they are re-evaluating them. We estimate simple econometric relations on the 1991-1997 period on a panel of industrial enterprises. The first section wants to investigate the way firms are evaluating the investment levels collected in the business surveys. The second tries to find factors that could lead to a change in the enterprise forecast.

Economic models usually describe investment as a derivation of simple comportment models of the firm : the firm is supposed to maximise its inter temporal profits under technical constraints (for example: production following a Cobb-Douglas function and capital accumulation constraint). Such models underline the impact of factors such as relative factor costs (in particular capital cost) and demand constraints on the level of the investment. Therefore, the fact that the firm expects an increase in its demand for the next periods will usually lead to an increase in its investment. These models also usually stress the fact that investment depends on the constraints encountered by the firm on its production side: the fact that the firm cannot increase its production because capital is not sufficient usually leads to an increase in its investment.

This study intends to explore these different aspects with the answers given by enterprises to two different business surveys in the French manufacturing industry: the investment business survey in industry and the business survey on activity in industry. The latter gives quantitative information on production capacities of the firm (capacity margins) and qualitative evaluation of the activity in the firm. It allows us to know whether the firm expects an increase in its demand. This study does not investigate financial factors of investment, mainly because it is hard to construct a good indicator of capital cost at an individual level.[1]

2 Investment Forecasts

When, in October, firm managers answer the business survey on investment they are asked to give a first evaluation of their investment amount for the next year. In later surveys, firms have to give successive evaluations of this same amount. With such a system, the firm has to give, in six different surveys, six evaluations of the investment amount it is planning for year n (one will note these investment amounts by : October n-1 / n; January n / n ...). In this section, one is looking for determinants of the investment forecasts compared to the perception the firm has of its situation.

Economists suggest that evolutions in the demand expected by the firm or an increase of the constraint on its productive capital could affect the level of the investment amount of the firm. To test these ideas, we are first going to estimate a linear econometric relation between variables from various surveys made at the same moment. A more general specification will take into account lags of some of the exogenous variables (table 23.3). We try to link the forecasts made by the firm for its annual investment amount with its capacity margin and its expected demand.

$$\mathrm{Log}(\mathrm{inv}_t^i) = \alpha.\mathrm{maps}_t^i + \beta.\mathrm{dem}_t^i + \mathrm{u}^i + \delta_t + \varepsilon_t^i \qquad (1)$$

In this equation, we note :

[1] We tried to introduce financial data from the treasury survey in industry, but unfortunatly the number of answers was too small to find any significant result.

inv_t^i : level of the investment amount that the firm i forecasts at survey t

$maps_t^i$: capacity margins with enrolment

dem_t^i : opinion of the firm on expected demand (see box 23.2 for the construction of this variable)

u^i : individual effect of the firm

δ_t : time dummies that take into account the macro-economic effects that are not already included in the other variables.

The error terms are supposed to follow the same null average law, and are independent among dates and individuals.[2]

In equation (1), we have introduced an effect u^i specific to the firm. This variable wants to capture the characteristics of the firm i that one cannot measure directly: the largest firms are also those which have large investment amounts (just for a scale effect), enterprises are not investing the same way from one sector to an other (the median investment rate (calculated as investment over added value) of the textile industry is of about 2% while it is of about 17% for the artificial fibres industry). Apart from these size and sector effects, the individual effect u^i can take into account behaviours that are more specific to the firm : a firm that increases its activity on the estimation period could invest considerably, independently of the general economic situation. Nevertheless, this specification is founded on a rather strong hypothesis : each enterprise has an average investment comportment during the whole period of estimation and only macro-economic shocks and exogenous variables explain the fluctuations of the investment level (see box 23.1 for estimation technique). One could have introduced an adaptive model, where the investment forecast would be explained by the investment amount of the previous year corrected by the variables we are using here (a similar approach is proposed in annex).

In equation (1), one is expecting that an increase in tensions on the production capacities of the firm and an increase in the demand expected by the firm will lead to an increase in the investment forecast. This influence should be patent when the firm decides to invest, thus in the

---

2 We could have specified this model with inter-temporal interdependance (which would have meant that the level of investment was influenced by the fact that the firm had invested a lot the previous year or not). We did not retain this specification in order to keep the model as simple as possible.

surveys when it proposes the first evaluations of its investment for a year of reference.

Table 23.1 - Investment and Capacity Utilisation, Annual Estimations

	October n-1 / n	January n / n	April n / n	October n / n	January n+1 / n	April n+1 / n
Constant	0.131	0.072	0.018	0.040	0.036	0.0024
	(3.50)	(1.85)	(0.49)	(1.02)	(0.82)	(0.05)
Capacity	**-0.0066**	**-0.0058**	**-0.0034**	**-0.0036**	-0.0025	0.00014
margins	**(-6.23)**	**(4.10)**	**(-2.82)**	**(-3.38)**	(-1.54)	(-0.10)
Demand	0.025	0.088	0.031	-0.029	0.025	-0.031
	(0.93)	(2.68)	(0.95)	(-1.06)	(0.68)	(-0.78)
No of firms	513	348	398	577	367	375

Source: Survey on investment in industry, survey on activity in industry (INSEE).

Note: This table gives *within* estimations for the period 1991-1997. The estimations noted October n-1 / n corresponds to the investment forecast for the next year, those noted January, April and October n / n for the current year, and the last two estimations refer to investment made the previous year. We have introduced temporal dummies to take into account macro-economic shocks. The estimation is made on the enterprises which have answered to 5 surveys out of the six possible. Students appear in brackets.

The estimations of table 23.1 are a partial confirmation of these ideas. It appears that the firms of the manufacturing industry take into account the level of their constraint on capacities, when they are forecasting their annual investment: small capacity margins, which means that the firm would have great difficulties to face a demand shock, leads to an increase in its investment amount. The fact that the correlation between the level of production capacity margins and the level of investment diminishes from the first estimation to the sixth suggests that when the status of the investment amount changes from a forecast for the first survey to quasi certain realisations for the last ones, the firm is gradually less influenced by the current level of its production capacities.[3] The fact that the correlation vanishes for the last surveys (in January and April n+1 / n) means that the answers of the firms are globally coherent: for this period the firm does not take into account the contemporary margins when it gives an evaluation of its amount of investment for the previous year.

Contrary to the capacity margins, the evaluation of demand variations given by the firm for the next three months (see box 23.2 on data) appear to have no significant effect on the level of investment. This result can

[3] The variance explained by model diminishes also from the first to the last estimation.

probably be linked with the data used for the demand proxy: firms are asked to answer to the question on demand on a very short basis. Three months are certainly too short compared to the commitment involved for the firm: an investment in usually supposed to last for a least a few years (even for computers). Thus, one cannot exclude that a variable that would take into account how firms appreciate a long term demand tendency would have an influence on the level of investment. One could introduce other proxies from the quarterly survey on activity for demand expectations but apparently none of these variables have any relation with the level of investment forecasts.[4]

Box 23.1 - Estimation Method

The introduction of an individual effect in equation (1) makes its direct estimation rather difficult. In order to rule out this technical difficulty, and if we don't want to specify more precisely this effect (fixed or random), it is classical to estimate this equation with a *within* estimator. Thus, we estimate an equation (2) where we have subtracted to (1) its average on the estimation period.

$$Log\left(inv_t^i\right) - Log\left(inv^i\right) = \alpha\left(maps_t^i - maps_t^i\right) + \beta\left(dem_t^i - dem^i\right) + \delta_t - \frac{1}{T}\sum_s \delta_s + \eta_t^i \qquad (2)$$

This new specification allows to evaluate the influence of the capacity margin and the expected demand of the firm on the level of investment relative to its average level. One can estimate equation (2) with ordinary least squares when one has annual investment amounts and quarterly data on expected demand and capacity margins.[5] The fact that the firm gives six successive estimations of its investment leads to six different estimations of equation (2).

---

[4] We tried proxies such as the expected tendency of production, order books in weeks, and general prospects.

[5] Formally, the error terms are not independant ($\eta_t^i = \varepsilon_t^i - \frac{1}{T}\sum_s \varepsilon_s^i$). One can establish that the within estimator is equal to the ordinary least squares estimator on model (1), but one should take this into account when one is estimating confidence intervals.

2.1 *Introduction of Capacity Investment*

The survey on investment in industry gives the possibility to split the total investment amount given by the firm in five distinct parts. The firm has the opportunity to give the share of each of the five following purposes for its investment: Renewal of old equipments, maintenance; Modernisation; Extensions of capacity; Introduction of new products; Other purposes (security, environment...). Unfortunately, these questions are only available for the surveys carried out in October and April. Hereafter, we want to take this information into account and we will consider that investments done for capacity extensions are the more likely to be influenced by the variables we have introduced in the estimations of table 23.1. Thus, we are estimating equations similar to equation (2) where the amount of investment corresponds to the investment amount dedicated to the increase of capacity.[6]

Table 23.2 - Extension Capacity Investments and Capacity Utilisation

	October n-1 / n	April n / n	October n / n
Constant	0.021	-0.174	0.024
	(0.15)	(-1.56)	(0.19)
Capacity margins	**-0.015**	**-0.010**	-0.006
	(-2.79)	**(-1.95)**	(-1.17)
Expected dema nd	0.009	-0.024	-0.154
	(0.07)	(-0.23)	(-1.50)
No of firms	84	109	112

Source: Survey on investment in industry, survey on activity in industry (INSEE).

Note: This table gives *within* estimations for the period 1991-1997. The estimations noted October n-1 / n corresponds to the investment forecast for the next year, those noted April and October n / n for the current year. We have introduced temporal dummies to take into account macro-economic shocks. The estimation is made on the enterprises which have answered to 4 surveys out of the six possible. Students appear in brackets.

The results obtained for these estimations are very similar to those we had for total investment (table 23.2). Tensions on capacities have a positive impact on the level of investment forecasts. This influence diminishes when the firm learns information on the amount it will finally make for the year concerned. And there is apparently no evidence of a relation between short term demand factors and capacity investment. The striking fact here is that the estimated parameter for capacity margins is significantly larger

[6] This corresponds to the share of extension capacity times total investment.

than the one we had when we were considering total capacity investment: this result is apparently consistent with the idea that tensions on capacities have a strong influence on investment via its share dedicated to capacity extensions. Thus, it is not surprising that the elasticity of investment to capacity margins is larger when considering investment dedicated to capacity extensions.

The previous estimations suggest that the relation between investment, expected demand and tensions on production capacity evolves from the moment when the firm makes its first forecast till the moment when the investment is actually already done (when the amount the firm gives in the survey is in fact an evaluation of the amount it has already invested). One can wonder whether the forecast given by the firm depends also on the constraints faced during previous trimesters. We test this idea with the estimation of equations similar to the previous ones but which takes into account the temporal aspects of the firm forecast. We are thus estimating equations with lags of the capacity margins.

Table 23.3 - Temporal Link Between Firm Investment Forecasts and Capacity Utilisation

	October n-1 / n	January N / n	April n / n	October n / n	January n+1 / n	April n+1 / n
Constant	0.040	0.026	0.023	0.065	0.054	0.031
	(0.87)	(0.63)	(0.53)	(1.36)	(1.14)	(0.58)
Maps(t)	**-0.0066**	**-0.005**	-0.001	-0.001	-0.003	0.0018
	(-2.56)	**(-2.31)**	(-0.63)	(-0.55)	(-1.29)	(0.67)
Maps(t-1)	-0.0015	-0.0012	**-0.0059**	-0.0036	0.0005	-0.0039
	(-0.60)	(-0.51)	**(-2.64)**	(-1.20)	(0.20)	(-1.49)
Maps(t-2)	-0.003	-0.0014	0.0014	-0.001	**-0.006**	0.0007
	(-0.13)	(-0.61)	(0.65)	(-0.41)	**(-2.24)**	(0.28)
Maps(t-3)	-0.0015	-0.0016	-0.002	-0.0023	-0.002	-0.035
	(-0.66)	(-0.74)	(-0.92)	(-0.84)	(-0.93)	(-0.34)
No of firms	323	328	342	365	355	335

Source: Survey on investment in industry, survey on activity in industry (INSEE).

Note: This table gives *within* estimations for the period 1991-1997. The estimations noted October n-1 / n corresponds to the investment forecast for the next year, those noted January, April and October n / n for the current year, and the last two estimations refer to investment made the previous year. We have introduced temporal dummies to take into account macro-economic shocks. The estimation is made on the enterprises which have answered to 5 surveys out of the six possible. Students appear in brackets.

When looking at the estimations of table 23.3, it appears that the forecast made by the firm is not always founded on the current estimation of its capacity constraint but also on the previous ones. Apparently the firm determines its level of investment considering the capacity margins that are prevailing at the moment when they have taken the investment decision. For the first periods, the firm uses the current margins in order to form its forecasts. For the following surveys, the firm uses constraints faced in the recent past. At the end of the period of estimation, it appears that the amount of investment depends on the margins the firm had the previous year.

3 Linearity of the Relation Between Investment and Capacity Margins

We have been estimating linear equations linking capacity margins of firms and their investment forecasts. These estimations show that a decrease in capacity margins, which would reflect an increase in tensions on production capacities, is a factor in the rise of the firm investment. Hereafter, we want to investigate whether this relation is linear or not, that is whether the firm is more sensitive to a modification of its production conditions when its capacity constraint is tight or loose.

We are estimating a non parametric relation between investment forecasts and capacity margins. The equation takes the general form :

$$\mathrm{Log}(\mathrm{inv}_i^t) = f(\mathrm{maps}_i^t) + \varepsilon_i^t \qquad (3)$$

In this equation, as we did in equation (2), we want to take into account specific effects of the firm and time dummies. Thus instead of equation (3), we are going to estimate an equation where we have subtracted to each variable the average over the firm (individual effect) and then the average over time of these first results (time dummies). The estimation technique is due to Nadaraya-Watson (see annex).

We are presenting estimations corresponding to those tested in table 23.1 (figure 23.1). These results are consistent with those we found for a linear specification. All functions have a negative slope which means that investment forecasts increase when capacity margins are diminishing. But the idea that tighter tensions on capital would lead to a more than proportional increase in investment is not really confirmed by such graphs. Apparently, there is no general results, and therefore it appears that more or less the linear specification we have adopted was a good one.

Box 23.2 - The Data

This study tries to confront the answers of firms to two different business surveys in the manufacturing industry. The data on the investment forecasts come from the survey on investment in industry, the variables on the production capacity and the demand expected by the firm come from the survey on activity in industry.

Business survey on investment in industry

This survey is carried out three times a year (in January, April and October). It polls about 4,000 industrial firms. It asks the managers to give three successive evaluations of their investment amount. Thus the first forecast for year n is done at the occasion of the survey of October year n-1. This estimation is then revised at each new survey, giving a total of nine successive evaluations of the same amount. Here, we have been using only the six firsts. It also gives (for April and October surveys) the destinations of investment amount : firms have to give the shares of five different purposes for two successive years.

Survey on the situation of activity in industry

This is a quarterly survey, carried out in January, April, July and October. It polls about 4,000 industrial firms. It asks the firm managers to give their opinion on different aspects of the firm activity and especially on its personal demand prospects ('evolution of demand: probable tendency for the next three months'). The firm answers for each of its products (or the main ones) on a qualitative basis (increase, stability, decrease). In order to have an opinion at the firm level, we have weighted the answers by the product sales. The capacity margins are estimated with the question 'could you increase your production if you hired new staff? If yes, how much could you increase your production with your current equipment?'.

A panel of firms

The estimation technique we have been using here requires us to set up a panel of firms of the French manufacturing industry on the period 1991-1997. Data on investment amounts come from the surveys spanning from October 1991 to October 1997 (the questionnaire was slightly modified at summer 1991, thus the data are not comparable before this date). The data coming from the investment survey were matched with those from the survey on activity in industry on the basis of the registration number of the firm.

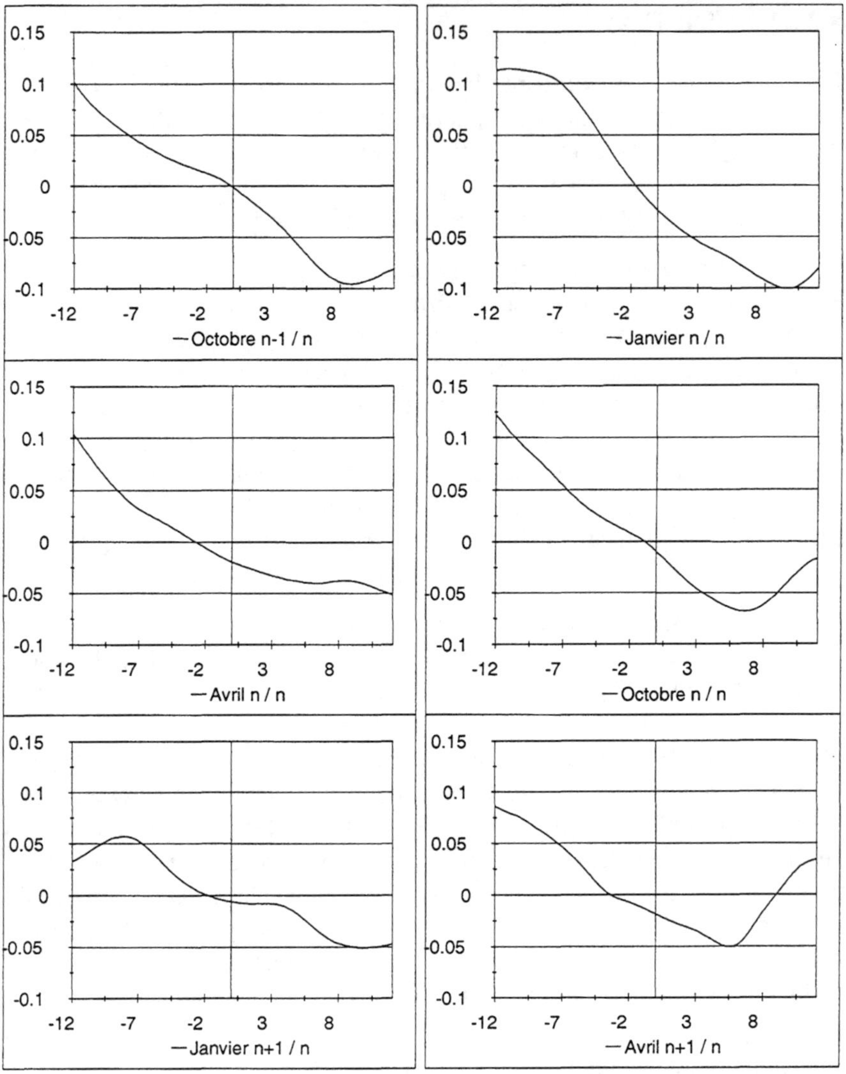

Note: These figures give estimations for the period 1991-1997. The estimations are using a Nadaraya-Watson kernel technique (see annex). The estimations take into account individual effects and time effect by subtracting averages on time and firms. The estimation is made on the enterprises which have answered to 4 surveys out of the six possible.

Source : Survey on investment in industry, survey on activity in industry (INSEE).

Figure 23.1 - Non-parametric Estimations: Investment Forecast vs Capacity Margins

4 Re-evaluations of Investment Forecasts

In the recent past, we have encountered large re-evaluations of the investment forecasts for industry onat least two occasions: in January 1995, firms have been expecting a rise of about 14% when three months earlier the estimated figure was of only 6%. A similar situation happened in January 1998, industrial firms were very timid in October and a lot more optimistic in January (the year on year rate of investment climbed from 4 to 11%). In this section, we are going to try to find some of the mechanisms leading to modifications in the firm investment evaluations from one survey to another. The previous sections have shown that when determining their investment forecasts, firms were taking into account their capacity margins. This section wants to investigate short term comportments: one wonders whether the re-evaluation of the investment amounts between two surveys are linked to the modifications in the opinion of the firm on demand or on its production capacities.

The estimation we are proposing here is very close to the one we have adopted in the previous section. One is estimating a linear relation (4) which links the re-evaluation of the investment forecasts to variations of the opinion of the firm.

$$\log(\text{inv}_t^i(\text{rev})) - \log(\text{inv}_t^i(\text{prec})) = \alpha.\Delta\text{maps}_t^i + \beta.\Delta\text{dem}_t^i + \delta_t + \varepsilon_t^i \tag{4}$$

The variations of capacity margins (maps) and the tendency of the expected demand (dem) correspond to the variations of these variables between two successive investment surveys (the interval could either be of three or six months depending on the month of reference one is considering, January, April or October). In this specification, we have not introduced any specific effect. If one had, this would have meant that the firm is re-evaluating its investment systematically by the same amount at the same moment of the year. It appears more reasonable to assume that on average, and everything else equal, firms are not re-evaluating their investment amounts.

Table 23.4 - Re-evaluations of Investment and Capacity Utilisation

	October – January n-1 / n n / n	January - April n / n n / n	April - October n / n n / n
ΔMargins	0.0003 (0.22)	-0.001 (-1.19)	-0.002 (-1.37)
ΔDemand	**0.038** **(1.96)**	**0.038** **(2.04)**	-0.030 (-1.39)
No of firms	395	406	454

Source: Survey on investment in industry, survey on activity in industry (INSEE).

Note: This table gives OLS estimations for the period 1991-1997. We have introduced temporal dummies to take into account macro-economic shocks. The estimation is made on the enterprises which have answered 4 surveys out of the five possible. Students appear in brackets.

When one is looking at the results of table 23.4, it appears that re-evaluations of investment forecasts are not linked to modifications in capacity utilisation rate. Thus, the firm does not increase its investment projects for the current year when it is confronted with a tighter capacity margin. That means that short term re-evaluations are not dependent of the level of capacity margins. It is apparently the short term character of these re-evaluations that explains this result. When one is estimating an equation similar to (4), but with variations on one year, it appears that investment evolves with the capacity margins (see annex for estimations).

These results also suggest that surprises on the expected demand could be a factor for these re-evaluations : a modification in the opinion of the firm for the expected prospects of demand for the next three months is linked with a modification in the investment amount. The fact that short term demand indicators have an influence on these re-evaluations is not surprising. It is probable that a firm decides on an investment project for a determined period, and that short term modification of the capacity margin does not affect the average amount the firm wants to invest. But one can infer from the previous estimations that the firm could modify its project on a residual basis when confronted with a different context. The fact that the re-evaluation does not depend on the modification of the expected demand between the surveys of April and October could be a signal that most of the current year investment is decided at that moment and that later surprises could not affect the actual final realisation.

5 Conclusion

The estimations of tables 23.1 and 23.2 show that the level of the investment forecast collected by investment surveys depends on the production capacity margins: the more the firm has capacity constraints, the more it wants to invest. The re-evaluations of investment forecasts during the year is apparently not linked with evolutions of tensions on production capacities but more probably to variations of the short term demand expectation of the firm. Thus, one finds on panel data some of the classical results that one can estimate on time series : an increase in expected demand, or an increase in capacity constraints lead to an increase in the firm investment.

In January 1998, firms of the manufacturing industry have drastically revised their investment anticipations for 1998 (the year on year rate rose from 4 to 11%). From October to January, utilisation rates and opinion on expected demand increased. Nevertheless, the evolution of these two variables cannot explain the total revision. Thus one can think that some elements of the macroecomic context (which is excluded of the models through the introduction of dummies) could have incited firms to have a pessimistic opinion on activity at the end of 1997. Uncertainty in this period, mainly due to crisis in Asia, could have led firms to adopt a careful strategy with limited engagements for the next year. Some of the information collected at the end of the year could have reassured managers on the future activity, which would have allowed them to start 1998 on a more optimistic basis.

6 Annex

A Non-parametric Regression: Nadaraya-Watson method

This method wants to estimate the function f in a model of the form:

$$y_i = f(x_i) + \varepsilon_i \text{ where } (x_i, y_i) \in R^d \times R \qquad (5)$$

When the (x_i, y_i) are n samples following a density law, we are looking for a function f that is solution of the program :

$$f(x) = \underset{m}{\operatorname{Arg\,min}}\, E(y_i - m(x_i))^2 \qquad (6)$$

Nadaraya-watson proposed to estimate f with an estimator of the form :

$$\hat{m}(x) = \frac{\sum_{i=1}^{n} y_i . K\left[\frac{X_i - x}{h}\right]}{\sum_{i=1}^{n} K\left[\frac{X_i - x}{h}\right]} \text{ and } K : R^d \to R \text{ "Kernel" such that}$$

$$\begin{cases} \int K(x)dx = 1 \\ \lim\limits_{\|x\| \to \infty} \|x\|^{d+1} . K(x) = 0 \end{cases} \tag{7}$$

where $h \in R^+$

A such estimator has *good* asymptotic properties (Härdle, Bosq and Lecoutre) :

For the estimations in this study, we took a kernel equal to :

$$K(x) = \frac{15}{16}(1 - x^2)^2, |x| < 1 \tag{8}$$

The choice of the window h is crucial for such estimators. Nadaraya and Watson suggest to use a window that is equal to $2.78.\text{std}(X_i).n^{-0.2}$.

One can show easily that this estimator $\hat{m}$ is solution of the program :

$$\underset{a_0}{\text{Min}} \sum_{i=1}^{n} K(\frac{X_i - x}{h}).(Y_i - a_0)^2 . \tag{9}$$

One can improve this estimator with the solution of

$$\underset{P}{\text{Min}} \sum_{i=1}^{n} K(\frac{X_i - x}{h}).(Y_i - P(X_i - x))^2 \tag{10}$$

where P is a polynom (this is the estimator used for figure 23.1 with deg(P)=1).

B *Year on Year Change in Investment*

We are going to estimate a relation on the panel of enterprises in order to try to show whether the annual evolution of the investment proposed by a firm is linked with the evolution on the same period of its capacity margins. Thus, we are estimating an equation such that :

$$\log(inv_t^i) - \log(inv_{t-1}^i) = \alpha.\Delta maps_t^i + \beta.\Delta dem_t^i + \delta_t + \varepsilon_t^i \quad (11)$$

We introduced no specific effect (as in equation 4). Investment amounts for period t correspond to forecasts proposed by the firm and those for period t-1 to the actual investment of the year preceding the forecast collected at the same survey.

Table 23.5 - Evolution of Investment and Capacity Utilisation

	October n-1 / n	January n / n	April n / n	October n / n	January n+1 / n	April n+1 / n
ΔMargins	**-0.0025**	**-0.0027**	**-0.0036**	**-0.0036**	-0.0033	-0.0019
	(-2.66)	**(-2.13)**	**(-3.09)**	**(-2.35)**	(-1.51)	(-0.82)
ΔDemand	0.029	0.015	0.022	0.023	0.043	-0.067
	(1.38)	(0.62)	(0.85)	(0.69)	(0.99)	(-0.17)
No of firms	456	414	426	393	258	252

Source: Survey on investment in industry, survey on activity in industry (INSEE).
Note: the estimation of April n / n uses investment forecasts for year n and estimation of investment for year n-1, capacity margins of April (n) and capacity margins of April (n-1).

These estimations confirm those from table 23.1. One can see that an increase in the capacity constraint leads to an increase of its annual investment amount. It also appears that when the estimation period covers correctly the time span of investment (the year of reference), it improves the estimated correlation. This result is consistent with the idea that investment amounts are not heavily revised after April. The fact that for the two last estimations the link is not significant means that the estimation period is too disconnected from the investment figures we are trying to explain.

C *Estimations with Annual Enterprise Surveys Data*

One can confirm some of the results obtained in table 23.1 with the estimation of equation (2) using data from the Annual Enterprise Survey. It allows the use of the actual amounts invested by industrial firms instead of the forecasts collected in the investment surveys.

Table 23.6 - Capacity Margins and Actual Investment

	January	April	July	October
Constan t	-0.007	-0.019	0.022	-0.021
	(-0.27)	(-0.75)	(0.85)	(-0.83)
Margins	**-0.0045**	**-0.0060**	**-0.0043**	**-0.0038**
	(-3.87)	**(-5.41)**	**(-4.43)**	**(-3.12)**
Expected demand	0.041	-0.040	0.0058	-0.044
	(1.27)	(-1.23)	(0.18)	(-1.45)
No of firms	494	529	532	583

Source: Annual Enterprise Survey, survey on activity in industry (INSEE).

Note: This table gives *within* estimations for the period 1990-1995. The equation links the actual investment of one year to the capacity margins declared to the four surveys of the year. We have introduced temporal dummies to take into account macro-economic shocks. The estimation is made on the enterprises which have answered to 5 surveys out of the six possible. Students appear in brackets.

The results are very similar to those we found with the forecasted investment amounts: it appears that the real amount the firm is making is linked with tensions on its production capacities and that it does not depend on the contemporary short term expected demand of the firm. Moreover, the fact that the correlation is stronger in April probably indicates that the level of capacity margins registered at that moment of the year is the one that gives the more information about the level of the final amount of investment for the current year.

References

Bosq, D. and J. P. Lecoutre (1987), 'Théorie de l'estimation fonctionnelle', *Economica,* Paris.

Dormont, B. (1989), *Introduction à l'économétrie des données de panel.*

Härdle, W. (1990), *Applied Nonparametric Regression*, Cambridge University Press.

Lejeune, M. (1985), 'Estimation Non Paramétrique par Noyaux: Régression Polynômiale mobile', *Revue Statistique Appliquée.*

Marfouk, A. (1989), 'Lien entre investissement et degré d'utilisation des capacités de production: le cas de la Belgique', *Cahiers Economiques de Bruxelles, 121*, pp. 4-32.

Morrison, J. (1985), 'On the economic interpretation and measurement of optimal capacity utilization with anticipatory expectations', *Review of Economic Studies LII*, pp. 295-310.

Price, S. (1995), 'Aggregate uncertainty, capacity utilization and manufacturing investment', *Applied Economics, 27*, pp. 147-154.

Price, S. (1996), 'Aggregate uncertainty, investment and asymetric adjustment in the UK manufacturing sector', *Applied Economics, 28*, pp. 1369-1379.

Sneesens, R. (1992), 'Contraintes de débouchés, capacités de production et chômage dans un modèle macroéconomique avec concurrence imparfaite, L'Actualité Economique', *Revue d'Analyse Economique, 68*, pp. 141-173.

Thollon-Pommerol, V. (1974), Les rectifications des prévisions d'investissement des entreprises, *Annales de l'INSEE, 15*, pp. 143-185.

24 Capacities and Capacity Utilisation from the Ifo Business Survey - Knowledge and Background

JÜRG DIETER LINDLBAUER

1 Definition and Calculation of Capacity and Capacity Utilisation

1.1 General Definition of Capacity Utilisation in the Production Area

The degree of capacity utilisation, a measure for the development of economic conditions, is one of the most widely observed results of the Ifo Business Survey. The question refers to the capacity of production facilities.[1] The general definition is:

$$U_t = \frac{Qr_t}{Qp_t} * 100 \qquad (1)$$

with:

U = degree of capacity utilisation, queried in percent,
Qr = actual production (in units, kg, DM, hours. etc.),
Qp = potential production or capacity (same dimension as Qr)
t = time index.

The problem of measurement is seen above all in the determination of capacity (Qp).

[1] The following question is asked four times a year at the end of each quarter: The utilisation of our plant for the production of XY (usual full utilisation = 100%) amounts to: up to 30/40/50/60/70/75/80/85/90/95/100/more than 100% being ...

1.2 On the 'Subjectivity' of the Definition of Capacity

The degree of *capacity utilisation* is one of the few questions for which quantitative reply categories are provided in the Ifo Business Survey. The space at the end of the scale in which the responder can supply the exact number when the utilisation degree exceeds 100% shows the variable 'capacity' cannot be defined as an absolute technical limit of machine capacity. Instead the basis is a firm's 'usual full capacity'. The definition of total capacity thus rests with the survey participant in the firm. The reasons for this are, firstly, that the participant should not be burdened with complicated calculation procedures which most likely do not coincide with the methods the firm uses and, secondly, it is not possible to formulate the question in such a way that it is applicable to all company particularities – this is evident already in the presentation on the differences in company size given below.

The necessary *individual determination of capacity* does, of course, present an area that attracts the main criticism. The level of the degree of utilisation is determined by the differing views of the survey participants of 'full capacity'. But even with an apparently exact definition of capacity, individual definitions, that some would derogatorily call 'subjective', cannot be ruled out. If we consider the simplest case of an individual mechanical production aggregate, even here the determination of the practically utilised maximum performance requires a weighing-up of production intensity and costs. If the enterprise takes greater wear-and-tear into consideration – it can usually place the performance limit higher than the use envisioned by the manufacturer of the equipment. What the enterprise decides depends ultimately on the urgency of demand and the prices it can command. This decision is without doubt subjective. The simple case is most likely rare in practice. If to some extent differing products are produced in the same facility, these will differ from each other in terms of cost and price and also margins. Primarily demand will, of course, determine which products receive priority in production – presumably products that bring more profits but other reasons are also possible such as entering new markets, delivery obligations, etc. What is the capacity of a facility if the maximum output per unit of time is different for each of the goods? What remains is again only a subjective or company-own determination.

1.3 Determination of Capacity Reserves or the Course of the Business Cycle?

Apart from these difficulties in giving an exact definition of capacity for the purpose of determining the 'exact' degree of capacity utilisation, the question arises as to what an *isolated number* tells us about the current degree of utilisation. Can we draw conclusions from this on capacity reserves or high/low costs per production unit caused by the fixed costs? This may be the case for individual facilities – if the unit cost developments are known. For aggregating results the following problems arise:

- The development of unit costs differ individually, in particular their minimum levels are not the same for all equipment at the same level of utilisation.
- The production units do not progress through the business cycle at the same pace. Whereas companies that benefited from exports reached their capacity limits fairly quickly in 1998, many other still lay in the shadows of weak domestic demand. Depending on the shifts in the cyclical phases between individual industries – which also differs from cycle to cycle – higher or lower levels are compensated more strongly or more weakly.
- Unit costs are not the only determinants for the decision on the intensity of capacity utilisation. If maximising profits or reducing losses is the primary goal, the price that can be obtained determines whether a firm can accept higher unit costs from stepped-up production or whether it decides to build up its order reserves. It will also tend towards lengthened delivery times if its main goal is to keep employment as stable as possible. Since 'a firm's typical full capacity' lies within the realm of increasing unit costs, here too one cannot speak of easily usable capacity reserves above a particular utilisation area – apart from organisational problems in the firm. In this case it is more likely to result, among other things, in an increase in order reserves, although full utilisation has not been reached.

The question about effects is also linked to the level of the degree of capacity utilisation. Will an enterprise invest (especially in expansion) if the utilisation degree has passed a particular threshold, will it hire personnel, etc.? How an individual enterprise ultimately reacts depends on numerous determinants, not least on the appraisal of whether the favourable demand situation will continue. Since the other influencing factors change, an enterprise can react differently at various times although capacity levels are the same. Moreover the reaction time can also vary. If an enterprise has great confidence in the future and favourable financing options it may expand as fast as is organisationally possible; without this confidence and if financing is difficult it will first wait until actual events force it to take action. Threshold levels of utilisation may be interesting in terms of the degree of attention with which further developments are being observed in individual cases but they probably contribute little to forecasting reactions. This does not mean, however, that such thresholds as a whole do not exist, i.e. in a statistical average by means of a number of individual decisions.

The main interest of the observer, regardless of the difficulties in finding a definition, is not aimed at an isolated number of a period but at the *development of the degree of capacity utilisation over time*. Here we have the advantage that the freedom of choice of reference for the time comparison plays a lesser role insofar as the responder sticks to the choice once it is made of the estimation method which had been assumed to be the case. If this is ensured, the results not only permit the recognition of whether the economic tension actually increases or decreases: the tension between the potential production and the real production induced by demand. Moreover, the data provide the possibility of comparing the cyclical situations in different periods e.g. different boom-phases, and from this the observer might derive an idea of threshold values.

1.4 The Implicit Production Potential

The production potential, that enterprises implicitly use to calculate the degree of capacity utilisation, results from (1):

$$Qp_t = \frac{Qr_t}{U_t} * 100 \tag{2}$$

If in place of the individual economic data on production and the degree of capacity utilisation we place the net production index and the utilisation degree of the manufacturing industry, we receive the development of the implicit production potential of the total aggregate. The term ‘implicit’ means that a series represents an aggregate of individually differing calculations of capacity.

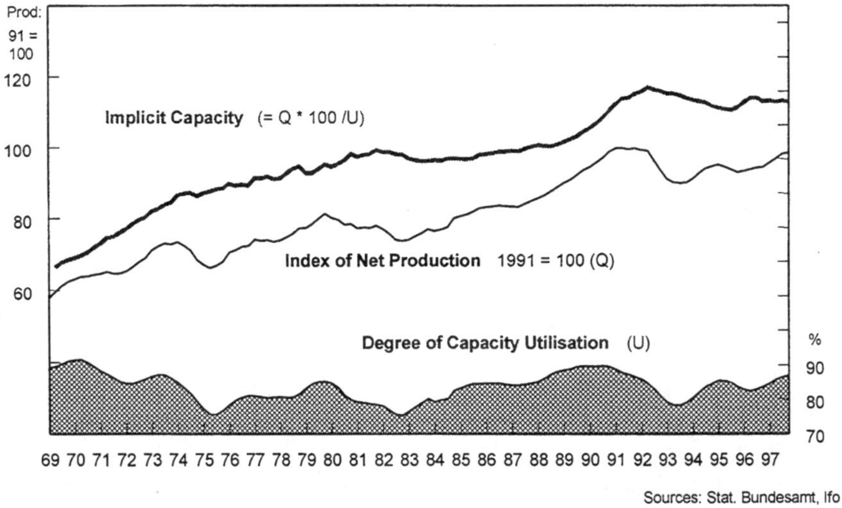

Figure 24.1 - The Implicit Capacity in West German Manufacturing

Figure 24.1 shows the result of such a calculation for the West German manufacturing industry.

2 Possible Contradictions between a Potential Calculation and Ifo Surveys

When other business cycle observers have opinions on the development of capacity utilisation that differ from the Business Survey results, they usually point to the 'subjectivity' of the survey respondents in determining their capacity. Recently, the German Institute for Economic Research in Berlin (DIW) issued a clear and lengthy statement on this topic:

> If, however, we look at the development of capacity utilisation according to Ifo over a longer period of time and if we analyse the development of production potential that is implicit in such an interpretation of the Ifo figures (difference between capacity utilisation and production), we come up with surprising results. The production potential that is assumed for the manufacturing industry sinks almost continuously since the beginning of 1992 although there was an investment boom in West Germany to the end of 1991 in the wake of German unification that was stronger than all investment revivals of past years... The permanent decline of production potential

that results from such a use of the Ifo figures shows that the Ifo capacity utilisation is not suitable for level comparisons.[2]

This objection calls into question not only the calculation of implicit capacity, it also criticises any type of temporal comparison of capacity data that go beyond the statements of a pure trend survey. It presupposes an insufficient temporal stability of the enterprise responses.

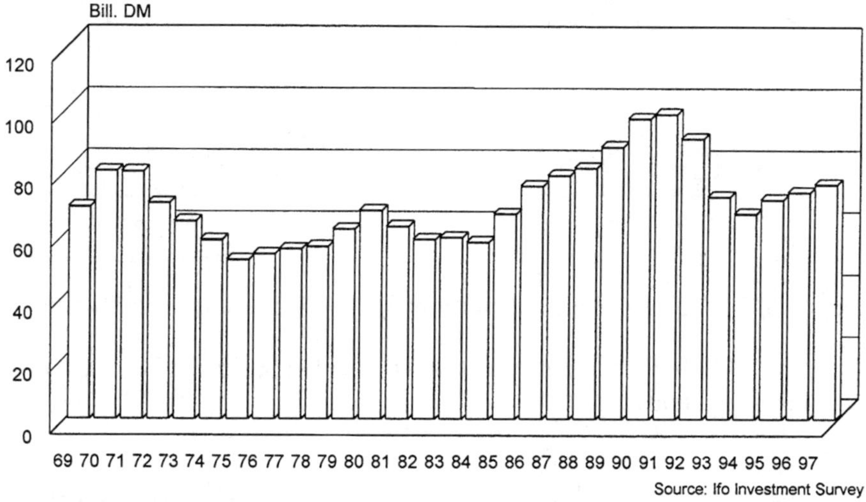

Figure 24.2 - Real Gross Fixed Investment, Manufacturing Industry, Germany West

Several months later, the DIW stated for 1996: 'Investment has been on the decline since as far back as 1992. The phase of contracting investment is without precedent in the history of the Federal Republic' and 'Given the far sharper contraction of investment here, potential output is currently actually declining [in manufacturing vs. the whole business sector]'.[3] In the article preceding this quotation, the curve calculated according to the capital-vintage model used by the DIW was on the increase up to the latest quarter (2nd quarter).

---

[2] Deutsches Institut für Wirtschaftsforschung (German Institute for Economic Research), Berlin, Zur wirtschaftlichen Lage in Deutschland im ersten Halbjahr 1995, DIW Wochenbericht v. 28. September 1995, p. 686, own translation.

[3] Deutsches Institut für Wirtschaftsforschung, Berlin, Medium-term Growth Path under Threat: Inadequate Investment in West Germany, DIW Economic Bulletin, January 1996, p. 21.

Both of these positions reveal a change, at least vis-à-vis the potential development. Nevertheless, the reference to very strong investments with necessarily strong capacity effects was not groundless. So, it seems necessary to find more support for the one or the other thesis by more investigation.

3 State of Knowledge on Utilisation Data

3.1 No Adequate Comparisons Possible

The simplest way of testing the explanatory power of a statistical series on the macro-level is the comparison with other time series. This is a problem for capacity utilisation insofar as there is official data on production development but not statistics from enterprise surveys on the development of active production potential or direct with regard to capacity utilisation.

Because of the significance of these factors, data on production potential and from this on the utilisation rate are estimated by various institutes, such as the DIW, from aggregated results, but mostly just for aggregate economic production potential – the Ifo Institute also determines this factor for the whole economy. This estimate is based on the 'capital stock' which is based on the plant and equipment (buildings and equipment) built up over the years minus retirements.[4] The former are determined via 'the most likely retirements'. For this kind of estimation, not only the correct inclusion of production start and finish of the equipment is decisive; problems are also presented by the potential capacity effects over the possible running times of the machines, independent of the flexibility of their employment. The use of such estimates as a criterion for the reliability of business survey data does not appear to be appropriate.

For this reason the analyst often turns to the method of trend adjustment of the production series. Assuming that an entrepreneur will not stray too far from a smoothed course of production, increased by a factor that allows for a certain amount of cyclical flexibility, the deviation of the actual production from its smoothed course should come close to the development

---

4 See: K. H. Oppenländer, Produktionspotential, in: D. Brümmerhoff (HRSG), Lexikon der volkswirtschaftlichen Gesamtrechnungen, München 1994, S. 287. M. Hummel, A. Müller, Modellrechnungen zur Höhe des gesamtdeutschen Kapitalstocks und Schätzung des Produktionspotentials, ifo studien zur strukturforschung 25, 1996, S. 61 ff. Sachverständigenrat zur Begutachtung der gesamtwirtschaftlichen Entwicklung, Wachstum, Beschäftigung, Währungsunion - Orientierung für die Zukunft, Jahresgutachten 1997/98, S. 254 ff.

of the rate of capacity utilisation. True, the course of the implicit capacity and the smoothed production series (Hodrick-Prescott Filter) differ considerably in cyclical terms (figure 24.3 – both series are based on the annual average of 1991). The differences, however, only state that investments in a boom phase exceed the target and are subsequently corrected – a corporate behaviour pattern familiar to business-cycle theorists.

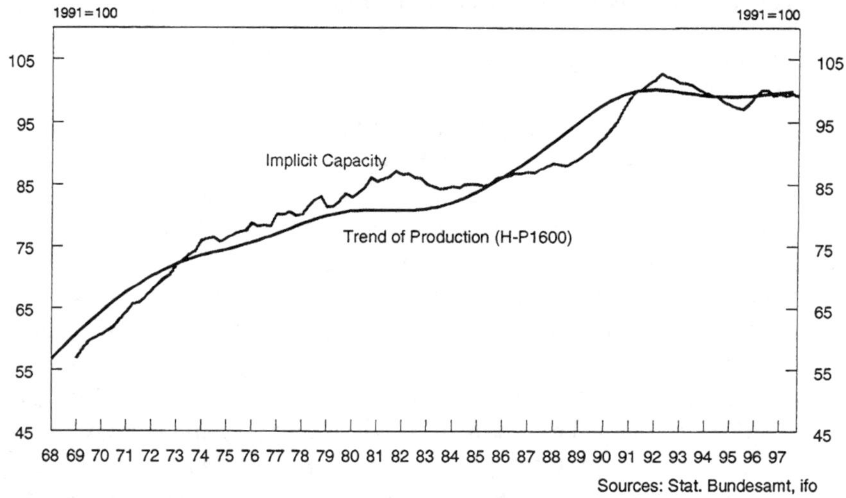

Figure 24.3 - Implicit Capacity and Production Trend

3.2 Additional Knowledge from a Special Survey

Another way to approach the explanatory power of statistical categories is to research the response base and how responses are decided on in the enterprises. In the October 1998 questionnaire for the monthly Ifo Business Survey in manufacturing, special questions were added. They were intended to provide information on the stability of the responses. Four special questions were added for West Germany and two for East Germany due to the short experience with this category (see annex 2). The return rate for such an unscheduled special question was high: 1580 responses from a total of 2600 returned questionnaires for the normal survey or a return rate of 60%; in East Germany 490 out of 670 responded which was more than 70%.

However, the possibilities of such surveys of a survey are limited for two reasons in particular. Too many and too detailed questions reduce the response rate, and statements on periods or points of time that are far removed are not only problematic in terms of the strains on memory but also if the responder at the enterprise has changed.

3.3 The Great Importance of Capacity Utilisation as a Reference Number

One basis for the comparability of capacity utilisation over a period of years is the constant responses to the Ifo questionnaire. In this aspect, the figures appear to be the most reliable if they are not estimated ad hoc for the Ifo questionnaire, possibly by different responders with their own ideas, but when the responding activity is firmly anchored in the management information system.

The growing importance of capacity utilisation as an indicator of production efficiency can also be seen in the fact that institutions such as industrial federations[5] or the Verein Deutscher Ingenieure (VDI, Association of German Engineers)[6] have issued guidelines to help enterprises cope with this difficult measurement.

If these guidelines were followed on a wide scale, this would be an indication that the enterprise calculations should display a certain uniformity. This in turn would be necessary to be able to answer more clearly the corresponding questions of the participants in the Business Survey. However, according to the results of the special survey question presented in Table 24.1, external guidelines have met with little interest thus far: only about 5% of the participants in the West and 12% of the participants in the East make use of such external suggestions.

Our question, however, provided no final answer on the actual use of these guidelines since the question was only directed at their use every month or every quarter whereas the complicated calculation guidelines are designed more for the annual planning.

Much more important for assessing the inter-temporal comparability was the response to the question on the primary user of this data: management or Ifo. According to Table 24.1 (see also Figure 24.4), the share of firms is quite high that calculate capacity utilisation quarterly or monthly for their own management: 82% for West Germany and 83% for East Germany, both weighted. The highest shares were reported from the basic materials

---

[5] For example: Zentralverband der Elektrotechnischen Industrie (ZVEI), Kapazitätsrechnung, Frankfurt 1978.

[6] Verein Deutscher Ingenieure, Auslastungsermittlung für Maschinen and Anlagen - Ascertainment of utilization rate for machines and production lines, VDI Richtlinie 3423, Düsseldorf July 1994.

and producer goods industry (89% West and 86% East) and the capital goods industry (82% West, 91% East). Lower rates were reported by the consumer goods industry (78% West, 72% East) and the food and drink industry (70% West, 65% East).

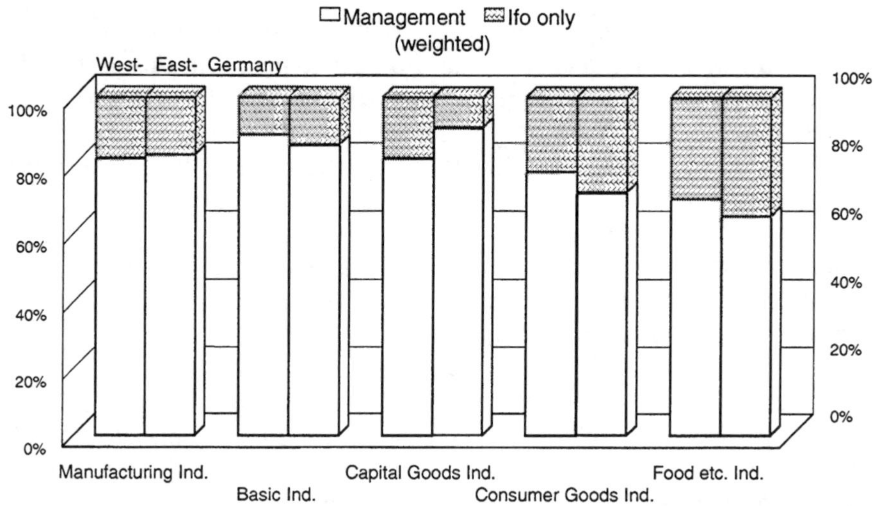

Source: Ifo Special Survey, 1998

Figure 24.4 - The Degree of Utilisation is Calculated Monthly or Quarterly

Dividing the results according to company size (Figure 24.5), we see that especially management in the larger enterprises is constantly informed about the utilisation rate. In West Germany there is hardly any difference in the size categories of more than 200 employees: almost 80% perform this calculation. In East Germany nearly 100% of the firms with more than 500 employees make the calculation – although there were only 34 responses in this category compared to nearly 500 in the West. Of the small firms with up to 49 employees, only half in the West and 70% in the East report this figure to management. For mid-sized firms (50-199 employees) management in the East (77%) is also better informed than in the West (69%).

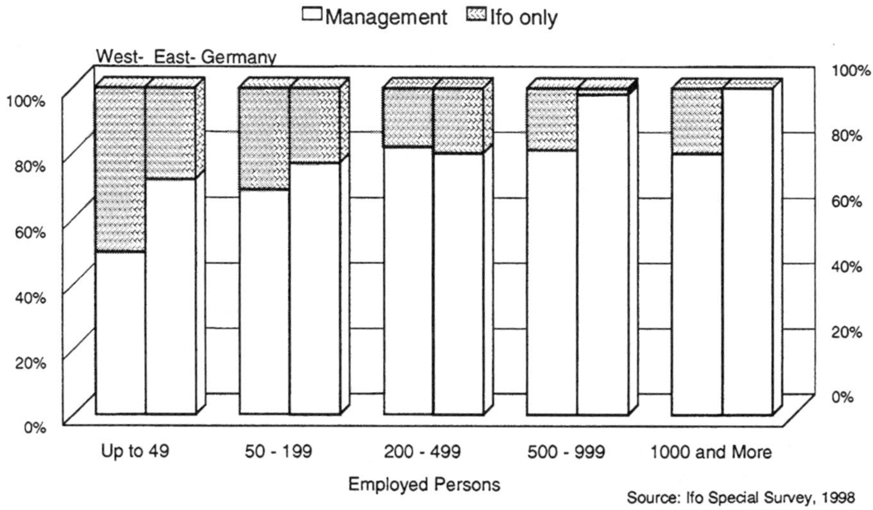

Figure 24.5 - The Degree of Utilisation is Calculated Monthly or Quarterly

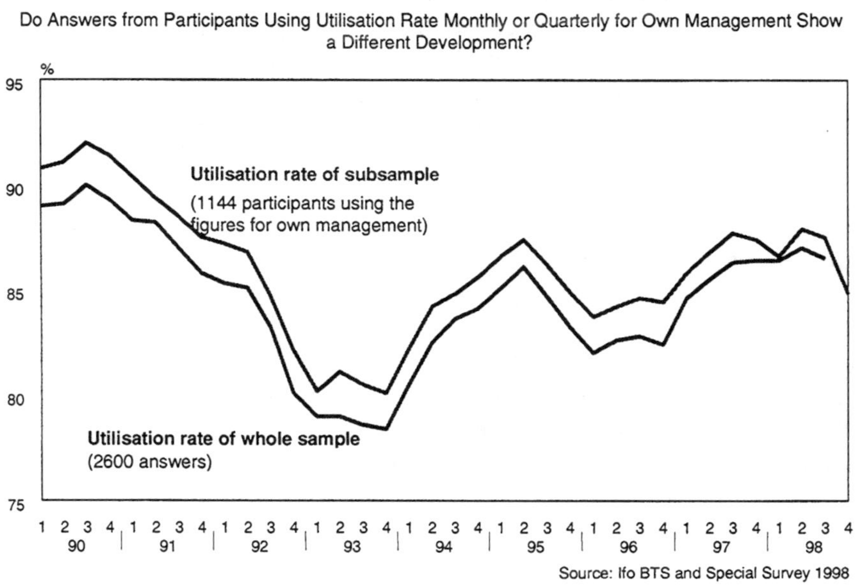

Figure 24.6 - Capacity Utilisation in Western Germany

For this reason the reliability of the response activity – at least for those firms that replied to the special question – can no longer be doubted.

The objection can, however, be raised that those firms that did not respond behave completely differently, but this is not conclusive in light of the insignificant differences in the curve of the average utilisation rates of all Business Survey participants and those who reported that they supply this figure to management (Figure 24.6).

3.4 The Reference Variables of the Companies' Calculations

The difficulty of calculating the utilisation rate is also dependent on the production structure of the enterprise in the product area included in the Business Survey. A response is at its simplest when it can be directly based on numbers, measurements and balances of always the same products, such as moulded pieces of the same type, quality, material, etc. This is possible not only when the production equipment is used just for one product but also for combined products with a constant programme. In these cases the departure point is overall results in quantities, values or working hours. It is difficult, however, in cases when the Business Survey product groups comprise one part of a possibly changing product programme for the same equipment. Here recourse is made to the utilisation of individual aggregates in comparison to the total utilisation of these aggregates, whereby the utilisation by individual products in the programme can only be determined by correcting the entire utilisation rate of the equipment used by the changing portion of this product within the programme. The utilisation of the entire production unit can be calculated as the sum of the individual aggregates or one must limit oneself to particularly important parts, such as a bottleneck. In the calculation of the utilisation rate more than one factor can also be included, for example machine times and working hours, quantities and values, etc.

The distribution of these responses is shown in Table 24.2 and Figure 24.7. It appears that the factors are also combined in practice, which is indicated by the high share of multiple answers (the sum of a line or the sum of shares in the bars in Figure 24.6 are more than 100%).

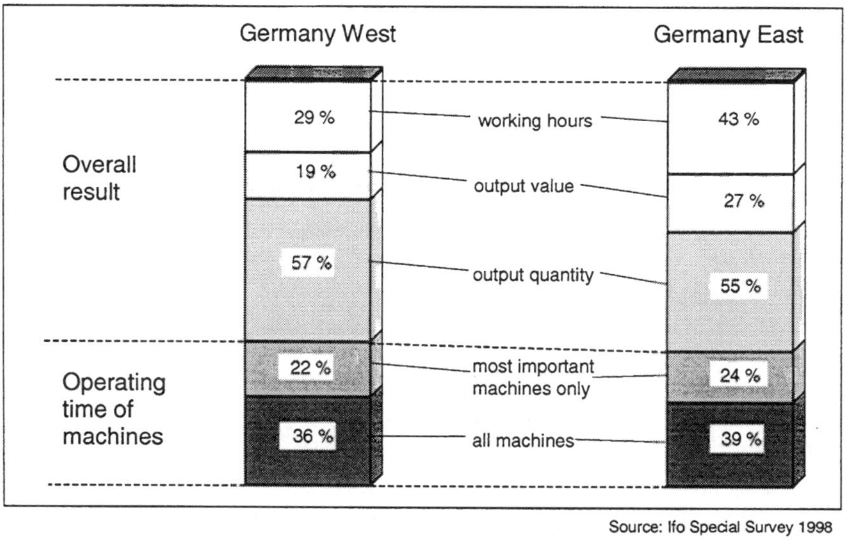

Figure 24.7 - Basis of Degree of Utilisation (Manufacturing Industry, Multiple Answers, weighted)

Most enterprises base their calculations entirely or partially on the quantitative overall results – especially in the food and drink industry. In second place in the West is the operating times of machines (the sum of all machines used) and in the East the working hours. In the consumer goods industry in the West quantitative results and machine operating times were equally strong.

In Table 24.2a the multiple responses were eliminated and only those enterprises listed that indicated only one of these methods (Figure 24.8). This led to a more pronounced profile. In the basic material and producer goods industry and in the food and drink industry the overall results were clearly dominant over machine operating times in the West, whereas in the consumer goods producing industry machine operating times dominated.

If the product group as defined in the survey consists of several products of which each has a different utilisation rate, these individual results must be aggregated using a weighting method. Weighting is not necessary in those cases in which either a similar product or a constant product programme is manufactured. The stronger the disaggregation of the product palette, the easier it is to arrive at such homogeneous product structures. With a division of total production into about 300 groups of similar products, the Business Survey makes it largely unnecessary for the participants to do the weighting themselves.

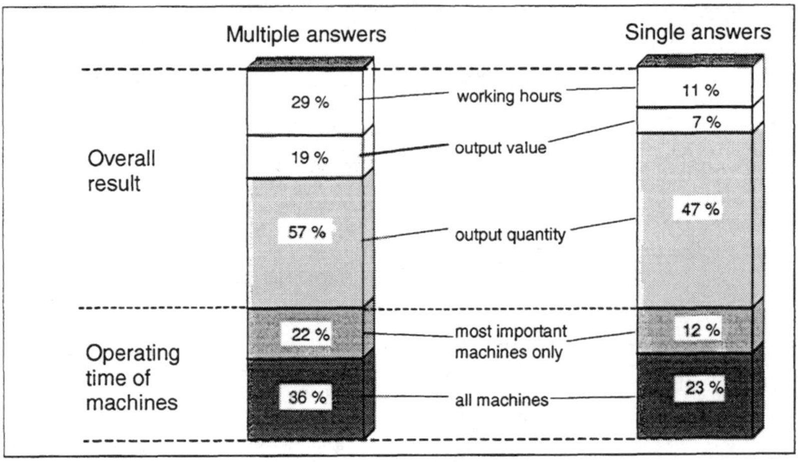

Source: Ifo Special Survey 1998

Figure 24.8 - Basis of Degree of Utilisation (Manufacturing Industry, Germany (West), weighted)

The weighting for production structure is carried out somewhat more frequently in the capital goods producing industry than in the consumer goods industry. This applies both for East and West Germany. No weighting was needed by about one quarter in the West and by about one third in the East (Figure 24.9).

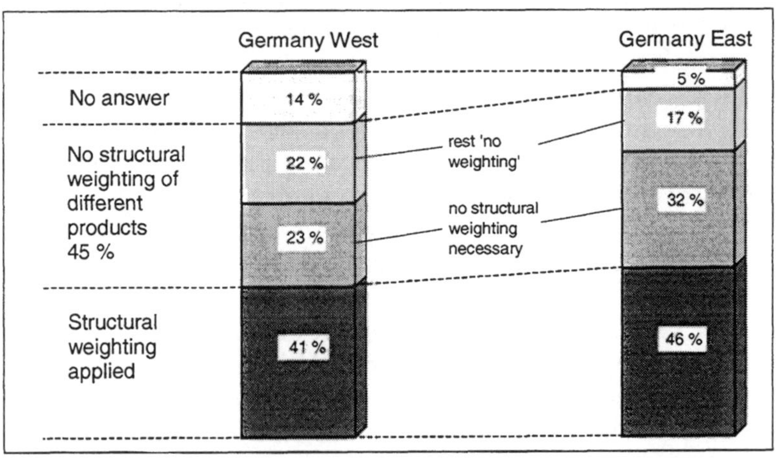

Source: Ifo Special Survey 1998

Figure 24.9 - Weighting for Structural Differences (Manufacturing Industry, weighted)

3.5 *Reporting Habits and Development in the 1990s*

3.5.1 The Results of the Questions: Rising Utilisation Rate A strong argument against the comparability of the Business Survey results on capacity utilisation is that reporting habits might have changed in recent years due to high productivity growth. Therefore we asked whether the reporting changed during the 1990s independent of the cyclical influences and how - up or down. As possible causes the questions suggested: changes of organisational or technological nature or a change of the method of calculation. In order not to overtax the respondents' memories and to improve the chances of obtaining answers, the question was limited to the years from 1990 onwards. Furthermore, the strong structural changes within the sample in East Germany suggested that this and the following questions not be asked in these regions.

The results in Table 24.3 show that the majority of the participants – between 54% for investment goods and 68% for food industries – did not change their reporting behaviour. On the other hand, the part of respondents that did change was not negligible. The shift was caused first of all by organisational or technological reasons. The result was a rising utilisation rate stated by about 36% of the total respondents (Figure 24.10). Differentiated by size groups, only the small companies changed notably less than the average.

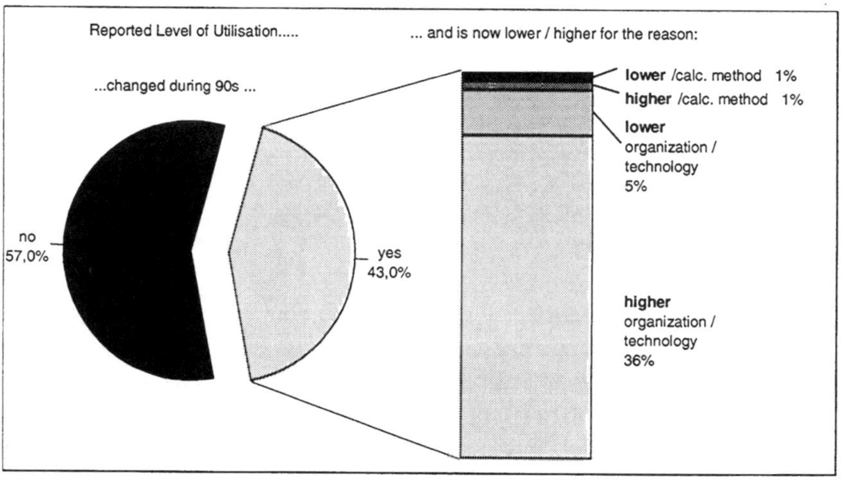

Source: Ifo Special Survey, 1998

Figure 24.10 - Changes in Reporting and Reasons

3.5.2 As Expected: Capacity Increasing Effects of Organisational and Technological Progress The replies were surprising at first glance. In the course of the last decades organisational and technological innovations caused enormous progress within the production sector, which possibly accelerated in the 1990s owing to increasing computerisation. Better process control together with more universally usable machines and finally CIM (computer integrated manufacturing) led to less loss of time. This is confirmed by Figure 24.11. While the utilisation rate held a more or less stable level – disregarding of course cyclical movements – over the last 30 years, the backlog of orders decreased.

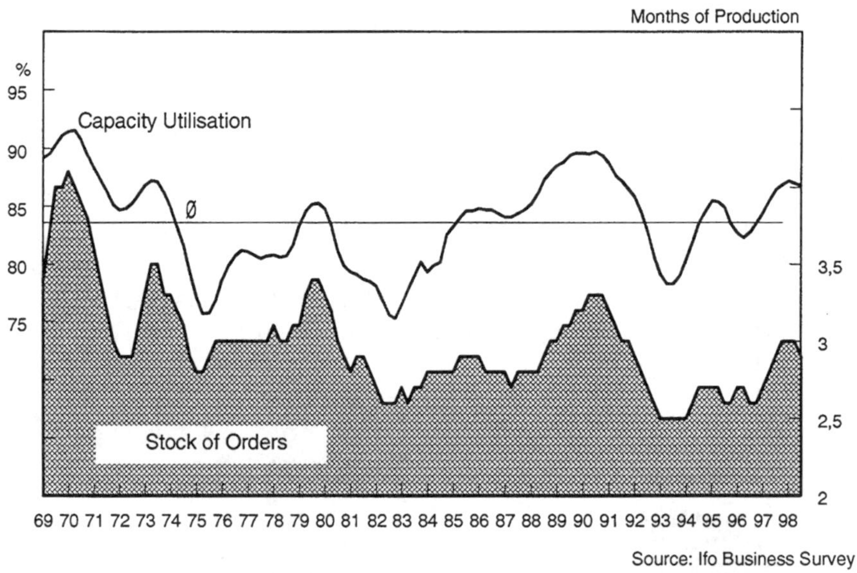

Figure 24.11 - Utilisation and Backlog of Orders in Months of Production

There is no doubt that this progress brought about a more efficient use of plant and therefore had capacity increasing effects. But does this also mean an improvement in capacity utilisation? That depends of course on the aim of the companies' calculations of the utilisation rate. They may want to control the total efficiency of the invested capital. In this case, they will set capacity in formula (1) at the highest level possible. For instance, if the machine should run for a full shift of 40 hours weekly but in reality only runs for 36 hours because of necessary servicing, repair and adapting, they would set the capacity at 40 hours. A new plant which needs only 2 hours for servicing, repair and adapting then would push up the upper limit of the utilisation rate from 36/40 (hours) = 0.9 or 90% to 38/40 (hours) = 0.95 or 95%. With this focus, the organisational and technological progress would have led to a higher utilisation rate. But if the entrepreneur concentrated upon cyclical effects only, he would have set the capacity first at 36 and then at 38 hours and thus the upper limit would have remained at 100%.

3.5.3 Reason for a Rising Utilisation Rate: Cost Reduction Figure 24.12 suggests another plausible explanation for an increase of the utilisation rate during the 1990s. Supposing the companies adjust their production – and with this their utilisation rate – according to the point where the curve of marginal costs cuts the price. A reduction of the unit costs (C_{90} to C_{98}) would have led to a rising utilisation rate. If the company produces according to the point of intersection mentioned, it can supply the same production (Q_r) in 1998 as it did in 1990 using lower capacity and a higher utilisation rate.

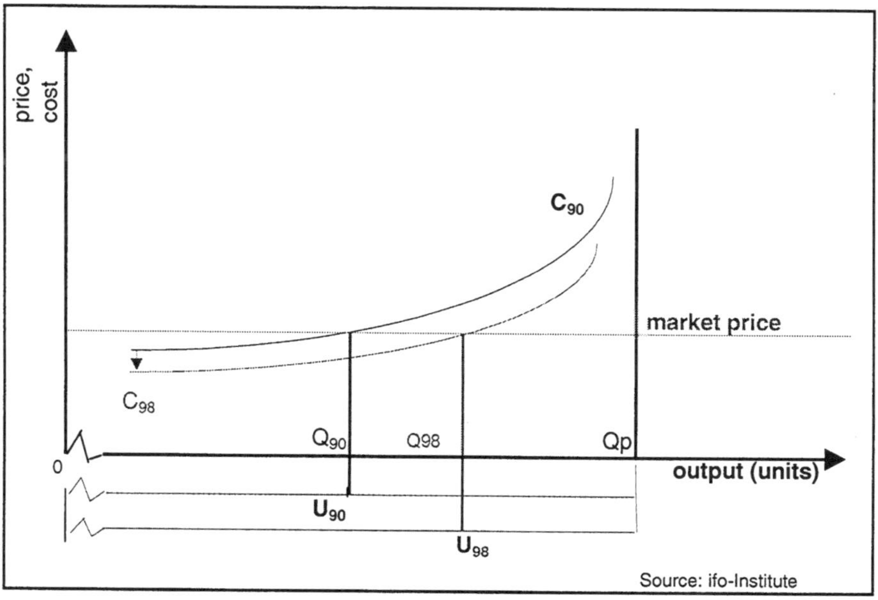

Figure 24.12 - Rationalisation Causing Higher Utilisation Rate?

According to the companies' reports, capacity utilisation in 1998, not taking the business cycle into account which means producing at the same level ($Q_{r98} = Q_{r90}$), was higher than at the beginning of the 1990s. The 'U' in formula (2) thus grew by ΔU within this period, signifying, this factor changed the potential production Qp between 1990 and 1998 as follows:

$$Q_{p98} = \frac{Q_{r90}}{\Delta U * U_{90}} = \frac{Q_{p90}}{\Delta U} \qquad (3)$$

From $\Delta U > 1$ follows $Qp_{98} < Qp_{90}$, the same production presumed. Thus, a rise of the utilisation rate could have caused the decline of implicit capacity in the 1990s.

3.5.4 Additional Cyclical Effects in the Period Analysed In the meantime a cyclical decline of production took place, which would have caused a still more pronounced decline in the utilisation rate had the companies not reduced their capacities.

A statement by an enterprise (supplier to the mechanical engineering industry) leads to this conclusion.

> Recession phases are periods in which innovations receive more impetus than in upswing phases. This means that at the beginning of an upturn new machines with better performance or new methods of metal processing are available, in general, at the same or lower prices than in the years before.[7]

A business cycle upturn usually takes place via new products and new production technologies. If accordingly an enterprise must fear that its product and the associated production technology will be obsolete in the next upswing, it will begin at an early phase of the downturn to assess the corresponding capacities as no longer (fully) utilisable and will immediately begin to reduce them – stock building in this case makes no sense.

Comparing the developments of the utilisation rate with the results of a regular special question about the assessment of the plant capacity with respect to the recent order stock and the new orders expected for the next 12 months, we first of all see a parallel course for both. The fact that the capacities received poorer scores for the troughs in the 1990s (1993, 1996) than for the troughs before 1990 compared to the utilisation rate might

[7] M. Müller, Analyse and Prognose von Nachfrageentwicklungen im Industriegeschäft auf der Ebene von Branchen, Geschäftsfeldern, Produktfamilien and Produktgruppen mit Hilfe von Konjunkturtestdaten, ifo Studien 1995, Berlin-München.

suggest that the companies recently reacted more sensitively and reduced their capacities more rapidly and to a larger extent – as the machines and the products aged at an accelerated pace due to accelerated computerisation (Figure 24.13).

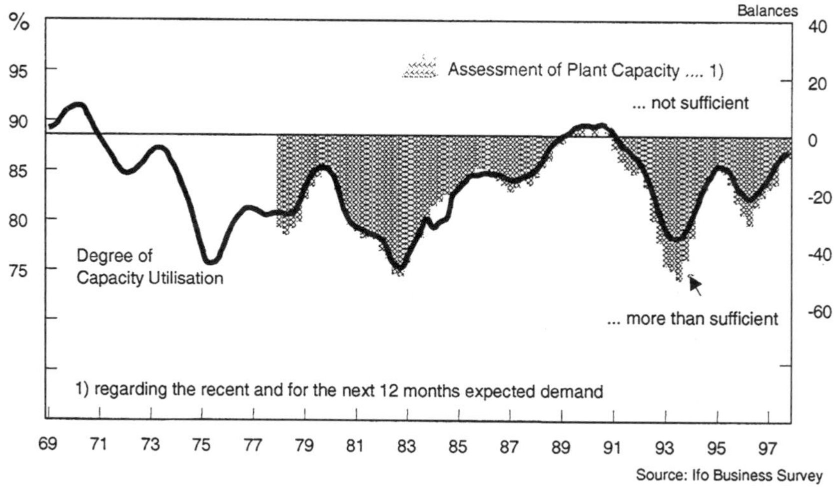

Figure 24.13 - Degree of Utilisation and Assessment of Capacities

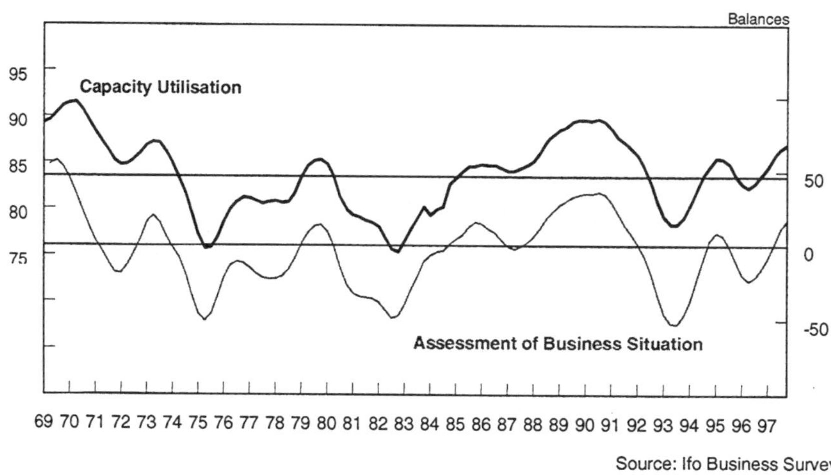

Figure 24.14 - Utilisation and Assessment of Business Situation

The comparison of the capacity utilisation with the assessment of general business situation shows similar results (Figure 24.14). Basically the two series took a parallel course but in 1993 an even higher utilisation rate was combined with a less favourable assessment of the business situation than in 1975 and 1982. The consequence should again be a relatively strong reduction of capacities in the 1990s.

3.6 Effects of Working Time Regime on Capacity

3.6.1 Influences on Utilisation Asking the firms for the utilisation rate has a clear advantage over calculating it using macro statistics. Only the companies know which plant and which machines can be included among the recent potential, even if they are – due to lack of demand – not used at the moment. The production potential is defined by the capacity of the machines, their working time per day, week, etc. and the production intensity. The company can react to demand fluctuations with any one of these variables. During an upswing they may possibly react in this sequence:

- Increase in intensity without a change of working time.
- More extra hours without a change of working time regime.
- Change of working time regime: Introduction of extra shifts, stepping up from one to two or from two to three shifts a day.
- During this phase, investment for rationalisation or replacement may also have capacity increasing effects.
- Investment for plant extension, take-over of other factories, etc.

The effects of these actions upon the utilisation rate are different. Thus a more intensive production, maybe even using more extra hours, will not be regarded as an increase in capacity. The degree of utilisation during this phase will therefore rise together with growing production. In the Ifo Survey, the participant has the possibility of reporting degrees of more than 100%. The introduction of a second or third shift, on the other hand, expands the potential and a higher capacity now is 'usual'. As it cannot be assumed that a parallel push in demand allows a company to raise production at the same rate, the utilisation rate will fall in the first instance.[8]

[8] The range of these capacity increasing effects by introduction of an extra shift might be wide, at least based on the calculations. Two examples: If a factory works with one shift and adds one complete second shift, the capacity grows by 100% and the utilisation rate decreases to one half (same production supposed). If three shifts during 5 days a week (120 hours) are expanded by 8 hours on Saturdays, the capacity grows by only about 7% and the utilisation is reduced by more or less the same rate. Each company will try to avoid these jumps and adapt better to demand. But that requires high flexibility of labour input which is more likely in big than in small companies.

During a downturn the opposite effects will be observed. Based on these considerations, the utilisation rate might show counter movements to the production cycle. As long as the higher capacity is held, the production is measured against a higher base, the utilisation rate necessarily turns out lower as if production were measured against the old, lower base. Also the increase of production must be corrected by the increase of capacity. Assuming that production Q_r grows by ΔQ_r, then according to (1):

$$\frac{\Delta Q_r * Q_r}{Q_p} = \Delta Q_r * U \qquad (4)$$

The utilisation rate equally grows by ΔQ_r. A parallel increase of capacity Q_p by ΔQ_p

$$\frac{\Delta Q_r * Q_r}{\Delta Q_p * Q_p} = \frac{\Delta Q_r}{\Delta Q_p} * U\,, \qquad (5)$$

increases the utilisation rate only by the quotient of these two factors.

During upturns production will rise, and with a certain lag also the base for calculating the utilisation will increase. In the course of a downturn the opposite will happen. By these effects the amplitudes of the utilisation rate will be reduced in comparison to production.

What might be the effect upon the calculation of the 'implicit capacity'?

There is no effect due to calculation because the lower utilisation rate reported by the participants (formula (1)) will give the higher capacity again, when related to the same production (formula (2)).

The real effect of capacity increases upon the series of utilisation rate cannot be clarified by one single question. We could therefore only try to learn something about possible counter movements caused by changes in work time.

3.6.2 Effects of a Change in Operating Time About two fifths of the respondents did not have to adjust working time to demand fluctuations or achieved a continuous adjustment during the 1990s. (Table 24.4, Figure 24.15).

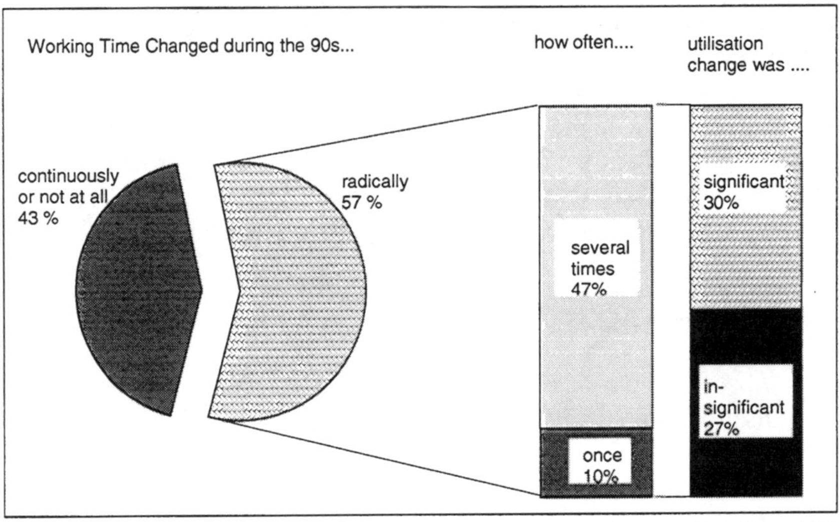

Source: Ifo Special Survey 1998

Figure 24.15 - Frequency and Importance of Changes in Working Time Regime

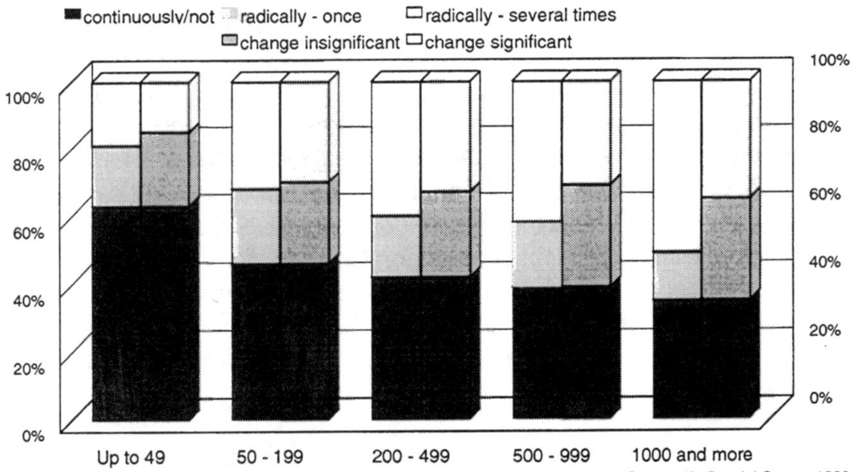

Source: Ifo Special Survey 1998

Figure 24.16 - Frequency and Importance of Changes in Working Time Regime by Size Groups

With this respect there is an obvious slope from the two thirds of small units (up to 49 employees) with only insignificant changes compared to one third of the big companies (1000 employees and more) taking no significant steps (Figure 24.16).

The rest, mostly big companies, adapted their working time by changes in the working time regime (by adding or removing shifts). Below average was the participation of basic materials and producer goods industries; investment goods producers were above average.

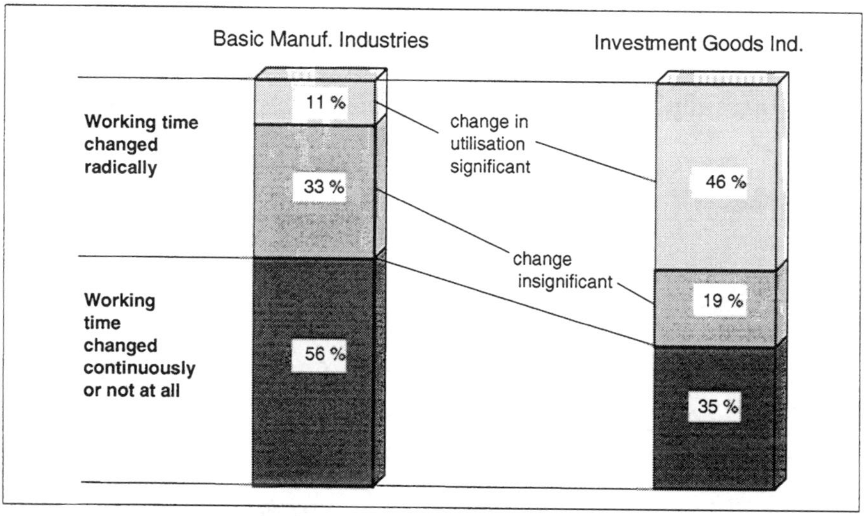

Figure 24.17 - Impact of Changes in Working Time Regime (Manufacturing Industry, weighted)

Nearly half of the participating factories changed their working time regimes several times during the 1990s – probably in keeping with the business cycle. Important for the possible occurrence of counter movements in the utilisation series is the strength of these changes from quarter to quarter. Out all the units 30% described the effects on the utilisation rate as significant (defined as 3% or more compared to previous quarter). But the portion of those reporting no significant changes had nearly the same size (27%). The significance for basic materials and producer goods was again below average. Among the investment goods producers nearly half of the participants stated significant jumps (Figure 24.17).

Among the size classes only the small ones distinguished themselves – only 15% felt significant changes (see Figure 24.16).

Summing up, these answers indicate that one should at least be aware of counter movements. Not all, not even a great part, of the companies will expand or contract their capacities at the same time. Thus these effects will in general smooth out. At least for mechanical engineering no decisive interruptions during up- or downswings can be seen (Figure 24.18; because of the re-structuring of the German statistical classification system according to the NACE scheme, there are no dates to update production for this industry after 1994). A relatively great part of the participants from mechanical engineering reported that their working time regimes changed several times during the 1990s and that the effects upon utilisation were significant.

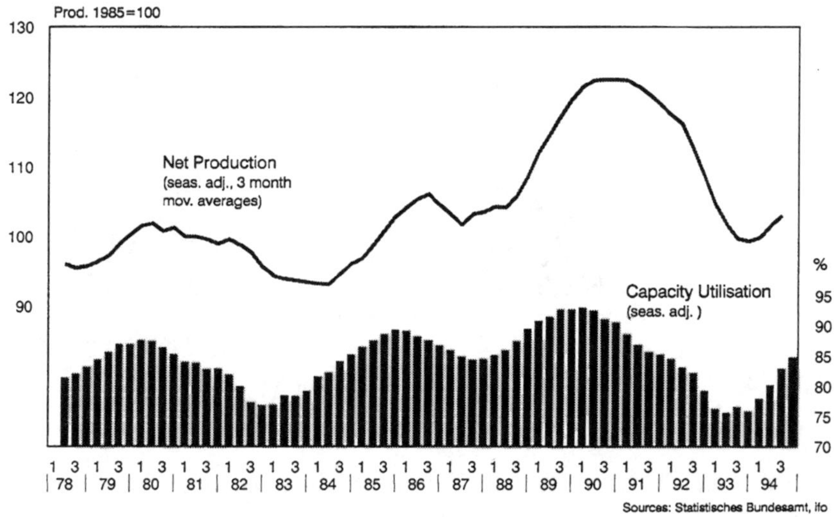

Figure 24.18 - Capacity Utilisation and Production in Mechanical Engineering

The question must be left open, however, as to why no counter movements could be seen: was it because of the smoothing effect of aggregation or because the respondents are actively smoothing the breaks?

4 Summary

The variable 'capacity utilisation' from the Ifo Business Survey is greatly important in business cycle observations as a measurement for business cycle development.

The absolute amount of plant utilisation is not the question but its development over time. The point is to determine which phases in the past can be compared to current values. To do this the company responses must have a corresponding stability.

If the results are not in accordance with the views of other business cycle observers, the critics like to question the stability of reporting. There were differences, for example, over the reality of the strong capacity declines in manufacturing as of 1992 as were presented in the 'implicit capacity' which can be calculated with the help of the utilisation rate based on the Business Survey and the official production index

In their models for estimating capacities the critics basically focus on the development of investments. In so doing they must make assumptions on capacity effects and the estimated retirements of plant and equipment – with assumptions of the median life expectancy of the machines.

A direct examination of the accuracy of the rate of capacity utilisation presented by the Ifo Business Survey is not possible because of the lack of other direct surveys such as official information gathering. The estimated data on the capital stock contain too many assumptions to be useful as an adequate measure for comparison

The only remaining possibility of gaining information of plausibility is indirect – via the course of measured factors or via a survey of the reporting behaviour of the Business Survey participants. In October 1998 a special question on this subject was added to the Business Survey, divided into West and East Germany. The response rate was good at 60% for West and 70% for East Germany, especially considering that these were not a normal supplemental questions.

The first of these questions sought to determine how seriously the enterprises themselves take these figures: do they use them for their own management or merely estimate them for the Business Survey? More than 80% of the participating firms calculate the figure monthly or quarterly for their own management. This is certainly an indication of stability.

Most of the enterprises base their replies primarily on machine operating times as well as on the overall volume of output; in third place they put working hours, but often they rely on more than one reference.

Since the stability of the responses has been called into question, what the companies say themselves is of particular interest: have they changed their reporting during the course of the 1990s? Since industry structure in East Germany underwent major change in this decade, the questions was limited to firms in the West. In all about a third of the participants reported that plant utilisation increased because of organisational or technical changes. A change in the method of calculating the degree of utilisation played almost no role in determining the rate.

What might have caused the increase? There are mainly two explanations. The first one is: the companies concentrate upon total capital efficiency and regard the loss of time for servicing, repair, adaptation of the line to another product or another product mix as loss of degree of utilisation. Then all the progress in avoiding those unproductive times - mainly from multipurpose machines, robots and EDP-controlled workflow - would show up as gain in utilisation rate. If in the contrary the 'normal' loss of time was excluded from the base this progress would not lead to an increase in the utilisation rate. A second possible explanation supposes, the entrepreneur produces up to the point where the costs of the last unit produced equals its price. Then the cost cut through the innovations would have allowed a higher production until the rising marginal costs reached the relatively stable market price again. All this of course without expanding the capacity, only by increased utilisation.

A now widely used possibility for reducing fixed costs is the flexibilisation of working time. A radical change of working time regime like introduction of an additional shift has abrupt capacity increasing effects and a sudden increase (or decrease during a downturn) could lead to a break in the series of utilisation. For this reason we wanted to know whether such fundamental changes have been brought about during the 1990s or whether no or only gradual changes were effected. In cases of radical changes in the working time regime, firms were to answer whether this has been once or several times and whether the firms consider the impact – in comparison to the previous quarter – as having been considerable or negligible. Radical changes were reported by 57% of the responding firms, nearly half changed several times in this period, and for less than a third the changes, according to the participants, had a clear impact on the utilisation rate.

The results of the inquiry suggested that an increase in the upper limit of the utilisation rate during the 1990s partly caused the decline of the 'implicit capacity'. But that is not the only possible reason. Nowadays a business cycle upturn usually takes place via new products and new production technologies. If accordingly an enterprise must fear that its product and the associated production technology will be obsolete in the next upswing, it will begin at an early phase of the downturn to assess the corresponding capacities as no longer (fully) utilisable and will immediately begin to reduce them – stock building in this case makes no sense.

The fact that enterprises directly link a falling rate of capacity utilisation with the future utilisability of the equipment proves the close connection – without time lags – between the development of the capacity utilisation rate and the appraisal of plant and equipment, taking into consideration current order books and the new order anticipated over the next 12 months.

Finally, some possible explanations for the deterioration of the 'implicit capacity' during the years since 1990 were found, of which the real de-investment probably had the highest weight. Nevertheless, further research should show the influence that cost reductions as well as organisational and technological progress exert upon the utilisation rate as determined by a business survey.

5 Annex

A Annex 1 - Tables

Table 24.1 - Prime User of Estimated Utilisation and Use of Guidelines

Answers in %	The degree of utilisation is calculated quarterly or monthly....								
	Total No. of answers	....for		....using an external guideline					
		Management use	Ifo Survey only	no	yes	if 'yes', edited by			n.a.
						association	VDI	other	
Germany West, weighted									
Manufacturing Industry	1566	82	18	85	5	2	0	3	10
Manufacturing Industry excl. Food etc.	1471	84	16	84	5	3	0	2	11
Basic Manufacturing Industries	245	89	11	70	4	1	0	3	26
Investment Goods Industry	679	82	18	91	5	2	0	2	4
Consumer Goods Industry	547	78	22	87	8	5	0	3	5
Food, Drink and Tobacco Industry	95	70	30	90	9	0	0	9	1
Size Groups (employed persons)									
-49	236	50	50	86	10	7	0	4	4
50-199	469	69	31	89	7	5	0	2	4
200-499	366	82	18	86	9	7	0	3	5
500-999	206	81	19	85	10	6	0	3	5
1000-	289	80	20	87	6	2	0	4	7
Germany East, weighted									
Manufacturing Industry	468	83	17	84	12	6	0	6	4
Manufacturing Industry excl. Food etc.	431	85	15	84	12	6	0	6	4
Basic Manufacturing Industries	114	86	14	94	4	1	0	3	2
Investment Goods Industry	185	91	9	81	16	7	0	9	3
Consumer Goods Industry	132	72	28	84	11	8	0	3	5
Food, Drink and Tobacco Industry	37	65	35	84	8	5	0	2	8
Size Groups (employed persons)									
-49	194	72	28	82	11	5	1	5	7
50-199	175	77	23	89	7	3	0	3	4
200-499	65	80	20	88	8	4	0	4	4
500-999	16	98	2	69	25	7	0	18	6
1000-	18	100	0	81	19	13	0	6	0

Source: Ifo Special Survey 98

Table 24.2 - Basis for Calculating the Degree of Utilisation

All Companies (including multiple answers) Answers in %	Calculation of utilisation is based upon: Total No. of answers	Operating time of machines: All machines	Operating time of machines: Most important	Overall result as: Output quant.	Overall result as: Output value	Overall result as: Work hours	Other variable	Weighting for consideration of product structure: yes	no: total	no: hom. prod.	n.a.
Germany West, weighted											
Manufacturing Industry	1579	36	22	57	19	29	1	41	45	23	14
Manufacturing Industry excl. Food etc.	1486	37	20	54	20	29	1	43	43	22	14
Basic Manufacturing Industries	246	34	9	64	18	19	0	32	40	20	28
Investment Goods Industry	690	32	27	47	20	36	1	49	43	20	8
Consumer Goods Industry	550	54	23	54	23	29	1	43	50	29	7
Food, Drink and Tobacco Industry	93	29	35	75	9	25	1	29	63	31	8
Size Groups (employed persons)											
-49	231	40	23	44	27	31	1	27	67	45	2
50-199	477	40	24	46	32	33	1	31	63	40	5
200-499	373	47	22	44	25	33	2	39	57	29	3
500-999	209	40	31	46	22	28	2	41	52	30	3
1000-	289	40	20	50	23	33	1	50	43	20	4
Germany East, weighted											
Manufacturing Industry	487	39	24	55	27	43	1	46	49	32	5
Manufacturing Industry excl. Food etc.	448	39	24	51	23	33	1	48	47	30	4
Basic Manufacturing Industries	118	33	23	69	20	12	1	35	62	36	3
Investment Goods Industry	188	40	24	39	28	63	2	54	41	27	5
Consumer Goods Industry	142	42	23	62	33	27	1	49	47	32	4
Food, Drink and Tobacco Industry	39	41	28	87	23	33	1	31	62	47	8
Size Groups											
-49	203	30	32	43	42	47	3	31	62	37	7
50-199	180	35	30	60	33	37	1	51	44	33	6
200-499	68	44	30	60	27	50	0	45	53	30	2
500-999	18	59	3	60	19	50	5	51	36	21	13
1000-	18	39	13	47	6	37	0	48	52	38	0

Source: Ifo Special Survey 98

Table 24.2a - Basis for Calculating the Degree of Utilisation

Companies giving only 1 answer Answers in %	Calculation of utilisation is based upon						
	Total No. of ans-we rs	Operating time of machines		Overall result			Other varia-ble
		All machi-nes	Most im-portant mach.	Output quant.	Output value	Work. hours	
Germany West, weighted							
Manufacturing Industry	731	23	12	47	7	11	0
Manufacturing Industry excl. Food etc.	690	24	11	45	8	12	0
Basic Manufacturing Industries	124	19	10	71	0	0	0
Investment Goods Industry	320	20	10	37	12	21	0
Consumer Goods Industry	246	47	18	16	10	9	0
Food, Drink and Tobacco Industry	41	12	15	70	0	3	0
Size Groups (employed persons)							
-49	105	26	13	31	16	13	0
50-199	190	26	12	25	23	15	0
200-499	183	37	19	19	12	13	1
500-999	108	31	23	27	7	12	0
1000-	145	29	10	35	13	11	1
Germany East, weighted							
Manufacturing Industry	168	22	8	30	12	27	0
Manufacturing Industry excl. Food etc.	159	23	7	29	12	29	0
Basic Manufacturing Industries	53	36	6	51	5	2	0
Investment Goods Industry	59	18	9	8	16	49	0
Consumer Goods Industry	47	11	5	49	13	22	0
Food, Drink and Tobacco Industry	9	20	20	53	0	0	7
Size Groups							
-49	65	24	7	19	20	28	4
50-199	55	17	14	36	15	18	0
200-499	29	30	16	33	9	13	0
500-999	7	34	0	10	0	56	0
1000-	12	19	0	35	11	36	0

Source: Ifo Special Survey 98

Table 24.3 - Change in Reporting Habits on Utilisation During 1990s

Answers in %	Total No. of answers	Reported level of utilisation changed					
		no	yes	Yes: for organis./technical changes, now		Yes: for change in calculating method, now	
				higher	lower	higher	lower
Germany West, weighted							
Manufacturing Industry	1366	57	43	36	5	1	1
Manufacturing Industry excl. Food etc.	1284	56	44	38	5	0	1
Basic Manufacturing Industries	219	58	42	40	2	0	0
Investment Goods Industry	594	54	46	41	3	1	1
Consumer Goods Industry	471	59	41	28	13	0	0
Food, Drink and Tobacco Industry	82	68	32	22	7	3	0
Size Groups (employed persons)							
-49	203	69	31	21	9	0	1
50-199	393	56	44	32	11	1	0
200-499	321	60	40	31	8	0	1
500-999	177	60	40	35	3	1	1
1000-	272	57	43	37	6	0	0

Source: Ifo Special Survey 98

Table 24.4 - Changes in Working Time Regime During 1990s

Answers in %	Working time changed...						
			radically				
	Total No. of answers	contin-uously or not at all	total	How often? (sum = 'total')		Resulting change in utilisation (sum = 'total')	
				once	several times	insigni-ficant	signi-ficant
Germany West, weighted							
Manufacturing Industry	1242	43	57	10	47	27	30
Manufacturing Industry excl. Food etc.	1169	44	56	10	46	26	30
Basic Manufacturing Industries	181	56	44	5	39	33	11
Investment Goods Industry	553	35	65	11	54	19	46
Consumer Goods Industry	435	46	54	16	38	25	29
Food, Drink and Tobacco Industry	73	40	60	13	47	30	30
Size Groups (employed persons)							
-49	169	63	37	18	19	22	15
50-199	373	46	54	22	32	24	30
200-499	307	42	58	18	40	25	33
500-999	156	39	61	19	42	30	31
1000-	237	35	65	14	51	30	35

Source: Ifo Special Survey 98

B Annex 2 - Questionnaire

1 **We quarterly (or monthly) calculate the degree of capacity utilisation for product x**

- for our management ☐
- only quarterly for the Ifo-Survey ☐

2 **We base the calculation of the degree of capacity utilisation for product x upon**

- operation times of the different machines
  - the sum of all used for x ☐
  - only the most important ☐
- the overall result as
  - output quantities ☐
  - output values ☐
  - working hours ☐
- other magnitudes ☐

Through weighting we take into account the structure of our production programme

yes ☐ no ☐

no weighting necessary for homogeneity of our production of x ☐

3 **Not regarding business cycle influences, our reported level of utilisation changed during the 90s**

yes ☐ no ☐

if 'yes':

- for organizational or technological reasons the degree of utilisation has
  - gone up ☐
  - gone down ☐
- for a change of our calculation method our reported utilisation got
  - higher ☐
  - lower ☐

4 **During the 90s**

- our regime of operating hours changed radically (e.g.by increasing/reducing the number of shifts per day)
  - once ☐
  - several times ☐

  for this radical change in regime the degree of utilisation changed
  - only insignificantly (about below 3%) ☐
  - (partly) significantly ☐
- our operating hours changed only continuously (e.g. working overtime) or not at all ☐

References

Deutsches Institut für Wirtschaftsforschung (1995), 'Zur wirtschaftlichen Lage in Deutschland im ersten Halbjahr 1995', *DIW Wochenbericht* v. 28. September, Berlin, p. 686.

Deutsches Institut für Wirtschaftsforschung (1996), 'Berlin, Medium-term Growth Path under Threat: Inadequate Investment in West Germany', *DIW Economic Bulletin*, Berlin, p. 21.

Hummel, M. and A. Müller (1996), 'Modellrechnungen zur Höhe des gesamtdeutschen Kapitalstocks und Schätzung des Produktionspotentials', *ifo Studien zur Strukturforschung 25*, p. 61.

Müller, M. (1995), 'Analyse and Prognose von Nachfrageentwicklungen im Industriegeschäft auf der Ebene von Branchen, Geschäftsfeldern, Produktfamilien and Produktgruppen mit Hilfe von Konjunkturtestdaten', *ifo Studien*, Berlin-München.

Oppenländer, K. H. (1994), 'Produktionspotential', in: D. Brümmerhoff (HRSG), *Lexikon der volkswirtschaftlichen Gesamtrechnungen*, München, p. 287.

Sachverständigenrat zur Begutachtung der gesamtwirtschaftlichen Entwicklung (1998), 'Wachstum, Beschäftigung, Währungsunion - Orientierung für die Zukunft', *Jahresgutachten 1997/98*, p. 254.

Verein Deutscher Ingenieure (1994), 'Auslastungsermittlung für Maschinen und Anlagen - Ascertainment of utilization rate for machines and production lines', *VDI Richtlinie 3423*, Düsseldorf.

Zentralverband der Elektrotechnischen Industrie (ZVEI) (1978), *Kapazitätsrechnung*, Frankfurt .

25 A Measurement of the Capacity Utilization Rate of the Mexican Firms in the Manufacturing Sector

RICARDO REYES-ARAIZA[1]

In this study information about the utilization of production capacity of the Mexican manufacturing sector, which was collected from a sample of business in this sector obtained through the Current Survey of the Banco de Mexico is used. The objective of this study is twofold: In the first place, it intends to explore the possibility of using results of utilization of production capacity, which were released by the Current Survey, as a reliable indicator of the future pressure of inflation in Mexico. Secondly, we try to find out whether the Banco de Mexico and the respondents of the survey have the same understanding of the term 'utilizaion of production capacity'.

Empirical evidence is found in the economic literature of various countries about the creation of inflationary pressures, after the utilization of production capacity has reached levels higher than a 'certain level' (which will be defined in the study). In that way the rate of the capacity utilized, for example in the manufacturing sector, is actually used as an indicator of inflationary pressures. The actual process is really quite simple, changes in the short run of production, initially reflect changes in the percentage of utilization of production capacity. In this way, if production increases, the competition for limited resources generates pressures relating to salaries and other production costs; workers with less experience are hired and less

[1] The analyses and conclusions are those of the author and do not necessarily reflect the views of the Banco de Mexico.

efficient equipment is used. Higher production costs will finally be passed on to the consumer.

The recent international discussion about this issue has been centering on the validity of the relationship between inflation and the utilization of production capacity, once the economies demonstrate a greater openness to the external market and to the flow of international capital. Also it should not be forgotten that for longer periods of time, production capacity can be increased in response to technological progress and to changes in the levels of investment in business, which are the factors that have important effects on productivity.

In the case of Mexico, the economic policy has been orientated towards a greater liberalization with respect to international commerce since its membership in GATT in 1986. The Mexican economy has also undertaken a profound restructuring of the industrial plant, based on the privatization of a number of important industries.

1 Analysis of Production Capacity-Inflation

In this study the percentage of the utilization of the production capacity measures the rate of the operation of the production capacity exclusively for the manufacturing industry. In this regard, the capacity is defined as the maximum amount of goods that can be produced for a unit of time with fixed plant supplies, equipment, labor and raw materials. Nevertheless, certain levels of production outside of efficient plant production are excluded, because they are unable to be sustained in a systematic way.

The inflationary pressures are evaluated comparung the utilization rate of the actual production capacity to a steady inflation rate-capacity use, which is called 'natural utilization rate'. From this point of view, inflation will increase to the degree to which the production capacity is above the natural utilization rate. In the same way, inflation declines when the utilized capacity is found to be below the natural utilization rate.

Figure 25.1 presents the positive relationship between the percentage of the use of production capacity and the inflation rate for a specific level of the expected inflation. In this case when the inflation and the expected inflation is 10%, the use of production capacity is found in the natural utilization rate (cu^*). A greater use of production capacity (cu') will lead to a higher inflation rate (15% in this example) because the movement is along the short-run curve. Without doubt, once the economic units make the required adjustment, the expected inflation will be 15%, returning the use of production capacity to cu^*. In this way the natural utilization rate is that rate at which the inflation equals expected inflation. A more familiar version of this process is that of the negative relationship between the unemployment rate and inflation for a given level of expected inflation.

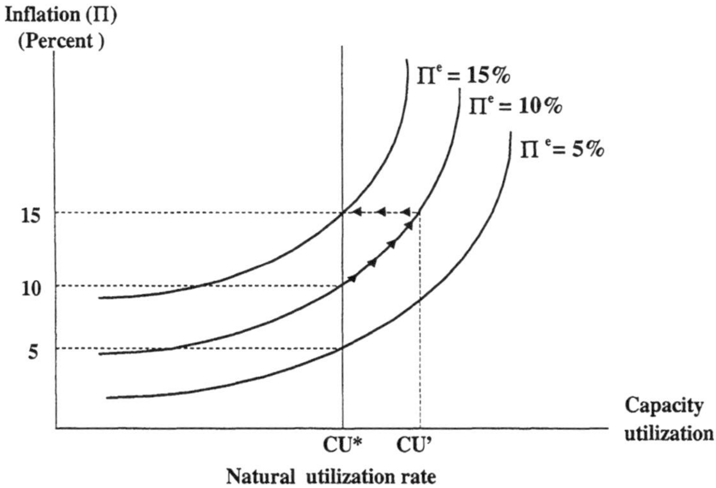

Figure 25.1 - Natural Utilization Rate

To derive the long term positive relation between changes in inflation and the use of production capacity, the majority of analyses incorporates a supposition about the formation of expected inflation, specifically that the rate of expected inflation in the following period is equal to a weighted average of past inflation, and the sum of these weights is equal to one.

The preceding relationship can be specified by means of equation 1 (below). In this case, lagging information is used to predict future changes in the rates of inflation, in addition to the difference between the percentage of the actual use of production capacity and the natural rate of utilization. This type of equation permits the incorporation of other determinants of inflation to make sure that the equation adequately describes the process of inflation. These variables have the characteristics of representing 'supply side shocks' and in this case the said variable was represented by the variation of the real exchange rate lagged one period (the real exchange rate of the Mexican peso in relation to the US dollar).[2]

---

[2] This part of the analysis is based on the studies done on the United States economy by Emery and Chih-Ping (1997), Garner (1994) and Finn (1996).

$$\Delta\Pi_t = b(cu_t - cu*) + \sum_{i=1}^{n} c_i \Delta\Pi_{t-i} + dtr_{t-1} + e_t \qquad (1)$$

where: $\Delta\Pi_t$: is the change in inflation from period t to period $t-i$.

cu_t: the rate of use of production capacity

$cu*$: the natural utilization rate

tr_t: the real exchange rate

e_t: the random term

Given that b and $cu*$ are constant, then $-bcu* = a$, leading to:

$$\Delta\Pi_t = a + bcu_t + \sum_{i=1}^{n} c_i \Delta\Pi_{t-i} + dtr_{t-1} + e_t \qquad (2)$$

Equation 2 is estimated using the procedure of 'ordinary least squares' for the period 1980-1998. The information utilized refers to the trimestral variation with respect to the same trimester of the previous year. Using the previous development it is possible to estimate the natural rate of utilization ($cu*$). Given that $a = -bcu*$, then $cu* = -\frac{a}{b}$; where a and b are estimated parameter.[3]

Table 25.1 demonstrates the main results utilizing three price indexes: consumer, producer and implicit deflator of the GDP. In the case of the consumer price index the use of production capacity explains more than half of the total variation of inflation. This variable is significant and has a positive sign. In this case the percentage of the use of production capacity that leads to a steady inflation rate is 71.3%; so that a higher capacity utilization rate than this level triggers an increase in inflation and a lower capacity utilization rate than this level triggers a reduction in inflation.

[3] Another interpretation consists in estimating the rate of the use of production capacity ($cu*$) that keeps the rate of the increase in prices steady. Said rate is obtained when we fix the determinants of the supply shocks to zero and solve for the capacity use. In this case: $0 = a + bcu$, from here we get $cu* = -\frac{a}{b}$.

Table 25.1 - Linear Regression Results* 1980-1998 Sample

	R^2	Constant	Coefficient			Stable Capacity Use
			Lagged Inflation	Real Exchange Rate	Plant Capacity	
Consumer Prices	0.553	-39.197 (-2.550)	0.462 (4.756)	0.252 (3.941)	0.550 (2.530)	71.3
Implicit Deflator of GDP	0.552	-36.844 (-1.999)	0.569 (5.407)	0.150 (2.437)	0.523 (1.982)	70.4
Producer Prices	0.535	-66.310 (-2.260)	0.473 (4.277)	0.253 (3.140)	0.946 (2.231)	70.1

* t-statistic in parentheses.

When we use the implicit deflator of the GDP, the results are very similar. In this case the adjusted R^2 is 0.552. The coefficient of the use of production capacity is positive, significant and of a similar magnitude as the result of the consumer price index. In this case the percentage of the use of production capacity that leads to a steady inflation rate is 70.4%.

When we incorporate the producer price index an important increase in the value of the coefficient of the use of production capacity is observed (value of 0.946), exceeding the reported values in the two previous regressions. This result was also found to be true for the United States economy (Emery and Chih-Ping, 1997), and there is a high probability that the causes are the same for both economies. The producer price index includes only the prices of goods, whereas the consumer price index includes the price of goods and services. In this case the steady rate use of production capacity-inflation is 70.1%.

In this way the evidence indicates that during the 1980-1998 period the use of production capacity is a useful indicator to predict changes in inflation. This relationship is maintained for the three price indexes incorparated in this study (consumer, producer and implicit deflator). In all three cases similar levels were obtained for the natural utilization rate, fluctuating from a minimum of 70.1% in the producer price index to a maximum of 71.3% in the consumer price index. The average value of the percentage of use that leads to a steady inflation rate was 70.6%, a level very similar to the average use of the production capacity rate that the companies reported for this period.

In order to analyze the stability of the relationship between the use of production capacity and inflation, some linear regressions were run for two periods: 1980-1987 and 1988-1998. Based on this analysis an attempt was made to discover if the relationship between the change in the use of production capacity and the inflation rate had changed in these periods. The criterion used to define these periods was the percentage of international trade with respect to the total volume of production. According to the international discussions, the use of the production capacity rate is a less reliable indicator of inflationary pressures as long as the economies have greater openness to foreign markets, due to the fact that greater imports generate a greater availability of goods, a situation which moderates inflationary pressures and weakens the link between the use of production capacity and inflation.[4]

Figure 25.2 - Measurement of the Opening of the Mexican Economy

In the case of Mexico, the international trade of goods and services has gained greater participation in the last ten years. Figure 25.2 demonstrates that not only the imports, but also the total commercial volume (both imports and exports) have systematically increased their participation in the Gross Domestic Product since 1988. It must be pointed out that economic policy began this orientation through a major opening in 1986, with the incorporation of Mexico into GATT, but the real effect on exterior commerce became apparent two years later in 1988.

---

[4] Under a flexible exchange rate system, a greater domestic expenditure for imported goods also generated inflationary pressures through the exchange rate. An increase in the demand for external goods generates a greater demand in currency transactions primarily with the US dollar, provoking a devaluation of the peso and a worsening of domestic inflation.

Table 25.2 - Stability Analysis Linear Regressions*

	R^2	Constant	Coefficient: Lagged Inflation	Coefficient: Real Exchange Rate	Coefficient: Plant Capacity	Stable Capacity Use
1980-1987 Sample						
Consumer Prices	0.623	-25.311	0.516	0.182	0.368	68.8
		(-1.870)	(2.792)	(2.017)	(1.950)	
Implicit Deflator of GDP	0.393	-28.063	0.532	0.106	0.432	65.0
		(-1.170)	(2.738)	(1.120)	(1.245)	
Producer Prices	0.703	-114.018	0.552	0.174	1.715	66.5
		(-2.921)	(3.257)	(1.875)	(2.928)	
1988-1998 Sample						
Consumer Prices	0.463	-83.426	0.427	0.308	1.174	71.1
		(-1.834)	(3.414)	(3.002)	(1.811)	
Implicit Deflator of GDP	0.555	-81.160	0.486	0.203	1.137	71.4
		(-2.338)	(3.723)	(2.358)	(2.303)	
Producer Prices	0.435	-103.11	0.388	0.307	1.451	71.1
		(-2.041)	(2.714)	(2.537)	(2.016)	

* t-statistic in parentheses.

In Table 25.2 the main results of the regressions for two periods of time are presented. In the case of the consumer price index, the explanatory power of the model is greater in the first period. The level of confidence in the coefficient of the use of production capacity declined to 90% in both periods, compared to the confidence level of 95% for the same coefficient in the larger regression (1980-1998). The natural rate of utilization raises from 68.8% in the first period to 71.1% in the second period.

When the implicit deflator of the GDP is used, the properties of the use of production capacity are less able to predict the changes in inflation during 1980-1987, the period in which the economy experienced a major orientation towards domestic markets. The adjustment showed better results for a time when the economy was more open to foreign markets (for the period 1988-1998). In this second period of time the natural rate of utilization was found to be 71.4%.

The coefficient of the use of production capacity remained significant in both periods when the production price index was applied. In addition, an remarkable change in the level of the natural rate of utilization was observed, resulting in a 66.5% level in the first period and a 71.1% level in the second period.

As can be observed, when inflation in Mexico is measured using the production price index or the deflator implicit in the GDP, the use of production capacity continues to forecast future changes in inflation in the period of greater openness. Incoporating the consumer price index reduces the level of confidence in the coefficient of the use of production capacity, although it continues being relevant in the model. One explanation of the good behavior of the use of production capacity during 1988-1998, in the case of Mexico, consists in the fact that 63% of national production are services that in the great majority are not traded in foreign markets. Thus, a great part of the economy is found to be insolated from the international markets and experiences inflationary pressures, even when there exists idle capacity in the foreign market. On the other hand, the natural rate of utilization resulted in an increase in the second period, indicating that the resources of the economy increased with market openness, a situation that permits to have a higher natural rate of utilization.

An alternative way of measuring unutilized resources in an economy is using the difference between the actual production and the potential production of the economy. In this study the deviation in percentage terms of the GDP with respect to its tendency was incorporated as a measure of inactive resources and its behavior is analyzed with respect to inflation. The deviation is estimated using the system of Hodrick Prescott (cyclical GDP). In the case of Mexico the development of the (production) capacity utilizaion rate is very similar to the development of the cyclical GDP with acoefficient of correlation of 0.73% (see Figure 25.3).

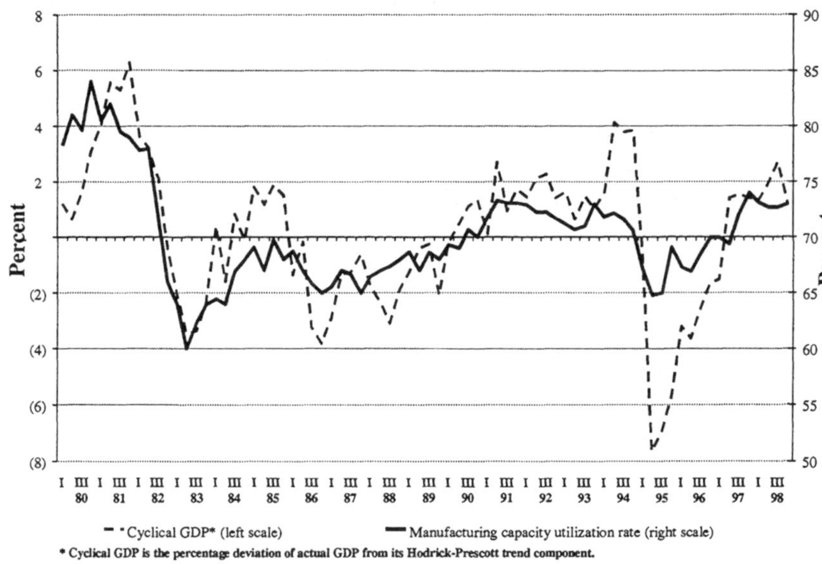

Figure 25.3 - Cyclical GDP and Capacity Utilization

Table 25.3 - Linear Regression Results Using the Cyclical GDP* 1980-1998 Sample

	R^2	Constant	Coefficient		
			Lagged Inflation	Real Exchange Rate	Cyclical GDP
Consumer Prices	0.584	-0.897	0.448	0.292	1.370
		(-0.980)	(4.792)	(4.584)	(3.514)
Implicit Deflator of GDP	0.570	-0.613	0.541	0.182	1.017
		(-0.686)	(5.179)	(2.878)	(2.626)
Producer Prices	0.560	-0.845	0.432	0.297	1.606
		(-0.744)	(3.928)	(3.626)	(2.943)

* t-statistic in parentheses.

Consequently, utilizing the cyclical GDP in substitution for the percentage of use of production capacity in the regressions leads to similar results as before (see Table 25.3).

2 Definition of the Percentage of the Utilization Production Capacity

In Mexico the available information about the manufacturing industrial production capacity and the percentage of use of such capacity comes from two sources: The Industrial Survery of the National Institute of Statistics, Geography and Information, which provides information for the period of 1994 to 1997, and the Current Survey of the Banco de Mexico, with available statistics for the period of 1983 to 1998. Although the questions included in the surveys are very similar, the meaning of capacity utilization in the responses of the business owners is not clear.[5] That is to say, it is unknown if the expression 'utilization of production capacity' is understood in the same way by the investigator and by the respondent. Therefore, in the questionnaires for the months of October and November of 1997 a group of questions was incorporated that should improve the respondents' understanding of the concept of 'utilization of production capacity.'

[5] The particular question of the INEGI is as follows: 'From the total production capacity of your establishment, point out the utilization percentage for your establishment for the month under study.' For its part, the Current Survey of the Banco de Mexico asks: 'What was the utilization percentage of the production capacity of your establishment in the month under study, in a range from 0 to 100%, where 100% indicates the full utilization of the production capacity?'

The utilization capacity can be defined as the maximum amount of goods that can be produced per unit of time with fixed plant supplies, equipment, labor and raw materials. Nevertheless, levels of production outside the area of efficient plant production are excluded because they are unable to be sustained in a systematic way.

The preceding definition incorporates the time lost due to repairs, maintenance, changes and speed in the processing of raw materials for production; the number of shifts per day; the number of operating days per week or per year; and in addition any capacity held in reserve, which is to say, any level of production capacity beyond that which is actually in use (generally speaking that capacity which is less efficient or represents processes of outdated technology), which is required to meet increases in market demand or when unforeseen changes of the market require greater capacity which can be established only after a significant period of time. However, it is doubtful whether the respondents include these concepts at the time of answering the questions about the utilization of the production capacity.

In tables 25.4 and 25.5 the answers that were obtained in October and November 1997 relating to the questions about utilization capacity, were averaged. The responses of each month were similar, so averaging is used in a way to save space in this document without altering the results. In the first instance the plants indicated that the average utilization of production plant capacity was 66% in the October-November 1997 bimonthly period. Within the same sector the percentage fluctuated from a rate of 60% for small firms to a maximum of 68% for large firms. In accordance with the orientation of the market, the major use of production capacity was reported for the export firms (69%).

The owners were requested to relate the unutilized capacity to the number of shifts in their firms. For 18% of the firms, the idea of the idle capacity refers to 'the plant capacity which can increase the number of work shifts', a situation which provoked a bias, thus diminishing the accuracy of the measurement of the production capacity and the utilization percentage of that capacity. This bias can be one of the factors which explains the low level of the capacity utilization of the Mexican manufacturing industry compared to the reported international level, only 47% of the firms understood 'the number of actual work shifts not fully utilizing their plant's capacity' as idle capacity, which is a correct interpretation.

Table 25.4 - Utilization Percentage of Production Capacity and the Meaning of Idle Capacity*

	Total	Large	Medium	Small	Export	Non-export
UTILIZATION PERCENTAGE OF PRODUCTION CAPACITY	66	68	67	60	69	63
MEANING OF IDLE CAPACITY (Percentages)						
- With the same plant capacity the number of shifts can be increased	18	11	12	34	23	10
- With the actual number of work shifts plant capacity not fully utilized	47	56	48	36	49	44
- Both concepts	35	33	40	30	28	37

* Percentages weighted for the number of workers in each firm. In each case they constitute the average of the responses of the October-November 1997 period.

Among the main factors which limit a higher use of production capacity is the lack of orders from the internal and external markets. Other important results indicate that 16% of the firms maintained a certain unutilized capacity level owing to the seasonal nature of product demand, and 8% pointed out that they do not use their plant capacity more intensively owing to the fact that maintaining higher inventories led to higher costs. Another 7% indicated that a better capacity use will be accompanied by higher investments to modernize the machinery. The answers given in table 25.4 and 25.5 indicate that the entrepreneurs have the same concept of capacity utilization as the investigators. Nevertheless, the error that was made is considering that the expansion of work shifts could increase capacity utilization, instead of answering the question concerning the utilization rate of capacity utilization given the actual number of work shifts.

Table 25.5 - Main Reasons for the Existence of Idle Capacity (Percentages)*

	Total	Large	Medium	Small	Ex-porters	Non-ex-porters
– Expenditures for the training of personnel	3	5	3	1	3	3
– Additional shifts to modernize machinery	7	2	7	11	10	4
– Additional investment to modernize machinery	7	6	7	9	7	8
– Additional financing	5	1	6	8	6	5
– Lack of material orders.	2	26	27	31	30	26
– Lack of orders in the external market.	12	11	14	7	8	14
– The idle capacity is composed of machinery of low productivity.	3	2	3	4	3	3
– Lack of managerial and board ability.	1	1	2	0	1	1
– Higher production implies higher costs to mantain larger inventories.	8	6	8	9	7	8
– Idle capacity is a response to a certain seasonal development in the demand of the product.	16	24	15	11	15	17
– In this period a certain level of production capacity is not used due to repairs and maintenance.	3	6	3	2	3	4

* Percentage weighted for the number of workers in each business. In each case they contitute an average of the responses in the October-November bimester.

In the long run there is a clear necessity to reduce bureaucratic reglementations, to increase public security, to improve the network of high speed roadways, and to modernize the railway system in order to achieve a greater use of production capacity.

3 Conclusions

The results obtained in this study indicate that in the case of Mexico, the production capacity in the manufacturing sector is a useful variable to predict future changes in the rate of inflation. The results demonstrate a greater consistency when inflation is measured through the producer price index, even though the consumer price index or the implicit deflator of the GDP continue to appear acceptable. The use of the production capacity is a relevant variable to analyze the period of greater openness to international trade. This is a logical result considering that the service sector, characterized by a high percentage of international non-commercial production, represents two thirds of the national GDP.

Finally, it must be pointed out that the information about the use of production capacity was established through a survey, whose major part is of a 'qualitative' type. In the said survey the business owners and the investigators that designed the survey did not understand the concept of the 'use of production capacity' in the same way. This might be one of the reasons to explain the low reported percentage of the use of production capacity in Mexican industry, with respect to international standards.

References

Emery M. Kenneth and Chih-Ping Chang (1997), 'Is there a Stable Relationship Between Capacity Utilization and Inflation?', Federal Reserve Bank of Dallas, *Economic Review,* First Quarter, pp. 14-20.

Finn Mary G. (1955), 'Is 'High' Capacity Utilization Inflationary?', Federal Reserve Bank of Richmond, *Economic Quarterly*, 81 (winter), pp. 1-16.

———. (1996) 'A Theory of the Capacity Utilization/Inflation Relationship', Federal Reserve Bank of Richmond, *Economic Quarterly*, 82 (summer), pp. 67-86.

Garner Alan C. (1994), 'Capacity Utilization and U.S. Inflation', Federal Reserve Bank of Kansas City, *Economic Reviews*, Fourth Quarter, pp. 1-21.

Humphrey Thomas M. (1986), *From Trade-offs to Policy Ineffectiveness: A History of the Phillips Curve*, Federal Reserve Bank of Richmond, October 1986.

Part VI

Stocks and the Business Cycle

26 Stocks and the Business Cycle: An Initial Examination of Business Opinion Survey Data

MATTHEW HASSAN and PHILLIP BRIGGS

Summary

Stocks or inventories are the difficult component of GDP – difficult to measure and difficult to forecast. Can the use of business survey data give us valuable insights into firms' behaviour regarding stocks? This paper looks at how firms behave when their expectations are not met. In particular it looks at how errors in expectations about output and costs influence stocks of finished goods. Results suggest that stocking responses are influenced by demand conditions, but not by supply conditions. An unexpected fall in output will result in higher than expected stocks, but an unexpected change in costs will not influence the stocks outcome.

1 Introduction

Stocks have always been a problem for economists:

1. They are difficult to measure: Most official stock series are based on accounting records. The standard approach used by accountants in assessing stocks is that they should be valued at the lower of their production cost or their present market value (See Institute of Chartered Accountants of New Zealand (1994)). Given this, there is inevitably going to be a degree of uncertainty about what the reported value of stocks is telling us. Then there is the problem of assessing the real level of stocks,

which is a job for the statisticians compiling national accounts data. If a firm's stockpile is large, and was built up over an extended period of time, which deflator is to be applied to the stocks? Ideally, an analyst needs to know the age of the stocks, in order to apply the appropriate deflator to each cohort of stocks. Information on the age of stocks is usually not available to analysts who are compiling the national accounts, and hence some assumptions have to be made about the age distribution of stocks in deriving estimates of real stocks.

2. The emphasis is on stock changes: The component that enters GDP is stock change, not the level of stocks. GDP is a flow variable, measuring output between two time periods. The difference in inventories between two time periods, which reflects the contribution to total output not captured by sales data, is also a flow variable, and is part of GDP. This emphasis on stock changes can itself be a problem. If stocks in the first time period are understated and stocks in the second time period overstated, the stock change can be way too high. The focus on stock change produces another problem. How is the change in the value of stocks over the period to be accounted for? For example, finished stocks produced just after time period one are likely to have a different value to those produced just before time period two. The normal way of handling this is to value stocks at the midpoint of the period. Hence, the stock change derived from the book value of stocks is adjusted by a stock valuation adjustment (SVA).

3. Stocks depend on both demand and supply: A stockpile is being used, and is being added to, all the time. The level of finished stocks will tend to reduce when demand increases, and increase when production increases. For some firms, demand and production may fluctuate markedly, even over a short time period.

Given these factors, it is not surprising that it has proved so difficult to produce robust models to explain stocking behaviour.

This paper focuses on the third factor listed above – the impact of demand and supply on stocks. In particular, we use similar techniques to those of Flood and Lowe (1995), who looked at changes in Australian manufactured stocks. Specifically, we use data from NZIER's *Quarterly Survey of Business Opinion* (QSBO) to assess whether an unanticipated change in output is associated with an unanticipated change in finished goods stocks. Similarly, we look at the impact of an unanticipated change in costs on the unanticipated change in finished goods.

2 The Role of Stocks

The relative importance of demand and supply influences have been debated over recent years. One view of stocks has been that they act as a buffer, so that unexpected changes in orders can be met from stocks, rather than having to drastically alter production levels. In effect, holding stocks allows production smoothing. However, this view has not always been in accord with the data. Production has often shown more variance than stock levels. It seems, therefore, that stocks may be playing another role besides production smoothing. It could be that stockpiling allows producers to vary their production to take account of favourable supply conditions. Suppose, for example, that the cost of production suddenly goes down because some inputs are more plentiful, and less costly, than usual. The producer may crank up production to produce stocks, which will be able to be sold later at a substantial profit.

We use QSBO data to look at two issues:

- whether an unanticipated increase in demand is associated with an unanticipated fall in finished goods stocks, and vice-versa; and
- whether an unanticipated fall in costs is associated with an unanticipated rise in finished goods stocks, and vice-versa.

3 The Data

The *Quarterly Survey of Business Opinion* was begun in 1961. It covers a number of sectors: manufacturers and builders, wholesalers and retailers, services, and architects. The data we are using are for manufacturers and builders. The questions we are looking at are of the form:

> What has been your firm's experience during the PAST THREE MONTHS and what changes do you expect during the NEXT THREE MONTHS in respect of the following (exclude seasonal variations by comparing three month period with the same period a year earlier):

Respondents then tick boxes marked 'Up', 'Same', 'Down' or 'NA' for the past three months, and for the next three months.

The data we will examine covers questions on 'Stocks - Finished Goods', 'Output', 'Average costs', and 'Average selling price'.

For a fuller description of the QSBO see Bowie and Easton (1987).

Figure 26.1 shows net balance figures for output. The net balance is the percentage of respondents answering 'up' minus the percentage answering 'down', with some adjustment for non response. Note that the net balance figure is an indicator of the change in a variable, rather than its level. We will refer to the series relating to the past three months as 'actual' values and the series relating to the next three months as 'expected' values.

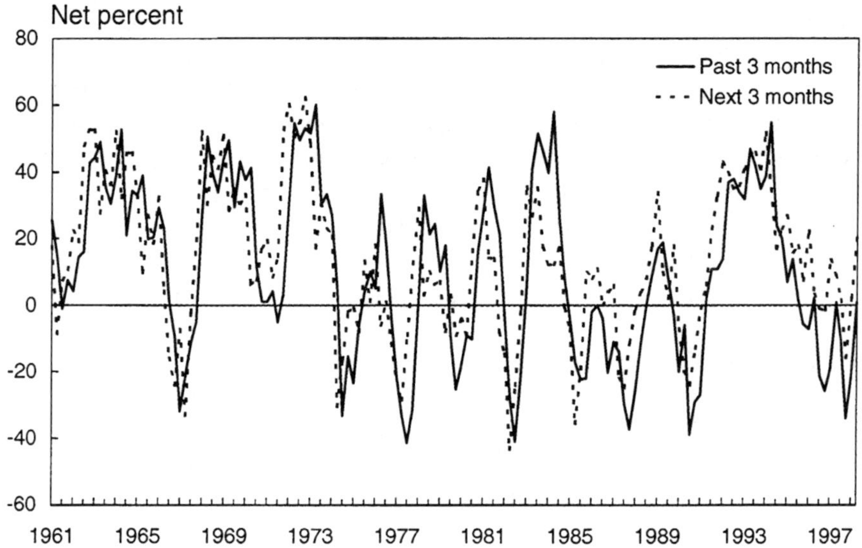

Source: NZIER

Figure 26.1 - Manufacturers and Builders – Output

As can be seen from Figure 26.1, the two output series give a clear picture of New Zealand's economic cycles. Figure 26.2 shows net balance figures for finished goods stocks. Again the cycles are evident, but not as clearly. As can be seen by comparing the two figures, the variation, or variance, in the net balance figures for output is greater than the variation in those for stocks. (The standard deviation for the actual output series was 26, while the standard deviation for the actual finished stock series was 12.) However, the stocks series is more volatile; it has more turning points.

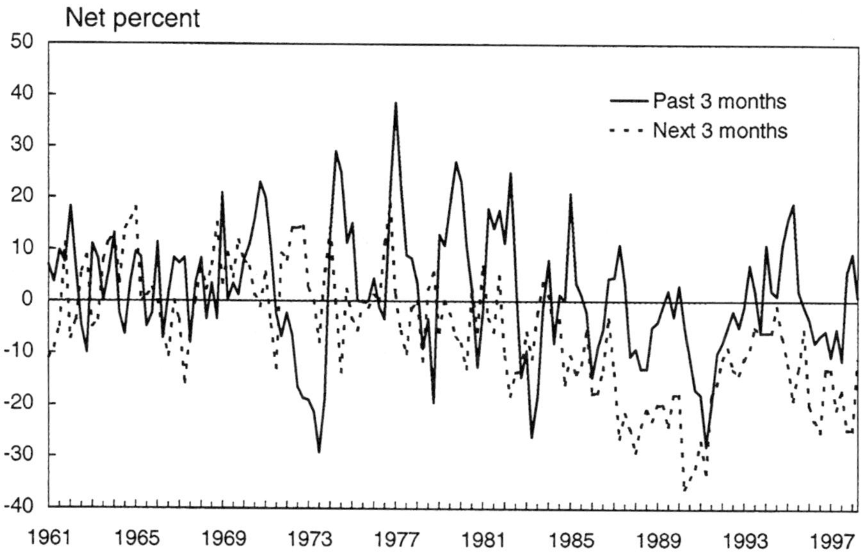

Source: NZIER

Figure 26.2 - Manufacturers and Builders – Finished Goods Stocks

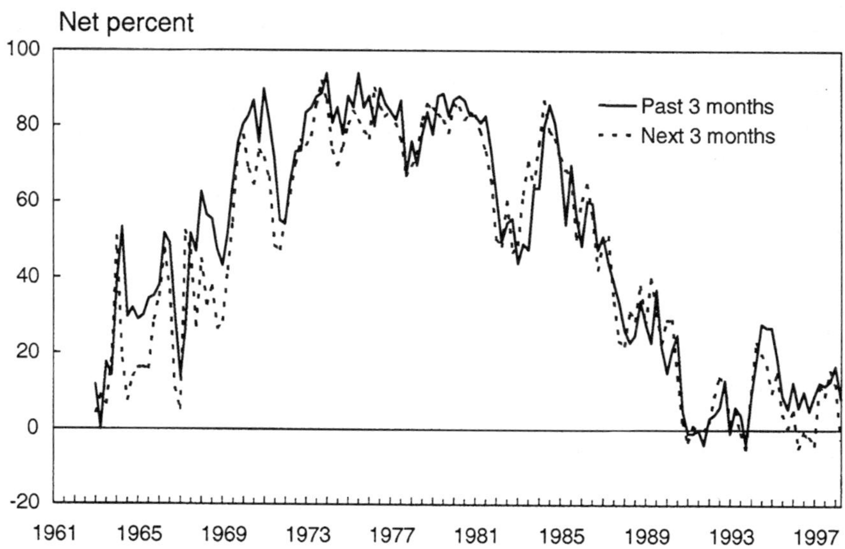

Source: NZIER

Figure 26.3 - Manufacturers and Builders – Average Costs

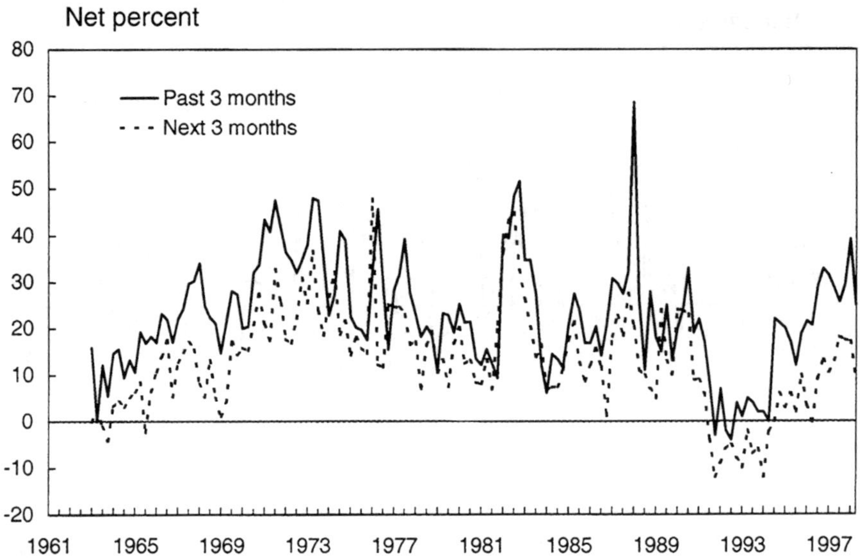

Source: NZIER

Figure 26.4 - Manufacturers and Builders – Real Costs

The average costs series (see Figure 26.3) show very high values between 1969 and 1987, reflecting the high levels of inflation over that period. The net balance series for expected costs was transformed to expected real costs by subtracting from it the net balance figures for expected average selling price. A similar transformation was used for the actual series, with actual prices being subtracted from actual costs. Figure 26.4 shows the resulting series.

4 Expectation Errors

Expectation errors were derived for three variables: finished goods stocks, output, and real costs. For each variable, the actual net balance was subtracted from the expected net balance for the preceding quarter.

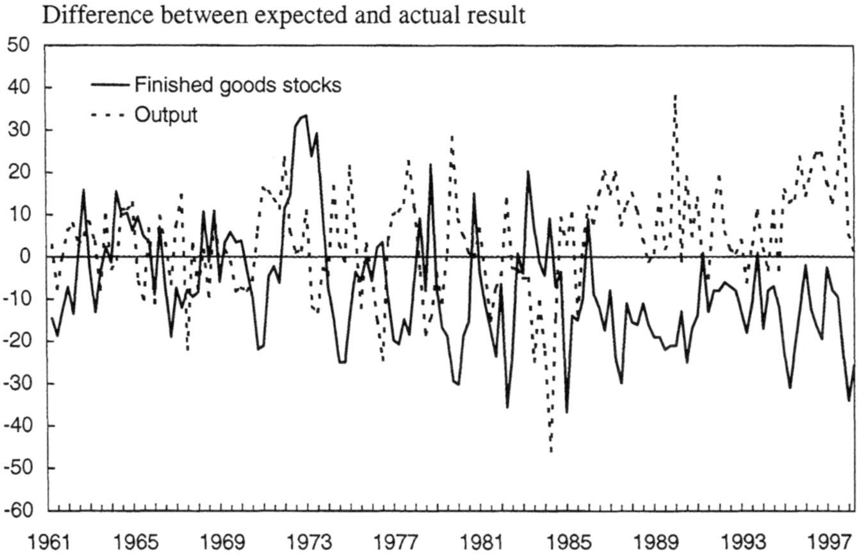

Source: NZIER

Figure 26.5 - Manufacturers and Builders – Expectation Errors

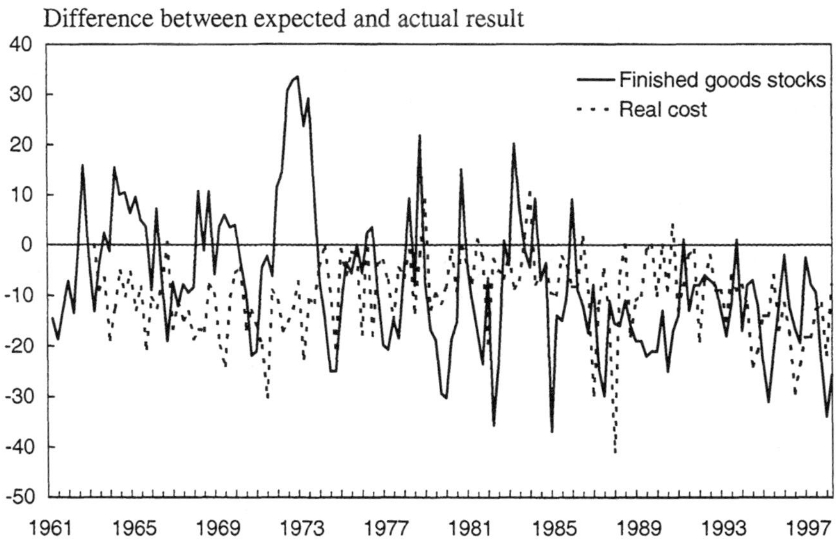

Source: NZIER

Figure 26.6 - Manufacturers and Builders – Expectation Errors

We looked at whether the variables were correlated. Figure 26.6 shows the expectation errors for finished stocks and output. There is a visible negative correlation between the two, with a rise in the output error being associated with a fall in the stocks error. However, the R^2 was not large, being only 0.091. Figure 26.5 shows expectation errors for stocks and real costs. There is no visible correlation here. The R^2 was 0.002.

A regression equation was derived using the three series:

$$\underset{}{\text{StockError}} = -7.993 - \underset{(-4.142)}{0.377}\ \text{OutputError} - \underset{(-1.402)}{0.203}\ \text{CostError} \qquad (1)$$

R^2=0.1120

Estimation period: December quarter 1963 to December quarter 1998

The t statistics, in brackets, show that the coefficient on the output error was significant, but the coefficient on the cost error was not.

We then tested for asymmetry in the effect of the two variables. We introduced four dummy variables:

D1	1 if output error > average output error, otherwise 0
D2	1 if output error < average output error, otherwise 0
D3	1 if cost error > average cost error, otherwise 0
D4	1 if cost error < average cost error, otherwise 0

D1 and D2 were multiplied by the output error to get two series: one containing greater than average output errors and zero values, the other containing less than average errors and zeroes. D3 and D4 were used similarly with the cost error series.

The following regression was derived:

$$\text{StockError} = -7.568 - \underset{(-2.677)}{0.392}\ \text{D1*OutputError} - \underset{(-1.956)}{0.354}\ \text{D2*OutputError}$$
$$-\underset{(-0.368)}{0.130}\ \text{D3*CostError} - \underset{(-1.317)}{0.196}\ \text{D4*CostError} \qquad (2)$$

R^2 = 0.1119

Estimation period: March quarter 1964 to December quarter 1998

Only the first coefficient, that on D1*OutputError, is statistically significant. As can be seen, the R^2 is lower than for the earlier equation.

So what do these results mean? Some conclusions:

- The equations showed the right sign on the cost error, with an unanticipated fall in costs being associated with an unanticipated rise in stocks. However the coefficients on the cost variables were insignificant. We therefore have no conclusive evidence that a supply side shock will result in an unanticipated change in stocks.

- The equations also showed the right sign on the output error, and the coefficient in the first equation was significant. However, the second equation suggests that the demand shock works only in a one sided fashion. An overestimation of output is associated with an underestimation of stocks. That is, an unanticipated fall in output will tend to result in an unanticipated rise in stocks. But we cannot say that an unanticipated rise in output will be associated with an unanticipated fall in stocks.
- The results contrast with Flood and Lowe's results for Australia. Their study showed that demand shocks had influenced inventories of finished goods, with a stronger effect when demand was unexpectedly high than when it was unexpectedly low. However, as for New Zealand, the coefficients on the real cost variables were negative but were insignificantly different from zero.
- The low R^2 values for our equations indicate that they have little explanatory power. What else could be accounting for the error in the expectations of stocks? Perhaps our survey respondents just are not that good at forecasting what will happen next quarter. If we look back at Figure 26.2 and Figure 26.6 we can see that respondents tend to underestimate finished stocks in the coming quarter.

5 Formation of Expectations

How do survey respondents actually form their expectations about stocks? Do they consider output and real costs when thinking about stocks?

We derived the following equations for expected goods stocks:

$$\begin{aligned} \text{ExpectedStocks} = -14.380 &+ \underset{(7.594)}{0.323}\ \text{ExpectedOutput} \\ &+ \underset{(3.380)}{0.294}\ \text{ExpectedCosts} \qquad (3) \end{aligned}$$

$R^2 = 0.295$

Estimation period: December quarter 1963 to December quarter 1998

The equation gives a low R^2 but both coefficients are statistically significant. Both coefficients have a positive sign. This makes sense for output: expectations of higher stocks are linked with expectations of higher output. But why should a rise in real costs be associated with a rise in finished stocks? In our earlier equations which linked stock errors with cost errors, we had been looking for a negative contribution from the cost variable. Whatever the reason for the positive sign on stocks in the above equation, again we have no evidence for the proposition that firms' expectations of lower costs will result in restocking.

6 Further Work

This work has been a preliminary examination only. We had originally intended to use firm level responses to build up a more detailed picture of expectation errors. However, we have, for this initial work, used aggregate results, i.e. net balance figures.

We have also limited the variables we have looked at. The QSBO collects data on other variables, such as productivity, which may affect the supply side response. However, there is uncertainty about how respondents interpret the questions. Do respondents think of productivity as labour productivity, or total factor productivity, or simply as a 'we're doing well' factor? Peters(1997) used only those survey records where the response to the productivity question was consistent with the responses to both the output and employment questions.

There are also doubts about the way we have interpreted the data in this paper. For example, we have been implicitly assuming that in their responses to the output question, and also to the stocks question, respondents have given us an assessment of real changes, rather than nominal changes. There is some tacit support for this assumption. Briggs(1998) found that the net balance figures for the QSBO question on 'export sales' were more highly correlated with official series for export volumes than with nominal exports.

There is also a question about the way we have handled the 'average costs' question. We have followed Flood and Lowe(1995) and derived a real cost series by subtracting the net balance figure for 'average selling prices' from that for 'average costs'. It may have been better to use both of the original series – the series for costs and the series for price – in the regression equations. After all, an unexpected rise in average selling prices may produce a supply side response, resulting in an unanticipated rise in finished stocks.

It seems likely therefore that when this work is pursued further, using firm level data, the emphasis will be on using the data 'as is', with a broader range of variables being tested for their impact on stocking behaviour.

References

Bowie, R. and B. Easton (1987), *Business opinion in New Zealand: the NZIER survey*, NZIER Research Paper No 36.

Briggs, P. (1998), *A presentation on using QSBO to forecast exports and investment*, NZIER working paper WP 98/6.

Flood, D. and P. Lowe (1995), 'Inventories and the business cycle', *The Economic Record*, vol. 71, No. 212, March 1995.

Institute of Chartered Accountants of New Zealand (1994), *Accounting for inventories*, Financial Reporting Standard No 4.

Peters, J. (1997), *Firm level price changes and productivity: an investigation using QSBO data*, report prepared for Treasury, NZIER.

27 Model for the Cyclical Trend in Stocks in Belgium

GEORGE VAN GASTEL, PIERRE CREVITS and
YVES DE LOMBAERDE

Changes in stocks have a significant influence on industrial output and economic growth. In the national accounts, this item is not estimated on the basis of exogenous variables but is simply taken as the difference between the aggregates obtained by the output approach and by the expenditure approach. To improve the estimate of this crucial economic variable, we should examine the possibility of validating this figure via other information sources. That is the aim of this paper.

1 Quantifying the Results of the Business Surveys

Within the strict deadlines for producing the quarterly national accounts, the only information available on stocks in Belgium comes from the business surveys. This concerns a qualitative appraisal of the volume of stocks of finished products in manufacturing industry (question 18 in the survey):[1] for each of the products which he makes, the manufacturer judges the level of his stocks of finished products by comparing them with the 'normal' level.

Our first instinct is to examine whether the answers to this question could not be used directly to estimate changes in stocks in the national accounts. This exercise is inconclusive. Figure 27.1 does not in fact reveal any apparent link between opinions on stocks and their levels in the national accounts.

[1] The question reads as follows: 'In your opinion, are your current stocks of this product higher than normal, normal or below normal?'

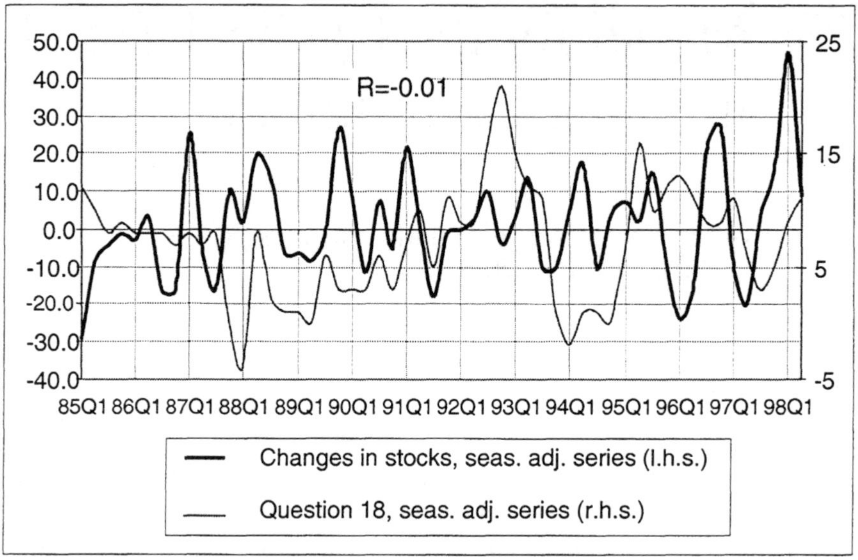

Figure 27.1 - Apparent Absence of Any Link Between Opinions on Stocks and Changes in Stocks as Estimated in the Quarterly National Accounts

There are two reasons for this problem of quantification: the difficulty lies partly in the question itself and partly in the characteristics of the national accounts.

1.1 Problem Connected with the Form and Content of the Question

The opinion on the level of stocks of finished products refers to a 'normal' situation, which is itself subjective, varying over time and according to the economic situation. That hampers the conversion of this qualitative information into quantitative data on the trend in changes in stocks.

Also, the question deals only with stocks of finished products held by a producer in manufacturing industry. But changes in stocks measured by the quarterly national accounts describe changes for all stocks in the economy:

- whoever holds them (be it the producer, another manufacturer incorporating them in his production process, or a wholesale or retail trader)
- and whatever their origin (goods produced in Belgium or imported).

However, studies in other countries (Germany; IFO-Institut) have shown that, even though they represent only one part, stocks of finished products fluctuate in a very similar way to overall stocks. Furthermore, it is changes in manufactured output that largely account for the economic cycle.

1.2 Problem Connected with the Belgian National Accounts

The series of changes in stocks in the quarterly national accounts is very uneven owing to its method of construction. Changes in stocks are not in fact estimated from external sources like the other national aggregates but are obtained as the difference between resources and uses.

2 Link Between Changes in Stocks and the Economic Cycle: Identifying a Stock Formation Model

Although it is difficult to use the results of the business surveys as an instrument for directly measuring changes in stocks, they can nevertheless help to update the link between changes in stocks and economic activity. Finding the model for the prevailing stock behaviour pattern in Belgium in itself provides us with a primary tool for validating the results obtained as a balancing figure in the national accounts, but above all it is the first step towards a genuine method of modelling stocks.

2.1 The Two Main Macroeconomic Models on Stock Formation

The macroeconomic models which provide an insight into stock formation behaviour are based on the reasons for building stocks found at microeconomic level. Four reasons have been identified:

- stocks may be held to eliminate or limit the marginal costs of production over time; in that case, stocks are used for maintaining steady output, serving as an adjustment variable to smooth out temporary fluctuations in sales;
- the second reason for holding stocks is based on the assumption that the enterprise can produce more efficiently under certain conditions or at certain times; it is therefore in the interests of the enterprise to take advantage of these situations favourable to productivity to produce more than necessary and build up stocks;
- the third reason for holding stocks is based on enterprises' aversion to the risk of failing to satisfy unexpectedly strong demand: building adequate stocks provides protection against goods being out of stock if demand exceeds output;

- the last reason for holding stocks is based on speculation: sometimes the enterprise may believe that it is more advantageous to stock-pile its production rather than sell it, if selling prices are expected to rise in the future.

There are two main macroeconomic models based on these reasons for holding stocks:

- the steady (smoothed) output model, based on the first reason for holding stocks: in this model, a strategy of minimising costs over time leads the enterprise to keep output steady relative to trends in sales; stocks therefore act as a buffer and follow a counter-cyclical trend;
- the stock accelerator model, based on the third reason for holding stocks: this model assumes that the enterprise holds a stock of finished products in proportion to its output level; when the economy is expanding, output is high and enterprises want to hold more stocks; conversely, when output falls, they run down their stocks proportionately; stocks therefore follow a pro-cyclical trend.

2.2 *Identification of an Annual Stock-holding Model*

Three sources of information are used to try to identify the stock-holding model which prevails in Belgium: the business surveys, the national accounts and the annual accounts of enterprises. The results obtained from these three sources tally.

2.2.1 Identification on the Basis of the Results of the Business Surveys A simple graphic analysis sheds light on the link between the qualitative appraisal of stocks in the business surveys and economic activity. Graph 2 reveals a very close link between the behaviour of stocks (described by the statistics obtained from the answers to question 18 in the business surveys) and the trend in economic activity (measured by the trend in GDP). When the economy is doing well, stocks are judged to be below normal, and vice versa.

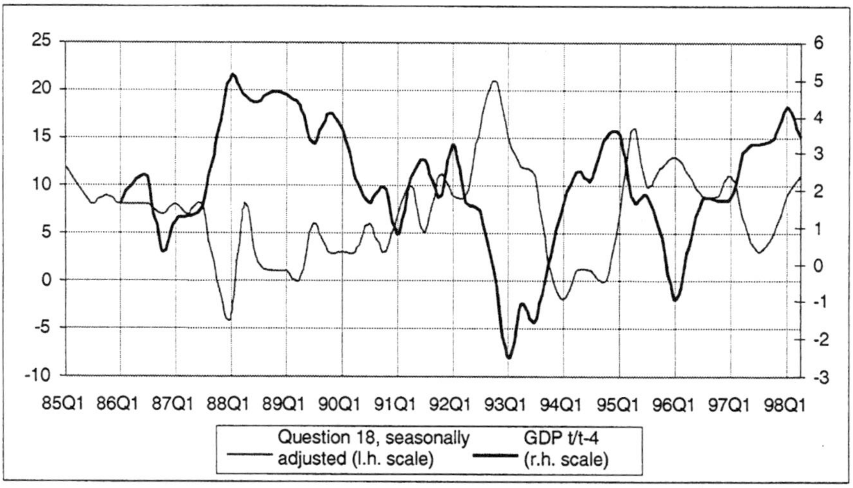

Figure 27.2 - Link Between the Trend in GDP and the Assessment of Stocks of Finished Products by Manufacturers

Figure 27.2 therefore suggests that Belgian stocks move according to the accelerator model, which assumes that stocks of finished products tend to adjust to anticipated demand. If a fall in demand observed when the economic climate is deteriorating shows stocks to be higher than normal, it is because the level of stocks considered 'normal' has declined in line with the observed fall in demand. Conversely, rising demand is reflected in a subjective lowering of stocks, since the desired stock level has increased.

2.2.2 Identification on the Basis of the National Accounts It is also possible to identify the stock-holding model prevailing in Belgium on the basis of the national accounts themselves. To do this, we used a linear regression on annual data to try to determine the statistical link between the rate of growth of GDP and the change in stocks (as a percentage of GDP). If Belgium has a stock formation pattern that conforms to the stock accelerator model, we would see a positive regression coefficient (significantly different from zero); a negative coefficient would indicate a steady output model.

The results of the regression are set out in table 27.1.

With a significantly positive coefficient, the results of this regression also imply that, on annual data, it is the accelerator stock model that prevails in Belgium. Moreover, the same analysis conducted for other

OECD[2] countries leads us to the same conclusion in the majority of cases, with entirely comparable regression coefficients.

Table 27.1 - Technical Characteristics of the Linear Regression of Changes in Stocks on the Trend in GDP (Period 1981-1997)

Regressor	Coefficient	Standard error	Student's distribution
Constant	- 0.18	0.12	- 1.48
GDP growth rates	0.11	0.05	2.11

Number of observations: 17
R^2 adjusted: 0.18
Durbin-Watson: 2.17

*2.2.3 On the Basis of the Annual Accounts of Enterprises*In annual terms, the change in stocks may also be measured on the basis of the annual accounts of enterprises recorded at the Central Balance Sheet Office.[3] Figure 27.3 shows that this third statistical source provides further confirmation of the accelerator behaviour of stocks.

This three-part exercise leads us to conclude, with little risk of error, that in annual terms Belgian stocks follow a pro-cyclical trend, i.e. they reinforce the economic cycle. This information is itself one of the initial factors needed for assessing the changes in stocks shown as a balancing item in the national accounts.

[2] Bouthevillain C. and Eyssartier D., The role of changes in stocks in the cycles of activity of the leading industrial countries, Review of the French Economic Observatory (OFCE), No. 62, July 1997.

[3] We confined our analysis to stocks of finished products as recorded in account 33 of the enterprise accounts. These stocks were aggregated for all enterprises in manufacturing industry submitting a complete presentation.

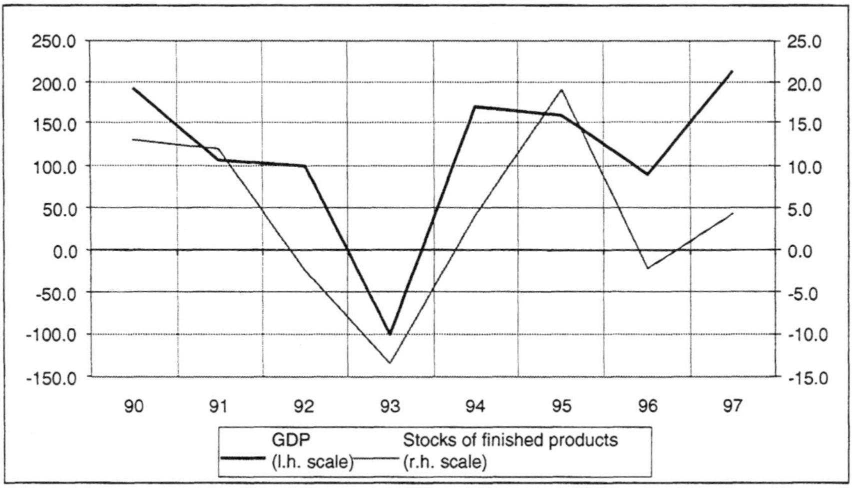

Figure 27.3 - Link Between the Trend in GDP and Stocks of Finished Products Noted in the Annual Accounts of Enterprises

3 Modelling Changes in Stocks in the Quarterly Accounts

This clear link established in annual terms between the trend in economic activity and changes in stocks encourages us to go further in modelling stock formation behaviour at quarterly level.

We focused on modelling changes in stocks rather than stock levels. The equation used was specified on the basis of the theoretical reasons for stock formation described earlier. The estimate was primarily obtained by taking account of the anticipated and unanticipated movement in demand excluding stocks. We ascertain anticipations via adjustment mechanisms and therefore assume that the anticipations are based solely on past and current trends in demand. In consequence, the determinants adopted are past changes in stocks (VS) and current and past changes in demand excluding stocks (VDhs).

$$VS = a + b\, VS_{-1} + c\, VDhs + d\, VDhs_{-1} + e\, VDhs_{-2} + f VDhs_{-3} + g\, VDhs_{-4} \qquad (1)$$

This equation is estimated on a quarterly basis by the ordinary least squares method. The results are set out in table 27.2.

Table 27.2 - Technical Characteristics of the Quarterly Modelling of Changes in Stocks (Period 1986 - 1998)

Regressor	Coefficient	Standard error	Student's distribution
Constant	2.18	2.19	1.00
VS_{-1}	0.36	0.17	2.08
VDhs	- 0.45	0.08	- 5.36
$VDhs_{-1}$	- 0.13	0.09	- 1.47
$VDhs_{-2}$	0.20	0.07	2.62
$VDhs_{-3}$	0.15	0.07	2.23
$VDhs_{-4}$	0.17	0.07	2.25

Number of observations: 49
R2 adjusted: 0.61
Ljung-Box[4]: 22.5 (χ_2 with 16 df = 0.127)

These results, estimated on a quarterly basis, shed new light on the stock behaviour prevailing in Belgium by identifying two stock-formation strategies which differ according to time-scales. The disaggregation into quarters revealed that stocks are used to maintain steady output in view of demand in the current and preceding quarters. This role may be interpreted as enterprises' response to unanticipated demand or as inertia in the production process, which takes time to adapt to demand. On the other hand, stocks adapt by acting as an accelerator in the light of earlier demand (dating from two or more quarters ago): this indicates how sales are expected to move, and therefore confirms the finding based on the annual figures.[5]

---

[4] The Durbin-Watson's one-lag autocorrelation d test is inapplicable when the lagged dependent variable is used as a regressor. The Ljung-Box Q' statistic, a more powerful variant of the Box-Pierce's Q test, is a global test of autocorrelation (H0: all ρk = 0); see Gujarati, D. N., Basic Econometrics, McGraw-Hill Intl Editions, NewYork 1995, 3rd edition, pp. 420, 421 and 717. In the case that we are concerned with, one cannot reject the hypothesis of the absence of autocorrelation.

[5] Only an accelerator effect appears in the annual analysis made previously. This may be because, in the case of annual data, part of the effects of any role which stocks have in maintaining steady output is picked up by the accelerator and it is therefore difficult to separate the part attributable to the steady output strategy from that conforming to the accelerator concept.

4 Method of Estimating Changes in Stocks in the Quarterly Accounts

The technical characteristics of this regression are satisfactory: the statistical adjustment is good (over 60% of the variance is explained) and, apart from the intercept and demand in the previous quarter,[6] all the variables have a significant influence. However, the predictive quality of this equation is insufficient for it to be taken on its own as a tool for forecasting changes in stocks in the quarterly accounts.

The method of estimating changes in stocks in the quarterly accounts must therefore be multi-modal and combine the use of all available information sources, namely:

- the balancing item necessary for reconciling the production and expenditure approaches in the quarterly national accounts;
- the results of the business survey on manufacturers' assessment of stocks;
- the results of the model based on past stocks and current and past demand.

Properly combined, this set of tools should make major improvements to the information supplied on stocks by the quarterly accounts. The study in this field is still going on.

5 Conclusion

The purpose of this paper was to compare all information available in the short term on changes in stocks and to analyse it in the light of macroeconomic theory on the subject. The ultimate aim was to improve the estimates of the quarterly national accounts.

The theory considers two apparently conflicting types of macroeconomic behaviour patterns which stocks may adopt: maintaining steady output, which justifies a counter-cyclical trend, and the stock accelerator, which explains a pro-cyclical trend. Our empirical study using the data from the Belgian quarterly national accounts reconciles these two approaches: using an elementary model of the behaviour of stock formation based on quarterly data, we find that stocks keep output steady in the very short term

---

[6] The non-significant influence of the previous quarter's demand is probably due to the transition taking place during that quarter between the steady output strategy and the accelerator behaviour.

and subsequently adopt accelerator behaviour. The latter predominates if annual data are used.

In conjunction with the replies to the question concerning the assessment of stocks in the business surveys, which - as we have seen - confirm the accelerator model, this method of modelling changes in stocks should prove to be a satisfactory tool for validating the quarterly balances between resources and uses, which are the first estimate of changes in stocks in the national accounts.

References

Bouthevillain C. and D. Eyssartier (1997), 'The role of changes in stocks in the cycles of activity of the leading industrial countries', *Review of the French Economic Observatory (OFCE), No. 62*, July 1997

Eurostat (1998), *Handbook quarterly accounts*, Luxemburg, preliminary version.

Gujarati, D. N., *Basic Econometrics*, McGraw-Hill Intl Editions, NewYork 1995, 3rd edition.

Part VII

Survey Data and Economic Forecasts

28 Economic Analysis and Short-term Forecasting with Qualitative Data from the Economic Survey International (ESI)*

HARALD A. HAUPT[a] and SANDRA M. WALLER[b]

Abstract

This paper examines whether qualitative survey data can improve the power of ex ante short-term forecasts of inflation. The models are based on expert expectations from qualitative economic survey data. The survey series are derived by checking carefully the information in disaggregated and aggregated answers. Empirical evidence is presented that passing classical rationality tests is no necessary condition for expert expectations to improve forecasting facilities. Additionally, as proposed by Maddala (1991) the results indicate that testing for rationality in the cointegration framework is more appropriate in the presence of price expectations data. Hence our conclusion is that it is important to examine whether there is a possibility of incorporating a learning process in the form of error-correction-terms in the forecasting models. Thus without a priori restriction

* Financial support from Verein der Freunde der Universität Regensburg e.V. is greatfully acknowledged.

a Corresponding author. *Harald.Haupt@WiWi.Uni-Regensburg.de*

b We thank the participants of the 24th CIRET conference and an anonymous referee for many valuable comments. Any remaining inadequacies that remain are our own responsibility.

of the survey expectations, cointegration analysis showed that the rationality restrictions are met by the equilibrium conditions between real and expected inflation. Despite other findings in the literature the results indicate that the predictive performance of vector-error-correction or autoregressive distributed lag models is superior to that of autoprojective models.

1 Introduction

Since 1981, the Ifo Institute for Economic Research in Munich has been conducting the worldwide Economic Survey International (ESI) amongst about 450 to 500 managers and economists in more than 70 countries.

Four times a year, questionnaires are sent to subsidiaries of transnational corporations, to local companies and to economic institutions whose representatives assess the present and prospective economic situation in their country[1] and return the questionnaire to Ifo. The methodology and evaluation technique of ESI is described in section 2.

After 18 years the ESI time series still are not sufficiently long for a comprehensive and indisputable time series analysis, but for a basic evaluation of the explanatory and predictive power of the survey by analysing the survey results with regard to their ability to track the development of a reference variable.[2] For this paper the inflation rates of Germany, the United States and Japan have been chosen to thoroughly investigate the performance of ESI data and to examine the relationship of the survey results and the quantitative series. The results of the analysis are presented in section 3.

2 Methodology and Evaluation Technique of the Economic Survey International (ESI)

ESI significantly differs from Ifo's monthly national business survey. In contrast to the business survey that is designed to reflect the economic developments of sectors, product groups and companies in Germany, ESI represents the economic situation of entire economies worldwide. It is,

---

1 Both foreign and native participants assess the situation for the relevant country.

2 In an earlier paper it has already been proved that ESI time series contribute to explaining and forecasting economic developments, see Brand/Pouquet (1995). However, a time series analysis of ESI series has not yet been done.

therefore, of great importance to find competent economic experts to participate in the survey. Since ESI is a survey among outstanding experts in the economic field, the question of representativeness in the conventional sense does not arise.

Quarterly[3] about 450 to 500 experts of transnational and national organisations in more than 70 countries are polled to receive up-to-date assessments of the economic situation prevailing around the world.

The questionnaire sent to the participants consists of 10 standard questions which are supplemented by regular questions and occasional questions of special interest.[4]

The standard questions are entirely qualitative and cover the following fields:

- Present and future economic situation including assessments on capital expenditure and private consumption
- Expected trade performance including exports, imports, and trade balance
- Expected inflation rate
- Expected short- and long-term interest rates
- Assessment of leading reserve currencies' values in relation to the relevant national currency
- Assessment of the value of the US-dollar in relation to the relevant national currency
- Expected level of domestic share prices
- Assessment of most important economic problems faced by the relevant country
- Assessment of the climate for direct foreign investments in the relevant country

In addition to the standard questions, regular supplementary questions are asked depending on the quarter surveyed:

- Expected economic-policy measures, asked in January and July
- Expected GDP growth for the current year, asked in April
- Expected GDP growth for the next three to five years, asked in October

Expectational questions always refer to a forecasting period of six months.

---

[3] The survey is conducted in January, April, July, and October. Up to and including 1987, the survey was conducted three times a year in February, July, and October.

[4] For example, questions concerning the introduction of the euro and the impact of the Asian crisis.

The usual scale used for the quarterly ESI report differs from the scale of Ifo's national monthly business survey. The answering scheme is threefold:

- The value of 1 is assigned to the replies 'bad', 'worse', 'lower' or 'deterioration'.
- The value of 5 is assigned to the answers 'satisfactory', 'about the same' or 'no change'.
- Finally, the value of 9 is assigned to the outcomes 'good', 'better', 'higher' or 'improvement'.

The individual replies graded in the described way are then combined to obtain the overall results for every country. The aggregated country result thus varies from 1 to 9.[5] Grades within the range of 5 to 9 indicate that positive answers prevail or that the majority of participants expects trends to increase. Grades within the range of 1 to 5 reveal predominantly negative assessments or expectations of decreasing trends. A result of 5 stands for indifferent answers, on average.

3 Analysis of the Explanatory and Forecasting Ability of ESI-Data

This paper examines whether the incorporation of ESI data in econometric models contributes to a significant improvement of the analysis and the forecast of economic developments. We start with an intensive data preprocessing, that is the statistical comparison of the real data (*rd*) and different survey data (*sd*) series in order to identify the *sd* series with the closest fit to the *rd* series. In the following section the time series properties of the *rd* and the selected *sd* series are investigated for all countries.

Since expectation formation plays an important role in theoretical and empirical economic modelling, we test the survey data for rationality, given that the corresponding *rd* and *sd* series are of the same order of integration.

Then cointegration tests are conducted in order to combine both short-run and long-run relationships between *rd* and *sd* series, which is important in the light of predicting the long-run behaviour and short run dynamics of the underlying economic series.

Finally, depending on the results of the cointegration analysis, vector-error-correction (VEC) and autoregressive distributed lag (ADL) models are installed to test the forecasting accuracy against the benchmark of autoprojective (AR) models.

[5] This interval is equivalent to the interval (-100, +100) in the Ifo Business Survey.

3.1 Data Preprocessing

We examine the problem of evaluating the analytical and projective value of survey data[6] on inflation. The subject of our considerations are quarterly times series on inflation rates for Germany, the United States and Japan between 1985 and 1998 ($T = 56$), both real[7] and survey data (*rd* and *sd*). The problem of finding the best method for processing qualitative survey data in order to get a good fit to reference time series is often addressed in the literature (see for example Öller, 1990). To eliminate the problem of badly scaled survey data, extensive research on the analysis of qualitative survey answers was done. Results show that there is no straightforward procedure of generating time series from survey data. We follow an approach proposed by Teräsvirta (1986) that uses the relative shares of the answers to the miscellaneous survey questions as independent time series and compare this disaggregated series with the usual ESI (weighted linear combination) series.

Table 28.1 - Correlations of Inflation Series

data sets	*Germany*	*United States*	*Japan*
ESI	−0.156	+0.504	+0.607
H	+0.221	+0.505	+0.626
S	−0.250	−0.459	−0.460
L	−0.058	−0.111	−0.412
ESI^s	+0.296	**+0.629***	**+0.756***
H^s	**+0.371**	+0.607*	+0.737*
S^s	−0.393	−0.585	−0.528
L^s	−0.177	−0.004	−0.499

* - rd series have been smoothed with an unweighted moving average technique.
^{s} - smoothed.

6 The transformation into quarterly data until 1988 was done analogously to Brand/Pouquet (1995), p. 3.

7 Sources: Germany: Quarterly consumer price index for all households, all items, Deutsche Bundesbank, Monthly Report; USA: Quarterly consumer price index, all items (wage earners), OECD Statistics, monthly Main Economic Indicators; Japan: Quarterly consumer price index, all items including imputed rent, OECD Statistics, monthly Main Economic Indicators.

In a first step we compare this disaggregated series and the usual ESI series with the real time series for all three countries by means of simple correlations in order to chose one survey series (for each country) for further analysis. The results are summarised in table 28.1.

The data sets are defined in the following manner:

ESI: Economic Survey International (weighted answers with weights 1 for *lower*, 5 for *about the same* and 9 for *higher*).

- *H*: share of respondents voting for *higher.*
- *S*: share of respondents voting for *about the same.*
- *L*: share of respondents voting for *lower.*
- *Germany: rd* for Germany.
- *United States: rd* for the United States.
- *Japan: rd* for Japan.

Since diagnostic instruments such as auto correlation functions (ACF) are based on the theory of stationary processes and the considered series are non stationary (see section 3.2), we base our series selection procedure on levels.[8] We consequently do not present autocorrelations or spectral densities.[9] Hence we simply and solely rely on sample correlations and visual diagnostics.

For unsmoothed inflation data we obtain the highest correlations between *sd* and *rd* for the *H* series uniformly for all countries, with correlations between 0.221 and 0.626. While the correlations for *ESI* data (United States and Japan) are only insignificantly smaller, the results change for seasonally adjusted series. The correlations are higher now (up to 0.756), but now *ESI* data performs better than the *H* series - except for Germany.

Moreover one should notice the strikingly higher correlations for the U.S. and Japanese data. Figures 28.1–28.3 show the graphs of the *rd* and the chosen *sd* series on inflation for all three countries. In summary one has to notice that especially for Germany the in-sample-correlations are quite low.[10] But when we took a closer look at the plot of the *rd* and *sd* series, we

---

8 Note that the ACF died out with medium pace.

9 See for example Öller (1990) who compares filtered (differences, seasonal differences and combinations) rd series with different sd series by means of autocorrelation functions, spectral densities and coherence functions.

10 Two major events responsible for the low in-sample-correlation for Germany could be detected: First, at the end of 1986, the price dampening effects of low commodity prices and the decline of the dollar phased-out earlier than generally expected. Second, the renewed increase in consumer prices at the end of 1991 due to significant rent raises and increases in fees for municipal services was unexpected.

could see a weakness for predicting turning points and a sometimes slow adjustment process. Splitting up the sample it becomes obvious that there are quite high correlations for different partial samples. Here, one major disadvantage of correlations becomes evident. Namely that correlations as selection criteria are only a good choice for short-term forecasting.

Beside that, due to the weak adjustment process in survey expectations, we do not use univariate distributed lag (DL) forecasting models. although this models would allow for longer ex ante forecasting periods. But, when modelling actual (and future inflation) it seems more appropriate to us, to incorporate both lagged real and expected inflation and eventually an adjustment process by use of error-correction models (ECM) in the context of autoregressive DL models.

As a result of our data preprocessing we choose the following *sd*[11] series:

- H^s for Germany,
- ESI^s for the United States and Japan.

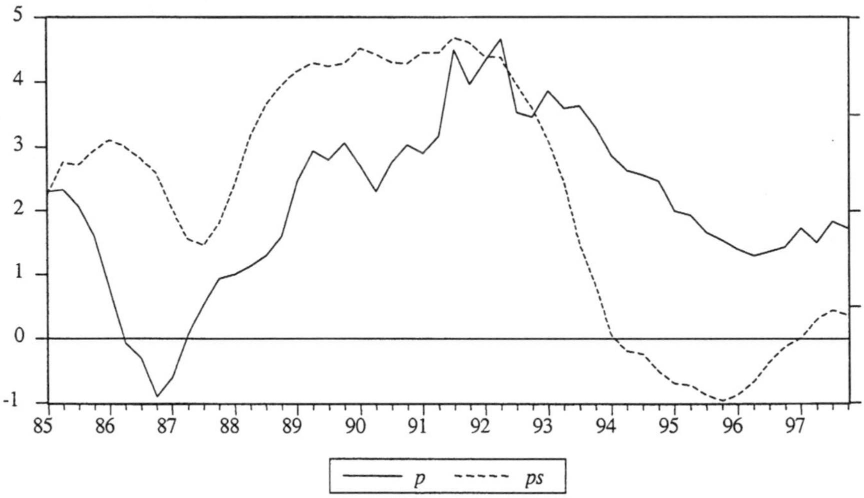

Figure 28.1 - Actual Inflation and ESI Expectations 1985:1 1997:4, Germany

[11] In the following the *sd* series are denoted by *ps*.

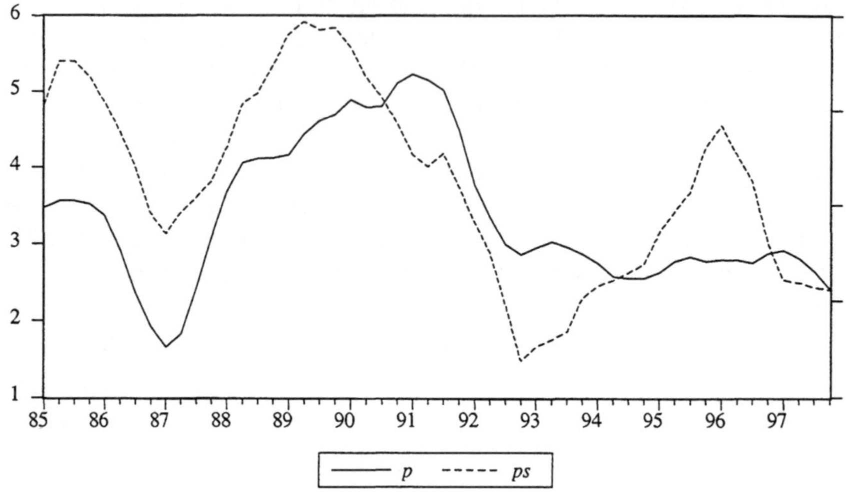

Figure 28.2 - Actual Inflation and ESI Expectations 1985:1 1997:4, USA

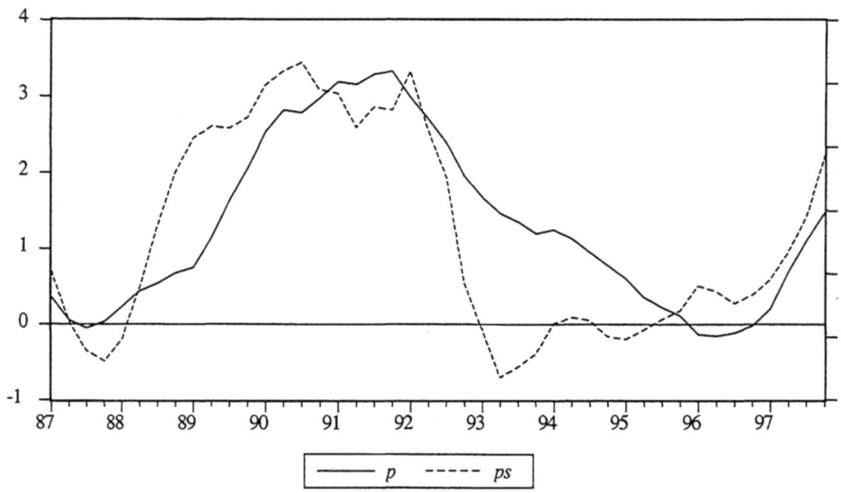

Figure 28.3 - Actual inflation and ESI Expectations 1985:1 1997:4, Japan

3.2 Investigating the Time Series Properties

Provided that the survey series were seasonally adjusted during the data preprocessing step and that there is no visible seasonal pattern in the inflation series, augmented Dickey-Fuller tests (ADF)[12] are conducted. In order to avoid the problems of Dickey-Fuller tests in the presence of I(2)-processes, AR(2)-models are estimated before testing for nonstationarity as proposed in Franses (1998, p. 87). Note that bounded series such as the *sd* series generally cannot have a unit root and that there are only asymptotically spurious results when regressing nonstationary variables.

Since we could neither detect a possible deterministic (time invariant) trend nor signs for a drift in the data, they are not included in any of the stationarity test equations.[13] Apart from that it seems more acceptable to have a weaker power of the tests than to lose control over the type I error, especially in the light of existing small-sample problems. Nevertheless it has to be said that 'the proper handling of deterministic trends is a vital prerequisite for dealing with unit roots',[14] but ''proper handling' of deterministic trend(s) is an impossible task' and 'to a humble *macroeconomist* it would seem that an edifice of asymptotic theory that depends crucially on *unknowable* quantities must be pretty useless in practice'.[15]

Often neglected in the literature, the number of lags included in the ADF-test equation is of great importance. Having too few augmentations, the null hypothesis can be rejected too often, whilst too many augmentations lead to the opposite effect[16] and is also contraproductive in the sense of parsimonious specification. So the augmentation choice is supported by Lagrange Multiplier tests (LM) for serial correlation, Bera-Jarque tests (BJ) for normality and White heteroskedasticity tests.[17]

The lag length is chosen in the sense of general to specific modelling, providing that the residuals of the test equation are white noise. During the

---

[12] The critical values are taken out of Charemza/Deadman (1997), p. 281-83.

[13] It is well known that the null hypotheses of DF tests do not imply restrictions on the coefficients of included deterministic trend components, and it is easily seen that including deterministic components in the test equations would constitute a model that nests both trend and difference stationarity. Thus, as an immediate consequence of our a priori exclusion of trend stationarity, neither drift nor trend components are included in the DF test equations.

[14] See Campbell/Perron (1991).

[15] See Cochrane (1991).

[16] See Charemza/Deadman (1997), p. 105, Maddala (1992), p. 584.

[17] Due to the small sample size no cross terms are included.

augmentation choice the AIC (Akaike Information Criterion) statistics are taken into account. In view of the low small sample power of the ADF test, controversal conclusions[18] are taken in favour of a parsimonious specification.

Time series of inflation p

Pre-estimation of AR(2) models for German and United States data showed no signs of I(2)-behaviour, i.e. coefficients which are not significantly different from (2, -1). The standard ADF test equation is given by

$$\Delta p_t = \delta p_{t-1} + \sum_{i=1}^{k} \delta_i \Delta p_{t-i} + \varepsilon_t \tag{1}$$

where ε_t is white noise. Providing white noise properties for ε_t, the appropriate lag length is $k = 3$ for Germany and $k = 6$ for the United States.

Since we cannot reject the null hypothesis $\delta = 0$ for both German and U.S. data, the next step consists of processing the first differences Δp and repeating the ADF test. The ADF equation is given by

$$\Delta\Delta p_t = \delta \Delta p_{t-1} + \sum_{i=1}^{l} \delta_i \Delta\Delta p_{t-i} + \varepsilon_t \tag{2}$$

where ε_t is white noise. White noise tests indicate an appropriate lag length of $l = 4$ for Germany and $l = 1$ for the United States. Now the t-values of Δp_{t-1} are -3.853 and -3.790, which is significantly negative respecting the critical values (see table 28.3 for a summary of the integration tests). Hence we can reject the null hypothesis and conclude that $p_t \sim$ I(1) for both countries.

We have taken a closer look at the Japanese data and report the results of the estimation of an AR(2) model for Japanese inflation (with standard errors in brackets),

$$\begin{aligned} p_t = 0.0803 + {} & \underset{(0.0755)}{1.8206}\, p_{t-1} - \underset{(0.0750)}{0.8762}\, p_{t-2} \end{aligned}$$

where the value of 2 is included in the 99% confidence interval ([1.6402, 2.0010] for 1.8206 and -1 is included in the 95% interval ([-1.0015, -

[18] In the sense of ambiguous results for different augmentation sizes.

0.7509]) for -0.8762. Note that the estimated residuals are white noise.[19] Hence we would suspect Japanese inflation to be I(2). But we have to consider both the possibly spurious results from the AR(2)-equation and the small sample problems concerning the significance level. As we would obviously commit a large type II error, we should not stick to a 1% or a 5% significance level here. Since we are quite unsure now if the Japanese data are I(1) or I(2), we start by testing I(2) against the alternative I(1). If the underlying process is I(2), we know from the literature that the critical values of the ADF test are no longer valid.

Now we follow an approach proposed by Dickey/Pantula (1987) (DP test) which is described as testing downwards starting with the highest sensible order of integration. Thus our initial test equation in conducting this test is given by

$$\Delta\Delta p_t = \lambda_1 \Delta p_{t-1} + \lambda_2 p_{t-2} + \omega_t, \tag{3}$$

considering that

$$\lambda_1 = \rho_1 \rho_2 - 1,\ \lambda_2 = -(1-\rho_1)(1-\rho_2)$$

is derived from the factorised lag polynomial constituting the underlying AR(2) process given by

$$(1-\rho_1 L)(1-\rho_2 L)p_t = \omega_t.$$

Hence our null hypothesis is $H_0 : \lambda_1 = \lambda_2 = 0$ which means that $p_t \sim$ I(2). Our alternative hypothesis is $H_1 : \lambda_1 < 0, \lambda_2 = 0$ which means that our lag polynomial has one root on and one root outside the unit circle, i.e. $p_t \sim$ I(1).[20] As $\lambda_2 = 0$ is valid for both hypotheses and we have to take care of ω_t to be white noise, our test equation is

$$\Delta\Delta p_t = \lambda_1 \Delta p_{t-1} + \sum_{i=1}^{k} \beta_i \Delta\Delta p_{t-i} + \omega_t. \tag{4}$$

---

[19] Of course a simultaneous confidence interval would be more useful and the results may be biased due to the nonstationarity of inflation, but the results should be interpreted only in an indicatory sense.

[20] See Charemza/Deadman (1997), pp. 111-112.

White noise tests indicate $k = 1$ and the *t*-value of -1.9098 means that our type I error lies between 5 and 10% (see table 28.3). Hence we decide to reject the null and continue with testing the null hypothesis of I(1) $H_0 : \lambda_1 < 0, \lambda_2 = 0$ against the alternative I(0)-hypothesis $H_1 : \lambda_1 < 0, \lambda_2 < 0$. Estimating equation (3),[21] we do not reject the null hypothesis since the *t*-value for λ_2 (-1.601198) is not significantly negative (see table 28.3). Thus we conclude now that Japanese inflation is I(1).[22]

Table 28.2 - Test Statistics ADF Test For p (and Δp)

	ADF test statistic			lower	upper
Germany	-0.9975	(-3.8527)	1% C.V.	-2.66	-2.55
USA	-0.3351	(-3.7903)	5% C.V.	-1.99	-1.91
			10% C.V.	-1.65	-1.58

C.V.=Critical Value

Table 28.3 - Test Statistics DP Test For p (and Δp)

	DP test statistic		lower	upper
Japan	-1.9098 (-1.6012)	1% C.V.	-2.66	-2.55
		5% C.V.	-1.99	-1.91
		10% C.V.	-1.65	-1.58

Time series of survey data on inflation ps

Now we test the *sd* series on inflation for stationarity. Again AR(2)-models have been estimated previously but gave no hint at integration of order two. Hence we continue with stationarity tests of the DF-type. White noise tests indicate an appropriate lag length of $k = 1$ for Germany and the United States and $k = 4$ for Japan. Ending up with a *t*-value well above the critical values (see table 28.4) we could not reject the null for all countries and consequently test the first differences Δp for nonstationarity. White noise

[21] Note that augmentation terms are included if necessary.

[22] Note that in contrast to our results, Grier/Perry (1998) recently found no unit roots in *monthly* inflation series from 1948 to 1993 for Germany, the United States and Japan. Their results indicated rejection of the null hypothesis at the 0.01 level for all three countries. They report that their augmented Dickey-Fuller test results which are not sensitive to the augmentation choice are supported by Phillips-Perron-tests.

tests indicate an appropriate lag length of $l = 3$[23] for Germany, $l = 0$ for the United States and $l = 7$ for Japan. The test statistics -2.978, -3.365 and -3.018 are significantly negative at the 0.01 level (see table 28.4). Relying on this results we assume that *ps* is I(1) for Germany, the United States and Japan.

Table 28.4 - Test Statistics ADF Test for ps (and Δps)

	ADF test statistic				lower	upper
Germany	-1.4397	(-2.9779)	1%	C.V.	-2.66	-2.55
USA	-1.0591	(-3.3650)	5%	C.V.	-1.99	-1.91
Japan	-0.1571	(-3.0183)	10%	C.V.	-1.65	-1.58

3.3 Classical Testing of Rationality of ESI-data

The purpose of this section is to test whether the ESI data for Germany, United States and Japan are rational. Taking a glance at the literature the elucidation of this question seems to be an important topic in investigating the practicability of survey data for the empirical modelling of macroeconomic hypotheses. There is a large theoretical and empirical body of literature concerning rational expectations and equally complex are the empirical results. So this paper will focus only on the basic ideas of the rational expectations hypothesis in Muthian sense as formulated for example in Pesaran (1987, p. 21-31), Maddala (1992, p. 434-36 and 1991, p. 323-26). Note that in our case rejection of rationality does not imply that the individual expectations are all irrational since we are testing for rationality of aggregated expectations.

The starting point is to test the *unbiasedness* of the expectations with the well known equation

$$p_t = \alpha + \beta ps_t + \zeta_t, \tag{5}$$

[23] The results for both the LM and the ADF test are ambiguous. The hypothesis of no serial correlation cannot be rejected for lag length 1 to 4, but since the hypothesis of a unit root can be rejected only for lag length 2 (on 5% level) and for lag length 3 (on 1% level), the Akaike and Schwarz criterion lead to the choice of three augmentation terms.

where the expected inflation is approximated by the survey data on inflation[24] ps_t and ζ_t is supposed to be white noise. The hypothesis is

$$H_{0,u} : E(\zeta_t | ps_t) = 0. \tag{6}$$

Considering the results of section 2 we know that OLS estimation of this equation would probably end up in spurious results since both series are nonstationary. But we are interested in the the long run relation in this case, so estimating equation (5) in first differences would not be consistent with theory. Hence in our opinion it does not make sense to correct for autocorrelation or heteroskedasticity here,[25] since the assumptions for the Wald test for parameter restrictions are not met anyway for equation (5). Thus we should proceed more pragmatically here.

The next step is to prove the *weak efficiency* of the survey data, i.e. to show that ζ_t is serially uncorrelated. Thus the corresponding hypothesis is

$$H_{0,e} : E(\zeta_t, \zeta_{t-j}) = 0, \forall j \geq 1. \tag{7}$$

To test this hypothesis we can use the LM test for serial correlation. If ζ_t exhibits serial correlation, this means that there was not an efficient learning process using the experience from former forecast errors for forming future expectations.

Note that strong efficiency would imply that there is no correlation between the forecast error and all (information) variables available to the (aggregated) forecasters.

Lastly we test the *orthogonality* of the survey data, i.e. that the conditional expectations of ζ_t given (p_{t-j}) and (ps_{t-j}) are equally zero $\forall j \geq 1$. Hence we test the hypothesis

$$H_{0,o} : E(\zeta_t | p_{t-j}) = E(\zeta_t | ps_{t-j}) = 0. \tag{8}$$

---

24 In order to be consistent with the theoretical values of α and β, the survey data time series on inflation was adjusted by the proportion between its mean value and the mean value of the real inflation series.

25 See for example Reckwerth (1997), p. 21, who applies the Newey-West procedure for estimating equation (5).

The results of the OLS estimation of equation (5) for all three countries (see table 28.5) and a Wald test of parameter restrictions ($\alpha = 0$ and $\beta = 1$) (see table 28.6) indicate a rejection of the unbiasedness hypothesis and hence of rationality for Germany and Japan. Additionally there is obviously severe autocorrelation present for all three countries and the already announced spurious regression problem. Hence further tests on efficiency and orthogonality could be neglected. Notice that these results do not only depend on the chosen variable but first of all on the selected sample.[26] This means both that evidence for rationality of a series must not last in time and that one has to be cautious in comparing different results.

Table 28.5 - Results of the Static Regression of p on ps (eq.(5)) (Standard Errors in Brackets)

	Germany	USA	Japan
α	1.3913 (0.3277)	-1.4150 (0.8770)	-2.2023 (0.4326)
β	0.3467 (0.1320)	1.4498 (0.2638)	2.6324 (0.3120)
R^2	0.1213	0.3765	0.5875
DW	0.1255	0.1020	0.1222

Table 28.6 - Wald Test for Parameter Restrictions

	Germany	USA	Japan
	Null hypothesis: $\alpha = 0, \beta = 1$		
F-statistic	12.2554	1.6767	10.9424
Proba-bility	0.0000	0.1973	0.0002
Chi-square	24.5107	3.3535	21.8847
Proba-bility	0.0000	0.1870	0.0000

[26] We performed some experiments in this stage, where for example estimation of (5) for German data from 1991:1 to 1997:4 led to more theory-consistent estimators, higher R^2, lower autocorrelation and not rejecting the null of ($\alpha = 0$ and $\beta = 1$).

For the United States we cannot reject the hypothesis of ($\alpha = 0$ and $\beta = 1$) whereas the residuals suffer from severe autocorrelation and consequently *ps* is inefficient. To complete our test we examine orthogonality with the following two regressions

$$\hat{\zeta}_t = \phi_0 + \sum_{j=1}^{p} \phi_j p_{t-j} + \upsilon_{1,t} \tag{9}$$

and

$$\hat{\zeta}_t = \varphi_0 + \sum_{j=1}^{q} \varphi_j ps_{t-j} + \upsilon_{2,t}, \tag{10}$$

where $\hat{\zeta}_t$ are the estimated residuals from equation 11 and $\upsilon_{1,t}$ and $\upsilon_{2,t}$ are white noise error terms. The expected results are that we can reject the null hypotheses of orthogonality ($\phi_i = \varphi_j = 0\ \forall i,j$), i.e. there are some ϕ_i and φ_j significantly different from zero.

We can conclude that our *sd* series are not rational. But, as mentioned by Maddala (1991), we should bear in mind that the '... failure of the tests for rationality does not mean that survey data are not useful' and 'especially with price expectations data ... estimation methods (may) account for the rejection of the rationality hypothesis'. For this reason we will perform further rationality tests in the framework of cointegration analysis in the next section.

3.4 *Cointegration Analysis*

Regarding the data on inflation we have two endogenous variables, each of which is first-order integrated. Consequently there can be either one or no cointegrating vector. If there is none, the standard time series analysis such as AR, VAR (vector autoregressive)[27] or ADL (autoregressive distributed lag) applies to the first differences of the data. Because there are two separate integrated elements driving the series, levels of the series do not appear in either the VAR or the ADL model. If there is one cointegrating equation, the model will need an error correction term involving levels of

[27] Note that we do not think that there is a straightforward implementation of MA (moving average) terms.

the series, and this term will appear on the right-hand side of the model equation (or both equations in the VAR case), which otherwise will be in first differences. The cointegration equation (if existing) can be determined by either the Engle-Granger two-step or the Johansen Maximum Likelihood procedure.[28] In the case that ADF tests showed that both series are integrated, but the Johansen tests show that the cointegrating rank is two, there is a contradiction. Some specification error (or the small-sample-weakness of unit-root-tests) might account for this contradiction.

Table 28.7 - Results of the Engle-Granger procedure

ADF cointegration test statistic[a,b]				**lower**	**upper**
Germany	-1.6024 (df = 47)	1%	C.V.	-5.29	-4.79
		5%	C.V.	-3.96	-3.85
		10%	C.V.	-3.40	-3.32
USA	-1.8071 (df = 49)	1%	C.V.	-5.35	-4.86
		5%	C.V.	-3.98	-3.87
		10%	C.V.	-3.41	-3.33
Japan	-1.9674 (df = 50)	1%	C.V.	-5.35	-4.86
		5%	C.V.	-3.98	-3.87
		10%	C.V.	-3.41	-3.33

[a] For critical values see Charemza/Deadman (1997), p. 284-289 interpolated.
[b] Degrees of freedom vary due to the augmentation choice.

For all three countries, *p* and *ps* seem to be integrated of the same order, exactly of order one. So there is the possibility of a linear combination of both variables to be stationary or formally *p* and *ps* are cointegrated of order (1, 1). As we have estimated the possible long-run relationships between *p* and *ps* in the previous section (see table 28.5), we now test the corresponding unrestricted (conditional) residuals for stationarity with the result that they are not stationary, neither for German nor for U.S. nor for

[28] See Johansen S. (1995).

Japanese data (see table 28.7). This means that the findings of equation (5) (table 28.5) do not represent a long run relation between inflation and expected inflation.

Considering the small sample weaknesses of the cointegration tests we alternatively use the Johansen procedure to estimate – if existing and unequivocal – the cointegrating vector and examine whether the normalised cointegrating vector is (1, -1).

Table 28.8 - Results for Johansen Cointegration Tests

		Germany		USA		Japan	
0.10		10.47	2.86				
0.05		12.53	3.84				
0.01		16.31	6.51				
H_0		none	at most 1	none	at most 1	none	at most 1
eigen-values	k=2	4.58	1.70	6.75	0.58	**17.03*****	**0.08**
	k=3	9.16	2.63	3.44	0.38	23.95***	0.13
	k=4	10.06	4.36**	3.05	0.33	10.21	0.10
	k=5	11.41*	4.18**	11.19*	0.72	11.71	0.18
	k=6	12.08*	2.46	**12.87****	**0.66**	19.33***	0.36
	k=7	24.02***	2.92*	4.80	0.46	20.20***	0.43
	k=8	**23.28*****	**1.82**	3.32	0.56	21.11***	0.97
normalized ci-vectors (std. errors)		k=8 **(1, -1.3263)** (0.1512)		k=6 **(1, -1.0500)** (0.0453)		k=2 **(1, -1.0235)** (0.1163)	

*, ** and *** denote significance at the 0.10, 0.05 and 0.01 level, respectively.

We processed the Johansen procedure for k ($k = 2, \ldots, 8$) difference terms and found ambiguous results for different values of k (for the results see table 28.8). But we found unequivocal cointegration relations for all three countries where the expected value of (1, -1) for the normalised cointegrating vector is exactly met for US and Japanese data, we conclude cointegration between *p* and *ps*.

3.5 Forecasting

We now specify and estimate VEC and ADL models for all three countries for 1985:1 to 1997:4 and then perform one-step forecasts for 1998:1 to 1998:4. We use the lag ordering proposed by the Johansen test for the VEC models and start our systematic specification search for the ADL model with eight lags. This may occur as a too intensive specification but the predictive power of the estimated models will shed light on the problem of possibly spurious relationships. According to Teräsvirta (1986) our estimated models should outperform benchmark autoprojective (AR) models[29] 'in order to be deemed useful'.

Table 28.9 - Results of One-Step Forecasts

	1998:1		**1998:2**		**1998:3**		**1998:4**	
	RMSE	MAPE	RMSE	MAPE	RMSE	MAPE	RMSE	MAPE
Germany								
VEC	0.3116	0.2066	0.2545	**0.1403**	**0.2840**	**0.2220**	**0.3057**	0.3065
ADL	**0.2744**	**0.1819**	**0.2317**	0.1481	0.3284	0.2807	0.3123	**0.3048**
AR	0.5222	0.3462	0.4264	0.2312	0.5081	0.4010	0.4717	0.4165
USA								
VEC	0.1851	0.0647	0.1993	0.0865	0.1748	0.0738	0.1784	0.0869
ADL	**0.0895**	**0.0313**	**0.1234**	0.0541	**0.1076**	**0.0446**	**0.1085**	**0.0519**
AR	0.1406	0.0492	0.1262	**0.0503**	0.1184	0.0522	0.1316	0.0671
Japan								
VEC	**0.0180**	**0.0073**	0.1685	**0.0620**	0.3148	**0.1399**	**0.2915**	**0.2418**
ADL	0.0938	0.0378	0.1823	0.0815	0.2768	0.1534	0.3486	0.3224
AR	0.0786	0.0317	**0.1657**	0.0731	**0.2547**	0.1402	0.3128	0.2865

[29] Here again we started our specification search with a maximum lag length of 8.

In a next step we calculated root mean square errors (RMSE) and mean absolute percentage errors (MAPE) in order to compare the perfomance of our rivaling models. The results, summarized in table 28.9, indicate a clear superiority of VEC and ADL models to the benchmark AR models. Notice that all models have a common tendency to overestimate future inflation.

4 Conclusions

We found that there is no straightforward way of transforming survey information, so we should let the data do the talking. For the United States and Japan the weighted complete survey information as represented in the ESI series contains more information on current inflation than any of the disaggregated series, whereas the shares of respondents voting for higher give the best explanation for German data.

All real and survey series under considerations are found to be I(1)-processes. Hence, as expected and often confirmed in practice, the classical tests for rationality fail or are misspecified. Nevertheless implementing the rationality restriction we found cointegration, and additionally the cointegration relations estimated with the Johansen procedure resulted in theory consistent estimators. These findings support the conclusion of Maddala (1991) that classical testing for rationality may account for rejection of rationality especially with price expectations data.

The forecasting results indicate a nearly unequivocal superiority of VEC models for Japan, VEC and ADL models for Germany and ADL models for the United States.

This means that models which incorporate survey information clearly dominate autoprojective models, i.e. the survey respondents have relevant information about future inflation.

References

Brand D. and L. Pouquet (1995), 'The Explanatory and Forecasting Power of the Economic Survey International', *CIRET studies* 49.

Campbell J.Y. and P. Perron (1991), 'Pitfalls and Opportunities: What Macroeconomists Should Know about Unit Roots', in: Blanchard O.J. and S. Fisher (eds): *NBER Macroeconomics Annual*, pp. 141-201.

Charemza W.W. and D.F. Deadman (1997), *New Directions in Econometric Practice*. 2nd ed.

Cochrane J.H. (1991), 'Comment on Campbell and Perron', in: Blanchard O.J. and S. Fisher (eds): *NBER Macroeconomics Annual*, pp. 201-210.

Franses P.H. (1998), *Time series models for business and economic forecasting.*

Grier K.B., M.J. Perry (1998), 'On inflation and inflation uncertainty in the G7 countries', *Journal of International Money and Finance* 17, pp. 671-689.

Johansen S. (1995): *Likelihood-Based Inference in Cointegrated Vector Autoregressive Models.*

Maddala G.S. (1991), 'Survey Data on Expectations: What Have We Learnt?', in: Nerlove M. (ed), *Issues in Contemporary Economics*, Vol. 2, pp. 319-344.

Maddala G.S. (1992): *Introduction to Econometrics*. 2nd ed.

Öller L.-E. (1990), 'Forecasting the business cycle using survey data', *International Journal of Forecasting 6*, pp. 453-461.

Pesaran M.H. (1987), *The Limits to Rational Expectations.*

Reckwerth J. (1997), *Der Zusammenhang zwischen Inflation und Output unter besonderer Berücksichtigung der Inflationserwartungen*, Diskussionspapier 5/97, Volkswirtschaftliche Forschungsgruppe der Deutschen Bundesbank.

Teräsvirta T. (1986), 'Model selection using business survey data', *International Journal of Forecasting* 2, pp. 191-200.

29 The Usefulness of Ifo Business Survey Results for Forecasting the German Share Price Index

GERNOT NERB and KURT STOCK

1 Problem Description

The Ifo Business Survey - like many related business surveys in other countries - was primarily designed to signal changes in advance in non-monetary areas such as monthly industrial production, monthly new orders in manufacturing, monthly export trends, or quarterly GDP. A number of studies confirm that business surveys have an outstanding performance in meeting these tasks.[1] An illustration of the predictive power of indicators based on business survey results is given in Figure 29.1. The Ifo Business Survey has also been very successful in forecasting short-term changes in sales prices as is demonstrated in Figure 29.2.

With the proved forecasting track record in quantitative changes and price trends, it is tempting to use the survey results also for forecasting profit trends in the economy. In actual fact convincing proof has been provided that business survey results, especially assessments of the current business situation and on the six-month business outlook, are suitable for accurately recording and also forecasting profit trends in the economy (Figure 29.3).

---

[1] See e.g. Gernot Nerb, 'The predictive power of selected indicators at cyclical turning points', in: Business Cycle Indicators, edited by Karl Heinrich Oppenländer, 1997 Aldershot.

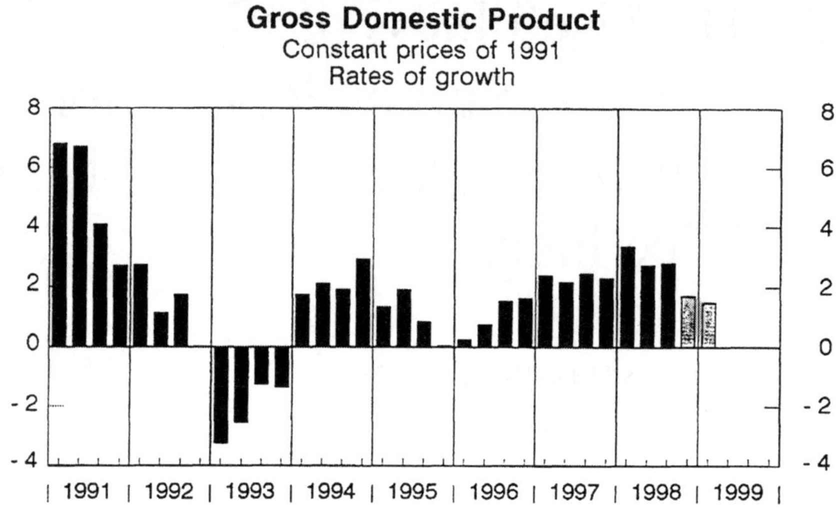

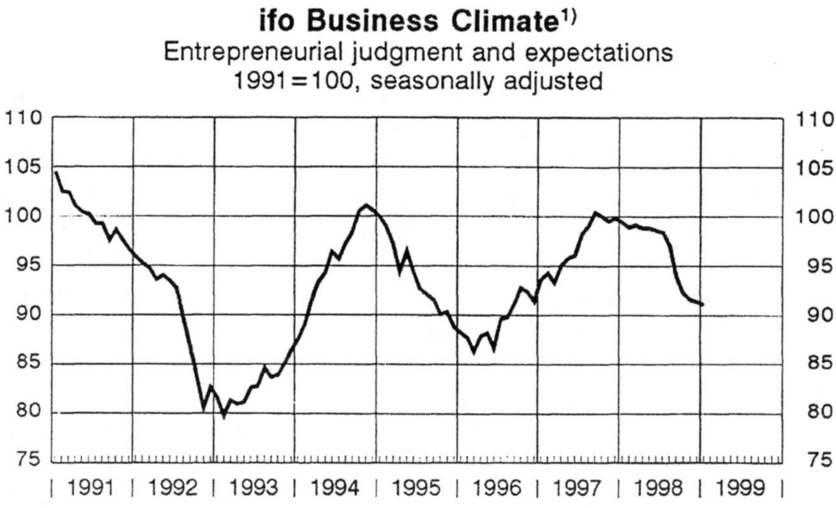

1) Trade and Industry.

Sources: Federal Statistical Office, Ifo Institute.

Figure 29.1 - Business Cycle Indicators (West Germany)

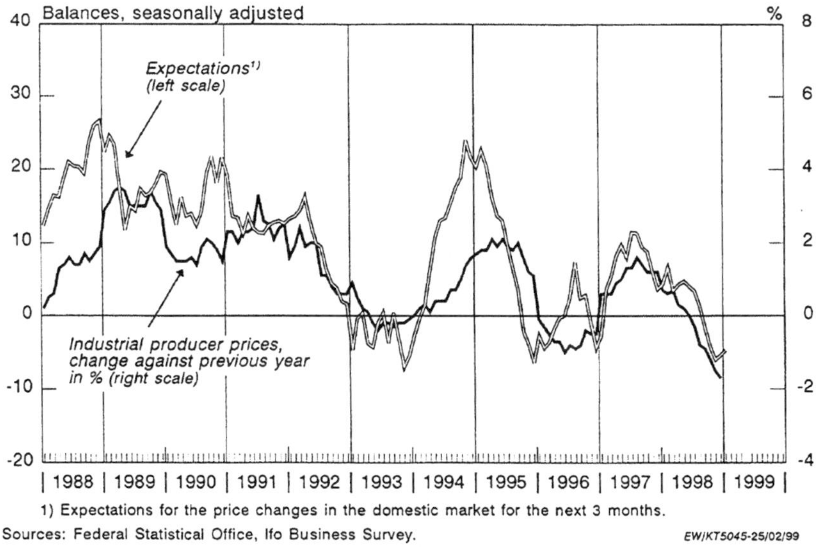

Figure 29.2 - Price Expectations and Price Development in Manufacturing Industry (West Germany)

From here it is only a short step to test the suitability of these data also for stock market analysis, since stock market trends primarily reflect the profit expectations of the investors.[2]

Of course, due to theoretical and practical considerations, even the best profit indicator alone is hardly able to explain and forecast stock market developments. Ultimately, for every stock market investor, in addition to the possible returns from a stock market investment, the relationship of stock market earnings and capital market interest rates is decisive: the higher the actual and/or expected yields from so-called safe haven investments, i.e. investments in the form of triple A (AAA) government bonds from countries like Germany or the United States, the higher the expected stock market return must be for an investment to be made here in light of the much higher risk of stock market investment. Thus, along with an indicator for overall corporate development, for stock market forecasts an indicator for the development of capital market interest rates - preferably

[2] See e.g. Th. F. Kempf, 'Measuring risk and expected return in portfolio management by using Ifo business survey data, in: Business Cycle Surveys with Special Reference to Pacific Basin Economies', papers presented at the 19th CIRET Conference Proceedings, Osaka 1989. Eds.: Oppenländer, Poser, 1990 Aldershot.

a leading one -must also be included. The clear inverse relationship of bond yields and share price development is shown in Figure 29.4

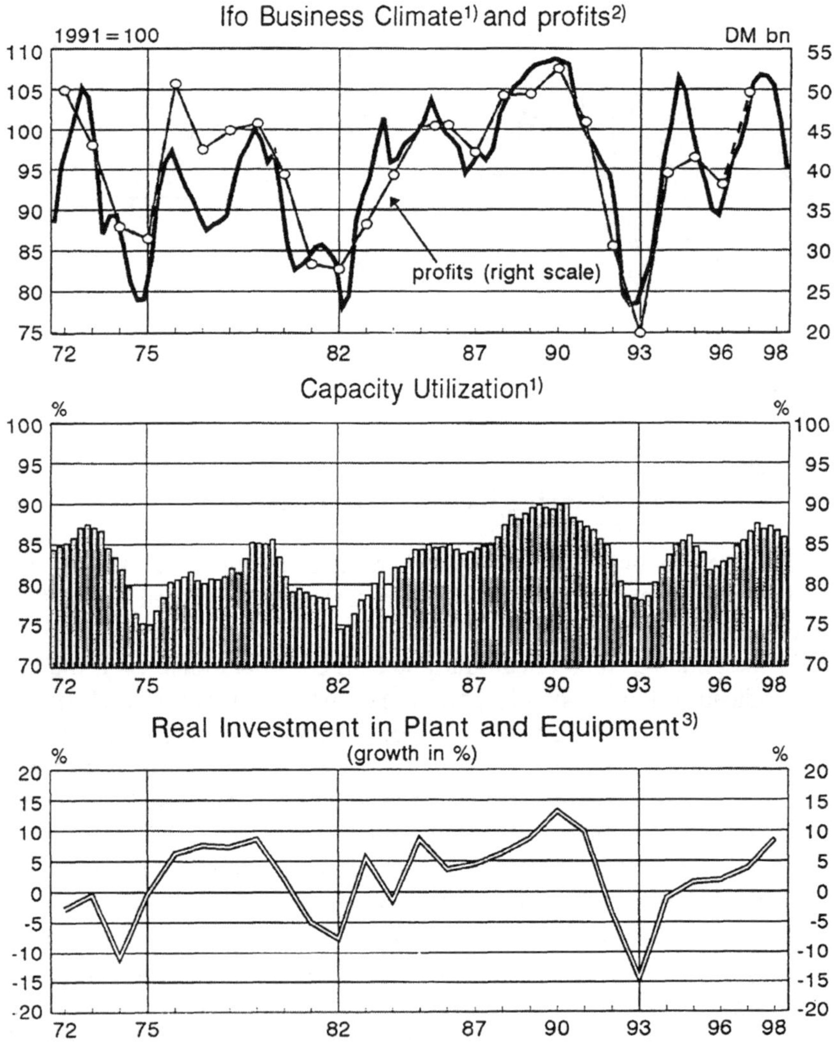

1) Manufacturing industry excl. food, beverages a. tobacco; West Germany
2) Annual net profit of western German enterprises, real.
3) Total investment in plant and equipment; after 1991 united Germany.

Sources: Federal Statistical Office, Deutsche Bundesbank, Ifo Institute. WL5007-15/02/99

Figure 29.3 - Determining Factors of Investments

The goal of this paper is not to forecast daily fluctuations of the share price index DAX but monthly changes. For this reason the study uses only the end of the month results for the DAX. Finally, the main goal of this attempt to forecast the stock market is to improve the lead time and the conciseness of this cyclical leading indicator. There is no doubt that a country's stock market index is one of its leading economic indicators. For this reason the stock market index is e.g. an important element in the indicator scheme of the OECD (Paris), the Conference Board in the US (in charge of the monthly publication of US leading indicators), and the EU Commission (monthly publications in Supplement B of the *European Economy*).

The appendix contains a survey of the applied methods.

2 Analysis and Forecast of the German Stock Exchange Index DAX

The target value is the German stock exchange index DAX is which the market rates of the 30 most important German corporations are compiled.

As was already stated, corporate profit expectations and capital market interest rates are important factors for stock market trends. Also the international capital market developments, especially the rate for ten-year US Treasury bonds, should influence stock market developments in Germany. Finally, due to the international dominance of the US stock market, German stock market rates are also closely connected with the Dow-Jones Index (see Figure 29.5). In line with these considerations, correlation diagrams were made between the DAX target values and all the potential influencing factors that have been mentioned, implying different lead-lag relations. The closest connection by far was between the Dow Jones and the DAX, with a three-month lead for the Dow Jones (table 29. 29.1). But also all the above-mentioned potential factors were statistically significant, with lead times, as a rule, of from two to six months.

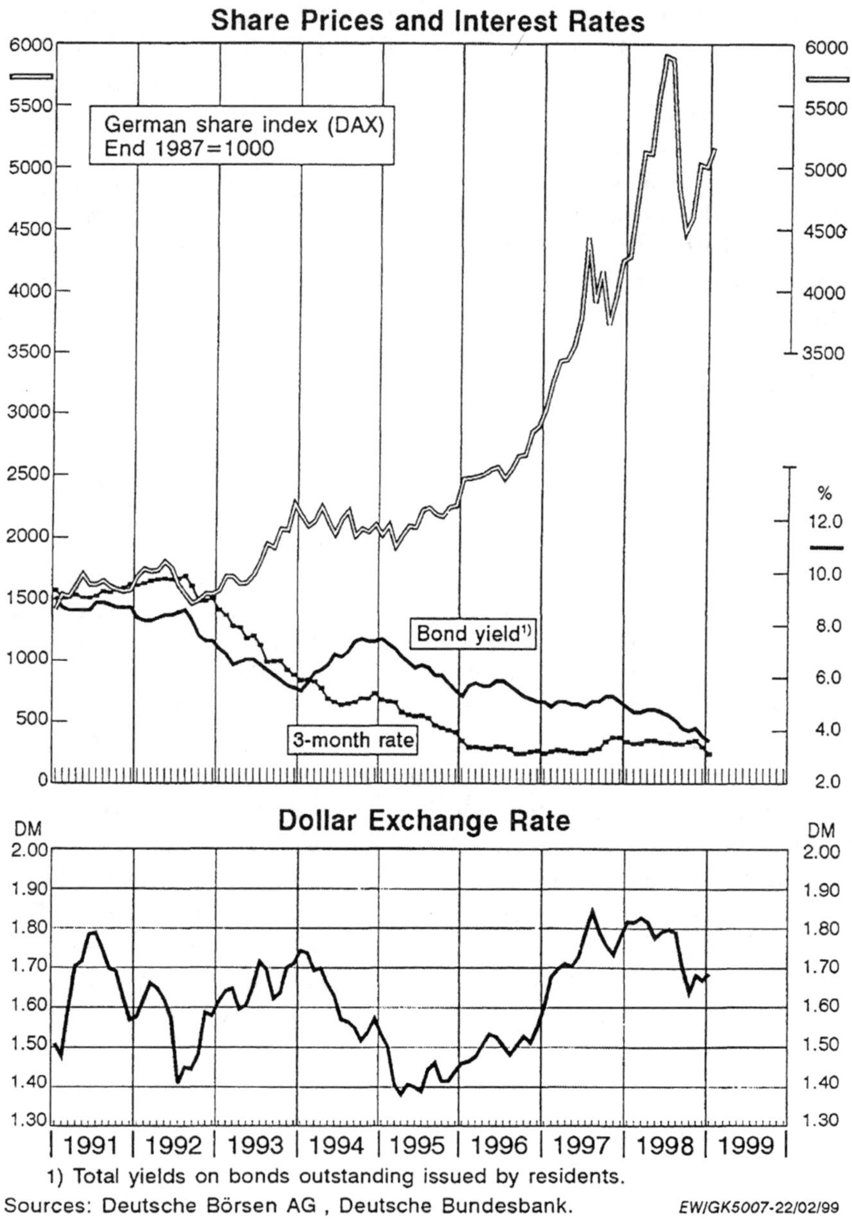

Figure 29.4 - Share Price and Interest Rate

Table 29.1 - DAX Stock Index[a)] - Monthly Correlation Analysis Until April 1998

Explanatory variables[b)]	Lead	r [d)]	Source[e)]
Orders received and interest rates (Germany)			
Yield on fixed interest bonds	-4	-0,64	BB
Money market interest rate	-6	-0,50	BB
Interest rate on 10 year government bonds	-3	-0,64	BB
Orders received by manufacturing industry (West Germany)	+3/-3	0,55/0,54	STABU
Exchange rates[c)]:			
DM vis-à-vis 18 industrial countries	-9	-0,50	BB
DM vis-à-vis the Dollar	-9	-0,31	BB
Survey series (West Germany):			
Business expectations	-2	0,42	ifo KT
Business climate	-3	0,27	ifo KT
Export expectations	-4	0,53	ifo KT
Regressors (USA):			
Dow-Jones-Index (30 stocks average)	-3	0,97	BB
Interest rate on 10 year government bonds	-4	-0,76	BB
Business climate in North America	-4	0,58	ifo ESI
Regressors (international):			
Leading indicators of the G7	-4	0,89	MAIN
International economic climate	-7	0,34	Ifo ESI

a) Original values. - b) 7-months-moving-average. - c) Difference to same month of previous year. d) Simple correlation coefficient. - e) BB = Monthly report of the Deutsche Bundesbank, Ifo KT = Ifo Business Survey, Ifo ESI = Economic Survey International of the Ifo Institute, MAIN = Main Economic Indicators of the OECD, STABU = Statistisches Bundesamt.

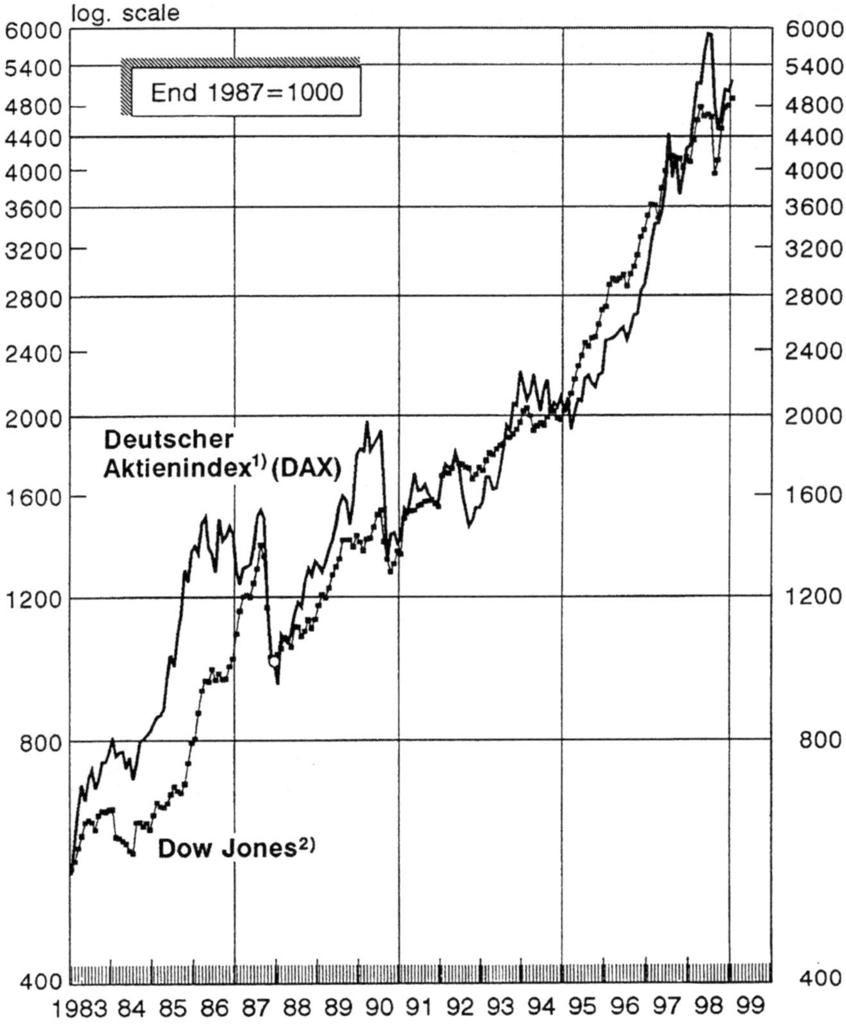

1) End of month.
2) Dow Jones Industrial, monthly average; rebased, december 1987=1000.

Sources: Deutsche Börsen AG, Dow Jones & Co., Inc. *EW/DAXDJ501-22/02/99*

Figure 29.5 - Share Price Development in Germany and the USA

As satisfying as the close connection with the Dow Jones is, it is only of limited use for a forecast of the DAX, for one reason because the lead time is relatively short (up to three months) and for another reason because especially for the most recent figures, which are crucial for forecasts, the connection is often not as close as for the long-year average. For this reason additional candidates for the forecast were sought that could prove suitable for covering the international side of factors influencing the DAX. The choice went to the OECD leading indicator for the G7 and to the international economic climate and the North American business climate measured by the Ifo Economic Survey International. As seen in table 29.1, especially the OECD G7 leading indicator with a lead of four months proved to be highly significant. In addition, the export expectations of manufacturing firms from the Ifo Business Survey were taken, which proved to be statistically significant with a lead of four months (see table 29.1 and Figure 29.6). The economic explanation for the importance of export expectations is that especially for the large companies in the DAX, exports are of key importance for business success. Probably for this same reason, the external value of the D-Mark against the 18 most important industrial countries (see Figure 29.7) proved to be very important for the course of the German stock market; the lead time here was as much as nine months.

The influence of orders received in manufacturing is also statistically confirmed, but the temporal link fluctuates between a lead of three months and a lag of three months (see table 29.1). For this reason this variable did not qualify for the inner circle of potential explanatory factors.

On the basis of this examination of individual variables, various regression approaches were tested. The three approaches shown in table 29.2 proved to be particularly suitable 29.. In the first case the bundle consisted of explanatory factors from the business expectations (according to the Ifo Business Survey for the west German business sector) (lead 3 months) and the return on German fixed-interest securities (lead 4 months). The second bundle contained, alongside the Ifo Business Climate for west German industry (lead 3 months), the return of German fixed-interest securities (lead 4 months), the effective DM exchange rate (lead 4 months) and the OECD leading indicators (4 month lead). In the third case, along with the business expectations for the west German business sector (3 month lead), the interest on ten-year German government bonds (3 month lead), the OECD leading indicators, and the Ifo business expectations for North America (the last two variables with a 4 month lead) were included. This third approach was used for ex-post forecasts and for the actual forecasting.

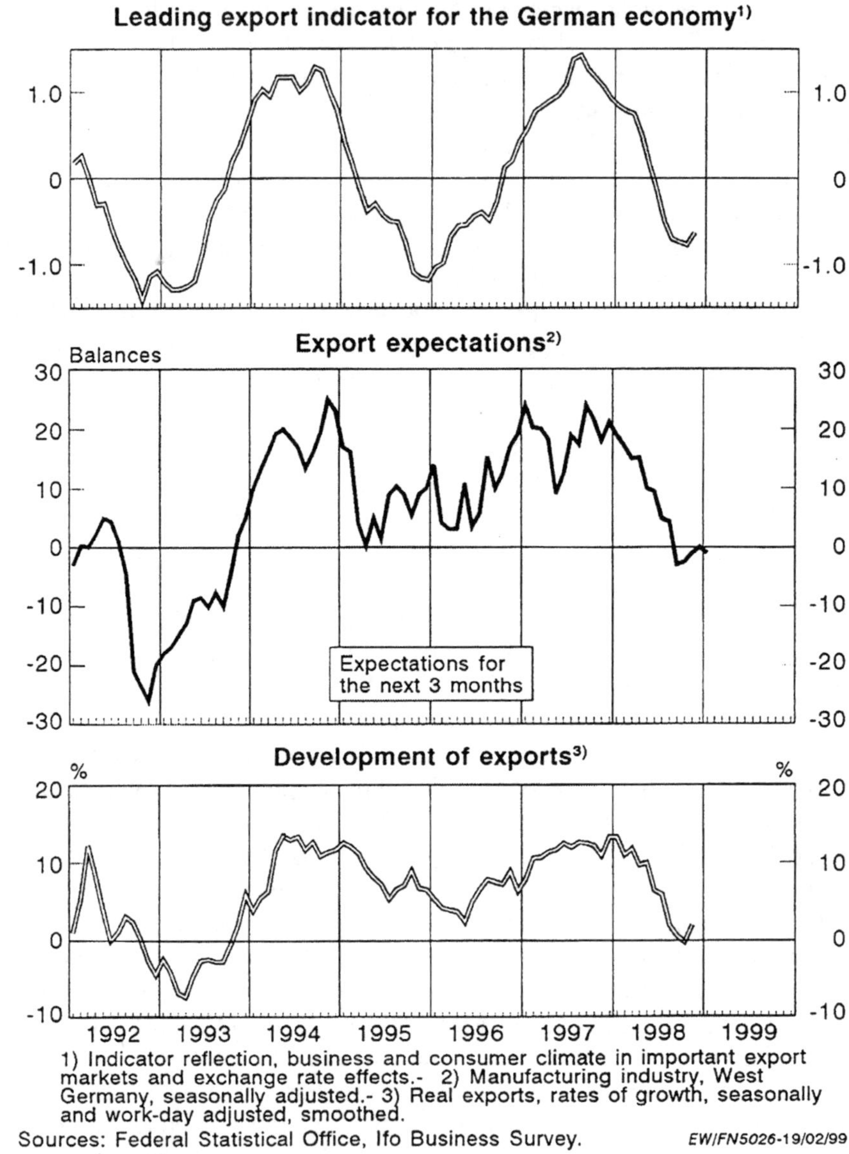

Figure 29.6 - Export Indicators

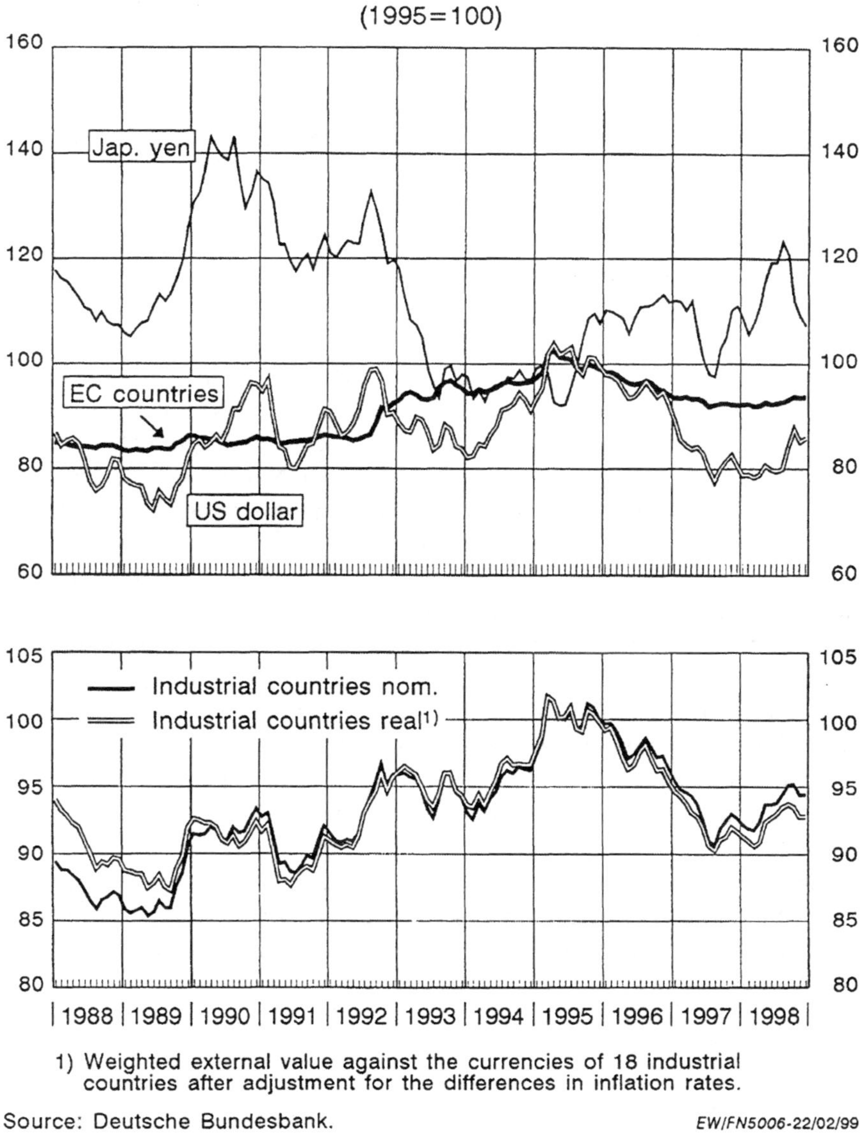

Figure 29.7 - External Value of the Deutsche Mark against Selected Foreign Currencies

The estimates made on the basis of the Ordinary Least Square (OLS) method were supplemented by a simultaneous structural and residual model and alternatively also by a combination of OLS with a successive residual model and by an Almon-model (see table 29.2).

The methodical refinement (simultaneous structure residual model, Almon approach, two-step approach) was superior to the OLS estimate. Within the refined approaches hardly any differentiation was possible.

For a genuine ex-ante forecast, concluded in mid-February 1999 for February and March, only the simultaneous structural and residual model of the third regression function (last line of table 29.2) was chosen; the OLS estimates serve as benchmarks (see Figures 29.8 and 29.9).

Another alternative to take care of the strong dependence of the German share price index DAX on the US share price index DOW JONES is to design a forecast function for the DOW JONES and to use these estimates as an input in a second step to forecast the DAX. Based on the US interest rate of 10 year government bonds and the OECD leading indicator for the G7 countries as well as the business climate for North America based on Ifo´s quarterly Business Survey International it was possible to design a relatively good estimation model for the DOW Jones index (see table 29. 29.3a). Putting in these estimates for the US share price development into a forecasting model for the German DAX - together with the German bond rate and the effective DM exchange rate (see table 29.3b and Figure 29.10) - resulted in good DAX estimates though not superior to results gained from the above mentioned 'refined' one step model, particularly the simultaneous structural and residual model .

Thus, it is proposed to apply mainly the third estimation type of table 29. 29.2 for practical forecasting (see table 29.4a). The results of ex-post forecasts based on a reference period ending in December 1994 respectively in April 1998 are presented in table 29.4.2b. Moreover, this table contains also genuine forecasts for the months February and March 1999 based on an extended reference period till January 1999 (see table 29.4.b, last two lines).

Table 29.2 - Comparison of Dynamic Regression Models for the DAX Index [a] - to April 1998

Explanatory[c] Variable	Constant term	DM exchange rate to 18 industrial countries	Business-expectations/-climate (West Germany)		Interest rate on 10 ear governm. bonds USA/BRD		Long term interest rate Germany	Leading Indicator of the G7	Business expec-tations N-America	Test statistics[b]			
Lag in months	-	-4	-3		-3		-4	-4	-4	AIC	R^2 adj	DW	K
OLS	7471,0 (26,5)	-	39,6 (9,7)	-	-558,0 (-15,4)	-	-177,7 (-5,2)	-	-	1985	0,75	0,4	20,5
OLS with successive residual model	-	-	-	-	-	-	-	-	-	1729	0,81	1,2	3,8
Almon-model with residual part[d]	5415,8 (2,2)	-	20,3 (2,6)	-	-120,1 (-3,1)	-	-	-	-	1766	0,98	1,8	3,0
Simultaneous structural and residual model	4485,7 (3,3)	-	14,3 (2,1)	-	-95,5 (-4,0)	-	-184,3 (-1,8)	-	-	1699	0,98	1,5	3,6
OLS	-9603,5 (-6,1)	-24,5 (-3,8)	-	6,3 (1,8)	-	-178,8 (-2,6)	-177,7 (-5,2)	169,7 (11,3)	-	2062	0,88	0,3	48,4
OLS with successive residual model	-	-	-	-	-	-	-	-	-	2034	0,97	2,0	5,1
Simultaneous structural and residual model	-8744,7 (-3,2)	*{Lag -7}* -20,6 (-1,9)	-	-	-	*{Lag -2}* -284,8 (-2,7)	-	*{Lag -9}* 128,3 (5,3)	-	1463	0,98	2,3	4,5
OLS	-8169,3 (-4,7)	-	12,6 (4,0)	-	-	-365,4 (-5,4)	-	124,4 (10,1)	189,4 (6,2)	1704	0,87	0,2	32,4
Simultaneous structural and residual model	-8987,9 (-3,0)	-	-	-	-	*{Lag -4}* -307,2 (-2,7)	-	*{Lag -6}* 131,5 (5,0)	-	1503	0,98	2,2	3,3

a) Original values. b) The symbols refer to: AIC = Akaike's criterion, R^2adj = adjusted R^2, DW = Durbin-Watson-statistic, K = Fisher's Kappa as White-Noise-test statistic. c) The same transformations of variables as in table 29. 29.1. d) Interest rates on 10 year government bonds polynomial-distributed-lag-model with lag length of 6 months.

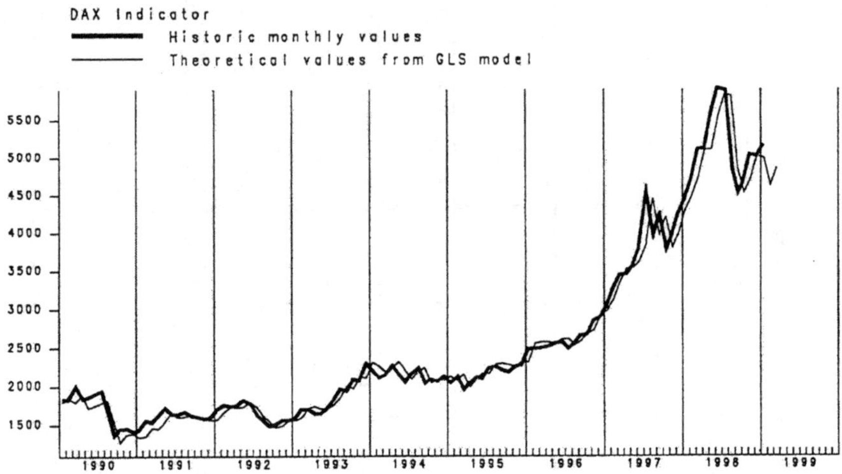

Figure 29.8 - Dax Indicator

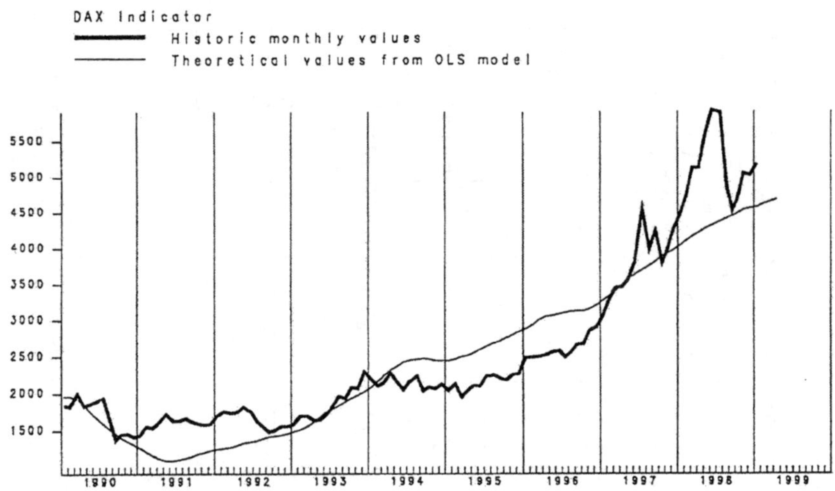

Figure 29.9 - Dax Indicator

Table 29.3a - Regression Models in a Two-Phase Process - to April 1998 - First Step: Explaining the Dow-Jones-Index[a)]

Explanatory[b)] variables	Constant term	Interest rate on 10 year governm. bonds USA	Business climate North America[c)]	Leading Indicator of the G7	Test statistics[d)]			
					AIC	R^2adj	DW	K
Lag in months		*-4*	*-3*	*-6*				
OLS	-18436,3 (-15,0)	-401,6 (-6,8)	163,7 (2,5)	250,5 (26,0)	1568	0,92	0,10	27,1
OLS with successive residual model	-	-	-	-	-	0,99	2,04	
Simultaneous structural and residual model	-17195,1 (-4,6)	-409,7 (-3,5)	-	240,5 (7,0)	1349	0,99	1,5	6,5

a) Original values. - b) The same transformations of variables as in table 29.1. - c) Growth rates to the same month of previous year. - d) AIC = Akaike's criterion, R^2adj = adjusted R^2, = Durbin-Watson-statistik, K = Fisher´s Kappa as White-Noise-test statistic.

Tabelle 29.3b - Regression Models in a Two-Phase Process - to April 1998 - Second Step: Explaining the Dax[a)]

Explanatory[b)] Variables	Constant term	Interest rate on 10 year governm. Bonds Germany	DM-exchange rate to 18 industrial countries[c)]	Dow-Jones-estimates (from successive model)	Test statistics[d)]			
					AIC	R^2adj	DW	K
Lag in months	-	*-4*	*-4*	*-6*				
OLS	2540,2 (3,2)	-213,5 (-5,8)	-4,5 (-1,3)	1,01 (18,2)	1464	0,91	0,65	18,4
OLS with successive residual model	-	-	-	-	-	0,97	1,98	-
Simultaneous structural and residual model	4193,4 (1,6)	-255,0 (-2,5)	-5,2 (-0,4)	0,51 (3,8)	1360	0,97	2,07	4,1

a) Original values. - b) 7-months-moving-averages. - c) Difference to same month of previous year - d) AIC = Akaike's criterion, R^2adj = adjusted R^2, DW = Durbin-Watson-statistic, K = Fisher´s Kappa as White-Noise-test-statistic.

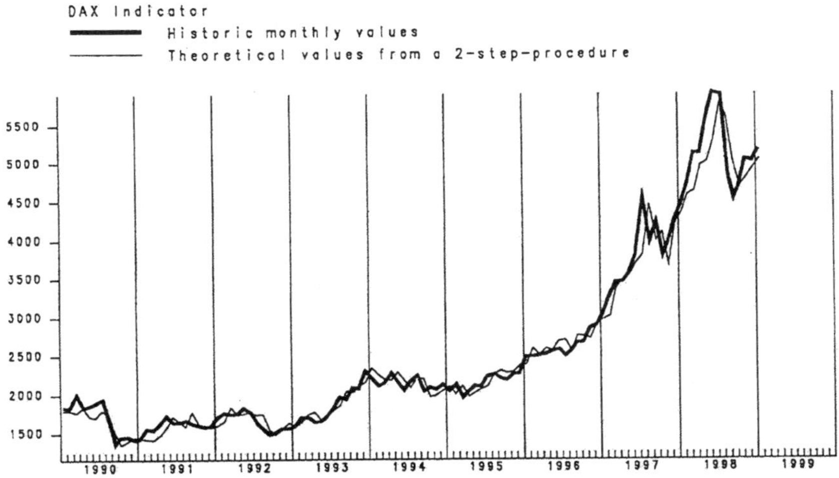

Figure 29.10 - Dax Indicator

In addition to the estimates of the total DAX value, an analogous attempt was made to explain and forecast DAX trends by industry (DAX road vehicles, DAX construction firms, DAX chemical firms and DAX consumer goods firms). The forecast quality – measuring by the Least Square (OLS) estimates – were only slightly worse than for the DAX as a whole, which indicates that good forecasting results can be achieved even with such a differentiated approach.

Such an industry refinement as well as the inclusion of other forecasting procedures, e.g. use of a neuronal network, is planned for the further course of the research project.

Table 29.4a - Final Assessment of Estimators
German Stock-Market-Index, Original Values -

Month of Ex-post-forecasting	Actual values	Theoretical values / estimated according to model[d)]			
		OLS	Simulta-neous structural-residual-model	Almon-model	Two-step-procedure
5/1998	5569,08	4377,42	5183,69	5243,65	5256,41
6/1998	5897,44	4421,01	5584,71	5719,21	5705,96
7/1998	5873,92	4463,84	5896,40	6036,59	6093,51
Relative error[a)]	-	23,53	5,04	4,12	4,32
U[b)]	-	1,0	0,04	0,03	0,03
Fisher´s Kappa[c)]	-	31,5	4,5	3,9	4,1

a) Root mean square percentage error. - b) U = Inequality coefficient according to Theil. - c) Test on white noise property of regression residuals. - d) Models to be compared: conventional least square approach (OLS), structural-residual-approach estimated by maximum likelihood, also an Almon distributed lag model and finally a procedure by which first the Dow-Jones is analysed and then, using the achieved estimated values, the DAX is forecasted. The causal structure is based on the second approach reported in table 29. 2.

Moreover, first results to forecast the capital market interest rates (yield on long-term government bonds) with the help of business survey results proved to be very successful. In this context the capacity utilisation appears to be suited to capture the output gap; moreover, companies' price expectations can be used for quantifying a risk premium that a typical capital market investor considers necessary before investing his money in long-term government papers. Though forecasting the capital market interest rate is an aim in itself, it can also help to lengthen the lead of the share price forecast as the yield on government bonds proved to be one of the most important influencing factors of share prices.

Table 29.4b - Test of Prognostic Ability[a]

Month of ex-post and ex-ante[b] forecast	Actual values	Theoretical value/estimated by model	
		OLS	Simultaneous structural-residual model
1/1995	2021,27	1919,15	2113,76
2/1995	2102,18	1920,32	2036,12
3/1995	1922,59	1965,21	2119,66
4/1995	2015,94	2038,34	1996,80
5/1995	2092,17	2068,60	2093,12
6/1995	2083,93	2069,42	2168,80
7/1995	2218,74	2046,50	2142,26
8/1995	2238,31	2083,20	2255,28
9/1995	2187,04	2093,03	2271,99
10/1995	2167,91	2072,42	2220,89
11/1995	2242,83	2075,51	2206,14
12/1995	2253,88	2093,59	2299,51
U[c]	-	1,0	0,46
5/1998	5569,08	3912,7	5154,9
6/1998	5897,44	3952,6	5585,4
7/1998	5873,92	3985.6	5888,1
8/1998	4833,89	4025,4	5876,0
9/1998	4474,51	4060,4	4891,9
10/1998	4690,99	4098,9	4559,2
11/1998	5022,70	4139,5	4752,3
12/1998	5002,39	4157,4	5060,1
1/1999	5160,00	4174,8	5042,9
U[c]	-	1,0	0.12
2/1999	-	4617,3	4613,1
3/1999	-	4648,2	4855,8

a) The figures refer to the second regression approach in table 29. 2. - b) The estimation period reaches from 1/1986 to 4/1994 or 4/1998.- c) U = inequality coefficient according to Theil.

3 Summary

Share prices - and also long-term government bond yields - have, in recent years, been very volatile, and despite an immense increase of the relevant literature, the explanations for these fluctuations remain unsatisfactory. Even more, forecasts in the financial markets have very often proved to be wrong.

This paper is certainly not a breakthrough in the field of financial market analysis. However, we think that especially the intensive exploitation of business survey results applied in this paper offers new insights in the field of share price fluctuations. This is not surprising as there is little doubt that those fluctuations are largely caused by investors' expectations of future trends of inflation, profits and the real economy.

4 Appendix

A Survey of Applied Methods

The solution procedure consists of three consecutive steps. In the following the main principles and some details will be briefly described.

1. Step: Search for promising explanatory variables and lead-lag-analyses

Bivariate coherency This problem allows us to check a large number of suitable 29. influences as explanatory variables both from a theoretical consideration and expert knowledge. The initial selection of promising indicators is done with the help of bivariate cross spectral analyses. The squared coherence between one of the explanatory variables X and the dependent variable Y:

$$K^2_{XY}(\lambda)=|f_{XY}(\lambda)|^2/(f_{XX}(\lambda)f_{YY}(\lambda)) \quad (1)$$

is a useful adjustment criterion in the frequency domain. The symbols $f_{xx}(\lambda)$, $f_{yy}(\lambda)$ denote the spectrum of the series X, Y and $f_{xy}(\lambda)$ the cross-spectrum to the frequency λ. The abscissa shows the wavelengths in decreasing order, the ordinate the associated coherence values. In this manner the strength of the linear connection can be measured for different frequencies (λ) or wavelengths.

This test is invariant facing linear transformations. An advantage is that there are the same results for differences or level values. But there is one constraint, which must be mentioned. Currently we do not have many observations from economic surveys; this is why the precision of the estimation can suffer.

Correlations Correlation calculations are also bivariate analysis methods but allocated to time domain. Their first duty is to check if indicator series can contribute to the explanation of the DAX.

The forecast goal requires that every explanatory variable is incorporated in the regression function with a sufficiently long lead time. For this reason the most important task of the selection phase is to determine the 'optimal' temporal distance to the dependent variable. The procedure generally used for this is serial correlation.

These bivariate analyses, however, concern only the two variables analysed. Nevertheless, the determined lead-lag structures were confirmed later in the trial regressions; deviations turned out to be rare or, if they occured, moderate.

2. Step: Regression analyses using the following methods

In the following, a regression structure will be established with the remaining indicator series.

The most frequently used econometric procedure to achieve a basic equation is the ordinary-least-squares-technique (OLS).

As there is only a limited number of regressors for the fundamentals of the stock market, it is not surprising that the regression residuals still contain systematic movements. That is why for example omitted market influences are reflected in the shock term. From this it is helpful to pay particular attention to these unexplained residuals.

Simultaneous estimation procedures (Harvey 1995) enable us to calculate all parameters for the structural and residual part together. This logical advantage is also expressed in a greater forecast suitability.

Almon models incorporate the influence of several periods in the past of one – or sometimes more – explanatory variables X_t. Apart from the basic structure, the lag length and the polynomial degree must be determined and justified. The first factor can be determined in the following indicator example a priori from economic considerations or from the above mentioned correlation analyses. The degree of the polynomials, however, must be determined formally in test calculations.

The high value of this parameter will be decreased step by step, the likelihood-ratio- or the t-statistic will be determined by model estimates. Finally the optimum will be chosen. The dynamic structure of this model type is therefore divided into three parts. These are: the distributed lag effects, the dynamics of the covariates and the dynamics of the residuals. The main advantage of the Almon polynomials is that only a few parameters have to be estimated (Davidson / Mac Kinnon 1993, pp. 647-676 and Hendry 1995, pp. 212-217). Due to the high flexibility the preferred equatation has to be chosen carefully with the aid of statistic criteria and insofar as available using economic a priori knowledge. For the residual part autoregressive specifications are most successful. This dynamic model with a distributed lag structure in one of the regressors lead to quite promising forecasts.

3. Step: Tests procedures and model selection

For every testing target the results of at least two statistical methods are compared.

In the table 29.s of the results section, two measures characterize goodness of fit of the estimates and help to select alternative approaches.

Adjusted R^2 is a statistic which correctively incorporates the number of k explanatory variables:

$$R^2_{adj}=1-[(T-1)/(T-k)]\,(1-R^2). \tag{2}$$

The symbol T denotes the length of the estimation period.

The alternative specifications of the regressions in this report form non-nested hypotheses. Akaike's information criterion (AIC) is thus suitable 29. for discrimination.

$$AIC=-2\ln(L)+2k. \tag{3}$$

In this formula L stands for the value of the likelihood function and k for the coefficients which have to be estimated. This decision rule includes the two criteria 'adjustment quality' (L) and 'efficiency in model parameters' (k). Therefore low dimensioned and simple models will be prefered. The approach for which the AIC is the smallest will finally be chosen.

The tests of misspecification used in this study tie up with the regression residuals. Model builders are interested in explaining the largest portion as possible of the systematic movement of a dependent variable. Thus a suitable 29. model should be characterized by approximately stochastic residuals. Furthermore it is advisable to consider the results of several procedures together.

The Durbin-Watson measure of first order is assigned to test autocorrelation in the regression table 29.. Second Fisher's Kappa K is calculated as the second statistic from the periodogram of the residuals. The value of the empirical testing variable should be lower than the critical value, tabulated by W. A. Fuller.

Detailed information displayed in graphs is, thirdly, an indispensable supplement.

All of the described tests have been derived from results of the estimation period. The forecast suitability of the models has priority in an indicator approach. Ex-post forecasts are decisive in the final selection. The estimation period is thereby shortened at the end in order to be able to forecast approximately as many periods as are necessary ex ante. This method compares the actual available values in the immediate past with the regression estimates and gives a hint of the accuracy. In all cases the dynamic methods explained could reduce the ex-post-predictive error.

In analyses with level values, the root mean square percentage error RMSPE is suitable 29. as a relative measure.

For a quick comparison of alternative estimation techniques the inequality coefficient U according to H. Theil will best be used:

$$U = (\sum_{t=1}^{T}(Y_t - YD_t)^2) / (\sum_{t=1}^{T}(Y_t - YB_t)^2) . \qquad (4)$$

This measure illustrates to what degree the forecasts YD_t from a dynamic model are more accurate than the prognoses YB_t of the accompanying basic solution of the OLS approach. A result less than 1 illustrates the degree of improvement. This measure is simple and therefore excellently suitable 29. for presentation.

References

Davidson, R. and J. G. MacKinnon (1993), *Estimation and Inference in Econometrics,* Oxford University Press, New York.

Harvey, A. C. (1995), *Zeitreihenmodelle,* 2nd edition, R. Oldenbourg Verlag, München Wien.

Hendry, D. F. (1995), *Dynamic Econometrics,* Advanced Texts in Econometrics, Oxford University Press, New York.

Kempf, Th. F. (1990), ‘Measuring risk and expected return in portfolio management by using ifo business survey data’, in: Oppenländer, K. H. and G. Poser (eds), *Business Cycle Surveys with Special Reference to Pacific Basin Economies*, Papers presented at the 19th CIRET Conference Proceedings, Osaka 1989, Aldershot.

Nerb, Gernot (1997), 'The predictive power of selected indicators at cyclical turning points', in: Oppenländer, K. H. (ed), *Business Cycle Indicators*, Aldershot.

Zimmerer, Th. (1997), *Künstliche neuronale Netze versus ökonometrische zeitreihenanalytische Verfahren zur Prognose ökonomischer Zeitreihen,* Regensburg.

30 Leading Indicators for the South African Building Industry: The Effect of the Reconstruction and Development Programme

JOHAN G. J. SNYMAN

Abstract

A *leading indicator* for the South African building industry was developed by the author[1] and presented to the CIRET conference in Singapore in September 1995. This composite index, called the MFA Qualitative Leading Indicator, is based on 33 survey indicators published on a quarterly basis by the Bureau for Economic Research (BER), University of Stellenbosch. The BER follows the *Konjunkturtest* methodology pioneered by the IFO-Institute, Munich, Germany. These 33 indicators were weighted according to the scoring system of the National Bureau of Economic Research, USA. During 1994 the new South African government published a policy framework entitled 'The Reconstruction and Development Programme (RDP)'. In this social upliftment programme subsidy funds would be allocated from the national budget for mass housing schemes. One million low-income housing units were to be built within five years. Whereas one would have expected great optimism, the *qualitative* leading

[1] The author is the director of Medium-Term Forecasting Associates (MFA), Building Economists, Stellenbosch, South Africa. He would like to thank Prof Eon v. d. M. Smit and Dr Carol A. Puhl of the University of Stellenbosch Business School for helpful comments on this paper.

indicator for the South African building industry shows that survey respondents are generally pessimistic about future business conditions. Furthermore, *quantitative* building investment data compiled by the South African Reserve Bank (SARB) are declining. When the movements in the MFA indicator are superimposed on the official Reserve Bank data it is evident that the survey data leads changes in the level of building activity. The analysis has certain policy implications which are discussed in this paper.

1 Introduction

To improve short-term forecasting in the South African building industry a qualitative leading indicator was developed by the author and presented to the CIRET conference in Singapore in September 1995. The new South African government came to power in April 1994 and announced an ambitious social upliftment programme, the Reconstruction and Development Programme (RDP). One of the cornerstones of the RDP entails the provision of mass housing schemes for the poor. A comparison is made in this paper between the course of the qualitative leading indicator and the annual percentage movement in investment in building data. The findings suggest that this low-income housing program has met with little success. In keeping with one of the topics of the 24th CIRET conference these findings also suggest that the survey data - on which the qualitative leading indicator is based – can be used for economic policy recommendations.

2 Composition of the Qualitative Leading Indicator for the South African Building Industry

The qualitative leading indicator, developed by Medium-Term Forecasting Associates (MFA), is based on 33 business survey indicators that reflect the economic activities of building contractors and sub-contractors. Included are survey variables such as the value and volume of work done, the availability of materials and labour, the degree of competition in tendering, and the cost and availability of finance, as well as general business confidence levels prevailing in the South African building industry. The survey data are gathered on a quarterly basis by the Bureau for Economic Research (BER) at the University of Stellenbosch, South Africa, according to the Konjunkturtest method developed at the IFO-Institute, Munich, Germany.

To compile a composite index from the available survey data the weights of the individual indicators were determined according to the scoring system developed at the National Bureau of Economic Research (NBER), USA. Six criteria are applied when assessing and selecting the indicators. These are (with their respective weights in brackets, rounded off):

- economic significance (16,7%);
- statistical adequacy (16,7%);
- timing at revivals and recessions (26,7%);
- conformity to historical business cycles (16,7%);
- smoothness (13,3%);
- currency or timeliness (10%).

To determine the median lead times of the MFA Qualitative Leading Indicator the reference cycle of the South African Reserve Bank (SARB) was used. This reference cycle depicts the overall economic performance of the building sector and is based on a diffusion index of construction activities. It was found that the median lead time at troughs varied between one and three quarters and that the lead time was longer at the upper turning points than at the lower turning points. This finding is in accordance with international experience (Strigel, 1981:20). The methodology is described in greater detail elsewhere (Klein,1990; Snyman, 1994; Snyman, 1995; Snyman, 1996; Van der Walt, 1982; Van der Walt and Pretorius, 1995; Zarnowitz and Boschan, 1975).

3 Objectives of the Reconstruction and Development Programme

The Reconstruction and Development Programme was announced after the new South African government came to power in April 1994. It claimed to be „an integrated, coherent socio-economic policy framework" (RDP, 1994:1). Its main objectives were the democratisation of South Africa, nation-building, the promotion of peace and security, economic growth and development. Housing formed a cornerstone of this social upliftment programme. The urban housing backlog was estimated to be 1.3 million units in 1990. Therefore, a key objective was to build one million low-income houses over a five year period, starting in 1994 (RDP, 1994:22). A mass housing programme could generate employment, skills and economic activity, both directly and indirectly, and should help to ensure peace and stability (RDP, 1994:23). Another goal was set, *viz.* to provide subsidy funds that were to reach not less than 5% of the national budget by the end of the five-year programme (RDP, 1994: 23).

4 Expectations and Outcome

At the time of the announcement of the RDP in 1994 there were great expectations that the mass housing programme would boost the fortunes of the building industry. The industry had suffered severely during the protracted 1989/1993 recession. In anticipation, manufacturers of building materials raised production levels and builders' merchants stocked up. Building contractors in the established sector joined forces with emerging small and medium-sized builders in anticipation of the housing projects which were to be put out to tender. Business confidence subsequently improved, and this was reflected in an improvement in the course of the MFA indicator. Please refer to figure 30.1. Shaded areas represent recessionary periods.

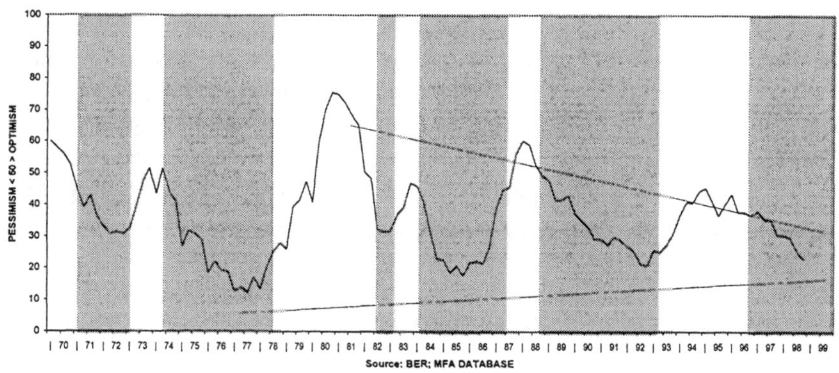

Figure 30.1 - MFA Qualitative Leading Indicator for the South African Building Industry

The indicator recorded a peak in the latter part of 1994. A second peak at a somewhat lower level was recorded in 1996. However, since then the indicator has been declining, thereby suggesting that the successful implementation of the RDP mass housing programme has not materialised. Indeed, the housing policy has only achieved 25% of its targets in four years (Pereira, 1998:14). Furthermore, according to the medium-term expenditure estimates of the Department of Finance for the fiscal year 1999/2000, public housing expenditure will only reach 2% of the national budget, falling short of the goal of 5% set in the RDP (Budget Review, 1998:6.2-6.3; Department of Finance Expenditure Estimates R.P.2-1998: Vote 18).

The following reasons have been proffered for the poor performance:

- rapid and uncontrolled mass urbanisation (Pereira, 1998:13);
- large-scale unemployment and retrenchments resulting from very low rates of economic growth (Gebhardt-Mann, 1998:16; Pereira, 1998:13);
- punitively high mortgage rates (Gebhardt-Mann, 1998:16);
- rental and bond repayment boycotts following the demise of the SA Housing Trust, a body set up by the previous government to facilitate mass housing delivery (Gebhardt-Mann, 1998:16);
- the unwillingness of banks and building societies to lend to low-income people because the risk of their defaulting on their mortgages is too high (Gebhardt-Mann, 1998:19; Pereira, 1998:13);
- the burgeoning bureaucracy surrounding low-income housing delivery; already 183 individual decisions and actions have to be taken after a state subsidy is approved and before building begins (Pereira, 1998:14);
- administrative capacity problems arising from inadequate training of new civil servants who have been charged with implementing the public policy decisions (Department of Housing Annual Report, 1997:8; Pereira, 1998:14).

Two further observations can be made regarding the cyclical course of the MFA indicator. Firstly, observe in figure 30.1 that the indicator leads the upper and lower turning points of the SARB reference cycle. In this presentation the downswing phases have been shaded to enhance the comparison. Secondly, observe also that the amplitude of the cyclical fluctuations in the indicator is diminishing. This finding suggests that the South African building industry is becoming more stable. The public policy implications of this stability are dealt with in Section 6.

5 Comparison: Survey Data with Quantitative Data of the SA Reserve Bank

Given the lacklustre response of the BER respondents to the RDP mass housing programme, it is useful to compare the MFA Qualitative Leading Indicator with official data compiled by the South African Reserve Bank. This is commonly referred to as an exogenous test in business survey literature. The BER frames its questions to reflect year-ago comparisons. The survey data, therefore, reflect trends, but not levels. In contrast, the SARB investment in buildings data reflect absolute levels. One has therefore to cast the investment data in such a form as to be compatible with the quarterly survey data. The time series chosen for this comparison is described by the SARB as 'Gross Domestic Fixed Investment By Type of Asset: Category Total Buildings, at constant 1990 prices' (SARB Quarterly Bulletin, December 1998). The quarterly seasonally adjusted data were smoothed with a three-term moving average. Subsequently, an annual percentage change was calculated to reflect the cyclical fluctuations in investment in buildings. This information is summarised in figure 30.2 below. In this figure the quantitative investment data are read along the left-hand axis and the business survey data are read along the right-hand axis.

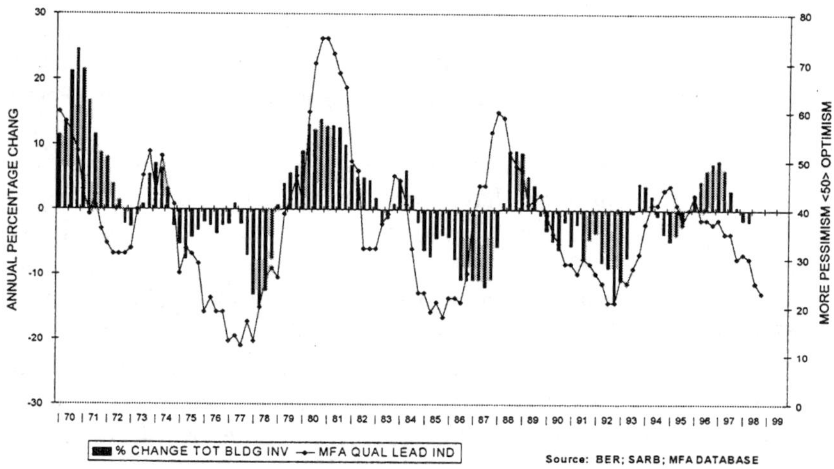

Figure 30.2 - Comparison: MFA Qualitative Leading Indicator and Annual Percentage Change in Total Investment in Buildings

This comparison yields a number of interesting features:

- the survey data capture most of the swings in investment;
- turning points in the survey data generally lead the upper and lower turning points in the investment data ; and
- finally, it shows that the cycle in investment in buildings is tending downward and that this is borne out by the deepening pessimism on the part of BER survey respondents.

6 Policy Implications

The downward course of the MFA Qualitative Leading Indicator, and the close correspondence this has with the decline in investment in buildings, has certain policy implications.

Firstly, the smaller amplitude of the cyclical fluctuations in this key indicator suggests that the building industry is becoming more stable. However, reference to absolute levels of investment in building data clearly shows that the industry is stabilising at a low level of activity. These findings have specific implications for two government departments dealing with public investment in buildings. In the case of the Department of Housing it is clear that their low-income housing projects have failed to boost the economy. The shortcomings of their policies should therefore be addressed to improve housing delivery. The analysis presented in this paper is also relevant to the Department of Public Works that is responsible for public investment in non-residential buildings (e.g. schools, hospitals, clinics, etc.). The findings of the analysis should be carefully considered in macro-economic stabilisation policies related to construction, currently being discussed but not yet implemented (Department of Public Works Green Paper, 1997:1-4). In this Green Paper it is suggested that improved macro-economic modelling and medium-term budgeting could counteract demand volatility (Department of Public Works Green Paper, 1997:5-8). It is in this context that the survey data and the leading indicator derived therefrom have a meaningful role to play in public policy recommendations.

Secondly, there is evidence to suggest that when compiling investment in buildings data, the SARB does not capture all building work undertaken in the informal sector of the economy. This refers in particular to low-income housing. A possible reason is that the Department of Housing is not obliged to pass a plan for a low cost housing project at the municipalities or local authorities (Taljaard, 1998:1). The SARB, in turn, relies on the municipalities or local authorities to capture the basic data of building plans approved or buildings actually completed. At this point there is no formalised system in place to capture ALL building work undertaken in the INFORMAL sector of the economy, which includes the rural regions of the country along with the urban regions.

Thirdly, the BER has an established database of building contractors and sub-contractors that forms the basis of their building survey responses. The MFA Qualitative Leading Indicator is, in turn, based on 33 of these survey variables. The trend in the MFA indicator therefore reflects perceptions in the established sector of the building market. To improve the survey coverage the BER should revise their sampling procedures to include emerging contractors in the informal building sector. New information technologies like e-mail and the Internet open up new ways in data collection and this is one of the themes of the CIRET Workshop being held on 16 March 1999.

7 Summary

This paper deals with two related topics that are included in the theme of the CIRET conference. These relate to the development of leading economic indicators and the use of survey data for economic policy recommendations. The (downward) course of the MFA Qualitative Leading Indicator for the South African building industry suggests that the mass housing programme implemented by the new South African government, in terms of the goals of the Reconstruction and Development Programme, has met with little success. This finding is supported by a comparison between the MFA indicator and the (downward) cyclical movement of SARB investment in buildings data. Three policy implications flow from these findings. Firstly, non-performance of the low-income housing sector, and the fact that the building industry is operating at well below peak capacity utilization, has important implications for macro-economic stabilisation policies in South Africa. Secondly, the SARB should endeavour to capture ALL building work completed in the country. Thirdly, the BER should revise their sampling procedures to include emerging contractors in the informal building sector. New information technology could assist the SARB and the BER in improving their survey coverage.

References

Department of Finance (1998), *Budget Review*, Pretoria, March.

Department of Finance (1998), *Expenditure Estimates (R.P.2-1998)*, Pretoria, March.

Department of Housing (1997), *Annual Report,* Pretoria.

Department of Public Works (1997), *Creating an Enabling Environment for Reconstruction, Growth and Development in the Construction Industry: Green Paper*, Pretoria, November.

Gebhardt-Mann, C. (1998), 'Houses and boycotts', *Finance Week*, Johannesburg, April, pp. 16 – 22.

Klein, P.A.(ed), (1990), *Analyzing modern business cycles: Essays honoring Geoffrey H. Moore*, M.E.Sharpe, London.

Pereira, P. (1998), 'How to house the poor', *Finance Week*, Johannesburg, April 30 – May 6.

RDP (1994), *The Reconstruction and Development Programme: A Policy Framework*, Johannesburg.

Snyman, G.J.J. (1994), *The development of leading indicators for the South African building industry using qualitative and quantitative data*, unpublished Ph.D. dissertation, University of Cape Town, Cape Town.

Snyman, G.J.J. (1995), 'New leading indicators for the South African building industry', *Business Cycle Surveys: Forecasting Issues and Methodological Aspects,* Selected Papers Presented at the 22nd CIRET Conference, Singapore.

Snyman, G.J.J. (1996), 'The development of leading indicators for the South African building industry', *Economic Management and Innovation, Productivity and Quality in Construction,* Volume 1, Papers presented at the CIB W55 Building Economics 7th International Symposium, Zagreb, September.

South African Reserve Bank (1998), *Quarterly Bulletin*, Pretoria, December.

Strigel, W.H. (1981), 'Essays on trade cycle surveys', *CIRET Studies* No. 30, Munich.

Taljaard, E. (1998), 'Low-income housing communication', *Building Industries Federation of South Africa*, Johannesburg, November.

Van der Walt, B.E. (1982), *The identification and evaluation of economic indicators for a study of business cycles in South Africa*, unpublished D. Comm. dissertation, Pretoria: Faculty of Economic and Political Sciences, University of Pretoria.

Van der Walt, B.E. and W.S. Pretorius (1995), 'Business cycles in South Africa during the period 1986 to 1993', *South African Reserve Bank Quarterly Bulletin*, Pretoria, March.

Zarnowitz, V. and C. Boschan (1975), 'Cyclical indicators: An evaluation of new leading indexes', *Business Conditions Digest*, Bureau of Economic Analysis, U.S. Department of Commerce, Washington D.C. May.

31 The Predictive Power of Finnish Business Survey among Industrial Sectors

KARI TAKALA and PEKKA TSUPARI

Abstract

This paper evaluates the predictive power of different responses given in the Finnish Business Tendency Survey (BTS) to forecast industrial production. The overall usefulness of surveys in predicting, e.g. aggregate industrial production has been confirmed in various studies in Finland and abroad (see EU report No. 7/1998). Here, we are in particular interested how helpful different business survey responses are for different industries. Since the predictive power differs quite a lot depending on industry, we try to select the most useful indicators for different industries and evaluate how much indicator value and predictive power is included into these questionairies.

In addition to industrial specific models, we evaluate system wide forecasting procedures based on multivariate structural time series models and Kalman filter estimation. We evaluate also the forecasting facilities for different industrial branches. A valid forecasting framework needs to take into account and signal for outliers, turning points and irregularities in seasonal variation. Therefore we pay some attention on these features in the data as well. The comovement and in particular leading indicator aspects among industries are in the focus of our interest. Our final purpose is to specify and estimate useful forecasting models for industrial sectors. We find out that confidence indicator, production expectations and business outlook indicator are particularly useful in forecasting production changes.

1 Introduction

In this paper we are interested in production expectations and other barometer response variables as means to help to predict the actual industrial production. With Finnish data the predictive ability of industrial confidence and business outlook variable on aggregate industrial production has been already established in several studies (e.g. Kangasniemi and Tsupari 1997, Teräsvirta 1986).

In particular, we are extending production forecasting to take into account disaggregated information about industrial branches (see also Kauppi and Lassila, 1997). This problem arises from the need of industrial sectors and branches to get a clear picture about the current and forthcoming activity within the production branch. This information may help them to smooth production and to improve investment timing or to find out their relative competitive position to their rivals. In Finland industrial statistics is published at about one and a half months lag, which forms a good basis for forecasting at the industry level.

Here we are also interested to find out dynamic dependencies between different industries. For this reason we employ multivariate structural models to take into account dependencies that may affect short-term forecasting. In Finland it is rather easy to see that apart from the overall business cycle that confronts aggregate industrial production and main industrial sectors there are also dependencies that link different industrial branches together. For example metal industry production is related to the investment activity in the paper and pulp industry because of a rising demand for large paper. Subcontracting within industrial sectors have been a growing tendency throughout the 1990s due to cost minimization and increased pressures for competitiveness. Ongoing globalisation on EU level has also increased price competition and put pressure for larger production units and horizontal industrial fusions. System estimation is employed to model these aspects between sector relationships.

A main theme in our analysis, however, is to search and use available barometer survey data in gaining better forecasts. To do this we have to go through and classify a number of barometer series in different industrial branches into leading, coincident and lagging indicators for industrial production.

Their predictive power is tested by bivariate Granger causality tests, which is the main tool in finding leading indicators for production.

As the diversification of industries has been pronounced and their short-term prospects have become more variable, it is even more important to evaluate performance of different industries. Therefore we finally estimate multivariate structural time series models for main industrial sectors in order to forecast the performance of individual industries. In particular we are looking for dynamic relationships between different industries to gain predictive power for short-term forecasting. Therefore we also take a brief look at potential cointegration relations between different industries, to see whether there exists any useful error-correction terms, which may contain additive predictive information.

The structure of the paper is as follows; In section 2 we represent major characteristics of the data, which may help to understand recent growth patterns in industrial production. Section 3 takes a closer look at correlation of industrial production both aggregate and by branch to various Business Tendency Survey (BTS) series. Granger causality tests for production expectation variables are presented in section 4. In the final section we present multivariate structural time series modelling results for industrial production by branch using BTS series as regressors.

2 Data Characteristics

In Finland aggregate industrial production follows quite closely the overall economic activity though the share of industrial production is below one third of the GDP (Figure 31.1). Figure 31.2 compares industrial production with GDP, where we can see the rapid growth in industrial production after the 1991 devaluation of the Finnish markka and the vigorous growth in electronics, which started sometime after 1992. We see that despite the prices of industrial products have been stable since 1990, the share of industrial production of GDP has been rising rapidly especially in real terms.

If we take a look at the industrial production by branch, we see that during our sample period for branches 1986 – 1997, there has been two major slowdowns or even recessions in the forest, chemical and textiles industries (Figure 31.3). These slumps in production were due mostly to the international business cycle and partly to the fall in paper and pulp prices. In the metal industry only one slump in the early 1990s can be observed. Strong growth in the electronics industry has been keeping up the metal industry production to the end of the 1990s.

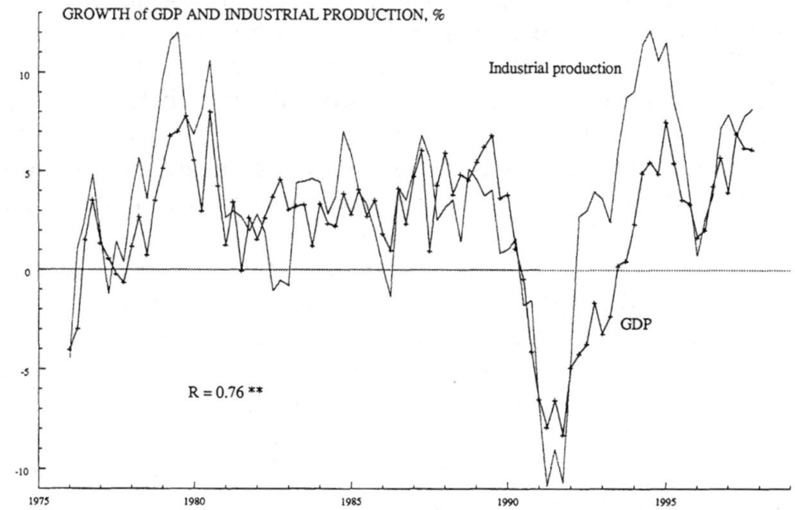

Figure 31.1 - GDP and Industrial Production, in percent

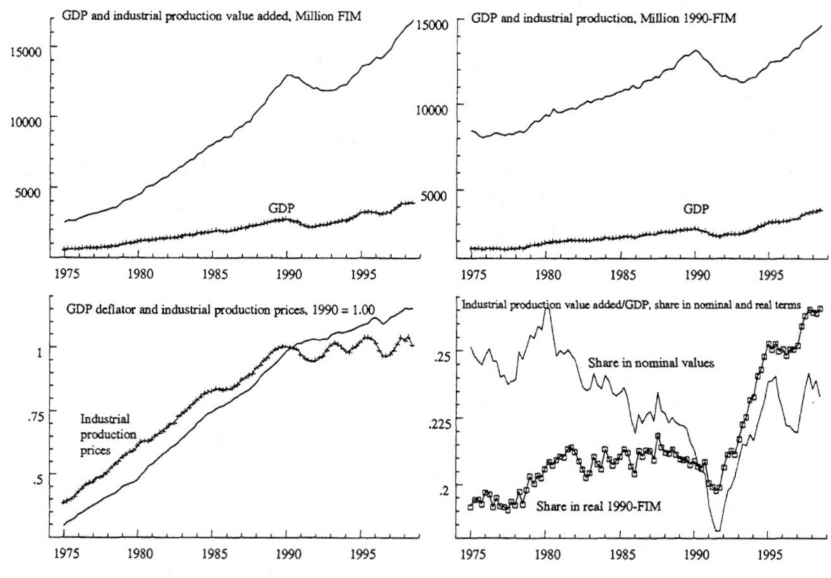

Figure 31.2 - Industrial Production in Relation to GDP

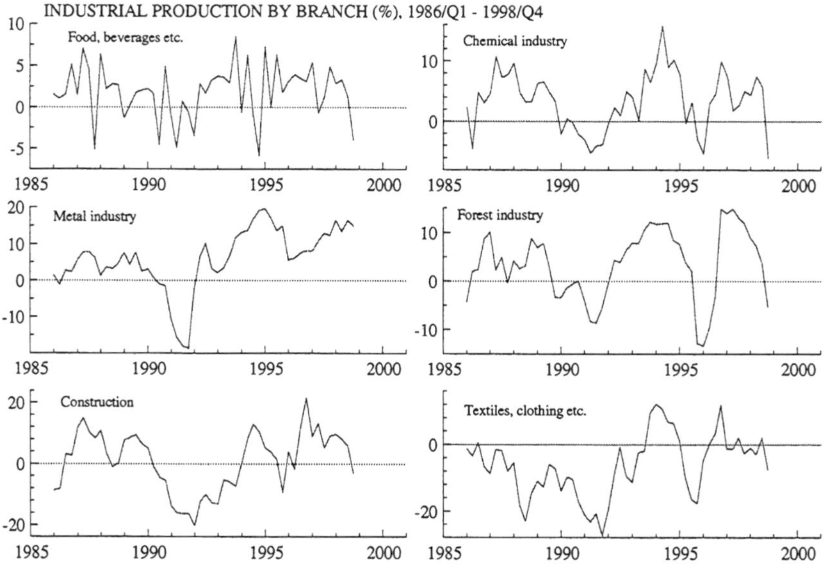

Figure 31.3 - Industrial Production by Branch

Growth rates by branch have been variable, although the main industries - metal and forest industry - follow relatively uniformly the aggregate economic activity. The growth has been especially volatile in the food, beverages and tobacco production. In 1995 Finland joined the EU, which led to a sharp decline in food and beverages prices for about 10-15%. Due to this profitability loss there was a decline in production as well. There have also been large structural changes within the industrial production along time and especially during 1990s mostly due to rapid growth in the metal industry and in particular in the electronics production in Finland. Table 31.1 presents the production shares of different industries. The first thing we observe is that the share of manufacturing production has revived in the mid 1990s from the slowdown in the end of 1980s. Manufacturing production varies inversely with the share of construction industry, which boomed at the end of 1980s as a consequence of financial deregulation increasing housing demand and went down after house price collapse (Tobin q effect) in early 1990s. The share of mining and quarrying production has remained relatively stable.

Table 31.1 - Processing Industries by Branch, % Distribution

	1980	1985	1990	1995	1996	1997
Mining and quarrying	1.4	1.2	1.1	1.1	1.1	1.0
Manufacturing	71.2	69.7	65.8	74.9	73.8	73.9
Food, beverages and tobacco	7.5	8.1	7.7	7.3	7.4	6.5
Textiles and clothing	6.0	4.9	2.5	2.1	2.1	2.0
Wood	6.2	3.5	4.1	4.0	3.4	3.9
Pulp and paper	10.9	9.6	8.4	14.0	11.1	10.8
Printing and publishing	4.7	5.7	5.3	4.8	4.9	4.6
Chemicals	8.5	7.7	7.4	7.7	7.7	7.3
Building materials etc.	2.9	2.8	3.2	2.1	2.2	2.2
Basic metals and metal products	6.7	6.5	6.9	8.7	8.5	8.5
Machinery and equipment, transport equipment	11.3	13.1	11.7	12.7	13.8	13.2
Electrical and optical equipment	4.0	5.4	6.2	9.9	11.1	13.2
Other manufacturing industry	2.6	2.4	2.2	1.7	1.7	1.6
Electricity, gas and water supply	7.3	7.8	5.9	7.5	8.0	7.2
Construction	20.1	21.4	27.2	16.5	17.1	17.9
PROCESSING INDUSTRY, total	100.0	100.0	100.0	100.0	100.0	100.0

Source: National Accounts, Statistics Finland

Within the manufacturing production we see business cycle swings particularly in the paper and pulp production, a decline in textiles and clothing and a rise in the basic metals and metal products and especially in electrical equipment production, which includes the exploding the production of mobile phones and telecommunication equipment. During the last years electric and electronics production has increased on average by 25% per year and its contribution to GDP growth has been rising rapidly. In 1997 the contribution of electric and electronics to GDP growth was 1.1% out of the 6% total increase. The contribution of Nokia alone was 0.6% of the annual Finnish GDP growth.

An obvious difficulty in using barometer responses is their volatility in the short run. Partly, this noise is related to the seasonality in quarterly responses though respondents are advised to take seasonal variation into account in their responses. However, it seems that seasonality is not always perfectly observed and it is hard to identify systematic seasonality in the aggregate production expectations or confidence series.

Table 31.2 presents the results from the outlier tests. In the actual production growth series numerous outliers were found in the food, beverages and construction time series. In other industries also the beginning of the recession during 1990-91 resulted into negative outliers.

On the other hand the construction industry was booming during 1986-87 as indicated by a couple of positive outliers. These 'surprises or innovations' in actual production do not match the outliers observed in the confidence series. Only in forest industry the drop in production in the fourth quarter of 1995 and the increase in production during 1993/Q3 in construction were coincidental. In the confidence series numerous individual outliers were found in chemical, textiles and clothing industries, but it seems that pairs of these irregular outliers do cancel themselves, and indicate no fundamental unstability of the production.

Table 31.2 - Outliers in Industrial Production and Industrial Branch Confidence

Branch	Industrial production outliers			Confidence outliers		
	Period	Value	Prob t	Period	Value	Prob t
Food, beverages and tobacco	1987.4	-2.3771	[0.0107] *	1991. 4	2.7978	[0.0037] **
	1994.4	-2.6172	[0.0059] **			
	1995.1	2.6872	[0.0049] **			
Chemical industry	1996. 1	-2.3513	[0.0114] *	1986. 3	-2.6621	[0.0053] **
				1992. 1	2.3555	[0.0113] *
				1993. 1	-2.3304	[0.0120] *
Metal industries	1991. 4	-2.1742	[0.0173] *	1989. 1	-2.2646	[0.0140] *
Forest industries	1995. 4	-2.2175	[0.0157] *	1995. 4	-2.0467	[0.0231] *
Construction	1986. 2	2.1157	[0.0186] *	1991. 2	-2.0051	[0.0253] *
	1987. 1	2.3826	[0.0097] **	1994. 3	2.7006	[0.0048] **
	1990. 1	-2.1660	[0.0165] *			
	1994. 3	2.5870	[0.0057] **			
Textiles, clothing, leather etc.	1991. 4	-2.0167	[0.0247] *	1987. 4	2.8665	[0.0031] **
				1990. 2	2.0589	[0.0225] *
				1991. 2	-2.1494	[0.0183] *
Industrial production	1991. 4	-2.1710	[0.0175] *	1996. 1	-2.0885	[0.0210] *

3 Aggregate Confidence and Industrial Production

Even though the industrial confidence indicator is rather volatile, it has been established that in the long-run the relationship is relatively stable. The instantaneous correlation is already very significant (0.63) between the aggregate industrial confidence indicator and annual growth in industrial production, but the relationship is even more convincing if annual moving average is applied to the series (Figure 31.4).[1] In most cases the confidence indicator peaks mostly a bit earlier or about the same time than actual production. Therefore it can be argued that the industrial confidence indicator might be a leading indicator of the actual production. Calculating cross-correlations between annual changes in industrial production and the confidence indicator showed also that the maximum correlation was found with one quarter lead during the period 1986-97, though the instantaneous correlation is of about the same size.

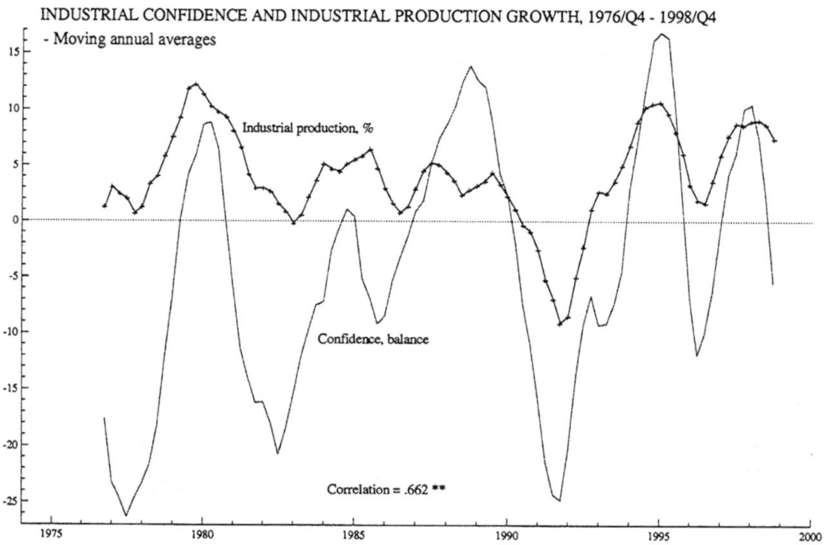

Figure 31.4 - Industrial Confidence and Production, Annual Moving Averages

Another feature worthwhile mentioning is that the mean of characteristic values is much lower than that of the observed growth in production. The mean of the confidence indicator was -4.7 during 1976-1997, while the

---

1 The industrial confidence indicator is calculated from the responses of manufacturing executives to three questions: production expectations in the next few months, order books as well as (as negatively signed) finished goods inventories compared to normal. Construction industry confidence is usually presented as a separate indicator from manufacturing barometer indicators. The confidence indicator for construction is calculated from answers to two questions: order books compared to normal and personnel expectations in the next few months.

mean of observed industrial production growth was 3.6, which indicates that about 8% growth has been assumed to be the 'normal balanced level' in industrial growth. It should be noticed also that the volatility of the confidence indicator is over twice as high as that of actual production.

The scatter plot between the confidence indicator and industrial production is shown in Figure 31.5.

In order to study the timing between industrial production and barometer responses, we calculate the cross-correlation functions. The correlation between the annual change and the business survey time series is calculated at time t for leads and lags of six quarters.[2] This allows an evaluation of relationships between the variables and the formation of an opinion on the internal relation of variables in a certain phase of the business cycle. The prime focus of interest is on variables that predict developments in manufacturing production and variables that indicate the business situation. If, for example, it turns out that the reference series is strongly correlated with some variable prior to time period t, this variable can be assumed to be a leading indicator of the measure in question. If the correlation is peaking approximately during the same time period, the variable is called a coincident variable.

One of the points of departure for this study is the assumption that the usefulness of the BTS has improved in Finland in recent years, as the survey has been expanded to cover all sectors better than before (see Kangasniemi and Tsupari, 1997). The usefulness has also been increasing by the fact that the survey is now conducted on a monthly basis in addition to the quarterly survey. Many of the studies conducted on the business survey were nevertheless done in the 1980s, when the coverage of the survey with respect to total manufacturing was much narrower than nowadays.

---

[2] Instead of quarterly changes, the analysis uses annual changes in the volume of manufacturing production as the reference series. One reason for the choice is that the annual series generates a better covariation with the business survey time series. The correlation coefficients are smaller when quarterly series are used in the comparison. The quarterly series have too much short-term variation while directional changes are more easily distinguishable from annual changes.

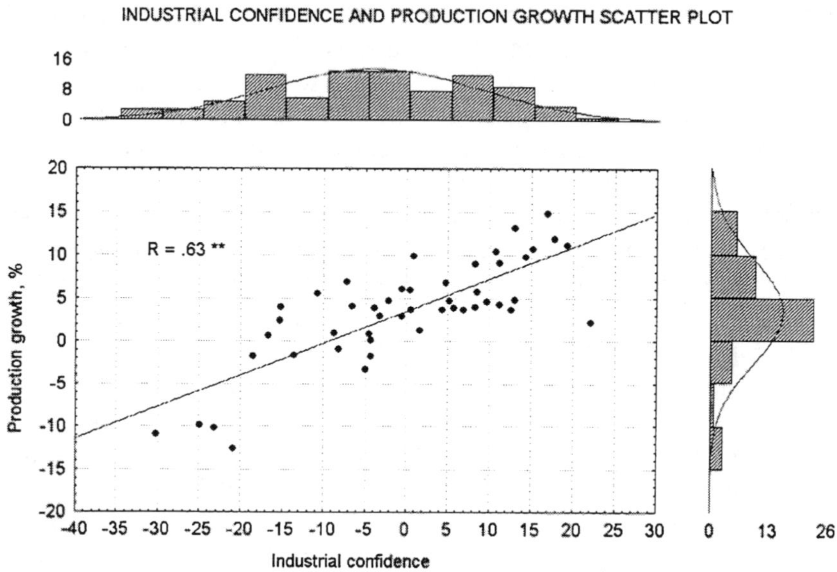

Figure 31.5 - Industrial Confidence and Production Scatter Plot

3.1 Cross-correlations Between the Manufacturing Volume and Business Tendency Series

On the basis of the coefficient analysis it can be seen that there is a strong correlation between the manufacturing production and the business trends survey variables. When we calculate correlations in different periods we find out that the correlation of the variables appears to improve after 1986. This study does not attempt to analyse closely the reason for this change, but it can be generally noted that part of this may be explained by the expansion of the business survey and changes that have occurred in the structure of manufacturing production.

Correlations between the manufacturing production and the BTS series during the period 1986-1998 are presented in table 31.3. Many of the variables correlate strongly over several successive lags. We will interpret the most significant lag for each variable as being the one where the absolute value of the correlation coefficient is highest. This holds for stationary processes.

Table 31.3 - Cross-Correlation Functions Between Industrial Production and BTS Series (BTS Variable List Presented in Appendix 1)

Correlation between the annual change of manufacturing production and BTS series at different lags, 1986-1998.

Variable	Correlation coefficient in different lags (quarters)												
101	-0.05	0.08	0.24	0.46	0.69	0.85	**0.92**	0.84	0.67	0.49	0.27	0.12	0.01
102	0.21	0.32	0.45	0.59	0.78	**0.86**	0.85	0.70	0.48	0.29	0.06	-0.08	-0.22
103	-0.39	-0.30	-0.17	0.00	0.19	0.37	0.55	0.65	0.71	**0.74**	0.70	0.69	0.64
104	-0.15	-0.06	0.11	0.30	0.47	0.63	0.73	0.78	**0.79**	0.77	0.69	0.61	0.51
105	0.30	0.38	0.43	0.51	0.66	0.70	**0.72**	0.60	0.40	0.23	-0.01	-0.18	-0.34
201	-0.03	0.14	0.32	0.55	0.76	0.83	**0.86**	0.68	0.47	0.31	0.11	0.07	0.01
202	0.23	0.41	0.52	0.67	**0.81**	0.76	0.73	0.50	0.34	0.17	-0.02	-0.09	-0.21
203	-0.29	-0.18	-0.02	0.19	0.39	0.57	0.73	0.78	**0.79**	0.75	0.67	0.62	0.54
206	0.25	0.40	0.58	0.75	**0.83**	0.82	0.70	0.46	0.29	0.14	0.03	0.03	-0.01
207	0.37	0.54	0.66	0.76	**0.81**	0.77	0.62	0.38	0.23	0.06	-0.04	-0.07	-0.14
208	-0.35	-0.28	-0.15	0.04	0.22	0.35	**0.44**	0.43	0.35	0.23	0.08	-0.07	-0.16
209	**-0.62**	-0.61	-0.56	-0.43	-0.27	-0.04	0.18	0.34	0.44	0.48	0.48	0.42	0.35
310	-0.07	0.06	0.18	0.37	0.55	0.70	0.82	**0.82**	0.77	0.70	0.59	0.49	0.39
311	-0.30	-0.17	0.02	0.25	0.50	0.70	**0.78**	0.76	0.66	0.55	0.41	0.31	0.22
312	-0.06	-0.15	-0.23	-0.32	-0.37	-0.29	-0.18	0.02	0.19	0.32	**0.38**	0.36	0.33
313	-0.40	-0.46	**-0.51**	-0.49	-0.48	-0.41	-0.24	-0.04	0.22	0.38	0.44	0.43	0.39
314	0.16	0.21	0.22	0.31	0.40	0.43	**0.43**	0.34	0.25	0.16	0.07	0.02	-0.07
315	**-0.75**	-0.66	-0.50	-0.34	-0.17	-0.03	0.08	0.16	0.20	0.20	0.20	0.19	0.18
316	-0.34	-0.23	-0.09	0.10	0.31	0.46	0.56	**0.60**	0.52	0.47	0.38	0.27	0.19
317	**0.66**	0.60	0.48	0.40	0.29	0.17	0.08	-0.06	-0.12	-0.20	-0.25	-0.24	-0.25
401	0.14	0.27	0.45	0.65	0.76	**0.84**	0.82	0.67	0.54	0.39	0.28	0.24	0.20
402	0.37	0.46	0.56	0.70	0.74	**0.78**	0.73	0.59	0.46	0.30	0.15	0.09	0.03
403	-0.26	-0.10	0.10	0.30	0.51	0.69	0.79	**0.83**	0.78	0.72	0.63	0.54	0.45
406	0.44	0.53	0.62	0.72	0.73	**0.78**	0.71	0.55	0.48	0.34	0.25	0.22	0.16
407	0.46	0.52	0.58	0.64	0.69	**0.70**	0.65	0.56	0.43	0.32	0.18	0.11	0.05
408	-0.19	-0.07	0.09	0.28	0.42	**0.53**	0.51	0.43	0.28	0.11	0.00	-0.11	-0.15
409	**-0.62**	-0.57	-0.46	-0.30	-0.13	0.11	0.27	0.34	0.39	0.34	0.30	0.26	0.17
501	0.31	0.46	0.57	0.63	0.71	**0.73**	0.72	0.59	0.50	0.36	0.25	0.25	0.17
502	0.54	0.62	0.66	0.66	**0.71**	0.68	0.64	0.55	0.41	0.28	0.12	0.01	-0.11
518	0.40	0.55	0.69	0.82	**0.89**	0.86	0.75	0.55	0.37	0.19	0.06	0.01	-0.03
604	0.17	0.29	0.48	0.64	0.74	**0.84**	0.81	0.73	0.59	0.44	0.30	0.17	0.07
605	0.64	0.68	**0.73**	0.73	0.63	0.46	0.22	0.00	-0.17	-0.30	-0.34	-0.33	-0.29
CI	-0.14	0.01	0.21	0.45	0.66	0.79	**0.80**	0.68	0.54	0.38	0.24	0.17	0.11
Lags	**-6**	**-5**	**-4**	**-3**	**-2**	**-1**	**0**	**1**	**2**	**3**	**4**	**5**	**6**

Many variables correlate strongly and predict the development of manufacturing production. The annual change of manufacturing production is best predicted with a lead of two quarters by BTS518, 'business outlook in the near future', with a correlation coefficient of 0.89. Also BTS206, 'order inflow compared with the previous quarter' (0.83) predicts production well. The correlation with a one quarter lead with respect to the volume of manufacturing production is as follows: for BTS604, 'investment expectation a year ahead' (0.84), for BTS206, 'order inflow compared with the previous quarter' (0.83) and for BTS202, 'volume of export compared with the previous quarter' (0.81). The confidence indicator (BTSCI) predicts the volume of production best with a lead of one quarter. The variable best capturing the development of manufacturing production at time t seems to be BTS101, 'production compared with the same quarter a year before'. The variables have a correlation coefficient of 0.92. Some of the business survey variables correlate with the reference variables with a lag. The variable depicting production capacity utilisation, BTS311, follows the level of production with a lag of one quarter.

The variable concerning the amount of personnel seems to follow the production volume with a lag. The variable BTS103, 'number of personnel compared with the same quarter a year ago' follows the trend in production best with a lag of three quarters with a correlation coefficient of 0.74. The variable 'number of personnel compared with the previous quarter', BTS203, follows production changes with a lag of two quarters. 'Personnel expectation for the next quarter' follows production with a lag of one quarter. One conclusion that can be drawn on the basis of this analysis is that all BTS series are highly correlated with each other. From this it can be decided that the business survey provides a relatively explicit picture of cyclical variations.

On the basis of the business survey, we can form a disaggregated picture of the economic situation. This is because, even though the BTS variables are correlated with each other, some of them genuinely predict the development of manufacturing production, while others do this with a lag. From the correlated variables we can thus select the best and monitor these BTS variables.

3.2 *Correlation Between the Manufacturing Volume and BTS Series in Different Branches*

In table 31.4 different industrial tendency barometer responses are investigated based on cross-correlations with the annual industrial production growth. The purpose of this analysis is to classify responses into leading, simultaneous and lagging indicators to find out the most efficient leading indicator for forecasting models. The table lists only response variables with significant correlations.

At afirst look there are some surprises in the correlations, e.g. for instance that the confidence indicator is a lagging indicator in chemical and construction industries. In food and construction industries there seems to be also a bias between confidence and actual production (Figure 31.6).

However, there are many intuitively reliable looking results as well. For instance production growth estimated by respondents (BTS101) receives a simultaneous significant correlation for most industries as it should. The same applies to production with respect to the previous quarter (BTS 201). However, production expectations in the next quarter (BTS401) show significant correlation only for total industry and construction industry. Production expectations for the second quarter ahead do not show a meaningful correlation for any industry.

Table 31.4 - Best Industry Specific Indicators for Industrial Production, 1986/Q1 - 1997/Q4

Branch	Leading indicators	Simultaneous indicators	Lagging indicators
Food, beverages etc.	206, 402, 408	518, 604	101, 207
Chemical industry	105, 206, 518	201	101, 311, CI
Metal industry	201, 206, 502, 518	101, 102, 403	103, 203, 310
Forest industry	206, 207, 313, 518	101, 102, 202	208, 310, 604
Construction	105, 209, 401, 403	101, 201, 206	103, 310, CI
Textiles, clothing	201, 407, 502, 605	102, 105, 518	101, 103, 203
Total industry	102, 206, 401, 518, 604	101, 201, 311, CI	104, 203, 310, 403

Variable explanations:

101 = Production compared to corresponding quarter previous year
102 = Exports compared to correspoding quarter previous year
103 = Personnel wrt corresponding quarter previous year
105 = Profitability wrt corresponding quarter previous year

201 = Production wrt past quarter
202 = Exports wrt past quarter
203 = Personnel wrt past
206 = New orders wrt past quarter
207 = New export orders wrt past quarter
208 = Selling prices wrt past quarter
209 = Expot prices wrt past quarter

310 = Production potential
311 = Order books wrt normal level
313 = Raw material inventory stocks

401 = Production expectations for next quarter
402 = Exports expectations for next quarter
403 = Personnel expectations for next quarter
407 = Export order expectations for next quarter
408 = Selling price expectations for next quarter

501 = Production expectation two quarters ahead
502 = Export expectations two quarters ahead
518 = Business expectations in the near future

604 = Investment expectations a year ahead
605 = Profitability expectations a year ahead
CI = Confidence indicator

One of the most important observations is that the question concerning business outlook in the near future (BTS518) is strongly correlated with forthcoming production changes, so we expect this variable to be an efficient predictor in forecasting models. It is very plausible and natural that the variable concerning new orders (BTS206, BTS407) will be a valuable predictor for future production also. Investment and profitability expectations seem worthwhile trying as explanatory variables for a couple of industries.

On the basis of the coefficient analysis carried out in different industrial branch series it can be seen that there is in general quite a strong correlation between the manufacturing production and the business trends survey variables. On the basis of the analysis we can already make a couple of additional remarks.

One important result, that we found out, was that there are certain discrepancies between industrial branches. Also in different branches different BTS variables get the highest correlation coefficient at time t. It seems that the best correlation between the production volume and business tendency series in different branches can be found in branches, in which respondents are more homogeneous. Those branches are e.g. machinery and equipment, metal products and construction. When we again calculate correlation coefficients in different periods, we find out that the correlation of the variables appears to improve with time. Many of the variables correlate well over the whole period, and in many cases the improvement was considerable.

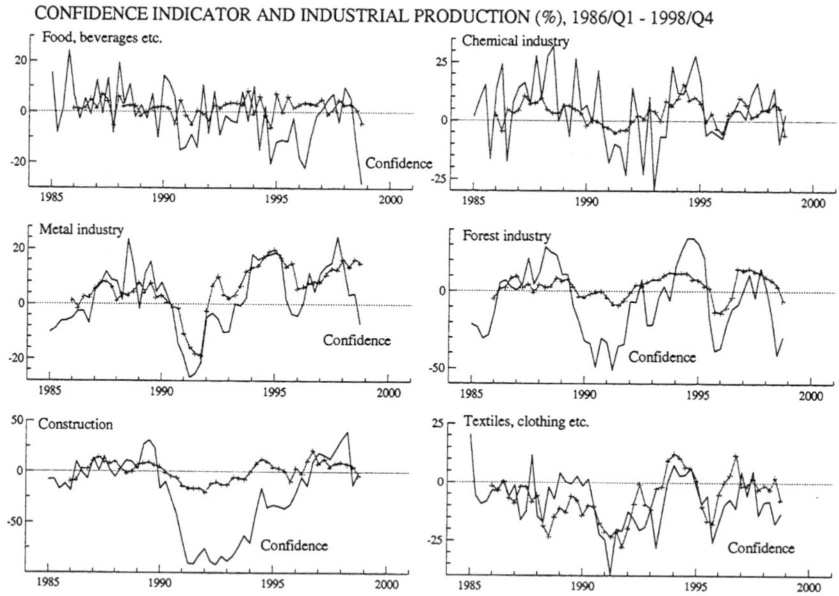

Figure 31.6 - Comparison of Industrial Confidence and Production by Branch

In table 31.5 we take a closer look at the production evaluation and expectation responses in the questionaire with respect to actual changes in production. First, we can notice the fact that the past is known better than the future in the form of decreasing correlation from the past year to two quarters ahead. The evaluation about the past year is very accurate for most industrial branches, only in food production this estimate seems to be a poor one. The past quarter is also rather accurately estimated in other industries apart from food and chemical industries.

Assessing the forthcoming production we notice a couple of interesting features. Predicting the production of the next quarter is a most difficult task in food and chemical industries of course, but for some reason the correlation is rather weak also for the forest industry. This seems a bit amazing since the paper industry, which forms the largest part of the forest industry, is a process industry where one would think that production would be relatively easily predictable. A couple of very low production expectations at 1990/Q3 and 1991/Q2 are mainly responsible for this. Anyway, the correlation for the next further quarter ahead is again pretty accurately estimated. It seems also somewhat surprising that extending production expectations for two quarters ahead does not deteriorate the fit very much.

Table 31.5 - Correlation Between Production Evaluations and Expectations to Actual Industrial Production, 1986/Q1 – 1997/Q4

Industrial branch	Past year	Past quarter	Next quarter	Two quarters ahead
Food, beverages etc.	0.341	0.166	0.128	0.139
Chemical industry	0.602	0.231	0.385	0.252
Metal industry	0.897	0.772	0.579	0.645
Forest industry	0.865	0.547	0.271	0.533
Construction	0.882	0.793	0.761	0.741
Textiles, clothing	0.798	0.694	0.599	0.529
Total industry	**0.921**	**0.627**	**0.538**	**0.604**

4 Causality Test for Barometer Variables

Even though we have already analysed the cross-correlation functions between barometer variables, it must be understood that correlation itself does not necessarily imply causation in any useful sense. Granger causality-tests can be helpful in finding genuine explanatory candidates for forecasting models. In Granger causality tests the question of causation from the point of predictive ability, namely the question whether x causes y, is approached by looking at how much of the current y can be explained by past values of y and then to see whether adding lagged values of x can improve this autoregressive explanation.[3]

Table 31.6 shows the correlations and Granger causality tests between production expectations of different industries and their actual respective production published in national statistics. The time periods of the expectations are matched to the corresponding periods concerned.[4] Correlations between expectations a quarter ahead and actual realized production quarterly changes vary a lot. Reasonably high correlations are achieved in metal, construction, textile industries and chemical industries. This result does not change concerning Granger causality tests at 5% significance level.

---

[3] Granger causality tests can be performed by two linear regressions, one containing the lagged values of the barometer variable in the equation and one without. Granger causality test is then based on an F-test for the lagged barometer response variables as a group. If this F-test is significant, we can conclude that the barometer variable reduces the forecast error of the industrial production variable and it therefore useful at least in an autoregressive model. It should be remembered that Granger causality does not mean any strict philosophical relation between cause and effect, but merely that one variable can be helpful in predicting another. In some sense forecasting ability is stronger a property than pure explanatory coincidence, since it requires controllable predictability between variables if all the 'third variable' links are eliminated from the framework. Granger non-causality i.e. absence of feedback from the dependent variable back to the independent variable has therefore an important role in econometric model building (see e.g. Hamilton, 1994).

[4] For instance as production expectations for the next quarter are investigated, the actual quarterly production change is lead to the corresponding period. However, in Granger tests only predictive i.e. lagged relationships with the production expectations are concerned.

Table 31.6 - Granger Causality Tests for Production Expectations in Different Industries

Industry	Correlation *Quarter ahead*	Granger test p-values *Expectations quarter ahead*		Correlation *Two quarters ahead*	Granger test p-values *Expectations two quarters ahead*	
		One lag	Four lags		One lag	Four lags
Food, beverages etc.	0.128	0.392	0.351	0.139	0.767	0.1771
Chemical industry	0.385	0.0225*	0.238	0.252	0.569	0.7732
Metal industry	0.579	0.0384*	0.116	0.645	0.231	0.5339
Forest industry	0.271	0.0971	0.23	0.533	0.0002**	0.9838
Construction	0.761	0.0013**	0.036*	0.741	0.057	0.3749
Textiles, clothing	0.599	0.0003**	0.004**	0.529	0.111	0.8365
Total industry	**0.538**	**0.0072****	**0.09**	**0.604**	**0.572**	**0.7049**

* = Statistically significant at 5% probability level, ** = Statistically significant at 1% probability level

Correlation columns present instantaneous correlations between production expectations (matched timing interval) and actual seasonally adjusted quarter-to-quarter changes in production

Production expectations look a bit different regarding the orrelations two quarters ahead. Correlations are surprisingly high still, but the Granger tests indicate that only forest industry and probably construction industries expectations have extra predictive power. Again the poorest performance is achieved for the food industry, where both simultaneous correlation and predictive power is weak.

5 Structural Model Estimations for Industrial Production

This section builds up the models, which are aimed at forecasting industrial production by sector. The main task is to evaluate how useful barometer responses are in forecasting production by branch. We use a structural time series model in this work since our interest is to get reliable and efficient short-term forecasts for the production series. By adding barometer variables as explanatory variables into the system, we get assessments of the predictive power of business tendency survey variables in a multivariate framework. One advantage of this framework is that we can get an idea of the stochastic behaviour of the industrial production series by looking at their stochastic level and slope terms as well as noise terms that describe the current state of the process. An important advantage is also that we can deal with nonstationarities i.e. unit roots in the original data within the same framework without taking differences. Another benefit of the structural time series models over Arima-models is that intervention variables with a desired effect on the dependent variable are much easier to be pecified as additional regressors.

Structural time series models (STM) are models, where the variation of the dependent variable is decomposed into time series components that have direct interpretation. Although these components are unobservable, they are based on the classical decomposition of trend, cycle, seasonal and irregular noise. Shortly a basic structural model can be written in an additive form

$$y_t = \mu_t + \psi_t + \gamma_t + \varepsilon_t,\ t = 1,\ldots,T \tag{1}$$

where μ_t is the trend, ψ_t is cycle, γ_t refers to the seasonal term and ε_t is the irregular noise component.

It is important to note that this family of models can be interpreted as regression models in which parameters are time-varying. If additive explanatory variables are added into this framework, they can be functions of time as well. The estimation of the variance parameters is based on a Kalman filter (see Harvey 1989).

The trend is defined as the best estimate of the long-run tendency forecast, which implies that trend should be essentially invariant to changes in the timing interval. The trend component can be further decomposed into e.g. random walk with a drift type of model

$$\mu_t = \mu_{t-1} + \beta + \eta_t \tag{2}$$

or even a more flexible stochastic trend model (see e.g. Harvey and Shephard 1993)

$$\mu t = \mu t\text{-}1 + \beta t\text{-}1 + \eta t \tag{3}$$

$$\beta t = \beta t\text{-}1 + \zeta t. \tag{4}$$

It should be noted that the irregular term ε_t and the local level noise η_t are assumed to be mutually uncorrelated white noise disturbances, which allows us to calculate the signal-noise ratio $q = Var(\eta_t)/Var(\varepsilon_t)$. This measure tells us how much systematic information there is in the trend component with respect to the irregular residual estimated conditional to the specified information set (past history in filtering, sample in smoothing). In general the larger is $Var(\eta_t)$ in comparison with $Var(\varepsilon_t)$ the greater is the discounting of the past observations relative to current observations. If $Var(\varepsilon_t)$ is zero, we have the limiting case that observations follow a random walk, which implies that the best forecast of the process is the latest observation y_T. In the alternative limiting case that $Var(\eta_t)$ and β_t is zero, the level μ_t is constant and the best forecast is the sample mean. If q ratio is zero i.e. $Var(\eta_t) = 0$, then the trend is deterministic. A standard regression model with deterministic time trend emerges when $Var(\zeta_t) = 0$. In the limiting case of no unobservable components structural time series models collapse into ordinary regression models, so regression models can be regarded as a subclass of STM models. On the other hand STM models can be classified to be a subclass of unobservable component Arima-models.

A multivariate structural time series model can be written as (Harvey and Shephard, 1993 p. 267)

$$y_t = Z_t\alpha_t + X_t\beta + \varepsilon_t, \quad t = 1,\ldots,T . \tag{5}$$

where y_t is a N x 1 vector of dependent variables, Z_t and X_t are N x p and N x k nonstochastic matrices respectively. The regression coefficients β are fixed and white noise terms ε_t have zero mean with innovation variance H_t. In the state space form regression coefficients α_t are allowed to evolve over time with the transition equation

$$\alpha_t = T_t\alpha_{t-1} + W_t\beta + R_t\eta_t , \quad t = 1,\ldots,T, \tag{6}$$

where again T_t (p x p), W_t (p x k) and R_t (p x g) are fixed matrices.

Model selection in a multivariate structural time series framework proceeds pretty much in the same way as in multivariate system modelling with exogenous explanatory variables. Model specification and selection heads towards a formulation which explains the characteristics of the data and give a structurally stable description of the data with parsimonious parametrization. When available explanatory variables do not explain all the nonstationary features of the dependent variable, stochastic trend components included will approximate these characteristics. Therefore stochastic trend components proxy for omitted variables in the regression.

When we are considering industrial production by branch, we obviously see that there is more or less distinct cyclical variation in each industry.

Partly these cyclical movements arise from the common business cycle in industrial production and overall economic activity.[5]

Before moving to the system modelling, we had a quick look at the time series properties of confidence indicators in contrast to those of the production series by industrial branch. Univariate structural time series models were first estimated without explanatory variables. The underlying processes are quite similar for production and confidence in terms of structural time series components, which was expected by the high correlation between the series. But there were differences also. For instance at the final state (i.e. the end point at 1997/Q4) construction has a significant slope, but in the confidence indicator we find some noise in the decomposition. The same applies to the textiles industry confidence, but we cannot identify that component in the actual textiles production. The coefficients of determination are quite similar for confidence and production series except in the textiles and chemical industries, but the prediction error variances are much higher for confidence structural models. The structural model identified for the total industrial production and its confidence indicator point out that these processes could be random walks without drift or even noise term.

In addition to the system structural time series analysis, we tested for cointegration between industrial branches and according to tests performed there could be one or two cointegrating relationships among six branches. The first cointegration relation involved food and chemical industries, the second cointegrating relation involved several sectors. However, error-correction terms calculated based on these relations did not prove to be significant explanatory factors in our system STM models, so they were not included into the final models.[6]

In table 31.7 the results from univariate structural time series models are given with potential explanatory variables as a benchmark for comparison. In addition to the structural components (level and slope) regressors we have included production expectations with the corresponding lags, the confidence indicator at present time and with one quarter lag, and the business outlook variable with two lags into the model. The level parameter

---

[5] It is possible to take these common features into account with common trend (cointegration) constraints. Similar cycles are also very plausible e.g. among metal and forests industries because of the common business cycle.

[6] It would be nice to have a theoretical explanation for these observed long-run relationships, which would make us more comfortable for using them, although we are aiming at only short-term forecasting models. In addition it should be remembered that our sample is not long enough to identify properly cointegrating relations.

indicates the current growth rate at the final state of the estimation, which was significantly differing from zero in chemical, metal, forest and construction industries. The slope term, which shows the short-term acceleration of growth was not significant for any sector at the end point.

The production expectations applied as explanatory variables did have additional predictive power in forest and construction industries. The confidence indicator was inevitably the strongest separate predictor for output in chemical, metal and forest industries. However, we notice that the lagged confidence indicator did not have additional predictive power in any branch. To our surprise the business outlook in the near future, which was used with two quarters lag, did not appear to be a reliable leading indicator for any industry. In general barometer response variables do increase significantly the overall explanatory power and predictive ability of the industrial production.

As a benchmark case, we may compare pure univariate structural time series models with univariate models with the above mentioned regressors. For all branches we see a significant increase in the coefficient of determination. System modelling can take into account the relationships between different industries. For instance, continuous growth in paper production (chemical forest industry) may generate paper machine investment that will certainly affect the metal industry as the major manufacturer for paper mills of Finnish firms. In a similar way a construction boom will increase orders for basic metals as in the construction of buildings steel and other metal inputs must be used.

In table 31.8 a structural time series system estimation is presented for six major industries. Applying system estimation with production expectations, confidence indicator and business outlook series as explanatory variables we can get a clear improvement in the R^2's for each branch. Coefficients of determination are in fact surprisingly high for metal and construction industries as we are modelling annual percent changes in industrial production and not the levels. Only the volatile production in the food production cannot be forecasted very efficiently.

Table 31.7 - Univariate Models With Production Expectations, Confidence and Business Climate as Explanatory Variables, 1986/Q1 – 1997/Q4 (t –Values Shown Below Parameter Estimates)

Industry	Explanatory variables (the number of lags used in parenthesis)							
	Structural parameters		Production exp. quarter ahead (1)	Production exp. two quarters ahead (2)	Confidence indicator	Confidence indicator (1)	Business outlook (2)	R^2
	Level	Slope						
Food, beverages etc.	**1.52**	**0.001**	**0.059**	**0.018**	**0.024**	**-0.099**	**0.012**	**0.087**
	1.51	0.017	1.86	0.71	0.64	-1.97	0.52	-
Chemical industry	**5.92****	**0.197**	**0.019**	**-0.003**	**0.08***	**0.065**	**-0.016**	**0.695**
	4.62	0.41	0.56	-1.16	2.47	1.59	-0.652	-
Metal industry	**5.66 ***	**0.053**	**0.098**	**0.007**	**0.184****	**0.058**	**0.065**	**0.886**
	2.22	0.11	1.19	0.113	2.75	0.567	1.54	-
Forest industry	**10.58****	**0.187**	**-0.02**	**.115***	**0.14****	**0.054**	**0.014**	**0.752**
	5.71	0.405	-0.36	2.53	2.94	0.89	0.041	-
Construction	**8.51****	**-1.51**	**0.037***	**0.001**	**-0.034**	**0.015**	**0.001**	**0.931**
	5.51	-0.65	2.59	0.08	-1.19	0.513	0.056	-
Textiles, clothing	**0.43**	**0.021**	**0.078**	**0.048**	**0.071**	**0.017**	**0.037**	**0.833**
	0.43	0.037	1.32	0.94	1.24	0.21	0.96	-

From the results we can conclude that production expectations for the next quarter ahead is a relatively strong indicator for forthcoming production of all industries but forest industry, where production expectations two quarters ahead seem to be a better indicator. The 'Business outlook in the near future'-variable was again used with two lags to extent the forecast horizon a bit further ahead.

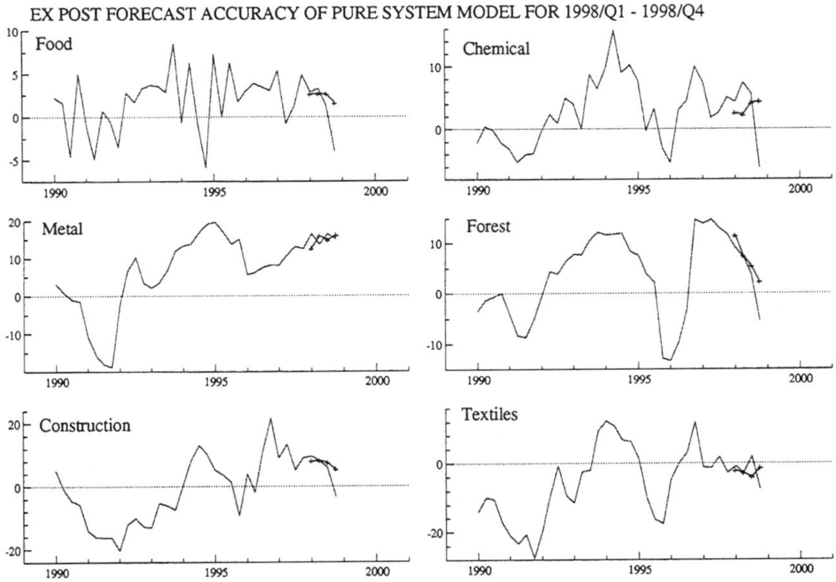

Figure 31.7 - Ex Post Forecast Accuracy of the Pure System Model Without Explanatory Variables

However, the ex post prediction tests performed for 1998 showed us few interesting features in addition to the improvement in forecasting ability from the benchmark univariate models. These tests are shown in table 31.9, where we notice however, that apparently year 1998 was somewhat exceptional. For pure STM forecasts ex post forecast accuracy proved to be very good for all branches but the chemical industry (see Figure 31.7). Although using barometer indicators seemed to be significant on average in the long run, ex post forecast errors for 1998 did increase significantly in food, metal, forest and construction industries. Of course, this may simply reflect the particular situation in 1998, but it causes some concern, since it may reflect the fact that in the short-run barometer indicators may divert the forecast from the recently observed actual variables. In some cases - e.g. production expectations two quarters ahead - it may be preferable to try to smooth the series by moving averages or other means to reduce the short-term noise.

As our major concern was to build up forecasting models for industrial production, we also calculated the ex ante forecasts for 1999 with different system models. These results are presented in table 31.10, which show a very wide range for possible forecasts depending on assumptions behind modelling.

6 Conclusions

In this paper we have tested the predictive power of Finnish Business Tendency Survey variables for industrial production by branch and measured their increment to the prediction accuracy of industrial production forecasts. We have found that we can clearly get considerably smaller prediction errors by using both system modelling for industrial branches and BTS series as explanatory regressors. In the long run it looks preferable to use system modelling with barometer indicators at the same time. However, our ex post forecast accuracy calculations for 1998 did not convince us that the barometer indicators were that useful. It might be the case that some smoothing could be helpful before the volatile barometer indicators can be used in forecasting work.

In the univariate time series models the best short-run predictor seemed to be the confidence indicator, while also production expectations are sometimes valuable. It came as some sort of surprise that the business outlook variable, which has a very high correlation with the production growth by branch otherwise, did not prove to be significant in our system models with two quarters lead. It is possible that the business outlook variable merely summarizes effectively the information, which is already included into other BTS responses.

In structural time series system modelling the confidence indicator was left out and the business outlook variable was applied as leading indicator in addition to production expectation variables. This system modelling exercise proved to be slightly better than system models with confidence indicators in terms of fit and model diagnostics.

In general it looks almost self evident that barometer indicators and other systematic assessments made by the actual economic agents performing the economic actions should be a useful aid in the forecasting work. Here we have used barometer variables directly connected to production for improving time series forecasts, and found clear evidence in favour for this type of modelling.

Table 31.8 - Multivariate Structural Time Series Model for Industrial Production, 1986/Q1 - 1998/Q4

Variable	Food Coefficient	Food t-value	Chemical Coefficient	Chemical t-value	Metal Coefficient	Metal t-value	Forest Coefficient	Forest t-value	Construction Coefficient	Construction t-value	Textiles Coefficient	Textiles t-value
Level	2.916	0.95	-2.320	-0.85	6.644	2.06	-6.730	-1.57	-14.085	-2.42	-15.029	-2.43
Slope	0.062	0.24	-0.623	-1.92	0.995	1.67	-3.880	-1.75	-1.935	-1.92	-2.797	-1.74
Production expectations one quarter ahead												
Textiles	0.016	0.30	0.004	0.08	0.014	0.27	0.058	1.04	0.069	0.81	0.177	1.76
Construction	-0.005	-0.16	0.057	1.81	0.046	1.36	0.062	1.60	0.139	2.48	-0.016	-0.24
Forest	0.013	0.32	0.070	1.76	0.067	1.54	-0.065	-1.32	-0.128	-1.82	-0.017	-0.21
Metal	0.039	0.56	0.133	2.00	0.054	0.75	0.021	0.26	0.116	1.00	0.236	1.72
Chemical	0.033	1.06	0.060	2.03	0.021	0.67	-0.014	-0.42	0.049	0.99	0.122	2.05
Food	0.040	1.20	0.072	2.32	0.083	2.44	-0.009	-0.22	0.039	0.68	0.085	1.29
Production expectations two quarters ahead												
Textiles	0.028	0.48	0.080	1.45	0.120	1.99	-0.106	-1.58	-0.128	-1.32	0.094	0.82
Construction	0.026	0.82	-0.086	-2.87	0.031	0.93	-0.060	-1.56	-0.088	-1.63	-0.013	-0.21
Forest	0.077	1.82	-0.012	-0.31	-0.030	-0.70	0.082	1.67	0.044	0.62	0.070	0.84
Metal	-0.240	-2.73	-0.089	-1.07	0.097	1.08	0.110	1.09	0.166	1.14	-0.030	-0.18
Chemical	-0.006	-0.18	-0.088	-2.75	-0.002	-0.07	-0.067	-1.75	-0.101	-1.80	-0.058	-0.87
Food	0.094	2.45	0.076	2.06	-0.117	-2.99	0.004	0.11	-0.028	-0.44	-0.054	-0.73
Business outlook in the near future (lagged two quarters)												
Textiles	-0.026	-0.51	-0.094	-1.92	0.019	0.35	-0.042	-0.74	0.045	0.53	0.107	1.06
Construction	-0.070	-2.12	0.035	1.13	-0.021	-0.64	0.022	0.56	0.098	1.72	-0.027	-0.42
Forest	-0.049	-1.34	0.023	0.68	0.061	1.57	0.147	2.93	0.092	1.43	-0.017	-0.23
Metal	0.140	2.71	0.063	1.31	0.005	0.09	0.048	0.73	-0.054	-0.60	-0.007	-0.07
Chemical	0.089	2.30	0.005	0.14	0.045	1.14	0.025	0.59	0.048	0.76	-0.020	-0.26
Food	-0.004	-0.09	-0.028	-0.68	-0.002	-0.05	-0.118	-2.39	-0.022	-0.30	0.058	0.68
PEV ratio	-	1.407	-	1.471	-	1.562	-	1.698	-	1.448	-	1.437
R^2	-	0.419	-	0.766	-	0.907	-	0.786	-	0.800	-	0.720
Rd^2	-	0.745	-	0.705	-	0.615	-	0.526	-	0.473	-	0.384
Rs^2	-	0.745	-	0.701	-	0.606	-	0.526	-	0.462	-	0.362

Table 31.9a - Ex Post Prediction Error Analysis for 1998

Food, beverages etc.

	Multistep extrapolations	RMSE	Ex post pure system	RMSE	Ex post system	RMSE	Statistic	P-value
1998Q1	0.20	3.58	0.20	3.58	3.35	3.00	-	-
1998Q2	0.72	4.03	0.62	3.58	-3.07	3.00	-	-
1998Q3	-1.29	4.57	-1.47	3.58	-6.02	3.00	-	-
1998Q4	-6.41	5.21	-5.60	3.58	-5.83	3.00	-	-
Predictive error Chow F(4, 46) test for pure STM system:							0.54	0.70
Predictive failure Chi2 (4) test for system estimation with explanatory variables:							10.12	.0384*

Chemical industry

	Multistep extrapolations	RMSE	Ex post pure system	RMSE	Ex post system	RMSE		
1998Q1	1.82	4.38	1.82	4.38	-5.00	3.03	-	-
1998Q2	5.80	5.74	5.20	4.38	3.10	3.03	-	-
1998Q3	4.91	7.43	1.52	4.38	2.30	3.03	-	-
1998Q4	-5.92	9.41	-10.55	4.38	-5.66	3.03	-	-
Predictive error Chow F(4, 46) test for pure STM system:							2.18	0.09
Predictive failure Chi2 (4) test for system estimation with explanatory variables:							7.85	0.10

Metal industry

	Multistep extrapolations	RMSE	Ex post pure system	RMSE	Ex post system	RMSE		
1998Q1	3.97	5.49	3.97	5.49	1.50	2.86	-	-
1998Q2	0.76	7.35	-2.44	5.49	-2.68	2.86	-	-
1998Q3	3.49	9.53	1.74	5.49	11.30	2.86	-	-
1998Q4	1.70	11.97	-1.19	5.49	12.60	2.86	-	
Predictive error Chow F(4, 46) test for pure STM system:							0.27	0.90
Predictive failure Chi2 (4) test for system estimation with explanatory variables:							36.31	.0000**

Table 31.9b - Ex Post Prediction Error Analysis for 1998

Forest industry

	Multistep extrapolations	RMSE	Ex post pure system	RMSE	Ex post system	RMSE	Statistic	P-value
1998Q1	-2.63	6.58	-2.63	6.58	-7.27	4.35	-	-
1998Q2	-3.27	9.99	-0.20	6.58	-0.33	4.35	-	-
1998Q3	-5.87	14.19	-1.68	6.58	1.53	4.35	-	-
1998Q4	-13.90	19.01	-7.58	6.58	-11.55	4.34	-	-
Predictive error Chow F(4, 46) test for pure STM system							0.61	0.66
Predictive failure Chi2 (4) test for system estimation with explanatory variables:							10.00	.0404*

Construction

	Multistep extrapolations	RMSE	Ex post pure system	RMSE	Ex post system	RMSE		
1998Q1	1.62	6.64	1.62	6.64	0.78	5.25	-	-
1998Q2	0.86	8.77	-0.09	6.64	-0.09	5.25	-	-
1998Q3	-0.68	11.34	-1.67	6.64	5.11	5.25	-	-
1998Q4	-9.02	14.28	-8.49	6.64	-18.51	5.25	-	-
Predictive error Chow F(4, 46) test for pure STM system:							0.47	0.76
Predictive failure Chi2 (4) test for system estimation with explanatory variables:							13.41	.0095 **

Textiles, clothing etc.

	Multistep extrapolations	RMSE	Ex post pure system	RMSE	Ex post system	RMSE		
1998Q1	1.24	7.63	1.24	7.63	-4.02	6.65	-	-
1998Q2	0.22	9.74	0.01	7.63	-4.41	6.64	-	-
1998Q3	6.08	12.16	6.08	7.63	13.40	6.64	-	-
1998Q4	-2.53	14.87	-6.07	7.63	0.85	6.64	-	-
Predictive error Chow F(4, 46) test for pure STM system:							0.34	0.85
Predictive failure Chi2 (4) test for system estimation with explanatory variables:							4.89	0.30

Table 31.10 - Comparison of Ex-Ante Forecasts for Industrial Production by Branch in 1999

Food, beverages etc.

	Pure STM system		System with expl. vars		Pure dynamic VAR-system	
	Forecast	RMSE	Forecast	RMSE	Forecast	Std.error
1999Q1	-1.44	3.58	-1.41	3.16	2.32	3.21
1999Q2	-2.21	4.03	-0.17	3.40	4.92	3.46
1999Q3	-2.99	4.57	-0.10	3.65	2.36	3.69
1999Q4	-3.77	5.21	-0.04	3.89	3.32	3.74

Chemical industry

	Pure STM system		System with expl. vars		Pure dynamic VAR-system	
	Forecast	RMSE	Forecast	RMSE	Forecast	Std.error
1999Q1	-3.60	4.38	-8.15	2.96	-4.36	3.19
1999Q2	-5.89	5.73	-5.18	3.11	-4.86	4.29
1999Q3	-8.19	7.43	-5.80	3.30	-2.86	5.01
1999Q4	-10.48	9.41	-6.43	3.51	1.51	5.32

Metal industry

	Pure STM system		System with expl. vars		Pure dynamic VAR-system	
	Forecast	RMSE	Forecast	RMSE	Forecast	Std.error
1999Q1	14.89	5.49	7.60	3.29	8.10	3.96
1999Q2	14.76	7.35	7.96	3.72	4.75	5.91
1999Q3	14.62	9.53	8.96	4.21	2.49	7.31
1999Q4	14.48	11.97	9.95	4.77	1.90	8.23

Forest industry

	Pure STM system		System with expl. vars		Pure dynamic VAR-system	
	Forecast	RMSE	Forecast	RMSE	Forecast	Std.error
1999Q1	-8.17	6.58	-22.66	4.20	-7.25	4.20
1999Q2	-13.08	9.99	-21.01	6.06	-8.45	5.72
1999Q3	-18.00	14.19	-24.89	8.38	-6.86	6.73
1999Q4	-22.91	19.01	-28.77	11.07	-3.19	7.33

Construction

	Pure STM system		System with expl. vars		Pure dynamic VAR-system	
	Forecast	RMSE	Forecast	RMSE	Forecast	Std.error
1999Q1	-4.30	6.64	-29.44	5.52	-2.84	5.94
1999Q2	-7.93	8.77	-28.08	6.38	-6.27	7.50
1999Q3	-11.56	11.34	-30.01	7.29	-4.13	8.96
1999Q4	-15.19	14.28	-31.95	8.26	-1.78	9.89

Textiles, clothing etc.

	Pure STM system		System with expl. vars		Pure dynamic VAR-system	
	Forecast	RMSE	Forecast	RMSE	Forecast	Std.error
1999Q1	-8.29	7.63	-11.63	6.36	-10.53	5.96
1999Q2	-10.80	9.74	-15.97	7.39	-12.94	8.03
1999Q3	-13.31	12.16	-18.76	8.74	-10.02	9.26
1999Q4	-15.82	14.87	-21.56	10.39	-5.63	9.82

7 Appendix

Business survey variables used in the research:

BTS101 Volume of production compared with the same quarter a year before
BTS102 Volume of export compared with the same quarter a year before
BTS103 Number of personnel compared with the same quarter a year before
BTS104 Volume of investment compared with the same quarter a year before
BTS105 Profitability compared with the same quarter a year before
BTS201 Volume of production compared with the previous quarter
BTS202 Volume of export compared with the previous quarter
BTS203 Number of personnel compared with the previous quarter
BTS206 Order inflow compared with the previous quarter
BTS207 Export order inflow compared with the previous quarter
BTS208 Selling prices compared with the previous quarter
BTS209 Production costs compared with the previous quarter
BTS310 Production capacity
BTS311 Backlog of orders compared to normal
BTS312 Stocks of finished products
BTS313 Stocks of raw materials
BTS314 Limits to production
BTS315 Lack of personnel
BTS316 Lack of capacity
BTS317 Weak demand
BTS401 Production expectation for the next quarter
BTS402 Export expectation for the next quarter
BTS403 Personnel expectation for the next quarter
BTS406 Order inflow expectation for the next quarter
BTS407 Export order expectation for the next quarter
BTS408 Selling price expectation for the next quarter
BTS409 Production cost expectation for the next quarter
BTS501 Production expectation two quarters ahead
BTS502 Export expectation two quarters ahead
BTS518 Business outlook in the near future
BTS604 Investment expectation a year ahead
BTS605 Profitability expectation a year ahead
BTSCI Confidence indicator

References

European Commission (1997); *The Joint Harmonised EU Programme of Business and Consumer Surveys*, European Economy - Reports and Studies, No. 6, Belgium.

Hamilton J. D. (1994), *Time Series Analysis*, Princeton University Press, Princeton, New Jersey.

Harvey, A.C. (1989), *Forecasting, structural time series models and the Kalman filter,* Cambridge University Press, Cambridge.

Harvey, A.C. and C.Fernandes (1989), 'Time series models for count or qualitative observations (with discussion)', *Journal of Business and Economics Statistics*, 7, pp. 407-422.

Harvey, A.C. and S.J. Koopman (1996), *Multivariate structural time series models*, London School of Economics and Political Science. Discussion Paper, No. EM/96/307.

Harvey A.C. and N. Shephard (1993), 'Structural Time Series Models', in: Maddala G.S., C.R. Rao and H.D. Vinod (eds) *Handbook of Statistics*, vol. 11, Elsevier Science Publishers.

Kangasniemi J. and P. Tsupari (1997), *Manufacturing Production and the Business Tendency Survey in Finland: The concept of Business Outlook*, Paper presented at the 23rd Ciret Conference, 30.7 – 1.8.1997, Helsinki.

Kauppi E. and J. Lassila (1997), *Forecasting Industrial Production with Business Survey Data: Lessons from the Finnish depression of the Early 1990s*, Paper presented at the 23rd Ciret Conference, 30.7 – 1.8.1997, Helsinki.

Teräsvirta, T. (1986), 'Model selection using business survey data', *International Journal of Forecasting*, Vol. 2, pp. 191-200.

Zimmermann, K.F. (1997), 'Analysis of Business Surveys', in: Pesaran and Schmidt (eds), *Handbook of Applied Econometrics*, Volume II. Microeconometrics, Basil Blackwell.

CIRET

CIRET, the Centre for International Research on Economic Tendency Surveys, is a forum for leading economists and institutions that *conducts and analyzes business and/or consumer surveys.*

Since 1953 CIRET promotes the exchange of knowledge not only of the theoretical but especially of the operational aspects of economic cycle research. As a platform it provides quick information often unavailable from official statistics such as plans, assessments and expectations of businesses and consumers. The overall aim of CIRET is to develop, encourage and improve communication, exchange and co-operation between scientists and institutions who use or conduct economic surveys. CIRET has links all over the world. The CIRET participants are scientists of economic as well as social research institutes, universities, financial institutions, central banks, firms, ministries, chambers of commerce and national bureaus of statistics, who regularly conduct or use surveys. Additionally, international organizations such as the OECD and supranational institutions like the European Commission take part.

The CIRET- weblink: http://www.ciret.org

The CIRET office is located at the

Swiss Institute of Business Cycle Research
Weinbergstr. 35
8092 Zurich/Switzerland
Info@ciret.org